Introduction

For persons not acquainted with the area west of Shreveport, a brief introduction is needed. Shreveport is located in the northwest corner of Louisiana. Fifty miles west of Shreveport is Marshall, Texas, and 150 miles farther to the west is Dallas. Jefferson—widely known for its bed and breakfast operations—is located 20 miles north of Marshall on Big Cypress Bayou (**fig. 1**).

Shreveport is located on the Red River. The Red connects with the Mississippi, which runs down to New Orleans. During the 1800s, Twelvemile Bayou entered the Red slightly above Shreveport and drained Soda Lake (now extinct) to the west. Soda Lake was connected with Caddo Lake; and entering Caddo Lake to the west was Big Cypress Bayou.

The waterbodies west of Shreveport provided an opportunity for steamboats to travel as far as Jefferson. This gave rise to a system of ports and landings, of which Jefferson was the most important, that tapped the market areas to the north and south and far to the west. The commercial relations of these ports and landings were with New Orleans, joined by St. Louis and Cincinnati in the early 1870s. These ports and landings were important factors in the commerce of New Orleans and played an important role in the development of Northeast Texas as far west as Dallas. Most of them have disappeared, and almost all have been forgotten.

In writing *Caddo Was . . . A Short History of Caddo Lake*, Fred Dahmer sensed that many steamboats must have passed in front of his property on Taylor Island at the western end of the lake, but he had no idea how many. In fact, at least 324 steamboats operated west of Shreveport, 288 of which went as far as Jefferson. Over 2,600 trips were taken to bring supplies to the emerging west and to carry out cotton and beef. The vast majority of these trips took place between 1840 and 1873, after which steamboat activity declined drastically and disappeared after 1905.

This is the story of what happened and why it happened. Chapters 1–4 deal with the peculiar circumstances that gave rise to the possibility of navigation west of Shreveport and the actions that were taken to realize that possibility. Chapters 5–15 deal with the origin of steamboat activity west of Shreveport, its development, its continuance in a modest fashion during the Civil War, and its expansion after the war. Chapter 16 presents the reason for the decline. Chapter 17 deals with the event that gave rise to a public misperception about the cause, and Chapter 18 supports Chapter 16 in demonstrating that this perception is false. The last three chapters bring the picture up to the present, revealing the continuity of development and why the past holds promise for the future.

A great deal of information on steamboats could not be incorporated into the text because it was topical or cumulative. This information is presented in Appendix A. Appendix B provides a year-by-year account of the activities of each steamboat. Appendix C lists the steamboats alphabetically. A bibliographical essay provides information on sources cited in each chapter.

For boat names, I have usually relied on the newspaper renditions, excluding shortened versions, nicknames, and additional names under which some boats were known. The names in the newspapers are generally compatible with the authoritative sources. In a few cases, the formal name rather than the running name is used. Because boats changed captains frequently, I have mentioned the names of captains only for the earliest years. The system for measuring tonnage changed after the Civil War. I have used the registered tonnages throughout. For compatibility, add forty-five percent to the tonnages before the Civil War. Errors in quotes and peculiarities of punctuation have been carried forward to maintain the flavor of the originals.

·1·
Navigation's Natural Setting

CHANGES

Normally in the presentation of a history of navigation it is only necessary to describe the physical features of a route in terms of factors that are readily observable today and then proceed immediately to a description of commercial activity. This is not the case for the Cypress Bayou and the lakes route. Much is in existence today that was not in existence when steamboats were operating along the route, and much was in existence when steamboats were operating along the route that is not in existence today. In addition, a great deal happened to transform the route as the level of waterborne transport increased. As a consequence, present circumstances do not offer much in the way of clues as to the conditions under which steamboats were operating during the 1800s.

With respect to new features, there are dams on Big Cypress Bayou and Caddo Lake. The dam on the former exercises a moderating influence on water levels, and the latter's dam is an impediment to any through traffic. During the steamboat period, the route was dominated by five large lakes (Soda, Shifttail, Clear, Caddo, and Cross). These lakes, as shown on C. W. R. Bayley's 1853 *New and Improved Map of Louisiana* (**fig. 1-1**), were hydrologically connected and were referred to collectively as Sodo by the Indians. These lake names were not constant. The name of the complex was eventually appropriated by one of its components in a corrupted fashion as "Soda," which says

1

Fig. 1-1. Sodo Lake complex. *Source: Courtesy of LSU Libraries Special Collections, Baton Rouge*

nothing about the chemistry of the area or early expeditions. Caddo Lake was generally called Ferry or, by corruption, Fairy. And designations for various portions of the complex shifted and were reversed.

Twelvemile Bayou was not the dredged and leveed channel greater than twelve miles in length that is found today, but rather a sinuous natural stream that served as an outlet to Soda Lake. During the steamboat period there were clearing and dredging operations conducted by private subscription, through state and federal projects, and by the steamboatmen themselves that transformed the natural landscape to make it more amenable to waterborne transport. The most visible of these are Government Ditch on the upper end of Caddo Lake and the various cuts along Big Cypress Bayou in the Benton Lake and Little Cypress Bayou areas.

In order to understand the conditions under which steamboats began operating along the route, it is necessary to reconstruct the natural setting and particularly to understand the singular event that gave rise to the peculiar hydrologic and vegetational features of the route.

THE VALLEY PERIOD

Until the end of the 1700s, the five lakes that formed the natural setting for steamboat operations did not exist. There was only Cypress Bayou, which began in the foothills west of present-day Lake O' the Pines and ended above the present mouth of Twelvemile Bayou. Cypress Bayou was a fairly rapid, cypress-fringed stream. Throughout most of its upper extent, it ran through a constricted valley. When reaching the area presently occupied by Caddo Lake, it cut south, entering a broad valley that was simply the expanded valley of Cypress Bayou (**fig. 1-2**).

From the north, another large valley entered the expanded valley of Cypress Bayou. Through this northern valley, a sizable stream flowed that in its earliest designation was known as Coushatta Jim's Bayou. This designation was eventually shortened to Jim's Bayou and corrupted to Jeems Bayou. It is rendered on some maps as James Bayou. On an upper portion of this bayou there was a small, deep lake formed by stream scour between bluffs that later came to be known as Monterey Lake. Before the 1800s, this was the only permanent lake in the region.

At the point presently occupied by the Caddo Lake dam, Cypress Bayou entered the valley of the Red River, where it was met by Black Bayou and Red Bayou from the north. Alternately hugging and diverging from the Albany line of bluffs, it passed through a shallow depression in the Red River floodplain that was eventually to become Soda Lake. Joining this depression were two other depressions that were to become Clear Lake and Shifttail Lake (a corruption of Cheftel). In an 1859 annual report of the Louisiana Board of Swamp Land Commissioners, the engineer William Washburn describes these depressions as cypress brake backswamps of the Red River that were infused with Red River water during the spring.

Below Grindstone Bluff, Cypress Bayou was essentially equivalent to the old channel of Twelvemile Bayou. This old channel diverged

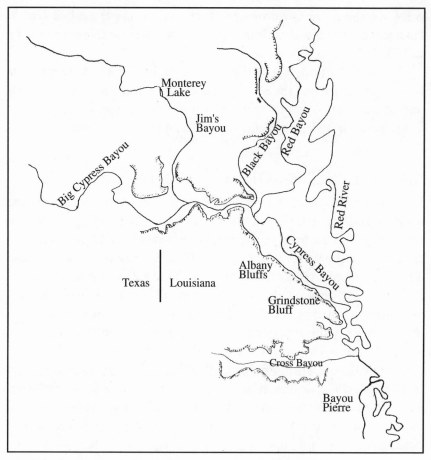

Fig. 1-2. Conditions prior to formation of the Sodo Lake complex

substantially from the present-day channel. It is readily observable on maps from the 1800s and can be seen on present-day topographic maps as a relict channel crossing the newer, dredged channel of Twelvemile Bayou. Cypress Bayou entered the Red River. Shortly below the mouth of Cypress Bayou, another stream entered the Red River from a broad valley to the west, which eventually was occupied by Cross Lake.

The upper valley presently occupied by Caddo Lake was an alluvial valley formed by Cypress Bayou. It sloped rapidly downward from the banks of Cypress Bayou and then gradually upward to the surrounding bluffs on the north and south. It was essentially flat bottomed and without lakes, although there were some swampy areas immediately downbank of the bayou that were replenished by spring overflows. At the northern end of the valley in the area presently occupied by Clinton Lake was an old backwater swamp of Cypress Bayou that in geologic times was the area through which the bayou passed. Evidence of the shifting of the ancient channel can be seen in the Alligator Thicket area of Goat Island.

The upper valley was occupied by a typical bottomland hardwood forest whose remnants can still be seen in the submerged logs and usually submerged stumps in the bed of Caddo Lake. The composition of this old forest was investigated through stump analysis by Arthur Veatch of the Louisiana Geological Survey in 1899 and by Lionel Janes of the Department of the Interior in 1914. The banks of the bayou that ran through the valley that eventually became Caddo Lake were covered with cypress. Immediately adjacent to the channel were cypress, water locust, and willow. Farther out were overcup oak, red gum, and cottonwood; and near the bluffs were loblolly pine and post oak.

Both the upper (Cypress Bayou) and lower (Red River) valleys were heavily forested. The best description of these valleys was given in 1904 by Capt. J. M. DeWare, president of the Jefferson Navigation Company, who provided testimony to Congress on the need to reestablish navigation to Jefferson that eventually led to the construction of the first dam on Caddo Lake. DeWare described the valleys of Cypress Bayou and the Red River on the basis of conversations with descendants of Indians who had lived in the area in earlier times: "At that time there was no chain of lakes. It was a dense forest—what the natives of the country called the 'first and second bottoms.' It was all kinds of oak and cypress, and it was the Indian hunting ground."

FORMATION OF THE LAKES

It was well known during the 1800s that the five lakes that formed the setting for navigation along the route had come into existence in recent, as opposed to geologic, times. In 1872, H. C. Collins, a geologist with the Corps of Engineers conducting a survey of Caddo Lake, which was then called Fairy Lake, reported the following:

> Fairy Lake is the entrance into Red River Valley of a large, wide valley from the northwest, which is probably as old as Red River Valley, and may be older. It was formerly traversed

by a deep sluggish stream called Cypress Bayou, which ran most of its distance between cypress swamps, the stumps and dead trees which are yet to be seen everywhere through the lake.

In Texas, a short distance west from the Louisiana line, is a portion of the bottom of the lake, now covered with 5 feet of water at the lowest stages, where the stumps are of yellow pine and white oak, proving that the relative positions of land and water have changed several feet, at least, since these trees grew.

Mr. Josey, living at Swanson's Landing, who is probably the most intelligent man in the vicinity, thinks there was a general subsidence of a very large tract, including bluffs as well as bottom, and that it took place since the removal of the Caddo Indians. He says that a few years ago, when a few of the Caddo Indians came back to visit the country, they told him that they used to cultivate corn-fields on land adjoining these oak and pine stumps, and now covered with water to the same depth, and that then the entire country was above overflow.

In 1849, Edward Smith, who was investigating sites for an English settlement, traveled throughout Northeast Texas, spoke to many people, and reported the following about the lakes west of Shreveport: "Sodo and Clear lakes are of recent formation, and many now living remember the period when the land was dry. The Indians informed Major Campbell, of Clinton, that the lakes were formed after a great earthquake, and the Major believes it to have been at the occurrence of the earthquake of 1812, when New Madrid, and other parts of the Mississippi valley disappeared." The traveler and journalist Josiah Gregg visited his brother, who lived five miles southwest of Shreveport, in November 1847 and reported the following:

> Another interesting feature in this region, is that of the great lakes (as they may be called here) of Caddo, including Cross & Clear lakes. Their outlet (about as large as the principal branch of Red River) is just above Shreveport. They extend 40 to 50 miles west, by the Cypress Bayous and from the North by (besides Jim's Bayou & others) Red Bayou, which comes out of Red R. above the Raft, and conveys near a third of the water of the river into the lakes. These lakes are said to be of recent formation—in fact, the great quantities of dead timber

still standing in some places, prove many portions of them to be so. But there are men now living who assert that they can recollect when the beds of those lakes, were, as other river & creek bottoms, traversed by the hunters. In this case they could scarcely be 50 years old—some say but little over 30. Whether formed by the sinking of their beds, or the rising of the bed of the river at their mouth, occasioned by the raft, is a somewhat interesting question for the geologist; however, I am of the opinion that it was the latter. There are similar lakes on the east side of Red River—formed, doubtless, in a similar manner: Lake Bistineau, etc.

As can be seen from these quotations, there were diverse theories from earliest times about how the lakes came into existence. The two primary theses concerning lake origins were that they owed their existence to the New Madrid quakes in the Mississippi valley, which began in December 1811, or to the actions of the Great Raft, an immense log jam on the Red River from time immemorial.

The earthquake thesis can be rejected on two grounds. First, there is no evidence of recent seismic activity in the area west of Shreveport. The issue was addressed directly in an 1893 Corps of Engineers report by Capt. J. H. Willard, who conducted soil borings in the area that was then occupied by Soda Lake, made observations with respect to the hardwood stumps in the lake, and concluded the following: "The borings also disprove the notion that these lakes were formed by the same convulsion that made those at New Madrid, the strata plainly being water deposits without contortions that upheaval or sinking would produce, and the oak stumps as well as the cypress are everywhere found to be vertical."

More importantly, there are two historic accounts indicating the existence of the lakes before the New Madrid quakes of 1811–12. In 1808, the Indian trader Anthony Glass visited the Coushatta village, which was located at Cedar Bluffs on the east side of the river above the site of what later became Shreveport. Glass reported that the Caddo Indians used to occupy the Coushatta site, "But now live about thirty Miles South West on the Lake." This could not have been anything other than the Sodo Lake complex.

The Freeman and Custis Red River expedition took place in 1806 under the sponsorship of Thomas Jefferson. To reach the upper Red

River from Natchitoches, it was necessary for Freeman and Custis to take an eastern route around the portion of the Red occupied by the Great Raft. They reentered the Red River at a point about nineteen miles below the Coushatta village, where Freeman reported the following: "On entering the River, we found a beautiful stream of 230 yards wide, 34 feet deep, and running with a gentle current; its banks are from 10 to 12 feet high, bordered by lofty trees, of the Cotton Wood, Oak and Red Cedar. On the right of the river, ascending, at the distance of from 50 to 100 yards, the land rises to the height of 50 feet above the banks, and is covered with Oaks, Hickory, Ash, and some Pine. On the left it is level and very rich; a large Prairie extending for several miles below the place where the party entered the River, and as far above. Beyond this Prairie there is a large lake, on the west of which, and nearly 30 miles from Red River, lies the principal Village of the Caddos."

It is now generally accepted that the lakes west of Shreveport during the last century owed their existence to the Great Raft. The raft was composed primarily of cottonwood trees, forming a dense mat whose interstices were filled with leaves and sediment, producing a solid mass through which the waters of the Red could barely penetrate. The logs were obtained from the banks of the Red, which cut back and forth across its alluvial plain, consuming immense quantities of timber. The noise of falling trees in spring was likened to the distant roar of artillery.

The raft was not stationary. It moved upstream at approximately one mile a year. This upstream movement was caused by the accumulation of logs at the head of the raft and decay of logs at the foot, which were carried downstream. Because the raft moved upstream about a mile a year and the materials of which it was formed took about eighty years to decompose, the raft maintained a fairly constant length of eighty miles in its upward movement.

As the raft moved upstream, it created a number of lakes along the Red River, most of which have disappeared. The exact mode of lake formation is a matter of controversy and may not be uniform. One common idea is that the lakes along the Red River were caused by the physical blockage by the raft of the outlets of tributary streams. This cannot have been the case for the lakes west of Shreveport (with the possible exception of Cross Lake), because the Freeman and Custis expedition of 1806 reported the head of the raft below Twelvemile Bayou when the lakes were already in existence. In addition, the lakes did not disappear after Henry Shreve removed the raft in the vicinity of Twelvemile Bayou in 1835.

Another idea is that the lakes west of Shreveport were caused by the ponding of water. Because the raft was fairly compact, it acted as a dam, causing upstream rises on the Red. When the raft neared the bluffs on which Shreveport came to be located, the upstream rise created backwater flooding on Cypress Bayou, forming the lakes. Although this may have been a factor in incipient stages of the lakes' formation, it should be noted that after Shreve removed the raft, it did not reform below the mouth of Twelvemile Bayou. The lakes continued in existence throughout the 1800s when upstream rises in the vicinity of Twelvemile Bayou were no longer a factor.

A third idea, and the one that appears most compatible with the available evidence, is that the lakes were formed by raft-induced distributaries of the Red River from the north. A distributary is an outflow channel and therefore the exact opposite of a tributary. The maze of distributaries leading off the Red River above Shreveport and feeding into the lakes are prominent on every old map of the area (see fig. 1-1). These distributaries formed progressively as the raft moved upstream, blocking the waters of the Red in its channel and forcing those waters to escape through the floodplains to the east and west and rejoin the Red farther downstream below the raft.

Most of the distributaries above Shreveport formed on the west side of the river because the river passes close to a series of bluffs on the east that prohibited water from escaping in that direction. The distributaries also tended in a northeast-southwest direction rather than simply paralleling the river around the raft, because the floodplain slopes to the west. The Red is a typical alluvial river carrying a high volume of sediment. When overbank flooding occurred, the water leaving the river dropped its heaviest sediments almost immediately, building banks that were much higher than the surrounding floodplain. Smaller particles dropped out progressively overland. These actions produced a floodplain profile of high riverbanks descending rapidly immediately away from the river and then with a gradual slope toward the bluffs to the west. The valley of Cypress Bayou presently occupied by Caddo Lake was even lower, as can be determined by comparing present-day Red River floodplain elevations to the elevation of the bottom of the lake.

At times during spring flooding season, the water rushed overbank and downhill into depressions, forming swampy areas such as the one that later came to be Soda Lake. But the spring floods could not produce permanent lakes, because the water quickly ran off through the channel of Cypress Bayou. What was needed was the replacement of overbank flooding by a break in the bank that would provide a continuous source of water to the lakes: in short, distributaries coming from the Red that would feed the lakes throughout most of the year.

These distributaries were produced by the raft. By acting as a partial dam, the raft backed up water for many miles on the Red, producing extreme pressures on its banks. These pressures were increased through the fallout of sediments in the Red, which occurred in the slackwater produced by the raft, raising the bed of the river and its corresponding water levels. These two phenomena created ideal conditions for breaks in the natural levee of the Red.

These breaks tended to occur at bends in the river. The potential for a break increased the farther out the bend thrust into the floodplain of the Red—the farther out the bend, the greater the difference between the water elevation in the river and the surrounding floodplain area. Where a break occurred, a distributary formed, with the channel following the line of least resistance into the floodplain depression, where shallow lakes formed. Because the bed of the Red had been raised by the actions of the raft, the distributaries and their recipient lakes were assured water from the Red River during most of the year. The water did not immediately flow off because the raft had restricted flows, which raised the bed and constricted the channel of the Red River downstream, and there was sediment deposition in the drainage channels of the lakes.

These processes gave rise to lakes all along the Red, as summarized by Capt. T. B. Linnard in a report on improvement of the Red River prepared in 1844:

> At some distant period the Red river . . . was a stream of broad channel. . . . The valley through which it takes its course is composed of deposits of very fine sand and alluvial substances, which are easily affected by the erosive action of the current. Changes in the direction of the channel sometimes take place with astonishing rapidity. The freshets of every year, abrading the banks, cause immense quantities of timber to fall into the stream, which, being dried by exposure to the sun during the summer, are taken up by the next flood and carried down stream.

Numerous snags must have lodged throughout the whole course of the river . . . and it is quite probable that the formation of the first raft was caused by deposits of trees . . . in sufficient number to arrest the drift timber brought down by subsequent freshets. A raft being once formed, the velocity of the current above it was diminished, and extensive deposits of the suspended soil were made on the bottom, decreasing the section of the channel until it became unequal to the discharge of all the water in full stages. The surplus at such times rushed through the depressions in the natural banquette of the river, and, receiving an acceleration of velocity in descending the slopes towards the borders of the valley, cut deep channels to points below the obstruction, where it reunited with the main stream. The floods of each season added two to three miles to the raft, which, in the course of years extended above the first formed lateral channels, and compelled the water to make other detours around the obstacle. The whole bed of the river, in which the raft had accumulated, having become elevated above its original height, the lowest points of the valley became permanently inundated; the cypress swamps and oak flats on either side were converted into lakes, in which the trunks and stumps of trees still remain.

With these general facts in mind, it is only necessary to describe the specific events that gave rise to the Sodo Lake complex west of Shreveport. In a report on the Red River and country adjacent prepared in April 1805 in Natchitoches, the Indian agent John Sibley indicates that Bayou Pierre was closed by the raft in 1798 or 1799. Bayou Pierre was a major distributary of the Red, leaving the river to the west at the bluffs on which Shreveport is presently located (**fig. 1-3**). The closure of this distributary created tremendous pressures upstream.

The first large bend above Shreveport reaches far out into the Red River floodplain. During the 1800s, there was a very large distributary known as Cottonwood Bayou that debouched from this bend (**see fig. 1-3**). Although it is little more than a drainage ditch today, Cottonwood Bayou is designated a crevasse channel on geologic maps, was said to be the first major distributary above Shreveport by the geologist Arthur Veatch in his 1899 report, and was said to be deep in the 1914 Department of the Interior report.

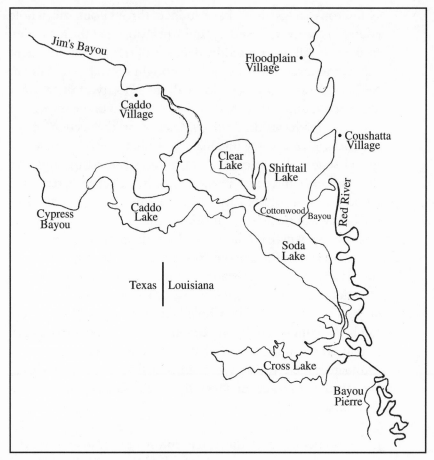

Fig. 1-3. Formation of the Sodo Lake complex

It may be hypothesized, therefore, that the Sodo Lake complex came into existence through a break in the first large bend above Shreveport, sending the water of the Red into the low depressions of its floodplain (forming Soda, Shifttail, and Clear Lakes) and into the valleys of Cypress Bayou (forming Caddo Lake) and Cross Bayou (forming Cross Lake). Given the closure of Bayou Pierre in 1798 or 1799, this event probably would have occurred in the spring of 1800. The year 1800 is confirmed by Sibley in a 28 November 1812 letter to his superior, William Eustis, the secretary of war: "The North West Corner of the State will be found in Lake Sodo, two or three miles to the West of Red River, Lake Sodo is between the Caddo Nation & Red River is Sixty or Seventy Miles long, & it is Said will average three

Leagues Wide & has been formed within about Twelve Years, it Stretches along Nearly parallel with Red River."

At the time the event occurred, the Caddo Indians were living on the Red River floodplain on the west side of the river to the northwest of the Coushatta village (see fig. 1-3). In his "Historical Sketches of the Several Indian Tribes," Sibley indicated that the Caddos moved from this site to their permanent home on Jim's Bayou in 1800 because of flooding induced by the raft. In speaking of the formation of Caddo Lake, the Caddos were supposed to have recounted that the earth trembled, the ground sank, and water poured over the land where the tribe had lived. This undoubtedly was a remembrance of the break in the bend above Shreveport, offering a second confirmation of 1800 as the year in which the Sodo Lake complex came into existence.

The earliest rendition of the Indian story that I have come across is in the 18 April 1867 Marshall *Texas Republican*. It was used then, as it is today, to suggest that Caddo Lake was formed by the New Madrid quakes of 1811–12. It is easy to understand why the earliest settlers interpreted what was said to them as a description of an earthquake:

> Many of the first settlers living near the lakes attribute their formation to the subsidence of the land during an earthquake, basing their belief on Indian tradition, which, though frequently marvelous, yet, when according with experience, is entitled to consideration. Credible individuals were informed by Indians that the ground "had a chill," and sank. A white haired Caddo chief stated to one of the early emigrants, that, in his boyhood, he went with several of his tribe on a hunting expedition on Sulphur Fork. While there they heard a "big noise." On their return, they were astonished to perceive the land covered with water near their usual crossing over the stream where Ferry Lake is now situated, and which then was a continuation of what is now called Big Cypress, and they were consequently compelled to cross the river further westward.

The 1914 Department of the Interior study, on the basis of textual analysis and tree ring dating, concluded that Caddo Lake had come into existence during the Revolutionary War period. This is incompatible with the remembrances of the people of the area, the latest of which were expressed in 1858 when there was a controversy over the draining of Cross Lake. According to the 25 September 1858 Clarksville *Standard*, "the chain of Lakes are mere submerged low lands, and the time when they were dry land is within the knowledge of persons now living." According to the Shreveport *Caddo Gazette*, as quoted in the same issue of the *Standard*, "There are persons now living in this vicinity who have a perfect recollection of the time when what now constitutes Cross, Soda, Clear, and Ferry lakes was dry land, not even subject to periodical overflows." The year 1858 is a bit too late for remembrances of events in the Caddo Lake area during the Revolutionary War period.

NAVIGATION CONSEQUENCES

With respect to navigation, hydrology is destiny. Little sense can be made of the concrete conditions of navigation on Cypress Bayou and the lakes apart from an understanding that the distributary system created and sustained the lakes, which meant that conditions on the route were intimately related to conditions on the Red River and ultimately to the raft as the causative agent. The hydrologic situation was even more complex because the lakes were superimposed on an existing bayou that brought water from the west. And the entire natural setting for navigation was highly peculiar because the lakes were formed in areas that were heavily forested.

The lakes were formed fully with the first break at Cottonwood Bayou. As the raft moved upstream, other distributaries were created, eventually establishing a complex distributary system. The original channel of Cypress Bayou disappeared beneath the waters of Caddo and Soda Lakes, with the downstream portion of Cypress Bayou becoming the historic Twelvemile Bayou. Because the Red was an alluvial river, tremendous volumes of sediment were carried by the distributaries into the area of the lakes, obliterating the old channel of Cypress Bayou in the upper portion of Soda Lake. The original forests were killed, including the cypress more gradually—even cypress cannot live in continuous high water. The new water regime created new cypress stands.

These basic events created the following conditions for navigation:

1. Without the raft, there would have been no lakes, and without the lakes, there would have been no navigation on Cypress Bayou. At least this was the opinion of the early engineers who surveyed the area. In an 1874 report on the improvement of Cypress Bayou, Capt. C. W.

Howell of the Corps of Engineers described the large basin formed by the Red River on the east and the bluffs to the west and stated that "the raft in Red River, along the eastern rim of this basin, deflected the greater portion of the river discharge above the raft into the basin, thus converting what before the advent of the raft was a cypress swamp, with a sluggish, unnavigable stream flowing through it, into a series of lakes, affording good navigation for the greater portion of each year." Similar comments were made by Capt. Charles Potter in a 1902 report: "Cypress Bayou evidently was an unnavigable stream until the advance of the Red River raft above Shreveport, acting as a dam, forced the water into its bottom lands and converted them into reservoirs, known as Fairy, Soda, and Cross lakes."

2. The navigability of the route was seasonally variable and unpredictable from year to year. This was because the navigability of the route was primarily dependent on the water supplied by the distributaries, which themselves were dependent on the Red River. Most of the water that came down the Red River was diverted to the area of the lakes by the raft. In general, when water levels were high on the Red, there was plenty of water on the route. Conversely, when the Red was low, the lakes were depleted. Water levels on the Red were heavily dependent on rainfall in its upper basin, which tended to be heavy in the spring, significant in the fall, modest in the winter, and practically nil in the summer.

As a consequence, the route was most usable in the spring and least usable in the summer. In the springtime, almost any size class of boats could use the route, at least within the range of length and tonnage operative on the Red River. During the summer, only the smaller class of boats could operate along the route. During extreme low-water months such as August, it was often the case that few, if any, boats could get through. Periods of extended drought on the upper Red River could produce circumstances in which the route was essentially closed for as much as a year.

The upward movement of the raft on the Red did not significantly affect the conditions of navigation. By the time boats began operating along the route in the early 1840s, the waters carried by the distributaries were concentrated at the foot of Caddo Lake, as shown in one of Lt. Eugene Woodruff's renditions of his 1872 *Map of the Red River Raft Region and Cypress Bayou* (**fig. 1-4**). Although the distributary system underwent modifications as the raft moved upstream, this condition

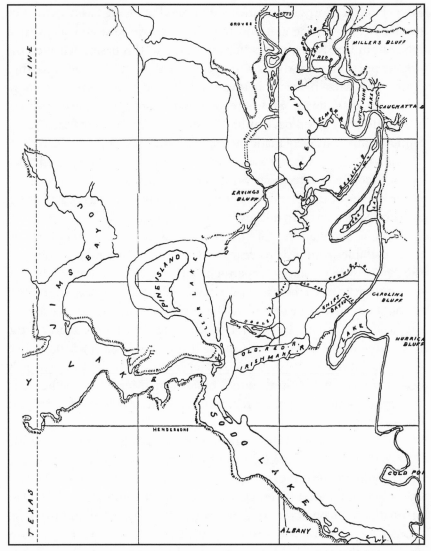

Fig. 1-4. Drainage patterns. *Source: LSU in Shreveport, Noel Memorial Library Archives*

did not change; and all of the waters of the Red were directed into the area of the lakes because bluffs on the east side of the river prohibited the formation of a competitive distributary system to the east.

3. Although Red River water through the distributaries was the major cause of the navigability of the route, the water supply of the

route was dual. A tremendous amount of water was brought into the system by Cypress Bayou and its tributaries, including the streams that flowed into Caddo Lake. These inputs were almost totally dependent on rainfall in the Cypress Bayou watershed.

The duality of water sources, not to mention variations in rainfall in the watershed, gave rise to volatile and highly unpredictable conditions for navigation. Generally, contributions to the route from the Red River outweighed contributions from the watershed. Under such circumstances, Red River water actually entered Caddo Lake, as reported by the geologist H. C. Collins in an 1872 survey report on the Red River and Cypress Bayou: "Stumpy Bayou is a deep channel between Shift-Tail Lake and the bluff, with 12 to 20 feet of water at a low stage, and not as strong a current as that in Shift-Tail Lake. Most of the water follows the bluff, and passes into Fairy Lake on its north side, the current running west up the north side of the lake about a mile, and depositing in it a large amount of mud. At times of a rapid rise of the river, there is a strong current up the lake to the west, so that sometimes Red River water is seen beyond the Texas line."

Normally, the force of Red River water backed up whatever water was in Caddo Lake, as reported, for example, in the 4 March 1873 *Shreveport Times*: "At Mooringsport the lake was rising by back water from Stumpy Bayou." This backwater effect often reached Jefferson, as reported, for example, in the 15 April 1873 *Shreveport Times*: "It will not be many days before there will be plenty of water in the lakes, and in all probability it will back up the bayou to Jefferson." Ideal conditions for navigation to Jefferson were obtained when rainfall in the upper Cypress Bayou Basin met incoming Red River water, as reported, for example, in the 23 June 1872 *Shreveport Times*, quoting the 21 June *Jefferson Democrat*: "The bayou has risen about ten inches at this point. The rise is from two causes. Red River is rising, and we have back water from that; and rain above here on the bayou, has caused a head rise."

When there was little rainfall in the upper Cypress Bayou Basin, but large quantities of water entering the area from the Red River, there was actually a reverse current up to Jefferson, as indicated, for example, in the 17 April 1873 *Shreveport Times*: "As there is no head rise in Cypress Bayou, it will take some time for the lake water to back up to the city wharf." When the lakes were full and water stopped entering the area from both ends, drainage moved in both directions, as reported, for example, in the 29 April 1875 *Shreveport Times*: "The lakes are plumb full, but on the fall—some water running this way and some hunting Jefferson. Good lakes those, to run both up and down, or any other way just to unload."

The situation was even further complicated by the fact that the Cypress Bayou drainage above Jefferson was small in comparison to the drainage area of tributaries to Cypress Bayou and Caddo Lake, producing circumstances in which local rainfall (e.g., north of Caddo Lake) could make significant contributions to the dual system. Taking all of these factors into consideration, the natural setting for navigation was obviously highly volatile and unpredictable, particularly for specific points along the route. As a consequence, information on navigation conditions along the route from the last boat down from Jefferson was a key element in reportage in the "River Intelligence" column of the Shreveport newspapers.

Even the latest news was not sufficient to give an exact picture of the conditions that would be encountered by the next boat up. And, for that matter, an up trip did not give a firm picture of what would be encountered on the return trip. Boats simply had to test the waters, sometimes returning to Shreveport, unable to get through Soda Lake, sometimes getting stuck for brief periods above Soda Lake on the way down. This led to wry comments on the part of the editor of the River Intelligence column, such as one concerning Soda Lake in the 6 August 1872 *Shreveport Times*: "Funny lake, that; somehow or other we can never get the straight of it. One day she is up and all right and the next day she is down and all wrong. Funny, but it must be so."

4. Water levels on Caddo Lake were generally higher than they are today. The exact difference cannot be determined because of a lack of comparable data. There are two measurements of normal high-water levels. The first is called ordinary high water, which is determined by observing shoreline escarpment and vegetational regimes that indicate the place that high water generally reaches. Such a study was conducted for Caddo Lake in 1914 by the Department of the Interior. This study determined that the ordinary high water on Caddo Lake during the 1800s was 173.09 feet.

Mean high water is determined by a period of record. For the period 1971 (when the new dam was built on Caddo Lake) to 1990, the mean high water level was 172 feet. Unfortunately, ordinary high water and mean high water are not necessarily comparable. There were no gauge stations on Caddo Lake during the 1800s. Therefore, the relationship between prior and present water levels cannot be determined with any degree of precision.

The old maps are not a great deal of help. Generally, they show areas as flooded that are not shown on present-day maps as flooded. However, the old maps were not based on a scientific analysis of water levels, and the areas shown as flooded are low and generally contain ponds and swamps today. The only survey of Caddo Lake during the raft period was one conducted by Lt. Eugene Woodruff in 1872. The survey map shows the water level on the lake at the time the survey was done. By comparison to a present-day topographic map, it can be seen that the water level on the lake was 2.5 to 3 feet higher than the lake as represented on a topographic map, which is based on dam height of 168.5 feet mean sea level.

Dual water sources during the 1800s suggest generally higher water levels. The best evidence is from the activities of the steamboats themselves, which were able to penetrate areas such as Clinton Lake and Monterey Lake through routes that are normally inaccessible to anything but airboats and canoes today. However, there is nothing in the record to suggest that these routes were normally open to steamboat passage, and careful attention must be given to newspaper accounts of navigation conditions at the time boats are recorded as having traveled to those areas.

Although water levels on Caddo Lake were probably generally higher than they are today, the difference should not be exaggerated. Passage into remote areas probably resulted from the boldness and tenacity of the steamboatmen as much as the availability of water. All things considered, it can be assumed the water levels on the lake were normally only a couple of feet higher than they are today for most of the year and that they were much lower than today in the summer. If water levels had been much higher than two feet, the older cypress trees on Caddo Lake would look much different than they do today. During the summer, the fixed-weir dam at the foot of Caddo Lake prohibits drainage and captures within the lake all of the available water. During summers in the 1800s, backwater force from the Red was diminished to practically nothing, allowing dramatic drainage of Caddo Lake.

That the dam exercises a moderating influence on lake levels is suggested by comparative data on average high water versus average low water, which is not affected by differences in measurement techniques. According to the Department of the Interior study, the average high water on Caddo Lake was 173.09 feet, the average low water was 165–66 feet, and the maximum low water was 163 feet. For the period 1971–90, the average high water was 172 feet, the average low water was 167.8 feet, and the maximum low water was 166.85 feet. This produces a difference between average high and average low water of 7.59 feet for the 1800s compared to 4.20 for the present, with a difference of nearly 4 feet between the maximum low-water figures. Put simply, water levels fluctuated more on Caddo Lake during the 1800s than they do today.

5. For the extremely shallow-draft vessels that operated on Cypress Bayou and the lakes, 2 feet of water was an important factor and helps to explain the accessibility of presently remote areas. However, generalizations with respect to water levels would have been a moot point as far as the steamboatmen were concerned, because they were always dealing with specific conditions of operation on specific days.

The conditions of operation were largely determined by external water levels, particularly at problem areas, and by the dimensions and draft of boats, the latter of which was partly dependent on what the boat was carrying. A boat 30 feet wide drawing 3 feet of water might be able to move through an area of Cypress Bayou 50 feet wide on a particular day, whereas one 40 feet wide drawing 4 feet of water would get stuck. This is why newspaper reports on navigability conditions tended to be highly specific. One example from the 1 February 1873 *Shreveport Times* concerned navigation conditions at a shallow, convoluted area slightly downstream of the confluence with Little Cypress Bayou: "At Daugherty's Defeat there were about twenty-eight inches for a wide boat." Nevertheless, the steamboatmen were not passive to these circumstances. Besides actions such as lightening (removal of cargo or passengers from a boat to reduce draft), the steamboatmen could make use of two natural features of the route that varied in importance in keeping with prevailing water levels. When water levels were high, high-water routes were used; the reverse occurred when water levels were low.

One high-water route was through Cross Bayou and up through The Pass into Soda Lake, as shown in Lt. Eugene Woodruff's 1872 *Map of the Red River Raft Region and Cypress Bayou* (**fig. 1-5**). The Pass was not a channel, but rather a floodway. During low-water periods

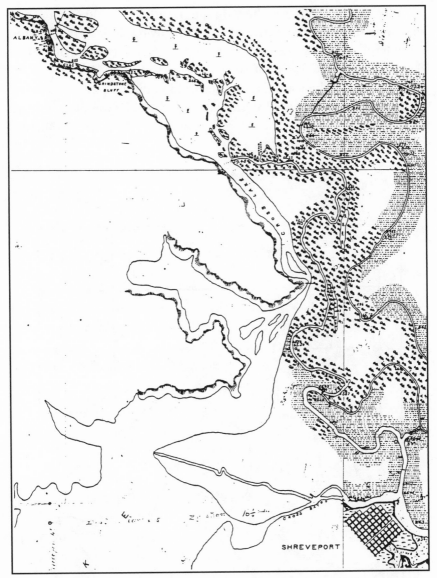

Fig. 1-5. The Pass. *Source: LSU in Shreveport, Noel Memorial Library Archives*

it was practically dry; but during high-water periods, it carried more water than the combined channels of Twelvemile Bayou and the Red River. Although The Pass afforded an opportunity to avoid the more tortuous Twelvemile Bayou passage, it was seldom used, apparently because currents were swift when it was usable.

When water levels were high on the lakes, boats could go anywhere they were not prohibited from doing so by living or dead trees. When water levels were low, they were restricted to the old channel of Cypress Bayou beneath the waters of Soda and Caddo Lakes. The old channel of Cypress Bayou beneath Caddo Lake within Louisiana was investigated by the Department of the Interior in 1914. A profile was prepared that included an old oxbow of Cypress Bayou as well as the submerged channel of Jim's Bayou (**fig. 1-6**).

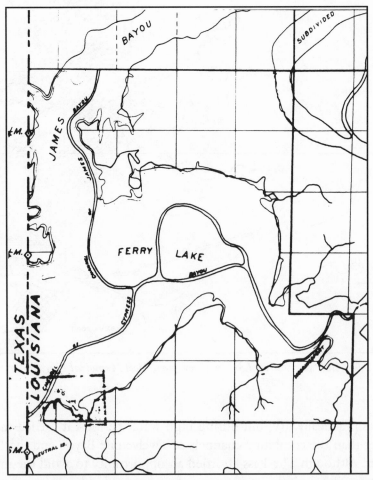

Fig. 1-6. Submerged channels. *Source: Courtesy of LSU Libraries Special Collections, Baton Rouge*

6. At times, backwater pressure on the lakes from the Red River distributaries produced flat-water, lake-like conditions as far up as Jefferson. However, under normal circumstances the pressure was exerted only up to the confluence of Big and Black Cypress Bayous, where the old town of Smithland was located. The six-mile stream segment between Jefferson and Smithland was much more influenced by rainfall in the upper portions of the Cypress Bayou watershed. In addition, the area above the confluence was much shallower than the area below the confluence.

These conditions were described by Woodruff in an 1872 survey report on Cypress Bayou in which he divides the navigation route in terms of geographic segments and then reconsiders the route in terms of flat-water conditions: "Considered as levels in some of which slackwater navigation may be desirable, the division is slightly different. Twelve-mile Bayou is a rapid stream, but deep and crooked, always affording tolerable navigation to Albany, at the foot of Soda Lake. Soda Lake may be considered a level for slackwater navigation from Albany to the head of Willow Pass, having a fall in that distance of 1.63 feet at the time of the survey. From Willow Pass the level of Fairy Lake extends throughout the whole lake and up Cypress Bayou to Smithland. From Smithland to Jefferson, a distance of six miles, the water is shoal, and its depth more dependent upon the stage of Cypress Bayou above this point than upon the lakes below."

Because there was a flat-water condition between Big Willow Pass (immediately below where the dam is at the foot of Caddo Lake today) and the confluence of Big and Black Cypress Bayous, the whole area was considered a lake and is so represented in texts and maps from the 1800s, such as T. S. Hardee's 1871 *Geographical, Historical and Statistical Map of Louisiana* (**fig. 1-7**).

The implications for navigation were dramatic. After passing though Soda Lake, boats faced essentially flat-water operating conditions and could proceed much more rapidly through Caddo Lake and Cypress Bayou than has generally been assumed. At no place in decades of newspaper navigation columns is there any mention of a boat getting into difficulties because of a current in this area.

The hydrologic break at Smithland and the shallowness of the area above Smithland gave rise to numerous navigation difficulties. During low-water periods, the landing, and later the wharf, at Jefferson could not be reached by steamboats on many occasions. As a consequence,

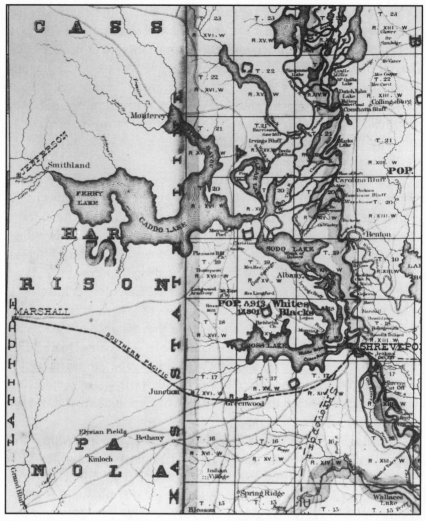

Fig. 1-7. Extent of Caddo Lake. *Source: Courtesy of LSU Libraries Special Collections, Baton Rouge*

boats stopped at various points downstream to offload and take on freight and passengers, giving rise to an overland and barge transport system in the vicinity of Jefferson.

7. When the lakes came into existence in 1800, the existing forests in the valleys of Cypress Bayou and the Red River were killed. By the time steamboats began penetrating Caddo Lake in the early 1840s, these dead trees were in various stages of decay, depending on differences

Fig. 1-8. Caddo Lake stumps. *Source: H. Doc. 488, 59th Cong., 1st Sess.*

in the hardness of the wood of the various species and their susceptibility to decay. It would have been a gloomy scene of immense destruction with numerous navigation impediments and hazards. The density of the decayed trees is illustrated by a photograph of their stump remnants taken by Arthur Veatch in the early 1900s **(fig. 1-8)**.

Contrary to popular opinion, cypress trees do not thrive in permanent water. The ones on the valley floor of Cypress Bayou would die gradually over many decades, but would still be hanging on in the early 1840s. The ones on the banks of Cypress Bayou would still be in good condition. All of those on the banks are now dead, with only a few standing trunks to mark the old channel of Cypress Bayou beneath the waters of Caddo Lake. There are only a few living examples of this old cypress forest, which are to be found at the northern end of the lake and upstream portions of tributary streams such as Harrison Bayou.

The new lakes produced a new stand of cypress trees similar to the dense stands that are found on Caddo Lake today. Cypress germinates in the zone between mean high water and mean low water. Because of the generally higher water levels in the 1800s, the stands would have been formed at slightly higher elevations than the dense stands of today.

The vast majority of the cypress trees on Caddo Lake today are a product of the water regime instituted by the 1914 dam. As a consequence, the first steamboats on Caddo Lake would have encountered dense stands of thin, tall cypress trees similar to the stands on the lake as they appeared in the 1950s. Mature examples of the early stands encountered by the steamboats can be seen in the large trees with flared buttresses along the shoreline at Uncertain, Texas, and in small clusters in the open lake.

The reason that there are not more examples is twofold. First, a tremendous number of trees were harvested, particularly in connection with the development of the offshore oil industry in Caddo Lake in the early decades of the 1900s. Secondly, the original stands were undermined by wave action coupled with dramatic water level changes on the lake, producing large trees with exposed root systems that

Fig. 1-9. Exposed-root cypress. *Source: Courtesy of LSU Libraries Special Collections, Baton Rouge*

eventually toppled over. Photographic documentation of these trees was produced through the 1914 Department of the Interior study (**fig. 1-9**).

Again, the steamboatmen were not passive to these natural conditions. Both dead and living trees were rapidly removed because they were obstructions to navigation and to save on distance and travel time. During low-water periods, trees would be cut down to the low-water line, so that during high water, steamboats could pass over the submerged stumps. This resulted in numerous major and minor "cutroads" on Soda Lake and Caddo Lake. Some of these provided extensive shortcuts; others were merely shavings at the edge of the main channel; and still others provided access to ports and landings.

8. Because the lakes formed in broad, shallow areas, wind was always an important factor in navigation, as it is on Caddo Lake today. Shallow lakes generate high wave action. Problems with wind were exacerbated by the fact that steamboats had large superstructures of decks above shallow-draft hulls that caught the wind, and the sail-like qualities of steamboats were increased when they were lined by solid walls of cotton.

Wind was dangerous under any circumstances and could easily drive a thin-hulled steamboat up onto a submerged stump or log. The best course of action was simply to lie inport until the wind subsided, as reported, for example, in the 7 February 1855 Shreveport *South-Western*: "The Jefferson Herald, of the 30th ult., says that the bayou continues to recede and has fallen eleven inches since our last. Sunday was the most boisterously windy day of the season. The wind on the lake blew a perfect hurricane, and all kinds of water craft were forced to lie in shore."

9. The Red River was an alluvial stream—it carried a tremendous amount of suspended sediments. After the distributaries formed, a great deal of sediment was carried down into the lakes. The current of Red River water observed by H. C. Collins in 1872 that entered into Caddo Lake brought with it Red River sediments that were deposited at the foot of the lake. The slackwater formed by Red River water confronting Cypress Bayou also produced ideal conditions for the deposition of sediments at the foot of Caddo Lake. These sedimentary deposits can be observed during low-water periods on the lake today and were instrumental in the survival of the lake when the distributaries were closed in the 1890s.

The sediments at the foot of Caddo Lake did not pose any navigation difficulties. Such was not the case farther downstream in Soda Lake, where most of the sediments were deposited, as reported by Capt. C. W. Howell in an 1874 survey of the area: "Soda Lake is the main settling basin for the Red River water passing through it. The deposit in this lake has been so great as to entirely cover the knees of the cypress trees yet standing. . . . The depth of such deposit was not ascertained, . . . but the covering of cypress knees indicates a thickness of several feet."

In the upper half of Soda Lake, the old channel of Cypress Bayou was obliterated by sediments. Steamboats ran a straight line in shallow water over these mud flats. A little farther down, at the foot of the lake above Albany Point, sedimentary deposition was even greater. This was also the area of greatest vegetative concentration from the old backwater swamp of Red River. Although a cutroad was formed through this area, low water and stumps were a constant problem. The old channel of Cypress Bayou was available slightly to the north during low-water periods but posed its own set of navigation problems.

The Albany Flats area was the greatest impediment to navigation during the steamboat period. It was the site of many wrecks, groundings, and hangups on stumps. It was the place where navigation generally came to an end during the summer. If boats could make it past the Albany Flats area, they could almost always travel upstream to at least the vicinity of Jefferson. This area also later proved to be the major impediment in plans for navigation improvements because of the peculiarity of its hydrology and topography.

THE RED RIVER CONNECTION

Cypress Bayou and the lakes, the Red River distributary system, wind, sediments, and vegetation old and new were the primary features of the natural setting for navigation along the route from Shreveport to Jefferson. However, the route did not exist in isolation. Most of the boats that traveled the route were from New Orleans and needed to go up the Mississippi and then up the Red.

The Red River was a treacherous stream, as witnessed by its great number of wrecks. At Alexandria there was an escarpment in the river that during low water formed a falls that could not be crossed by steamboats. Closure of the Red to steamboat traffic was not an absolute impediment to steamboat traffic on the Cypress Bayou route because steamboats from New Orleans could transfer freight and passengers at Alexandria to steamboats operating above the falls. However, the route was heavily dependent on Red River water, so closure of the Red generally corresponded with closure of the route. Conversely, there were many points during the steamboat period in which boats could reach Shreveport but not Jefferson.

The Red made one last contribution to the peculiarities of the hydrologic situation. During periods of high water, the Red River below Shreveport was unable to accommodate the combined discharges of Twelvemile Bayou and Cross Bayou. As a consequence, water flowed upstream above Shreveport and below the foot of the raft, draining to the east through an old distributary named Willow Chute, as indicated in an 1855 survey report on the Red River by Col. Charles Fuller: "The channel of the Red River, from the head of the present raft to Shreveport, . . . exhibits such an entire deficit of width, depth and fall, that *up stream* currents are found through more than one half of its distance during every freshet."

Although these upstream flows were undoubtedly used by steamboats during the springtime to travel from Shreveport up the Red River and into Twelvemile Bayou, they were not mentioned in the navigation columns because they were a curiosity with no implication for boat movements. Nevertheless, that the Red River should flow backward is a fitting testimony to the unique, unpredictable, and somewhat bizarre conditions that constituted the natural setting for navigation on Cypress Bayou and the lakes.

·2·

People of the Wilderness

CADDO LOCATIONS

The formation of the Sodo Lake complex in 1800 and its sustenance by the Red River distributary system provided the potential for navigation on the Cypress Bayou and the lakes route. However, this potential was not to be realized for many decades. Navigability was of little use without settlement, and settlement was restricted by the occupation of the lands south and west of the Red River by the Caddo Indians. In addition, navigability on the route was pointless without access to the Red River, and this was prohibited by the existence of the Great Raft. Both of these impediments were overcome in April 1835 through the Caddo Indian Treaty and through the removal of the raft up to the mouth of Twelvemile Bayou by Capt. Henry Shreve.

The Kadohadacho, or Great Chiefs, of the Caddo Nation were the head of a loosely joined group of tribes speaking the same language, deriving their authority from tradition and from sustained wise judgment. From time immemorial, according to their legends, they lived on the south side of Red River in the great bend, as shown on Nicholas King's map of the Freeman and Custis Red River expedition, which was sponsored by Thomas Jefferson in 1806 (**fig. 2-1**). Although the area in which Shreveport eventually came to be located was part of their hunting range, they did not reside there until 1795 and did not

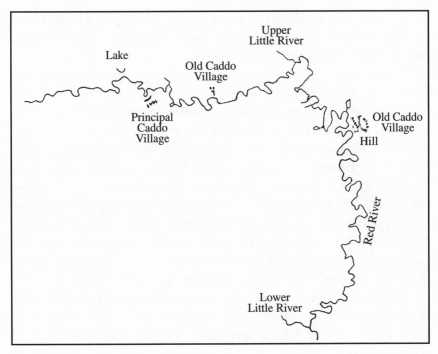

Fig. 2-1. Upper Red River Caddo locations

take up their last independent residence on Jim's Bayou, which enters
Caddo Lake, until 1800.

As with other Native American tribes, they had no natural resistance
to European diseases and were continually devastated by them after
contact had taken place. They were further weakened by continuous
attacks by the Osages, a traditional enemy farther to the west composed
of very large, very aggressive warriors. As a consequence, in 1788 they
moved farther east and in 1790 took refuge with a related tribe, the Petit
(or Little) Caddo, as recorded in a 27 March 1790 letter from Louis de
Blanc, the commandant at Natchitoches, to Esteban Miro, the Spanish
governor in New Orleans: "The Great Caddo tribe of Indians found
itself obliged two years ago to change the location of its village on account
of the continual war being waged on them by the Osage tribe. Being
persecuted incessantly by their enemies, these Indians were obliged last
month to take refuge in the village of the Little Caddo."

The historian Dan Flores interprets the Little Caddo village to be
the lowermost of the three upper Red River Caddo Indian villages.

This interpretation is almost certainly correct. The Kadohadacho would have moved initially as far away as possible from their enemies within the confines of their traditional villages.

The move to the area presently occupied by Shreveport did not take place until 1795, again because of disease and attacks by the Osage. There are two accounts of this move. The first is by Indian Agent John Sibley in his April 1805 "Historical Sketches of the Several Indian Tribes," which was written in Natchitoches. Sibley is clearly speaking about the site marked "Principal Caddo Village" on King's map when he writes about the Caddos: "They formerly lived on the south bank of the river, by the course of the river 375 miles higher up, at a beautiful prairie, which has a clear lake of good water in the middle of it, surrounded by a pleasant and fertile country, which had been the residence of their ancestors from time immemorial." Sibley also writes that "the Indians left it about fourteen years ago, on account of a dreadful sickness that visited them," adding, "They settled on the river nearly opposite where they now live, on a low place" before moving to the Jim's Bayou site, which, according to Sibley, had been occupied only since 1800.

The second account is by Peter Custis of the Freeman and Custis expedition in a July 1806 record from the Coushatta Indian village at Cedar Bluffs, clearly referring to the Jim's Bayou site: "The Caddoes reside about 50 miles from this according to some accounts & not so far according to others/on a small Creek emptying into a lake which communicates with the River a little above the Raft. It has been 11 years since they came to that place.—They formerly lived on the River in a large Prairie said to be 150 leagues above this.—They were driven thence by the Osage Indians who have always been at war with them."

Sibley appears to be in disagreement with de Blanc on the abandonment of the original village (de Blanc: 1788; Sibley: about 1791) but in agreement if it is assumed that Sibley is writing about the abandonment of the Petit Caddo village (de Blanc: 1790; Sibley: about 1791). Sibley does not mention the Petit Caddo village. Instead, he says that the Caddos moved immediately from their original village to a Red River floodplain village directly east of the Jim's Bayou site.

Sibley disagrees with Custis on the date of movement to the Jim's Bayou site (Sibley: 1800; Custis: 1795). Custis does not mention the Petit Caddo village or the Red River floodplain village, saying that the

Caddos moved directly from their original village to the Jim's Bayou site.

To complicate matters, Sibley prepared a list of distances upriver on the Red for the Freeman and Custis expedition that is appended to their report. In this list, Sibley provides yet another intermediate location for the Caddos—the Cedar Bluffs site occupied by the Coushattas: "To Conchetta villages where the Cadoux lived, 9 years ago." Sibley contradicts himself (not one, but two, intermediate sites); and, by appending the list, Custis opposes himself (not direct, but at least one intermediate site).

These problems can be resolved by keeping a few simple points in mind:

1. Neither Sibley nor Custis was attempting to present a detailed account of the movements of the Caddo Indians.

2. Sibley and Custis were both drawing on the same source: the Indian trader Francois Grappe, who lived in Campti and operated a cattle ranch on Lake Bistineau. Grappe was Sibley's informant on the Caddos and on the middle Red River. He was also the guide and interpreter for the Freeman and Custis expedition.

3. Both accounts center on the abandonment of the traditional villages, the move south, and the establishment of the final village on Jim's Bayou. The disagreements arise out of different pieces of information that were used by Sibley and Custis to present the same story and the varying implications that were drawn from them. The total story was, in fact, quite complex, involving six sites and five moves.

The original village of the Caddos was the one, according to Sibley, on the south bank of Red River where the French had a post. This was the "Principal Caddo Village" on King's map. In 1788, the Caddos moved from this village to another village farther away from their enemies, probably to the first downriver "Old Caddo Village" marked on King's map. In 1790, they moved to the Petit Caddo village, almost certainly the next downriver "Old Caddo Village" marked on King's map.

In 1795, they abandoned their traditional villages and moved downstream to the vicinity of what later became Shreveport (**fig. 2-2**). This is the significance of Custis's statement, "It has been 11 years since they came to that place." It is easy to understand why Custis would have misunderstood what Grappe was relating verbally (that they had come eleven years ago), because the Caddo had just come

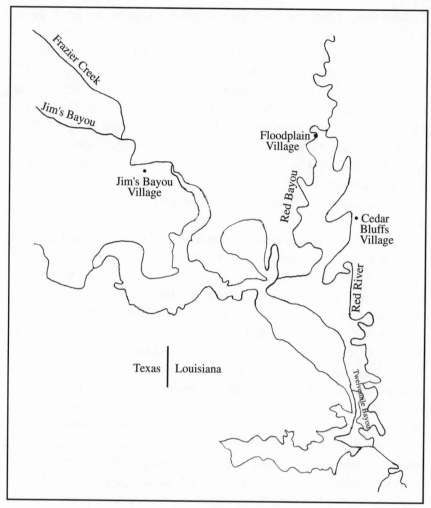

Fig. 2-2. Caddo locations in the Sodo Lake area

from their Jim's Bayou village. There were two intermediate steps unknown to Custis but that were related by Grappe and independently verified.

When the Caddos came to the Shreveport area in 1795, they located first at Cedar Bluffs, as recounted by the Indian trader Anthony Glass, who visited the Coushatta village at Cedar Bluffs in 1808 and reported the following: "Camped and found we were within one mile of the Conchetta village.—On the East Bank of Red River. . . . these Conchettas (as they are called) are Emigrants from the Creeks. have not long lived here. They are friendly with the Caddoes who own the Country & who used to occupy the same spot; But now live about thirty Miles South West on the Lake the Caddoes left the place on account of having lost many of their People by the Small Poxe it being a custom to abandon a Village where many have died. This place is nearly in North Latitude 32,50: and distant from Nackitosh by the usual Road about 120 miles in a rich beautiful place."

The Cedar Bluffs site was abandoned because of disease (Glass) in 1797, as per Sibley's account of river miles upstream provided to the Freeman and Custis expedition in 1806: "To Conchetta villages where the Cadoux lived, 9 years ago." The site was then occupied by the Coushattas in 1803 or 1804 according to the Freeman-Custis journal account, which says that the Coushatta village they were visiting in 1806 had been built within two or three years.

When the Caddos abandoned Cedar Bluffs in 1797, they did not go immediately to Jim's Bayou, but rather occupied a site on the Red River floodplain. Sibley describes the floodplain site in relation to the Jim's Bayou location (which was occupied at the time that Sibley was writing in 1805) in the following terms: "They settled on the river nearly opposite where they now live, on a low place, but were drove from there on account of its overflowing, occasioned by a jam of timber choking the river at a point below them."

Glass confirmed this intermediate site. After he left the Coushatta village, he proceeded across the Red River to its western floodplain and then traveled north and slightly west for nine miles through rich prairies until he saw the "remains of Caddo Huts and many Peach trees." From the description, it is obvious that this was not a temporary encampment. It had been occupied sufficiently long enough for peach trees to have been cultivated (the Caddos were fond of peaches), and it had not been abandoned for very many years when Glass saw it in July 1808.

Of additional interest is the fact that the directional figures and mileage recorded by Glass terminate in an "Indian Village" at the confluence of Red Bayou and Stumpy Dam Bayou marked on R. E. Jacobs's 1935 map of *Routes of Steamboats to Surround Rafts in Red River* (fig. 2-3). Sewell 1831 is given as the source. Despite the misspelling, this was Washington Seawell, who conducted a navigation improvement project in that area during the early 1830s. The ultimate source of this particular piece of information must have been one of Seawell's field reports (which are in the National Archives), because no

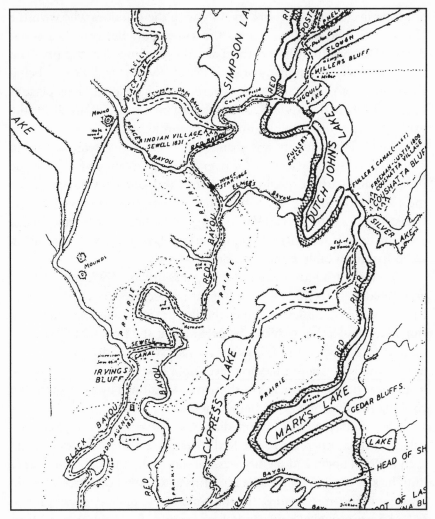

Fig. 2-3. Caddo floodplain village. *Source: LSU in Shreveport, Noel Memorial Library Archives*

mention is made of an Indian village in the published reports on Seawell's project.

The floodplain village was abandoned in 1800 in favor of the Jim's Bayou site. Referring to this site, Sibley writes in 1805, "They have lived where they now do, only five years." Sibley also gives the reason for the move when he says that the Caddos were driven from the floodplain of the Red River "on account of its overflowing, occasioned by a jam of timber choking the river at a point below them." This jam of timber was obviously the Great Raft, whose head would have been a few miles below Twelvemile Bayou in 1800.

The Caddo Indians related a story about the formation of the Sodo Lake complex: "The earth trembled, the ground sank, and water poured over the land where the tribe had lived." The tribe was saved by the actions of a wise chief who had a premonition of the disaster and moved his people to higher ground. Although embellished, this story was rooted in the real experience of the Caddos in their floodplain village on the occasion of the break in the bend in the Red River in 1800 that brought the Sodo Lake complex into existence. The Caddos were too high up to be in the direct path of the flood, but they were near enough that the rushing waters precipitated a retreat to high bluffs on the newly formed Caddo Lake.

THE JIM'S BAYOU VILLAGE

The final home of the Caddos in the Shreveport area was on Jim's Bayou (also James Bayou or Jeems Bayou). The first description of this site is by Sibley, who writes in 1805 that the Caddos "Live about thirty-five miles west of the main branch of Red river, on a bayou or creek, called, by them, Sodo, which is navigable for pirogues only, within about six miles of their village, and that only in the rainy season." The general location is established by Sibley in relation to the floodplain village, which was said to have been on the Red River nearly opposite the site that he was describing. Looking at Sibley's comment from the perspective of the floodplain village, Jim's Bayou is nearly opposite the floodplain village that Glass saw and fits the description of a waterbody that is pirogue navigable during the rainy season, at least for the unflooded portion above Monterey Lake. Sibley cannot have been referring to Cypress Bayou, because it is much too large. Sibley's description makes the important observation that the village was located on the bayou proper rather than the flooded valley of Jim's Bayou that constitutes the northern extension of Caddo Lake. It is not surprising that the Caddos called the bayou Sodo—the various waterbodies that formed the complex were thought of as a single entity.

A second description of the site is given by Peter Custis in 1806, writing in relation to the Coushatta village: "The Caddoes reside about 50 miles from this according to some accounts & not so far according to others/ on a small Creek emptying into a lake which communicates with the River a little above the Raft." The key piece of information in this account relates to the raft. The "communication" with the Red River that was a little above the head of the raft in 1806 must have been Twelvemile Bayou, because Sibley reports that the raft had closed Bayou Pierre about 1799. Given the unified conception of the Sodo Lake complex at the time, Custis is apparently talking about Jim's Bayou, which entered Sodo Lake, which communicated with the Red River through Twelvemile Bayou.

The two other contemporary descriptions of the site are by Glass and Thomas Freeman, the other half of the Freeman and Custis expedition. Writing in relation to the Coushatta village, Glass says that the Caddos "live about thirty Miles South West on the Lake." The Freeman and Custis expedition bypassed the raft to the east and reentered the Red River at Willow Chute (above Shreveport). Freeman reports that to the west of the river above and below the point of reentry there was a large prairie (what came to be known as Caddo Prairie) extending for several miles: "Beyond this Prairie there is a large lake, on the west of which, and nearly 30 miles from Red River, lies the principal village of the Caddos."

From these accounts it can be concluded that the Caddos lived on a small bayou or creek that flowed into the west side of the Sodo Lake complex, with Jim's Bayou as a likely candidate. The mileage figures are in obvious disagreement; but the major problem that they cause lies in the conception that they give of a village located at a substantial distance from the Red River (in one case, almost to Jefferson). It should be kept in mind that these were not straightline miles, but rather estimates based on horseback transport on winding trails through hilly areas. Furthermore, the estimates were given by men on the basis of secondhand information during a period in which people were not even careful about the spelling of their own names.

The Freeman and Custis party was visited by the Caddos at the Coushatta village. The Caddos left their village in the morning and arrived at the Coushatta village at noon, traveling at a leisurely pace and preceded by a runner who had been sent to determine why they had not arrived the day before. These events suggest a village much closer to the Red River than is given by the mileage figures interpreted as straightline distances. It is therefore necessary to turn to other sources of information to determine a more exact location.

The Caddo village is shown on William Darby's 1816 *Map of Louisiana* (**fig. 2-4**) on the south side of a stream entering Clear Lake from the west. No such stream ever existed. The stream pattern is clearly that of Jim's Bayou and its tributary Frazier Creek (**see fig. 2-2**). Darby obviously transposed the stream to Clear Lake from the flooded portion of Jim's Bayou. Such a mistake is perfectly understandable given the fact that Darby was the first to map Northwest Louisiana, operating under the most primitive of conditions and piecing together bits of information from various sources.

Darby's map shows the Caddo village well to the east of the Louisiana line. This is not the present-day Louisiana line, which runs through the middle of Caddo Lake. In 1816, it was actually the boundary between the United States and New Spain, which, by preexisting convention, was a line running directly north from the point at which the thirty-second parallel of latitude crossed the Sabine. Darby was the first to determine this point and run this line. With respect to the location of the Caddo village, the important problem is that what appears on the map is not what Darby discovered on the ground, as is

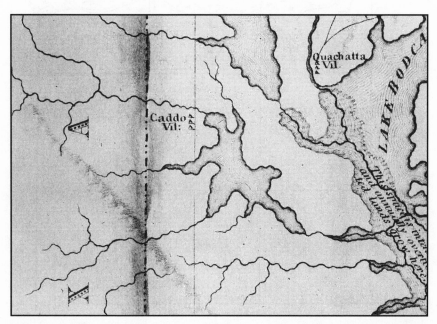

Fig. 2-4. Darby's Caddo village. *Source: Courtesy of LSU Libraries Special Collections, Baton Rouge*

indicated in a 28 November 1812 letter from Sibley to William Eustis, the secretary of war: "Mr. William Darby a Mathematician has been for Nearly two years Employed in Collecting Materials for publishing a Map of the State of Louissiana, he left this place about Six Weeks Ago to ascertain the 32 deg. of North Latitude on the River Sabine & to Measure from thence One Degree or Sixty Nine Miles to the Intersection of the Parallel of 33 degrees of North Latitude, which is the North West Corner of this State. Mr. Darby found the 32° on the Sabine a few Miles below the Nandaco Village Near a Large Bayou called Nassosette, & in Running the North line, both the Nandaco & Caddo Towns are left out of this State, the line passing about Six or Eight Miles to the Eastward of them both, greatly to the disappointment of the Indians."

An "Indian Village" is shown immediately south of Jim's Bayou on an 1839 Louisiana General Land Office map for Township 21 North,

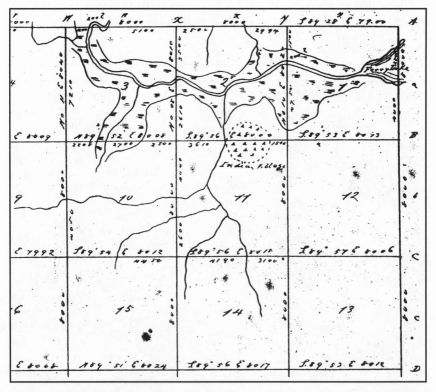

Fig. 2-5. Jim's Bayou Caddo village. *Source: Louisiana State Land Office, Division of Administration*

40

Range 16 West (fig. 2-5). The village site is actually about three miles into Texas and was covered by the Louisiana surveyors because the boundary between the United States and the Republic of Texas was indefinite until 1841. This appears to be the Caddo village identified by Darby (south of Jim's Bayou and a few miles into Texas, with the mileage discrepancy accounted for by the inexactness of Darby's survey).

Although the Caddos had sold their land in 1835, a few years before the Land Office survey was conducted in the fourth quarter of 1838, they did not leave the Caddo Lake area immediately. The surveyor

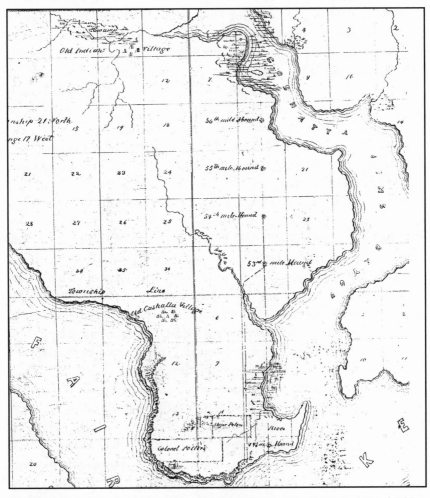

Fig. 2-6. Abandoned Caddo village. *Source: Courtesy Texas General Land Office, Austin*

visited the village, but his notes do not indicate who, if anyone, was there. Nevertheless, the village was apparently occupied. It would have been represented on the map as abandoned if that had been the case. This village was apparently abandoned by 1842, because it is designated as an "Old Indian Village" on an anonymous map (**fig. 2-6**) produced after the United States–Republic of Texas boundary survey in 1841 and before the death of Robert Potter in March 1842 (Potter's home is shown on the map and the inscription suggests that he was still alive).

Maps and contemporary accounts indicate that there was a trail between the Caddo and Coushatta villages and that this trail branched off to the south to Shenix's Ferry at Stormy Point on Caddo Lake. This trail is mentioned in a 1 June 1841 journal inclusion by the United States–Republic of Texas boundary surveyors in conjunction with the establishment of the fifty-eighth and fifty-ninth mile markers upward from the Sabine: "after a most circuitous day's journey, encamped at a spring of delicious water, on an old Indian trail leading from Caddo prairie to the Coushatta village, and a short distance west of the boundary." This trail is shown on the survey map (**fig. 2-7**) as running just north of what would be Monterey Lake on a contemporary map and leading directly into the general area of the Indian village shown on the Land Office map.

The historic evidence for a Jim's Bayou location for the Caddo Indian village is firm. It can be supplemented by two additional pieces of verifiable evidence. Sibley says that the Caddo agricultural operations were on a flat prairie of white clay soil. This prairie, which is immediately north (across the bayou) from the Indian village on the Land Office map, can be seen about two miles west of the Louisiana-Texas line off the old Vivian airport road. In addition, the Caddos called their village "Timber Hill." The site shown on the 1839 map is occupied by a large timbered hill that would have contained a virgin pine forest in 1800.

In his "Historical Sketches of the Several Indian Tribes," Sibley says that in the year that they moved to the Jim's Bayou site, "the small pox got amongst them, and destroyed nearly one half of them; it was in the winter season, and they practiced plunging into the creek, on the first appearance of the irruption, and died in a few hours." Three years later, "they had the measles, of which several more of them died." By 1805 when Sibley was writing, their numbers had been reduced to 450 adults, including a few strangers, although they continued to exercise a great deal of authority over related tribes: "The whole number

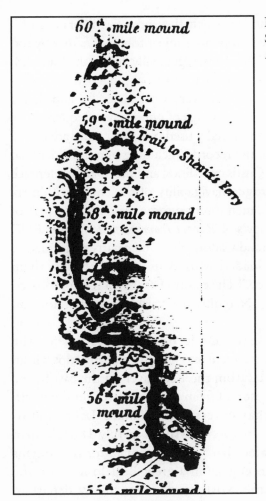

Fig. 2-7. Caddo trail to Shenix's Ferry. *Source: S. Doc. 199, 27ᵗʰ Cong., 2ⁿᵈ Sess.*

of what they call warriors is now reduced to about one hundred, who are looked upon somewhat like Knights of Malta, or some distinguished military order. . . . Besides these, there are of old men, and strangers who live amongst them, nearly the same number; but there are forty or fifty more women than men. This nation has great influence over the Yattassees, Nandakoes, Nabadaches, Inies or Tackies, Nacogdoches, Keychies, Adaize, and Natchitoches, who all speak the Caddo language, look up to them as their fathers, visit and marry among them, and join in all their wars."

Sibley also describes agricultural activities and the country surrounding the Jim's Bayou site: "The Caddoes raise corn, beans, pumpkins, &c. but the land on which they now live is prairie, of a white clay soil, very flat; their crops are subject to injury, either by too wet or too dry a season. . . . The country, generally, round the Caddoes, is hilly, not very rich; growth, a mixture of oak, hickory, and pine, interspersed with prairies, which are very rich, generally, and fit for cultivation. There are creeks and springs of good water frequent."

Although the Caddo undoubtedly used pirogues, there are only a few mentions of such use in the records, including minor incidents in the journal of the Freeman-Custis expedition and the oblique reference by Sibley regarding the pirogue navigability of the bayou within six miles of the village. Specific mention of pirogue usage on the part of the Caddos is given in Sibley's *A Report from Natchitoches in 1807*, which records that "The Grand Caddo Chief and a party of 15 men of that Nation in Perogues loaded with skins arrived. I gave them Provisions & a carrot Tobacco." The carote (French for roll) of tobacco was apparently of the fine Natchitoches variety and therefore an expensive present.

Horses were the preferred mode of transportation for the Caddos, particularly for the frequent and lengthy hunting trips within their territory, which ranged from the Red River on the east to the Blackland Prairie on the west and from the Red River on the north to the Cypress Bayou that enters into Wallace Lake (below Shreveport) on the south. In a letter written in July 1831, Indian Agent Jehiel Brooks indicated that "It is customary for the Indians of this Agency generally to engage in a great Buffalo hunt on the Prairies which lie far to the Northwest. They chiefly depart in November and return in the April following."

SETTLERS AND AGENTS

Sovereignty over this territory was always split during the period of Caddoan occupancy, at first between France and Spain and then, after the Louisiana Purchase of 1803, between the United States and New Spain, Mexico (New Spain's successor in 1821), and the Republic of Texas (Mexico's successor in 1836). Although dual sovereignty caused some problems for the Caddos because of conflicting calls on their allegiance, it did little to affect movement within their territory. This was a wilderness area, difficult to control because of its remoteness and lacking a formal jurisdictional dividing line until the United States–

Republic of Texas boundary survey in 1841, only four years before Texas entered the Union.

The remoteness of the area is well illustrated by Darby's map **(fig. 2-8)**. There are no towns in Northwest Louisiana in 1816, only the villages of the Caddo, Coushatta, and Yatassee. Settlers are so few that they are shown individually. The raft dominates the landscape, flooding the Red River bottomlands and thereby prohibiting their settlement; and the course of the river is lost in innumerable watercourses, prohibiting its navigation and further restricting the opportunity for settlement. The Caddos lie in the center of a vast wilderness.

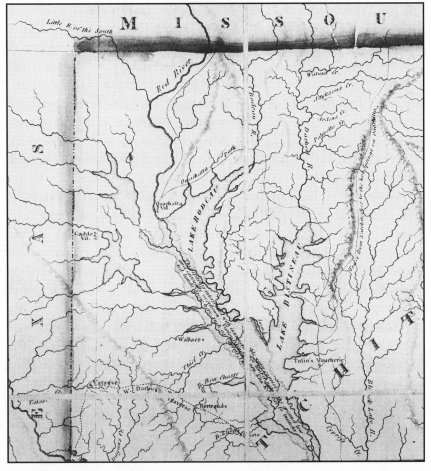

Fig. 2-8. Northwest Louisiana in 1816. *Source: Courtesy of LSU Libraries Special Collections, Baton Rouge*

The closest settlers are the brothers Thomas and Jacob Wallace, who moved to the south shore of Wallace Lake in 1805 from the Bayou Pierre settlement farther downstream on the floodplain of the Red River. Jacob was the first and Thomas the third son of an English family that emigrated from Virginia to Louisiana in 1776. Thomas was born in 1780 at Opelousas and served in 1826 as a guide for the first federal survey of the Sodo Lake area. Thomas also provided testimony to Joseph Paxton concerning the head of the raft in relation to Lake Bodcau in Paxton's famous 1828 "Letter in Relation to the Raft of Red River." The Wallace house was designated the first Caddo Parish courthouse by the Louisiana Legislature in 1838.

Tulin's Vaucherie on the east shore of Lake Bistineau was the cattle ranch of Francois Grappe, friend of the Caddos and known affectionately as Touline. Grappe was born in 1747 at the French post adjacent to the Caddos' upriver village. His mother was half Indian, although apparently not Caddo. When the post closed in 1763 (when Spain acquired Louisiana), his father, Alexis, took the family to Campti. Alexis was one of the few Frenchmen licensed by the Spanish to trade with the Indians. Francois served as his father's assistant in this trade until Alexis died around 1775, after which Francois continued the trade business, while at the same time acting as an interpreter for the Spanish and the Americans.

Grappe lived in Campti but operated a spacious cattle ranch on Lake Bistineau, with 1,500 head of cattle in 1812 according to John Maley's journal. Because of its location on the eastern bypass around the Great Raft, the vaucherie was a stopping place for persons traveling north such as Glass and Maley. Because Grappe was intimately acquainted with the middle Red River and the various Indian tribes in the area, he was a major informant for Sibley in the sketches of Indian tribes and the Red River country and served as a guide and interpreter for expeditions such as that of Freeman and Custis. The Caddos granted a large tract of land to Grappe's heirs in the 1835 Caddo Treaty in remembrance of the kindnesses that Grappe had extended to them.

On the American side of the Caddos' territory, the United States government established Indian agents and agency houses at Natchitoches (1805–21), on the Sulphur Fork of Red River (1821–25), on Caddo Prairie a few miles northeast of Clear Lake (1825–31), and at Peach Orchard Bluff on Bayou Pierre (1831–34). The function of the agents was to protect the Indians, a responsibility they fulfilled diligently until the later years. In conjunction with the agency houses, "factories" were developed to trade with the Indians and to provide services such as blacksmithing, both to gain allegiance and to diminish the deleterious influence of traders who plied the Indians with whiskey to strike better bargains for their goods.

Apart from the Indian agents, two of the most prominent people connected with these operations were Larkin Edwards, who was employed as an interpreter for the Caddos, and his son-in-law, Jacob Irwin, blacksmith and gunsmith for the Caddos from 1813 to 1835. Edwards was from Tennessee and first appears in the historic record for the Red River area in June 1820, when he briefly took care of the Sulphur Fork trading house in the absence of Captain Fowler, who had become ill, closed the trading house, and gone to Natchitoches, where he died of consumption.

Edwards abandoned the trading house in January 1821. When Fowler's replacement, Major McClellan, arrived, he found the furs, goods, and structures in a deplorable condition and that Edwards had taken most of Fowler's furniture and all of his belongings. He ordered Edwards to return the property and refused to settle accounts with him until he did. As it turned out, Edwards had been justified in his actions because he did not receive any pay while he was taking care of the trading house.

Edwards had been married to an Elizabeth Lovelace in Tennessee. They were separated in 1815, and she died in 1820. Edwards later married a Caddo Indian who was said to be daughter to the chief. Edwards is recorded to have had three daughters and four sons, including Mary, who married Jacob Irwin, and John, who also served as interpreter for the Caddos and died shortly after the treaty was signed. Apparently none of these children were products of the marriage to the Caddo woman. Progeny from the second marriage probably would not have been recorded, particularly if the marriage did not take place through a civil ceremony.

As an interpreter for the Caddos and one who had married into the tribe, Edwards was a close friend of the Caddos. As a consequence, he was granted a parcel of land (640 acres) at Bennett's Bluff through the treaty. This land was sold to Angus McNeill in 1836 and became the nucleus of the city of Shreveport. Edwards died in 1842 at his home on Coates' Bluff, which was the next bluff downriver from Bennett's Bluff.

SHENIX'S FERRY

The first white family to live on the Cypress Bayou and lakes route was that of James Shenick (also Shemick, Schinnick, Shennick, Shinnick, Scheunick, Shenix), who operated a ferry across Caddo Lake from at least 1824 to at least 1841. This ferry operation was the second instance of navigation along the route (the first being Caddo pirogues), and the operation and its owner were to make lasting contributions to the nomenclature of Caddo Lake.

The ferry operation is shown on the 1839 Land Office map for Township 20 North, Range 16 West **(fig. 2-9)**. The ferry ran between Stormy Point on the north shore of Caddo Lake in a southwesterly direction slightly southeast of where the power line is today. Structures are shown on the north and south shores, with "Shenix's Improvement" designating the structures. "Improvement" was a common term on these early maps to denote any habitations or areas under cultivation. The ferry is shown with a pointed bow, a square stern, and a sweep at the rear for guidance. She was probably propelled by oars.

Further information on the ferry is provided by May notations in the journal of the surveyors who determined the boundary between the United States and the Republic of Texas in 1841:

> 21st.—Despatched Mr. Conway, United States surveyor, in search of a boat to transport the party and baggage train across the lake. . . .
>
> 22nd.—The party sent with Mr. Conway in search of a boat arrived in charge of a large ferry scow, and were engaged in repairing her the remainder of the day.
>
> 23d, 24th, and 25th.—Employed in transporting men, baggage, provisions, wagons, &c., across the lake. . . .

Given the nature of what was transported, this must have been a very large vessel. That she was a scow means that the bow was square at the waterline. The pointed bow above enabled easy access at landings.

The evidence for the existence of the ferry from at least 1824 is given in a 1 October letter from Indian Agent George Gray, writing from the Sulphur Fork Agency to Thomas McKenney in Washington, D.C.: "The number of whites within the immediate vicinity of this

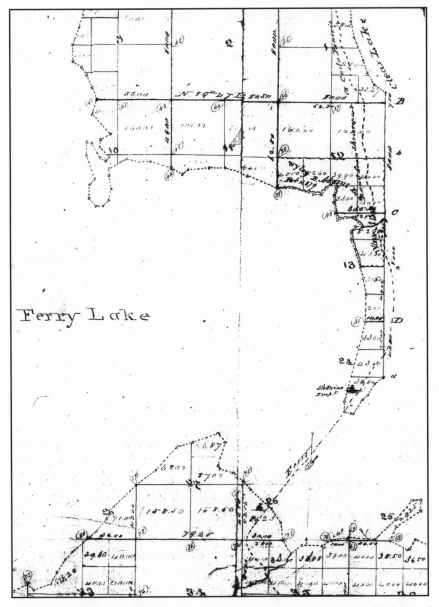

Fig. 2-9. Shenix's Ferry. *Source: Louisiana State Land Office, Division of Administration*

Agency, are two families one Settled on a large Lake, for the purpose of Keeping Ferry, for the accommodation of the Indians and Travellers, and the other on a large Creek or River, for the same purpose, Red

River is the largest stream within the limits of the Agency, and is navigable for a long distance, for Keel Boats, in high water."

The ferry is mentioned occasionally in the letters from the Indian agents for the 1820s and 1830s. During the 1820s, Gray disbursed funds for "ferryage over Caddo Lake." The first disbursement recorded was $100 for 1827. In early 1831, Indian Agent Jehiel Brooks, giving reasons for relocating the agency from Caddo Prairie to Peach Orchard Bluff (on Bayou Pierre below Shreveport), pointed out that "the Indians will meet with no obstructions at any time in their visits thereto, the distance to travel from their Villages shortened very considerably, with a free Boat navigation at any season of the year and the expense of transportation materially diminished." Conversely, Brooks spoke disparagingly of "the Sodo Lake ferry (which is particularly inconvenient to the Agency, and Indians alike owing to the frequency of high winds)." After the agency was moved, Brooks said that $100 a year had been saved because the Indians no longer needed to be ferried across Sodo Lake.

The Land Office map shows the ferry operation as continuous with the "Road from Shreveport to Caddo Prairie." Shreveport was not in existence in 1824 when the ferry was first in operation. The trail went south to Natchitoches, where the Indians traded, and by 1839 it branched east to Shreveport after going around the western end of Cross Lake. The trail also went north, branching to the Caddo village to the west, as shown on the 1841 boundary survey map (see fig. 2-7), and to the east to the Coushatta village at Cedar Bluffs, as mentioned in the survey journal.

Prior to the formation of Caddo Lake in 1800, the place at which the ferry came to be operated was apparently the traditional crossing of Cypress Bayou and its valley by the Indians. After the lake was formed and before the ferry was in operation, it was necessary to pursue a circuitous route to the west of the Sodo Lake complex, with Cypress Bayou forded in the vicinity of present-day Highway 43. Stormy Point, as its name implies, was not a hospitable place for a ferry crossing, which was better accommodated by the short distance and protected environment of the Mooringsport peninsula area. Evidently the ferry was located at Stormy Point because this was the traditional crossing.

From these texts, it is apparent that the ferry was started in the 1820s and maintained at least through the early 1830s for the sake of the Indians, whose passage was paid by the federal government as part of the benefit package to maintain their allegiance. The ferry replaced the circuitous western route around Caddo Lake as shown on Henry Tanner's 1820 *Louisiana and Mississippi*, which also correctly delineates the stream and flooded portions of Jim's Bayou and the location of the Caddo village (**fig. 2-10**). Because the ferry is not listed as government property, it was a private enterprise, with the operator receiving $100 a year from the government for the transport of Indians and miscellaneous fees for other services and the transport of occasional travelers and traders.

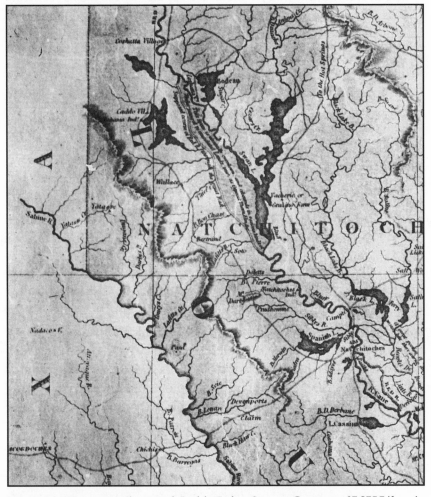

Fig. 2-10. Western trail around Caddo Lake. *Source: Courtesy of LSU Libraries Special Collections, Baton Rouge*

The linkage between the ferry and James Shenick is provided by the Land Office map. No one by the name of Shenix appears in any of the records of the period. However, a James Shinnick (or Schinnick) is mentioned occasionally in the 1830s correspondence file for the Indian Agent Brooks. In January 1831, Larkin Edwards, James Shinnick, John W. Edwards, and Jacob Irwin provided testimony on the flooding of Caddo Prairie, which was used in support of Brooks's contention that the agency should be moved to Peach Orchard Bluff.

James Schinnick was paid $66 on 7 April 1831 for the March transport of materials from the abandoned Caddo Prairie Agency to Peach Orchard Bluff. The payment was apparently for transport across Caddo Lake; other people are mentioned as being involved in the land transport of materials. The receipt was signed by Larkin Edwards, John W. Edwards, and James Schinnick. "X, his mark" was used in conjunction with Schinnick's signature, indicating that he was illiterate.

It is easy to see how the name Shenick could have been corrupted through verbal transmission to Shenix. It is not, at first glance, easy to see why a white man with a family would have located in the Caddo Lake wilderness in 1824 to transport Indians across the lake. The answer is given by Indian Agent Brooks in a deposition concerning the Caddo Treaty in response to a question concerning when he had last seen Larkin Edwards: "I was at Coats's Bluff in the month of February, 1838, where I saw Larkin Edwards, at the house of his son-in-law, a Mr. Scheunick. He appeared to be very infirm and imbecile; and the said Scheunick so represented his situation to me at the time."

Although it was Edwards, not Shenick, who lived at Coates' Bluff, the key piece of information is that Shenick was Edwards's son-in-law. James Shenick was married to Edwards's daughter Emily. Another daughter, Ann, was married to an Abner Shemick, apparently James's brother. James was able to operate the ferry on Caddo lands with government support because he was Edwards's son-in-law, and Edwards was a friend of the Caddos and an employee (as interpreter for the Caddos) of the Indian Agency. A woman with children would have been comfortable under such circumstances because she was afforded special protection through a family relationship.

The last indication of the existence of Shenix's Ferry is John LaTourette's 1845 *Reference Map of the State of Louisiana*. The ferry operation was sold in about 1846 to S. D. Pitts, who ran it under his own name as a strictly commercial venture until about 1857, when it was superseded by a ferry at Mooringsport slightly downstream. Shenick moved to Myrtis, Louisiana, which is above Vivian, where he built a home (ca. 1850) at Myrtis Mill Pond and died in 1863, as indicated by a succession notice in the 14 January 1864 *South-Western*. He left two legacies to the Caddo Lake area:

1. "Ferry Lake" was the official name for Caddo Lake until the early 1900s. Although there is no firm evidence, it is obvious that Ferry Lake was named for Shenix's Ferry.

2. "Jeems Bayou" on contemporary maps is a corruption of "Jim's Bayou," which is mentioned by name in the survey journal and designated "Coushatta Jim's Bayou" on maps of the period (**see fig. 2-6**). The bayou was named after James Shenick, who was nicknamed Coushatta Jim because of his close association with the Indians.

The last mention of Shenick is given in an 1899 report by the geologist Arthur Veatch covering Stormy Point and Dahahuit, the last great chief of the Caddos (who died early in 1833 according to a contemporary account by Jehiel Brooks):

> *Stormy point, Ferry lake.* A cellar dug near the end of Stormy point by Col. S. D. Pitts in 1885, disclosed quite an amount of pottery at a depth of from four and one-half to five feet. One large pot, when found, was full of living ants, evidently attracted there by something the pot contained. A smaller pot was filled with children's bones. An iron tomahawk, two iron rifle barrels and an iron knife about eight inches long were also found.
>
> About 1870 high water washed out the bluff on the southwestern corner of the point and exposed a skeleton. The forehead was covered with a thin highly ornamented piece of silver bent to fit the skull. On the back of the head was a circular piece of silver. These pieces are said to have been analyzed by a local jeweler and pronounced virgin silver. On the shoulders were thin crescent shaped pieces of metal. They were described as having been coated with green, and are hence inferred to have been copper.
>
> The son-in-law of Larking Edwards, the interpreter and friend of the Caddoes, "Old James Shemick," from whom the place was bought, stated several years before the skeleton was found that the last chief of the Caddoes was buried somewhere in that vicinity.

This point was a favorite place for the collecting of the Caddo Indians when they desired to start for Shreveport. They crossed the lake at Newport point and their trail from there to Shreveport is said to have been quite visible as late as 1860.

OTHER TRIBES

From 1800, when the Caddos occupied the Jim's Bayou site, until 1835, when they sold their land to the United States, the territory occupied by the Caddos was a catchment area for tribes and tribal remnants driven west by continuous white pressure. In a June 1827 letter, the Indian Agent Gray describes Caddo Prairie as a "whirlpool that is sucking within its bosom, the restless and dissatisfied, of all nations and languages." The Caddos welcomed these groups, apparently out of sympathy for their plight. The most important of these tribes, and the ones closest to the Caddos, were the Coushatta, Alabama, and Quapaw (fig. 2-11).

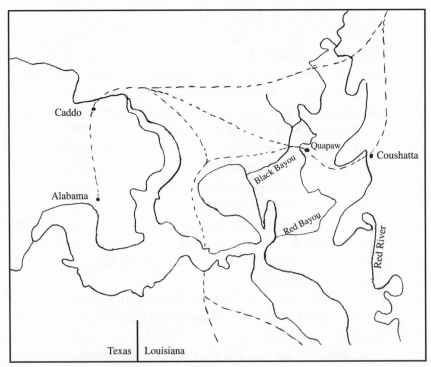

Fig. 2-11. Indian villages in the Sodo Lake area

The Coushattas were not located at Coushatta Bluffs but farther downstream at Cedar Bluffs on the Red River, as shown on King's map of the Freeman and Custis expedition (**fig. 2-12**). Sibley describes the people, but not this village, because he was not aware of its existence when he was writing in April 1805. He came to know of its existence late in 1805. This is known to be the case because Sibley used the Caddo floodplain village as an identifier in his 1805 list of distances upriver on the Red and then switched to the Coushatta village in his early 1806 modification of this list for the Freeman and Custis expedition. If Sibley had known of the Coushatta village in 1805, he would have used it as an identifier because, in contrast to the Caddo village, it was on the banks of the Red.

The Freeman and Custis journal indicates that the Coushatta village formed in 1803 or 1804 and that by 1806 it consisted of "6 or 8 families of stragglers from the lower Creek nation." It is not surprising that Sibley was not aware of this ragtag band that obviously located on the Red late in 1804, particularly because they moved from the Sabine (their location according to Sibley's 1805 description).

The Coushattas were Creeks who, according to Sibley, arrived in Louisiana in 1795 and consisted altogether of about two hundred men in dispersed settlements. The Red River village is shown on Capt. George Birch's 1826 map of the Sodo Lake area as just above Coushatta Bayou,

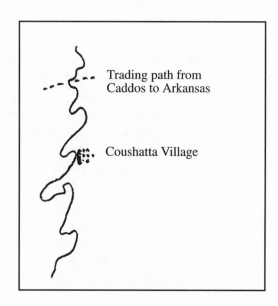

Fig. 2-12. Location of the Coushatta village

but on the wrong side of the river (if the inscription is meant to indicate location rather than general area). That Coushatta Bayou left the Red River just below Cedar Bluffs is known because it is shown, as "Coshatta Chute," on Land Office maps.

Writing in 1837, Lt. A. H. Bowman, who acted in a review capacity for Henry Shreve's raft removal effort, stated that when the work of improvement began (i.e., in 1832 or 1833), the head of the raft was five miles below the Caddo village. Bowman was obviously speaking of the Coushatta village, because there was no Caddo village on the Red River. The village is not shown on Shreve's 1833 survey map and probably ceased to exist by 1833—it is not mentioned in the letters of the Indian agents after 1831.

Closely related to the Coushattas were the Alabamas, another Creek tribe who, like the Coushattas, spoke the Muskogean dialect. The Alabamas were described by Sibley in 1805 in the following terms:

> ALABAMAS, are likewise from West Florida, off the Alabama river, and came to Red river about the same time of the Boluscas and Apalachies. Part of them have lived on Red river, about sixteen miles above the Bayou Rapide, till last year, when most of this party, of about thirty men, went up Red river, and have settled themselves near the Caddoquies, where, I am informed, they last year made a good crop of corn. The Caddoes are friendly to them, and have no objection to their settling there; they speak the Creek and Choctaw languages, and Mobilian; most of them French, and some of them English. There is another party of them, whose village is on a small creek in Opelousas district, about thirty miles northwest from the church of Opelousas; they consist of about forty men; they have lived at the same place ever since they came from Florida; are said to be increasing a little in numbers for the past few years; they raise corn, have horses, hogs, and cattle, and are harmless, quiet people.

The village near the Caddos was located on the northwest side of Potter's Point about seven miles directly south of the Jim's Bayou Caddo site and is shown (marked "Coshatta Village") on an 1839 Land Office map about five miles from Robert Potter's property (**fig. 2-13**). John Salmon "Rip" Ford was in the area early in 1838 and reported: "Not

Fig. 2-13.
Location of the
Alabama village.
*Source: Louisiana
State Land Office,
Division of Ad-
ministration*

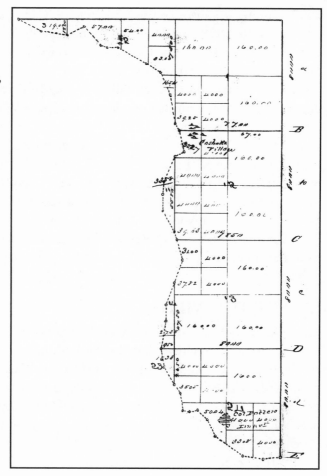

far from Colonel Potter's residence the Muscogees had a settlement between Caddo Lake and the Red River." This village was formed in 1804 according to Sibley's testimony, during the same year that the Coushattas located on Red River. This village was apparently abandoned by 1842 and is designated "Old Cashatta Village" on the anonymous map produced after the 1841 boundary survey and before Potter's death in March 1842 (see fig 2-6).

The Quapaws were a Siouan-speaking tribe forced by treaty to give up their land in Arkansas, where they had been primarily hunters. They moved to Caddo Prairie in March 1826 to a site agreed upon by the Caddos, who were provided a small annuity to compensate for the inconvenience. They tried their hand at agriculture; but the Great Raft was beginning to cause extensive flooding on Caddo Prairie. The corn crops of 1826, 1828, and 1830 were wiped out by flooding, and there was a drought in 1827. The Quapaw were starving to death, and most of them returned to Arkansas in 1830.

The location of the Quapaw village cannot be determined precisely on the basis of the published historic texts. The village was located on a Bayou Treache on the Red River floodplain one-half mile from the Caddo Prairie Agency, which was also affected by the flooding. When George Gray moved the agency from Sulphur Fork to Caddo Prairie, he said that the agency house would be located on the road between the Coushatta and Caddo villages near a navigable waterbody. The agency was apparently located between Black Bayou and Red Bayou, as shown on Jacobs's map (see fig. 2-3), but the direction of the village from the agency is unknown.

END OF THE WILDERNESS

The isolation of the Caddos from the pressure of white settlers did not last very long. The Great Raft, by prohibiting effective waterborne commerce on the middle Red and to the upper Red and by flooding potentially settleable rich bottomlands, afforded a great deal of protection to the Caddos. However, it could not stop the progressive movement of whites into the western territories opened by the Louisiana Purchase of 1803.

By the middle of the second decade of their location in the Shreveport area, the Caddos found themselves caught in a pincer movement from the north and south. To the north was the Arkansas Territory, expanding rapidly to the southwest, with thrusts over the Red River into the old tribal areas of the Caddo beginning in 1811. To the south was the old Bayou Pierre French settlement that emanated from Natchitoches and Campti and stretched out on the fertile lands between Bayou Pierre and the Red River, moving progressively upward and joined by an occasional Anglo settler and merchant. By at least 1817, Samuel Norris was well established on the Red River floodplain just below what later was to become Shreveport; and by at least 1832, Jim Coates was operating a store on one bluff removed from the future site of Shreveport. The Indian agents were diligent in expelling intruders at the north and south, but they simply slipped back into Caddo territory after the troops had left.

By the 1830s, the Caddos knew that the relentless pressure of white settlement was unstoppable. As Tarshar, their chief in 1835, said: "*My children*: For what do you mourn? Are you not starving in the midst of this land? And do you not travel far from it in quest of food? The game we live on is going further off, and the white man is coming near to us; and is not our condition getting worse daily? Then why lament for the loss of that which yields us nothing but misery? Let us be wise, then, and get all we can for it, and not wait till the white man steals it away, little by little, and then gives us nothing."

That the white man was coming was well known to everyone in April 1835 when the Caddos sold their land to the United States. Henry Shreve began to remove the raft on the Red River in April 1833 and by June had reached the Indian Agency at Peach Orchard Bluff. Writing in 1834, the Indian Agent Brooks, who consummated the treaty with the Caddo Nation, was clear about the implications of Shreve's activity: "Since the practicality of removing the obstructions to the navigation of Red River has been established, much excitement has been manifested respecting the river lands throughout the region of the raft, embracing a considerable scope of the Caddo territory, and is already a fruitful source of trouble to me and uneasiness to the nation. This state of things was anticipated by me from the first, and was the occasion of my suggesting to the President, when last in Washington, the necessity of extinguishing the Indian title to all such land prior to the removal of the raft."

Coincident with the treaty, Shreve cleared the Red to the mouth of Twelvemile Bayou in April 1835, opening the bluffs on which Shreveport was founded and opening the Cypress Bayou and the lakes route to New Orleans, the locus of all commercial activity in the Mississippi River valley. The Great Raft, which had brought the Sodo Lake complex into existence and afforded protection to the Caddos, was on the verge of destruction. As Tarshar recognized, it was time for the people of the wilderness to move on, for the wilderness was fast disappearing.

·3·

The Great Raft

A UNIQUE PHENOMENON

The second major impediment to the use of the Cypress Bayou and the lakes route was the Great Raft on the Red River. As long as the raft blocked the mouth of Twelvemile Bayou and occupied the channel of the Red below Twelvemile Bayou, the route was a navigable channel from nowhere to nothing. Navigability was pointless without access to the Red, and access to the Red was pointless as long as the Red was not navigable. The key element in the eventual commercial flowering of the area west of Shreveport was the linkage through the Red and the Mississippi to New Orleans, the import and export center for the whole of the Mississippi River valley. This linkage was not achieved until April 1835 with the removal of the raft up to the mouth of Twelvemile Bayou by Capt. Henry Shreve.

A secondary effect of the raft on the area west of Shreveport was that it was an impediment to settlement. Waterways helped people to get from one point to another; but more importantly, they were channels by which settlements could be supplied and by which they could export agricultural commodities during a period in which roads and the vehicles that traveled on them were inefficient. Even if the Caddo Indians had never occupied Northeast Texas, there would have been little in the way of settlement in the area west of Shreveport had the raft remained on the Red downstream of the mouth of Twelvemile Bayou.

Although there have been many log jams on many rivers, the Great Raft on the Red River was a unique phenomenon. There were small log jams all along the Red River, but these did not constitute the Great Raft. It was a unitary phenomenon, as its name suggests, that began at a particular point on the Red, grew to a size that was fairly constant throughout its history, and then began moving upstream by the accumulation of debris at its head and the decay of old materials at its foot. As it moved upstream, it transformed the adjacent landscape, determined settlement patterns, and controlled the range in which boats could operate. It is not surprising that it was personalized by many observers.

The Red River is many thousands of years old, and the conditions for raft formation may always have been available. As a consequence, there is reason to believe that there was more than one raft on the Red River throughout its geologic history. Evidence for the existence of more than one raft is given by the geologist H. C. Collins in an 1872 Corps of Engineers report on the Red River in the region of the raft in which he takes note of multiple beach ridges in the Clear Lake area:

> Clear Lake is a very muddy, shallow lake, containing an island of about 2,000 acres, called Pine Island. . . . Pine Island consists of a long, low, narrow ridge of yellow land, with sandy soil just like that on the bluffs, and not like the bottom soil, surrounded by a slough from 50 to 200 feet wide, filled with Cypress and gum trees, and in which the water is seldom less than a foot deep. This is surrounded by a ridge which has evidently been a beach, as it is filled with the washed shells and very old driftwood, (cedar and cypress), and contains many flint implements and some broken pottery. It is from 20 to 50 feet wide. This in turn is surrounded by a slough, and this by a beach very like the other, until there are four distinct beach ridges, and even this last one, which is probably not quite so wide as it will become, has many flint arrowheads in it, and pottery also. . . . Each ridge must have formed during a long period of high water. With the falling of the water the trees would grow down along the exposed bank, keeping as near the water as they could, without being washed up by waves or killed by high water. Then another gradual rise of the water for a long period would float in drift, and form another beach, and

make it steep on the island side, and a long slope on the outside, just as it is now. It is quite probable that in this valley will be found the record of four or five rafts having slowly moved up this valley, and reached some point at the head of any possible accumulation, the river changing its bed more or less between the limits of the hills, or the raft decaying or washing away.

Be that as it may, during the historic period there was only one Great Raft; or, to be more precise, two installments of the same raft with entirely different historical repercussions. At the beginning of the 1800s, the Great Raft extended from Campti, Louisiana, to the vicinity of what later became Shreveport. By the time Henry Shreve began his raft removal activities, the raft extended from about eight straightline miles below the site of Shreveport to about seventeen straightline miles above, with debris downstream and a raft segment far downstream.

This raft was completely removed by Shreve in 1838. It reformed, but not in the area from which Shreve had removed it. That improvement was permanent. The place where the head of the raft had been when Shreve removed it became the place where the foot of the second raft installment was formed. This place was near present-day Belcher, Louisiana. This new installment gradually built up, extending nearly to the Arkansas line when it was removed by Lt. Eugene Woodruff in 1873, marking the end of the influence of the raft on the history of the Red River valley.

CHARACTERISTICS

The best analysis of the raft remains the August 1828 "Letter in Relation to the Raft of Red River," which was written by Joseph Paxton of Hempstead County, Arkansas, to Ambrose H. Sevier, delegate to Congress from the Territory of Arkansas. At the time that Paxton was writing, the foot of the raft had advanced to sixty or seventy miles above Natchitoches. He reports that "the time is yet within the memory of some of the oldest inhabitants in and near Natchitoches, when the lower end of the raft was still below that place; and that the then Governor ordered out the troops in command, to break down and cause to float off, all the part then below."

Because the raft was snaking its way upriver at a little less than a mile a year, Paxton realized that it must have had an origin somewhere below Natchitoches at a time that would have enabled its foot to have been near Natchitoches when the governor of Louisiana ordered its removal by the troops stationed at the post. Paxton found a likely explanation for the formation of the raft through conversations with steamboatmen who pointed out that rises on the Mississippi caused an eddy on the Red up to the rapids at Alexandria and that within this eddy there was always an accumulation of driftwood. This accumulation was never great because the raft upstream prevented larger logs from reaching the eddy. But Paxton concluded that it was within this eddy that the first large logs became embedded in the Red, giving rise to the Great Raft; and, working backward from the position of the foot, Paxton also concluded that the Great Raft came into existence about 1530.

The Great Raft did not, of course, emerge full blown. Throughout its history, it maintained a fairly constant length of about eighty river miles. This is because the raft was composed of materials that took about eighty years to completely decay. With the first deposit of raft materials in the eddy, the raft began to form progressively upstream, less than a mile each year. Within about eighty years, the raft was fully formed about eighty miles long; but it was at this point that the decayed logs at its lower end began to slough off, to be carried down to the Mississippi and out to the Gulf of Mexico. As new logs accumulated at its head and old logs disappeared at its foot, the Great Raft moved upstream, maintaining a fairly constant length.

The raft was composed primarily of cottonwood logs and branches, but also of much smaller amounts of oak, ash, willow, sweet gum, cedar, and bois d'arc. These materials were derived from the banks of the Red above Shreveport. Throughout most of its course from the Great Plains, the river flows through a narrow channel with high banks and then through a lightly forested prairie. But when it reaches Northeast Texas, it enters the Gulf Coastal Plain, where it begins to meander, cutting through the soft alluvium that the river itself has deposited and forming large bends that are, like the river itself, in constant state of movement over the valley floor.

In earlier times, the alluvial banks of the Red were heavily forested between Shreveport and Paris, Texas. As the river meandered back and forth over its floodplain, it cut into these forested areas, consuming immense quantities of timber. The green trees would fall into the water from the caving banks, making a sound that reminded Lt. Eugene Woodruff of the distant roar of artillery. They would be exposed for a season or two while they dried and grew lighter and would then be carried downstream by spring floods, losing most of their branches on the way and producing well-trimmed materials for the waiting raft below.

The materials that composed the raft were of varying ages, with the oldest materials at the foot and the youngest at the head. As a consequence, the raft was not homogeneous. The upper portion of the raft was composed of floating materials. The middle portion was composed of water-logged materials that extended to the bottom of the river. These materials were choked with sediment, small branches, and leaves, and on their surface grew vines and small willows (**fig. 3-1**). The bottom of the raft was composed of materials in an advanced state of decay; and below the raft proper for many miles downstream there was floating debris and submerged raft remnants.

The raft was not continuous, but rather segmented (**fig. 3-2**), with segments tending to form at bends in the river. The raft acted as a dam, raising water levels for many miles upstream. Immense pressure was exerted at bends in the river upstream of the raft because the bends reached out into the alluvial plain of the Red, which sloped downward

Fig. 3-1. Red River raft. *Source: LSU in Shreveport, Noel Memorial Library Archives. Photographer: R.B. Talfor*

toward the bluffs to the east and west. When enough pressure was exerted, a break would form in the natural levee of the bend, sending the water into the alluvial plain. As the water flowed out at the break, a slackwater condition would be created between the break and the head of the raft. Debris quickly accumulated in the slackwater area near the break, forming a new raft segment, which eventually closed the break and exerted further pressures upstream.

LOCATIONS

In this stepwise fashion, the Great Raft moved upstream. The various locations of the post-Shreve raft can be determined precisely because it was the subject of many state and federal reports concerning proposed navigation improvements from the 1840s through the 1870s and was mapped using scientific survey principles by Lt. Col. Stephen H. Long in 1841, by Col. Charles A. Fuller in 1855, and by Lt. Eugene A. Woodruff in 1872. For the period prior to the 1840s, it is necessary to rely on hints in various texts and uncertain maps.

Fig. 3-2. Open water between raft segments. *Source: LSU in Shreveport, Noel Memorial Library Archives. Photographer: R.B. Talfor*

There are five accounts of the foot of the raft:

1. The first evidence for the existence of the raft is J. F. Broutin's 1722 *Carte des Natchitoches*, which is reproduced in Germaine Portre-Bobinski and Clara Smith's *Natchitoches*. The map, which is restricted to the immediate vicinity of Natchitoches, shows a small raft segment immediately above the settlement in Cane River (a primary channel of the Red at that time). Natchitoches was founded as a French trading post in 1714. Because the raft was the determinative factor in upriver settlement, it can be presumed that the foot was somewhere in the vicinity of Natchitoches in 1714, particularly in the light of Paxton's comments on the removal of a segment below the town in the 1760s. Broutin's map shows Old River to the west of Cane River as the route out of Natchitoches to New Orleans, confirming that there was at least one segment on Cane River below Natchitoches prior to the 1760s. It is obvious that the foot of the raft when Natchitoches was founded in 1714 was somewhere on Cane River between its upstream and downstream intersections with Old River.

2. In his 1805 account of the Red River and adjacent country, John Sibley, writing of the Campti plantation houses, reports that "the upper end of this settlement is the last on the main branch of Red River, which, straight by land, does not exceed twenty-five miles above Natchitoches. At the Upper House, the great raft or jam of timber begins; this raft chokes the main channel for upwards of one hundred miles by the course of the river; not one entire jam from the beginning to the end of it, but only at the point, with places of several leagues that are clear." The upper house of the Campti plantations was occupied by Francois Grappe at Grappe's Bluff, about five miles west of Campti and immediately across the river from Powhatan. The lowest portion of the raft was constituted by a small raft segment that was blocking the entrance to a stream that entered Red River at Grappe's Bluff. Heeding advice from Sibley, the settlers in the area removed this raft segment.

3. Nicholas King's map of the 1806 Freeman and Custis expedition shows three raft segments between Campti and Lake Bistineau, with the lower one at Grappe's Bluff. The lower one was the first above the stream mentioned by Sibley and only a short distance above the location of the segment whose removal Sibley had secured in late 1805.

4. Reporting in 1828, Paxton said that the foot of the raft was 60 or 70 river miles above the point below Natchitoches where it was

ordered removed by the Louisiana governor.

5. Henry Shreve's 1833 sketch of the Red River shows the raft as 140 miles long, with its foot a short distance above Loggy Bayou, which is now the southern boundary of Bossier Parish.

Accounts of the head of the raft (**fig. 3-3**) are more numerous:

1. In his 1805 account, Sibley writes of the western, Bayou Pierre, passage around the raft: "Six or seven years ago, boats used to pass this way into the main river again, its communication with which being above the great raft or obstruction; but it is now choked, and requires a portage of three miles." The mouth of Bayou Pierre was thus closed by the head of the raft in 1798 or 1799. This was the old mouth of

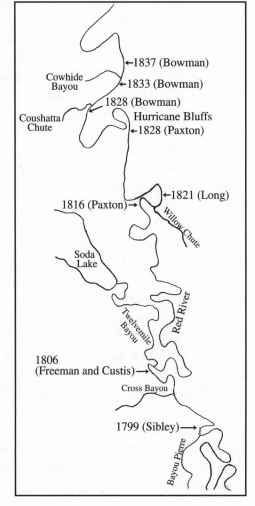

Fig. 3-3. Locations of the head of the raft

Bayou Pierre, extending out of a bend of the Red River that has since been cut off.

2. The Freeman and Custis Red River expedition of 1806 reports that the head of the raft was just below Twelvemile Bayou. This was not the present mouth, but rather the old mouth about one and one-half miles northwest of the present mouth on a bend of the Red River that has since been cut off.

3. Paxton, writing in 1828, states: "It is a fact well known in this part of the country, that when the first keel boat ascended Red river through the raft, its head was then immediately below and in sight of the well known outlet called Bee Bayou. At this time, twelve years since, the head of the raft is twelve miles above said point." Bee Bayou was an old name for Willow Chute, so named for the numerous beehives in the decaying cypress trees that lined its banks. Subtracting twelve years from 1828, Paxton is saying that the head of the raft was just below Willow Chute in 1816. This was an old mouth of Willow Chute, extending from a bend that has since been cut off.

4. In an 1841 report, Lt. Col. Stephen H. Long states: "In 1820, it is said, that the raft removed by Captain Shreve from that part of the river above the outlet of Willow Chute had no existence, the channel above that point being then open and unobstructed." Long indicates that the head of the raft had passed beyond the mouth of Willow Chute in 1821, which is compatible with the position given by Paxton for 1816.

5. Writing in 1828, Paxton says that "the head of the raft has now arrived at a point where the river washes the left bluffs. The course of the keelboats which have hitherto brought up supplies, has been to the left of the channel; but it is now thought that they can no longer get out on that side on account of the bluffs." Paxton is describing the left-descending bluffs and the imminent closure of the eastern route around the raft. The head of the raft in 1828 was at Hurricane Bluffs.

6. Lt. A. H. Bowman, who acted in an oversight capacity for Shreve's effort, writes in an 1837 report: "When I visited the raft in 1828 it reached within a very short distance of Cushatte chute; it now extends three miles above that point, making the average annual increase less than half a mile. The yearly extension of the raft near its present head has been lessened by the immense quantity of drift that is carried into Lake Sheodo through several large bayous, which in that vicinity have broken from the river into the lake." Coushatta Chute (also called

Coushatta Bayou) was an old name for Peach Orchard Bayou. Bowman conducted his survey in the summer of 1828, and Paxton was writing in August of that year, so they appear to contradict, with Bowman placing the head of the raft many miles above Hurricane Bluffs. However, given the leap-frogging tendencies of the raft, Coushatta Chute was the next logical place for the formation of a raft segment above Hurricane Bluffs. Because Bowman was writing from personal observation and Paxton from delayed word of mouth, it is apparent that the head had already advanced beyond Hurricane Bluffs in 1828.

7. Bowman also states: "That portion of Red River usually denominated the 'raft' at the period when the work of improvement commenced, extended from the mouth of Loggy Bayou to a point five miles below the Caddo village." Bowman is speaking of the Coushatta village and the inception of Shreve's effort in 1833. Given his prior indication that the raft had advanced only three miles in the nine years from 1828 to 1837, the head of the raft was just below Cowhide Bayou in 1833. The slow upward movement of the raft is compatible with the fact that the head of the raft was just above Cowhide Bayou when Shreve broke through the head in 1838.

EFFECTS

As the raft moved upstream, it dramatically transformed the Red and its adjoining landscape. Slackwater conditions immediately upstream of the head caused rapid deposition of suspended sediments, raising the bed of the river and constricting its banks. Water levels were raised for many miles above the advancing head, and there was dramatic flooding on both sides of the river, producing the extensive inundation area shown on Darby's map. The raft and attendant flooding obliterated the channel of the Red, so that it is usually designated on the old maps such as Maxfield Ludlow's 1818 *Map of the State of Louisiana* as "supposed course of the river through the great raft" (**fig. 3-4**). This inundation area in the 1820s was described by Timothy Flint:

> About thirty leagues above Natchitoches commences the Raft, which is nothing more than a broad swampy expansion of alluvion of the river to the width of 20 or 30 miles. The river, spreading here into a vast number of channels, frequently shallow of course, has been for ages clogging with a compact

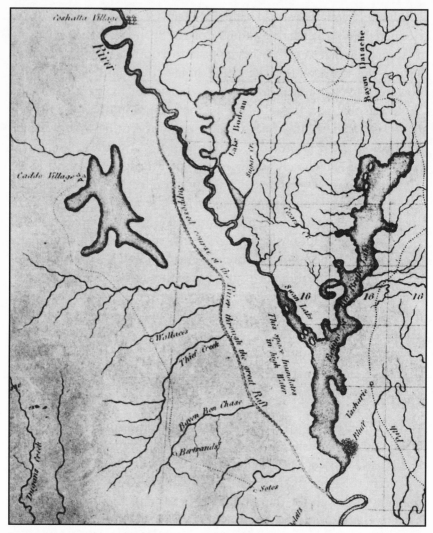

Fig. 3-4. Supposed course of Red River. *Source: Courtesy of LSU Libraries Special Collections, Baton Rouge*

mass of timber, and fallen trees wafted from the upper regions. Between these masses the river has a channel, sometimes lost in a lake, and found by following the outlet of that lake back to the parent channel. There is no stage of water, in which a keel boat with an experienced pilot may not make her way through the raft. The river is blocked up by this immense mass of timber for a length, on its meanders, of between 60 and 70 miles.

There are places where the water can be seen in motion under the logs. In other places, the whole width of the river may be crossed on horseback, and boats only make their way, in passing these places, by following the inlet of a lake, and coasting it to its outlet, and thus finding the channel again. Weeds, flowering shrubs, and small willows have taken root upon the surface of this timber, and flourish above the waters. But in all these places the course of the river, its outline and its bends are distinctly marked by a margin of forest trees, which grow here on the banks in the same manner, as they do where the channel is open.

The second major effect of the raft was the formation of distributaries. The raft acted as a dam, permitting very little flow on the river. The hydrologic force of spring floods was vented through breaks in the natural levee of the river. When breaks occurred, the water would seek the bluffs to the east or west, because the floodplain of the Red sloped downhill away from the river. Bends pointing east produced eastward distributaries and vice versa for those pointing west, because the breaks occurred on the outside of the bends. The water would then rush southward on the inclined plane of the Red, usually reentering the river at a point downstream where the river struck a bluff and the distributary water had no place to go other than back into the main channel.

The distributary system on both sides of the river was complex and in a constant state of change. New distributaries formed progressively upstream of the advancing raft, and old distributaries would be blocked by raft segments. When a new distributary formed, it might pursue an independent course or cut into or across an older distributary or ancient bayou on the Red River floodplain. Some of the distributaries were large and long, carrying a substantial portion of the flow of the Red and paralleling the river for many miles. Together, the distributaries formed braided patterns on the Red River floodplain that were constantly changing because of the dynamic nature of the raft.

These braided patterns were segregated into subbasins of the Red River valley. As the river pursues its course downstream, it alternately strikes bluffs to the east and west, forming large, crescent-shaped subbasins extending north to south from one eastern bluff to the next and one western bluff to the next and east to west from the Red to the encompassing bluffline of the valley (**fig. 3-5**). On the west side of the river there was a subbasin that extended from Blanton's Bluffs at the Arkansas line down to the bluff on which Shreveport was located.

The distributary system within this subbasin fed into the Sodo Lake complex and discharged through Twelvemile Bayou and Cross Bayou. From the Shreveport bluffs down to the Natchitoches bluffs, there was another subbasin on the west side of the river that was dominated by Bayou Pierre. On the east side of the river there was a subbasin extending from far into Arkansas down to Miller's Bluffs a few miles below the Louisiana line. Also on the east was a subbasin that extended from Hurricane Bluffs down to past Coushatta, Louisiana. The first major distributary at the northern end of this subbasin was Willow Chute, and its major outlet at the southern end was Loggy Bayou.

The third major effect of the raft was the formation of hundreds of lakes on both sides of the river. The largest of these are shown in a composite by geologist Arthur Veatch (**fig. 3-6**). However, not all of the lakes shown on Veatch's map were contemporaneous. Each came into existence at a particular point in time, developing sequentially

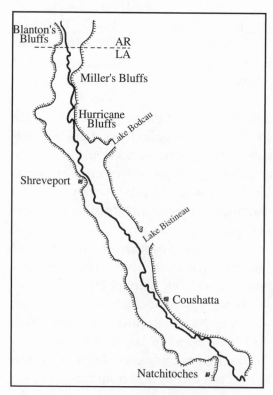

Fig. 3-5. Subbasins of the Red River valley

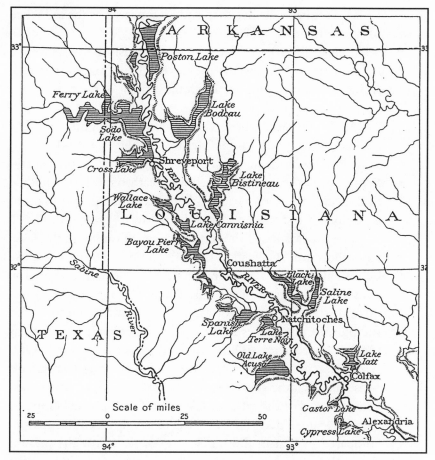

Fig. 3-6. Raft-formed lakes. *Source: H. Doc. 488, 59th Cong., 1st Sess.*

upstream as the raft moved upstream over hundreds of years; and each began to disappear as the raft moved above them or was removed by man.

The appropriate designation for these waterbodies is raft-formed lakes. That they were products of the raft and not the result of some other natural mode of formation is known by four facts:

1. No lakes formed along the Red River above the zone of raft influence.

2. There were witnesses to the formation of many of the upper lakes, providing testimony to their sequential development in conjunction with the upward movement of the raft.

3. The lakes sequentially declined and disappeared as the influence of the raft was removed from each of them.

4. Variations in the state of decay of the preexisting forests were a clear indication to contemporary observers like Paxton that lake formation was correlated with upstream movement of the raft:

> A Mr. Wallace, whose veracity no one doubts, who has resided many years in the vicinity of the raft, and is well acquainted with it, states, and is willing to testify, that thirty-five years ago the head of the raft was nearly opposite the middle of Bodeau Lake, then a beautiful prairie. At this time, this point is computed to be thirty-five miles below its present head.
>
> The appearance of the state of decay of timber in this lake, and others near the head of the raft, compared to that in those below, also proves their more recent formation, and the consequent progress of the raft. The raft, as it ascends, chokes up and stops the mouth of the bayous, as they descend from the hills, forming lakes in their valleys, gradually enlarging as the raft approaches, killing the timber in them as the water rises, first in the middle where the surface is lower, and subsequently near the margin, where, in this lake and others near the head of the raft, the timber still retains small limbs, in a partial state of decay; proving the relatively recent formation, compared to that in those below, even far below the present site of the raft, when, as in lake Noir, there is scarcely a vestige of it remaining. The state of decay of timber in all of them, being always advanced in proportion to, and is an index of their distance below the present head of the raft, leaving no room to doubt as to the mode, time, and cause of their formation.

The exact mode of formation of each of these lakes could only be determined through individual analyses. It is obvious that many were formed through the process described by Paxton involving initial ponding of water and then physical blockage of stream mouths by the raft. Such lakes disappeared fairly quickly after the foot of the raft passed the stream mouth. Others, such as the Sodo Lake complex, were formed by distributaries that continued to feed water into them after the raft foot passed an outlet channel such as Twelvemile Bayou.

Whatever their exact mode of formation, all of the lakes in the Red River valley owed their formation to the peculiar conditions generated by the Great Raft. Veatch summarizes the implications: "Indeed, it is very safe to assume that had there been no raft there would have been no large lake in Red River Valley, and that any classification of lakes by origin must regard these temporary bodies of water as unique." Another possible implication, which was drawn by various litigants in land dispute cases, is that they had never been lakes at all, but rather mere temporary bodies of water constituted and destroyed by the dynamism of the raft.

In this process of creation and destruction, distributary-formed lakes such as the Sodo Lake complex were more resilient than those that had been formed by the blockage of stream outlets. When Henry Shreve removed the raft from the mouth of Twelvemile Bayou in 1835, the Sodo Lake complex did not drain. Water continued to be thrust through the distributaries into the lake area by the raft above. Even after the raft was completely removed in 1873, water continued to be diverted into the distributary system because the distributaries were strong and deep and able to compete for Red River water. In addition, raft-induced sediment fallout had raised the bed of the Red, making the distributaries even more competitive for Red River water. Lastly, sediment deposits at the foot of such lakes as Caddo and Soda and within the old drainage channels such as Cypress Bayou formed natural dams that continued to hold water long after the raft had been removed from the Red.

Many of the lakes shown on Veatch's map have disappeared forever, including Soda, Shifttail, and Clear—within the Sodo Lake complex. Many others disappeared and were recreated by dams, including Cross Lake. Caddo Lake was on the verge of disappearance when a dam was erected in 1914. It appears to be the only lake in the Red River valley that maintained a continuous existence from the raft period, and in this lies its uniqueness. It is a naturally formed, artificially maintained lake whose hybrid nature is best described by the oxymoron "natural reservoir."

PASSAGES

The movement of boats on the Red River was determined by the Great Raft. The Red was accessible throughout its length below the raft, and this length changed constantly as the raft moved upstream. Although the raft was not completely impenetrable, as a practical matter boats could not move through it. Speaking about the decayed lower end of the raft, Paxton says, "Pirogues are known frequently to pass this old river channel, to and from a small settlement near the head of the raft, and are constantly in the habit, while passing, to move the loose timber to form themselves a passage." In addition, Capt. George Birch penetrated the raft in a skiff in 1825 up to Cross Bayou, but that was in conjunction with a federal survey. The general situation with respect to navigation on the Red was expressed by Francois Grappe to the 1806 Freeman and Custis expedition when he said that "it was absolutely impracticable to pass the great raft in boats of any kind; as neither Red nor White men had attempted it for 50 years before."

The texts of the early 1800s such as that of Timothy Flint sometimes refer to persons as having gone through the raft, but that actually meant

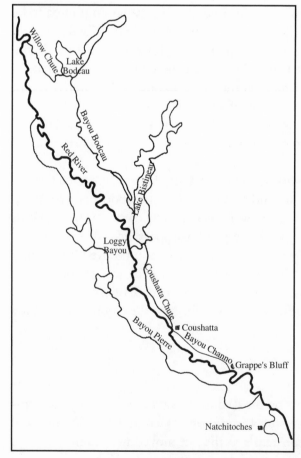

Fig. 3-7.
Routes around the raft

around the raft. That the term "the raft" included the inundation zone as well as the raft proper is demonstrated by Paxton's description of the raft's dimensions: "The raft is eighty miles long, and will average twenty in width." Passages were available around the raft proper in the inundation zones on the east and west sides of the river. These passages were constituted by the distributary and lake system. The western passage was the first in time and was through Bayou Pierre, which extended from the bluffs on which Shreveport was eventually founded down to the vicinity of Natchitoches **(fig. 3-7)**.

Writing about Bayou Pierre in 1805, Sibley explains: "Six or seven years ago, boats used to pass this way into the main river again, its communication with which being above the great raft or obstruction; but it is now choked, and requires a portage of three miles." This statement contains four important pieces of information: (1) boats were able to bypass the raft through Bayou Pierre; (2) the Bayou Pierre passage was closed in 1798 or 1799; (3) the head of the raft had reached the Bayou Pierre outlet in 1798 or 1799; and (4) boats were still using the route, but with a portage, in 1805. Sibley does not indicate the nature of these craft, what they were carrying, or where they were going, but it is probable that they were large river pirogues carrying trade goods to upriver Indian settlements and that one of the users was Francois Grappe.

With the closure of the Bayou Pierre route, attention shifted to the opportunities afforded by the distributaries and lakes on the east side of the river. The first description of this passage is given by Sibley in the context of a discussion of the raft in relation to the Campti settlement:

> The upper end of this settlement is the last on the main branch of Red river, which, straight by land, does not exceed twenty-five miles above Natchitoches. At the Upper House, the great raft or jam of timber begins; this raft chokes the main channel for upwards of one hundred miles by the course of the river; not one entire jam from the beginning to the end of it, but only at the point, with places of several leagues that are clear. . . . The first or lowest part of the raft is at a point or bend in the river, just below the upper plantation; at which, on the right side, a large bayou, or division of the river, called Bayou Channo, comes in, which is free of any obstructions; and, the

greater part of the year, boats of any size may ascend it into lake Bistino, through which, to its communication with the lake, is only about three miles; the lake is about sixty miles long, and lies nearly parallel with the river; from the upper end of which it communicates again with the river, by a bayou called Daichet, about forty miles above the upper end of the raft; from the lake to the river, through Bayou Daichet, is called nine miles; there is always in this bayou sufficient water for any boat to pass; from thence, upwards, Red river is free of all obstructions to the mountains.

The only problem with this route was a small raft segment that blocked the river just below the Bayou Channo outlet. Sibley suggested to the settlers in the area that they remove the raft segment. This was done, and the route described by Sibley became, with upstream modifications, the route around the raft prior to Shreve's efforts (see fig. 3-7).

Sibley indicates that Bayou Channo entered the Red River at Grappe's Bluff and that it extended three miles from the Red River into Lake Bistineau, which paralleled the Red River and was sixty miles long and which afforded passage through the nine miles of Bayou Daichet back into the Red River above the raft. Sibley's Bayou Channo was the last portion of a stream that extended downward from Lake Bistineau and included present-day Coushatta Bayou (which ends at Coushatta, Louisiana) and present-day Nicholas Bayou (which ends at Red River downstream of Coushatta). The nearly full extent of this stream can be seen on C. W. R. Bayley's 1853 *New and Improved Map of Louisiana*. At the time Sibley was writing, what is now Nicholas Bayou extended downstream to Grappe's Bluff. Remnant portions of this three-mile stream portion designated Bayou Channo by Sibley can be seen on contemporary topographic maps, but the stream itself has disappeared because the entire area described by Sibley is no longer influenced by the raft and the Red River has shifted its course.

Sibley's statement that Bayou Channo was three miles long and was the outlet for the sixty-mile-long Lake Bistineau is understandable given the extraordinary hydrologic conditions resulting from the raft. The eastern passage could be conceptualized as a single sheet of water, as it was in Darby's 1816 map; as a series of lakes and streams, as in the Freeman and Custis account; or as a lake with bayous at both ends, as it was with Sibley. All of these conceptualizations were correct, depending on the amount of overflow from the Red.

SIBLEY VINDICATED

Sibley's description has sometimes been deprecated, with the particular claim that he was in a state of confusion about Bayou Dorcheat, which enters Lake Bistineau from the north. In addition, the mileage figures mentioned in the description were part of an extensive mileage table appended to Sibley's report and also supplied to the Freeman and Custis expedition in 1806. These mileage figures appear to be very much off base. Nevertheless, in the introduction to his report, Sibley indicates that he had been to the head of the raft and, more importantly, that his information on the Indians and middle Red River had been obtained from Francois Grappe, a reliable source: "I have invariably found, that whatever information I have received from him, has been confirmed by every other intelligent person having a knowledge of the same, with whom I have conversed."

Sibley was not confused about the location of Bayou Diachet at the upper end of the eastern passage. Bayou Dorcheat, which enters Lake Bistineau from the north, was a transposition from this earlier usage. Bayou Diachet was the earliest designation for Willow Chute, for which Bee Bayou was the middle term. This is apparent when the various texts of the period are assimilated.

One early source that relies heavily on Sibley but contains sufficient additional information to indicate that it is an independent account is Samuel Brown's 1817 *The Western Gazetteer*. In describing the eastern bypass around the raft, Brown uses the Bayou Channo, Lake Bistineau, Bayou Diachet nomenclature, with the latter stream providing reentrance to the Red River above the raft: "Bayou Channo, leading into Lake Besteneau, affords a pretty good navigation; and by passing through the lake and bayou Dacheet, boatmen gain several miles, as the meanders of the river are very tedious. The medium depth of this lake, is from fifteen to twenty feet, and never less than twelve, though the remains of cypress trees of all sizes, now dead, most of them with their tops broken off, are yet standing in the lake. From bayou Dacheet to the mountains, the river is free of obstructions."

Brown was the last to mention Bayou Channo. As the raft moved upstream, access to the eastern bypass was achieved through other streams. The first in time was Coushatta Chute, which enters the Red River at Coushatta, Louisiana. Coushatta Chute was used by Claiborne Wright in 1816 and is mentioned often in the texts of the 1820s. In an 1841 Corps of Engineers report, Lt. Col. Stephen H. Long says, "Prior to the removal of the old raft, the channel through which the keelboats were conducted past this formidable obstruction, led successively through Loggy Bayou, the southern extremity of lake Bistineau, bayou Bodeau, lake Bodeau and Willow Chute; at the head of which last it united again with the present navigable channel, which was then unobstructed by the raft." Loggy Bayou, which presently forms the southern boundary of Bossier Parish, is a channel coming out of Lake Bistineau that enters immediately into the river (see fig. 3-7). It is mentioned in texts from 1825 as an alternate channel to Coushatta Chute.

Dochette was a variant of Diachet that was used by Sibley in a list of river miles upstream as the reentrance to Red River above the raft. This second Sibley list, which was very similar to the first, was submitted to the Freeman and Custis expedition in 1806. Freeman and Custis reentered the Red River above the raft at Willow Chute; therefore, it is obvious that Sibley's Dochette (Diachet, Daichet) was an early name for that stream. Freeman and Custis also mention that the downstream entrance into the eastern bypass that they took was called Datche by the Indians and that its current was very rapid because Datche was "the discharge for the water which runs out above the great raft."

It is apparent from the Freeman and Custis description of Datche and their movement up the Red River through three raft segments that this was a prior name for Loggy Bayou. Thus, Datche, Dochette, Daichet, and Daichet were various renderings of a single stream that led out of Red River, entered Lake Bistineau, and discharged into the Red through a small stream segment. (Freeman and Custis say the segment was five miles long.)

Sibley, through Grappe, would have been aware of the Datche (i.e., Loggy Bayou) passage that was taken by Freeman and Custis. However, this particular segment of the eastern passage does not appear in either of Sibley's two lists, which use Diachet solely for the nine-mile passage back into the Red River above Lake Bistineau and recommend the Bayou Channo entrance to the passage around the raft.

The reason should be obvious. When Sibley was writing in 1805, the Red River between Bayou Channo and Loggy Bayou was obstructed by three raft segments, as shown on Nicholas King's map. In providing instructions for the Freeman and Custis route in 1806, he would not have recommended going up the Red River through three raft segments and then into Loggy Bayou, but rather the lower and easier route through Bayou Channo. The difficulties experienced by Freeman and Custis in traversing the three raft segments is testimony to the correctness of Sibley's recommendation.

The nomenclature for the upper portion of this single stream called Diachet was then dropped in favor of Bee Bayou, with Datche probably continuing to be used for the lower portion. The use of Datche for this lower portion disappeared by at least 1833, when it is named Loggy Bayou on Henry Shreve's survey map. With the acceptance of this nomenclature, Dorcheat was then transposed to the stream that enters Lake Bistineau to the north. This transposition was reasonable given the fact that Bayou Dorcheat empties into Lake Bistineau, which, in turn, is drained by Loggy Bayou.

The various renderings of Dorcheat are never used for the upper portion of the eastern bypass after Samuel Brown in 1817. That portion came to be known as Bee Bayou and is so used by Paxton in 1828, Capt. George Birch in a federal raft survey in 1826, and A. Hanscom of Miller County, Arkansas, in an 1825 letter to George Izard, governor of the Territory of Arkansas. The reason for the name is given by Hanscom, who says that the bayou is infested with stumps of trees that had been cut to obtain honey. By 1835, when Shreve wrote his annual report for that year, the name Bee Bayou had been changed to Willow Chute.

The other problem in the interpretation of Sibley's texts lies in his various renditions of river miles, which appear to be grossly exaggerated. These exaggerations are common in the texts of the period, appearing, for example, in Hanscom's letter. The reason for the appearance of exaggeration is that these are not river miles in the modern sense, which are measured at center stream using sophisticated procedures to take curves into account. Early navigators and early observers such as Sibley had no capacity to compute such river miles. Rather, they relied on a point system from shore to shore that was based on the use of eddies to facilitate the movement of watercraft. The contrast between real river miles and this point system was described by Lieutenant Northrup in an 1845 Corps of Engineers report:

From New Orleans to Alexandria, it is 360 miles.
To Grand Ecore, it is 95 miles higher.
To Shreveport, it is 110 miles higher.
To Fulton, it is 120 miles higher.
To Fort Towson, it is 160 miles higher.
The distances I believe to be correct, though it is usually called 250 miles from Grand Ecore to Shreveport; the same from thence to Fulton, and 300 miles to Fort Towson. These estimates are based on the number of points from shore to shore, averaging the distances between them at two miles, which is evidently too much, though kept up by the boatmen generally.

This point system was used by steamboatmen well after the Civil War, as indicated by a Corps of Engineers account of distances on the Arkansas River, which appeared in the 11 August 1869 Shreveport *South-Western* with the following notation: "The table of distances, as given below, may be relied upon. It necessarily differs from the distance run by steamers, which, at low water, cross from side to side, in order to follow the channel." The discrepancy and its relative magnitude continued to be noted as late as 1873 in connection with Lt. Eugene Woodruff's survey of the raft region, as indicated in the 13 May *Shreveport Times*: "Steamboatmen variously estimate the distance from Shreveport to Carolina Bluffs at fifty, sixty, and seventy miles, but the actual survey makes it only thirty-five miles—quite a difference, which we will not now stop to explain away. Suffice it to say, it has knocked all our theory of steamboat miles into place."

The earliest indication of this system is Sibley's 1805 description of the Red River and adjacent country. Because Sibley derived his river mileage figures from Grappe, and Grappe never navigated craft other than pirogues, it is apparent that there was continuity in the use of this system from the pirogues of the 1700s through the keelboats of the 1800s and late into the steamboat period. The resiliency of this system resulted from the fact that it reflected the real conditions of river navigation, which proceeded by zigzags and for which centerline distances were irrelevant.

Sibley's mileage figures are useful if divided by two and if two things are kept in mind: (1) that the point system averaged two miles, meaning that any particular distance figures could be somewhat above or below the average; and (2) the Red River of today is not the same river it was in 1805. In order to correct, as best as possible, for the second factor, reference can be made to the 1886–92 Corps of Engineers *Survey of Red River and Tributaries*, which provides the earliest rendition of legitimate river miles.

Sibley indicates that Bayou Daichet left the Red River twenty miles (i.e., forty miles adjusted) above the head of the raft. Freeman and Custis reported the head of the raft just below the old mouth of Twelvemile Bayou only a year later. According to the survey map, the distance between the Willow Chute outlet and the old mouth of Twelvemile Bayou was about twenty-three miles. This confirms that Diachet and its variants were old names for Willow Chute and demonstrates that Sibley's "river miles" can be used for approximate locations.

Sibley also indicates that the Caddos' floodplain village was forty miles (i.e., eighty miles adjusted) above Daichet. The survey map gives thirty miles as the distance, to which must be added five miles for the Willow Chute cutoff and Shreve's Hurricane Bluffs cutoff. This places the floodplain village nearly opposite the Jim's Bayou site and in the approximate location indicated by Glass's journal.

EARLY BOAT MOVEMENTS

When Henry Shreve removed the raft up to the mouth of Twelvemile Bayou in 1835, he provided an opportunity for boats to pass around the upper portion of the raft through Soda Lake and Black and Red Bayous. Before that time, boats traveling to the upper Red River were restricted to the western (Bayou Pierre) and eastern (Bayou Channo/ Coushatta Chute/Loggy Bayou–Lake Bistineau–Willow Chute) bypasses. The first of these in time was the Bayou Pierre route, which was utilized by river pirogues and smaller craft until it was closed by the raft in 1798 or 1799, after which a portage was used for a few years.

With the closure of Bayou Pierre, boats shifted to the eastern bypass, which is described in its fullness moving downstream by Hanscom in his 1825 letter to Izard:

> The route pursued enters Bee Bayou; this is a large Bayou, the current of which is gentle, and the channel deep, and nothing at present to obstruct the free navigation thereof by

steamboats, except the numerous dead cypress trees which stand in it, and also a great number of stumps from which some of these trees have been cut for the purpose of obtaining honey. Numerous branches of considerable size are put out of this Bayou, and many also come in on the right. The computed distance of the route in this Bayou is forty miles, and conducts into Badcaw Lake. The route crosses the lake in a direction a little South of East, to a handsome Bluff on the East side near the entrance of Badcaw Bayou; the distance across the Lake is eight miles.

The Badcaw Bayou resembles and answers the description given of the Bee Bayou, (except that there are frequently bluffs of high land on the left,) until within ten or twelve miles of the lower end, where several large branches come in from the right, one of which, called the Red Shute, is very rapid, and the Badcaw becomes rapid from its junction with this shute to its entrance into Swan Lake. The length of the route in this Bayou is estimated at sixty miles. Swan lake is from one to two miles in width; the length I have never heard computed. It is entered on the West side, and turning to the right run down it about ten miles to where there is a pass from thence to Lake Bistino. There are handsome bluffs or hills along the left or Eastern shore of Swan Lake; crossing Lake Bistino, which is here from six to eight miles in length, there are several passes from thence to the coal banks, the distance to which is above eight miles.

At and a little above the coal banks there are considerable branches coming in from the right, and at this place a considerable portion of the waters of the North side of the raft seems to be united; but immediately below, it divides itself into two principal branches; the right denominated the Old River; the left the Coshattee Shute; the former being open and free of any obstructions, is always navigated by boats descending; the latter is frequently taken by boats ascending in consequence of the distance being shorter. At the distance, from the Coal Banks, of fifty miles, by Old river, and about thirty by the Coshattee Shute, these branches again unite, and their junction is denominated the lower end or foot of the raft. From the foot of the raft to the mouth of Bayou Pierre, the country to the right appears much intersected with Bayous, frequently putting out and coming in on that side.

The route at present pursued is near the left or Northern side of the extensive overflow occasioned by the raft, as bluffs or high ground frequently present themselves on that side. On the right or Southern side, dry land is never seen in time of high water . . . ; but the growth of timber thereon being green, indicates that the country is generally overflowed only in high freshets.

Keelboats had been operating on the lower Red River back into the Spanish period. However, it was not until 1816, according to Paxton's 1828 letter to Sevier, that the first keelboat ascended the Red River around the raft using the eastern bypass, apparently on military business: "It is a fact well known in this part of the country, that when the first keel boat ascended Red river through the raft, its head was then immediately below and in sight of a well known outlet called Bee Bayou. At this time, twelve years since, the head of the raft is twelve miles above said point, and has continued to progress every intermediate season since, at about the same rate. This boat was conducted by Major Moss, who is known to you."

Prior to the passage of the first keelboat through the eastern bypass, the route was used by small pirogues and large river pirogues. The larger craft were used by the middle Red River Indian tribes such as the Caddos, Alabamas, and Coushattas to transport trade goods to and from Natchitoches. Although the Indians preferred horses for personal transport, large trade goods such as bundles of hides could only be transported by water. Because the Caddos' river pirogues would have been too large to penetrate Jim's Bayou in the vicinity of the village, they were probably fleeted downstream on the flooded portion of Jim's Bayou.

The eastern route was used by the Freeman and Custis Red River expedition, which departed from Natchitoches on 2 June 1806. This expedition, which had been commissioned by Thomas Jefferson to explore the upper Red River, used two experimental craft built under the direction of William Dunbar in New Orleans. These were flat-bottomed boats twenty-eight feet long drawing sixteen to twenty-nine inches when loaded, with curved gunnels at the bow and stern and cabins for the expedition leaders. The expedition also used five large river pirogues built from cypress trees, with a carrying capacity of thirty barrels.

After passing through three rafts on the Red River, the expedition reached the mouth of Loggy Bayou, where they were met by Grappe, who with a hired Indian served as guides through the eastern route. Loggy Bayou was found to be only five miles long before entering Lake Bistineau **(see fig. 3-7)**. The passage taken by Freeman and Custis around the raft is described in detail by Dan Flores in *Jefferson and Southwestern Exploration*. Given the intricate and convoluted description of the passage provided by Freeman and Custis, generosity is required to describe this passage as a route. Nevertheless, in Freeman's words, "after fourteen days of incessant fatigue, toil and danger, doubt and uncertainty, we at length gained the river above the Great Raft, contrary to the decided opinion of every person who had any knowledge of the difficulties we had to encounter." The party reentered the Red River through Willow Chute (not named by them), noted the existence of a large lake to the west on which the Caddos resided, and proceeded upriver to the Coushatta village at Cedar Bluffs.

Another notable passage was taken by Claiborne Wright and his family in 1816 to become the first settlers to arrive by boat in the Red River portion of the Arkansas Territory. The passage was taken in a twelve-foot by sixty-foot keelboat named the *Pioneer* with the assistance of an Indian guide. The trip was described in later years by Claiborne's son, George, who was seven at the time of passage: "To look back and just imagine all the meandering that had been made and it did really seem to have been impossible to have made all those turns and to have got safly through into the River again. It was one continuous chain of bayous and Lakes from the time that we left the River at Coshatto shoot until we passed out of the Last Willow shoot into the main River."

Coushatta Chute was taken rather than Loggy Bayou because all ascending boats took that passage to save time, according to Hanscom's 1825 letter to Izard. George Wright maintained that this was the first keelboat passage around the raft. However, credit for that accomplishment must go to Major Moss, also in 1816, because Paxton was writing about facts well known in Hempstead County, Arkansas, in 1828 and to a person who was well acquainted with Major Moss. The Wright passage was the first to be accomplished by a keelboat that was not on government business.

The foot of the raft established the upper limit of steamboat navigation on the Red River. Robert Fulton is credited with the creation in 1807 of the first steamboat to operate successfully as a commercial venture in American waters. The *New Orleans*, in 1812, was the first steamboat to operate on the Mississippi River. The first steamboat to operate on the Red River was Henry Shreve's *Enterprise*, which arrived at Alexandria in January 1815 carrying volunteers from the Battle of New Orleans. The *Beaver* reached Natchitoches in March 1820 and established a lucrative Red River trade, making ten or eleven trips during that year. In 1825, the *Governor Shelby*, *Kentucky*, *Rapide*, *Hornet*, *Superior*, *Eliza*, *Natchitoches*, *Florence*, *Louisville*, and *Neptune* made thirty-six trips to Natchitoches.

There is no record of any steamboat ever having taken the eastern or western bypasses fully around the raft. However, it is known that Ben Milam's *Enterprise* (not the same boat as Shreve's *Enterprise*) ascended the Red River around the raft through a portion of the eastern bypass, reaching the Arkansas Territory in June 1831, followed by the *Rover* in 1834. These passages were intimately connected with federal modifications to transport routes undertaken by Washington Seawell and Henry Shreve in the 1830s and are more appropriately discussed in the next chapter. In addition, the first documented passage of a steamboat through Bayou Pierre was the *Bolivar* in 1836; but this had nothing to do with bypassing the raft, which had been removed up to the mouth of Twelvemile Bayou in 1835 by Shreve.

The eastern route from 1816 through 1834 was almost entirely a pirogue and keelboat route. It does not appear to have become an important route for keelboats until June 1824, when Fort Towson was founded on the upper Red River; keelboats were the preferred mode of military supply transport on difficult passages such as the Red River in the 1820s. Although steamboats probably ran on the Red River above Natchitoches as the raft retreated, there is nothing to suggest penetration of Coushatta Chute or Loggy Bayou prior to the 1831 voyage of the *Enterprise*.

CLOSURE OF THE EASTERN BYPASS

The critical weakness of the eastern route around the raft was not its difficulty, but rather its vulnerability to the raft as it moved upstream. In an 1841 Corps report, Lt. Col. Stephen H. Long states: "In 1820, it is said, that the raft removed by Captain Shreve from that part of the river above the outlet of Willow-chute had no existence, the channel above that point having been open and unobstructed." This means that Willow Chute was closed by the raft in 1821. The eastern route was still usable through upward extensions formed by new outlet channels created by the raft and by canals cut by the keelboat men (particularly the government component) in the small pocket of opportunity afforded by the Red River floodplain between Willow Chute and Hurricane Bluffs (fig. 3-8).

The upward extension of the eastern route is described in Hanscom's late 1825 letter, when a new outlet named Willow Bayou formed above Willow Chute:

> In descending the Red River, the route at present leaves the river and enters the Willow Bayou, the head of which is about six miles in a straight line from the head of the raft; this Bayou is deep and rapid; it has increased in size at least one half within the last three years, in consequence of the raft having caused an elevation of the river at the head of it. The navigation of this Bayou is continued for about six miles, in which distance it divides its channel in numerous places, the principal left hand one of which is followed and conducts into a small lake known by the name of Stump Lake, about one mile in diameter. Before entering Stump Lake the principal branch of the Willow Bayou is left to the right; from Stump Lake, there is a pass of about four miles, the navigation of which is similar to that of Willow Bayou, into another small lake called Mud Lake, in which the water is shallow; the distance through it is one mile. From Mud-Lake, the route pursued enters Bee-Bayou.

Human efforts to deal with the situation are presented by Capt. George Birch in his 1826 survey report:

> From lake Bodkeau boats enter Bee Bayou, which has a circular course and is fifty miles in length; at the head of it is Muddy lake, a short distance from Red River above the raft. In 1822, Capt. Berryman of the 7th Infantry, cut a canal from the river to the bayou only one hundred and twenty-seven feet in length, through which he passed with his keelboat, and which

until last year had been the only communication from the river above to the keelboat navigation below. A Mr. Harrison passed up with a keelboat last winter and found that the river had rafted up to the outlet cut by Capt. Berryman and had also choked up the canal. Mr. Harrison was then obliged to cut an outlet higher up the river, through which this spring a number of boats have passed down with facility. The great objection to this route is that owing to the filling up of the river with driftwood every year at least two miles ascending, in a short time the raft forms above and chokes up the canal previously cut, and renders the cutting of another necessary, higher up the river and above the driftwood.

The upper limit of the potential for human and natural modifications of the eastern route was set by Hurricane Bluffs. That upper limit was reached when the raft arrived at Hurricane Bluffs in 1828. In Paxton's

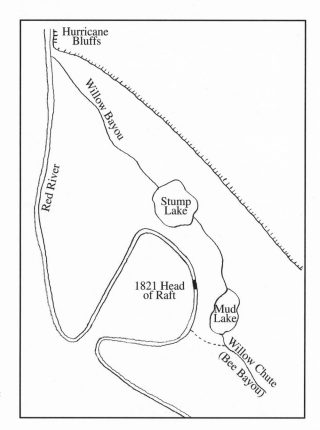

Fig. 3-8. Outlet channel after closure of Willow Chute

words: "The head of the raft has now arrived at a point where the river washes the left bluffs. The course of the keel-boats which has hitherto brought up supplies, has been to the left of the channel; but it is now thought that they can no longer get out on that side on account of the bluffs." By the late 1820s, the eastern bypass around the raft had exhausted the gamut of its possibilities. It was time for the federal government to intervene.

·4·
Shreve's
Accomplishment

EARLY FEDERAL EFFORTS

Federal interest in the navigability of the Red River and the Great Raft as an impediment to navigation and settlement extends back to the Louisiana Purchase in 1803 and Thomas Jefferson's desire for westward expansion. In seeking to understand the conditions for expansion, Jefferson sent out expeditions such as Lewis and Clark in 1804 and Freeman and Custis in 1806 and secured information from locally knowledgeable sources. One of these was John Sibley, resident of Natchitoches, Louisiana, and newly appointed Indian agent, who was asked to provide an account of the Red River and adjacent country. This resulted in an April 1805 letter to General Dearborn, the secretary of war, which was published as part of the Lewis and Clark Papers.

According to Sibley's account, the Bayou Pierre route to the west of the Red River had been closed by the raft in 1798 or 1799, but the Willow Chute route to the east was still open. The foot of the raft was at the upper cabin of the Campti settlement above Natchitoches, and the head was about twenty miles (forty miles corrected) below the Willow Chute exit from the Red River. Sibley recognized the raft as an impediment to navigation. Although he was later to become an advocate of raft removal, in 1805 he apparently did not think that removal was necessary, pointing out that bayous and lakes on the east side of the river offered adequate passage around the raft for small boats.

Arkansas became a territory in 1820, and Fort Towson was founded in May 1824 on the Red River in what is now southeastern Oklahoma. These events spurred federal interest in the raft as an obstruction to navigation and settlement. The Willow Chute exit was blocked by the raft in about 1821. The eastern route was still usable by keelboats through upward extensions of the route formed by Red River overflow and through canals cut progressively back to the Red River as the raft moved upstream. However, it was obvious that within a few years the head of the raft would reach Hurricane Bluffs, prohibiting any access to the Red River from the east.

Overland transport was extremely tedious and costly, and Fort Towson needed supplies. In conjunction with the founding of the fort, the commanding officer of the Western Department was instructed by the Department of War on 25 March 1824 to find a solution to the navigation problem. A survey was initiated, which was conducted by Capt. George Birch of the Seventh Infantry late in 1825. This was the first federal survey of the Sodo Lake area.

Birch left Natchitoches on 25 October with his subordinate (a Lieutenant Lee), a guide by the name of Wallace, and twenty-five men in a keelboat. On reaching the foot of the raft, he left the keelboat and, accompanied by Lieutenant Lee, Wallace, and six men in two skiffs, traveled through the raft up to Cross Bayou. This is the only report of anyone having actually ascended the Red River through the raft, a necessity for understanding the nature of the obstruction, but nevertheless a feat requiring boldness and tenacity: "I left the keel . . . and pursued the course of old Red River, through its meanderings a distance of ninety-six miles, passing in my route 168 rafts of timber, from 100 yards to one mile in length, composed of logs of all sizes, and so closely connected as to preclude the possibility of removal. The labor and difficulty encountered by us on the route was immense, having to drag our skiffs around all the obstructions, most of them a quarter, and some a mile long, through thick wood and cane brake."

Birch did not think that removal of the raft was possible. The objective of the survey was to determine whether the old Bayou Pierre route could be reopened by tying it into one of the Red River distributaries that flowed into Soda Lake. This distributary was referred to as Coushatta Bayou by Birch, so named because it left the Red River in the vicinity of the Coushatta Indian village at Cedar Bluffs. Coushatta

Bayou, which joined Cottonwood Bayou before emptying into Soda Lake, was later to be known as Peach Orchard Bayou **(fig. 4-1)**.

Birch left the Red River and the raft through Cross Bayou and entered Cross Lake, proceeding north through the hydrologic connection between Soda Lake and Cross Lake that was known as The Pass during the steamboat period. He then entered Twelvemile Bayou, which he called Sheodo Bayou, proceeding thence into Soda Lake, which he called Lake Sheodo. The water was shallow, and Birch was unable to locate Coushatta Bayou, though he was fully convinced of the efficacy of the route because it had previously been used during higher water by one of his men accompanied by Wallace. His most significant encounter was with the tremendous sediment deposits that were building up in Soda Lake and that were later to prove hazardous for steamboat navigation: "In our endeavors to find this Bayou (which forms the most important link in the chain of the proposed communication by way of Bayou Pierre river, and Red river, 30 miles

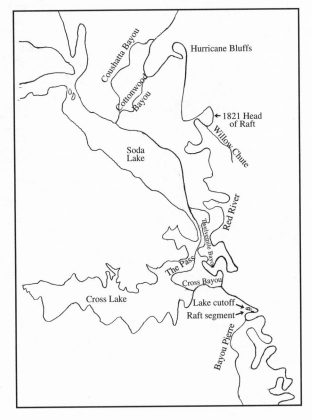

Fig. 4-1. Birch's plan of action

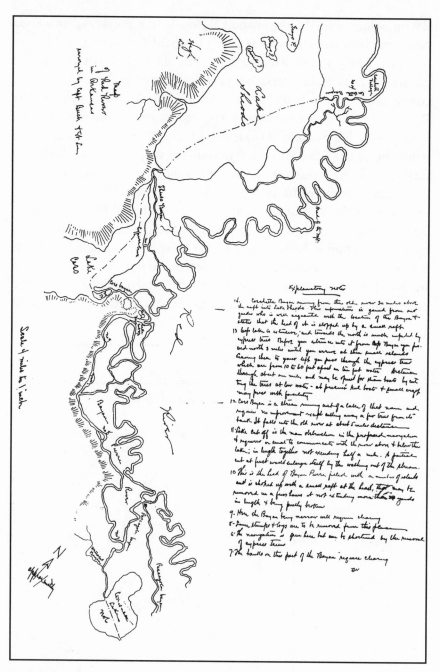

Fig. 4-2. Birch's survey map. *Source: LSU in Shreveport, Noel Memorial Library Archives*

above the head of the raft,) we spent three or four days along the shore where its entrance was said to be located, but owing to the shoalness of the lake our skiffs were rendered useless, and the mud so soft, that, in attempting to coast the lake around on foot, we frequently in the distance of half a mile, sunk up to our waists in the mud. Being nearly out of provisions, and no appearance of a rise of water, I concluded to return, not without however being perfectly satisfied as to the practicability of passing through the Coshatta Bayou at a high stage of water."

Birch's proposed route is displayed on a map accompanying his report (fig. 4-2). This was the first survey map of the Sodo Lake area. However, Birch was interested in bypassing the raft, and his map extends only over to the two islands at the west end of Soda Lake that formed Big and Little Willow Passes. No improvements would be needed to Coushatta Bayou other than the removal of a small raft at its head. Tree removal would be needed in Cross Lake and Cross Bayou. Between Cross Bayou and Bayou Pierre, the Red River was nearly free of obstructions. However, there was a raft segment in the Red River loop out of which Bayou Pierre ran (see fig 4-1). To bypass this obstruction, two canals would be needed incorporating a small lake (designated Lake Cutoff) on the Red River floodplain. A small raft needed to be removed at the head of Bayou Pierre, and occasional tree clearing would be required on Bayou Pierre all the way down to the vicinity of Natchitoches.

Birch was adamant that the Great Raft could not be removed and that his proposed route would secure adequate passage for steamboats to the upper Red River: "With the foregoing view of the survey, and by reference to my map, it may be safely calculated that the communication by way of Bayou Pierre River can be opened for steam boats, and that the raft of Old River can never be removed."

The General Assembly of the Territory of Arkansas was quick to respond to the opportunity offered by federal concern for the supply of Fort Towson. A copy of the 1824 Department of War order was secured, and a memorial (now lost) was submitted to the U.S. Congress "asking the appropriation of a sum of money for the removal of certain obstructions in the navigation of Red River." The memorial was referred to the Committee on Roads and Canals, which immediately began to obtain information, resulting in the March 1827 report on "Navigation of Red River" and the subsequent essay by Joseph Paxton.

The 1825 letter from A. Hanscom of Miller County discussed the relative merits of improvements to the eastern and western bypasses, favoring the latter. A letter from B. Bullett, a citizen of Louisiana, submitted by Henry W. Conway, delegate to Congress from the Territory of Arkansas, came down decidedly in favor of raft removal because it would reclaim lands inundated by raft-induced flooding as well as providing through navigation for steamboats.

The staunchest advocate of raft removal was Joseph Paxton of Hempstead County. In his 1828 letter to Ambrose H. Sevier, delegate to Congress from the Territory of Arkansas, Paxton emphasized defense, the supply of Fort Towson, land reclamation, and, most importantly, protection of the Arkansas planters from the impending destruction of their lands by the upward-moving raft, drawing a parallel with the previous destruction of Bodcau Prairie:

> Bodcaw prairie alone contains an area of four hundred square miles. It is represented to have been exceedingly beautiful, and thirty years since was the resort of immense herds of buffaloes. It is now a stagnant lake, but would then be, with all its former beauty and enhanced fertility, reclaimed.
>
> Opening the raft would prevent an immense destruction of United States' property. It must not be forgotten that the raft is not standing still, but is gradually progressing upward, like a destroying angel, spreading desolation over a most lovely country, partially surveyed, purchased up, and settled, at the appalling rate of nearly one hundred thousand dollars in each ten years. These are not chimeras, but truths that can be substantiated. Most of the inhabitants in this devoted section are known to you, and from you, as their representative, they are expecting relief. I am acquainted with them all. Some of them are my intimate friends; they have ventured their all here in this once delightful country, without being aware of the catastrophe that awaited them. Very lately their true situation presented itself; but every season now adds proof of the insensible but irresistible and gradual approach of their fate. They are gazing in torpid despair on the ruin that awaits them, and which they can neither resist nor escape. The lands that they have purchased, with all their additional improvements, will now command no price. Thus, all those beautiful prairies

above the raft, the representation of what Bodcaw was once, and now the pleasant abode of man, must become in rotation what Bodcaw is now, or the loathsome habitation of the reptile. These reflections excite feelings that are not in unison with dispassionate representation.

The Committee on Roads and Canals responded favorably to the memorialists with a paean to federal responsibility for dealing with the problems posed by the raft, stating:

> That, after much examination of the object of the memorialists, the committee appreciate highly the importance of improving the navigation of one of the largest rivers of North America, bordering on the territory of the United States, for several hundred miles, and running through it for a considerable distance. The interest which the Memorial of the Legislature of Arkansas inspired, is increased by a consideration of the small extent of this line of navigation which requires its obstructions to be removed, in order to bring the whole into effective and beneficial use, in peace, for commercial purposes, and in war, for those of military defense. In the former, not only the United States have a deep interest, as a proprietor of an extensive territory, to be disposed of for their benefit and that of the future purchasers of their right of soil—but the state of Louisiana, through which the produce of the extensive and fertile region of country on the waters of this river must, hereafter, reach its market, whether it ascend or descend the Mississippi.
>
> In the latter, every interest of the United States is involved, since the Federal Government is the shield of the security of all its members. And this view suggests the more urgent call upon the Union, in favor of the proposed improvement, from the consideration that both Louisiana and the Territory of Arkansas present exposed frontiers, both to civilized and savage foes.

Nevertheless, the committee didn't know what to do. The Territory of Arkansas was clearly in favor of land protection as well as navigation, and the former could be achieved only through raft removal. However, Congress at this time had authority over defense and navigation, but not over flood control, much less over the imminence of flooding. The committee also had in hand a report recommending the needed improvements from a federal perspective, which did not entail raft removal.

As a consequence, the committee responded favorably to a request by Alexander Macomb, the chief of engineers, for $25,000 to effect the needed improvement, with a stipulation that the situation be restudied. The requested funds were appropriated through the River and Harbor Act of 23 May 1828, with the wording left vague to allow for the possibility of dealing with the raft either through removal or through improvements to a bypass.

Capt. W. H. Chase, commanding engineer of the Gulf of Mexico, was placed in charge of the effort. In the summer of 1828, an examination was made of the portion of the Red River occupied by the raft, and a project was proposed for navigation improvements. Although the results of this survey are not available in the published records, the survey was conducted by Chase's assistant, Lt. A. H. Bowman, and Bowman's proposed plan of action is evident from the nature of the work that actually transpired.

Bowman's plan of action was a modification of Birch's proposal. In an 1837 report concerning his oversight of Henry Shreve's raft removal activities, Bowman indicates that he visited the raft in 1828 and that at that time the head of the raft reached within a very short distance of Coushatta Bayou. Birch's proposal to utilize Coushatta Bayou was no longer tenable. Bowman found another distributary, Red Bayou, much farther upstream, and his plan of action was to provide improvements to Red Bayou, link Red Bayou with Black Bayou (which entered into Clear Lake), and then proceed through Soda Lake and Twelvemile Bayou, incorporating the Lake Cutoff channel proposed by Birch (**fig. 4-3**).

The work effort was placed in the hands of Lt. Washington W. Seawell (not Sewell as it is spelled in all secondary sources), who was commissioned in the Seventh Regiment of Infantry in 1825 and assigned to engineer duties. Seawell's effort was limited to the construction of small canals and to cutting down and removing standing and fallen timber in the selected route. The work began in the winter of 1829 at the upper end. By June of the next year, twelve of the nineteen miles between Clear Lake and the Red River outlet of Red Bayou had been "cleared out and rendered navigable for boats."

Fig. 4-3. Bowman's
plan of action

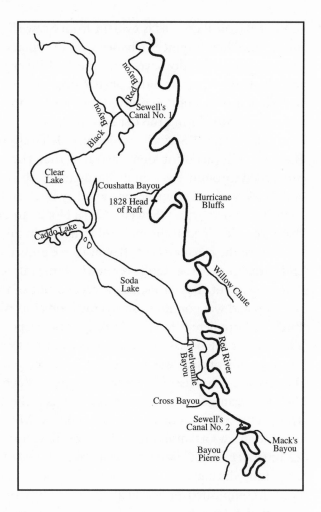

The latter part of the first period of operations undoubtedly included the construction of Sewell's Canal, linking Red Bayou with Black Bayou in 1830 (see fig. 4-3). This was not a conventional canal. In the early 1920s, the canal was inspected by a team from the Department of the Interior in conjunction with litigation concerning the navigability of Black Bayou. The DOI determined that Sewell's Canal was not really a canal, but rather an ancient natural channel linking Red Bayou and Black Bayou. Seawell's effort was apparently limited to tree removal and some deepening.

By September 1831, fifty-three miles of improvements had been completed, incorporating the area from the head of Red Bayou to the head of Bayou Pierre, as is evident from Seawell's final report on the project to Chief Engineer Charles Gratiot: "Black Bayou, Clear Lake, Sheodo Lake, Sheodo Bayou and the Red River from Sheodo Bayou to Lake Cut-off, are without obstruction—the canal from Red River to Lake Cut-off is not completed, but is so nearly so, as to have been passed by boats during the last season."

In this account, Seawell, like Birch, calls Twelvemile Bayou "Sheodo Bayou." The account demonstrates that the completed project proceeded through Twelvemile Bayou rather than through Cross Lake and Cross Bayou as originally proposed by Birch and that it incorporated the Lake Cutoff bypass (Sewell's Canal No. 2) around the raft segment that Birch identified as the major obstruction in the Bayou Pierre route.

Before the canal was cut, Bayou Pierre proceeded out of the lower end of the loop of the Red River in which the raft segment was located. After it was cut, Bayou Pierre proceeded out of the Red River above the loop and was contiguous with the loop at its western edge; and, as Birch had predicted, Bayou Pierre quickly deepened its new channel, allowing for the passage of steamboats and keelboats.

Seawell's project was important for three reasons. Even without the proposed downstream improvements to Bayou Pierre, it allowed the first steamboat, the *Enterprise*, to reach the upper Red River in 1831. This boat was owned by Benjamin R. Milam, who was later to become an important figure in the Texas Revolution. According to the 22 June *Arkansas Gazette*, Seawell was on board. The trip was made in May–June during an extreme low-water period and could only have been accomplished under such circumstances by a very small vessel such as the *Enterprise*, which weighed thirty to forty tons and drew twenty to twenty-four inches loaded. The event was described in a 24 June letter from James S. Conway of Lafayette County, Arkansas, which was published in the 6 July *Arkansas Gazette*:

> *Dear Sir*—I have the satisfaction of informing you, that, on the 16th inst., the citizens of Long Prairie, in Lafayette county, had the great satisfaction to witness the landing of the steamboat *Enterprise*, (formerly the Alps) at the first settlement on Red river, above the Great Raft. It is difficult to imagine the powerful effect this circumstance had on the feelings of the citizens. Men, women, and children, were elated almost to intoxication. For this novel and cheering sight, we are indebted

to the daring enterprise of Col. BENJAMIN R. MILAM, who recently became the owner, for this express expedition—and set out from Natchitoches about the 23rd May, with the avowed intention of bringing her through, or sinking her in the attempt. The former he accomplished, though not without considerable labor, in opening the numerous narrow bayous through which she had to pass; much of which labor was occasioned by the extreme low stage of the water, which was scarcely ever known so low at the same season of the year. Her passage was very much prolonged in consequence of having two very large keel boats in tow, and all the way from Natchitoches having to cut and use green wood.

Her passengers are Col. MILAM, Lt. HAYWOOD, of the U.S. Army, Capt. HAWLEY (of the boat), Capt. R. H. FINN, Messrs. T. J. WRIGHT, STEEL, SAVAGE, SIMON, BLOCK, and her crew; all of whom join in saying, that their passage was much more agreeable than could have been anticipated on the first steam-boat passage through the Great Raft of Red river; and that the trip would have been performed in half the time, with a favorable stage of water.

The route taken by the *Enterprise* from Natchitoches to Long Prairie is not described in the newspapers. However, another steamboat, the *Rover*, made what undoubtedly was a similar passage in 1834, proceeding through Coushatta Chute, Lake Bistineau, and Mack's Bayou (see fig. 4-3). The *Rover* then proceeded up Red River through Lake Cutoff, thence into Twelvemile Bayou and the remainder of the route opened by Seawell. The voyage of the *Rover* is described retrospectively in the 3 July 1872 *Shreveport Times*:

Speaking of the navigation of Mack's Bayou, it may not be out of place to state that it was navigated many years ago. We learn from Capt. Jim Crooks that his uncle Capt. Ben Crooks, in 1834, had a government contract to carry government stores from New Orleans to Fort Towson. He loaded the steamer Rover and started up in the spring of that year. Owing to the raft in the river between this point and Grand Bayou, he left the river and went up Coushatta Chute, across Loggy bayou, then filled with patches of raft, to Lake Bistineau, thence up

Red Chute to Sniders' Bluff on Lake Bodceau, where a canal connects with Mack's bayou, thence up Red river to Twelve Mile bayou, through Soda, Shift Tail and Clear lakes to Black bayou and Red bayou into the upper river. Before the raft formed above Willow chute the boats used to go up Lake Bodceau to where Willow chute puts into the lake, and passed into Red river that way. It will be seen that the early navigators of Red river had as good, if not a better knowledge of this country than we have at the present time. A thorough account of the trials and hardships of the early attempts to navigate Red river would be very interesting at this time. Who is equal to the occasion?

The only steamboat to have ever taken the full Seawell route, including the unimproved Bayou Pierre portion, appears to have been the *Bolivar*, as indicated in the 1843 report of the Louisiana state engineer: "During the high water of 1836, the steamer Bolivar with a large keel in tow passed through the Pierre on her way to Jonesboro. She made it through the bayou in three days, losing one day in Spanish lake. This was before a log had been removed or a tree cut from the channel, and the boat left but slight trace of her passage. I noticed but five or six trees cut on the upper part."

The second reason that Seawell's project was important was that the route opened by Seawell through Twelvemile Bayou, Soda Lake, Clear Lake, Black Bayou, and Red Bayou was to remain—with minor modifications—the only passage to upper Red River until the raft was finally destroyed in 1873. Contrary to popular opinion, the upper Red River trade was very large. If the route had not been opened by Seawell, ports and landings on the northern edge of the Cypress Bayou and lakes route would have captured much of this trade, and minor landings such as Monterey would have become places of considerable commercial importance.

Third, and most importantly from the perspective of the present study, the downstream portion of Seawell's project constituted by Twelvemile Bayou and Soda Lake was the first leg of the Cypress Bayou and lakes route. Seawell provided the first of many improvements to this route, though obviously not for the sake of passage to the west, which was inhabited only by Indians at the time. The exact nature of Seawell's improvements to Soda Lake and Twelvemile Bayou cannot be determined from the published sources. However, given the general nature of his activities, it is almost certain that he removed standing timber in Soda Lake, establishing the route that was used throughout the steamboat period.

In spite of the elation over the opening of steamboat commerce to upper Red River, the citizens of Arkansas were not pleased with the results of Seawell's effort. On 7 November 1831, they submitted another memorial to Congress indicating that commerce through the Seawell route had already reached $300,000 annually but complaining of its dangers and consequent exorbitant insurance costs and requesting $25,000 for raft removal.

Seawell responded to this memorial by arguing for the safety of the route, pointing out that raft removal would be costly and probably only temporary because of the continuous accumulation of drift. He requested an additional appropriation to complete and improve the work. This request was granted, but the funds became available too late in the season to begin operations. In his 1832 annual report, Chief of Engineers Charles Gratiot said that this was just as well, because new information had led to a reversal of policy:

> The appropriation for overcoming the obstructions presented to the navigation of Red river by the Great Raft became available at too late a period in the season to make the necessary preparation for continuing the work on that river during the past summer, as almost all the supplies for the support of the force requisite for their prosecution can only be forwarded to the point at which they would be required in the season of high water. . . . This is less to be regretted, as it is believed from the reports received at this department, as well as from verbal information entitled to great credit, that the plan of operations heretofore pursued is not such as to afford, even in its accomplishment, any lasting benefit to the navigation of that river. Instead of deepening the bayous and connecting them by short canals, and thus opening a communication around the raft, it is the opinion of persons, who have had opportunities of judging, that the raft itself might be removed through the agency of one or two of the steamboats at present employed in improving the navigation of the Mississippi and Ohio rivers at an expense not exceeding that which would attend the execution

of the plan already adopted. This being the opinion also of people residing in the neighborhood of the raft, it was deemed advisable to suspend further operations till one of the boats alluded to could be dispatched, without injury to the service on which she is at present engaged, to ascertain by trial the possibility of effecting its removal. In addition to the benefit which the removal of the raft would confer upon the navigation of the river, it would reclaim by drainage an immense tract of valuable land which otherwise must lie waste till the water with which it is at present covered is carried off through its natural channels.

SHREVE ATTACKS THE RAFT

Foremost among the persons to whom Gratiot referred as having had "opportunities of judging" was Capt. Henry Miller Shreve, after whom Shreveport was named. Shreve was one of those energetic nineteenth-century figures who achieved distinction in a number of different areas. Shreve was an entrepreneur of navigation—a businessman who made important contributions to steamboat technology, built boats, engaged in commerce, established new routes, and was instrumental in breaking the back of the Fulton steamboat monopoly. He was also a public servant who made significant contributions to snagboat technology and implemented that technology as superintendent of Western River Improvements for the Corps of Engineers, a position to which he was appointed in 1826.

Shreve had been highly successful in his operations on the Ohio, Mississippi, and Arkansas, which involved snag removal and channel straightening; and as superintendent of Western River Improvements, raft removal fell within his jurisdiction. In September 1832, Gratiot wrote to Shreve, who was his immediate subordinate, asking his opinion on the feasibility of raft removal and his willingness to undertake the task. Shreve responded immediately to the challenge, without ever having seen the raft.

In February 1833, he proceeded to Louisville to outfit the expedition. The snagboat *Archimedes* and the steamboats *Java*, *Souvenir*, and *Pearl* were given minor repairs; 159 men, including officers, mechanics, cooks, and laborers, were obtained; the approximately $22,000 left over from Seawell's project was acquired from Gratiot because the remoteness of the raft region made the receipt of monthly installments impractical; and additional information was obtained on the raft, which led Shreve to note: "I find public opinion much against the probability of removing the raft; but I am of a different opinion, and believe that I shall succeed."

The entire expedition arrived at the first deposits of drift on the Red River on 11 April 1833 and immediately began work. The situation confronted by the work party is ably represented in Shreve's *Rough Sketch of that part of Red Rivir* [sic] *in which the Great Raft is Situated*, which was submitted by Shreve in 1833 in conjunction with his report on the first year of work **(fig. 4-4)**. The area up to Coates' Bluff was visually inspected by Shreve, and the area above was delineated on the basis of received information. The map was not based on a formal survey and is obviously not drawn to scale. It was, like Birch's, a working map intended for informing higher authorities and Congress about the dimensions of the effort and the general approach that would be taken.

Shreve's map shows the entire raft at an estimated 140 miles, with the midpoint constituted by the Caddo Indian Agency on Bayou Pierre slightly above its confluence with Sand Beach Bayou. Although the raft is shown as extending all the way down to Loggy Bayou, the ease of Shreve's progress on the lower half indicates that he was dealing with accumulated debris and that the raft proper did not begin until the midpoint, about eight straightline miles from downtown Shreveport.

The position of the head of the raft cannot be determined from the map. However, an exact position is given in Lt. A. H. Bowman's 1837 report on Shreve's progress. Bowman says that when the work of

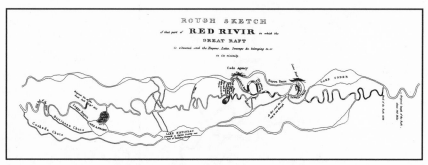

Fig. 4-4. Shreve's rough sketch. *Source: H. Doc. 98, 23rd Cong., 1st Sess.*

improvement began (i.e., in 1833), the head of the raft was five river miles below the Caddo village, obviously referring to the Coushatta village at Cedar Bluffs. This would place the head of the raft in the vicinity of Cowhide Bayou **(fig. 4-5)**.

Key geographic locators on Shreve's map are the Indian Agency and Coates' Bluff, because the location of both is known. The Sodo Lake complex is merely sketched—Shreve was not interested in the area, and no hint is given of a bayou to the west. Willow Chute and

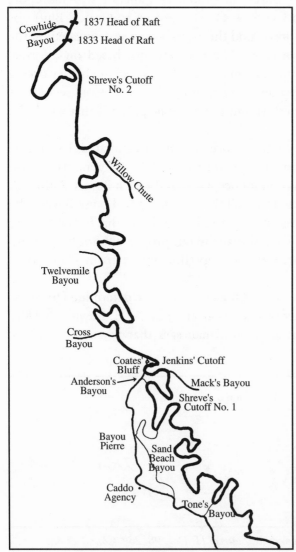

Fig. 4-5.
Shreve's project

(farther down) Mack's Bayou are shown as leaving the river to the east; and Tone's Bayou is shown as Norris' Small Bayou. Two possible cuts are shown, only the lower of which was eventually made.

The general plan of action was to use the *Archimedes* to pull and dismember logs, with stumps disposed offchannel and floatable logs either left instream to be carried down by the next rise or else stored offchannel. Some of the debris was used to block the mouths of distributaries so that flows would be concentrated in the main channel. The work of debris movement was conducted by the three steamboats and, later, a crab that pulled stumps on shore. Shoreline trees were cut to reduce the potential for reformation of rafts. Mud islands produced by the raft were simply allowed to be washed away by increased flows; but cuts were to be made at key points to reduce navigation distance, bypass some raft segments, and produce storage areas for debris.

The activities of the work party in 1833 extended only from 1 April through 23 June. Shreve had been instructed by Gratiot not to exceed his allocation, and within a little less than three months the funds were exhausted. During this time, Shreve was able to clear the river of obstructions up to the Indian Agency, which was the halfway point in the project. The ease with which the downstream decayed raft materials were removed led Shreve to underestimate the dimensions and costs of the task at hand.

During the second week of April, he estimated that the whole raft could be removed in sixty-six days, noting, however, that he was "not informed of what may yet be found above." By June, he was more cautious, particularly after having seen some of the upper portions of the raft and recognizing that the work would be greatly increased at the head where the timber was undecayed. Nevertheless, he remained highly optimistic, stating that the raft could be removed in nine months of concentrated effort at a cost of $10,000. He asserted that his initial success had already demonstrated that raft removal was feasible: "That the removal of the raft can be accomplished there is no doubt. Nothing is required but the necessary funds in the hands of an individual who possesses the requisite skill with sufficient energy to put that skill in operation."

Funding arrived too late for any work to be done until the end of 1834. This was not a problem for Shreve because he had much more important duties on other western rivers, particularly the Mississippi and Ohio. The timing of work on the Red and the allocation of men and boats to raft removal was always subordinate to these other activities.

Shreve closed his operations on the Ohio in November 1834 and proceeded to the Red River with the steamboats *Java, Souvenir,* and *Pearl,* three keelboats, three machine boats, and 300 men, officers, and mechanics. Arriving in December in the area where the raft had been removed in 1833, the party moved upstream cutting bank timber and removing remaining debris, a task that was finished in January 1835. The party was then joined by the *Archimedes,* which had been working on the Mississippi, and work commenced on the raft above the Indian Agency.

By 14 March, the raft was removed up to the point on Shreve's map marked for the first cutoff. The bend that was to be cut off was bow-shaped rather than the loop shown on Shreve's map and caused a detour of nearly eight miles. The neck, which was only 261 yards wide, was excavated, producing the area in Shreveport designated as Shreve's Island on contemporary maps (**see fig. 4-5**). The abandoned channel was used for storage of raft materials.

The *Souvenir* then proceeded from the cutoff bend, through Anderson's Bayou, into Bayou Pierre, and thence into the northern portion of the bend cutting into Coates' Bluff where Seawell had isolated a raft segment by constructing his canal. This raft segment was removed in fifteen days, and by 13 April the whole river was cleared up to Twelvemile Bayou, which Shreve called Soda Bayou.

By the time work stopped on 25 May, the raft had been removed to within six miles of Benoit's Bayou, with an estimated twenty-three river miles of raft remaining. Shreve was still highly optimistic, yet he was much more cautious with respect to estimates of time and cost. Particularly time consuming was the need to stop up numerous distributaries to insure sufficient flow in the main channel to carry off loosened raft materials. Nevertheless, Shreve believed the work could be completed in one season with an additional appropriation.

Shreve returned to Louisville, the base for all of his river improvement operations, in June 1835. The snagboat and the three steamboats were repaired, sent to work elsewhere, then returned to the Red River in December and began work on 7 January 1836. Shreve surveyed the remaining raft during that month, this being the first time that he had seen its upper portions. There were thirty-three rather than twenty-three miles of raft to be removed, the increase caused in part by an accumulation of five miles during high flows at the end of 1835.

Shreve also noted that the raft between Twelvemile Bayou and Willow Chute, part of which had already been removed, caused the greatest difficulties because of its compactness and that work above Willow Chute to the head of the raft would be easier. The problem of raft removal in the difficult area was increased by the fact that the Red River below Twelvemile Bayou had not sufficiently scoured to carry the flows from the Sodo Lake area. As a consequence, water entering the Red at Twelvemile Bayou flowed upstream into Benoit's Bayou, making it impossible to float loosened logs downstream on the Red. Obviously, Benoit's Bayou would need to be closed.

In January, Shreve projected completion of raft removal by 25 May, when the work was to be closed. Shreve was only able to reach one mile above Willow Chute, partially closing Willow Chute and Benoit's Bayou with raft materials. The remainder of the raft had proved to be far more intractable than Shreve had calculated, and much time was lost because of sickness among the workers. He was reluctant in his July report to estimate the time and cost for completion. Nevertheless, estimates were necessary; thus, he projected completion of raft removal by the end of the next season of work.

In 1837, Shreve nearly reached his goal, arriving within 440 yards of the head of the raft at the close of work on 25 May. The work was facilitated by a new snagboat, the *Eradicator*. All of the distributaries were sufficiently stopped, with the exception of Willow Chute, and a canal was excavated across a narrow point of land, cutting off a bend. With only 440 yards of raft remaining, Shreve had the end of the project in his sights: "I can now make a calculation, that I am willing to stake my reputation on, that the whole obstruction can be removed in three months."

A DIVERSION

The canal that was constructed in the first half of 1837 has given rise to a long-standing misinterpretation of Shreve's activities during that year. It has been assumed that this cut was the one adjacent to Coates' Bluff on Shreve's map and that the purpose of the cut was to isolate the Coates' Bluff settlement from the Red River in favor of the bluff a few miles upriver that was to become the site of Shreveport in which Shreve was to be an investor.

The assumption was made because the 1837 cut was not described and only two projected cuts are shown on the 1833 map: the Coates' Bluff cut and the Shreve Island cut, which was made in 1835. In addition, Lt. A. H. Bowman, who conducted a review of Shreve's progress, stated strongly in an April 1837 letter that this particular feature of Shreve's initial plan of action should be completed in the present season of work: it would save distance, avoid two sharp turns, redirect flow away from Bayou Pierre, enlarge the dimensions of the Red, and decrease the potential for raft formation.

Nevertheless, the Coates' Bluff cut was not made by Shreve in 1837; and if it were made by him at all, it was not within the context of his activities as a federal agent. Shreve ended his 1837 activities in the raft area in May and wrote the report in which the completed cut is mentioned in Louisiana in August. The Louisiana General Land Office contracted on 18 October for a survey that included the bend in the Red River fronting Coates' Bluff. This survey was completed in the fourth quarter of 1837. The bend is clearly shown, but there is no cut.

The cut referred to in Shreve's 1837 report was made far above the site of Shreveport in a secondary bend contiguous to the first large bend in the Red River above Shreveport (see fig. 4-5). It could not have been represented in Shreve's 1833 map because Shreve was not acquainted with this area of the raft. However, it is shown on a map and described as Shreve's cut in an 1841 report by Lt. Col. Stephen H. Long, who replaced Shreve as superintendent of Western River Improvements (fig. 4-6).

That this was Shreve's 1837 cut is obvious from Long's description. Long says that the bend was about three miles long and its neck about 150 yards wide and that the cutoff bend was used for the storage of raft materials. In his 1836 report, Shreve discusses the proposed cut in the context of work on the upper portion of the raft and describes it in the following terms: "I contemplate cutting through a point of land one hundred and sixty yards, which will shorten the river seven miles, and facilitate the removal of the remainder of the raft." The cutoff bend facilitated removal of the raft by serving as a materials storage area as is shown on Long's map. The correct length of the bend is given in Shreve's August 1837 report, after the cut was completed: "A canal was also excavated across a narrow point of land, through which the whole channel of the river now flows, and shortens the distance three miles."

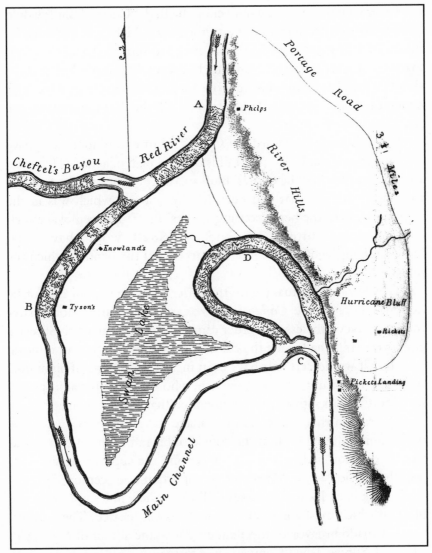

Fig. 4-6. Shreve's upper cutoff. *Source: S. Doc. 64, 27ʰ Cong., 1ˢᵗ Sess.*

Shreve does not mention any other cuts in his annual reports through 1840, when his jurisdiction over the raft came to an end. Nevertheless, it is obvious that the cutoff at Coates' Bluff was made before early 1839 and that Shreve was involved, as is indicated by a Shreveport *Caddo Free Press* article that appeared in the 19 February 1839 *New Orleans Commercial Bulletin* describing what a steamboat passenger would see moving upriver on the Red: "Coattes' Bluffs would next be noticed, as they jut out into the river, which now, however, by means of a "cut off," has left them never to return. An attempt was made by some persons at Natchitoches to build a town here, which should rival Shreveport, but it proved a failure, and the canal cut by order of Capt. Shreve has destroyed all the fond hopes of the speculators."

Shreve's attitude toward the Coates' Bluff cutoff appears to have changed over time. It was part of his original plan of action. However, when Shreve reached the Coates' Bluff area in 1835, he sent the *Souvenir* to remove the raft that had been left by Seawell, which was in the north portion of the bend fronting Coates' Bluff. This removal effort, which required fifteen days and cost $520, would have been incomprehensible if Shreve intended to cut off the bend in which the raft was located.

That Shreve eventually gave the order to make the cut cannot be doubted, because the *Caddo Free Press* article appeared shortly after the event. Nevertheless, the order cannot have been given to Shreve's employees. If he had made the cut in connection with the raft removal activities, it would certainly have been mentioned in one of his annual reports, particularly because Bowman, who was the official inspector for Shreve's work, strongly recommended that the cut be made.

The reason that Shreve did not make the cut in 1835 when the opportunity offered itself in the course of his raft removal efforts was that no decision had been made concerning the appropriate site for a port that obviously would become an important trade center. This port could have been located at Coates' Bluff or a few miles upriver at the bluff on which the Bennett and Cane store was located. The decision was not made in favor of the Bennett and Cane site until May 1836 when the Shreve Town Company was formed.

Action with respect to potential competition was not needed until 5 May 1837 when an agreement for the development of a settlement at Coates' Bluff was filed in Natchitoches. Shreve closed work on the raft on 25 May and went back to Louisville. The cut isolating the incipient Coates' Bluff settlement had not been made by the fourth quarter of the year. This cut was apparently made in the spring of 1838, under promptings by Shreve, but by Bushrod Jenkins, who was owner of the Red River property near the bend and also an investor in the Shreve Town Company.

This cut was not made by the *Eradicator*, which was not a dredge but a snagboat. No special equipment was needed. The Shreve Island cut was made in 1835, apparently by hand labor and before the *Eradicator* was put in service. Little would have been required to make the Coates' Bluff bend cut, because Bowman indicated in 1837 that the neck of the bend was only 34 yards wide. The Coates' Bluff bend cut is always designated "Jenkins Cutoff" on old maps and was identified as such by Long in 1841 in the same report that provides the map of Shreve's upper Red River cut: "From the inlets of Caddo and Cross-lake bayous, downward, the channel is sufficiently capacious and the current sufficiently rapid for a distance of nine miles, to Jenkins's cut-off, which leads across the gorge of a bend three miles below Shreveport, the circuit of which has an extent of about three miles, and its gorge about one hundred yards. Midway of the bend just mentioned is the outlet into bayou Pierre, which conveys from the main channel nearly or quite three-fourths of the water that passes Shreveport. A very considerable portion of the water thus withdrawn is restored again to the main channel at Shreve's cut-off, six miles below Jenkins's cut-off."

DENOUEMENT

At least one of Shreve's predictions was realized—the work of raft removal was completed in 1838. The breakthrough was achieved by the *Eradicator* and the *Pearl* and a new steamboat named the *Laura*, which began work in December, January, and February, respectively. On 7 March, one of the steamboats forced her way through the remaining section of raft. By the twenty-ninth, five commercial vessels had passed through the area on the way upriver. Two steamboats (the *Black Hawk* and the *Revenue*) were lost to snags in April before the *Eradicator* had completely removed debris; but by 1 May, "the navigation through the whole extent of the raft was considered safe, and was navigated by the largest class of boats trading in that river, with full cargoes, at the rate of seven miles an hour up stream, and twelve down, without damage to the boats."

The raft had been defeated; but Shreve's success was to be short-lived. Shreve had recognized as early as 1836 that maintenance work would be needed to keep the river open. In July 1838, a new raft of about 2,300 yards formed in the vicinity of the previous raft's head, an ideal place for new raft formation because of the constricted nature of the channel and slackwater conditions created by the numerous distributaries to the west. Work on this obstruction began in December and was completed by February 1839. Another raft of about 2,150 yards formed in April. Finding himself in an emergency situation with exhausted appropriations, Shreve completed removal of this raft in May with personal finances and an advance from the Real Estate Bank in Washington, Arkansas (both of which were later reimbursed).

Yet another raft of one mile formed in August 1839 at a point about four miles below the head of the original raft. Arkansas citizens raised a sum of money to employ two steamboats for raft removal. This effort was successful, but only for a few weeks, when a new influx of raft materials closed the channel. The State of Louisiana attempted to remove this raft, which was about a mile in length, but was unsuccessful.

In October 1840, Shreve reported navigation permanently closed pending additional congressional appropriations, which he considered critical in order to prevent raft buildup. The appropriations were not forthcoming. In 1841, with a change of administrations in Washington, Shreve was relieved of his appointive position as superintendent of Western River Improvements and replaced by Lieutenant Colonel Long.

Although the problem of the raft was to be addressed almost continually in subsequent years, beginning with Long, it was not permanently removed until 1873. The one-mile raft segment attacked unsuccessfully by the State of Louisiana is the lower segment on Long's map. This segment was the foot of a new raft that built progressively upward, transforming the landscape and the conditions of navigation on the Red and around the raft and nearly reaching the Arkansas line before it was destroyed by a man even more impressive than Henry Shreve.

ASSESSMENT

The best assessment of Shreve's effort was given by Lt. A. H. Bowman in his oversight report of 16 April 1837, when the work was still in progress: "It is difficult to form a just conception of the magnitude of this work. . . . The indefatigable industry, zeal, and perseverance of the superintendent have triumphed over difficulties well calculated to intimidate him; bayous have been closed with masses of timber; islands of huge logs, for centuries imbedded together, and covered with living trees, have been removed; the timber composing them has been dragged on shore, or, being cut up or cast upon the current, has passed away. Indeed every mile in ascending bears evidence of the immense labor bestowed upon its improvement."

Nevertheless, Shreve should not be romanticized. He was not a visionary but a federal employee who had been given a job to do and sufficient men and equipment to accomplish the task. Although there were many skeptics concerning the possibility of raft removal, there were also many supporters, particularly in Arkansas and Louisiana, who were instrumental in securing the needed appropriations. Congress was consistent and generous, with substantial appropriations during almost every year of the life of the project, resulting in a total cost of $325,800. Although the raft was unique, its removal was merely a technical problem, and the measures employed by Shreve were not qualitatively different from those that he was using on other rivers. Finally, his dismissal was a normal political act, and Congress immediately provided appropriations for the continuance of the raft removal effort by Shreve's replacement.

Although the raft removal effort extended across six years, work was conducted during only twenty-two months by a person with more pressing duties elsewhere, and the breakthrough at the raft's head was actually accomplished in seventeen working months. It was Shreve's skill and energy that produced the desired results. Yet the project as a whole must be judged a failure, for the objective was not to remove the raft temporarily, but rather to open the upper Red River to permanent navigation. This failure was more than compensated for by benefits resulting from Shreve's effort that were not part of the official project purpose.

The raft never reformed in the area in which it had been removed. This provided conditions for rapid settlement below the new raft, a point about which Shreve was justly proud: "In that part of the river where the raft was located, there was not the trace of a man to be seen from its foot up to Rush island, near the Caddo agency, when the work was commenced in 1833, and which is now a continued line of cotton plantations, extending to the town of Shreveport, a distance of 115 miles. From that place to the head of the raft there are many large improvements, and preparations now in progress to put in cultivation a large portion of the land on that part of the river."

The effect on navigation of raft removal on the lower Red was instantaneous, with steamboats following in the wake of Shreve's progress, as indicated, for example, in Shreve's 1836 report: "There have been twenty-seven trips made this year, from January 1 to May 25, by steamboats as high as Coates's Bluff, which is 115 miles above the foot of the original raft." By the end of the project, the whole area between Carolina Bluffs and Loggy Bayou was open to navigation. The area mentioned by Shreve that was above Shreveport and below the foot of the new raft constituted a special component of Shreveport's steamboat activity designated the Old River trade.

Shreve also made an important contribution to the upper Red River trade. Throughout the decades when steamboats were most active on the Red, it was Seawell's route that provided access to the upper Red River. Although the lower portion of this route through Bayou Pierre was developed by the State of Louisiana in the 1840s, Bayou Pierre does not appear to have ever attained the ease of passage provided by the Red. Clearance of the Red up to the entrance to Twelvemile Bayou was thus a major improvement to the Seawell route, probably generating a much higher volume of upper Red River trade than would otherwise have been sustained.

Shreveport would probably never have come into existence, and most certainly not under that name. The continued existence of the raft above and below the site that eventually became Shreveport would have allowed for modest development of waterborne commerce in Northwest Louisiana and Southwest Arkansas. The Coates' Bluff settlement, situated strategically at the outlet of Bayou Pierre from the Red River, would have become the center of this trade, but no town of importance would ever have developed.

From the perspective of the present study, Shreve's most important accomplishment was the removal of the raft up to the mouth of Twelvemile Bayou, which was achieved in April 1835. Shreve had no interest in the area west of the Red River, except insofar as the distributaries that fed the Sodo Lake complex were impediments to his raft removal efforts. Nevertheless, by removing the raft up to that point, he provided through navigation on the Red into the Cypress Bayou and the lakes route, linking the area west of Shreveport with New Orleans, which was the center of commerce for the entire Mississippi River valley.

·5·
The Advent of Steamboats
1840-44

MISSING PIECES

With the removal of the raft up to the mouth of Twelvemile Bayou in April 1835, the Cypress Bayou and the lakes route was formally open to navigation. However, no boats went in that direction because there was as yet no settlement and attendant commercial activities to capture the attention of steamboats. The raft was removed to open Red River and particularly the Arkansas Territory on the upper Red, not to open the area west of the emerging town of Shreveport. The advent of steamboats on Cypress Bayou and the lakes was contingent on the development of the area and particularly on the inception of cotton agriculture.

Steamboat activity on the Red River followed closely in the wake of Shreve's progress upstream. In January 1834, the *Chesapeake* arrived at New Orleans "from the raft in Red River." The raft was removed up to the Coates' Bluff settlement (an early competitor of Shreveport, but now part of the city) in March 1835. Shreve reported on 6 June 1836 that twenty-seven trips had been made by steamboats as far as Coates' Bluff between 1 January and 15 May. The most active was the *Privateer*, which is reported in the 26 March *New Orleans Price Current* as having returned to New Orleans from Coates' Bluff, the first mention of this settlement in the navigation record.

Boats such as the *Privateer, Velocipede, Brian Boroihme,* and *Nick Biddle* are shown as returning from Coates' Bluff in the latter half of

1836. The 10 January 1837 *New Orleans Commercial Bulletin*'s record of the return of the *Nick Biddle* from "Shreve Port" marks the earliest reference to this emerging town. In an April 1837 report on Shreve's progress (which was within six miles of the head of the raft), Lt. A. H. Bowman reports that in the area in which obstructions had been removed, "Merchant boats are constantly passing and repassing" and therefore would prevent the reformation of any large raft.

During the first three months of 1838, the *Black Hawk, Brian Boroihme, Romeo, Revenue,* and *Livingston* arrived back at New Orleans from Shreveport. On 7 March, Shreve's steamboat broke through the head of the raft, and Shreve reported that five merchant vessels had passed through the cleared area by the nineteenth. Boats like the *Brian Boroihme, Livingston,* and *Cochuma* began arriving back from places like Fulton, Fort Towson, and Lost Prairie.

In 1839, the following boats are listed in the *New Orleans Commercial Bulletin* as having made at least one trip to Shreveport: *Athenian, Brian Boroihme, Campte, Cochuma, Columbian, Davy Crockett, Echo, Florida, Hannibal, Livingston, Manchester, Mariner, South Alabama, Swiss Boy,* and *Washington*. Boats traveling above Shreveport to various points up to Fort Towson included the *Brian Boroihme, Cochuma, Columbia, Echo, Florida, Liberty, M. Tarver, Manchester,* and *Mariner.*

The last boat from New Orleans that passed through the raft area before she reformed was the *Liberty* in June 1839, on her way to Fort Towson. The area above the raft was accessible through the old Twelvemile Bayou–Soda Lake–Black Bayou–Red Bayou route, but no boats were reported to have taken that passage in late 1839 or in 1840. The downstream portion of the Red above Shreveport was still open to navigation to the foot of the raft at Carolina Bluffs. Boats to Shreveport and to the foot of the raft in 1840 included the *Bogue Houma, Brian Boroihme, Caddo, Campte, Claiborne, Hannibal, Osceola, South Western,* and *Washington.*

The route west of Shreveport through Cypress Bayou and the lakes was poised for use pending settlement of the area. Commercial interest in the area northwest of Shreveport began to be expressed by returns from Caddo Prairie by the *Choctaw* in June 1836, the *Denmark* in February 1939, and the *Kansas* in January 1840, which is shown in the *New Orleans Price Current* as having returned on the eleventh with 232 bales of cotton. However, these trips were almost certainly to the Red Bayou–Black Bayou area and probably also upriver on the Red below the raft.

The area west of Shreveport does not appear to enter the newspaper navigation record until 1841. The 16 January *New Orleans Price Current* shows the *Miami*, with a McClure as captain, as having returned from "Caddo" on the ninth carrying 134 bales of cotton. That this was an abbreviation for Port Caddo is suggested by the fact that the 24 February 1842 *Daily Picayune* shows the *Star* as having returned from Caddo, and the 26 February *New Orleans Price Current* shows the same boat as having returned from Port Caddo.

On the same day that the *Miami* may have returned from Port Caddo, the *Brian Boroihme*, with John Smoker as captain, advertised in the *Daily Picayune* for Port Caddo. This was the first advertisement for any port or landing on the route. It was followed by a 15 June 1841 *Daily Picayune* advertisement for the *Farmer*, with A. Edwards as captain, to Benton and Port Caddo; by a 17 December 1841 *New Orleans Commercial Bulletin* advertisement for the *Vermillion*, with Arnold as captain, to Port Caddo; by a 9 January 1842 *Daily Picayune* advertisement for the *Echo*, with A. Wheeler as captain, to Port Caddo; by a 5 February 1842 *Daily Picayune* advertisement for the *Star*, with Ruter as captain, to Port Caddo; and by a 25 February 1842 *Daily Picayune* advertisement for the *Star*, with Ruter as captain, to Smithland and Port Caddo.

The navigation record suggests that steamboats first began operating on Caddo Lake up to Port Caddo in early 1841, that steamboats were carrying cotton out of Port Caddo by early 1841, and that there was a progressive movement upstream on Cypress Bayou to Benton in the middle of 1841 and to Smithland in early 1842. All of these points are tenuous. There are early texts that suggest that steamboats were operating on Caddo Lake before 1841. The assumption that the *Miami* returned to New Orleans from Port Caddo rather than Caddo Prairie is problematic. As will become clear in later chapters, advertisements are not firm indicators that a boat actually made a trip. The *Brian Boroihme* may not have traveled to Port Caddo in January 1841; the *Farmer* may not have traveled to Benton in June 1841; and the *Star* may not have traveled to Smithland in February 1842. There is, in fact, no firm evidence that any steamboat went beyond Port Caddo prior to 1845.

The first unequivocal evidence for the penetration of Caddo Lake by a steamboat is a 24 February 1842 *New Orleans Commercial Bulletin* record for the *Star* as having returned from Port Caddo on the twenty-third carrying 567 bales of cotton. This is also the first record of cotton export from the area. However, it cannot provide a starting point for a discussion of steamboat activity west of Shreveport because it disregards the significance of the advertisements for boats to Port Caddo and even Benton in 1841. It is therefore necessary before presenting a detailed analysis of the navigation record to consider the operational nature of steamboats, the general development of the area, evidence for boat activity prior to 1841, and the emergence of the earliest ports and landings.

NAVIGATIONAL CONTEXT

Steamboats were commercial freight and passenger carriers that went where business opportunities led them. There was no transport demand without people, so steamboats traveled to populated areas. Throughout the South, the primary functions of steamboats were to carry agricultural exports such as cotton and to bring supplies to producers. Steamboats traveled to areas where cotton was being produced by farmers and planters. The level of steamboat activity was generally proportional to the amount of cotton produced.

Steamboats were always preceded by people engaged in agriculture. In the earliest development of any particular area with water access, there was usually a brief period in which there were few people and no cotton production or production in such small amounts that the interest of the steamboat community was not stimulated. Transport needs might be satisfied by ox-wagons and by watercraft such as flatboats and keelboats. Steamboats were the most efficient carriers of cotton and plantation supplies. Consequently, increased population and production always gave rise to a spurt of steamboat activity, unless the waterbody was unusable for some reason.

Steamboats could stop anywhere for offloading and loading freight, which was done by the extension of a plank to the shore. However, they only stopped at demand points for freight services. These demand points were ports and landings. A landing served the needs of a specific plantation or a small group of plantations and usually included storage facilities of some sort such as a shed. Ports were larger—with more sophisticated storage facilities—and were maintained by mercantile establishments that served the needs of the farmers and planters within the region of the port's dominance.

The Cypress Bayou and the lakes area did not begin to be settled until the late 1830s, after Shreve removed the raft up to Twelvemile Bayou in 1835 and before the boundary between the United States and the Republic of Texas was established in 1841. The earliest description of this area is contained in a 28 March 1839 article in the Shreveport *Caddo Free Press* and reads as follows:

> EASTERN TEXAS.—Soda Lake, Port Caddo, Tuscumbia.
> Though the Parish of Caddo and Eastern Texas are divided by the political relations, they are in all other respects one and the same. The nature of the country, the quality of the soil, the staple products and means of communication are identical. The rapid settlement therefore of our neighbors is viewed by our citizens with great interest and gratification.—It is not generally known that Soda Lake is one of the most extensive and beautiful sheets of water in the south. Its fertile and picturesque shores are now cloathed with many a log cabin, and ere many months, the primeval forest must give way to the cultivated fields. Port Caddo and its vicinity, of which we have before spoken (and we are glad to perceive our notice generally copied in the city papers), continues to increase and improve at a rate, which in any other country would be deemed wonderful. Tuscumbia is a new town just laid off at the head of navigation on the Cypress Bayou, and must become a point of some importance. The tide of Anglo Saxon population is setting steadily and with no ebb to the west. Wave will follow wave until the towers and palaces of Mexico shall be submerged, the Rocky Mountains swallowed up and the stream of life flow uninterruptedly from the Atlantic to the Pacific.

This article indicates that in early 1839, the Sodo Lake area, which the article calls Soda in keeping with the conventional designation of the period, was just beginning to be settled. Many log cabins had been established, but the forest had not been cleared, and no crops had been planted. Port Caddo and Tuscumbia farther upstream on Cypress Bayou are mentioned. Reference to "Port Caddo" indicates some type of navigation, but it does not necessarily mean that steamboats went to that place by early 1839. Reference to Tuscumbia as "at the head of navigation" does not indicate any realized navigation, because the term commonly referred to the point farthest upstream on a navigable waterbody. "The city" was a conventional term for New Orleans during the period. New Orleans was informed about the development of the area because it was the import and export center for the lower Mississippi valley and would be interested in new market opportunities.

The earliest indications of steamboat travel on Caddo Lake are contained in two 1840 descriptions of Texas. The first in time was probably George W. Bonnell's *Topographical Description of Texas*, which was published in April 1840. Under the section "Red River," Bonnell provides the following description of the area: "Lake Soda is a body of water of twenty miles in length, by eight in width. It is surrounded on every side by a rich body of land. It is in the disputed territory, and we do not yet know whether it is in the United States or Texas. Steam boats pass from Red river into this lake. Caddo river is a branch of lake Soda; it is about forty miles in length, and navigable for steam boats a short distance. The land upon it is good. . . . Cypress Bayou is a branch of Caddo river, about thirty-five miles in length, which enters it from the north-west. It contains extensive bottoms of rich land, but is not navigable."

One possible reading of this text is that it is a description of the area known as Soda Lake between Big Willow Pass and the head of Twelvemile Bayou. However, it is much more probable that the text is referring to the entire Sodo Lake complex, which included Caddo Lake. "Sodo" had apparently been corrupted to "Soda" by 1839, and the latter term was soon to be applied to the first component of the complex out of Shreveport. Navigation in Soda Lake immediately west of Shreveport would have been of no interest to a reader of a book on Texas, because that navigation was to the north rather than to the west; and the overall description of the area does not make much sense unless Bonnell is referring to a waterbody that included Caddo Lake. On this reading, "Soda Lake" includes Caddo Lake and "Caddo river" means Cypress Bayou. Cypress Bayou in Bonnell's text obviously refers to Black Cypress Bayou—it enters Cypress Bayou from the northwest and is not navigable.

The second earliest suggestion of steamboat traffic on Caddo Lake is Francis Moore's *Map and Description of Texas*, which was published sometime in 1840, accompanied by Austin's *Map of Texas*. The "Lakes" section on Red River County contains the following information: "Along the course and near the Red River, are scattered a great number of small lakes, which probably have been formed by the waters of this stream, which has been set back by the immense raft which formerly blocked up its channel; the largest of these lakes is Caddo or Soda lake, near the south-eastern boundary. It is about one hundred and fifty miles long, and from two to twenty broad; most of it is quite shallow, and many trunks of the decaying trees, which formerly grew upon its present bed, still project from its bosom, rendering its navigation quite dangerous. Small steamboats are almost constantly plying between the shores of this lake and the portion of Red River below."

Given the immense size of the lake described (150 miles long), it is obvious that Moore is referring to the entire Sodo Lake complex and that he is designating the upward limit of Caddo Lake as the confluence of Big and Black Cypress Bayous, as was common during the period. Steamboat traffic on the lake appears to have been quite large, as is indicated by the term "constantly plying." However, the text is referring to the Sodo Lake complex: steamboats did not necessarily frequent the shores of Caddo Lake. Most of the boats that were "constantly plying" were probably operating on Soda Lake to Caddo Prairie and the upper Red River.

These texts suggest that steamboats were operating on Caddo Lake by at least 1840, that they were probably operating as far as Port Caddo (as "Caddo river" was said to be "navigable for steam boats a short distance"), and that they were not operating on Cypress Bayou much above Port Caddo, if at all. The texts should not be understood to indicate that boats began operating on Caddo Lake in 1840. That determination must await a review of other evidence.

Although the level of activity in 1840 is unknown, it was probably minor. The population was small, and agriculture was just beginning. In addition, conditions for navigation were not good. The lake had only been in existence for about forty years, and the remains of the bottomland hardwood forest that occupied the valley of Cypress Bayou before the lake came into existence must have posed formidable difficulties for steamboat access.

These boats were not carrying out cotton. If they had been, there would be at least a few records of returns in the New Orleans newspapers. They were probably carrying supplies to the new settlers, among whom were those who occupied the earliest ports and landings, which included Port Caddo, Benton, and Smithland on Cypress Bayou and Swanson's Landing on Caddo Lake, all of which emerged in the late 1830s (fig. 5-1).

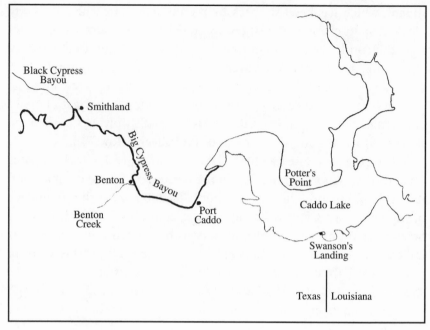

Fig. 5-1. Early ports and landings

EARLY PORTS AND LANDINGS

Port Caddo was by far the most important port along the route until the emergence of Jefferson in the late 1840s. Three letters—contained in *The Papers of Buonaparte Lamar*—were posted from Port Caddo during November 1838. The correspondence pertained to the invasion of Caddo Parish by Republic of Texas troops under Gen. Thomas Rusk to chase out a remnant of the Caddo tribe. In addition, the 29 November 1838 agreement between Rusk and Charles Sewall, the Indian agent, concerning the settlement of the dispute stipulates that two of the Caddo Indians "are also allowed to go to Port Caddo to hunt for one of the citizens of that place."

The designation "Port Caddo" does not necessarily mean that steamboats were going there by November 1838. In February 1838, the Land Office of the Republic of Texas was opened, and John Salmon "Rip" Ford was appointed deputy surveyor with a district in Harrison County. He proceeded to the Caddo Lake area and observed the following: "The locality where Post Caddo was afterwards laid off was reached. A few settlers were nestled around it. They obtained supplies by hauling on wagons from Shreveport and by flat boats which navigated lake Caddo. . . . This body of water was at that time full of fish. In half an hour one could hook enough fine trout or bass for a meal. Alligators were plentiful, and mainly of large size."

Because Ford was a surveyor, his observations can be trusted. It is obvious from his description that the settlement did not have a formal status and that this status was not achieved until General Rusk used it as a base in November. A post office was established at Post Caddo in January 1839; Port Caddo is listed as part of the mail route from San Augustine from October 1839; and a post office was established at Port Caddo in November 1840.

Most importantly, Ford indicates that no steamboats had traveled to the Port Caddo area by early 1838, because the settlement obtained supplies by hauling overland from Shreveport or by flatboats that navigated Caddo Lake. The flatboats could not have been of the large variety that traveled with the current down the Mississippi to New Orleans. The Caddo Lake flatboats must have had some means of propulsion. There was no current to carry them to the Port Caddo area. They were probably very small craft that were poled, and they almost certainly were operated by itinerant merchants.

The article on Port Caddo that had been originally published in the *Caddo Free Press* and picked up by the New Orleans newspapers would probably resolve the problem of whether steamboats were arriving at Port Caddo by early 1839. Unfortunately, a review of all of the New Orleans newspapers for January through March 1839 did not uncover the article, even though the *Caddo Free Press* is liberally quoted.

Benton was only a few miles upstream of Port Caddo and was reached through a portion of the bayou that was deep and free from obstructions. It was situated on a peninsula formed by Benton (now Beckum) Creek and Cypress Bayou in the vicinity of present-day Benton Lake, a little less than halfway between Port Caddo and Smithland. Very little is known about this place, partly because, like Smithland, it had no potential for larger development after the rise of Jefferson.

After Rip Ford left Port Caddo in early 1838, he stopped at Wray's Bluff, which he describes as "a small town not far from the head of the lake" where "Dr. Sanderson kept a boarding house which he called a hotel." An 1880 Texas General Land Office map of Harrison County by C. Meyer shows Ray's Bluff at the confluence of Ray's Creek and

Big Cypress Bayou (**fig. 5-2**), indicating that Ray's Creek was a former name for Beckum Creek and that Ray's Bluff was a former name for Benton. That this was a very early designation is confirmed by the fact that a Ray's Bluff on Big Cypress Bayou below its confluence with Little Cypress Bayou is shown on a 24 October 1840 map of Harrison County prepared for Richard Cooper, the county surveyor. According to Ford's testimony, the settlement at Ray's Bluff was more townlike than Port Caddo in early 1838, but no mention is made of navigation.

A short distance from Ray's Bluff was the town of Tuscumbia, which the March 1839 *Caddo Free Press* article described as newly laid out. Tuscumbia was located on the south bank of Little Cypress Bayou, which was never navigable. A 1901 Texas General Land Office map of

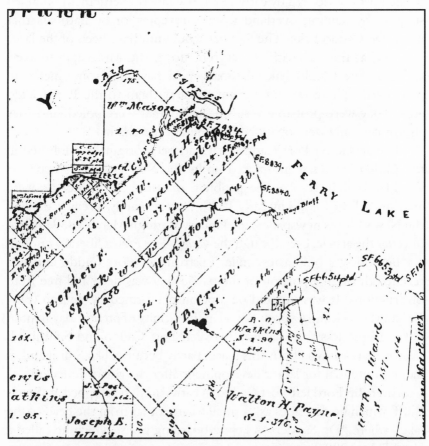

Fig. 5-2. Ray's Creek and Ray's Bluff. *Source: Courtesy Texas General Land Office, Austin*

Marion County by J. W. Legg shows an "Old Tuscumbia Crossing" over Little Cypress Bayou slightly west of present-day Highway 134. Tuscumbia had a post office in October 1839 that generated small revenues under its postmaster, Levi Jordan. Service was discontinued toward the end of 1840.

Smithland was located at the confluence of Big and Black Cypress Bayous, below the present town of Smithland. The land in this area was first surveyed in 1838 by James Baker. A post office was established at Smithland in September 1839, with L. R. Cherry as postmaster. A 640-acre plot was surveyed in 1840 by William F. Johnson, who records in his March field notes that the plot is located along Big and Black Cypress Bayous "immediately below the mouth of Black Cypress, including as is now known the town of Smithland." The emerging town was visited in August 1841 by the traveler and journalist Josiah Gregg, who reports the following:

> Arrived at Smithland on Ferry Lake on the 21st—This village has lately been founded, and is handsomely situated on a bluff which makes up the north side of the lake, at or near, as is said the head of navigation. If this is the case, it must some day become a clever town: for when steam boats can come up Red R. below the Raft, they can enter the lake and come up this high. Hence they must have almost at all times a free outlet from here to N. Orleans, which gives this part a great advantage over the upper Red River country, which I fear will ever be embarrassed by the Raft. Some say, however, that with some labor the head of this lake may be made good navigation as far up as the proposed site of Jefferson, six or 7 miles west. If this should prove true Jefferson would take all the western business, unless it should be embarrassed by some unpropitiousness of its location. Of this I know nothing as I have not visited its site. Smithland, as well as all the country bordering the lake and either branch of the cypress must always be very unhealthy, owing to the stagnancy of the waters, and the marshiness of their borders.—Smithland as yet has not over half a dozen houses in it, and not that many families.

Like Moore, Gregg is describing Caddo Lake (Ferry Lake was an early name for Caddo Lake) as extending up to the confluence of Big and Black Cypress Bayous. Smithland is said to be located on the prominent bluff that is readily observable today. It was recently founded and had six houses, but not that many families. This was a town of considerable size for Northeast Texas in 1841. The degree of development and the suggestion of expansion indicates a high level of commercial activity for the period, either realized or imminent.

No conclusions about realized commerce can be drawn from Gregg's use of the term "head of navigation," and his account demonstrates that the texts of the period were using the term to mean the upper limits of navigability on a stream rather than the existence of boat traffic. Smithland is not described as the head of navigation, but rather as "at or near" the head of navigation. The status is problematic because the head could be extended farther upstream by improvements to Cypress Bayou.

Swanson's Landing was located where Swanson's Landing is today, on the south shore of Caddo Lake and slightly west of the Louisiana-Texas line. Peter and Amelia Swanson and their sons Thomas and Walter were among the earliest settlers on Caddo Lake. Texas General Land Office records indicate that Peter Swanson came to Texas in February 1838. No property ownership is shown in the Swanson's Landing area in an 1839 Louisiana General Land Office map, which was based on a survey in the second quarter of 1838. Land patents were not available in the territory in dispute between the United States and the Republic of Texas until January 1841. The twenty acres in the landing area were surveyed for Swanson in July 1843, with the surveyor's notes indicating that the area was already known as Swanson's Landing. The landing was probably established in late 1838 or early 1839.

THE FIRST STEAMBOAT

Rip Ford made the acquaintance of Robert Potter when he stopped at Ray's Bluff in early 1838, and he mentions that "Not far from Colonel Potter's residence the Muscogees had a settlement between Lake Caddo and the Red River." The Muscogees referred to were the Creek Alabama Coushattas whose village was on the Potter's Point peninsula in the vicinity of Kitchen's Creek. Ford's text suggests that Potter was living on Caddo Lake by early 1838.

Potter was a figure of historic importance. Born in 1789, he was elected to the North Carolina Legislature at the age of twenty-seven.

After serving two terms, he was elected to the U.S. House of Representatives. He signed the Texas Declaration of Independence, was appointed the first secretary of the navy of the Republic of Texas, and was elected to two terms in the Congress of the Republic of Texas. He became involved in the violent dispute between factions who disagreed on how the problem of crime should be addressed in the no-man's-land formed by the indefinite boundary between the United States and the Republic of Texas and was killed on Caddo Lake on 2 March 1842.

Robert Potter and Harriet Page (later Ames) were the first white settlers on Caddo Lake, if by settler one means a person who has established a permanent residence and has cleared land for agriculture. Although sometimes referred to as the Potters, the Texas Supreme Court determined in 1875 that they had never been married. In any case, they lived together at a home on the north shore of Caddo Lake at a place known as Potter's Point (see fig. 5-1). Although land was cleared for agriculture, Potter apparently never put in a crop, as is evident from a letter that he wrote to Harriet on 18 January 1841.

Harriet wrote her memoirs at the age of eighty-three in New Orleans. In her account, she indicates that Potter had preceded her to Caddo Lake to build the house they were to occupy, and that when she moved to Potter's Point, the only people in the area were Indians. Potter was instrumental in helping other people to settle in the area. Harriet mentions Sandy Miller, Stephen Peters, and, later, James Rives. She also says that "Mr. Rieves moved his family near the Point; he and my brother chartered a little steam-boat and came down to the Point in that way. It was the first steam-boat that had ever entered the lake."

The chartering of steamboats was highly unusual. When Harriet says "came down to the Point," she is apparently referring to her brother and Rives rather than to the boat. There are no accounts of any steamboat ever having landed at Potter's Point. The boat apparently dropped the two men off at the site of what was to become Rives' Landing on Jim's Bayou, and they went overland the short distance to Potter's house (fig. 5-3).

Harriet's memoirs are an important document in the navigation history of the area, because they concern the arrival of the first steamboat on Caddo Lake. Unfortunately, Harriet does not provide a year, and it is not even obvious when she came to Potter's Point. It is apparent from her description that she arrived in the spring (muddy roads, flowers

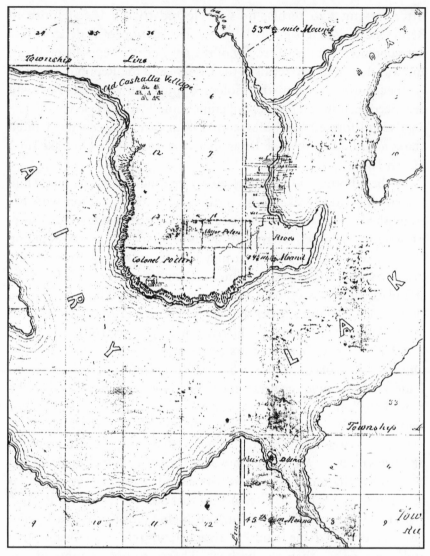

Fig. 5-3. Potter's residence. *Source: Courtesy Texas General Land Office, Austin*

in bloom). She mentions that during her first year at Potter's Point, one of her children by Potter was born. Given the sequence of events recounted, this must have been Lakeann, who was three when Potter was killed in 1842. Assuming that Lakeann was born in the latter part of the year in which Harriet arrived, that would place the arrival in the spring of 1838. This would be compatible with Ford's observation from early 1838 concerning Potter's residence in relation to the Muscogees.

Again, given the sequence of events described by Harriet, this would seem to place the arrival of the first steamboat on Caddo Lake in 1840. However, given the vagueness of Harriet's account, this is only an educated guess, and the year 1839 is also a possibility. Nothing is said about where this boat had come from or where it was going. It is unlikely that the charter would have been out of Shreveport—this would have been extraordinarily expensive. It is more reasonable to assume that the boat was on a commercial venture to some other point on the lake.

In her plan to escape from Potter's killers in 1842, Harriet mentions Amelia Swanson on the south shore of Caddo Lake. Swanson's Landing was across the lake from Potter's Point and was in existence from the late 1830s. It is highly probable that the first steamboat on Caddo Lake was destined for Swanson's Landing and was chartered for an initial stopoff at the area that later became Rives' Landing on Jim's Bayou. The year 1840 is also highly probable. In 1852, merchants and planters in the Cypress Bayou and Caddo Lake area issued a formal protest against New Orleans increases in steamboat insurance rates, pointing out that no steamboats had been lost during the twelve years in which boats had been operating in the area. Although the name of the boat may never be known, it was probably one of the many boats that advertised for Shreveport during that period.

THE NAVIGATION RECORD

The year 1841 is the first year for which there are any newspaper navigation records regarding steamboat activity west of Shreveport. The *New Orleans Price Current* shows the *Miami*, with McClure as captain, as having returned from "Caddo" on 9 January carrying 134 bales of cotton. This was the first appearance of the term "Caddo" in the navigation record. It may have covered Caddo Lake up to Port Caddo and was used to differentiate this area from previous trips up to Caddo Prairie. However, in addition to the vagueness of the record, the development of the area appears to have been insufficient to generate cotton export in early 1841.

On the same day that the *Miami* returned from Caddo, the *Brian Boroihme*, with John Smoker as captain, advertised in the *Daily Picayune* for Port Caddo:

> FOR PORT CADDO, FOOT OF THE RAFT, *Shreveport,*
> *Natchitoches, Alexandria and all intermediate landings.*—The
> well known steamboat BRIAN BOROIHME, J. Smoker,
> master, will leave for the above and all intermediate landings
> on MONDAY, the 11th inst., at 4 o'clock, P.M. For freight or
> passage, apply on board, foot of Customhouse street.

This was the first official recognition of Port Caddo in the navigation
record. However, there is no evidence that this boat reached its intended
destination, because there is no return record.

On 15 June, the *Farmer*, with A. Edwards as captain, advertised in
the *Daily Picayune* for Benton and Port Caddo:

> FOR FOOT OF THE RAFT, BENTON, PORT *Caddo,*
> *Shreveport, Natchitoches, Alexandria and all intermediate*
> *landings.*—The superior steamer FARMER, A. Edwards,
> master, will leave for the above ports on TUESDAY, 15th inst.,
> at 4 o'clock P.M., positively. For freight or passage apply on
> board at Customhouse street wharf, or to
> SAML. S. COBB & CO.,
> 15 New Levee.

For Benton to have been featured in a newspaper advertisement in
June 1841, it would need to have already been known. Although Benton
was to appear later in thousands of steamboat advertisements, this was
the only one in which it was listed first, suggesting initial enthusiasm
over a new commercial outlet. However, there is no evidence that this
boat reached either Benton or Port Caddo.

On 17 December, the *Vermillion*, with Arnold as captain, advertised
in the *New Orleans Commercial Bulletin* for Port Caddo. This
advertisement was changed to Shreveport and the foot of the raft on
the twentieth; and this boat is shown as returning from Red River,
with Wilson as captain, on 7 January 1842.

On 9 January 1842, the *Echo*, with A. Wheeler as captain, advertised
for Fort Caddo in the *Daily Picayune*. There is no record of a return
for this boat. The use of Fort Caddo as an alternate to Port Caddo
occurred intermittently through the 1850s. The 1 February *Daily
Picayune* shows the *Star*, with Ruter as captain (also spelled Rutter,
Rooter, and Bouter in other records), as having arrived from Caddo.

This boat immediately (on 5 February) advertised for Port Caddo in the *New Orleans Commercial Bulletin*. On the same day, the *Georgia* advertised for Caddo.

The 24 February *Daily Picayune* shows the *Star* as having returned from Caddo on the previous day, and the *Commercial Bulletin* of the twenty-sixth shows the *Star* as having returned from Port Caddo on the twenty-third carrying 567 bales of cotton. This is the first firm record of a steamboat on the route and the first unequivocal record of a steamboat transporting cotton out of Port Caddo. This boat immediately (on 25 February in the *Daily Picayune*) advertised for various points on Red River and west of Shreveport in the following manner:

REGULAR PACKET.
FOR SMITHLAND, FORT CADDO, FERRY, *Clear and Soda Lakes, Foot of the Raft, Shreveport, Campte, Natchitoches, Alexandria, and all landings on Red River.*—The superior A1 and fast running steamer STAR, Rooter, master, having been built expressly for the above trade will leave on SATURDAY, the 26th inst., at 4 o'clock, P.M. For freight or passage, apply on board, foot of Canal street, or to
SAML. S. COBB & CO., 15 New Levee.

This advertisement is interesting for three reasons. It provides the first mention of Smithland in an advertisement and the only listing of Smithland first, indicating that in February 1842 Smithland was considered the head of navigation. Ferry (the old name for Caddo Lake), Clear, and Soda Lakes are differentiated, and multiple points along the route had taken on importance. The *Star* is listed as a regular packet, meaning that she intended multiple trips to the same area. This was apparently the first boat to be built expressly for the Cypress Bayou and the lakes trade and the first to commit to fairly regular runs from New Orleans to Port Caddo.

The *Star* was a 138-ton sidewheeler measuring 141 feet by 22 feet that was built in 1841. She arrived back in New Orleans from Port Caddo in January and February 1842 and issued the advertisement to Smithland on 25 February. She is shown in the 19 March *New Orleans Price Current* as having returned from Port Caddo on the seventeenth carrying 342 bales of cotton. Whether this boat actually reached

Smithland cannot be determined from the record. The *Star* immediately (on 18 March) advertised for Port Caddo, Ferry and Soda Lakes, and above the raft. This boat appears in the navigation record in connection with Port Caddo only in 1842 and was out of service by 1847.

Along with the *Echo*, the *Georgia*, and the four trips made by the *Star*, the only other boat to Port Caddo in 1842 was the *South Western*, with Cheatham as captain, which is shown in the 8 April *Daily Picayune* as having arrived from Caddo. That makes a probable seven trips for 1842, at least in terms of those that were recorded or advertised, and all of these trips occurred during the first few months of the year.

The 21 January 1843 *Daily Picayune* shows the *Telegraph*, with Cummings as captain, as having returned from Fort Caddo carrying 861 bales of cotton. The 9 April *Daily Picayune* shows the *Ontario*, with Caruthers as captain, as having returned from Port Caddo carrying 426 bales of cotton. The *Ontario* advertised for Port Caddo again on the seventeenth and is shown in the 10 May *Daily Picayune* as having returned from Port Caddo carrying 116 bales of cotton.

There does not appear to have been any activity west of Shreveport in the middle of the year, and there is only one record of a return toward the close of the year. In the 1 November *Caddo Gazette and De-Soto Intelligencer*, the *Elizabeth* issued a provisional advertisement saying that she would run as a regular packet between Shreveport and Alexandria until there was sufficient water in the area west of Shreveport to enable her to run to Port Caddo. The same advertisement appears in a 7 February 1844 issue of the *Caddo Gazette*. Therefore, it is likely that the *Elizabeth* never made it to Port Caddo in 1843.

On 13 November, the *Beaver* advertised for Port Caddo in the *Caddo Gazette and De-Soto Intelligencer*, and the same issue mentions that the *Beaver* was at Shreveport (along with an unnamed boat) waiting for papers from New Orleans to enable her to travel to Port Caddo (which was within the Republic of Texas and hence in foreign waters): "There are two queer-looking steamboats at our landing (one named Beaver, the other seems to be without a name) which we are told are intended for the Port Caddo trade. They came up with their fingers in their mouths, unprovided with the documents requisite for the prosecution of a trade between the United States and Texas and will be compelled to wait until they can be provided with them from below."

The *Beaver* never made it to Port Caddo. An account of this voyage is given by the clerk, Florence Findren, in the *St. Louis Republican*, as quoted in the 16 December 1881 *Shreveport Times*. The account describes the *Beaver* as "a small boat with a recess wheel, open hold and no deck aft of the boilers." The recessed sternwheel and other peculiarities were the reason the *Beaver* was described as "queer-looking" when she arrived at Shreveport. According to the account, the *Beaver* went to upper Red River and on returning to Shreveport, burned at the landing. An account of the fire is given in the 7 February 1844 *Caddo Gazette*.

The *Swan* advertised for Port Caddo in the *Daily Picayune* on 16 November. There is no record of her departure. However, an 11 November advertisement says that the *Swan* will leave for the Sabine River after returning from the Red River. The *Swan* is shown on 29 November as having cleared for the Sabine, so it is probable that the trip to Port Caddo was made.

The *Robert T. Lytle*, with Joseph F. Lodwick as captain, advertised for Port Caddo on 5 December and is shown on 6 December as having cleared for Port Caddo and on 20 December as having arrived back in New Orleans from Port Caddo carrying 154 bales of cotton. The *Robert T. Lytle* also advertised for Port Caddo on the twentieth, cleared for Port Caddo on the twenty-fifth, and is shown on 7 January 1844 as having arrived back from Port Caddo carrying 205 bales of cotton.

The *Bois d'Arc* is shown on 21 December as having cleared for Port Caddo and on 5 January 1844 as having arrived back in New Orleans from Shreveport carrying 755 bales of cotton. The captain was John Smoker, who was also captain of the *Brian Boroihme*, the first steamboat to advertise for Port Caddo. The *Bois d'Arc* was a 182-ton sidewheeler measuring 136 feet by 26 feet that was built in Ohio in 1842 and named after the bois d'arc tree. Although she was operative along the route only through 1845, she left a lasting imprint by opening the high-water passage at the northern end of Caddo Lake that came to be known as Bois d'Arc Pass.

The *Bois d'Arc* was also the first boat to register a high number of trips to Port Caddo, making at least nine trips to that port from January through June 1844 and carrying out 4,408 bales of cotton. On the second trip, the *Bois d'Arc* is shown in the *Daily Picayune* as having cleared for Port Caddo on 29 January and as having arrived back in New Orleans on 12 February. What happened in between is indicated by the 7 February *Caddo Gazette*, which is one of the few extant issues of a Shreveport newspaper from this early period.

The Steamboat Register, which records arrivals and departures from Shreveport for the previous week, shows that the *Bois d'Arc* arrived from New Orleans on 3 February and departed for Port Caddo the next day:

STEAM BOAT REGISTER.
ARRIVED.
Jan. 31, *Belle of Red River*, DAVIS, from N.O.
Jan. 31, *Planter*, SMITH, from New Orleans.
Feb. 2, *Bois d'Arc*, SMOKER, from N. Orleans.
Feb. 3, *Robert T. Lytle*, LODWICK, from N.O.
DEPARTED.
Jan. 31, *Planter*, SMITH, for Fort Towson.
Feb. 3, *Bois d'Arc*, for Port Caddo, Texas.

Passengers occasionally provided formal statements in the newspapers expressing thanks for particularly pleasant trips. This was the case for the second trip of the *Bois d'Arc* to Shreveport on the way to Port Caddo:

A CARD.
We, the undersigned, passengers on board the steamer *Bois d'Arc*, on her trip from New Orleans to Shreveport, adopt this method of tending our thanks to *Captain John Smoker*, for his very urbane and courteous conduct during the passage; and we cannot withhold the expression of our admiration of the vigilance and care manifested by himself and officers on all occasions, and their assiduity in rendering those under their protection at once comfortable and contented.

Lathan Garlick,	Willis Pollard,
Wm. E. Dufy,	Wm. Garrett,
C. S. Beasly,	V. H. Jones,
H. J. G. Battle,	George N. Butt
Wm. M. Burns,	A. Vanvay,
H. Rugeley,	John M. Massie,
R. C. Oglesby,	Wm. T. Scott,
Preston B. Rose,	John H. Roper,
James Wells,	James W. Begran,
John D. Fulford,	Enoch Backs,

Augustus Mosely,	Barnett Levy,
Jesse Parchance,	E. Attaway,
Henry Breazeal,	John Speake,
W. J. Hotchkiss,	James S. Broles,
W. H. Preston.	

Steamer *Bois d'Arc*, Feb. 2, 1844.

The *Sabine*, with Isaac Wright as captain, was another boat that frequented Port Caddo in 1844. The *Sabine* was a 106-ton sidewheeler measuring 108 feet by 21 feet that was built in Kentucky in 1843. She advertised for Port Caddo in May 1844, saying that she had taken the place of the *Republic* (also captained by Wright during that year), and in June, saying that she had taken the place of the *Bois d'Arc*, both of which were larger, heavier boats. The *Sabine* made four recorded trips to Port Caddo during the low-water period from June through August and carried out 142 bales of cotton.

The *Robert T. Lytle*, with J. F. Lodwick as captain, made one recorded trip to Port Caddo and one to Caddo Lake, carrying out 766 bales of cotton. The *Planter*, with M. W. Lodwick as captain, advertised for Port Caddo in May and made one recorded trip to Soda Lake in June, with J. N. Cummings as captain, carrying out 63 bales of cotton. The *Republic*, with Wright as captain, made one trip to Port Caddo at the end of May and advertised for Port Caddo in June. The *Elizabeth* continued to advertise provisionally for Port Caddo during this year, but there is no evidence that she ever made a trip. Finally, the *New Brazil*, with Cummings as captain, advertised late in December for Port Caddo, but there is no evidence that she made a trip during this year.

Of the boats mentioned in the navigation record in connection with Port Caddo during the 1841–44 period, it can safely be said that the *Star*, *Bois d'Arc*, *Robert T. Lytle*, *Ontario*, *Telegraph*, *Republic*, and *Sabine* went to that port. The *Miami*, *Planter*, and *South Western* are possible, and the *Planter* definitely went into Soda Lake. The *Brian Boroihme*, *Farmer*, *Echo*, *Georgia*, and *Swan* are evidenced only by advertisements, but may have made the intended trips. The advertisements for the *Vermillion*, *Elizabeth*, and *New Brazil* are too uncertain for these boats to be included in a listing for Port Caddo.

Of the fifteen boats for which there is reason to believe that they went to Port Caddo, all were sidewheelers. The largest was the *Robert*

T. Lytle, at 159 tons and measuring 158 feet by 22 feet. Of the fifteen boats, ten had records or near records of travel to Port Caddo, producing a cumulative record of twenty-eight trips, most of which were in 1844. The most active boat was the *Bois d'Arc*, with ten recorded trips in 1843 and 1844.

All of these boats traveled to places other than Port Caddo, including the major Red River ports of Natchitoches, Alexandria, and Shreveport; and some went much higher on the Red River above the raft. The normal trip from New Orleans to Port Caddo and back appears to have taken a couple of weeks. Trips above the raft sometimes involved months of absence.

With the exception of the advertisements for the *Farmer* and the *Star*, there are no advertisements for the 1841–44 period that mention Smithland or Benton, and no boats are listed as departing to or arriving from those ports in the New Orleans newspapers. This does not mean that other steamboats did not travel to those ports during that period. On the other hand, the advertisements should not be taken as proof that steamboats went to Benton and Smithland during the 1841–44 period.

Steamboat return records always listed only one port in the "arrived from" column, and that was always the dominant port in the area to which the steamboat had traveled. Almost all steamboat return records for the Cypress Bayou and the lakes route are for Port Caddo and then Jefferson. Secondary ports along the route do not begin to appear in steamboat advertisements until 1851. The advertisements for the *Farmer* and *Star* are important because they are anomalous, indicating that Benton had assumed commercial importance by June 1841 and Smithland had assumed commercial importance by February 1842, even if steamboats did not reach those points during those years.

THE COTTON TRADE

The boat list for the period 1840–44 is obviously not inclusive, because at least some boats were operating on Caddo Lake in 1840 whose names are unknown. This incompleteness is a matter of little importance. The earliest penetrations into the area in 1840 were side trips from Shreveport to supply the newly emerging farms and plantations and did not involve cotton export. If steamboats would have been restricted to such activities west of Shreveport, the area never would have established a navigation history.

The key event in the 1840–44 period was the beginning of cotton transport out of Port Caddo, which may have been signaled by the arrival of the *Miami* in New Orleans from Caddo in January 1841 carrying 134 bales of cotton. However, the first unequivocal record for cotton transport out of Port Caddo was the *Star* in February 1842. Nevertheless, the advertisements for the *Brian Boroihme* and *Farmer* in 1841 indicate that the area west of Shreveport was fully recognized by the New Orleans newspapers during that year. In addition, cotton was a summer crop, with the first bales taken out in the fall. There is a firm record for cotton export in February 1842; it is highly likely that cotton was being taken out of Port Caddo by steamboat in the latter part of 1841.

The rapid growth of steamboat activity on the route was intimately related to the inception and expansion of cotton agriculture. Boats returning to New Orleans from Port Caddo carried 134 bales in 1841, 909 bales in 1842, 1,557 bales in 1843, and 6,391 bales in 1844. Not all of this cotton came from the Cypress Bayou and the lakes area; some would have been picked up at points along the Red River on the return trip. However, Port Caddo would not have been listed as the point of return had not a substantial portion of the cotton been brought from the area.

Throughout most of the period prior to the Civil War, Port Caddo was the primary water outlet for the cotton of Harrison County, and Harrison County was always one of the largest cotton producers in Texas. By 1849, according to the census figures, Harrison County was producing 4,581 bales of cotton, making it the second largest cotton producer (after Colorado County) in Texas. It was this rapid development of Harrison County—particularly its northeast sector—that set the stage for the flowering of Port Caddo as a cotton exporter.

The navigation events of the early 1840s were, therefore, directly connected with the general development of cotton agriculture in the area and particularly with the emergence of large cotton plantations northeast of Marshall in the late 1830s and early 1840s. Settlers had begun arriving in the vicinity of Marshall in 1837 as part of the general immigration initiated by the formation of the Republic of Texas in 1836. By 1839, persons such as William Scott and John Webster arrived who were to establish a planter class, many with holdings in the thousands of acres.

The sequence of events leading up to the explosion of commercial activity can be reconstructed on the basis of early maps and texts. The Louisiana General Land Office maps for the Caddo Lake area, which were published in 1839, were based on surveys extending from the fourth quarter of 1837 through the first quarter of 1839. These surveys extended into Texas, but not as far as Port Caddo, because the boundary between the United States and the Republic of Texas was indefinite until 1841.

The maps show very few property owners and practically no development. The only structures represented are the ferry facilities of James Shennick on the north and south shores in the vicinity of Stormy Point. "Col. Potter's Improvement" is shown on Potter's Point on the basis of a survey conducted in the first quarter of 1839. The term "improvement" probably indicates structural development, which is compatible with Rip Ford's mention of Potter's residence in 1838. Two land patents are shown for James J. Rives west of Jim's Bayou. To the north and across Jim's Bayou, patents are shown for James Cannelly and Sarah K. Peters, widow of William Peters. On the south shore of the lake are shown Mooring's Clearing, below present-day Mooringsport, and farther to the west, Davis Field and Johnson's Field, all of which were small.

The March 1839 *Caddo Free Press* article indicates that a number of log cabins had been built on the lake, but that little had taken place in terms of land clearing, and no crops had been cultivated. A modest number of settlers resided there by early 1840, encouraging boats to ply the shore of the lake and bring supplies. Extensive land clearing took place from late 1839 onward. The first cotton crop was planted in the spring of 1840 and harvested in the fall. Steamboats began to carry it out in 1841.

Port Caddo no longer exists, and there is little other than historical evidence to indicate that there was ever anything of importance on the land contiguous to Caddo Lake State Park. As a consequence, it is difficult to believe, but nevertheless true, that Port Caddo was once featured in the New Orleans newspapers, providing the initial linkage of the Cypress Bayou and the lakes area to the international cotton market. Port Caddo was to remain an important cotton exporter until shortly before the Civil War, but its status as a primary destination for steamboats on the route was soon eclipsed by the rise of Jefferson.

·6·
The Birth of Jefferson

A TOWN DE FACTO

Throughout most of the steamboat period, Jefferson was the head of navigation on the route, meaning simply that it was the point farthest upstream on Cypress Bayou. The site chosen for Jefferson both was and was not a good place for a port. Because the route was primarily an import and export channel for the area to the west, it was well known that the point farthest west would dominate commercial activity in the region, as is indicated, for example, by Josiah Gregg's comments from Smithland in August 1841.

Jefferson was founded at the highest practical point on Cypress Bayou. The bayou above was very restricted, and any point farther upstream would have required extensive channel widening and deepening, which would have been impractical in the 1840s. It was founded on a high bluff generally above the inundation zone, but subject to periodic floods in the springtime. It was situated at a point where Cypress Bayou was split by Saint Catherine's Island, where the north and south branches rejoined to form a natural embayment that was an ideal place for docking and turning. Streets were oriented toward the waterfront, confirming that the town was envisioned as a port (**fig. 6-1**).

Although in many respects an ideal place for a port, Jefferson had one major drawback. The six miles of Cypress Bayou between Jefferson and Smithland were shallow, which caused innumerable, though not

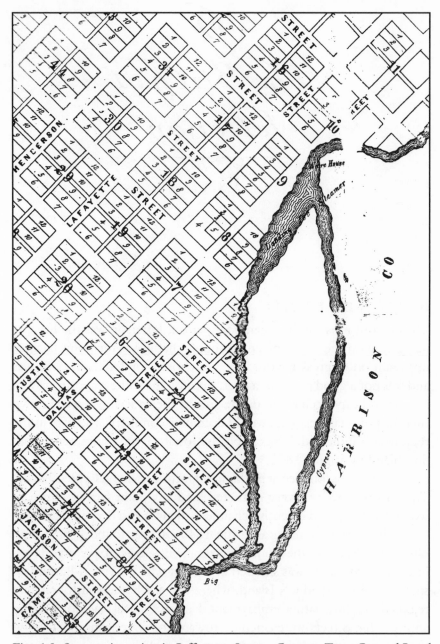

Fig. 6-1. Street orientation in Jefferson. *Source: Courtesy Texas General Land Office, Austin*

insurmountable, difficulties for steamboats attempting to reach Jefferson during low-water periods. Smithland was a much better place for a port because it was at the headwaters of Caddo Lake and therefore almost always easily accessible to steamboats. Nevertheless, six miles closer to western markets proved to be a decisive competitive advantage for Jefferson given the difficulties involved in overland transport; and once Jefferson's commercial infrastructure was in place, Smithland had no capacity to compete even for northern markets.

Allen Urquhart, Jefferson's founder, appeared before county commissioners in August 1838 to claim a headright of 1,280 acres. Urquhart chose 640 acres on Cypress Bayou and the other half of his headright in Daingerfield, where he was to reside. Jefferson is first mentioned as a town site by Josiah Gregg in August 1841 when he visited Smithland and speaks of the "proposed site of Jefferson, six or 7 miles west." The Cypress Bayou tract was surveyed by Urquhart in November 1841. The survey map indicates that a ferry was already in existence, which was operated by Berry Durham for Urquhart at the foot of Houston Street according to the 1 September 1876 *Daily Jimplecute*.

Buck Barry, Texas Ranger and frontiersman, was a witness to Jefferson at its inception. Barry arrived by steamboat at Jefferson in April 1845 and reports in his reminiscences that at the time of his arrival, "There were several houses under construction but there was only one finished. It was a log cabin built without a nail in it." The rations on the steamboat had all been eaten, so it was necessary for Barry to obtain breakfast on shore. He was directed to where smoke was coming from brush about 200 yards from the boat. In company with a young Tennesseean, he made his way through the brush to the smoke "where a man served us with meat, bread and black coffee, using a very large pine log for a table. This was my first meal on Texas soil."

The finished cabin was apparently unoccupied. Barry does not mention it as a possible place for breakfast, and he was forced to seek lodging with a farmer named Steward, who was at Jefferson but who lived twenty miles away. Barry does not mention any people in Jefferson other than Steward and the man who served breakfast, who was probably Berry Durham, operating an open-air concession near the landing. Barry's account of the status of Jefferson in April 1845 is confirmed by an 1849 report by Edward Smith, an Englishman who traveled throughout East Texas investigating sites for a colony. Smith states: "Jefferson four years ago possessed only three log houses." Because Smith was writing in 1849, the three log houses mentioned by Barry had been completed and were occupied by at least the end of 1845.

Jefferson was a relative latecomer in the development of ports and landings on Cypress Bayou. It was preceded by Port Caddo, which was established as a military post in late 1838 and acquired a post office in early 1839; by Benton, which operated under the name of Ray's Bluff in 1838 and is mentioned by name in the 1841 advertisement for the *Farmer*; and by Smithland, which had a post office from late 1839. And, given the fact that Jefferson was a planned town at least as early as 1841, it may seem surprising that only a few log houses were completed by 1845. This sequence of events and Jefferson's relative lateness were not accidental, but rather the result of a navigation problem.

Difficulties would have been encountered in achieving navigation through Caddo Lake and up Big Cypress Bayou to its confluence with Black Cypress, where Smithland was located. The area on Big Cypress above the confluence was more than difficult—it was a barrier to navigation. Caddo Lake extended up to Smithland, providing reasonable water depths and a wide channel. Beyond that point, the six miles upstream to the town site of Jefferson were shallow and constricted. During the early 1840s, this area would have been filled with obstructions, making navigation extremely difficult for any watercraft and probably impossible for steamboats.

For a town envisioned as a port, no investments would have been made in the building of commercial or residential structures until the impediments to navigation access were overcome. The existence of the problem and its likely resolution were recognized by Josiah Gregg when he visited Smithland in August 1841. At that time, Smithland was at the head of navigation with steamboat access whenever there was sufficient water in Red River for steamboats from New Orleans to reach Shreveport. Jefferson was as yet an isolated town site, but with a capacity to assume its rightful place as the head of navigation if Cypress Bayou were cleared out.

This clearing took place at the end of 1844 on the basis of private funding. The project was initiated on Tuesday, 9 April 1844, by a meeting in Daingerfield of interested parties in the southern portion of Red River County:

MEETING OF THE CITIZENS OF THE SOUTHERN DIVISION OF RED RIVER.

At a meeting of the citizens of the Southern Division of Red River, in the Town of Daingerfield on the 9th last, for the purpose of devising a plan through which the Cypress may be cleared of obstructions to navigation from Smithland to Jefferson.—The object of the meeting was briefly, and ably explained by Dr. M. W. Mathews, Col. B. H. Martin, and Dr. Tabor. Isaac Hughes Esq. was called to the chair, and B. W. Gray appointed Clerk.

After the organization of the meeting, the following gentlemen were appointed as a committee, who should devise the best and most expeditious plan for accomplishing the object of the meeting: Isaac Hughes, M. W. Mathews, E. G. Rogers, J. D. Crawford, B. Gooch, Allen Urquhart, B. W. Gray, W. Peacock, and Mr. Withee.

After deliberation, a motion was made and seconded, that a committee of three be appointed to examine the Cypress, and to make some examination of the amount of money necessary to remove the obstructions to navigation, and report to the committee of nine, in Daingerfield, on the second Monday in May.

It was then moved and seconded, that the meeting adjourn; and that the two committees meet in the town of Daingerfield, on the second Monday in May 1844.

This account appeared in the 17 April 1844 Clarksville *Northern Standard,* with the following commentary by the editor, Charles DeMorse:

On Tuesday a meeting was held at Daingerfield, to take means to clean out the obstructions to the navigation of Big Cypress to Jefferson, or as much further as it may be found practicable, the proceedings of which will be found in another column. The citizens of that section feel a laudable desire to improve their facilities for the exportation of cotton, and the importation of such necessary articles as cannot conveniently be produced at home, and there is every reason to believe that a little energetic action, and the expenditure of a small amount of means, to be obtained by general contribution, will effect the object easily and speedily. The obstructions from Smithland to Jefferson are said to be trifling, and the importance of having a point of shipment and commercial business as high up as practicable, is obvious enough to any body.

The committee met as planned and reported a favorable recommendation to the larger group on Monday, 13 May 1844, as reported in the 12 June *Northern Standard*: "At a meeting of the citizens of the Southern Division of Red River county, at Daingerfield, on the 13th May 1844, Isaac Hughes in the chair, and B. W. Gray Secretary, to receive the report of a committee appointed at a former meeting, to examine the Cypress and Lake Sodo, from Jefferson to Port Caddo, and to report the probable amount of expense to render the same navigable for Steam Boats—the committee having performed the service assigned them at the former meeting, reported favorably believing that the amount of expense would not exceed two thousand dollars." The committee's recommendation was approved and a bid advertisement submitted to the *Northern Standard* for work that was to begin on 4 July 1844 and be completed by 25 December: "A motion was made and carried, that Maj. Charles DeMorse, with his usual courtesy, publish in the Northern Standard, that the clearing out of the Cypress will be let to the lowest bidder, at Daingerfield, on the 4th day of July next, to be paid for in cash or cotton, on the 25th day of December next."

Cypress Bayou between Smithland and Jefferson was obviously not navigable for steamboats at the time the project was initiated. The deliberations were not concerned with removing impediments to existing navigation on Cypress Bayou, but rather with what would be needed to "open the navigation" and "render the same navigable for Steam Boats." The persons who met for this discussion were planters and merchants with an interest in securing more efficient means for the export of cotton and the import of goods, as well as promoters of the good of the county, as explained in the 17 April article concerning the initiation of the project: "At present, those who wish to procure goods or realize something immediately for their cotton, are obliged to haul it to Port Caddo or Shreveport, either of which are at an inconvenient distance. Aside from the distance and expense of hauling to those points, the citizens of the Southern division, feel a wish, which is the result of both pride and interest to trade within their own limits, and rear up among themselves, rather than among strangers, a place of trade. In such case, part of the profits which their business affords, will be expended in their county; and they will reap the benefits of mutual trade and expenditure, of which they have nothing when they trade beyond their own limits."

There is no documentation concerning who conducted the work or what the work entailed, other than that it concentrated on the removal of obstructions to navigation between Smithland and Jefferson and that the work effort was initiated in July 1844 and completed in December. There is nothing to suggest that any digging was involved. The obstructions in need of removal would have included trees that had fallen into the water from the banks (as they do today), embedded and floating logs, stumps, mats of branches and small logs, and living cypress trees on the fringes of the channel. The work was conducted during the low-water season, the only period when such work was feasible, and the sawed and chopped timber that was floatable would have been left inchannel to be carried down by the spring rise on Cypress Bayou.

The reason that the meetings concerning the project were held in Daingerfield rather than in Jefferson was that Jefferson was only a planned town in 1844. However, as soon as the initial meeting was held to consider the clearing of Cypress Bayou and it was obvious to the meeting participants that action would be taken, concrete plans for the construction of facilities at the Jefferson town site began to be made, as reported in the 17 April *Northern Standard*: "Whenever, as is now projected, warehouses shall be built at the place, and establishments of goods, offering the usual trading and advancing facilities shall be established, Jefferson commanding the trade of a large and fertile section of country, will necessarily become a point of importance. Such houses we are informed will be established within the next six months."

By October, as the work progressed, houses began to be erected at the Jefferson town site, as reported in the *Northern Standard* for the sixteenth: "We are told that several houses are now going up at this point, which, our readers will recollect, is the head of navigation on Big Cypress, and several stocks of goods will be opened there within the next two or three months. Jefferson is, we think, destined to be a place of considerable trade. It must necessarily command all the business which has hitherto gone to Shreveport and Port Caddo, from the section of country north and west of the lake."

By January 1845, the planned town was emerging into reality, as reported in the *Northern Standard* for the sixteenth: "The town of Jefferson, in the Southern Division of our own County, was but yesterday a mere name upon paper, and now we are told, quite a number of buildings are going up—several persons will have goods there directly—the navigation of the Cypress has been cleared, so that the first rise of water will take out the logs and leave the passage free to steamboats of moderate size, and a town will be there immediately; a town *de facto* and one destined to concentrate a large inland commercial business."

It is apparent that the project of clearing out Cypress Bayou was completed on schedule in December 1844. As the work progressed, several houses were under construction by October of that year. By January 1845, the "mere name upon paper" was becoming "a town *de facto*." When Buck Barry arrived in April, two houses were under construction and one was completed, but it was not yet occupied. It can be inferred from Smith's comments in 1849 that these three houses were completed and occupied by the end of 1845, the year in which Jefferson can rightfully be said to have come into existence.

Jefferson was conceived as a port and founded as a port to realize the competitive advantages that would accrue to the highest navigable point on Cypress Bayou. It was envisioned as a commercial center oriented on navigation and particularly on the transport possibilities offered by steamboats. None of this would have come to pass had Cypress Bayou between Smithland and the town site of Jefferson not been cleared out by private action at the end of 1844. As a consequence, Jefferson owed its existence to a navigation project.

ARRIVAL OF THE *LAMA*

The clearance of Cypress Bayou by the end of December 1844 and the implications of that clearance for navigation as discussed in the Clarksville *Northern Standard* create a very strong presumption that the first steamboat arrived at Jefferson in 1845, contemporaneous with the town's birth. However, this is not necessarily the case. A steamboat could have penetrated Cypress Bayou to the town site prior to 1844, after which the bayou became impassable. In addition, it is obvious that the first arrival could have been in 1846 or afterward.

The 17 April 1844 *Northern Standard* reports that "there has already been boated off from Jefferson, the present season 340 bales of cotton and there are 60 more bales to ship." The "season" referred to in this text was the commercial season, which was equivalent to the cotton transport season. This season extended from September through August, because September was the month in which the first cotton was normally brought to market and also the month in which the fall rise in water levels made the transport of cotton by water possible. Thus, the text is referring to the first transport of cotton from the town site of Jefferson by water between September 1843 and April 1844.

This cotton does not appear to have been transported by steamboat. The quoted article continues: "At present, those who wish to procure goods or realize something immediately for their cotton, are obliged to haul it to Port Caddo or Shreveport, either of which are at an inconvenient distance." This could be taken to mean that a steamboat made a trip to the Jefferson town site between September 1843 and April 1844 and that for some reason the channel had become closed. A more probable reading is that the 360 bales were transported by small flatboats or barges to Port Caddo, which was well established as a cotton exporter by late 1843, and that the most feasible means of transport was overland to Port Caddo. As a consequence, nothing definite can be concluded from the text about the arrival of the first steamboat at Jefferson.

By local tradition in Jefferson, as recounted by Fred Tarpley in *Jefferson: Riverport to the Southwest*, the first steamboat to Jefferson was the *Llama*, with W. W. Withenberry as captain, which arrived at Jefferson in late 1843 or early 1844. This local tradition concerning the name of the boat and its captain is supported by three texts that were written at a time when there were still people around who would have known at least some of the facts. The first is from the *Biographical and Historical Memoirs of Northwest Louisiana*, which was a popular work published in 1890: "The following are some of the noted captains of the river service: . . . Capt. W. W. Withenbury, who commanded the 'Llama,' George Alban pilot, the first steamer that ever passed from Red River through Cypress Bayou to Jefferson, in 1845."

The second is from the 20 March 1872 *Shreveport Times*, quoting the *Jefferson Daily Democrat* of the seventeenth of that month: "The steamer Lama was the first boat that ever arrived at Jefferson. She was commanded by Captain Withenbery, with Geo. Alban as pilot, and _____ Wortham as chief engineer. This was on the 17th day of

June 1844. On her return to Shreveport, she was obliged to anchor out in the stream, to avoid being seized upon by the United States Commissioner for having crossed the line."

The third is from the 1 September 1876 *Daily Jimplecute*: "The first steamboat that ever landed at Jefferson was the Lama, Capt. Withinberry, in the winter of 1844–5, (the exact date we cannot ascertain from the fact that the records of the town, or many of them, was burned during J. S. Elliott's administration as Mayor). . . . Capt. Wm. Perry met her at Shreveport and assisted in bringing her through. John Speake, Amos Ury and a few other citizens were also on board of her."

In these accounts, there are obvious discrepancies in dating (1843, 1844, or 1845) and the spelling of names, including the name of the boat (*Llama* or *Lama*) and the captain (Withenberry, Withenbury, Withenbery, or Withinberry). The name of the boat is easily resolved. William Lytle's authoritative *Merchant Steam Vessels of the United States, 1790–1868*, which is based on a review of federal boat enrollments, does not have any listing for a *Llama*. However, there is a listing for a *Lama*, and the following information is provided: sidewheel; 68 tons; built in 1844 in Cincinnati, Ohio; first home port, Cincinnati, Ohio; exploded, Camargo, Mexico, 29 May 1847. The *Lama* was, in fact, a well-known boat in the Red River and Cypress Bayou trades, and this is the spelling that is always used in the numerous steamboat advertisements and port records that mention the *Lama* when she was active in the 1840s.

In addition, there never was a steamboat captain by the name of Withinberry (or any of the other numerous variants). There was, however, a very famous captain by the name of W. W. Withenbury who was active in the Red River and Cypress Bayou trades from the 1840s until the Civil War. His first name, Wellington, was used only in legal documents, for obvious reasons. George Alban, who is identified as the pilot of the first boat to Jefferson, was also well known in the same trades during the same period. Both are mentioned in the 21 March 1872 *Shreveport Times* as being among the oldest living persons who had operated on the Red River.

Given the popularity of Withenbury and Alban, it is inconceivable that the traditions concerning the captain and pilot of the first boat to Jefferson are incorrect, particularly because at least one was recorded (in 1872) when both were still alive. In addition, it is inconceivable that the *Lama* was not the first steamboat to Jefferson. All sources agree that a boat by that name (or something similar) was the first boat to Jefferson. All of these sources ultimately go back to persons who were alive when the event occurred, and some were written when persons with direct knowledge of the event were still active in the steamboat business or still living in Jefferson. Assuming that the *Lama* was the first steamboat to Jefferson, the newspapers of the 1840s enable us to follow her movements in great enough detail to determine the year and month at which she arrived at Jefferson.

Boats under construction during the 1800s were often described in newspapers. Because Lytle lists 1844 and Cincinnati as the year and place of construction of the *Lama*, a search was made of the Cincinnati newspapers for information on construction activity. Although no information was found, the Steamboat Register in the 24 September 1844 *Cincinnati Gazette* records the arrival of the *Lama* at the Port of Cincinnati from the shipyard within the previous three days. The 23 September date may be used as a proxy for the date of launching because completed steamboats always entered immediately into some trade. This excludes the *Jefferson Daily Democrat* date of 17 June 1844 as a possible time of arrival for the *Lama* in Jefferson.

It was a federal requirement that all boats more than twenty tons be enrolled if traveling within the United States or registered if traveling to foreign ports. Steamboats established a record of enrollments and registrations based on the ports from which they ventured and their destinations. The National Archives in Washington, D.C., contains the enrollment documents for the first home port of each vessel, which is the primary basis for the Lytle list. The *Lama*'s Cincinnati enrollment (**fig. 6-2**), which was obtained from the National Archives, indicates that the *Lama* was sixty-eight tons, 100 x 24 x 3 feet 8 inches, with one deck and cabin below. The captain was W. C. Caldwell, and the owner was T. N. Muir of Pearson & Home, Grand Gulf, Mississippi.

Because time was money, steamboats immediately left on maiden voyages. Advertisements were published in anticipation of the date of launching to secure the earliest possible date for departure. The first advertisement for the *Lama*, which appeared in the 10 September *Cincinnati Gazette* and ran through the eighteenth, reads as follows: "FOR NEW ORLEANS.—The steamer LAMA, H. C. Caldwell, master, will leave as above on Monday, Sept. 16, at 4 P.M." A modified advertisement indicating that the *Lama* would carry mail appeared on

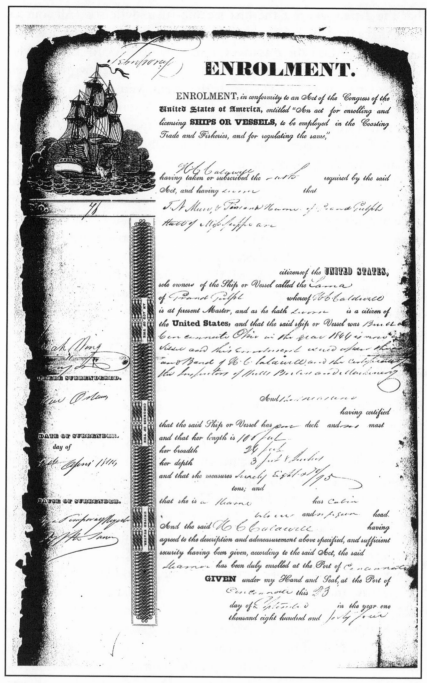

Fig. 6-2. *Lama*'s enrollment. *Source: National Archives*

the twenty-first, then again on the twenty-fourth, with that date being the expected date of departure. Then, on 26 September, the *Gazette* shows the *Lama* as having departed for New Orleans within the previous two days with Caldwell as captain. The story is then carried forward by the New Orleans newspapers. The *Daily Picayune* records that the *Lama* reached New Orleans from Cincinnati on 27 October 1844, with Caldwell as captain and carrying 87 bales of cotton.

It is at least theoretically possible that the *Lama* could have gone to Jefferson on her maiden voyage from Cincinnati to New Orleans in the period from 26 September through 27 October. The normal trip from Cincinnati to New Orleans in 1844 was a week to ten days; but the *Lama* was on her maiden voyage and would have taken longer. The hypothesis of a side trip to Jefferson involving Withenbury as captain would have difficulty explaining how the *Lama* arrived in New Orleans with the same captain (Caldwell) as she left Cincinnati. Most importantly, in January 1845, the Clarksville *Northern Standard* was still looking forward to the spring rise that would clear out the debris from the channel clearing effort and open a passage for steamboats up to Jefferson.

On 27 October 1844, the day of her arrival in New Orleans, the *Lama* advertised as destined for Williams' Landing on the Yazoo River in Mississippi, with the notation that she drew only twenty-four inches of water. She arrived back in New Orleans on 14 February 1845, from Belmont, Mississippi, with Caldwell as captain. Aboard were 223 bales of cotton.

On the basis of these records, it is obvious that the *Lama* could not have gone to Jefferson in 1844. She left Cincinnati in September and arrived at New Orleans in October with a captain who was not Withenbury and during a period when the channel between Smithland and Jefferson was not yet clear for the passage of steamboats. After she arrived in New Orleans in October, she immediately entered the Mississippi trade, from which she returned to New Orleans early in 1845. That leaves 1845 as the only possible year for the first trip to Jefferson among the years suggested in the sources that were closest to the event.

On the same day the *Lama* arrived back in New Orleans from Mississippi (15 February 1845), she advertised as a regular packet to Vermillionville (now Lafayette) on the Vermillion River in Louisiana with Henry V. McCall as captain. This was a short trip—the 24 February

New Orleans Price Current shows the *Lama* arriving back in New Orleans on that date. Then, on 26 February, a retraction was issued in the *Daily Picayune* saying that the *Lama* had been taken out of the Vermillionville trade and that her place would be taken by the *Gazelle* with McCall as captain.

There is no mention of the *Lama* in the issues of the *Daily Picayune* for March 1845. However, we know that she was in the vicinity of Jefferson during that month because of a bill of lading for the *Lama* signed by W. W. Withenbury on 23 March 1845 at Smithland for 154 bales of cotton to be delivered to New Orleans **(fig. 6-3)**. That this was the Smithland on Cypress Bayou below Jefferson is evident from the fact that the printed words "Port Caddo" were crossed out and replaced by "Smithland." March is a possibility for the first trip to Jefferson because the *Lama* could have gone there before picking up the cotton in Smithland, which was only six miles distant, and cotton from a downstream port was always picked up on the return trip.

The next mention of the *Lama* in the *Daily Picayune* was on 13 April, when she is recorded as having cleared for Port Caddo on the previous day, with Withenbury as captain. According to the *Ship Registers and Enrollments of New Orleans, Louisiana*, 12 April was also the day on which the *Lama* was registered at the Port of New Orleans, with the following information provided: "Registered (temporary), No. 34, Apr. 12, 1845. Owners: Thomas N. Muir, Pearson & Home, Grand Gulf, Miss. Master: W. W. Withemburt. Register secured by John McDougall, New Orleans, agent for the owners."

Registration was appropriate because the *Lama* was traveling to Port Caddo, which in April 1845 was within the Republic of Texas and therefore in foreign territory. The *Lama* arrived back in New Orleans from the Red River on 20 June after an absence of more than two months. This was an extended trip: going not just to Port Caddo, but also to the upper Red River. The Saturday, 14 June, Clarksville *Northern Standard* reported: "The Lama arrived at our landing on Saturday of last week, and passed up to Fort Towson"; on returning to New Orleans, the *Lama* reported having seen the *Hempstead* and others above the raft.

The *Lama* could have proceeded to Jefferson after stopping at Port Caddo in April. Indeed, Jefferson could have been the intended destination, in spite of the fact that the April registration was for Port Caddo. Jefferson was only an incipient town at the time and would not have been recognized by the federal authorities in New Orleans. Port

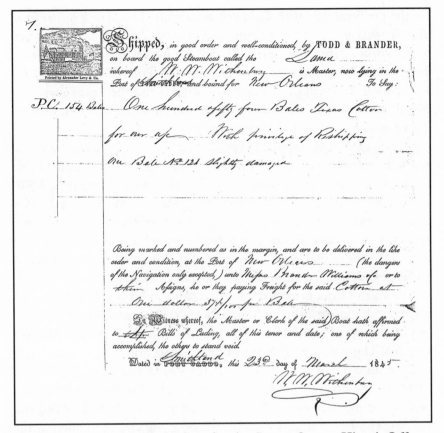

Fig. 6-3. Smithland bill of lading for the *Lama*. *Source: Historic Jefferson Foundation*

Caddo was well known and officially recognized by 1842. Any boat that went to Jefferson in 1845 would have been recorded as destined for Port Caddo, Shreveport, or Red River.

There are no other indications of the *Lama* having traveled in the direction of Jefferson. After returning from her extended Red River trip on 20 June, she is reported on 9 July as having cleared the Port of New Orleans for the Yazoo River on the previous day, with Witenburg as captain. An advertisement on 9 July also shows the *Lama* as going to Williams' Landing on the Yazoo River, with W. W. Withenbury as captain.

After returning to New Orleans, the *Lama* advertised for Pensacola on 1 August and was listed on 2 August as having cleared for Pensacola on the previous day, with Caldwell as captain. The *Ship Registers and Enrollments of New Orleans* indicated that the *Lama* was "Registered at the Port of Pensacola on July 31, 1845. Owner: Robert C. Caldwell, Pensacola, Florida. Master, C. C. Caldwell." The registration was for foreign travel, which in this case was Mexico and the Texas coast. Pat Kelley in *River of Lost Dreams: Navigation on the Rio Grande* lists the *Lama* as active in the Rio Grande trade.

Ownership may have been transferred in 1846, because the *Lama* was advertised for sale in the *Daily Picayune* during the middle of that year. William Lytle in *Merchant Steam Vessels of the United States, 1790–1868* reports that the *Lama* exploded at Camargo, Mexico, on 29 May 1847. Camargo was about one hundred miles from the coast on a tributary to the Rio Grande that extended into Mexico. May 1847 was just a little more than three years from the time the first boat to travel to Jefferson emerged from the shipyard in Cincinnati.

From this brief history of the *Lama*, it can be concluded that she arrived in Jefferson either in March 1845 (the month of the Smithland bill of lading) or April 1845 (the month of her registration for Port Caddo). There are no other possibilities. Years prior to 1844 are ruled out, because it was in that year that the *Lama* was built. The end of 1844 and the first two months of 1845 are ruled out because the *Lama* was operating elsewhere. The months after April 1845 are ruled out because the *Lama* returned to the Yazoo trade and then entered the Rio Grande trade.

The choice between March and April is resolvable. Buck Barry, who departed from New Orleans, says that he was on the second boat to Jefferson: "I had to wait nearly a week before I caught a boat going up Red River. It not only went up Red River but made her way through Soda and Caddo Lakes into Texas to a landing then and now called Jefferson. There were a hundred and thirty odd passengers aboard. . . . This was the second boat that made its way to Jefferson. A majority of the passengers, like myself, were going to Texas." Barry also provides an exact date for his arrival. At the end of the chapter "Gone to Texas," he writes: "We returned to San Antonio and spent the fourth of July, 1845. I had been from the 12th of April, the time I ate my first meal on the pine log at Jefferson, to the latter part of June, making my way across the frontier of Texas." This meal was the breakfast in the brush, which took place the morning after Barry's boat arrived at Jefferson: "Upon arriving at Jefferson, the captain notified us that we would have to look out for our own breakfast, as we had eaten all the rations on board. Going ashore next morning, I enquired where to get my breakfast." The breakfast was eaten on the twelfth; thus, Barry arrived on the night of the eleventh.

The day on which Buck Barry ate his breakfast in Jefferson was also the day on which the *Lama* was registered in New Orleans and cleared for Port Caddo. Because Barry arrived in Jefferson the night of 11 April on the second boat to Jefferson, the *Lama*'s April voyage to Port Caddo—initiated on the twelfth—cannot have been her first voyage to Jefferson. With April excluded, that leaves March as the only possible month for the *Lama*'s first voyage to Jefferson.

The March voyage is shrouded in mystery. The only real evidence for its existence is the bill of lading signed at Smithland on the twenty-third. There is no report of the departure from or return to New Orleans for this trip, only the bracketing cancellation on 26 February of the Vermillionville trip and the clearance for Port Caddo on 12 April. The reason why there is no newspaper account was that the trip was illegal: no registration had been obtained for foreign travel, and Smithland was in the Republic of Texas.

The previously quoted clipping from the *Jefferson Daily Democrat* notes that when the *Lama* returned to Shreveport after having made the first voyage to Jefferson, "she was obliged to anchor out in the stream, to avoid being seized upon by the United States Commissioner for having crossed the line." Crossing the line between the United States and the Republic of Texas was impermissible without registration, and goods brought into the United States illegally were subject to seizure by federal authorities. The *Daily Democrat* ties this incident to the *Lama*'s first voyage to Jefferson, confirming that the March voyage entailing Smithland was the first voyage to Jefferson.

It is peculiar that registration was secured for the *Lama* in April and not in March. Lacking registration and an advertisement, the *Lama* probably did not carry much in the way of freight or passengers to Jefferson on the first trip. Return freights were subject to seizure at Shreveport and New Orleans, into which the cotton was almost certainly carried clandestinely (it was never reported as having been officially received at New Orleans). The advertisement indicating the last-minute replacement of the *Lama* by the *Gazelle* in the Vermillionville trade was also peculiar. A management decision had been made whose rationale remains hidden.

Withenbury was readily available to make the voyage. He was operating as a steamboat captain out of New Orleans at least as early as November 1842, when the *Daily Picayune* notes his arrival on the sixth aboard the *Relief* from Yazoo City, and the *Relief* is advertised on the ninth as a Red River packet to Alexandria with Withenbury as captain. In addition, the 9 November 1843 *Daily Picayune* reports the arrival of the *Waverly* at New Orleans from Cincinnati with Withenbury as captain.

From the available evidence, it can be concluded that the *Lama* was the first steamboat to Jefferson and that she arrived at Jefferson on an illegal voyage in March 1845, with W. W. Withenbury as captain and George Alban as pilot.

The arrival of the *Lama* in March 1845 is directly related to the clearance of Cypress Bayou. This project was completed in December 1844, with sawed logs and other debris from the clearing effort left inchannel to be taken out by the spring rise on Cypress Bayou, which, according to the 16 January 1845 *Northern Standard*, would "leave the passage free to steamboats of moderate size." The spring rise occurred early in 1845—the logs and other debris floated out, and the information that the channel was open and that cotton was awaiting shipment was conveyed to persons in New Orleans who were in charge of the operation of the *Lama*. The planned trip to Vermillionville was canceled in late February, and the *Lama* soon embarked for Jefferson, where she arrived in March 1845, the earliest possible time at which any steamboat could have traveled through the now-free passage upstream of Smithland.

The 1 September 1876 *Daily Jimplecute* reports that William Perry met the *Lama* at Shreveport to provide guidance for the trip upstream. Although there is no documentary evidence for who cleared out Cypress Bayou in 1844, Perry is mentioned in a 27 September 1849 article in the *Texas Republican* in connection with additional efforts to clear out Cypress Bayou and Caddo Lake and was always the preferred contractor for such activities. It is thus highly probable that he was the contractor for the 1844 project and that he met the *Lama* in Shreveport to provide direction through the newly opened passage between Smithland and Jefferson because he was the only person intimately acquainted with that portion of the route and the difficulties it might pose for the first steamboat passing through it.

·7·
The Growth of Commerce
1845-55

EIGHTEEN FORTY-FIVE

After the *Lama* reached the emerging town of Jefferson in March 1845, Buck Barry arrived on the second boat to Jefferson on the night of 11 April. Barry must have been on the *Gazelle*, the boat that took the place of the *Lama* in the Vermillionville trade at the last minute, enabling the *Lama* to travel to Jefferson. The *Gazelle* arrived back in New Orleans from Vermillionville on 27 March, according to the *Daily Picayune* of that date, and is advertised the next day for Port Caddo with S. W. Vandergrift as captain.

The *Gazelle* is shown in the 3 April issue as having cleared for Port Caddo on the previous day, which would have been the designated destination for any boat that went to Jefferson in 1845. A 2 April departure would have allowed sufficient time for the *Gazelle* to reach Jefferson on the night of the eleventh. This is the only boat that cleared for Port Caddo during the appropriate period, and her close association with the *Lama* made such a voyage possible.

The third boat to reach Jefferson was almost certainly the *Lama* in her April trip to the area. After leaving Jefferson on the March trip, the *Lama* stopped at Smithland to pick up additional bales of cotton, which were signed for by Withenbury on 23 March. The *Lama* would have immediately proceeded downstream, arriving at Shreveport a day or two later and then arriving at New Orleans at the beginning of the next month. Registration was secured for travel to Port Caddo on 12 April, and the *Lama* cleared the Port of New Orleans the same day. Although there is nothing definite to indicate that the *Lama* went as far as Jefferson, it is highly unlikely that she would have terminated her trip at Port Caddo after having made the first thrust into the Jefferson area in March, particularly because the water was high in April, and the April trip lasted more than two months, with the *Lama* proceeding to the upper Red River.

Thus, for 1845 it is probable that the *Lama* made two trips to Jefferson and the *Gazelle* made one. Four other boats (*Bois d'Arc, Maid of Kentucky, Rodolph,* and *Yazoo*) are recorded as departing from New Orleans for Port Caddo, and six others (*Col. Harney, Douglas, J. E. Roberts, Little Yazoo, New Brazil,* and *Panola*) advertised for Port Caddo. Any of the boats that departed or advertised for Port Caddo after the second boat, the *Gazelle,* arrived at Jefferson on 11 April could have proceeded to Jefferson. These include the *Yazoo, Bois d'Arc, Maid of Kentucky, Rodolph, Col. Harney, Panola,* and *J. E. Roberts.*

Of particular interest among the boats operating in 1845 are the *Bois d'Arc, New Brazil, Little Yazoo,* and *Rodolph.* The *Bois d'Arc* made nine recorded trips to Port Caddo in 1845, continuing to operate from the previous years of 1843 and 1844 under the captaincy of John Smoker, who also captained the *Brian Boroihme* in 1841, the first boat to advertise for Port Caddo. The *Little Yazoo* appears in an advertisement for the *New Brazil,* saying that the latter will transfer freight at Shreveport to the former, which draws only fourteen inches light, for transport to the "Head of the Lakes," apparently meaning Port Caddo. The *New Brazil* also advertised independently of the *Little Yazoo,* suggesting that she went to Port Caddo during this year. Lastly, the *Rodolph,* with M. Welch as captain, began advertising in October as a regular ten-day packet from New Orleans to Port Caddo, the first to commit herself to a regular schedule, at least on paper.

The year 1845 was also the year in which Port Caddo was established as the seat of a district for the collection of tariffs on freight brought into the Republic of Texas by steamboats and on personal property brought in by immigrants. The Soda Lake Collectoral District was created on 29 January, with L. H. Mabbitt as collector of customs, comprising "all the counties of Red River and Bowie lying south of Sulphur Fork, with Harrison and Rusk, and all of Nacogdoches lying west and north of Rusk County." This was an extremely unpopular measure among the steamboatmen and the immigrants. A customs house was supposed to be established at Port Caddo; but Mabbitt was forced to reside in Marshall and was unable to exercise any authority, as is evident from a letter in the *Texas Treasury Papers* written by Hamilton Bee in Marshall on 25 April 1845:

> I found Col. Mabbitt the Collector of the Sodo Lake District, residing at this place, the state of public feeling preventing his residence at Port Caddo from all I can learn from conversations with different gentlemen, I am satisfied that the Citizen's of Harrison will not pay the Tariff unless compelled by force. . . . the situation of Col. Mabbitt is exceedingly unpleasant, he informs me that threats are continually made against his life—they have forced his deputies to resign, and even the Captains of the steamboats plying on the Lake, openly set his authority at defiance, and he is in the mortifying position of a high minded, chivalrous man, forced to submit to every species of indignity in his attempts to discharge his duty—he informs me that he has written to the Department for authority to call on the Colonels of the Regiments in his district, which will enable him to take possession of goods, sold openly in this place and Port Caddo, without the duties paid on them.

This action was not taken because Texas was well on its way to statehood, after which the tariff issue was moot. Texas was offered statehood in March 1845 and formally admitted to the Union in December. During the brief period in which the collectoral district was operative, small amounts were collected from immigrants; but it is unclear whether steamboats ever paid tariffs at Port Caddo. It should be noted that Bee's 25 April letter does not mention Jefferson, even though the *Lama* had made two trips and the *Gazelle* one trip to that town by that date. Jefferson was not yet known as a point of destination.

The open defiance of the tariff authorities by the steamboatmen was paralleled by their unwillingness to register at the Port of New Orleans for travel into the Republic of Texas from Shreveport. Of the twenty-six steamboats that should have registered from 1842 through 1845, only nine did. The *Lama* at first made an illegal trip and then gained registration. Almost all of the boats that traveled to the Republic of Texas without the appropriate papers advertised their trips in the

New Orleans newspapers, attesting to the fact that enforcement was a perennial problem on the frontier.

By at least the close of 1845, Jefferson was beginning to be recognized as a steamboat port. The only extant issue of a Shreveport newspaper for 1846 is the 11 February *Caddo Gazette*. This issue contains an advertisement for the *Express Mail* that is dated 17 December 1845 and that mentions Jefferson on the proposed itinerary for the next year:

> EXPRESS MAIL, JOHN SMOKER, Master,
>
> This substantial and elegant steamboat will run as a regular packet between New Orleans and Shreveport and as high up as Port Caddo and Jefferson in Texas, commencing her trips as soon as Red River becomes navigable for boats of her class.
>
> The *Express Mail* has been purchased by the old proprietors of the Bois d'Arc, and they bespeak for the former the same liberal patronage which has been bestowed upon the latter, pledging themselves to use every exertion to merit its continuance.
>
> The *Express Mail* will not be surpassed by any boat in the Red River trade in point of capacity for carrying freight and passengers. She will stow about 1,800 bales of cotton, and has thirty-eight large state rooms.
>
> She may be expected as soon as the water will permit.
>
> LEWIS & HOWELL, AGENTS.
> Shreveport, December 17, 1845.

This is obviously a provisional advertisement. It was not uncommon for such advertisements, particularly when they involved an announcement for a new boat in a trade, to run for many months, with the date of the initial submission of the advertisement recorded at the bottom. Whether this promise was fulfilled is unknown. The *Express Mail* advertised three times in the *Daily Picayune* in 1846, but all of these trips were to Port Caddo, and Jefferson is not mentioned.

EIGHTEEN FORTY-SIX

The year 1846 was the first year in which a steamboat advertised for Jefferson with a specific departure date. This is also the first year in which a boat is recorded as having arrived in New Orleans from Jefferson. The advertisement is for the *J. E. Roberts* in the 27 March *Daily Picayune*, and the record is for her return from that advertised trip on 16 April. It is particularly fitting that this boat was owned and captained by W. W. Withenbury. The *J. E. Roberts* was advertised in the Port Caddo trade in 1845, with J. E. Roberts as captain. However, when she was enrolled in New Orleans on 8 March 1846, Withenbury is shown as owner and captain, having purchased the boat sometime after 19 February 1846, the last date for which the *J. E. Roberts* advertised for Port Caddo with D. Roberts (J. E.'s brother) as captain.

The 27 March 1846 advertisement for the *J. E. Roberts* reads as follows:

FOR FORT TOWSON, FULTON, PORT *Caddo,* *Jefferson, Shreveport, Natchitoches and Alexandria.*—The very well known, light and fast running steamer J. E. ROBERTS, W. W. Whitenburg, master, will leave for the above and all intermediate landings on FRIDAY, the 27th inst., at 4 o'clock, P.M. For freight or passage apply on board at the foot of Customhouse street, or to T. B. SMITH, 14 Poydras St.

This boat is shown on 16 April as having returned from Jefferson carrying 947 bales of cotton. She advertised on the same day for Fort Towson, Jefferson, and Port Caddo. Other boats that advertised for Jefferson in 1846 were the *Yazoo, Belle of Red River, Belle of Ouachita,* and *Vesta.* It is uncertain whether the *Belle of Red River* actually traveled to Jefferson. The *Daily Picayune* advertisements for this boat do not mention any transfer arrangements. However, a provisional ("as soon as the water will permit") advertisement for the *Belle of Red River* appears in the 11 February 1846 *Caddo Gazette,* and a companion advertisement for the *Live Oak* declares: "This splendid light draft boat will run throughout the season in conjunction with the *Belle of Red River,* from Shreveport, Port Caddo, Jefferson and all intermediate landings on the lake, and also to all Landings on Cross Lake, as soon as the water will permit." It cannot be determined whether the *Live Oak* operated in this transfer capacity because there are no other extant Shreveport newspapers for 1846.

Of the boats that advertised for Jefferson in 1846, the *Belle of Red River, J. E. Roberts* (with D. Roberts as captain), and *Vesta* also advertised for Port Caddo. The *Enterprise, Jim Gilmer*, and *Yalobusha* are recorded as having arrived from Port Caddo. The 22 September 1880 *New Orleans Daily Democrat* says that the *Latona* brought a load of 1,549 bales of cotton from Port Caddo in 1846. The *Express Mail, Frankland, Rodolph, Yazoo*, and *Wheel of Fortune* advertised for Port Caddo. The *Enterprise* was captained by Withenbury in May after his April trip on the *J. E. Roberts*, and the *Latona* was captained by John Smoker in December after his April trip on the *Express Mail*.

The year 1846 was also a year that produced three excellent accounts of the area west of Shreveport. The first is by the Rev. John H. McLean, whose family had come to Texas in 1839 and eventually settled a few miles north of Jefferson. When Buck Barry arrived at Jefferson in April 1845, the town contained only one completed log house, two under construction, and apparently no inhabitants. When McLean visited Jefferson as a small boy in 1846 (or perhaps 1847), the commercial activity generated by steamboats was already beginning to have a profound effect:

> Jefferson was the first town I ever saw. There were a few boat landings on the lake, as Port Caddo, Swanson's Landing and Smithland, with a solitary store, but no town until Jefferson sprang up in 1846 at the head of navigation on Big Cypress near where it empties into Caddo Lake. There were three or four stores and shops of different kinds, with a population of probably fifty or sixty people. I had on my first hat, somewhat on the plug order; and, as I went gazing about at the new and the strange things, a shower of rain came suddenly upon me. My first thought was for my hat, and, placing it under my coat, I made at full speed for the nearest shelter, much to the amusement of bystanders. As I recall, these were among the first merchants: Speak & Willard, Perry Graham, and Jeff Crawford, father of Col. Crawford of Dallas.

The second account for 1846 is by A. W. Moore, who traveled from Daingerfield to Jefferson and from Jefferson to Greenwood, Louisiana, at the end of June:

> 25th from Dangerfield to Jefferson 30 miles. for the first 10 miles some red Land mostly gray the timber on both kinds verry

fair. Water good and plenty. the next 20 gray sand with a rotten mulatto clay foundation. timber such as has been described except we occasionally [saw] some pretty extensive groves of Pine. from Dangerfield the country may be called broken but not Mountainous or in other words beautifully undulating sufficiently rolling to drain itself and is perhaps a fair country for farming purposes Jefferson being the shipping point, for produce, cotton etc. the prospect for health good until within a few miles of Jefferson then very sickley. Jefferson is a small town just springing into existence situated at the head of Caddo Lake made by the junction of the two Cypress and almost surrounded by Lakes of various sizes and has the appearance of being as sickly a place as exists under the sun. It is nevertheless destined to be a place of considerable business being the highest navigable point below the raft. Population 2 or 3 hundred.

Moore apparently crossed Cypress Bayou at Jefferson and then proceeded south toward Greenwood: "26th to camp 28 miles through a low filthey oak and Pine country for ten miles full of Lakes Ponds and muddy dead running streams. the soil in places pretty fair then a high rolling oak and hickory land of a better quality for the bal. of our days Journey. some good water a plenty for stock. our course now lays pretty much with the course of Caddo Lake and therefore cannot be said to be healthey although we saw no local cause of sickness after the first 10 miles but the appearance of the setlers and the emblems of mourning we saw bore indubitable evidences that the hand of death would never be stayed whilst one solitary subject remained to prey upon. what few crops we saw here looked extremely well."

The third account for 1846 is by William McClintock, who visited Daingerfield at the beginning of September and traveled southwest, describing the desolate area west of Jefferson:

> 8th. Arose at light this morning and found all our horses gone except two—found them all but three by 9 o'clock— although the rain had obliterated all traces of them for two miles, I struck their trail in the tall grass at last, and followed on till I overtook them. The other three we found in the evening, and rode ten miles. This town of Dangerfield, consists of three or four cabins scarce fit for pigsties. We staid at Ellison's, and

there learned that the ferry boat, on big Cyprus had sunk and we must swim. We succeeded in raising the boat and dragging her ashore, by swimming in and fastening a grape vine to the bow, which was only 4 or 5 feet under water. The stream is only 40 or 50 feet wide, and 15 or 20 deep. We baled the water out of the boat and cut up some rope halter to cork her. Got over safely by 11 A.M. I pushed on for little Cyprus. These streams, the bottoms and bayous on them, abound with alligators, besides many other reptiles common to Texas. Reached Little Cyprus late in the evening. I had fallen behind with Burchill; who was sick. When I came up, most of the horses were loose and running through the woods. They could not get them to swim it. Peters was raving, swearing and scolding most vociferously, and not doing or likely to do anything else. I dismounted from my horse, stripped myself and horse and mounted him, entered the stream telling the rest if they would drive theirs in they would follow. Some of them did and got their horses over. I then swam back and took another. In this way we were soon over. In less than half a mile, we had to strip and swim another stream, or slough. After getting over, we had not gone a mile, before we came to a creek, the bridge over which had washed away by the recent rain. It was now quite dark and to find a crossing place in the dark night was impossible. The beds of these streams are often much deeper than wide. We unsaddled. I hobbled my horse and turned him out to grass. Spread my blankets and lay down to sleep. None of us had a bite to eat, nor had had since sunrise.

EIGHTEEN FORTY-SEVEN

In 1847, the number of trips made by steamboats to points west of Shreveport appears to have increased, at least if the advertisements are to be trusted, even though there was little activity during the second half of the year. The *Ellen*, with John Graham as captain, advertised as a regular packet to Jefferson and Port Caddo in January and appears to have fulfilled the commitment. She was a regular advertiser and made two recorded trips to Jefferson and one to Port Caddo.

The *Monterey*, under Captain Withenbury, made one recorded trip to Jefferson and advertised six times for Port Caddo. The *Buffalo* and

Vesta advertised for Jefferson, and the *Victress* made one recorded trip. In addition, the *Belle of Illinois*, *Latona*, *Rodolph*, and *Victress* advertised for Port Caddo, and the *Yazoo City* made one trip. The *Latona*, with John Smoker as captain, and the *Rodolph* and *Vesta* were holdovers from the previous year.

Josiah Gregg, in his diary for November 1847, describes the growth of Shreveport, which was the hub for all boats traveling west toward Port Caddo and Jefferson and north to the upper Red River: "The town of Shreveport was named for Capt. Shreve—indeed, I believe, founded by him about the close of his labors upon the raft. When I first knew it (in 1841) it was a very insignificant place; and, indeed, when I visited in 1844, it appeared to me, to contain scarcely 200 souls. But it has rapidly increased since; so that I suppose it must now contain 1000. The truth is, it appears to me to bid fair to become a city of some importance."

EIGHTEEN FORTY-EIGHT

The year 1848 was a slow year, with only a few boats operating in the direction of Jefferson, and five others going only as far as Port Caddo. The *Creole* recorded one trip to Jefferson and the *Caddo* two trips to Port Caddo. The *Monterey* and *Latona* advertised for Jefferson and Port Caddo, and the *Monroe*, *J. T. Boswell*, *Vesta*, and *Belvidere* advertised for Port Caddo, which continued to dominate the trade west of Shreveport.

The *Caddo* was operated by John Graham, who had run the *Ellen* in 1847. An advertisement for the *Caddo* that appeared in the 30 January 1850 Shreveport *Caddo Gazette* provides a glimpse of the boat and her master:

> *Shreveport, Port Caddo, and N.O. Packet,*
> CADDO,
> JOHN GRAHAM, Master.
> This elegant and well known steamer, which has been entirely renovated, will regularly maintain her position in the trade between New Orleans and Shreveport, and the latter place and Jefferson, and intermediate landings, throughout the season. The Caddo is one hundred and fifty feet long, thirty-one feet beam, six and a half hold, two engines, seventeen and

a half inches diameter of cylinder, seven feet stroke, very strongly built, and will carry fifteen hundred and fifty bales of cotton.

Captain Graham, thankful for past favors, hopes to renew and merit a continuation of his accustomed patronage.

Nov. 7, 1849.

EIGHTEEN FORTY-NINE

The year 1849 was a swing year in which the number of boats to Jefferson equaled the number to Port Caddo. The trade was dominated by the *Monterey*, with Withenbury as captain, which made five recorded trips to Jefferson and two to Port Caddo; and by the *Duck River*, with Sam Applegate as captain, which made eight recorded trips to Jefferson and one to Port Caddo. The *Corinne*, *W. A. Violett*, and *Shamrock* are recorded as having made trips to Jefferson, and the *Caddo* and *Dime* advertised for Jefferson. The *Caddo*, *D. B. Mosby*, *Latona*, and *Tallahatchie* recorded trips to Port Caddo, and the *Belvidere* advertised for Port Caddo.

Edward Smith was an Englishman sent in 1849 to evaluate potential colony sites in Texas, and his *Account of a Journey Through North-Eastern Texas* is a compendium of information on transportation routes, natural resources, agricultural production, labor, and security. Smith left New Orleans on 17 May on a steamboat and reached Shreveport on the twenty-first after a seventy-five-hour voyage. Unable to obtain horses in Shreveport, he took another steamboat on the twenty-third through an "interesting chain of lakes to Jefferson, situated at the head of Navigation, on Cypress Creek." Arriving on the twenty-fourth at Jefferson, he obtained horses and embarked on an extensive reconnaissance of the northeast corner of the state, providing the following account of the towns through which he passed:

> Chief towns. The chief towns are, with few exceptions, unimportant places, from the very limited period which has elapsed since their foundation.
>
> Jefferson four years ago possessed only three log-houses; now it is well laid out, and has somewhat near sixty good houses, and several large well-supplied stores, also one warehouse for the shipment of merchandise, and a small saw and grist steam mill.

Dangerfield is a very small place, but it is said to be rapidly rising. They have just determined to found a college there.

Tarrant consists of twelve or fifteen houses congregated on a very large prairie, from which there is no line of separation.

Clarkesville is said to be the most flourishing town in N.E. Texas, containing, probably, three hundred families.

Paris and Bonham are of fair size, with two hundred and fifty or three hundred inhabitants each. The courthouse is built of brick, but the other houses are neatly constructed of pine boards.

McKinney was founded but a year or two ago, and is small.

Dallas is a rising town, well situated for commerce, on a tongue of land on the very banks of the Trinity.

On our return route, we passed through no country town, except Marshall, the most flourishing place through which we traveled. An iron casting furnace, two saw mills, and other useful works, with several large hotels, and many stores, testify that enterprise and wealth abound amongst the people.

With respect to Jefferson in particular, Smith reports the following:

This is situated in Texas, on Cypress Creek, and in 32° 46 of lat. It is approached from Shreeveport by the Red River, and the 12 mile Bayou, and a long chain of lakes, and enters farther to the West than Shreeveport, and consequently is a more convenient port to the settlers in the interior. Steam boats have plyed these lakes during the past four years, but no regular line had been established until the present season. We arrived at Jefferson in the middle of May, and found that ours was the twenty-first arrival during that season. This Port bids fair to seriously injure Shreeveport, but the cost for transit from Jefferson induces many to take their produce sixty miles further to Shreeveport; but as the quantity of produce increases, it is probable that the rates of freight from Jefferson will diminish.

When speaking about steamboats plying the lakes, Smith obviously means up to Jefferson, because he would have been aware of boats traveling to Port Caddo. The statement about the establishment of the first regular line to Jefferson in 1849 is problematic. If Smith is talking about a regular New Orleans–to–Jefferson packet, the statement is questionable: the *Ellen* appears to have established this role in 1847. He may have been referring to a boat operating strictly between Shreveport and Jefferson, and this might have been the boat that he took to Jefferson, which he does not name. However, it is more probable that he is referring to the *Duck River*, which made regular trips to Jefferson in 1849 and advertised as a regular packet to Jefferson, as, for example, in the 20 July 1849 Marshall *Texas Republican*:

> STEAMER DUCK RIVER,
> *Regular Red River packet, for Alexandria, Natchitoches, Shreveport, Port Caddo and Jefferson*, J. APPLEGATE, Master, will make regular trips throughout the season. Her accommodations are good, her officers are attentive, and it is the desire to make her in every respect worthy of patronage.
> July 20, 1849.

EIGHTEEN FIFTY

By 1850, the number of boats shown as going to Jefferson exceeded the number shown as going to Port Caddo. The *Duck River* continued to dominate the Jefferson trade, with eight recorded trips. The *Monterey* and *R. C. Oglesby* made recorded trips to Jefferson, and the *Caddo* and *New Latona* advertised for Jefferson. The *Medora* made seven and the *Monterey* five recorded trips to Port Caddo. No boats are shown as operating on the route during the second half of the year because of low water on the Red River.

The *New Latona* was a replacement for the *Latona*, although the latter continued to operate on the route. The *New Latona* advertised to Jefferson and Port Caddo in the 21 December 1850 *Texas Republican*:

> STEAMER NEW LATONA.
> This new and splendid boat, SMOKER, Captain, will run regularly throughout the business season, between *Jefferson, Port Caddo, and New Orleans*, touching at all intermediate landings. She has been built expressly for this trade, and for safety, and the character of her accommodations, cannot be surpassed by any boat on the river. Her cabin is large and

commodious, and neatly fitted up. It is intended she shall combine safety, and comfort.

Dec. 14, 1850.

This boat was nearly 200 feet in length and weighed nearly 400 tons and was later described as the largest boat ever seen at Shreveport during her day. In spite of the clarity of the advertisement, it is possible that the *New Latona* never went to Jefferson or Port Caddo. She is shown in the *Daily Picayune* as a regular visitor to Shreveport, but not to Port Caddo or Jefferson. However, this boat went as far as Soda Lake in March 1851 to secure cotton from the wrecked *Jim Gilmer* during a high-water period.

The December 1850 advertisement for the *New Latona* was the last mention of John Smoker in connection with the Cypress Bayou and the lakes route. Smoker was captain of the *Brian Boroihme*, the first advertised boat for Port Caddo, and operated the *Bois d'Arc* to Port Caddo from 1843 through 1845, the *Express Mail* to Port Caddo in 1846, and the *Latona* to Port Caddo and Jefferson from 1847 through 1849. The *Latona* continued in the Jefferson trade in 1851, but under the captaincy of Thomas Hunt.

Other familiar names in 1850 were John Graham, Sam Applegate, and W. W. Withenbury. Graham captained the *Ellen* in 1847 and the *Caddo* from 1848 through 1850. Applegate captained the *Duck River* in 1849 and the *Duck River*, *Medora*, and *Southern* in 1850. Withenbury captained the *Lama* in 1845, the *Enterprise* and *J. E. Roberts* in 1846, and the *Monterey* from 1847 through 1850. Besides being responsible for the first boat to Jefferson, Withenbury was also responsible for the first wreck in connection with the trade west of Shreveport. In May 1850, the *Monterey*—on her way to Port Caddo—struck a snag in Soda Lake and sunk with the loss of one life and the total cargo.

The primacy of Jefferson over Port Caddo by 1850 suggested by the navigation record is confirmed by the newspaper commentaries, which speak of Jefferson's growth, the consolidation of its market area to the north and west, and its future prospects. Robert W. Loughery, the editor of the Marshall *Texas Republican*, was a resident of Jefferson when he first came to Texas and made periodic trips to Jefferson over many years, as well as reporting information on Jefferson obtained from others. One of his earliest accounts is in the 14 March 1850 *Texas Republican*: "We are gratified at the accounts we receive of the increasing prosperity of our sister town. There are now, we understand, nine or ten mercantile establishments at Jefferson, that are doing an excellent business. Not a bale of cotton, it is said, has, during the last year, passed by there, and the lake navigation has been uninterrupted during the business seasons. Merchants from the interior, and particularly from the Red River counties, as well as the planters, now go there for their supplies, and are accommodated on the best terms. The lands surrounding it are rapidly filling up with that kind of population most desirable."

A second account for the year was written to Loughery by a Marshall resident and appeared in the 28 March *Texas Republican*:

> I was much pleased with the improvement which Jefferson has made in the last six months, both in appearance and commerce. She commands the highest navigation for an extensive section of new and fertile country, which is settling and improving rapidly. Her houses are filled with goods and groceries sufficient in quality and quantity for the entire demand of her extensive patronage, and her merchants are liberal. . . .
>
> Her position gives her a double advantage over any other point in Eastern Texas. She has the benefit of being interior, and at the same time at the head of navigation. This may safely be accorded to her without detracting in the least from any of her neighboring commercial points. Artificial helps may give her a rival, but not a competitor. She alone will command almost the entire trade of a territory sufficient in extent and agricultural resources to make her one of the first towns in the State.

A third account for the year was written to Loughery by a Jefferson resident and appeared in the 20 June *Texas Republican*: "Our town is improving. Several large buildings are now in progress of completion. The trade also of this place is at this time quite brisk. Wagons from the country are continually blocking up our streets; and the speculation in beef cattle has almost become a mania. The lake is still in fine boating order. Next week look for the '*Oglesby*,' which never fails to roll up '*like winken*,' and as regular as 'tea time.'"

EIGHTEEN FIFTY-ONE

During 1851, the *Caddo*, *Corinne*, *Latona*, *Tallahatchie*, and *W. A. Violett* continued to make trips to Jefferson and Port Caddo. The *Red River* made one trip to Port Caddo, and the *Osceola*, with R. H. Martin as master, made a record eleven trips to Jefferson. Withenbury was operating a new boat, the *Echo*, which recorded five trips to Jefferson and one to Smithland. The latter is the only record in the *Daily Picayune* of a boat showing Smithland as her place of departure to New Orleans. This was a new *Echo*, built in 1850, not the one operating to Port Caddo in 1842. A provisional advertisement in the 6 September 1851 *Texas Republican* informed the public that the *Jefferson* was being built as a lake packet; but this boat never got to operate in the area because she was wrecked at Grand Ecore on the Red River on her maiden voyage from New Orleans, according to the 13 March 1852 issue.

The *Southern*, with Sam Applegate as captain, began advertising in the 21 December 1850 *Texas Republican* that she was built as a New Orleans-to-Jefferson packet and that she would begin running in that trade as soon as water conditions permitted, which would not have been until 1851. A companion article says that this boat was 183 feet by 31 feet. The provisional advertisement continues into 1851. This boat never appeared at New Orleans and nothing is known about it.

Apart from the 1841 advertisement for the *Farmer* to Benton and the 1842 advertisement for the *Star* to Smithland, none of the hundreds of advertisements that appeared in the New Orleans, Shreveport, and Marshall newspapers from 1841 through 1850 mentioned any port or landing on the Cypress Bayou and the lakes route other than Jefferson and Port Caddo. This is not because there were no other ports and landings. Instead, the boats that advertised did not consider places other than Jefferson and Port Caddo to be of sufficient commercial interest to be worthy of mention.

Things changed in 1851. On 4 February, the *Osceola* advertised in the *Daily Picayune* for Port Caddo, Benton, Smithland, and Jefferson. On 23 April, the *Osceola* advertised as a regular Red River and Lake packet to Shreveport, Port Caddo, Benton, Smithland, and Jefferson. On the same day, the *Echo* advertised for Shreveport, Port Caddo, Benton, Smithland, and Jefferson. The *Echo* is listed as returning from

Smithland on 18 June. Then, on 6 September, the *Jefferson* issued its provisional advertisement in the Marshall *Texas Republican* with a proliferation of landings:

LAKE PACKET.

THE steam boat *Jefferson*, BEN MCKINNEY, master, (now being built at Cincinnati expressly for the trade), will commence making regular trips as soon as the water permits, to Jefferson, Smithland, Port Caddo, Clinton, Reeves, Swanson, and all other landings on the Lake.

The *Jefferson* will carry about 1500 bales of cotton, and her accommodation for passengers will be unsurpassed by any boat in the trade.

August 16, 1851.

R. W. Loughery, the editor of the *Texas Republican*, visited Jefferson twice in 1851. The first trip in 1851 occurred in March and is reported in the issue for the twenty-ninth:

We had not been in Jefferson for eighteen months, and were consequently surprised and delighted at the improved condition of the place; not only in the town, but in the country immediately surrounding it. The place no longer presents the appearance of a dull plodding village, but has grown into a point of extensive commercial importance. It has now many large wholesale houses; steamboats arrive and depart weekly, heavily freighted; wagons from the surrounding country are to be seen pouring into the place, houses are going up; and everything betokens present and future prosperity. Six years ago, Jefferson had scarcely an existence; and when it was first laid out as a town, and it was proposed to navigate the Cypress with steamboats, the scheme was looked upon by almost everyone as ridiculous. The navigation of this Bayou and the Lake now having been established beyond question, the town with a back country to support it, is destined to grow with rapidity.

We were particularly struck with the improved condition of the country on the road leading to Daingerfield. It looks almost like a village, with neat cottages, and buildings of a more pretending character. Many of these residences are owned by the businessmen of Jefferson, and are well improved. This region is called "Paradise;" a name given it, we suppose, from the fact that it contains a majority of the young ladies.

Loughery's second trip to Jefferson in 1851 was made in September during the summer low-water season and is reported in the issue for the twenty-seventh: "The navigation being closed, we did not find business as lively as it was when we were there last spring; such, of course, was not to be expected. But we found the town rapidly going ahead in improvements, and preparations making for the winter, when business will open no doubt with more animation than it has ever done before. Among the new houses, going up, we noticed a large building in progress owned by Messrs. J. M. & J. C. MURPHY, who intend opening a large store in that place. The merchants at Jefferson, are doing at present, a very fair business, and the trade will soon increase as the crops of cotton begin to arrive."

EIGHTEEN FIFTY-TWO

In 1852, eleven boats made at least thirty-one trips to Jefferson and Port Caddo. Boats recording trips to Jefferson included the *Cleona*, *Caspian*, *Echo*, *Frances Jones*, *Grenada*, *Pitser Miller*, *Post Boy*, *Red River*, and *Storm*. The *Caddo No. 2*, with John Graham as master, took the place of the *Caddo* and advertised for Jefferson. The *Cleona*, *Red River*, and *Storm* also went to Port Caddo and the *Pitser Miller* to Caddo Lake. The only boats that went exclusively to Port Caddo were the *Lucy Robinson* and *Swan*, which registered one trip each.

With respect to ports and landings, the advertisements for the *Caspian*, *Storm*, and *Cleona* are pertinent. The *Caspian* and *Storm* both advertised on 14 April in the *Daily Picayune* for Jefferson, Smithland, Benton, Port Caddo, Mooring's Landing, and Albany. In the 17 January issue of the Marshall *Texas Republican*, the *Cleona* advertised as a regular lake packet for Albany, Mooring's Landing, Swanson Landing, Rives' Landings, Monterey, Clinton, Port Caddo, Benton, Smithland, and Jefferson.

The *Cleona* arrived back in New Orleans on 22 July according to the *Daily Picayune*, and there were no boats west of Shreveport during the next three months of the summer low-water period. Cotton receipts at Port Caddo were low in September and the first half of October according to the *Texas Republican* of the sixteenth: "We have received a letter from Port Caddo, dated the 15th inst., from which we learn that there is eight or ten inches more water in the Lake than there was when the Cleona made her last trip. The amount of cotton received at Port Caddo this season has not been very large, which is perhaps owing to the fact that planters are not aware that there is a chance of getting it off. Our correspondent thinks if shipments of cotton were made immediately, a boat would soon be induced to visit the Lake and take it off."

EIGHTEEN FIFTY-THREE

In 1853, eleven boats made at least thirty-four trips to points west of Shreveport, in spite of the fact that there was no activity after July because of low water on the Red River. The *Cleona* made nine recorded trips to Jefferson. The *Alabama, Grenada, John Strader, Pitser Miller, S. W. Downs, Texas Ranger,* and *Venture* also recorded trips to Jefferson, and the *Caddo No. 2* and *St. Charles* advertised for Jefferson. The *Cleona, S. W. Downs,* and *St. Charles* also recorded trips to Port Caddo. The only record for a boat traveling solely to Port Caddo was for the *Compromise.* The *Post Boy* recorded one trip to Fairy Lake, a corruption of Ferry Lake, the old name for Caddo Lake derived from Shenix's Ferry.

The *Venture* was a small boat of only sixty-one tons, with a length of 102 feet. She was captained by James Crooks of Caddo Parish, who first appears in the record concerning activities west of Shreveport as captain of the *Post Boy* in 1852, which he continued to operate in 1853. The *Venture* appears only once in the record and apparently was a local boat operating out of Shreveport. She was at Jefferson on a special mission, as recorded in the 23 April *Caddo Gazette*:

> The steamer Venture brought down from Jefferson, the other day, a company of five or six men, having in their charge a prisoner who it seems killed a man in Hopkins County, Ky., by the name of Walden, some time back. One of the party was the brother of the murdered man, and had brought the others along to assist in taking the prisoner wherever they should find him, without any requisition, however, from the Governor of

Kentucky. At Jefferson, some eight or ten men endeavored to effect the rescue of the prisoner, but the citizens with praiseworthy spirit, determined that he should be carried back for trial. The scene, we are informed, was quite exciting. The citizens turned out with guns—some old flint-lock rifles that had figured probably in the time of the Moderators and Regulators, being conspicuous—pistols, &c., and escorted the prisoner through the street to the Venture, whose officers were in arms ready to receive him. Our informant tells us that his attention was attracted by a rough old customer in the crowd, who was intensely excited by the occasion—swore it reminded him of old times. No doubt he would have considered it fine to hang the man to a lamp-post, provided our sister city enjoys such a luxury. We believe the captain of the Venture (our favorite by the bye) was heard to say that he wished to see something like "old times" himself, and to express profound regret that the mob had not executed him summarily, in accordance with the frontier honored laws of Judge Lynch—even at the loss of his passage money down. This innocent gratification was not, however, afforded, and the gentleman was landed, with his attentive escort, opposite our town—in Bossier parish—safely out of the reach of habeas corpus—which, however, would have been of little service to him, as his captor avowed his determination to shoot him, if anything of the kind was attempted, swearing that his brother's death must and should be avenged.

They left Wednesday evening on the St. Charles.

Loughery visited Jefferson in January and notes the continuing progress of the town in the 28 January *Texas Republican*: "Jefferson is improving. A number of elegant buildings are going up, and business is lively. The Lake at present is quite low, not being more than enough water for a small boat. The merchants, however, anticipate a speedy rise, which is much needed as a large amount of cotton on the Lake has not yet been shipped, and many of the merchants expect large stocks of goods shortly."

In November, many of the captains who operated boats in the Red River and the Cypress Bayou and lakes trades met in New Orleans to establish a steamboat combination that would fix freight rates. This was the first of many attempts to set rates by joint action. Most of these attempts were short-lived because captains were highly competitive, and it was impossible to establish monopoly power in a free-entry system. The attempt was forcefully opposed throughout Northeast Texas, partly on principle, but mostly because the stipulated rates were exorbitant. The planters and merchants of the area agreed to support liberally any boats that would buck the combination. They found a ready response in Captain Alexander of the *Pitser Miller*, joined by Captains Sweeny and Withenbury. William Brooks of Jefferson purchased the *Belle Gates* to join in the opposition, and Richard Crump of Jefferson started a company to purchase another boat. The combination disintegrated early in 1854.

EIGHTEEN FIFTY-FOUR

In 1854, nine boats made at least thirty trips to Jefferson and Port Caddo, six of which were holdovers from the previous year. The *Cleona* recorded eight trips to Jefferson. The *B. E. Clark*, with Withenbury as captain, and the *Allen Glover* (fig. 7-1), *Belle Gates*, *Caddo No. 2*, *Grenada*, *St. Charles*, and *Storm* made recorded trips to Jefferson. The *C. Hays*, *Ruby*, and *Unicorn* advertised for Jefferson. The *Unicorn* had a calliope on board. The *Caddo No. 2* and the *Texas Ranger* made recorded trips to Port Caddo. Besides three trips to Jefferson, the *Belle Gates* recorded one trip to Benton. This is one of the few arrival records indicating Benton as the primary destination.

Most of the advertisements for this year list Benton and Smithland as destinations along with Port Caddo and Jefferson, and many other ports and landings are included in *Daily Picayune* advertisements. On 24 May, the *Caddo No. 2* advertised for Smithland, Benton, Port Caddo, Swanson's, Perry's, Low's, and Morning's; and a companion advertisement for the same boat lists Swanson's Landing. On 1 June, the *Storm* advertised for Port Caddo, Monterey, Benton, and Jefferson; and the *Ruby* advertised for Port Caddo, Monterey, Benton, Clinton, Smithland, and Jefferson. On 29 June, the *Grenada* advertised for Jefferson, Smithland, Benton, Port Caddo, Swanson's Landing, Perry's Landing, and Lowe's.

No boats went to Jefferson from August 1853 through February 1854. Loughery visited Jefferson in January and notes the lull in the issue of the *Texas Republican* for the twenty-eighth: "Jefferson was some

Fig. 7-1. *Allen Glover* at Demopolis, Alabama, with Allen Glover's store and warehouse in background. *Source: Joseph Merrick Jones Steamboat Collection, Special Collections, Tulane University Library*

what duller than usual, owing to the want of navigation. For a day or two previous, we were assured that there had been a number of wagons from above, and business was quite brisk. The business men appear sanguine. A number of new buildings are going up, and everything bids fair for an active business season, so soon as the river opens."

Navigation conditions were still not good in early March. The *Texas Republican* of 17 March references the *Jefferson Herald* to the effect that "there are 9,000 bales of cotton in the warehouses of Jefferson, and large stocks of hides, peltries, and bois d'arc seed, awaiting shipment." The break occurred in late March and lasted through July; but the conditions for navigation were not ideal. Loughery visited Jefferson again in May during the interim when boats had begun traveling on the Red River and Cypress Bayou and reports on his trip in the 20 May *Texas Republican*:

> We had the pleasure of spending a day or two during the present week at Jefferson, and as usual were much pleased with our trip. There is always a spirit of enterprise and improvement in our sister town which we admire. New buildings are going

up, and business is ever on the increase. We found it duller than we have ever known it at this season in the year, owing to the low water in the Lake. The water was rising very rapidly, however before we left, and the Cleona's whistle resounded in our ears just as we were starting for home.

We indulge the hope that the present rise in the Lake may last several weeks, so as to enable our Jefferson friends to get off their cotton—of which there are, we understand, six or eight thousand bags in the various warehouses—and to get up the large stocks of merchandise and groceries which they expect to introduce into that market. The merchants and business men seem very confident that the rise in the Lake will continue sufficiently long for their purposes.

Wharves were uncommon on the waters of the Mississippi River and its tributaries because of the great disparity between high-water and low-water levels. Steamboats usually accessed landings by running the bow into the shore and placing a plank between the boat and the shore. Jefferson was unusual in that it invested heavily in wharves over the decades, with the first wharf built in 1854. There are no descriptions of the previous dirt landing, but it must have been similar to the one at Shreveport described in the 14 February 1866 *South-Western*: "We have had another week of cold, wet, disagreeable weather, which has made it anything but pleasant to those who had business at the landing. Our levee is so much out of repair, that, in wet weather, it is next to impossible for pedestrians to navigate without going knee-deep in mud. The boats find it impossible to receive and discharge their cargoes during these wet spells with anything like dispatch. As these boats have to pay pretty dear for the privilege of landing at our mud wharf, it is nothing more than right that a part of this money should be expended in keeping the landing in something like decent order. As it is now, it is a disgrace to our city and a libel to our citizens."

Care must be exercised in determining the existence of a wooden wharf, because, as the quote indicates, dirt landings were commonly referred to as wharves. Shreveport never had a permanent wooden wharf. A structure was erected after the Civil War, but apparently lasted only one season. Neither did dockage fees indicate the existence of a dock. Shreveport, like Jefferson, had a dockage fee from the earliest years that was much resented by the steamboatmen, who brought the issue to a decision in their favor in the courts. The first mention of a wharf at Jefferson is in the 18 March 1854 Clarksville *Standard*: "From Jefferson we learn that Brooks and Bros., have bought the 'Bell Gates,' carrying 2500 bales of cotton, the finest boat ever in the Lake trade, and Capt Crump was in treaty for another boat for that trade. The people of Jefferson are determined to be free from extortionary combinations, and have taken the proper course to succeed. The Lake is now navigable, and boats have doubtless arrived at Jefferson before this. Jefferson is still improving with the constant pace which it has kept for three years past. A fine wharf has been erected, giving facility for the loading and unloading of boats."

That this was a wooden wharf is suggested by its description and confirmed by Linda Prouty in an overview of Jefferson's wharves prepared in conjunction with a report on archaeological testing related to the 1872 wharf. Prouty says, on the basis of a review of city and county documents, that various wharves and docking structures were built between 1850 and 1860 and that by 1860 the wharf area extended from Polk Street to the alley between Soda and Washington. These facilities were made of yellow pine and cypress boarding and were constantly in need of repair because of the impact of boats against pilings placed in unstable silt. The 1854 wharf, which was not specifically identified by Prouty, was a city facility.

EIGHTEEN FIFTY-FIVE

The rise in the lake noted by Loughery in May 1854 continued, but it was soon terminated by the worst navigation period in the history of the Cypress Bayou and the lakes route. No boats are listed in the *Daily Picayune* after July 1854 and through 1855 as having arrived at New Orleans from points west of Shreveport. This is because an extreme low-water situation developed on the Red River and the Cypress Bayou and the lakes route that was not to be overcome until January of 1856. Navigation conditions on the route are described in the 9 May 1855 Shreveport *South-Western*, referencing the *Jefferson Herald*: "The Jefferson Herald, of the 1st inst., informs us that the bayou at that point is too low 'for mud turtle navigation,' and thinks that 'the advantages of Jefferson as a *shipping* point are just next to nothing at all.' Our Texas friends have most assuredly had a hard time of it during the past year."

The *South-Western* reports only four boats operating in the direction of Jefferson in 1855. The *Alida, Augusta, Grenada,* and *Sodo* completed one trip each to Jefferson. The *Sodo* attempted to reach Jefferson again and made it only as far as Smithland. Even the little *Augusta,* which was only twenty-seven tons, had difficulty completing her trip. She is reported on 28 February as having run aground somewhere between Shreveport and Jefferson. The situation was so bad that steamboat captains began operating keelboats on the Red River, and cotton was barged from Jefferson to Shreveport.

Loughery visited Jefferson in February, when a break in the drought was still expected, and reported on the seventeenth about the continuing expansion of Jefferson even in the absence of commerce: "We visited Jefferson the first of the present week, and remained two or three days. Business was dull owing to low water, but the prospect was fair for an active commencement as soon as navigation is opened. There are several thousand bales of cotton and an immense quantity of peltries, hides, etc., awaiting shipment. A number of new stores, warehouses, and private residences have been erected since we were there last."

SUMMARY

After excluding the *Belle of Red River, New Latona,* and *Jefferson* as questionable, there were seventy-two boats for which there is a record or advertisement that they were in the Cypress Bayou and lakes trade from 1845 through 1855 (excluding boats advertised in the *Daily Picayune* in 1855). Of these, forty-eight went to Jefferson or advertised for Jefferson. The lightest boat that made a recorded trip was the *Augusta,* at 27 tons, and the heaviest was the *St. Charles,* at 311 tons. The average tonnage was 170 for boats that made recorded trips. The smallest boat was probably the *Augusta,* but her dimensions are not known. The next smallest was the 46-ton *Little Yazoo* at 80 feet by 20 feet. The largest was the *Red River* at 174 feet by 29 feet.

All of these boats, with the exception of the *Ellen, Alida, Augusta,* and *Sodo,* were sidewheelers, and the latter three are not recorded as having operated on the route until 1855. The year 1855 marked the beginning of the incursion of sternwheelers into a trade previously almost restricted to sidewheelers. Sternwheelers did not begin to dominate the trade until after the Civil War, giving rise to the common and quite understandable misperception that sidewheelers were uncommon in the Jefferson trade.

These boats made more than 200 recorded trips to points west of Shreveport and well over 300 if advertisements are taken into consideration. The number of boats operating along the route fluctuated over the eleven-year period, increasing from six in 1845 to nine in 1854, if only boats recording trips in the *Daily Picayune* are included. The number of trips increased gradually from twenty *Daily Picayune* recorded trips in 1845 to thirty in 1854, with significant limitations produced by low water in the second half of many years. Commerce appears to have been accelerating fairly rapidly during the closing years of the period, with nine to eleven boats making about thirty trips a year, in spite of an absence of commerce in the second half of 1853 and 1854. The year 1855 was anomalous because of extreme low water, and the upward trend in number of trips was resumed in 1856, with a large increase in the number of vessels operating along the route.

Although this characterization can be considered reliable, and the boat list is representative of the Cypress Bayou and the lakes trade for the period 1845–55, care must be exercised in the use of discrete pieces of information. An evaluation of the data reveals that there are problems in the record that cannot be completely resolved.

Extant issues of the Shreveport *South-Western* do not begin until 23 August 1854 with the first issue of volume three. Afterward, the Shreveport newspapers offer a fairly complete record, with the exception of 1857–60 and the war years. The Shreveport newspapers are the only completely reliable source on boats and trips to points west of Shreveport, and they contain invaluable information on navigation conditions on the Cypress Bayou and the lakes route that is not available in the New Orleans newspapers. Unfortunately, prior to 1855 only scattered issues of the Shreveport newspapers are available.

Before 1855, it is necessary to rely on the New Orleans newspapers and particularly the *Daily Picayune*, which contains many different sources of information on steamboats, including departures, arrivals, boats leaving on the day of publication, freight consignments, and advertisements. Of these, the arrivals column is the most reliable in the sense that a boat listed as returning to New Orleans from Port Caddo or Jefferson can be assumed to have actually visited those ports.

Unfortunately, the arrivals column does not achieve any degree of consistency until 1849, and attempts to supplement the record with advertisements produce another set of difficulties. Of the seventy-two boats for which there is evidence that they went west of Shreveport from 1845–55, nineteen are based on advertisements, fourteen of which are from the 1845–48 period. Some of these boats undoubtedly went to Port Caddo and Jefferson, but advertisements provide no certainty. This can be demonstrated by reference to the year 1855.

The 1855 issues of the *Daily Picayune* show almost continuous advertisements to Jefferson for the *St. Charles* and *R. W. Powell* and additional advertisements for the *Storm, Swan, Belle Gates, Caddo No. 2, Lone Star,* and *Victoria*. However, it is doubtful that any of these boats made it to Jefferson in 1855 because of extreme low water on Red River, which severely restricted passage over the falls at Alexandria. Most are correctly shown in the arrivals column of the *Daily Picayune* as having returned from Alexandria.

These were not bogus advertisements. Freight and passengers were portaged around the falls to another set of boats operating between Shreveport and Alexandria that advertised constantly in the *South-Western* in 1855. These boats could either proceed to Jefferson, offload at Shreveport for another boat to Jefferson, or offload at Shreveport for overland transport to Jefferson. Thus, advertisements were not a promise that a boat leaving New Orleans would necessarily arrive at a particular port, but rather indicators that the requisite services for transport would be rendered. Promises could never be given with respect to the Cypress Bayou and the lakes route because the ability to pass beyond Shreveport could not be determined until a boat from New Orleans reached Shreveport and gained knowledge of the conditions of navigation.

Although 1855 was an anomalous year, the implications for the use of advertisements to establish a record for the arrival of a particular boat at a particular port should be clear. Advertisements are uncertain. Boats advertised and never left New Orleans for the intended port. Some wrecked on the way. Many transferred freight and passengers at Shreveport. Given the significant number of transfer arrangements in 1855, it is obvious that advertisements cannot be used to establish a list of boats that arrived at a particular port such as Jefferson. Nevertheless, advertisements for boats to Jefferson indicate that these boats were in the Jefferson trade, even if they only went as far as Shreveport and engaged in freight transfers.

There are only a few boats on the list for 1845–55 that are derived from sources other than the *Daily Picayune*. Many boats are mentioned in the Marshall *Texas Republican*, in scattered issues of the Shreveport newspapers, and in journal accounts such as that of Edward Smith. But almost all of these are covered by the *Daily Picayune*. This suggests that the boat list for 1845–55 is fairly inclusive. However, there are also problems with inclusiveness, which again can be demonstrated by reference to the year 1855.

The *Daily Picayune* shows a great number of advertisements but no arrivals from Jefferson in 1855 because of the low-water situation. On the other hand, the Shreveport *South-Western* records the *Alida*, *Augusta*, and *Grenada* as having made one trip each to Jefferson, and the *Sodo* is recorded as having made one trip to Jefferson and one to Smithland. The reason that these boats are not listed in the *Daily Picayune* is that they did not go to New Orleans in 1855, but rather operated out of Shreveport to points west.

Again, although 1855 was abnormal, this indicates that the New Orleans newspapers are not an inclusive source for boats west of Shreveport during the 1845–55 period. More importantly, it points to the existence of particular types of boats that were not directly involved with the Port of New Orleans. One type was a class of small boats operating out of Shreveport and Jefferson between those two points and on Cross Lake, on the middle Red River, and on Black and Red Bayous into Caddo Prairie. They were often locally owned and operated and sometimes locally built. Although they often established regular routes to places such as Hurricane Bluffs, they were also opportunistic carriers, particularly thriving as transfer operators when low water made it impossible for the New Orleans boats to pass west of Shreveport.

These boats did not advertise in the Shreveport newspapers, but they appear in the Shreveport newspaper navigation columns from 1855 onward. Before that time, they must be discovered accidentally, such as in the advertisement for the *New Brazil* that mentions the 46-ton *Little Yazoo* as the transfer partner at Shreveport or an article on the transport of a prisoner between Jefferson and Shreveport that mentions the 61-ton *Venture*. The 27-ton *Augusta* and the 108-foot *Sodo* were members of this class. Collins and Claflin, the owners of the *Sodo*, were Shreveport businessmen mentioned by name in connection with the building of the boat at their Red River yard in the 13 December 1854 *South-Western*; and the local orientation of the boat is emphasized in the subsequent issue: "The new steamer Sodo made a trial trip on Saturday, and fully met the expectations of her builders. The ladies of Shreveport, through Mr. Wihans, presented a beautiful silk flag to the boat, accompanied with a few appropriate remarks, which were responded to by Mr. A. Slaughter, on the part of the owners, in his usual felicitous style. The Sodo was built to navigate the lakes and bayous above this port, and is in every respect the best low water boat afloat. With wood, water, and provisions on board, she draws less than 11 inches; and left here for the falls, with 151 bales cotton, drawing under 18 inches. Notwithstanding which her hull is unusually staunch. We hope that her owners will be richly rewarded for the enterprise they have displayed."

Another class of boats that did not advertise in the New Orleans newspapers comprised the regular packets that operated between Shreveport and Jefferson. These boats were somewhat larger than the opportunistic carriers, advertised in the Shreveport newspapers, and often switched to the New Orleans trade on a seasonal and even a yearly basis. Such boats generally made scheduled appearances at Jefferson. They are difficult to identify for the period 1845–55 because of the scarcity of extant Shreveport newspapers. The *Live Oak* was probably of this class: she advertised for Port Caddo and Jefferson, operating out of Shreveport in conjunction with the regular New Orleans and Shreveport packet *Belle of Red River*.

The existence of the opportunistic carriers and the Shreveport-to-Jefferson packets indicates that *Daily Picayune* notices provide undercounts of trips west of Shreveport. This helps to explain why Edward Smith reported that his arrival in May 1849 at Jefferson was the twenty-first arrival of the navigation season, which extended from the previous September. The count of arrivals in New Orleans from Jefferson during this period was ten, which meant that the New Orleans records accounted for only half the trips. The remainder may have been constituted by boats operating out of Shreveport, although some boats shown as having arrived from Port Caddo in the *Daily Picayune* may actually have gone as far as Jefferson.

In the departures and arrivals column of the *Daily Picayune* for 1845, all records are for Port Caddo, and Jefferson is not mentioned. By 1855, the opposite is the case. It is apparent that Jefferson had replaced Port Caddo as the primary area of commercial interest by 1850. However, Port Caddo's decline was relative rather than absolute, and it actually increased in commercial importance during the period. Advertisements for boats to Jefferson almost always included Port Caddo, and almost all boats that went to Jefferson stopped at Port Caddo. As a consequence, Port Caddo's commercial importance increased along with the general rise in steamboat activity during the 1845–55 period. What is surprising is Port Caddo's resiliency, because even ten years after Jefferson was founded, some boats operating out of New Orleans were still showing Port Caddo as their primary destination.

Although Jefferson rose to prominence during the 1845–55 period, the most distinctive feature of the period was the emergence of the system of ports and landings that was to form the base for steamboat activity on the Cypress Bayou and the lakes route through the early 1870s. The lull in commercial activity induced by low water in 1855 provides a convenient pause in the historic record to discuss ports and landings and the route.

·8·
Ports and Landings

THE EVIDENCE

By 1855, the following ports and landings west of Shreveport were appearing in steamboat advertisements: Jefferson, Smithland, Benton, Port Caddo, Clinton, Swanson's, Rives', Monterey, Perry's, Low's, Mooring's, and Albany (**fig. 8-1**). Although Pitts' Landing does not appear in an advertisement until 1857, it is mentioned in the 14 February 1855 *South-Western* in connection with the raising of the *Alida*, a steamboat that had wrecked on Caddo Lake. These ports and landings, with the possible exceptions of Perry's and Low's, about which little is known, were the primary commercial centers prior to the Civil War. The only important additions were the beef packery below Jefferson, which began shortly after the war; Bonham's Landing, which began serving as an outlet for Capt. Ben Bonham's plantation in the 1870s; and Shanghai Landing, which first appears in the navigation record during the early 1870s.

Rocky Point, Anna Glade, Red Bluff, and Selters appear in landings lists in the late 1870s and early 1880s, but they were probably part of a different commercial activity. Rocky Point, for example, was a source of street paving materials for Shreveport in 1874. Notably absent are Uncertain and Potter's Point, neither of which is ever mentioned in connection with steamboat activity. There does not appear to have been even a minor landing in the Uncertain area, which would have been

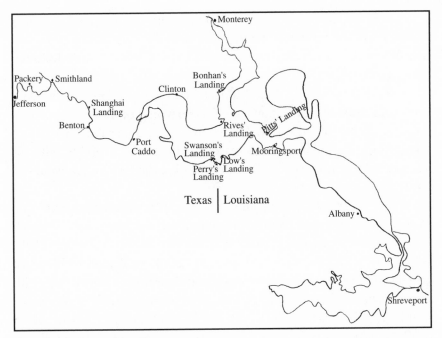

Fig. 8-1. Ports and landings

redundant given the proximity of Port Caddo. Plantations on the Potter's Point peninsula were serviced by Rives' Landing and Bonham's Landing, and Potter's Point itself was inaccessible during low water because the old channel of Cypress Bayou was near the south shore of Caddo Lake. Jeter's Landing is first mentioned in the 24 April 1888 *Shreveport Times* as a destination for the *Alpha*; but this was long after the cotton trade ended, and the freight carried by the *Alpha* is not described.

The relative importance of the thirteen advertised ports and landings did not change very much until immediately before the Civil War when the influence of the railroad to Swanson's Landing began to be felt, because the level of commercial activity sustained by each was largely determined by fixed import and export market areas. The two most important commercial centers were Jefferson and The Packery. Jefferson's market area extended far to the west. The Packery was a special case because it was not a typical port or landing but a processing center for animal products. It is never included in steamboat advertisements because it was not a passenger destination and imported little other than salt and barrels for the packing operations.

Steamboat advertisements in the New Orleans newspapers almost always mention Jefferson, Smithland, Benton, and Port Caddo and usually Swanson's Landing, Mooring's Landing, and Albany. Monterey and, to a lesser degree, Clinton were also important, but because they were off the main route, they appear in advertisements only when a boat wished to emphasize that a special trip would be made. Monterey's importance fluctuated seasonally, depending on upper Red River water levels. Swanson's Landing increased in importance briefly when it became a rail terminal in 1858; Mooring's Landing eventually achieved a port status.

Many of the ports and landings other than Jefferson and The Packery were places of considerable commercial importance. The only comparative commercial statistics are from the *Texas Almanac* for 1859, which shows the following exports for commercial year 1857–58 of cotton bales for ports and landings along the route: Jefferson, 25,000; Smithland, 5,000; Benton, 8,000; Port Caddo, 5,000; Swanson's Landing, 8,000; Monterey, 1,500; and "5 or 6 Landings on the Lake," 8,000. Among these five or six landings were probably Clinton, Rives' Landing, Pitts' Landing, Mooring's Landing, and Albany.

Although these are point-in-time estimates given by a Jefferson resident, they are probably generally reflective of relative importance, particularly because they single out Jefferson, Smithland, Benton, Port Caddo, and Monterey for special mention. The relative importance of Swanson's Landing vis-à-vis Port Caddo probably reflects the fact that the rail from Swanson's Landing was within a short distance of Marshall by October 1858, which would have cut into Port Caddo's commerce. The number of bales exported through Jefferson grew substantially in later years, but this was by increased cotton production to the north and west rather than capture of the commerce of the other ports and landings.

Steamboats did not require any infrastructure for landings and could stop anywhere that a bank could be reached and a plank extended from the boat to the shore. Temporary landings of this sort were probably not common along the route because the permanent ports and landings were fairly close to each other, were collecting points for merchandise, and were serviced by roads. What little evidence exists with respect to stopping places suggests that boats centered their activities on the established ports and landings on the main route (Albany, Mooring's, Swanson's, Port Caddo, Benton, and Smithland)

and that they generally stopped at all of them, if only briefly, on the way to and from Jefferson.

A major exception to the generalization concerning temporary landings was the area between Jefferson and Smithland. There was a road between these two points that closely followed the bayou, with a ferry crossing at Black Cypress Bayou. During low-water periods, especially during the summer, it was often impossible for steamboats to reach Jefferson. Boats would move as far upstream as possible given water levels and the draft of a particular vessel and then stop to discharge and receive freight, which was transported by barge to and from Jefferson and by wagons on the road paralleling the bayou.

As a consequence, the area between Jefferson and Smithland was almost a continuous landing during low-water periods. It is obvious that the road was heavily used by wagons—it is observable today and is heavily indented in the landscape. That this was a low-water transport road rather than a connecting road between Jefferson and Smithland is evident from the fact that much of it is submerged during high-water periods. Although almost any point along the road could serve as a landing for a steamboat, the primary points mentioned in the newspapers were Potato Bend, above The Packery; Boon's Bend, below The Packery; and Smithland and The Packery, all of which served as temporary landings for Jefferson freight during low-water periods.

Although the ports and landings were important to commercial activity along the Cypress Bayou and the lakes route, their dimensions should not be exaggerated. Most were modest, with some sort of warehousing and a few structures. Only Jefferson and Swanson's Landing had wharves. Jefferson, Smithland, Benton, Port Caddo, Monterey, Mooringsport, and Albany are shown on state maps. Smithland and Monterey had town plans but never achieved a status other than that of small villages. Swanson's Landing aspired to town status and changed its name to Petersburg but also never achieved its aspirations.

The continuity of the major ports and landings throughout the steamboat period is well established by the various formal lists that appeared after commerce had declined dramatically by the middle 1870s. Louis Adam's 1877 *Adam's Directory of Ports and Landings* lists Albany, Pitts' Landing, Swanson's Landing, Port Caddo, Benton, Smithland, and Jefferson. J. Frank Glenn, who was a clerk on various steamboats, prepared a private "List of Landings on Red River" in 1879 that includes some of the later ports and landings on the Cypress Bayou and the lakes route that were part of a different commercial activity. Proceeding out of Shreveport, Glenn lists Cross Bayou, Mrs. Cain, Cedar Bluff, Albany, Williams Landing, Pitts Point, Mooringsport, Rocky Point, Swansons, Anna Glade, Port Caddo, English's Woodyard, Benton, Smithland, Red Bluff/Jackson's Woodyard, Packery, Rail Road, and Jefferson.

Frank Clayton's 1881 *Landings on All the Western and Southern Rivers and Bayous* provides an extensive list, including distances from St. Louis. I have converted Clayton's mileage figures to distances from Shreveport, including distance to next landing, which appear to be estimates, as indicated by the obvious incorrectness of the distance from Smithland to Jefferson. It should be noted that this list was prepared after the navigation route had been reduced in length by various cuts along Cypress Bayou and at the head of Caddo Lake:

Landing	Distance Above Shreveport	Distance to Next Landing
Albany	19	7
Williams'	26	3
Moorings Port	29	1
Pitt's Point	30	5
Rocky Point	35	5
Swanson's	40	5
Anna Glade	45	5
Port Caddo	50	5
Benton	55	5
Smithland	60	5
Red Bluff	65	15
Selters	80	10
Jefferson	90	

J. Frank Glenn also prepared a set of "Private Memoranda" in 1886 that describes the route from Shreveport to Jefferson in detail, with the exception of Soda Lake and Caddo Lake. With respect to ports and landings, Glenn mentions Albany, Anna Glade, Port Caddo, Benton, Smithland, Packery, Saw Mill, and Jefferson. Mooringsport is mentioned in a later section on "Marks—Caddo Lake."

By the beginning of the 1900s, the system of ports and landings that had served as the base of operations for steamboats west of

Shreveport had nearly disappeared. Writing in 1904, Capt. Charles Potter of the Corps of Engineers mentions only Jefferson and Mooringsport as still in existence, stating, "Jefferson is the only place of importance on the 65-mile water course to Red River which forms a part of the boundary between Marion and Harrison counties in Texas and crosses Caddo Parish, Louisiana. Years ago there were about 20 small landings scattered along this route, few of which ever attained the distinction of a village, and most of which have now disappeared."

The history of the ports and landings along the route has not previously been covered in a comprehensive fashion. Although Jefferson as a port has been addressed in various books, there are only a few pamphlets and articles on other ports and landings. As a consequence, the history of navigation facilities along the route must be reconstructed from bits of evidence in maps, newspaper articles and advertisements, and the navigation record.

The navigation record is obviously of immense importance, but it is also extremely misleading if used in isolation. Records of steamboat returns at Shreveport and New Orleans do not list intermediate stopping places. As a consequence, there are only a few records of returns for places other than Jefferson and Port Caddo. Nevertheless, detailed memoranda for Red River craft indicate that steamboats generally stopped at most of the ports and landings between New Orleans and Shreveport, of which there were more than fifty. As a consequence, it can be assumed that all boats that are listed as having arrived back at Shreveport from Jefferson stopped at all of the ports and landings on the main route, which from Jefferson downstream included Smithland, Benton, Port Caddo, Mooringsport, and Albany.

It has already been demonstrated that steamboat advertisements in the New Orleans newspapers cannot be used to determine travel west of Shreveport. Nevertheless, they do indicate boats participating in the Cypress Bayou and the lakes trade, and they offer, collectively, the only complete list of ports and landings on the route. Unfortunately, no steamboat ever advertised for all of the ports and landings at which it would stop. A full listing can be achieved only by gathering information from various advertisements.

Most importantly, advertisements cannot be used to establish a commercial record for a particular port or landing. Many of the ports and landings along the route appear in advertisements only during the 1850s, but there is sufficient evidence from other sources that steamboats continued to visit them beyond that period. Advertisements during the 1840s were dominated by Port Caddo and from the late 1850s onward by Jefferson. The Jefferson advertisements usually mention major ports and landings along the route such as Benton and Smithland, but others are covered by the phrase "and all intermediate landings."

With the emergence of Jefferson as an important factor in the trade of New Orleans, there was a brief period in which the elements of the newly consolidated route needed to be brought to public attention. After the Jefferson trade was well established, advertisers could assume that everyone knew of the minor ports and landings, so that only the majors needed to be included. As a consequence, the 1850s offer the only window on the full range of secondary landings along the route; and their disappearance from advertisements does not necessarily indicate that they were no longer functional.

SHREVEPORT

Boats leaving New Orleans went upriver on the Mississippi, then upriver on the Red to Shreveport, stopping at many landings, including the major Red River ports of Alexandria and Natchitoches. All boats traveling west or north of Shreveport stopped at Shreveport on the way up and the way down. Boats traveling in the direction of Jefferson generally had up freights that were partially discharged at Shreveport. Down freights were generally enhanced at Shreveport before a boat returned to New Orleans.

Shreveport was the center of four different trades. First, and most important from the city's perspective, was Shreveport's direct trade with New Orleans. Second, there was the Cypress Bayou trade that centered on Jefferson. Third, there was the Old River trade, which serviced the Red River plantations below the foot of the raft at Carolina Bluffs and the middle Red River plantations above the raft that transported cotton overland to Carolina Bluffs. Fourth, there was the upper Red River trade, which proceeded around the raft to the upper Red River ports such as Pecan Point, Logansport, Kiamichi, Little River, Jonesboro, Lanesport, and Fulton.

The Old River trade was open whenever boats could reach Shreveport, because Old River was simply the largely static portion of Red River above Shreveport and below the raft. The upper Red River trade fluctuated violently with the rise and fall of the Red River, which was heavily dependent on regional rainfall. The dimensions of these two trades in relation to the Cypress Bayou trade were highly variable, but much larger than has generally been thought. March–May 1867 is representative for conditions when navigation above the raft was good. During that period, there were forty-three Cypress Bayou arrivals at Shreveport, compared to twenty-seven from the upper Red River and ten from Old River.

Boats such as the *Enterprise* (1831) and *Rover* (1834) that reached the upper Red River before Shreve removed the raft almost certainly would have stopped in the vicinity of the future site of Shreveport, particularly because the lower Coates' Bluff settlement was in existence from at least 1832. However, it was not until 1836 that the *Privateer* arrived officially in New Orleans from Coates' Bluff and not until 1837 that the *Nick Biddle* is listed as having arrived from Shreve Port, the first mention of this emergent city in the steamboat record. Shreveport then appears on Thomas Bradford's 1838 *Louisiana* (**fig. 8-2**).

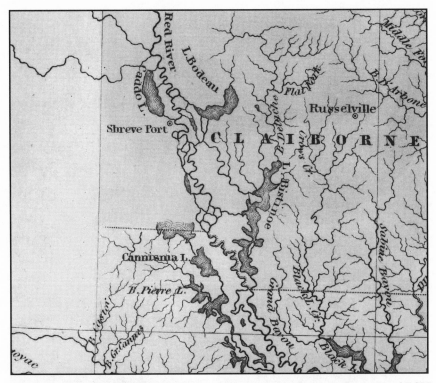

Fig. 8-2. First map representation of Shreveport. *Source: Courtesy of LSU Libraries Special Collections, Baton Rouge*

Shreveport was strategically located on the first high bluffs at the southern end of the Red River floodplain subbasin that began at the Arkansas line and formed the setting for the distributary system that fed into the Sodo Lake area. This system provided access to the upper Red River above the raft. Shreveport was located at the confluence of Cross Bayou and the Red River and only a short distance downstream from the confluence with Twelvemile Bayou. Shreveport would have been an important port under any circumstances, serving as a depot for plantation supplies, a jumping-off point for immigrants, and a collection point for cotton, particularly from the southwest.

Early Shreveport is shown in detail in H. Brosius's 1872 *Bird's Eye View of Shreveport, Louisiana* (**fig. 8-3**). Shown in the sketch from left to right are the *Maria Louise, John T. Moore, Henry M. Shreve*, Shreveport ferry, and *Clifford* instream and the *Little Fleta, Texas, Era No. 10, Belle Rowland*, an unidentified boat, and *Flavilla* at the landing. A description for the same period is given in the 17 January 1872 *Shreveport Times*:

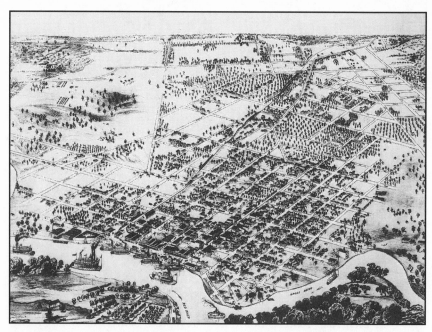

Fig. 8-3. Shreveport in 1872. *Source: Library of Congress*

We are willing to back the business appearance of the levee yesterday forenoon against any other levee of its size in the world. The wharf was lined with the elegant steamers D. L. Tally, Anna, Lockwood, Belle Rowland, Flavilla, Hamilton, and the Clifford, all busy as bees but one, and even that steamer showed signs of life. The landing was packed with freight from one end to the other, which innumerable drays were endeavoring to carry off, but judging from the progress they made, it will take them two or three days to do it. Every description of freight, from a box of matches to a steam cotton press with its intricate and cumbersome machinery, could be seen scattered broadcast. Huge piles of flour, bacon, whisky, lard, pork, hay, oats, bran and corn could be seen in front of the Lockwood while the Anna made a beautiful display of furniture of all kinds from a trundle bed to a set of parlor furniture. All this was flanked by rows of cotton and bales of hides for the loading steamers. The landing was so packed with freight that the Belle Rowland had to put her cotton off on the point near the ferry before coming along side the Lockwood to take on her Jefferson freight. The Gladiola was forced to put off her freight above the foot of Milam Street. From the terminus of the railroad to the steam cotton press was one field of cotton bales undergoing locomotion, a matter of some trouble. The streets, alleys and all the available space around the different warehouses was blocked with cotton, and the street proper was jammed with cotton wagons which did not move off so quickly as is generally the case when the market is fair and active. The sidewalk was one dense mass of people, moving to and fro as best they could midst the thousand and one packages of freight tumbled in and out of the stores. The cotton sellers with their samples in hand were as thick as fleas on a mangy dog, hunting after the buyers, who appear to have almost deserted their favorite thoroughfare. To one posted with our ways and means of doing business it is an infallible sign that the cotton market is depressed. The blacking man was out and did a lively business with the amendments. Take it all in all, it was a bully sight, and almost enough to make a poor man feel rich.

The term "wharf" was used in the 1800s to refer to any landing. Shreveport never had a wharf (a single construction effort resulted in failure)—only a dirt embankment. Fall rains accompanied by moderate commerce produced quagmires, as reported in the 12 September 1866 *South-Western*: "Since our last issue the rainy weather has put in a full week, without any discount. For seven days and nights it has 'reigned,' and at the present writing we see no dethronement of our unwelcome monarch. . . . Business on the landing for the past week was not overly brisk, although a good deal of hard labor was performed. The mud was knee deep, and slippery at that. We saw persons with more enterprise than caution, in undertaking to reach a steamboat, have to set down to rest, while others actually laid down right in the mud. It occurred to us that people who would do that must be 'powerfully' exhausted."

Boats leaving Shreveport and heading to Jefferson traveled through Soda Lake and Caddo Lake and then up Cypress Bayou. All boats carried up freights and down freights whenever possible. Where a boat stopped depended on what she was carrying upstream and where that freight was to be discharged. Down freights were picked up on the return trip. It can be presumed that most boats made two stops at each port and landing during the round-trip, with the exception of Jefferson, which was inaccessible during low water, and places like Clinton and Monterey, which were off the main route and required side trips.

For convenience, the sixteen ports and landings that were active during the steamboat period through the 1870s will be discussed in the order of movement upstream, with the caveat that this suggests nothing about focus, particularly because some boats operated out of Jefferson, and others operated out of Shreveport to places like Monterey. Because of its importance, Jefferson will not be included in this chapter. Subsequent chapters include running accounts of year-by-year Jefferson navigation activities.

ALBANY

Albany was located about nineteen river miles from Shreveport on the bluffs fronting Soda Lake on the southwest and served boats traveling west toward Jefferson and north through the Black Bayou–Red Bayou route around the raft. Albany was strategically situated just below Albany Flats, which was the greatest impediment to boats moving west and north. It probably served as an information point for navigation conditions, enabling steamboats to determine whether they should take the cutroad across Albany Flats or the longer route in the channel of Cypress Bayou beneath Soda Lake, as shown on Capt. Eric Bergland's 1885 *Map of Cypress Bayou and the Lakes* (**fig. 8-4**).

In a 1988 unpublished paper titled "Relationship of Grindstone Bluff to Albany Landing," J. Ashley Sibley says that the first land purchase in the area was by Mary McCain in September 1846 at Grindstone Bluff, two miles below the landing. He also indicates that there was a warehouse, store, and sawmill at the landing. The warehouse was used to store plantation supplies and cotton awaiting downstream shipment. Cotton was brought from as far west as Texas, and cotton, corn, and cattle were brought from plantations on the Red River

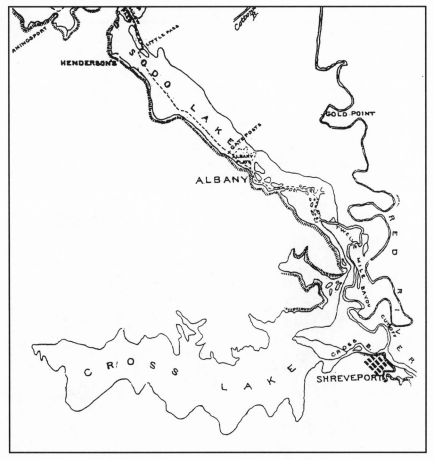

Fig. 8-4. Albany. *Source: H. Ex. Doc. 103, 48ᵗʰ Cong., 2ⁿᵈ Sess.*

floodplain north of the lake and transported across the lake by a ferry at the landing.

Citizens of Caddo Parish held a meeting at Albany in January 1850 to discuss construction of a railroad or plank road from Albany to Marshall, as reported in the *Texas Republican* of the twenty-fourth. Although resolutions were passed with enthusiasm, nothing appears to have resulted in the way of concrete action. Albany first begins to appear in steamboat advertisements in 1852. The first mention is for the *Cleona* in the 17 January *Texas Republican*, followed by the *Caspian* in the 30 March *Daily Picayune* and the *Storm* in the 14 April *Daily Picayune*.

Albany was one of the places visited by the *Banjo*, a party boat, in 1857, as reported in the 11 March *South-Western*: "Ned Davis and his

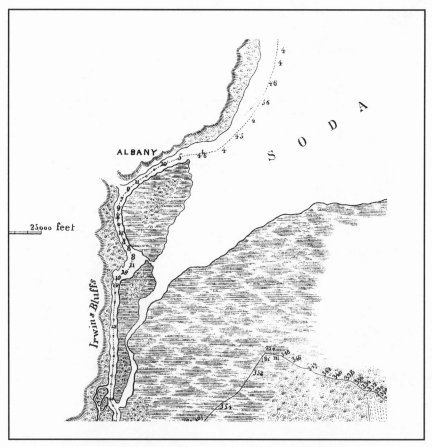

Fig. 8-5. Fuller's Albany. *Source: S. Ex. Doc. 62, 33rd Cong., 2nd Sess.*

Ethiopian minstrels drew crowded audiences at Albany, Mooring's, Benton, Jefferson, etc., and were received with unbounded applause."

There are only a few other mentions of boats specifically in connection with Albany. The 1857 *Daily Picayune* records the *Osprey* and *Alida* as having returned from Albany, the latter with George Alban as captain; and the 1861 *South-Western* shows the *W. Burton* as having returned to Shreveport from Albany. In addition, the *Shreveport Times* indicates that the *Clifford*, *Frank Morgan*, and *Royal George* made trips to Albany in 1874 to obtain rock for paving Shreveport's streets. As with the other ports and landings between Shreveport and Jefferson, the scarcity of records indicates nothing about the level of commerce, because intermediate landings are not shown in the records of boats returning to Shreveport or New Orleans.

J. W. Dorr with the *New Orleans Crescent* made a horse-and-buggy tour of Louisiana in the spring and summer of 1860 and reports in "A Tourist's Description of Louisiana in 1860" that Albany was "a shipping point of some note" and that business was done there by the merchants Hare and Hawkins. Albany was not noteworthy enough to be included on any antebellum state maps, although it does appear on T. S. Hardee's 1871 *Geographical, Historical and Statistical Map of Louisiana*. Its first map appearance is on Col. Charles Fuller's January 1855 *Map of Red River With Its Bayous and Lakes In the Vicinity of the Raft* (**fig. 8-5**).

Albany served as a benchmark site for Capt. J. H. Willard's 1890–91 survey of Cypress Bayou and the lakes. A benchmark map from Willard's 1893 report provides a good representation of the likely dimensions of the landing during the steamboat period (**fig. 8-6**). Albany appears in steamboat advertisements after the Civil War, in Adam's 1877 landings directory, Glenn's 1879 landings list, Clayton's 1881 landings directory, and Glenn's 1886 memoranda. That it was still an important commercial center at the end of the high point of steamboat activity in 1873 is indicated by the fact that it appears on Lt. Eugene Woodruff's 1872 *Map of the Red River Raft Region and Cypress Bayou*, which was concerned with navigation.

MOORINGSPORT

Mooringsport was generally referred to before the Civil War as Mooring's Landing or simply Mooring's and occasionally as Mooring's

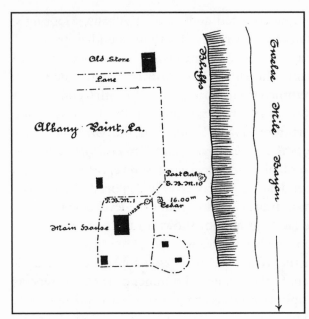

Fig. 8-6. Albany. *Source: Annual Report of the Chief of Engineers, 1893*

Point. By corruption, it was sometimes referred to as Morning's or Morning's Port. It was located on a strategic peninsula jutting into Caddo Lake in deep water shortly above the entrance to the lake. Mooringsport does not appear on the 1839 Louisiana General Land Office map. However, a Mooring's Clearing is shown a few miles south of the peninsula on the survey map for Township 17 North, Range 16 West (fig. 8-7). According to the 1976 *Profile of Mooringsport*, the town was named for Timothy Mooring (1801–80), who arrived with his brother John in 1837; and the peninsula was homesteaded by Isaac Croom in 1842. This is compatible with the map evidence and the general development of the area.

Mooring's Landing first appears in connection with navigation in an advertisement for the *Cleona* in the 17 January 1852 *Texas Republican*, followed by an advertisement for the *Caspian* in the *Daily Picayune* for 30 March of the same year. It achieved early importance, indicated by the fact that it appears in the 19 February 1853 *Texas Republican* as one of the areas (with Jefferson, Smithland, Benton, Port Caddo, Marshall, and Swanson's) in which planters and merchants should be willing to contribute money for lake improvements. The earliest advertisement using the designation "Mooringsport" was for

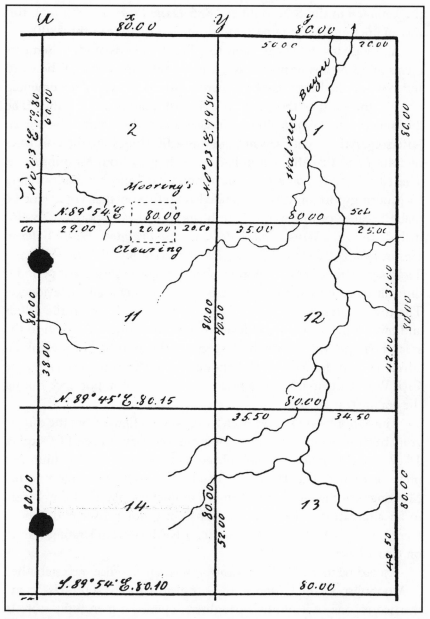

Fig. 8-7. Mooring's clearing. *Source: Louisiana State Land Office, Division of Administration*

the *Camden* in the 8 November 1856 *Daily Picayune*, although this was an uncommon designation until the last quarter of the 1800s.

Although it would be possible to collect hundreds of advertisements mentioning Mooringsport and it can be presumed that all boats to Jefferson stopped at the landing, there is little in the way of documented arrivals, and most of these are from the last quarter of the 1800s. The 29 January 1868 *South-Western* indicates that the *Dixie* arrived from Jefferson on the twenty-seventh carrying 4,000 hides and forty-six bales of cotton and that the cotton had been shipped from Mooringsport. The 10 July 1875 *Shreveport Times* shows the *Lotus No. 3* as traveling to Mooringsport on a trip intended to Jefferson that could not be made because of low water. Late boats to Mooringsport (1878–96) include the *Blue Wing, Caddo Belle, Cornie Brandon, Frank Willard, Gussie, John G. Fletcher, Lessie B., Ranger, Rosa Bland, Thornbush,* and *Vicksburg.* The status of Mooringsport during the steamboat period is difficult to reconstruct on the basis of the readily available evidence. The town's present structure did not emerge until late in the 1800s and owes much more to oil development on Caddo Lake than to the steamboat period. Nevertheless, given the number of steamboat advertisements for Mooring's Landing in the 1850s and even after the Civil War, it obviously was a place of commercial importance during the era of steamboats.

Tim Mooring must have been a well-known figure from the earliest years because an advertisement for a runaway slave in the 11 October 1849 *Texas Republican* and subsequent issues mentions him as a previous owner. The 10 March 1860 *Texas Republican* reports that Mooring shot and killed Daniel Smith, another resident of Caddo Parish, in an altercation. Mooring was apparently not prosecuted. The 8 December 1874 *Shreveport Times* reports Mooring operating a ferry on Cross Lake.

According to the *Profile of Mooringsport*, a post office was established at Mooringsport on 1 August 1854. Calvin Croom, son of Isaac and married to one of Timothy's daughters, opened a mercantile store in 1852, which corresponds to the first steamboat advertisements. The 4 September 1861 *South-Western* reports that Calvin Croom had been an early resident of Shreveport, but that he had been living on the lake for twelve to fifteen years, which would place his appearance at Mooringsport between 1846 and 1849. The 26 October 1854 *Texas Republican* reports that Croom had been a printer until 1850 or 1851, after which he became a farmer with only two or three slaves, one of which was stolen in February 1854. Croom's marriage to Margaret Mooring is recorded in the 25 January 1851 *Texas Republican*. The 6 December 1874 *Shreveport Times* reports Calvin Croom still living at Mooringsport.

Mooringsport was not as commercially important as Jefferson, Smithland, Benton, Port Caddo, Monterey, and even Swanson's Landing after it became a rail terminal in 1858, because Mooringsport was not listed independently as a cotton exporter in the 1859 *Texas Almanac*. The apparent reason was that Mooringsport did not have a large trade area to the south. It was situated between Albany and Swanson's Landing and restricted by a road fifteen miles to the south that provided direct access to Shreveport. A ferry apparently established in the middle 1850s and operated by Croom was an important commercial enterprise, enabling freight transport to and from the north shore of Caddo Lake and above.

Mooringsport's rise to modest importance in the cotton and hide trade was occasioned by the development of a market area to the north of Caddo Lake, which was dependent on the establishment of a ferry and the supplanting of Pitts' Landing with its ferry on the north shore of Caddo Lake at the old Shenix's Ferry crossing at Stormy Point. The initial situation is shown in the 1839 Louisiana General Land Office map of the Shenix's Ferry crossing; and the final situation is represented by a captured Confederate map of Caddo Parish, which shows a ferry at Mooringsport, a road to Lewisville, Arkansas, heading north, and the road to Shenix's Ferry as extinguished (**fig. 8-8**).

The supplanting of Pitts' Landing by Mooringsport can be followed in the minutes of the Caddo Parish Police Jury, which are available in the *South-Western* from 1855 on. At that time, private citizens were responsible for the maintenance of public roads, and assignments were made in June. The ferry at Mooringsport was in existence by at least June 1856, but the road to the north was not. Land traffic to and from Mooringsport moved through Pitts' Landing on the east-west road shown on the Confederate map. Pitts' Ferry, which had replaced Shenix's Ferry, disappeared sometime after June 1857, and the road running north from the landing (which was called the Old Pitts' Ferry Road) was abandoned as a public enterprise by June 1859. Mooringsport became dominant over Pitts' Landing, but it was unable to establish a large market area to the north because of the existence of Monterey, which was much higher.

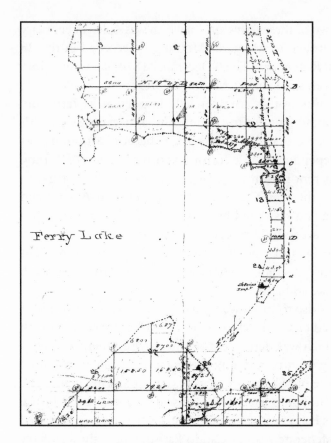

Ferry Lake

Fig. 8-8. (top)
Shenix's ferry.
*Source: Louisiana
State Land Office,
Division of
Administration*

(right)
Mooringsport area
crossings. *Source:
Louisiana Secretary
of State, Division of
Archives, Records
Management and
History*

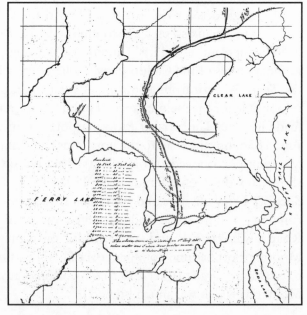

Mooringsport appears on the Union Army's *General Topographical Map* and on a captured Confederate map of the upper Red River, but not on John Colton's 1860 *Colton's Louisiana*. It can also be found on T. S. Hardee's 1871 *Geographical, Historical and Statistical Map of Louisiana* and on Lt. Eugene Woodruff's 1872 *Map of the Red River Raft Region and Cypress Bayou*. The stores operated by Calvin Croom and J. S. Noel are shown on a benchmark map prepared by Capt. J. H. Willard in connection with his 1890–91 survey **(fig. 8-9)**. Croom's warehouse was used by J. Frank Glenn as a navigation reference point, as indicated in his 1886 memoranda: "From Mooringsport, get head on Little Island and stern on 'Crooms' warehouse for Stormy Pt."

Glenn's memoranda also indicate that, at least for the late navigation period, the landing was at Noel's Point at the end of Croom Street, as pointed out in the *Profile of Mooringsport*. The Confederate Caddo Parish map shows the ferry landing at Noel's Point, and Glenn's "Marks" for entering Caddo Lake indicate that the ferry landing was also the steamboat landing: "When you circle out from the 3 stumps, get stern on Island and head on lone cypress, quit (?) open on the right hand point. Run these mks until abreast of 'Coopers' house, then get stern on house, and head on point at Mooringsport Ferry Ldg."

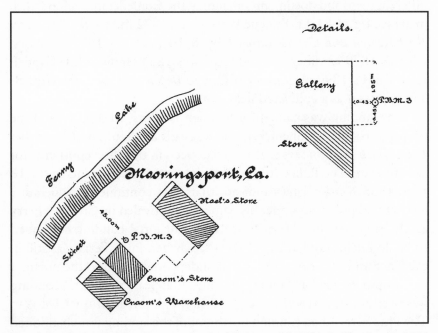

Fig. 8-9. Mooringsport. *Source: Annual Report of the Chief of Engineers, 1893*

PITTS' LANDING

Pitts' Landing, also referred to as Pitts' Point or simply Pitts', was located at Stormy Point, which was the old crossing for Shenix's Ferry. It appears in newspaper advertisements in Shreveport and New Orleans and much more frequently than Low's or Perry's. Examples include the *Lafitte* (*Daily Picayune*, 26 February 1857); *Reub White* (*Daily Picayune*, 25 August 1857); *Rescue* (*South-Western*, 1 December 1858); *Joseph Holden* (*Daily Picayune*, 10 May 1858); and *Fleta* (*South-Western*, 6 March 1861). Although Pitts' Landing is not mentioned in an advertisement until 1857, it was in existence by at least 1854, because it is mentioned in the 14 February 1855 *South-Western* as the place in which the *Alida* had sunk in January.

Given the landing's geographic position, it probably served as an outlet for commodities from the upper Red River area, particularly cotton and animal products, performing a function similar to that of Monterey and increasing in importance when Monterey was inaccessible because of low water. It does not appear to have been as important as Monterey because it is not shown on state maps and is not listed independently in the 1859 *Texas Almanac* as a cotton exporter. However, it was advertised fairly frequently and appears in many different maps and documents, including the Confederate Caddo Parish map **(see fig. 8-8)**, Lt. Eugene Woodruff's 1872 *Map of the Red River Raft Region and Cypress Bayou* **(fig. 8-10)**, Adam's 1877 directory, Glenn's 1879 landings list, and Clayton's 1881 landings list. Capt. J. H. Willard's 1890–91 *Survey of Cypress Bayou and the Lakes* **(fig. 8-11)** depicts it as a cultivated field.

The landing was named for Stephen D. Pitts, who purchased the property from James Shenick, perhaps as early as 1846. The 10 October 1866 *South-Western* says that Pitts had been in the Shreveport area for twenty years. The Police Jury road maintenance assignments in the 13 June 1855 *South-Western* indicate that Pitts continued to operate a ferry at that point but under his name. It was rivaled by Croom's Ferry at Mooringsport by at least June 1856; but Pitts' Landing continued to be dominant until at least June 1857, when Pitts' Ferry was still in existence and Mooringsport had an independent road to the north.

In spite of the late landings listings, it appears that Pitts' Landing was overtaken by Mooringsport before the outbreak of the Civil War. The Pitts Ferry Road running north out of the landing was abandoned

Fig. 8-10. Pitts' Landing.
*Source: LSU in Shreveport,
Noel Memorial Library
Archives*

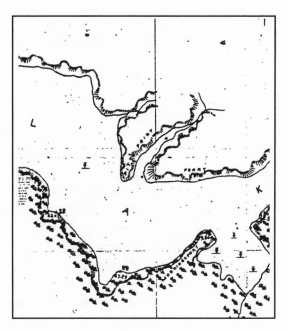

Fig. 8-11.
Abandoned
Pitts' Landing.
*Source:
Louisiana
Department of
Transportation
and
Development*

as a public enterprise by June 1859, and Pitts became the owner of the Battle House in Shreveport in October 1866.

MONTEREY

Monterey, or Point Monterey, was located on William's Bluff on the east shore of present-day Monterey Lake. Early postal route records indicate that the town was originally named William's Bluff, apparently after William Browning, an early resident; and the name change may have been related to the activities of the steamboat *Monterey*, under Capt. W. W. Withenbury, which was prominent in the lake trade in the late 1840s. Although Monterey Lake was a very old lake preceding Caddo Lake by probably thousands of years, it was not designated as an independent entity during the steamboat period, being the upper end of the flooded portion of Jim's Bayou. The present-day lake apparently derived its name from the landing after the waters of Caddo Lake receded and Monterey Lake reappeared as an independent entity.

Daniel Boon in *Monterey* provides a brief overview of the town on the basis of documents and interviews. A Masonic Lodge was established at Monterey in 1848. Monterey was used as a reference point for land patents by John Collom on 31 January 1849 and by Charles Ames on 29 November 1850. A post office was established at Point Monterey on 16 August 1851 with Norphlet Gupton as postmaster. This was part of the Jefferson mail route, which was under contract to Eli Ussery. The office was discontinued on 23 January 1867, reestablished on 1 August 1878, and finally extinguished on 30 June 1900.

Boon provides an undated *Plan of the City of Monterey, Texas*, showing a public square and the steamboat landing on the western edge of the proposed city (**fig. 8-12**). Although city status was never achieved, development was not inconsiderable. There was a blacksmith shop near the landing in 1847. Gupton ran a mercantile business and a saloon in a two-story building near the landing. Jim Noel operated a store prior to 1870. William Browning's store was open between 1870 and 1876, as well as his sawmill, grist mill, cotton gin, and large cotton warehouse. Between 1877 and 1879, S. L. Williams owned and managed a store, which was purchased by R. H. Harrell in 1879. This was the last store to operate in Monterey.

Monterey was less than a town and more than a landing and was correctly designated by the post office as a village. This intermediate

Fig. 8-12.
Monterey city plan.
Source: Daniel Boon,
Monterey

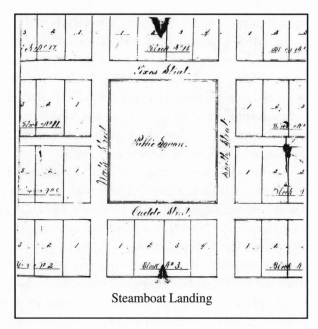

Steamboat Landing

status was determined by the level of trade. Monterey was established at the upper end of the flooded portion of Jim's Bayou to tap the trade of the extreme northeastern corner of Texas. This trade area was shared by the other ports and landings on the north side of Cypress Bayou and Caddo Lake and by Mooringsport on the south through its ferry. The level of trade fluctuated with the ability of steamboats to reach Monterey and to travel above the raft, thereby avoiding costly overland transport to and from places like Monterey.

Boon provides an account of an early steamboat arrival at Monterey, although the name of the boat is unknown. According to a family Bible notation, Rube Harrison arrived at Monterey by steamboat on 7 July 1847; both an R. R. Harrison and a J. R. Harrison are shown as officers of the Masonic Lodge in 1848. That steamboats were traveling to Monterey at least as early as 1847 is reasonable given the existence of the village by at least 1848.

Monterey's importance was recognized from the earliest years. It is named in the 3 December 1853 *Texas Republican* as one of the areas (along with Swanson's Landing, Port Caddo, Benton, Jefferson, Smithland, and Clinton) whose merchants and shippers should be interested in opposing a freight-rate price-fixing scheme by the steamboatmen; and it is listed independently in the 1859 *Texas Almanac* as an 1858 exporter of 1,500 bales of cotton. Most importantly, Monterey was recognized at the state level, because Jim's Bayou was included in a 7 February 1853 Texas navigation improvements appropriation measure, the text of which appears in the 2 July 1853 *Texas Republican*. Surprisingly, the residents of Monterey voted overwhelmingly against the appropriation measure according to the 13 August 1853 *Texas Republican*.

Monterey's importance is further illustrated by the fact that it is included on J. DeCordova's 1851 *Map of the State of Texas*, Colton's 1860 *Colton's Louisiana*, and Hardee's 1871 *Geographical, Historical and Statistical Map of Louisiana*. Its exact location is best illustrated by a captured Confederate map of Caddo Parish, which shows the village immediately west of the Louisiana line and about one-third of a mile from the northern boundary of Township 21 North **(fig. 8-13)**. This would place the town at the northern end of present-day Monterey Lake **(fig. 8-14)**. The road leading into the village is observable today immediately east of Monterey Cemetery.

Monterey's importance is confirmed by the steamboat record. The first advertisement listing the village is for the *Cleona* in the 17 January 1852 *Texas Republican*, followed by the *Pitser Miller* in the 14 May 1853 *Jefferson Herald*, the *Ruby* and *Storm* in the 1 June 1854 *Daily Picayune*, and the *Swan* in the 12 December 1856 *Daily Picayune*. There was a proliferation of advertisements for Monterey in the *Daily Picayune* in 1857 and 1858, including the *Afton, Jr., Belle Creole, Caddo Belle, Col. Edwards, Duke, Grenada, Hope, Joseph Holden, Marion, Reub White, St. Charles, Southern, Sunbeam*, and *Swan*.

Given the problem of transfers at Shreveport, boats advertising in the *Daily Picayune* must be excluded from an analysis of the nature of the craft that actually docked at Monterey. Probable arrivals would include boats advertising in local newspapers, where transfer is not an issue: *Cleona* (*Texas Republican*, 17 January 1852); *Pitser Miller* (*Jefferson Herald*, 14 May 1853); and *Rescue* (*South-Western*, 1 December 1858). These three boats advertised as regular packets to Monterey and other ports and landings on Cypress Bayou and the lakes.

There were six boats with documented trips to Monterey. According to various issues of the *South-Western*, the *Larkin Edwards* made ten trips from Shreveport to Monterey in the first three months of 1859. According to the 29 February 1860 *Daily Picayune*, the *Vigo* made

Fig. 8-13. Monterey.
*Source: Louisiana
Secretary of State,
Division of Archives,
Records Management
and History*

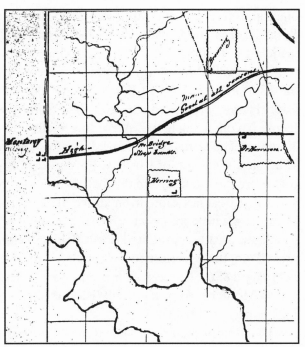

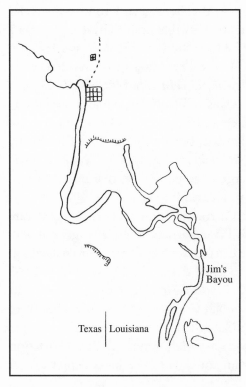

Fig. 8-14. Monterey

one trip to Jefferson and Monterey. According to the 23 January 1867 *South-Western*, the *L. Dillard*, known affectionately as the *Rantidotler*, made a trip to Jefferson, offloaded at Shreveport, and "put out for a settlement called Monterey, situated on Jeems' bayou." According to the 13 March 1867 *South-Western*, "The elegant stern wheeler Irene, Capt. Harvey Heth, came in from Jefferson by way of Monterey, on Jeem's bayou, flying light." According to the 23 February 1870 *South-Western*: "The Lotus No. 2 came down from Monterey last night with 450 bales of cotton, of which 150 were for this place. Two hundred bales were those taken from the Texarkana at the mouth of Black Bayou when that boat last came from above the raft. The boys on board the Lotus gave a little 'blow out' to the denizens of the Monterey region, which was greatly appreciated by the denizens aforesaid, who no doubt proved on the occasion to be regular lotus-eaters." Lastly, the 12 February 1876 *Shreveport Times* reports that the *May Lowry* made a trip to Monterey to pick up 100 bales of cotton on a return trip from Jefferson.

The three probable arrivals and the six recorded arrivals were mostly mid-sized to tiny craft. The *Lotus No. 2*, a 230-ton sidewheeler measuring 135 feet by 26 feet, and the *Irene*, a 211-ton sternwheeler measuring 156 feet by 32 feet, were sizable craft. The *Cleona* was a 185-ton sidewheeler at 128 by 27 feet; the *Pitser Miller* was a 158-ton sidewheeler at 126 by 26 feet; and the *Vigo* was a 144-ton sidewheeler at 130 feet by 26 feet. The *Rescue*, *Larkin Edwards*, and *L. Dillard* were very small craft. The *Rescue* was a 77-ton sternwheeler, and the *L. Dillard* was a 56-ton sternwheeler at 107 by 19 feet. The characteristics of the *Larkin Edwards* are unknown, but by the nature of her many local trips out of Shreveport, she was obviously a tiny opportunistic carrier. The *May Lowry* was a large boat at 196 feet that made a single trip under very dramatic high-water conditions.

Monterey apparently played a role in the export of Confederate cotton to the west during the Civil War, particularly because government cotton sheds are known to have existed downstream on Jim's Bayou in the vicinity of present-day Cottonshed Arm. The 17 November 1863 *Semi-Weekly Shreveport News* reported that ten Negroes in government employment burned the home of Nat Graham in Monterey. They were confined to jail in Jefferson, and all but three were released.

Monterey was the vicinity of a widely reported Reconstruction incident. A white man by the name of David Reed had opened a voter registration office and apparently trained freedmen, at a price, for rebellion against the existing social conditions. One black and one white man were reported killed in the ensuing controversy. Reed claimed that he was innocent of all charges, including those based on evidence provided by six freedmen.

The February 1876 trip by the *May Lowry* is the last participation of Monterey in recorded navigation activities and the last mention of cotton export by boat. Mention is made of Monterey in the 18 November 1877 *Shreveport Times*, but it is in connection with the observation that boats were not needed up that way because of a lack of business opportunities. The village in decline is pictured by Boon in terms of an 1878 visit by Sam Williams, son of S. L. Williams, who noted that besides his father's store, there were seven or eight vacant houses. Boon's source indicated that Williams came up on the *Hornet*, a distinct possibility given the fact that this 39-ton screw propeller made many recorded trips to Jim's Bayou in the early 1870s.

By 1911, the fact of navigation to Monterey had been largely forgotten, and it was necessary for litigants seeking information on historic water levels on Caddo Lake to secure affidavits from persons such as Frederick A. Leonard, who swore: "That in 1859 he was clerk on a steamboat, plying between Shreveport and Monterey, which was a town then located on Jeems Bayou; the said boat running on Ferry Lake and making all stops and calls on said lake, as well as on Jeems Bayou; that since that date he has frequently been passenger on steamboats, running between Shreveport and Jefferson on Ferry Lake, and between Shreveport and Monterey on Ferry Lake and Jeems Bayou." The boat on which Leonard was clerk in 1859 was the *Larkin Edwards*, which made ten recorded trips to Monterey and seventeen trips to Jefferson during that year.

BONHAM'S LANDING

Bonham's Landing was located on Jim's Bayou and has maintained a continuous existence up to the present. Ben B. Bonham was a famous steamboat captain in the Red River and Cypress Bayou trades. The *Gossamer*, which made many trips to Jefferson in the 1860s, was one of the boats that he captained. When he retired in the early 1870s, he began a plantation on Jim's Bayou. His first cotton crop was carried out by the *Hornet* in March 1873, according to the *Shreveport Times* of the fourteenth: "The Hornet came in from Jeem's bayou with 105 bales of cotton. Capt. Ben Bonham, an old time river man, but now a planter on Jeem's bayou, or in that neighborhood, came down on the Hornet with his crop."

This event probably marked the beginning of Bonham's Landing. Whether the landing served purposes other than those relating to Bonham's plantation is unknown. Bonham went back into the steamboat business. The 1 January 1882 *Shreveport Times* reports that his new boat, the *Lessie B.*, left Cincinnati for Shreveport and would run between Shreveport and Jefferson. The *Lessie B.* made many trips during that year until she wrecked on Cypress Bayou in March. Bonham also operated the *Alpha* in the late 1880s. Bonham is buried in the Greenwood Cemetery in Shreveport, with the headstone showing a birth date of 11 August 1825 and a death date of 24 September 1898.

RIVES' LANDING

Rives' Landing was located on the west side of the flooded portion of Jim's Bayou far downstream from Monterey. The Rives family was one of the first to settle on Caddo Lake. Two land patents are shown for James J. Rives in the 1839 Louisiana General Land Office map for Township 21 North, Range 16 West (**fig. 8-15**), and a Rives plantation is shown farther downstream at the entrance to Jim's Bayou on the 1841 United States–Republic of Texas boundary survey map (**fig. 8-16**). Harriet Ames says that Robert Potter was helpful in bringing a James Rives to the Caddo Lake area and that Rives arrived with Ames's brother on the first steamboat on Caddo Lake. This would have been sometime before 1842, the year in which Potter was killed.

There are only two mentions of Rives' Landing in the navigation record. The first was for the *Jefferson*, appearing in the 6 September 1851 *Texas Republican*:

> LAKE PACKET.
> The steam boat *Jefferson*, BEN MCKINNEY master, (now being built at Cincinnati expressly for the trade,) will commence making regular trips as soon as the water permits, to Jefferson, Smithland, Port Caddo, Clinton, Reeves, Swanson, and all other landings on the Lake.

Fig. 8-15. Rives'
land patents.
*Source: Louisiana
State Land Office,
Division of
Administration*

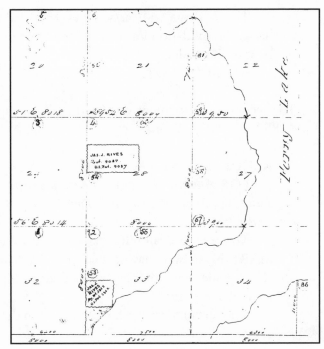

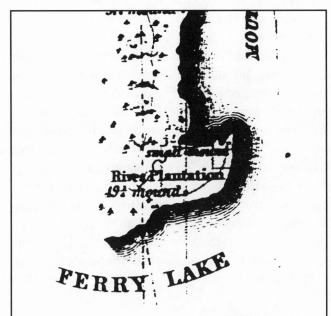

Fig. 8-16. Rives'
Landing. *Source:
S. Doc. 199, 27th
Cong., 2nd Sess.*

The *Jefferson* will carry about 1500 bales of cotton, and her accommodation for passengers will be unsurpassed by any boat in the trade.

August 16, 1851.

The second advertisement was for the *Cleona*, appearing in the 5 June 1852 *Texas Republican*:

REGULAR LAKE PACKET, CLEONA.

FOR *Albany, Mooring's Landing, Swanson Landing, Rives' Landings, Monterey, Clinton, Port Caddo, Benton, Smithland, and Jefferson.*

The fine fast running Passenger Packet, Cleona, R. H. MARTIN, master, having been purchased expressly for the above trade, will commence her regular trips as soon as the water will permit.

Shippers may rely on her remaining in the trade during the entire season.

Jan. 10, 1852.

Of the thirteen ports and landings that appear in advertisements, Rives' Landing is the only one that appears only in local newspapers. The *Jefferson* and *Cleona* were built for the New Orleans-Jefferson trade. The *Jefferson* was wrecked on her maiden voyage. The *Cleona* made many trips to Jefferson but did not advertise for Rives' Landing in the *Daily Picayune*. The limited focus of the available advertisements suggests that Rives' Landing was a matter primarily of local interest. This should not be surprising given the fact that Monterey captured trade to the north, and Rives' Landing probably only serviced plantations in the vicinity of the Potter's Point peninsula.

Unless this is a typographical error, the advertisement for the *Cleona* indicates that there was more than one Rives' Landing. If this is the case, the landings were probably located at the plantation on the 1841 map and at the lower of the land patents on the 1839 map. The upper landing was probably a predecessor to Bonham's Landing. Rice's Pocket on contemporary maps is a corruption of the lower Rives' Landing.

LOW'S LANDING

Low's Landing is mentioned in only two steamboat advertisements: for the *Caddo No. 2* in the 24 May 1854 *Daily Picayune*; and for the *Grenada* in the 29 June 1854 *Daily Picayune*. Advertisements generally list ports and landings in downstream order. Low's is mentioned in the advertisements after Swanson's and Perry's Landings and before Mooringsport. It was located on the south shore of Caddo Lake somewhere on the Rocky Point peninsula.

The minutes of the Caddo Parish Police Jury in the 13 June 1855 *South-Western* indicate that Low's Landing was located in Ward One at the lake terminus of the Union Academy Road and that it was operated by John Low and his son, John, Jr. The 25 June 1856 issue indicates that John, Sr., had died in the interim. The 3 June 1857 issue indicates that the landing was still in existence. June 1858 issues are missing, and the landing is not mentioned thereafter.

The Harrison County Commissioners Court minutes for 1854 and 1855 indicate that the Union Academy was located at the northern end of the State Line Road below Buzzard Bay and that Union Academy Road ran within Harrison County from Port Caddo to the academy. Because the road continued into Caddo Parish, it apparently ran below Buzzard Bay into the Rocky Point peninsula, where it terminated at Low's Landing. Jeter's Landing is not mentioned in the navigation record until 1888 and was an ideal location; it is probable that Low's Landing was a predecessor (**fig. 8-17**). The demise of Low's Landing appears to be connected with the rise of Swanson's Landing and particularly with its establishment as a railroad terminus in early 1858.

PERRY'S LANDING

Perry's Landing appears in the same two advertisements as Low's and was located between Swanson's Landing and Low's Landing. The Harrison County Commissioners Court minutes for 1854 and 1855 indicate that Joshua and Levin Perry were connected with the landing and that the Perry's Landing Road ran from the Central Academy to the landing. Given the fact that Perry's Landing was below Swanson's Landing and within Texas, the only possible location is the west shore of Buzzard Bay.

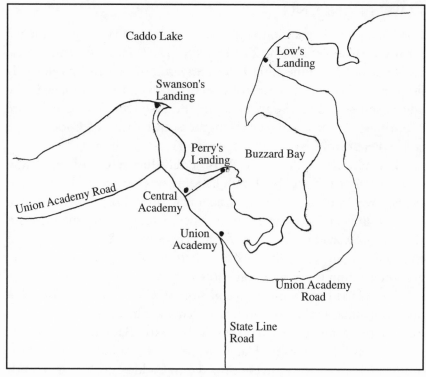

Fig. 8-17. Low's Landing and Perry's Landing

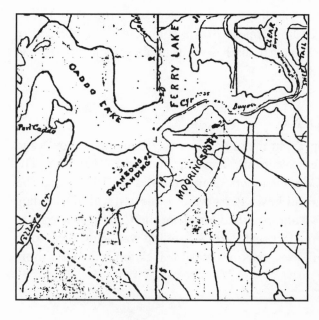

Fig. 8-18.
Swanson's Landing.
*Source: Louisiana
Secretary of State,
Division of Archives,
Records
Management and
History*

The Central Academy was apparently located northwest of the Union Academy on the Union Academy Road. The Perry's Landing Road branched to the east off the Union Academy Road, terminating at Perry's Landing on Buzzard Bay immediately adjacent to the state line (see fig. 8-17). Although Perry's Landing tied into the railroad to Swanson's Landing with a tram, it had no capacity to compete for commerce with the larger and better-situated landing on Caddo Lake and remained a minor factor in the navigation picture.

SWANSON'S LANDING

Swanson's Landing was founded by the planter Peter Swanson and was located on the south shore of Caddo Lake in the area of present-day Swanson's Landing. Although probably originated to serve the needs of the Swanson plantation, it was ideally located to provide a cotton outlet for the other rich plantations of Harrison County. The old channel of Cypress Bayou hugged the south shore of Caddo Lake; consequently, Swanson's Landing was accessible even during low-water periods. Because it played such an important role in the development of the Southern Pacific Railroad, more is known about Swanson's Landing than about every other port and landing on the route with the exception of Jefferson.

Sam Touchstone, in an article on the *Mittie Stephens* and Swanson's Landing, suggests that the original landing was located to the southeast on Buzzard Bay, citing as evidence the Confederate map of the upper Red River (fig. 8-18). Although this is a valid inference, the map would have shown the location of the landing after the construction of the rail terminus and its attendant wharf. The official *Map of the Southern Pacific Railroad Through Harrison County, Texas*, filed with the Texas General Land Office by W. T. Scott in 1860, shows the rail terminating on Caddo Lake (fig. 8-19). The old grade is still in existence and can be seen running to the end of the point on which present-day Swanson's Landing is located. The pre-rail landing was probably located where the postrail landing is shown on Capt. J. H. Willard's 1890–91 *Survey of Cypress Bayou and the Lakes* (fig. 8-20).

According to the 6 October 1860 *Texas Republican*, the wharf extended "far out into the water, so that boats can land and discharge freight without difficulty." The major freight discharge was railroad iron, which required greater drafts of boats. The wharf extended out

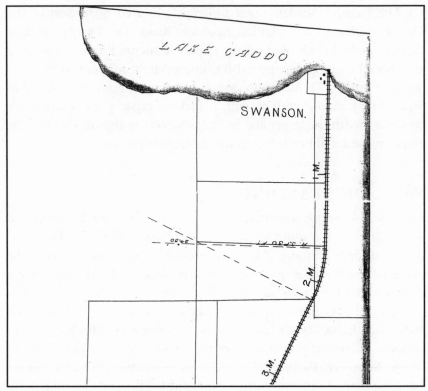

Fig. 8-19. Railroad to Swanson's Landing. *Source: Courtesy of Texas General Land Office, Austin*

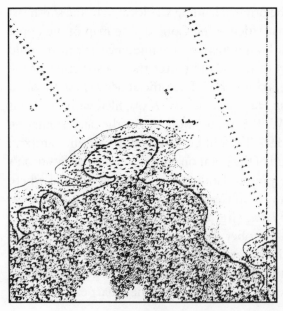

Fig. 8-20. Swanson's Landing. *Source: Louisiana Department of Transportation and Development*

into Caddo Lake near the end of the point to tap the old channel of Cypress Bayou, which was less than a quarter of a mile from shore, rather than the shallow waters of Buzzard Bay. Still, the bay would have provided an ideal place for laying up during windy conditions on the lake. It may be that the structures shown on the Confederate map included the home of Dr. W. C. Swanson, which the 15 April 1859 *Texas Republican* describes as a magnificent mansion in a splendid grove of towering oaks about half a mile from the railroad.

The Swansons were among the earliest settlers on Caddo Lake. No property ownership is shown in the Swanson's Landing area in an 1839 Louisiana General Land Office map, which was based on a survey during the second quarter of 1838. Texas General Land Office records indicate that Peter Swanson came to Texas in February 1838. When the landing began cannot be documented because it was in the area in dispute between the United States and the Republic of Texas. Land patents in this area were not available until January 1841 through an act of the Congress of the Republic. Swanson secured a judgment for 640 acres from the Panola County District Court in January 1842, and 20 acres in the landing area were surveyed for Swanson in July 1843, with the surveyor's notes indicating that the area was already known as Swanson's Landing. The landing was probably established in late 1838 or early 1839. Swanson took the remaining 620 acres of his headright in Smith County northeast of Tyler.

Harriet Ames mentions Amelia Swanson in connection with her plans to escape from Potter's killers in 1842. In a letter on file at the Marshall Museum, Eudora Hodges indicates that Swanson built a log house at the landing, that the Akin family from Alabama arrived at the landing by steamboat in 1846, that Peter died in 1849, and that he left two sons, Dr. W. C. Swanson and Thomas F. Swanson. The year of Peter Swanson's death is confirmed by Edna White in *East Texas Riverboat Era and Its Decline*, who notes that Swanson, his wife Amelia, and some of his children and slaves are buried in the little family cemetery near the town of Leigh and that Swanson's headstone reads: "Born September 24, 1789. Died December 4, 1849."

Swanson's Landing was obviously one of the earliest ports and landings on the route and first appears in the navigation record through an advertisement for the *Jefferson* in the 6 September 1851 *Texas Republican*. Other early advertisements include the *Cleona* (*Texas Republican*, 17 January 1852); *Caspian* (*Daily Picayune*, 30 March

1852); *Caddo No. 2* (*Daily Picayune*, 24 May 1854); and *Grenada* (*Daily Picayune*, 29 June 1854). However, the advertisements are deceptive. The landing was certainly in existence prior to the 1850s, and all boats that went to Port Caddo in the 1840s would have stopped there.

The only record for cotton export from the landing is in the 1859 *Texas Almanac*, which shows the landing as an 1857–58 exporter of 8,000 bales of cotton; but this was after the railroad had begun to play an important part in the landing's commerce. The pre-railroad level of commerce is unknown, but it must have been significant, because Thomas Swanson began advertising as a receiving and forwarding merchant in the 4 January 1851 *Texas Republican*:

WAREHOUSE.
The subscriber is now prepared to receive cotton and merchandise. Instructions in every case in reference to the shipping of cotton, will be strictly obeyed. As far as his interest is concerned, he hopes that those who patronize him will be pleased in every respect.

T. F. SWANSON,
Forwarder and Receiver,
Swanson's Landing, Jan. 4, 185(1).

Swanson appears to have been a simple receiver and forwarder of merchandise—he did not advertise plantation supplies. The operation was successful to such a degree that Swanson proposed a town at the landing that would be named in honor of his father, as indicated by an advertisement in the 9 October 1852 *Texas Republican*:

PETERSBURG, FORMERLY CALLED SWANSON'S LANDING.
THE undersigned is now prepared to receive cotton and up freight. He has got a fine wharf, so that no boat shall be delaid in her landings at this point. All pains will be taken in shipping and reshipping; also, in storing; Cotton will be stored at 25 cents per bale; barrels will be stored at 12½ cents per barrel for the first month, half price after the first month. Clear receipts will be given for all cotton in good order.
Thankful for the liberal patronage which has heretofore been extended to me, I can confidently promise that business

will be strictly attended to. This place is situated 18 miles south east of Marshall.

THOMAS F. SWANSON.

Oct. 9, 1852.

It should be noted that the location given in the advertisement should be northeast of Marshall. The reference to a wharf apparently indicates the existence of a wooden structure, although no firm conclusion can be drawn. The proposed name change was not immediately accepted. Swanson's Landing is mentioned in the 19 February 1853 *Texas Republican* as one of the areas that should be interested in contributing to navigation improvements. It does not appear to have been a settlement. The article speaks of planters and merchants "in the neighborhood of Swanson's." On the other hand, a resolution signed by Thomas F. Swanson (among others) in the 3 December 1853 *Texas Republican* speaks of the "merchants and shippers of Swanson's Landing, Port Caddo, Benton, Jefferson, Smithland, Clinton, Monterey, and all other landings on the Lake" as among those who should be opposed to a freight price-fixing scheme by the steamboatmen.

Swanson's Landing was apparently growing into a settlement, and Swanson used the designation Petersburg in an advertisement that appeared in the 28 July 1855 *Texas Republican*, noting additional charges for transfers of cotton, weighing and marking, and taking bills of lading. The name change was endorsed by at least one boat: the *Victoria* advertised for Jefferson in the December 1855 *Daily Picayune* and is shown as arriving back from Petersburg, Texas, on 31 January 1856. However, it was not until the advent of the railroad that the settlement grew into prominence.

The Southern Pacific was chartered in Texas, with a stipulated completion date in early 1858 for the first twenty miles of track. It was envisioned as an east-west line that would run below Caddo Lake from the Louisiana state line to the west. The easiest way to build a railroad was by extension of an existing line that could carry materials. The Southern Pacific wanted the Vicksburg, Shreveport & Texas Railroad to build a temporary connection between Shreveport and the Texas line so that work could begin at that point. When this connection was not forthcoming, it was necessary to pursue another course of action.

Railroad materials could have been brought overland from Shreveport to the Texas line by wagon and the Southern Pacific begun at the intended point; but that would have been difficult and costly. Steamboats had the capacity to transport railroad iron efficiently. More importantly, they had the capacity to transport locomotives (apparently both on towed barges). Because the rails and locomotive had to be transported from New Orleans by steamboat under any circumstances, it was decided that the best course of action was to build a north-south spur line from Swanson's Landing to Jonesville, where the track would be extended to the west to Marshall and beyond.

That Swanson's Landing was chosen as the point of departure for the spur line was a matter of considerable importance to the landing but not to the railroad company. The railroad was not interested in establishing the landing as a commercial center, only in obtaining a place for the waterborne importation of railroad materials, as explained in the 9 May 1857 *Texas Republican*: "The Southern Pacific, will for the present, have its Eastern terminus at Swanson's Landing, on Caddo Lake; not as a matter of choice by the company, but as a matter of necessity. From that point, the iron can be laid down without being hauled on wagons. Some of the iron is on the ground, and the balance . . . is at Albany."

The work effort got underway in the spring of 1857, with Albany serving as a temporary depot for the heaviest railroad iron. Materials were brought up to Swanson's Landing and Albany by the *Osprey* and the *Alida*, the latter under Capt. George Alban, the pilot of the first boat to Jefferson. Rails were brought up from New Orleans to Albany by the *St. Charles* and *Empress*. The Southern Pacific contracted with the *Wabash Valley* to tow barges loaded with railroad iron to Swanson's Landing. The first locomotive arrived in Shreveport in late July, as is indicated by a *South-Western* article on the twenty-ninth entitled "CLEAR THE TRACK!": "The steamer Alida brought up the locomotive Louisiana and its tender for the Pacific railroad. In a few days our friends in the neighborhood of Swanson's Landing will be edified with the shrill music of the iron horse."

The *Alida* apparently did not bring the locomotive to Swanson's Landing, because she is shown in the 4 August 1857 *Daily Picayune* as having returned from Albany. The *Alida* towed the barge carrying the locomotive to Albany, where it almost certainly was transported to the landing by the *Wabash Valley*. A letter from a Dr. Taylor in Marshall dated 25 July 1857 confirmed that the locomotive reached the landing in July and served as a materials carrier as track was laid to the south and west on a prepared grade that was soon to extend beyond Marshall. Dr. Taylor's letter appeared in the 5 August *South-Western*: "Three weeks will complete the grading of our road from Swanson's landing to a few miles beyond this place; making several miles more than we expected to have completed, and for that portion of the road the crossties are nearly all procured and delivered. Iron for twenty-eight miles is at the lake terminus, and we have a locomotive on the ground ready for use. The road will now advance rapidly to the westward."

Only twelve miles of track had been completed by December. With time running out on the stipulated completion date, a public appeal was made for assistance. This appeal was met, and the twenty miles of track between Swanson's Landing and Jonesville were completed on 11 February 1858. By 27 February, R. W. Loughery, the editor of the *Texas Republican*, was able to report on a railroad trip to Caddo Lake from Scott's Depot, seven miles east of Marshall. Finally, by October the rail extended to Marshall Depot, one and one-half miles to the east. Late advertisements for the Southern Pacific in the *Texas Republican* indicate that this was its farthest extent and that the rail never actually entered Marshall before the Civil War.

In conjunction with these events, the name "Petersburg" was increasingly used. The 27 May 1857 *Texas Republican* reports: "Contracts for most of the grading and crossties, for the section of road between this place and Petersburg, (Swanson's Landing,) have been made with responsible parties, who are to complete this work early in the autumn." Boats such as the *Reub White* (25 August) and *Bonita* (17 November) began advertising for the termination of the Southern Pacific Railroad in 1857 shortly after the locomotive was brought up aboard the *Alida* and *Wabash Valley*. In early 1858, the *Governor Powell* (16 March) and *Joseph Holden* (10 May) advertised for Petersburg, and the name was used in freight bills for the railroad during at least the same year **(fig. 8-21)**.

The height of this development was probably reached in January 1858 when Thomas Swanson and his mother, Amelia, offered Petersburg for sale. The advertisement that appeared in the *Texas Republican* states: "This town which is the eastern terminus of the S. P. R. R., on Caddo Lake, is now laid out in lots and for sale, cheap for cash." The advertisement notes that the lots were 33½ feet in front and

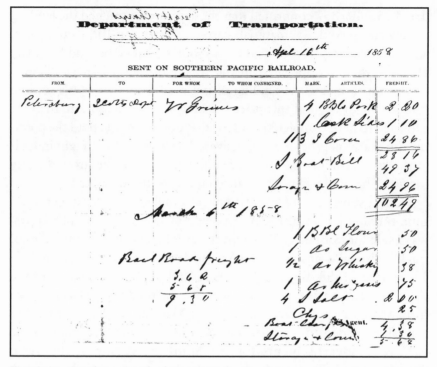

Fig. 8-21. Southern Pacific freight bill for Petersburg. *Source: Dewey Somdal Collection, LSU in Shreveport, Noel Memorial Library Archives*

166½ feet in depth. This was an obvious attempt to capitalize on the increased land values created by the railroad. Whether anything came of the offer is unknown.

"Petersburg" never attained common usage, was outweighed by "Swanson's Landing" when it was used, and does not appear after 1859. When Loughery took another trip on the Southern Pacific in January 1860, he no longer used Petersburg: "On Sunday last, in company with A. R. Mitchell, of the Upshur Democrat, and a number of our citizens, we took a trip over the Southern Pacific Railroad to Swanson's landing." Freight bills similar to the one from Petersburg to Scott's Depot in 1858 were issued from Swanson's Landing to Scott's Depot in 1859 (**fig. 8-22**).

The railroad had an immediate and profound impact on Swanson's Landing and its environs. This impact began when only a dozen miles of track had been laid. The 19 December 1857 *Texas Republican* notes: "Twelve miles of track are finished, and over this distance we learn that

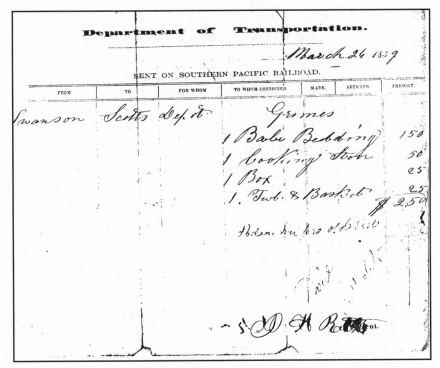

Fig. 8-22. Southern Pacific freight bill for Swanson's Landing. *Source: Dewey Somdal Collection, LSU in Shreveport, Noel Memorial Library Archives*

cotton is already being carried." On the same day, an advertisement signed by James M. Curtis, who was connected with the Southern Pacific Railroad, established rates for cotton transport to Swanson's Landing from whatever point the rails might have been completed when the cotton was transported:

SOUTHERN PACIFIC RAILROAD.

The undersigned begs leave to inform his friends and the public generally, that he has leased for a time the entire warehousing privileges at Petersburg, the Eastern Terminus of the S. P. R. R., on Caddo Lake, where he is prepared to store and ship cotton. Send to him by Railroad, or otherwise, also up freights of all sorts at the usual prices charged at other warehouses on the lake. Cotton deposited on the line of the Railroad will be taken to the Lake, and goods forwarded by the cars to any point as the track progresses, at the following rates:

For cotton bales, between 5 and 10 miles, 25 cents
For cotton bales, between 10 and 15 miles, 33 cents
For cotton bales, between 15 and 20 miles, 40 cents
For cotton bales, between 20 and 25 miles, 55 cents
For cotton bales, between 25 and 30 miles, 60 cents
Wet barrels, same distances, will be charged same prices as cotton bales.
Dry barrels, 20 percent less.

JAMES M. CURTIS.
Petersburg, Dec. 14th '57.

Loughery traveled the seven miles from Marshall to Scott's Depot by buggy on 20 February (as reported a week later), where he took the train to Petersburg and found that the railroad was beginning to serve as a collecting point for the cotton in the vicinity:

> On Saturday last, in company with Major Blanche, and Messrs. John K. Yerger and Thomas B. Lincoln, we left Marshall for a trip on the Railroad. The day was one of the loveliest of the season. A pleasant drive of seven miles and a half brought us to Col. W. T. Scott's, to which point the cars are now running. We remained at the terminus until late in the evening, when we took the cars, and arrived at Petersburg, on the Lake. The ride was exciting and pleasant, enhanced by the novelty of being on a Texas railroad. At Petersburg we were hospitably entertained by Capt. J. M. Curtis, with whom we remained until the next morning, when we returned. . . .
>
> The road is laid with the very best iron, and in our judgment, well finished. In fact, it is a very good new road. Several hundred bales of cotton were at this end of the road awaiting shipment, and we observed several small lots on the road side as we were going down.

In the same issue as Loughery's article, Curtis advertised that the Southern Pacific was receiving cotton and other freight at Scott's Depot, with B. H. Scott at the depot as forwarder and Curtis at Petersburg as receiver. Curtis's monopoly on the warehousing facilities at Swanson's Landing was short-lived. Thomas L. Lyon and Thomas F. Swanson began advertising in the *Texas Republican* on 17 April 1858 as receiving, forwarding, and commission merchants, with a wide array of goods. Lyon and Swanson offered cash advances on cotton and other produce consigned to the firm for shipment:

> THOS. L. LYON   THOS. F. SWANSON
> THOS. L. LYON & CO.,
> SWANSON'S, TEXAS.
> RECEIVING, FORWARDING AND COMMISSION MERCHANTS,
> General Dealers in Groceries, Sugar, Coffee, Molasses, Whiskey, Tobacco, Flour, Pork, Salt, &c.,
> Staple and Fancy Dry Goods,
> Hardware, Castings, Nails, Hoes, Axes, and Cutlery, &c.,
> Shoes and Boots for Ladies and Gents, Hats and Caps, &c.
> A General assortment of Clothing, Coats, Pants, Vests, Shirts, and Drawers, of all kinds and qualities, ploughs and points, which we will sell LOW for the CASH, or on time to prompt and punctual paper.
> THOS. L. LYON & CO.
> Special attention to all consignments, advances of Cash or Groceries on cotton or produce in store for sale or shipment.
> Swanson's, April 17, '58.

Thomas L. Lyon & Company issued a new advertisement in the 3 December 1848 *Texas Republican* indicating that they also dealt in boat and bar stores and that they gave advances on cotton consigned to Winston, Harrison & Company, apparently a New Orleans firm. Charges on cotton are given at $0.25 per bale and on barrels at $0.125 cents per barrel, with $0.06 more for drayage.

C. E. Hynson, the general superintendent of the Southern Pacific, prepared an advertisement on 15 October 1859, establishing freight rates for various distances between Swanson's Landing and Marshall, with a promise that full service would begin on the twentieth. The advertisement establishes rates to and from (reading from the landing) Perry's crossing, Jefferson crossing, Scott's Depot (also designated Scottsville), and Marshall, guaranteeing that "the Company will be prepared to take cotton and other produce from the end of the track, one and one half miles east of Marshall and other depots on the road. Good shelters are prepared for the protection of cotton, and back freights, and an agent will always be in attendance for receiving and forwarding. . . . It is expected that there will be a connection formed between this Road and a line of steam packets that will take cotton without delay or expense of trans-shipment, to New Orleans."

A follow-up advertisement, dated 4 December 1859 and appearing in the *Texas Republican* on the tenth, says that the Southern Pacific Railroad was then making daily trips to and from Marshall to Swanson's Landing carrying freight and passengers. The company was "now amply prepared with Warehouses and Sheds for the reception and storage of cotton, and all kinds of Freights, and Boats Landing at Swanson's will find a good wharf, and any amount of warehouse facilities. There is a competent and careful agent at all the depots and stations, and shippers may rest assured that all business entrusted to their care shall have strict attention and careful handling." A price of $0.75 per bale was given for the freight, storage, commission, and handling of cotton delivered on board the boats. This advertisement also suggests the existence of a wooden wharf, but it is more likely that it is referring to one under construction that was observed by Loughery as nearly completed in January 1860.

By the end of 1859, the railroad was becoming a conduit for the export of regional cotton production, as is indicated by the 3 December *Texas Republican*: "Cotton is carried on the railroad each trip. Not only our own planters, but several of the planters of the surrounding counties are sending their cotton over the road." When Loughery traveled from the Marshall Depot to Swanson's Landing in January 1860, he found that sheds and a warehouse had been erected at the Marshall depot for storing cotton and that Scott's Depot and Jonesville bore striking resemblances to villages. On a similar trip in March, he found cotton awaiting shipment all along the route: "There was quite a quantity of cotton at the Marshall depot; I should suppose between fifteen hundred and two thousand bales, and a considerable number of bales at every other station on the route." These were impressive figures for depots serviced by a train making daily runs.

At the landing itself, Loughery found in January that there was a large frame warehouse, sheds sufficient to store any amount of cotton, and all the other buildings needed by the railroad company. In March, he found that "the landing was covered with cotton. I would suppose there was enough on hand to load several steamboats, and it continues to arrive as rapidly as it is taken off." In January, two steamboats had left shortly before Loughery arrived, and the *Sallie Robinson*, which he calls "a very respectable size boat," landed. In March, the *W. A. Andrew* arrived at noon and began taking on cotton, which detained her into the night; and at 10 P.M., the *National* arrived.

Loughery also found in January a "nearly finished" wharf that was expected to be completed in a week. However, he also reported in March that there were "a number of hands engaged in constructing a new wharf." The wharf, which definitely was constructed of wood, is described after completion in the 6 October 1860 *Texas Republican*: "The wharf at the Lake terminus of the S.P. Railroad Company is finished, and it is said to be an excellent one, extending far out into the water, so that boats can land and discharge freight without difficulty. There has been one boat at Swanson's landing during the past week. The railroad company has excellent warehouses for storing cotton and back freights. Send in your cotton, therefore, and have it transported without delay, as navigation is expected at an early day." The wharf extended far out into the water because its primary purpose was to receive railroad iron, which produced greater boat drafts.

Swanson's Landing had become an important feature in the navigation picture before the advent of the railroad; but the railroad gave the landing prominence. It was the central point for the U.S. mail route serviced by the *Fleta* thrice weekly, apparently to bring mail to Marshall, and it was a party and picnic spot for the citizens of Marshall, with regularly advertised excursion trips by the Southern Pacific. The rails were soon to take away what they had given and more, and the landing nearly disappeared shortly after the Civil War. The advertisement issued jointly with Thomas Lyon in 1858 appeared under Swanson's name alone in the 25 February 1860 *Texas Republican*. By the next year, Swanson was dead, with his wife, Mary, appointed as executrix for the estate in April. The north-south portion of the rail that had given Swanson's Landing prominence was removed during the Civil War and relaid toward Shreveport, never to return.

Swanson's Landing continues to appear in steamboat advertisements through at least 1866; but in that year, the rail was completed from Shreveport to Marshall, then extended west to Hallsville in 1868 and Longview in 1871. From 1866 onward, the east-west rail dominated the transportation system south of Cypress Bayou and Caddo Lake.

The landing was reduced to an isolated servicer of agricultural enterprises in its immediate vicinity, which would have happened even if its spur line had not been removed. After having received heavy coverage prior to the Civil War, the landing is never mentioned in a non-navigation newspaper article after the war.

Nevertheless, steamboats continued to stop at the landing, perhaps frequently because of its location. The 26 February 1868 *South-Western* reports: "Late in the afternoon the sternwheel packet Flicker, Capt. Taylor, arrived at our wharf from Swanson's Landing, on the lake, with 200 bales of cotton and a few passengers." The 24 December 1871 *Shreveport Times* reports the *Wash Sentell* laid up at Swanson's because of high winds. The last mention of the landing in the navigation record is in the 30 March 1872 *Shreveport Times*.

CLINTON

Clinton was located on the north shore of Clinton Lake slightly west of Pine Island Slough, as shown on the Texas General Land Office's 1901 *Map of Marion County* by J. W. Legg, which contains historic information (**fig. 8-23**). The route to the landing from Cypress Bayou is shown as Clinton Chute on Lt. Eugene Woodruff's 1872 *Map of the Red River Raft Region and Cypress Bayou* (**fig. 8-24**). Clinton Chute was in the approximate location of present-day Clinton Ditch. After entering the lake, boats proceeded through Withenbury Slough, named after Capt. W. W. Withenbury, who almost certainly developed the passage to Clinton. The name has been corrupted to Whistleberry on contemporary maps, and Clinton Chute has been transposed to Cypress Bayou.

Clinton Lake is not mentioned in any old texts and makes its first appearance on Woodruff's map, encompassing present-day Carter's Lake. The name of the lake was apparently derived from the landing. The landing appears to have been named by and for Clinton J. Willard, one of the original landholders in the area. If it had been named by steamboatmen, it would have been called Clinton's Landing rather than Clinton. The distinction is important because it indicates that Willard envisioned the area as a potential site for a town. The anticipated level of development was not achieved because Clinton was off the main boat route and between the major northern ports of Monterey to the east and Smithland to the west. In addition, Clinton's immediate

Fig. 8-23. Clinton. *Source: Courtesy Texas General Land Office, Austin*

market area was dominated by the much older and well-established Port Caddo, which was located on the main route and connected to the north shore of Cypress Bayou by a ferry.

When Edward Smith traveled throughout Northeast Texas in 1849 looking for a site for an English colony, he interviewed many persons. One of these was "Major Campbell, of Clinton, near Jefferson, Texas," who lived "upon the line of navigation" on the "Big Bend on Lake Caddo." Campbell indicated that he had brought part of his family from Missouri to the area in 1843 and that he had recently begun to cultivate tobacco, from which he expected production at 700 pounds per acre selling at $0.10 per pound, with one hand capable of raising ten acres per year. Campbell recommended to Smith that the colony

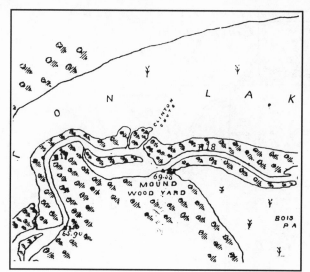

Fig. 8-24. Clinton Chute. *Source: LSU in Shreveport, Noel Memorial Library Archives*

be located at the Big Bend if it expected to pursue commerce because "above all it is upon the line of navigation." The Big Bend on Caddo Lake was one of the three areas that Smith particularly recommended to immigrants. Even so, the colony was located elsewhere, only to fail.

The person interviewed by Smith was John P. Campbell, listed in the 1850 Cass County Census as a forty-seven-year-old farmer born in North Carolina, with a forty-year-old wife, Louisa, born in Tennessee. Their five children (Leonidas, Sarah, James, Thomas, and Samuel) were born in Missouri and ranged in age from seventeen years to six years. There was another child, Louisa M. McKinny, age two and born in Missouri, apparently named for the wife. The Campbell estate was valued at $7,000, a considerable sum of money in 1850. The census enumeration for Campbell also lists as residents on the plantation James M. McCord (mechanic, forty-four, born in North Carolina), Thomas Roper (overseer, thirty-nine, born in Tennessee), and William H. Roberson (physician, thirty-five, born in Alabama).

The plantation was offered for sale in the 4 October 1851 *Texas Republican* by John A. Campbell of Jefferson, with the initial probably a misprint:

BY JOHN A. CAMPBELL.
Fourteen Hundred and Thirty-Six Acres of Land for Sale!!!
520 ARE in cultivation—all fresh land; good negro quarters, all weatherboarded; good cotton gin, press, and screw—all new; good stables and cribs—all hewed logs and sheded; good mule sheds, lots, etc.; comfortable hewed-log dwelling house, store rooms, carriage house, &c.; smith and wood shops, smith tools, farming utensils; 2000 bbls corn, 15 stacks fodder, oats, peas, potatoes, &c. A large stock of cattle and hogs;—and—geering, etc., will be sold with the place, if desired by the purchaser, or any part of the above named property. Six never failing springs on the premises, and very healthy; 15 miles east of Jefferson; 3½ miles north of Clinton, in Cass county. For terms apply to

JOHN A. CAMPBELL, or to
THOMAS ROPER, on the place.
Jefferson, Texas, Sept. 23, 1851.

The settlement of which the Campbells were a part was not important enough to merit a post office, but it was important enough to be included on the congressionally established postal routes between Fulton, Arkansas, and Jefferson and between Port Caddo and Moore's Ferry on the Sulphur Fork of Red River, as reported in the 9 December 1848 *Northern Standard*. Clinton may have served briefly in 1848 as the site of the Masonic Lodge established at Monterey during the same year; and its commercial activities were significant enough for it to be mentioned (along with Swanson's Landing, Port Caddo, Benton, Jefferson, Smithland, and Monterey) in the 3 December 1853 *Texas Republican* as one of the areas that should be concerned about a freight price-fixing scheme by steamboatmen.

Clinton is included in four different steamboat advertisements: *Jefferson* (*Texas Republican*, 6 September 1851); *Cleona* (*Texas Republican*, 5 June 1852); *Pitser Miller* (*Jefferson Herald*, 14 May 1853); and *Ruby* (*Daily Picayune*, 1 June 1854). The advertisements for the *Jefferson* and *Cleona* appear in the section for Rives' Landing. The advertisement for the *Pitser Miller* appeared under the names of prominent Jefferson businessmen:

REGULAR PACKET
FOR Port Caddo, Benton, Smithland, Jefferson, Clinton,

and Monterey, and all landings on the Lake.

Steamer *Pitser Miller*, E. ALEXANDER, Master, will run regular for the above landings during the season throughout.

WM. M. FREEMAN, SPEAK, SAUFLEY & NIMMO,

Agents, Jefferson.

The *Jefferson*, *Cleona*, and *Pitser Miller* advertised in local newspapers as regular packets to Clinton. The availability of these advertisements is significant because steamboats seldom advertised in the *Texas Republican*, and there is a near absence of antebellum Jefferson newspapers. The lone advertisement in the *Daily Picayune* indicates that Clinton was at least a recognized name in the New Orleans trade: "For Shreveport, Port Caddo, Monterey, Benton, Clinton, Smithland, Jefferson and Fort Towson—The superior light draught steamer RUBY, D. Glascock, master, will leave for the above and all intermediate ports on THURSDAY, the 1st day of June prox. For freight or passage apply on board, or to SMITH & FIMISTER, 16 Canal street."

An advertisement that appeared weekly in the Shreveport *South-Western* beginning on 18 October 1854 indicates that there were commercial services at Clinton:

H. E. CURTIS & CO.,
RECEIVING and Forwarding
Merchants, Clinton Landing,
Lake Caddo, Texas.
Oct. 18.

The later history of Clinton, if any, is unknown. Curtis's advertisement disappears after the first few months of 1855, which may indicate that the business itself disappeared during the regional commercial disaster precipitated by an absence of navigation during that year. Clinton does not appear in any documents after 1855, and the Campbells are not listed in the 1860 census. It would not have appeared on late landings lists because it was off the main route. Glenn's memoranda mention "Clinton bayou on right" shortly after passing "Mound Fish Ground" going upstream; but this indicates nothing with respect to continuing commerce at the landing.

PORT CADDO

Port Caddo was the earliest of the ports and landings on the route and the most important until the rise of Jefferson. It was the only one of the ports and landings other than Jefferson that could be called a town. Its location is shown on Lt. Eugene Woodruff's 1872 *Map of the Red River Raft Region and Cypress Bayou* as being immediately north of the hills now occupied by Caddo Lake State Park (**fig. 8-25**). The landing is shown as extending along the bayou in an 1893 benchmark map prepared by Capt. J. H. Willard in conjunction with his 1890–91 survey of Cypress Bayou and the lakes (**fig. 8-26**). The town was spread out to the north and east of the gentle rise adjacent to the hills; the landing fronted the town and extended upstream below the bluffs.

T. C. Richardson in his *East Texas: Its History and Its Makers* suggests that the site of Port Caddo was previously occupied by the settlement of Macon, which was formed by J. Haralson and Henry Martin, who brought their families from Macon, Georgia, about 1833. This could not have been the case. In January 1840, the postal route between San Augustine and Port Caddo was extended to include Macon, demonstrating that the sites were not equivalent and suggesting that Macon came into existence after Port Caddo. An auction sale advertisement for a plot of land in Harrison County owned by Julia

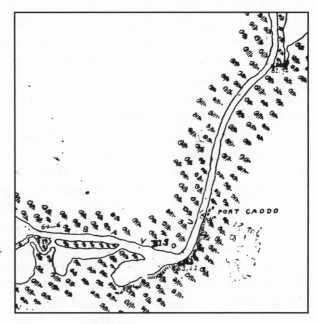

Fig. 8-25. Port Caddo. *Source: LSU in Shreveport, Noel Memorial Library Archives*

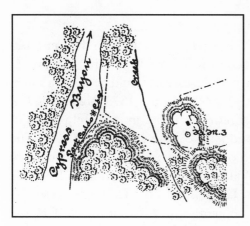

Fig. 8-26. Port Caddo. *Source: Annual Report of the Chief of Engineers, 1893*

Field appeared in the 24 November 1866 *Texas Republican*. It mentions that the land adjoined and included the site of Old Macon and embraced one of the best boat landings and woodyards on Caddo Lake, apparently referring to the woodyard at Mound Pond. The location of the land for sale is given as sixteen miles from Marshall and eighteen miles from Jefferson, from which no conclusion can be drawn. Macon was probably downstream from Port Caddo in the vicinity of Anna Glade Bluff.

Before the Shenix's Ferry crossing was established at Stormy Point in the early 1820s, the Caddo and other Indians needed to travel around the west end of Caddo Lake to reach Natchitoches. Map delineations of this trail suggest that it could have passed through the area that eventually became Port Caddo. However, this is not the case. A land sale advertisement in the 28 November 1865 *South-Western* states that the land was adjacent to the old Indian crossing and located one and one-half miles above Port Caddo. This would place the trail in the vicinity of present-day Highway 43.

John Arrowsmith's 1841 *Map of Texas* shows a branch of Trammel's Trace passing through Port Caddo from the north over Big Cypress Bayou. The trace, which extended from Jonesboro, Texas, to Nacogdoches, Texas, was blazed by Nicholas Trammell in 1820 and was equivalent in part to an even older trail that ran between Arkansas and Nacogdoches. The trail from Arkansas joined the trail from Jonesboro near Hughes Springs, northwest of Jefferson, and crossed over Big Cypress Bayou a few miles west of Jefferson. The branch shown in Arrowsmith's map does not appear in any maps prior to the existence of Port Caddo and was obviously an extension to accommodate a new settlement rather than a prior crossing on which Port Caddo came to be founded.

Port Caddo was not founded on the site of a pre-existing trail or settlement but rather in a new area that was selected because it was the first point on Cypress Bayou that afforded sufficient land for a town. Rip Ford visited the area in early 1838 and writes of the "locality where Post Caddo was afterwards laid off," around which a few settlers were nestled who obtained supplies by wagons from Shreveport and by flatboats that navigated Caddo Lake. This settlement was not a town, was apparently not named, and was not visited by steamboats. This is incompatible with V. H. Hackney's contention in *Port Caddo—A Vanished Village* that Port Caddo was so named by the end of 1835 and that it had been visited by the *Indian* and *Nicholas Biddle*. Unfortunately, Hackney does not provide a source, and I have been unable to find any newspaper records to support his contention. The *Indian*, at least, could not have arrived by 1835: she was not built until 1836.

Hackney also indicates that Port Caddo was first laid out as a town through a land grant of 660 acres by the Republic of Texas to Obediah Hendrick, Jr., on 7 July 1838, with the land described as being in "Shelby County on the South of Ferry Lake embracing Taylors Bluff." Hackney does not give a year for when the town was developed. The town was incorporated and divided into 1,000 lots, indicating the dimensions of Hendrick's vision. Hackney lists lot purchasers such as William H. Cobbs, who played an important role in Port Caddo's commerce, but years of purchase are not given.

Port Caddo was used as a base for the Texas Militia in November and December 1838 for launching an attack on a remnant of the Caddo tribe. Although the boundary between the United States and the Republic of Texas was indefinite at the time, the area in which the Caddos were located was recognized by everyone involved as within the United States. Thus, the attack on the Caddos was a foreign invasion. The Caddos had always been pacific and friendly to whites. In 1838 they were destitute, having been dispossessed of their lands and cheated in the compensation. Republic officials were apparently duped into thinking that the Caddos were engaged in depredations by influential rabble-rousers like Robert Potter, whom Ford characterized as a powerful rhetorician with an interest in clearing out the Indians. When the battle began, the Caddos requested a parley and explained their situation. General Rusk quickly recognized his error with respect to the Caddos and an amicable settlement was reached. Nevertheless, the United States' animosity over the invasion of its territory continued.

When Ford writes about the locality where Post Caddo was laid off, he is not suggesting that the port developed as a military post rather than as a town. Letters written by Adjutant General Hugh McLeod from the base in November and December use "Port Caddo" rather than "Post Caddo," and the port was selected as a post because it was the nearest Texas settlement to the Caddos. "Port" and "Post" were used interchangeably in the texts of the period, including in steamboat advertisements, a convention that did not disappear until at least 1857.

Port Caddo was a town by the end of 1838. A post office was established at Post Caddo in January 1839; Port Caddo is listed on the mail route from San Augustine beginning in October 1839; and a post office was established at Port Caddo in November 1840. It is probable that 1840 was also the year in which the first steamboat arrived at Port Caddo. At least one mercantile store was in operation by that time, because Hackney includes a sight draft signed by James Wadsworth at Port Caddo on 10 May 1839. Although steamboats could have traveled to Port Caddo in 1840, the first advertisement designating the port was for the *Brian Boroihme* in the 9 January 1841 *Daily Picayune*.

Port Caddo is not shown on H. Groves's 1837 *Map of the Republic of Texas*. The first map representation I have been able to find is Henry Tanner's 1839 *A New Map of Louisiana with its Canals, Roads & Distances from place to place along the Stage & Steam Boat Routes* (**fig. 8-27**). This map is particularly interesting because it shows Port Caddo well within the boundaries of Louisiana, an error that was not to be corrected until the 1841 United States-Republic of Texas boundary survey. Tanner's earlier map, published in 1833, shows neither Shreveport nor Port Caddo.

Hackney also presents excerpts from a letter dated 15 February 1841 purporting to show that the murder of John Campbell in Port Caddo was indicative of the attitude of some of the residents toward taxation. This letter was written by L. H. Dillard, sheriff and tax collector of Harrison County, to the secretary of the treasury of the Republic of Texas and appears in *Texas Treasury Papers*. The full text of the first paragraph of the letter indicates that Campbell was not murdered in his function as tax collector but in his function as acting sheriff: "It

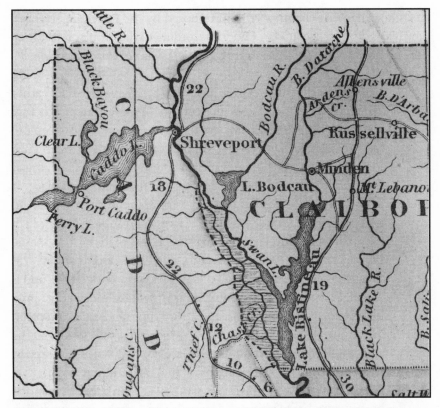

Fig. 8-27. Port Caddo. *Source: Courtesy of LSU Libraries Special Collections, Baton Rouge*

becomes my duty to lay before you a statement of facts in relation to the collection of taxes in this County. Dr. John B. Campbell late Coroner and acting Sheriff had collected about one fourth the amount of Taxes due the Republic from this County previous to the 23rd Jan. last on which day he was assassinated at Port Caddo and robbed of all his official papers including his Tax Book. It is reported that he was shot by one Reece Hughes who was backed by an armed mob of criminals whose recognizances he (Campbell) held for their appearance at Court on a charge of murder. It is also reported that the said mob made a bon-fire of his papers and consequently the Tax Book is destroyed."

Moreover, the Rev. John McLean in his *Reminiscences* says that Hughes was revenging the unjustified killing of his brother Isaac by Campbell. This is not to say that the people of Port Caddo were accepting of taxes. A tax considered onerous by merchants, immigrants, and steamboatmen was the import tariff imposed by the Republic of Texas, which was disregarded at Port Caddo, according to the Houston *Morning Star*, as quoted by the 27 March 1844 Clarksville *Northern Standard*:

> FREE PORT.—A free port in Texas may sound rather startling upon the ears of the officers of government who are watching with so much anxiety to ascertain how large a sum can be collected from imposts, to fill the coffers of government. The idea of a free port in Texas under the present tariff system, almost necessarily includes the idea that a revolution has taken place. It is nevertheless true that there is a free port in the republic, in which are to be found two or three large mercantile houses which annually sell more goods than are consumed by the whole population west of the Colorado. This free port is situated in Harrison county, at the head of navigation on Caddo lake, and is styled Port Caddo. Steamboats are plying almost constantly between it, and Red River, and many thousand bales of cotton are annually shipped from it to New Orleans, and goods to the amount of many thousand dollars are annually imported free of duty, and sold to the planters of the surrounding country, at prices twenty-five or thirty per cent lower than those demanded by any merchants who are compelled to pay the impost duties. No collector has ventured to enforce the law at this port, and importations are made in defiance of law as freely and openly as they are made in Shreveport or Nachitoches. Owing to the facilities thus offered for procuring supplies of foreign goods, at a cheap rate, the country in the vicinity is rapidly filling up with emigrants, and new farms are opening in all directions around the town. It is even said that several families from the western settlements have removed eastward and settled near the Lake owing to the advantages of the free trade. We can no longer wonder that so few emigrants have passed through the eastern counties into the middle and western sections of Texas, during the last two or three years—The advantages offered in the Eastern counties for smuggling cotton into the United States, and obtaining cheap smuggled goods in exchange, are so great that few emigrants will desire to remove to the less favored west. We have no cause however to blame the eastern representatives or senators for this state of things, for the late veto of the tariff bill,

which was intended to remedy part of these evils, was sustained by the votes of two Senators of the western and middle counties.

Six collectoral districts were created in January 1837; but the area west of Shreveport was not one of them, which is another indication that steamboats were not operating on Cypress Bayou as early as 1835. The Soda Lake Collectoral District was created in January 1845, encompassing the counties west of the Sulphur River. A customs house was to be established at Port Caddo, but universal opposition forced the collector to reside in Marshall, where his efforts were negligible. Of the $349,871.40 collected in the eight Texas districts during the fifteen months following 31 July 1844, only $866.54 was collected in the Soda Lake District. This issue became moot with the entrance of Texas into the Union in December 1845.

Port Caddo was the most important of the ports and landings along the route through 1850, when Jefferson assumed primacy—if advertisements and arrivals records are good indicators of relative importance. Port Caddo was the primary cotton outlet for the rich plantations of Harrison County and captured a significant portion of the trade north of Cypress Bayou through its ferry. It was also one of the primary points of immigration. An example suggesting the magnitude of immigration is given in the 6 May 1846 Clarksville *Northern Standard*, quoting the Marshall *Soda Lake Herald*: "The Steamer Jim Gilmer, ORRICK Master, arrived at Port Caddo on the 18th inst., bringing about 400 emigrants, also a great deal of property, besides."

Randolph Campbell in *A Southern Community in Crisis* points out that Port Caddo was the only antebellum town in Harrison County other than Marshall to be large enough to be included in the census. The census indicates that at least fifty people lived in Port Caddo in 1850, including four merchants, three grocers, and a tavern keeper. An advertisement for 200 lots for sale in Port Caddo appears in the 10 August 1849 *Texas Republican*, indicating something of the dimensions of the town. The most well known of the merchants was William H. Cobbs, who was postmaster in Port Caddo from May 1846 through May 1848 and first appears in the *Texas Republican* of 15 June 1849 as a financial contributor to a proposed effort to clear Cypress Bayou of obstructions.

Cobbs was not the first merchant in Port Caddo. The firm of Todd & Brander was operating out of Port Caddo prior to March 1845, when it issued a bill of lading for the cotton that was to be carried out of Smithland by the *Lama*. Brander was from a family of merchants in New Orleans. J. D. Todd & Company of Port Caddo is mentioned in the 16 August 1849 *Texas Republican*. This was James D. Todd, who later became the primary merchant at Smithland. The firm of Perry & Spell, composed of N. B. Perry and Marshall Spell, is mentioned in an advertisement in the 8 June 1849 *Texas Republican*. This firm was dissolved on 1 March 1852, with Perry settling the remaining business. Another early merchant was R. A. Boggass, who appears in the 2 May 1850 *Texas Republican* as the local contact for Cowan, Dykers & Spauldings, cotton factors in New Orleans.

On 11 October 1849, R. W. Powell, a cotton factor in New Orleans, advertised in the *Texas Republican* with William H. Cobbs and J. H. Fyffe as the local contacts in Port Caddo. James D. Todd advertised in the 31 August 1850 *Texas Republican* that he had moved to Smithland and that anyone who wished to ship cotton by him through Port Caddo should refer to William H. Cobbs. Cobbs's operation flourished along with the town, and he was able to build a new warehouse in 1851, as is indicated in a 6 September *Texas Republican* advertisement:

> NEW WAREHOUSE AT PORT CADDO.
> WILLIAM H. COBBS & CO., Receiving and Forwarding Merchants, are prepared to store cotton and merchandise consigned to their care.
> Having a large and commodius warehouse and shed, and facilities for carrying on the business, they trust by attention and promptness, to receive a liberal patronage from their many friends and acquaintances, and the public generally.
> THOMAS H. COWAN, WILLIAM H. COBBS,
> Port Caddo, August 28, 1851.

In 1852, Cobbs appears as an agent for the *Red River* in an advertisement in the 13 March *Texas Republican*. A similar advertisement that does not mention Cobbs appears in the 6 March *Daily Picayune*. What is particularly interesting about these advertisements is that Port Caddo would have been listed without Jefferson as late as 1852. The *Texas Republican* rendition, which apparently was published through the Shreveport *South-Western*, reads as follows:

NEW ORLEANS & PORT CADDO PACKET,

The new fast running passenger steamer RED RIVER, Capt. HENRY V. MCCALL, has been purchased expressly for the trade, and will run as a regular packet during the entire season. The Red River has just been newly furnished throughout, with new beds, bedding, carpeting, &c., &c.

The "*Red River*," from her great speed and superior accommodation for passengers and shippers offer fine inducements.

For freight or passage apply on board or to W. H. COBB, *Agent, Port Caddo.*

Shreveport, March 13, 1852.

W. H. Cobbs & Company advertised in October 1852 as carrying a large assortment of dry goods and groceries. Cobbs advertised an even larger stock of goods in April 1853 and served as postmaster again from April through August. In December, Cobbs informed the public that his warehouse and shed were nearly filled, that cotton could not be shipped because of an absence of navigation, and that future cotton receipts would be stored outdoors under tarpaulins. Cowan died in April 1854, and the firm was reorganized under Cobbs's name alone, with the previous stock of goods sold at auction. An example of the type of agricultural enterprises with which Cobbs did business is given in the 24 December 1858 *Texas Republican*:

FOR RENT.

A VALUABLE PLANTATION, the late residence of Peter Baugh, deceased, about two miles below Port Caddo. There are four hundred and fifty acres of open Bottom Land under good fence, fresh and equal to any in Harrison county. There is a good family house, negro house, all the necessary out-houses, a good well of never failing water in the yard. The place has also upon it a Gin House, with screw, etc., etc.

Persons desiring to secure a valuable place, would do well to apply while there is a chance, for it is land that will be soon taken.

W. F. BALDWIN, Adm'r.

Dec. 24, 1858.

In August 1854, Cobbs retired from the receiving and forwarding portion of his business, selling his warehouse and cotton shed operations to an employee, William H. Farley. This exchange of ownership was covered in four advertisements in the 26 August 1854 *Texas Republican*. In January 1855, Farley became postmaster at Port Caddo and purchased the rest of Cobbs's business, advertising staple and fancy dry goods, the exchange of goods for hides and pelts, and cash advances on cotton. In February, Cobbs requested all debtors to the old firm to pay up; and by May, he was spending most of his time in Marshall, where he would reside permanently. In May 1856, Cobbs advertised that he was bankrupt and that he would be able to get back in business if the debts owed to him were paid.

Farley brought his brother into the business in 1856, advertising under the name of W. H. Farley & Company in the 6 September *Texas Republican*:

> W. H. FARLEY   J. A. FARLEY
> W. H. FARLEY & CO.,
>   RECEIVING, *Forwarding and Commission Merchants*, Port Caddo, Texas, keep on hand a general assortment of groceries, also Bagging and Rope.
>   Cash advances made on cotton in store.
>   Sept. 6, 1856.

W. H. Farley & Company was dissolved in 1857. William Farley relinquished his office as postmaster in September 1858 and offered his town residence for sale in the 15 October 1858 *Texas Republican*:

> VALUABLE TOWN PROPERTY FOR SALE.
>   WM. H. FARLEY & CO. of Port Caddo, Harrison County, Texas, are now offering, and will sell their town property in that place, on the lowest terms that any business man will ask for, if application is made soon. The property consists of a well finished Store House and Dwelling House, with all necessary outbuildings, kitchen, stables, garden, horse lots, a small orchard, and a never-failing well of the best water on the premises. Apply to the undersigned, on the premises.
>   WM. H. FARLEY & CO.
>   Refer to J. J. WILLIAMS, Marshall.
>   Port Caddo, Oct. 14, 1858.

The last mention of William Farley in the newspapers is a 7 January 1859 *Texas Republican* advertisement in which Farley says that his business affairs and the sale of his residence had been placed in the hands of John F. Williams of Marshall and that any debtor who had not paid by the end of January would be sued.

William Farley's place in the mercantile establishment was taken by A. J. T. Carter, who operated with J. A. Farley under the name of Farley & Carter, as advertised in the 21 March 1857 *Texas Republican*:

> J. A. FARLEY, A. J. T. CARTER,
> FARLEY & CARTER
> (*Formerly W. H. Farley & Co.,*)
> RECEIVING, *Forwarding, and Commission Merchants*, Port Caddo, Texas, will attend promptly to all business with which they may be entrusted, and respectfully solicit a continuance of the public patronage which has been lately bestowed upon the house of which they are the successors. Port Caddo, as is well known, is one of the most elegible points on the Lake. The roads leading to it are good, and are always accessible. No other place has a better, or more commodious warehouse. The navigation to this point is excellent. The best steamers can get there, at this time, without difficulty.
> March 21, 1857.

Farley then dropped out of the firm, which was operated by Carter alone until 1860, when it was purchased by the Hope brothers, as reflected in a 6 October *Texas Republican* advertisement:

> WAREHOUSE AT PORT CADDO.
> The undersigned have purchased the Warehouse formerly owned by Mr. A. J. T. Carter, at Port Caddo, on the Lake, and are prepared to receive cotton and back freights. Every attention will be paid to business entrusted to their charge. The most perfect reliance may be placed in their punctuality, promptness, fidelity, and strict attention to business. They solicit a share of the Forwarding and Commission business, promising that nothing shall be wanting on their part, to merit a continuation of it.
> A. & A. HOPE,
> Oct. 6, 1860.

Adam Hope served as postmaster at Port Caddo from March 1860 through November 1866. He was a member of Lane's Regiment during the Civil War, attaining the rank of captain. The cotton warehouse at Port Caddo was still in existence during the war, because Hope advertised in the 1 April 1863 *South-Western* that, being away from home, he would not be responsible for damage to cotton caused by leaks in the warehouse. Business does not appear to have been resumed after the war. The facilities came into the ownership of Rene Fitzpatrick, who offered an obviously unused building for rent in the 16 March 1866 *Texas Republican*:

> FOR RENT.
> Caddo, Harrison county, Texas. It is 68 feet long, 30 feet wide, contains a fine large dry goods room, with well finished, large counters, and is capable of containing and properly displaying a stock of from fifty to seventy-five thousand dollars worth of goods. It also has a fine counting and a fine sleeping room. The store house is situated in one of the best country neighborhoods in the State. For further information enquire of the undersigned.
>
> RENE FITZPATRICK.
> March 9, 1866.

By 1850, the number of steamboats shown as arriving at Shreveport from Jefferson exceeded the number arriving from Port Caddo. The last two boats arriving at Shreveport from Port Caddo that had not gone to Jefferson were the *Caddo No. 2* and *Texas Ranger* in 1854. Although Jefferson's rise was absolute, Port Caddo's decline was only relative. Although there is no possibility of documentation, the volume of commerce through Port Caddo probably increased during the 1850s and 1860s as cotton production expanded in Harrison County and the level of trade through Marshall increased.

The assumption that Port Caddo declined as Jefferson rose to prominence is based on a misconception of their respective commercial activities. Port Caddo and Jefferson were never in competition because they tapped different market areas. Port Caddo was a major outlet for Harrison County cotton, and if Port Caddo had not existed, the commerce would have been carried on by Benton and Swanson's Landing. In addition, the flow of commodities and immigrants through Marshall was through Port Caddo and Shreveport rather than Jefferson, as indicated by two *Texas Republican* articles, the first of which appeared on 9 November 1850: "The large quantities of cotton which are continually carried by, en route to Shreveport and Port Caddo, prove that the crops have turned out better than was anticipated." The 10 December 1853 issue reported: "Immigrants are passing through our town almost daily. Wagons are on the streets during all hours, cotton wagons are passing thick and fast for Shreveport and Port Caddo."

Port Caddo was hurt by the low water of 1854–55, which diminished commerce through the suspension of navigation. This was the apparent cause of Cobbs's bankruptcy in early 1856. The construction of the Southern Pacific in 1858 from Swanson's Landing to the vicinity of Marshall would also have hurt Port Caddo, because it would have cut into the direct trade with Marshall, and some Harrison County planters would have found it easier and cheaper to use the rail line rather than transporting by wagon to Port Caddo. Nevertheless, with the overall increase of trade in the region, Port Caddo would not have experienced an absolute decline. This was why there was a continuity of facilities and services at Port Caddo for cotton growers up to the Civil War, even with the rapid changes in ownership.

Port Caddo was not defeated by Jefferson or by the rail to Swanson's Landing, which in any case had been removed during the war. Commerce at the port had nearly ceased during the war. It did not revive after the war, as Jefferson's did, because the Southern Pacific was completed from Shreveport to Marshall in July 1866, and there was no point in transporting overland to Port Caddo by wagon when the rails offered direct access to the Port of Shreveport. Steamboats stopped advertising to Port Caddo in 1866, and the post office was discontinued in November of that year.

Nevertheless, Port Caddo did not disappear in 1866. Its resiliency is demonstrated by the fact that it appears in Adam's 1877 directory of ports and landings, Glenn's 1879 landings list, Clayton's 1881 landings list, and Glenn's 1886 memoranda. It also appears on all the major Corps survey maps, including Lt. Eugene Woodruff's 1872 *Map of the Red River Raft Region and Cypress Bayou*, Capt. Eric Bergland's 1885 *Map of Cypress Bayou and the Lakes*, Capt. J. H. Willard's 1890–91 *Survey of Cypress Bayou and the Lakes*, and even Capt. W. P. Wooten's 1907 *Cypress Bayou & the Lakes*.

The level and nature of commerce during this late period cannot be determined. However, it is unlikely that Glenn would have included Port Caddo on his 1879 landings list and in his 1886 memoranda had not some form of commercial activity continued—Glenn's notes are those of a working steamboatman. This late commercial function is confirmed by the 14 August 1875 *Shreveport Times*, which mentions Port Caddo, Benton, Smithland, and Jefferson as the commercial centers on Cypress Bayou. A bill of lading in the Joseph Jones Collection at Tulane University in New Orleans indicates that the *May Lowry* picked up two bales of cotton in Port Caddo on 5 March 1877; and the 18 November 1877 *Shreveport Times* indicates that Port Caddo had no need of water because of a lack of business. By that time, a rail system had developed throughout Northeast Texas that captured almost all of the trade that previously had passed through ports.

BENTON

Benton was located on a small peninsula formed by the confluence of Beckum Creek and Cypress Bayou. It is shown on Capt. W. P. Wooten's 1907 *Map of Cypress Bayou and the Lakes* (**fig. 8-28**), which itself was derived from Willard's 1890–91 survey. Willard provides a detailed map in his 1893 report because Benton was used to establish a survey benchmark (**fig. 8-29**). The accompanying description indicates that

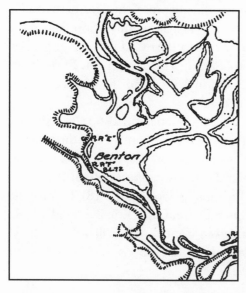

Fig. 8-28. Benton. *Source: H. Doc. 20, 60ᵗʰ Cong., 1ˢᵗ Sess.*

Fig. 8-29. Benton. *Source: Annual Report of the Chief of Engineers, 1893*

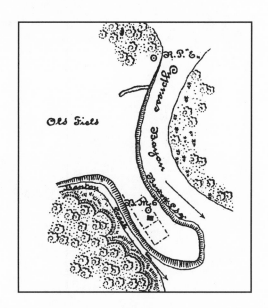

the benchmark was within a fenced yard and near a house, as shown on the map. The map shows the landing itself as being on Cypress Bayou. Although the geographic extent of Benton is not known, it probably encompassed only the peninsula and its immediate vicinity. The only remaining indication of its existence is Benton Lake, which is shown on contemporary maps, and the corruption of Benton to Beckum in the naming of the creek **(fig. 8-30)**.

Shortly after Rip Ford visited the Port Caddo area early in 1838, he traveled to Ray's Bluff, which he described as "a small town not far from the head of the lake." Here Ford met Robert Potter at Dr. Sanderson's boarding house, which he called a hotel. It is clear from Ford's description that Ray's Bluff was much more developed than the site of the future Port Caddo and that he considered the former a town and the latter a settlement. Ray's Creek was a former name for Beckum Creek; the settlement at Ray's Bluff that was to become the nucleus of Benton was more sophisticated than the settlement in the Port Caddo area in early 1838.

The name "Benton" does not appear in any texts until 1841, when it was used in an advertisement for the steamboat *Farmer* in the 15 June *Daily Picayune*, which indicates that Benton would have been known among the New Orleans merchants by that time. Although hundreds of advertisements were to list Benton during the

Fig. 8-30. Benton Lake area

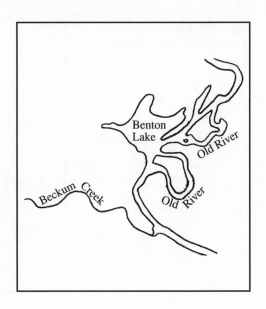

following decades, no others listed Benton during the 1840s, and this was the only advertisement to list Benton first. Benton does not appear again until the *Osceola* advertised for Port Caddo, Benton, Smithland, and Jefferson in the 4 February 1851 *Daily Picayune.* Nevertheless, it can be assumed that most of the boats that listed for Port Caddo and all of the boats that listed for Jefferson in the 1840s stopped at Benton.

Beginning in 1851, Benton appears regularly in advertisements with Jefferson. Although Benton was a stopping place for all boats that went to Jefferson, there are only a few records of boats having arrived from Benton. The 27 April 1854, *Daily Picayune* shows the *Belle Gates* as having arrived in New Orleans from Benton, and the 23 February 1856 *Daily Picayune* shows the *St. Charles* as arriving from Benton. The 17 December 1856 *South-Western* mentions that the *Storm* had arrived back at Shreveport from Benton. But this was accidental. The *Storm* had departed for Jefferson but was only able to get as far as Benton because of low water.

Benton was one of the three (along with Port Caddo and Swanson's Landing) primary outlets for Harrison County cotton and captured a portion of the trade that flowed through Marshall. Although Willard uses the designation "Benton Landing" in his 1893 report, it was never referred to as anything other than Benton in the steamboat literature and was obviously a place of commercial importance. The 5 January 1856 *Texas Republican* describes Benton as "an excellent shipping point; the road leading to it is good, and it is only 15 miles from Marshall." The planters and merchants at Benton are mentioned as among those who should be interested in navigation improvements in the 19 February 1853 *Texas Republican*; the 3 December 1853 *Texas Republican* includes Benton as among the ports and landings that should be concerned about the steamboatmen's price-fixing scheme; and it was one of the places that drew large crowds for Ned Davis's minstrels in March 1857.

The Texas Western Railroad, which was the predecessor to the Southern Pacific, chose Benton as a site for the spur line from Caddo Lake, as is indicated by a *Galveston News* article quoted in the 26 August 1854 *Texas Republican*: "The first section of the road, sixteen miles in length, has been located and surveyed from a place called Benton, on the northern extremity of Lake Caddo, to Marshall. This section is to be constructed solely for the purpose of connecting the main road with Red River, so as to enable them to procure the iron and other supplies by that river, Benton being the nearest point of navigation at which such connection can be made."

The 1858 *Texas Almanac*, which describes the condition of the state in 1857, contains an account of Harrison County by B. H. Martin of Benton. Martin writes that "Benton and Fort Caddo are shipping points upon the lake, with but few inhabitants; about 10,000 bales of cotton are shipped annually from those points, by steamers to New Orleans, the freight being from $1.50 to $1.75 per bale; insurance two per cent." Benton is then mentioned in the 1859 *Texas Almanac* as having shipped 8,000 bales in 1858 at the same time that Smithland and Port Caddo were shipping about 5,000 bales apiece.

The first recorded merchant in Benton was Charles C. Mills, who began advertising in the 15 November 1851 *Texas Republican*:

BENTON.
   THE *Warehouse* at this place is ready for the reception of cotton, and the road to it in fine order.
   Mr. WM. PRESTON, will attend to the business in my absence, and on my return, my personal attention will be given to the business. And a constant supply of Family Groceries kept on hand.

A liberal patronage will be thankfully acknowledged by the subscribers.

CHAS. C. MILLS.
Nov. 15th, 1851.

The B. H. Martin who wrote the Harrison County article for the 1858 *Texas Almanac* was previously a partner with L. P. Alford in the firm of Alford & Martin, commission merchants in New Orleans, who advertised in the 27 June 1850 *Texas Republican*. Martin served as the postmaster at Benton throughout the entire life of the post office, which extended from September 1854 through December 1857. He was also the most prominent businessman in Benton, advertising in the 24 September 1853 *Texas Republican* as newly established through the purchase of a pre-existing cotton warehouse (apparently the one operated by Mills) and offering cash advances on cotton to planters willing to deal with cotton merchants in New Orleans with whom Martin had a business relation:

WAREHOUSE, AND COMMISSION BUSINESS.
B. H. Martin has taken the Ware House at Benton, six miles above Port Caddo, on Soda Lake, and respectfully tenders his services to the Merchants and Planters of the surrounding country in the above business.

Benton is located about fifteen miles from Marshall, and as a shipping point, more accessible than any other point on the Lake—being of shorter distance and a better road.

Boats can come to Benton whenever they can to Port Caddo. The rate of freights and Insurance are the same to both places.

Cash and advances made on cotton, if desired, when shipped to our friends in New Orleans. When navigation opens, a good supply of Groceries will always be on hand, which will be sold at a small advance on cost. The rate of charges will conform to those of other Ware Houses.

Mr. Martin's experience and strict attention to business, induces a hope that he will merit and receive a due proportion of patronage. Cotton will be received by the 15th of October, or earlier if desired.

September 10, 1853.

The type of agricultural enterprises with which Martin did business is suggested by an advertisement in the 9 August 1856 *Texas Republican*:

> 360 ACRES OF VALUABLE LAND FOR SALE.
> I will sell on exceedingly favorable terms, a valuable plantation 8 miles Northwest of Marshall, on Little Cypress, containing Three Hundred and Sixty Acres of as choice land as can be found in Harrison County. Seventy acres of this land is cleared and under fence. A good Dwelling House, all necessary out-houses, good orchards, a most excellent well and several fine springs, affording as good water as could be desired. Title unquestioned.
> I have also a Land Certificate for 120 acres, which I will also sell.
> Apply to Major Samson McCown, who is fully authorized to dispose of the above mentioned property.
> GEO. W. MATTHEWS
August 2, 1856.

On the same day that Martin advertised acquisition of the warehouse at Benton, L. P. Alford advertised as the new owner of the Planter's Hotel in Marshall. Perhaps by the end of 1853, the old partners reassociated in the firm of B. H. Martin & Company in Benton. This firm was dissolved in December 1855 by limitation, a mutual agreement to part company within a specified time period. Martin continued to operate under his own name, as is indicated by an advertisement in the 2 August 1856 *Texas Republican*:

> WAREHOUSE, BENTON, TEXAS.
> B. H. MARTIN,
> RECEIVING, Forwarding and Commission Merchant. Has now on hand and to arrive, a large lot of Sugar, Coffee, Pork, Bacon, Salt, Iron, Nails, Castings, Bagging, Rope, Rice, Molasses, Candles, Whiskey, Apple Vinegar, etc., which are offered for a small advance on cost for cash, or to good customers as an advance on cotton.
> Aug. 2.

However, Martin desired to leave the business because of long-standing ill health, as is indicated by a companion advertisement:

A GREAT CHANCE!
I PROPOSE to sell, on very reasonable terms, owing to constitutional bad health for many years, my Benton property. It is too well known to require minute description. I consider it the best location in Eastern Texas for a man of business habits and facilities to make money.
My stock of Groceries will be sold with the place, if desired.
B. H. MARTIN
Benton, Texas, Aug. 2, 1856.

This sale evidently did not take place immediately, because the advertisement for B. H. Martin as receiving, forwarding, and commission merchant continued to appear through 1859. As indicated by a 9 July 1859 *Texas Republican* advertisement, the establishment was eventually sold to Jules Norsworthy and William Kennedy:

JULES A. NORSWORTHY   WM. N. KENNEDY
NORSWORTHY & KENNEDY
RECEIVING, FORWARDING, COMMISSION, AND GROCERY MERCHANTS,
BENTON TEXAS.
HAVING purchased of B. H. Martin, his Ware-House and Cotton-sheds, together with his entire stock of GROCERIES, tender their services to the public as his successors in the above business, and pledge their unremitted exertions to give satisfaction to all who may favor them with their patronage. They will give their personal attention to receiving and forwarding goods with dispatch. Their rates for storage and commission will be the same as heretofore charged by Mr. Martin. They will endeavor to keep a large supply of Groceries on hand, for which they will make advances on cotton in store. They solicit your business, knowing they can give you entire satisfaction.
July 9, 1859.

Martin moved to Marshall, where he became an agent for Peeler's Patent Ploughs in November 1861. He reacquired the Benton facility in January 1862, advertising as a receiving, forwarding, and commission merchant. He was back in Marshall by at least the end of 1865, where he opened a dry goods store on the south side of the public square.

Although Benton does not appear in the census, it was important enough to be included in various state maps, including John Colton's 1860 *Colton's Louisiana*. Like Port Caddo, it would have been harmed by the emergence of Swanson's Landing as a rail terminus and most particularly by the completion of the rail between Shreveport and Marshall in 1866. However, it appears in steamboat advertisements at least as late as 1866 and was still shipping cotton during that year, as is indicated by a bill of sale for twelve bales of cotton by S. M. Swenson in New Orleans on 5 April 1866. The cotton was received from W. P. Watson and shipped out of Benton aboard the *Lizzie Hamilton* (**fig. 8-31**). The 18 November 1877 *Shreveport Times* mentions Benton as a place that did not have a need for water because of a lack of business. Benton is mentioned in Adam's 1877 landings directory, Glenn's 1879 landings list, Clayton's 1881 landings directory, Glenn's 1886 memoranda, and even maps into the 1900s, indicating that it continued to serve some commercial function late in the history of steamboat activity.

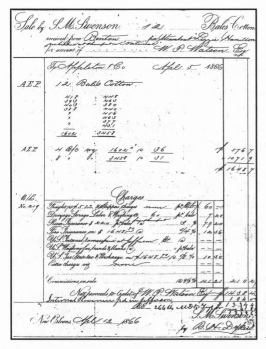

Fig. 8-31. *Lizzie Hamilton* bill of lading. *Source: Historic Jefferson Foundation*

SHANGHAI LANDING

A 1903 Corps report on improvements to Cypress Bayou indicates that Shanghai Landing was two miles above Benton. At that time it was frequented by a small gasoline boat that made many trips between Jefferson and the landing and the landing and Benton moving large quantities of cord wood, lumber, and telephone poles. The only other mention of the landing is in the 10 January 1872 *Shreveport Times*, which reports that the *Wash Sentell*, while descending Cypress Bayou, was damaged by striking the bank about two and one-half miles above Shanghai Landing and continued until just below the landing where she was grounded.

Shanghai Landing extended back to the period of large-scale cotton export and lasted for at least thirty years. However, it is not mentioned in connection with any activities related to cotton export, does not appear in any newspaper advertisements or boat records, and does not even appear in any late landings lists when it obviously was in existence. As a consequence, it can be assumed that this landing was not a part of the cotton trade and that it always operated as part of the lumber industry. If so, it was probably located on the bluffs on the north bank of Cypress Bayou a couple of miles above Benton and served as an outlet for the timber of the area.

SMITHLAND

Smithland was located at the confluence of Big and Black Cypress Bayous below the present town of Smithland at the upper limit of the Sodo Lake complex, as shown on T. S. Hardee's 1871 *Geographical, Historical and Statistical Map of Louisiana* (**fig. 8-32**). A post office was established at Smithland in September 1839, with L. R. Cherry as postmaster. It is mentioned in William F. Johnson's March 1840 survey field notes, was visited in August 1841 by Josiah Gregg when it had six houses but not as many families, and became part of the postal route from Nacogdoches to Epperson's Ferry in November 1841. It first appears in the navigation record in a 26 February 1842 *Daily Picayune* advertisement for the *Star* as a regular packet for Smithland; Fort Caddo; Ferry, Clear, and Sodo Lakes; and various points on the Red River.

In the 1950s, the old town of Smithland was the subject of extensive legal investigations in connection with *Thomas Jordan, Inc.,*

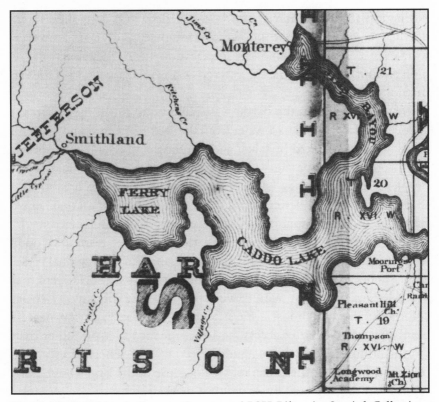

Fig. 8-32. Smithland. *Source: Courtesy of LSU Libraries Special Collections, Baton Rouge*

et al. v. Skelly Oil Company, et al. The information contained in the appellees' brief is fundamental for understanding the origins and development of the town. However, one of the fundamental contentions of the appellees was that the town was located on the Cypress Bayou floodplain below the bluffs. Although it is unquestionable that the floodplain was the site of the landing and of at least one warehouse, Gregg expresses clearly that the village of Smithland in 1841 was located on the bluff.

Smithland appears to have derived its name from an early property owner and merchant named George Smith. The site was obviously chosen because of the commercial opportunities offered by waterborne transport. There was a lake-like condition between the foot of Caddo Lake and the confluence of Big and Black Cypress Bayous. The only navigation impediment was the fairly shallow and convoluted area downstream of Smithland known as Dougherty's Defeat. However, whenever steamboats could get into Caddo Lake, they could get as high as Smithland, and the site offered access to a large market area to the north and west.

Above Smithland, the bayou was shallow and much more affected by local rainfall than by backwater from the Red River; and until the end of 1844, it was choked by fallen and standing timber and other debris that prohibited the passage of steamboats. Given the low-water access problems experienced by Jefferson throughout its history, it is obvious that Smithland was a better place for the head of navigation on Cypress Bayou, if navigation conditions alone were the determining factor.

Nevertheless, Gregg recognized that whatever port developed farthest upstream would become the dominant factor in regional trade. This was because steamboats were part of a transportation system that included ox-wagons, which were slow and expensive. Export commodities were almost always taken by ox-wagon to the nearest point that offered water access, and that meant Jefferson rather than Smithland for the vast area extending to the west. Jefferson also came to dominate the northern market area because of the large commercial infrastructure generated by its western markets.

If advertisements are considered an indicator of commercial importance, Smithland, like Benton, was only briefly the center of attention—the February 1842 advertisement for the *Star* was the only one to list Smithland first. Nevertheless, it was always one of the most important points on the route, appearing regularly in steamboat advertisements for Jefferson when Port Caddo and Benton are mentioned, which was common practice before and immediately after the Civil War. It continued to play at least some role in commercial activity until the last steamboats operated on the route.

Smithland achieved prominence before Jefferson. Lt. W. H. Emory's 1844 *Map of Texas and the Countries Adjacent* shows Smithland, Port Caddo, Daingerfield, Marshall, Greenwood, and Shreveport, but not Jefferson. Sidney Morse and Samuel Breese's 1844 *Map of Texas* shows Jefferson as well as Smithland; but Smithland is clearly dominant. Roads lead from Clarksville and DeKalb through Smithland and across Cypress Bayou and down to Marshall. Jefferson stands alone and isolated, suggesting a planned town status **(fig. 8-33)**. There was obviously a ferryboat at Smithland by at least 1844.

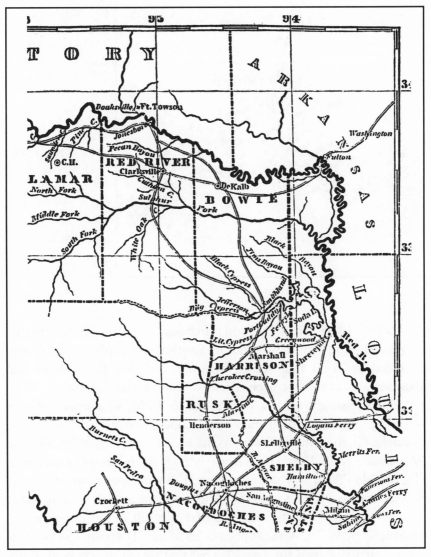

Fig. 8-33. Roads to Smithland. *Source: Historic Jefferson Foundation*

By at least June of 1844, Dr. John Woodley lived in Smithland, practicing medicine and operating a mercantile store with George Smith. When Woodley died in January 1846, his estate was comprised of 1,077 acres of land; personal items such as books; a large lot of medicine, furniture, and stock; and a thoroughbred horse. Smith, who acted as administrator of Woodley's estate, bought the ferry for $11.

263

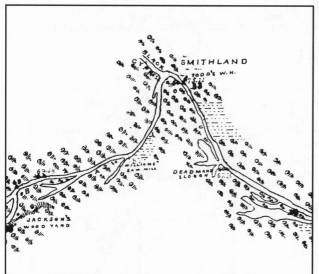

Fig. 8-34.
Smithland. *Source:*
LSU in Shreveport,
Noel Memorial
Library Archives

Early in 1849, James D. Todd purchased 570 acres nearby. He also purchased from Smith two lots in Smithland "south of storehouse occupied by Todd and erected by Smith and Woodley." Smith and Woodley appear to have been strictly in the mercantile business. They rented (or perhaps sold) a warehouse to Todd, who operated as a receiving and forwarding merchant. Todd's warehouse was on the floodplain immediately adjacent to the bayou, as shown on Lt. Eugene Woodruff's 1872 *Map of the Red River Raft Region and Cypress Bayou* (**fig. 8-34**). Todd was shipping cotton out of Smithland under the auspices of his Port Caddo establishment from at least March 1845. This is demonstrated by the fact that the bill of lading signed at Smithland by W. W. Withenbury on 23 March 1845 for 154 bales of cotton carried aboard the *Lama* on her first trip from Jefferson shows the Port Caddo firm of Todd & Brander as the shippers. Todd moved permanently from Port Caddo to Smithland in August 1850.

Todd was the most important businessman in Smithland, where he lived with his wife Susan and their daughters. The 15 June 1849 *Texas Republican* lists Todd as one of the monetary contributors to proposed navigation improvements. In January 1851, Todd posted a letter from Smithland to his daughter Ada in New Orleans, complaining, "I am so annoyed by persons coming in that really I scarcely have time and opportunity wherein to discharge my business duties." The letter was hastily finished and sent aboard the *Echo*, which made many trips to Jefferson during that year and was captained by W. W. Withenbury. In June 1853, Todd and his wife mortgaged their Smithland property, including "open warehouse, ferry boat, ferry privileges, the storehouse and steamboat landing and warehouse privileges."

Smithland is mentioned in the 19 February 1853 *Texas Republican* as one of the places whose planters and merchants should be interested in contributing to navigation improvements and in the 3 December 1853 *Texas Republican* as one of the places whose merchants and shippers should be concerned about a price-fixing scheme by the steamboatmen. The 1859 *Texas Almanac* shows Smithland as exporting 5,000 bales of cotton in 1858. The type of agricultural enterprises served by Todd is suggested by a 7 January 1859 advertisement in the *Texas Republican*:

A FINE PLANTATION FOR RENT.
   THE Plantation of the late J. C. Ward, eight miles east of Jefferson, on the Lake—500 acres cleared and fresh, new fence, elegant framed dwelling house, gin-house, quarters, stables, cribs, orchard, garden, on a public road, and in a fine neighborhood, three miles from the steamboat landing at Smithland. The whole, or a part, will be rented for this year, on very reasonable terms. Apply to Dr. A. S. Johnson, Marshall, or R. H. Ward, Jefferson, Texas.
   N. B. The above place, of 1232 acres, will be sold on good terms. Apply as above.
   January 7th, '59.

There is a long-standing contention that the early residents of Smithland moved to Jefferson at its inception because of a faulty land title. There is nothing in *Thomas Jordan v. Skelly Oil* to suggest that this was the case, and the story probably originated in the move to Jefferson in the 1850s of prominent Smithland merchants such as Todd and John Pitkin. The town grew modestly before the Civil War, and the post office was not discontinued until January 1867. What is surprising is that Smithland managed to survive so long just a few miles downstream from Jefferson. Even the extinction of the post office did not signify the end of Smithland's commercial activity.

According to a bill of lading cited in *Thomas Jordan v. Skelly Oil*, Stevens & Seymour of New Orleans shipped a case of merchandise to S. F. Mosely at the Port of Smithland on 2 May 1866. A freight bill for the estate of W. P. Watson was prepared by the clerk of the *Golden Era* at Smithland on 5 February 1869 (**fig. 8-35**). The *Flavilla* mentions that she passed the *C. H. Durfee* at Smithland in the 24 December 1871 *Shreveport Times*. Smithland is included in all late landings lists and appears on numerous maps.

Verbal evidence in *Thomas Jordan v. Skelly Oil* presented by residents of Smithland from the 1870s and 1880s indicates that the town on the bluff seen by Gregg in 1841 soon became centered on Todd's commercial facilities, most of which were on the floodplain of Big Cypress Bayou near the landing. One of the witnesses, Bennie Johnson, who was born in 1880, remembered the steamboats coming up the bayou: "Why, they stopped there at a landing, my father and mother lived right up there at the foot of the hill, and that steamboat would blow for what we called the Smithland stretch, and I would tear out down the hill, me and the rest of the children, and by the time it got to the landing we would be there. Of course, we wasn't allowed down there where they was working, we had to set up there on the hill."

Anna Emory, born in 1872, remembered the excitement generated by steamboat landings because of the potential for commercial spills:

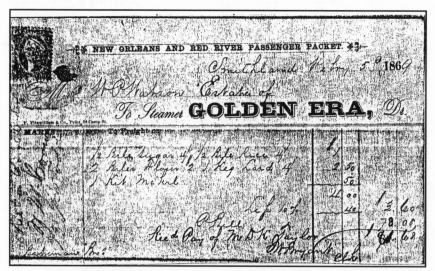

Fig. 8-35. *Golden Era* bill of lading. *Source: Historic Jefferson Foundation*

"We looked at the men rolling the barrels and unloading the different boxes and things they brought up there for Todd's house. We would stand way up on this little hill, wasn't any trees there then, we would stand up there and look at the men rolling those barrels and was happy when one would roll out and bust. Well, when some of them would hit and bust and whatever it was, sugar or apples or things, we was proud to see that. Because they gave us that wasted stuff."

THE PACKERY

The Packery was located a few miles upstream of Smithland and a few miles downstream of Jefferson and is shown on Lt. Eugene Woodruff's 1872 *Map of the Red River Raft Region and Cypress Bayou* (**fig. 8-36**). This was a slaughterhouse and meatpacking plant that imported salt and barrels and exported tremendous quantities of beef and other animal products. Next to cotton, beef and animal products were the most important export commodities from the Jefferson area. A number of packeries were located in the Jefferson area prior to and during the Civil War, the first of which was started by Harvey Black in September 1857. The packery shown on the Woodruff map was the one that played an important role in postwar navigation. It was started by Wilson and Stoner in 1866, continued by Wilson, sold to Elliott, and expired in 1870.

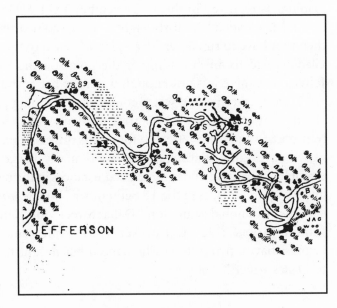

Fig. 8-36. Beef packery. *Source: LSU in Shreveport, Noel Memorial Library Archives*

TEMPORARY LANDINGS

In addition to the permanent ports and landings, there were a number of temporary landings that were used during low-water periods, which generally occurred during the summer. If boats could pass through Soda Lake, they almost always could get at least as far as Smithland because of the lake-like condition and deep water below that point. Above Smithland, the bayou was shallow, and it was usually the case during the summer that boats destined for Jefferson were forced to stop at various points between Smithland and Jefferson, depending on a particular boat's draft and the water level on the bayou at the time of the trip.

One of the most prominent stopping places was only two hundred yards downstream from the wharf, access to which was often blocked during low water by a sandbar that was eventually removed by Jefferson's dredge. An example for an incoming boat is given in the 27 July 1871 *Daily South-Western*, quoting the *Jefferson Times and Republican* of the twenty-fifth: "The bayou has declined in the forty-eight hours ending yesterday evening at 5 o'clock, near one and a half inches. The recent rains have had little or no effect on the falling waters of Cypress bayou. The water is dead low, and the boats find it impossible to get to our wharf. They come as far as the bend, about two hundred yards below town, and there discharge and receive freights."

The stopping place was also used by departing boats to finish loading, as reported in the 19 December 1871 *Shreveport Times*: "It now takes a loaded boat forty-eight hours to come from Jefferson, and then they have to run all the deep places known to the best pilots. The Gladiola had to finish loading at the point on the bayou just below Jefferson as there was not enough water for her at the main wharf."

During extreme low-water conditions, stopping places were used all the way down the bayou to Smithland. That required freight transport to and from Jefferson for points downstream. One approach was to use skiffs, flatboats, and particularly barges. Most of the examples of barging under these circumstances in the navigation record involve up freights, as in the 18 September 1867 *South-Western*, which uses the common designation "Dallas Street" for "Jefferson": "Capt. John T. Roots' sidewheel packet T. D. Hine came in today from Cypress bayou flying light. She barged her freight from the packery to Dallas street."

Freights were also conveyed to and from Jefferson by ox-wagons. There were two roads between Jefferson and Smithland. A normal transport road ran on high ground north of the bayou, and a low-water road hugged the bayou. These roads joined at Black Cypress Bayou, which was crossed by Nesmith's Ferry. The low-water road was used for freight transport during low-water periods because it was contiguous to the bayou with its temporary landings. A portion of this road can be seen as a heavy indentation in the landscape immediately southwest of The Packery property. That it was a low-water road is indicated by the fact that portions are submerged during high-water periods.

There are actually only two examples in the navigation record of ox-wagon transport on the low-water road. The 15 September 1869 *South-Western* reports the following about the *Lotus No. 2* at Shreveport, from Boon's Bend below Jefferson, and on its way to New Orleans: "The Lotus No. 2, Thornton Jacobs, master, Tom Jacobs, clerk, came down from Boon Bend, some three miles below Jefferson, this evening. She brought 30 bales of cotton at $5 per bale. After taking on board at this point 126 bales of cotton at $2, and some 46 head of cattle, she let herself out for the city. Cotton is now hauled from Jefferson to Boon Bend."

Another example—the 26 August 1868 *South-Western*—also mentions the cypress brake on Soda Lake: "The Kouns-Line packet Era No. 8, Capt. Truslow, arrived to-day from Boon Bend, on Cypress bayou, with one bale new cotton. Her officers report scant two feet of water on the 'brake.' Capt. Truslow says he made close connection at Boon Bend with a double-geared ox-wagon for Jefferson, ten miles distant, for the last time this season."

Because the low-water road followed the bayou, and steamboats did not require any infrastructure for the discharge or loading of freight and passengers, boats wishing to use the road for transport of freight to and from Jefferson could stop anywhere. In addition, boats wishing to transport freight by barge had no difficulty in stopping at any point on the confined bayou. As a consequence, the entire stretch between Jefferson and Smithland served as a temporary landing during low-water periods, with boats simply getting as high upstream as they could and then stopping. An example from the 11 December 1867 *South-Western* uses "slaughter house" for "packery": "The Shreveport and Dallas Street packet Flicker, Capt. Wilkinson, arrived to-day from

Cypress bayou, with only a light freight. The Flicker succeeded in reaching a point just above the slaughter-house, which shows that Jefferson is almost accessible to navigation."

The most common practice, however, was for steamboats to stop at designated temporary landings, which are recorded in the Shreveport navigation columns as points for which boats are destined and from which they have returned. Smithland and The Packery became temporary landings for Jefferson freight during low-water periods. Fleta Landing also appears regularly in the navigation record as a low-water landing. Although the evidence for its location is vague and contradictory, it appears to have been fairly close to Jefferson and most probably was just below the shoal in the bayou one-half mile from town.

The most important temporary landings were Boon's Bend and Potato Bend. Boon's Bend was located immediately southeast of The Packery (see fig. 8-36). This bend is currently not a part of Cypress Bayou because it was cut off by Jefferson's dredge in 1872, and this cutoff was improved by the Corps of Engineers in the late 1880s. Potato Bend was immediately southwest of The Packery and is identified on Woodruff's map (see fig. 8-36). It is currently not part of Cypress Bayou because it was cut off by Jefferson's dredge in 1871.

An example of departure for Boon's Bend appears in the 22 September 1869 *South-Western*: "The fleet and high-headed George let herself out this evening with a fine trip for Jefferson. Capt. Jim only contracts to 'stand and deliver' at Boon Bend. For an additional consideration he *might* be induced to barge up to the city." An example of return from Potato Bend appears in the 3 November 1869 *South-Western*, which uses "Esculent Bend" as an equivalent for "Potato Bend": "Early this morning the low water packet Fleta, Capt. Wm. Gillen, A. C. Green, clerk, came in from Esculent Bend with 330 bales of cotton belonging to the Dallas street merchants."

WOODYARDS

In addition to the permanent and temporary landings, there were three woodyards along the route. Steamboats burned wood at a fairly rapid rate, and it was necessary to replenish stocks about every 150–200 miles. These three woodyards were evenly distributed along the route, with one above Shreveport, one below Jefferson, and one in the center at the head of Caddo Lake. These operated twenty-four hours a day, because steamboats traveled at all hours of the day and night.

The lowest of these was Williams' Woodyard. In Lt. Eugene Woodruff's 1873 survey report on the Red River and Cypress Bayou, his assistant, H. C. Collins, indicates that Williams' Woodyard was on Twelvemile Bayou at the head of Cross Lake, obviously referring to The Pass, which was the hydrologic connection with Soda Lake and is marked as Cross Lake on various maps. The second woodyard upstream was Mound Woodyard, which is shown on Woodruff's 1872 map (**fig. 8-37**). The one closest to Jefferson was Jackson's Woodyard, which is shown halfway between Smithland and The Packery (**fig. 8-38**).

Glenn's 1879 landings list includes English's Woodyard and Jackson's Woodyard. English's is listed between Port Caddo and Benton and apparently was a late facility. Willard's 1893 report used Keene's Woodyard as a survey benchmark site. This appears to have been a successor to Jackson's Woodyard.

There are no accounts of any steamboats stopping at woodyards along the route. Their importance and some idea of the frequency of refueling can be gained from a *Bart Able* memorandum for a quick 690-mile trip, as given in the 29 April 1868 *South-Western*: "Left New Orleans Tuesday evening at 20 minutes past 5 o'clock; landed at Baton

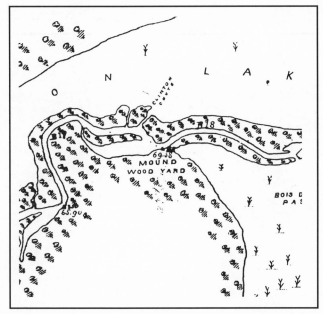

Fig. 8-37. Mound Woodyard. *Source: LSU in Shreveport, Noel Memorial Library Archives*

Rouge twice; landed at Lobdell's store and took on board fifty cords wood; at the mouth of Red river took on board freight and passengers; landed at Barbin's, S. K. Johnson's and reached Alexandria at 25 minutes past 12 o'clock; landed at Durant's and reached Grand Ecore at 25 minutes past 9 o'clock; wooded at Campte and put off freight at Armstead's, and reached Grand bayou at 5 minutes past 4 o'clock; put off freight at Marston's, Powell's, George Robinson's and wooded at Lattier's, reaching Shreveport at 10 minutes past 4 o'clock on the morning of the 24th, making the time from port to port in 58 hours and 50 minutes—the quickest time on record."

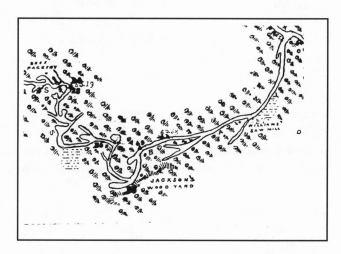

Fig. 8-38. Jackson's Woodyard. *Source: LSU in Shreveport, Noel Memorial Library Archives*

·9·
The
Route

OVERVIEW

The paths taken by steamboats engaged in trade west of Shreveport included the main route to Jefferson as well as the secondary routes to Monterey and Clinton. The upper terminus of the main route was the turning basin at Jefferson. No steamboat ever went above Jefferson, although there is evidence for intermittent use of Cypress Bayou above Jefferson by smaller craft for downstream transport of commodities when roads were impassable. The secondary route to Clinton split off from the main route on Cypress Bayou near Mound Pond and terminated at the northern edge of Clinton Lake. The secondary route to Monterey split off from the main route in Caddo Lake and proceeded up to the northern end of the flooded portion of Jim's Bayou.

The route developed over time. The first leg through Twelvemile Bayou and Soda Lake was established by Washington Seawell in 1828–31 and was first used by the *Enterprise* in 1831. However, this portion of the route was developed in conjunction with the upper Red River trade. The portion of the main route up to Port Caddo was in service by at least 1840; but the full route was not functional until the arrival of the *Lama* at the town site of Jefferson in March 1845, enabled by the bayou-clearing efforts of William Perry in late 1844. The channels to Monterey and Clinton do not appear to have become part of the route until the late 1840s.

Throughout most of its history, the route to Jefferson was part of much larger routes. From the beginning, Jefferson and the other ports and landings along the route were part of the commercial activity of New Orleans. Boats from New Orleans traveled west of Shreveport and then returned to New Orleans, or else offloaded or loaded at Shreveport to and from boats operating to the west. In either case, the Jefferson trade was part of the New Orleans trade, incorporating the Mississippi and Red Rivers. In the 1870s, the Midwestern cities of St. Louis and Cincinnati became important factors in the Jefferson trade, tying the route to the upper Mississippi and its tributaries. By the 1880s, with the decline of steamboat activity, the route became largely a regional stream, with boats operating locally out of Shreveport to places like Mooringsport.

From the late 1830s through the early 1870s, the first leg of the route played double duty, accommodating boats moving north to the upper Red River, as well as boats moving to points west of Shreveport up to Jefferson. This unified path included Twelvemile Bayou and Soda Lake. At the head of Soda Lake, boats heading west went through Big Willow Pass into Caddo Lake. Boats heading north split off into Stumpy Bayou, thence into Clear Lake, Black Bayou, Seawell's Canal, and Red Bayou, then back into the Red River above the raft. There were also modifications to this northern route as the raft moved upstream. With the removal of the raft in 1873, it was no longer necessary for upper Red River boats to share the first leg of the route with those engaged in the Jefferson trade.

The route to Jefferson was modified over time by cutroads and cutoffs. Cutoffs involved excavation across narrow points of land to bypass convoluted bends. The most important cutoffs before 1873 were the upper and lower Benton cutoffs, which were made by William Perry in the late 1850s, and the Potato Bend and Boon's Bend cutoffs between Jefferson and Smithland, which were made by Jefferson's dredge in 1871 and 1872, respectively. A series of cutoffs, as well as improvements to the existing cutoffs, was made by the Corps of Engineers in the 1870s and 1880s, including Government Ditch at the northern end of Caddo Lake. However, the Corps cutoffs did not play an important role in steamboat activity, which had entered a state of rapid decline.

During low-water periods, in-stream trees (primarily cypress) were cut down to the low-water level. When the water rose, boats could pass over the stumps, saving valuable travel time. These stump passes were called cutroads. The most important cutroads were Martin's Cutroad in the Albany Flats area and Withenbury Cutroad at the northern end of Caddo Lake. Both of these cutroads were made by Capt. Robert H. Martin at the end of 1854 under a contract to clear the route from Albany to Port Caddo. There were also numerous minor cutroads in Soda Lake and Caddo Lake. It can be assumed that there was an important cutroad from Bois d'Arc Pass down to Withenbury Cutroad, probably also made by Martin in 1854.

These improvements reduced the length of the route significantly. An 1880 Corps report on the improvement of Cypress Bayou lists the cutoffs and indicates that they produced a reduction in the distance from Shreveport to Jefferson from ninety-six to sixty-five miles. Because these figures do not include the cutroads, it can be assumed that the pre-improvement route was ninety-six actual river miles. And, because the cutroads and probably Perry's Benton cutoffs could not be used during low water, it can be assumed that the low-water channel was approximately ninety-six miles long throughout the decades when the route was most heavily used by steamboats.

The route should not be thought of as a static line that was affected only by navigation improvements. Significant variations in the route were produced by water level fluctuations, which were seasonally dependent. During the higher water periods, boats could enter Soda Lake through Cross Lake rather than Twelvemile Bayou, run Martin's Cutroad at Albany Flats and Withenbury Cutroad at the northern end of Caddo Lake, and enter Cypress Bayou through Bois d'Arc Pass. During lower water periods, boats were generally confined to Twelvemile Bayou and to the old channel of Cypress Bayou beneath Soda and Caddo Lakes.

The navigation columns of the Shreveport newspapers offer a running commentary on the changing nature of the route. A few examples will be used to suggest seasonally induced route variations:

> There appears to be no end to the water that has fallen about Jefferson. . . . The lakes this side are plumb full and rising fast. There is no trouble about navigation, as boats can run anywhere. (*Shreveport Times*, 3 April 1875)
> The lakes, bayous, lagoons, etc., this side are falling fast and will soon be too low for the largest class of boats to run the

high water channel, that is to take the straight chute across the lakes. Of course the serpentine route will still be available for some time yet. (*Shreveport Times*, 8 May 1875)

The officers of the Durfee, the last boat out from Jefferson, report the bayous and lakes falling, with five feet in Cypress Bayou, three feet eight inches in Bois d'Arc Pass, and three and a half feet over the stumps in the cut road across Albany Point. . . . Loaded boats now have to follow the channel through the lakes, which makes it slow and tedious work. (*Shreveport Times*, 29 February 1872)

The route taken by any particular boat was heavily dependent on the water level conditions, but also on the size and draft of the boat, the weight of her load, and the risk-taking propensities of her captain. A particular boat might take alternate routes on the up and down trips, and boats with differing loads and dimensions might follow different variations of the route at the same time, as in this example from the 30 March 1873, *Shreveport Times*: "Mr. Ike Hunter, pilot of the Belle Rowland, reports three feet four inches on the Albany flats and the water falling. . . . The Belle Rowland, Bossier and Clifford came out light, and run the cutroad across Albany point. The Lotus No. 3 had part of a load, and had to run the channel around it."

In addition to path variations, the character of the route changed dramatically with water level fluctuations. The 11 April 1872 *Shreveport Times* reports "oceans of water in the lakes for any kind of steamer." The issue for the thirteenth describes the quality of the route: "Our largest class of boats with full loads find no trouble in running all the cut-offs and short cuts, plantations and forests between here and Jefferson. No land in sight on the route after leaving Albany, till Dallas street looms in the distance." The 23 December 1871 *Shreveport Times* describes the other side of the coin: "Between this city and Jefferson there is a wide expanse of shallow water interspersed with deep holes, bayous, islands, morasses, and dead cypress which gives the boats or rather the officers a great deal of trouble. When the water is high they skim the surface like a gull, but unfortunately such is not the case now. The water is low and navigation slow and tedious. Mud is not yet well adapted to steamboat navigation, and we doubt very much that it ever will be."

With the advent of low water, which usually occurred during the summer, the operational length of the route contracted and Jefferson was no longer the head of navigation. The formal inception of low-water navigation was defined by the 18 August 1869 *South-Western* as thirty-three inches at Albany Flats. This was the point at which the normal class of boats dropped out of the Jefferson trade, which was then dominated by the low-water craft. When water levels decreased to thirty inches at Albany Flats, Jefferson was still accessible to a small class of boats with light loads according to the 25 August 1869 *South-Western*.

However, when there was twenty-six inches on Albany Flats, steamboats were no longer able to reach Jefferson according to the 8 September 1869 *South-Western*. At this stage of water, steamboats began stopping at various points below Jefferson. The point of stoppage moved progressively downstream as water levels became even lower, with variances depending on the running drafts of particular boats. As steamboats stopped at various points below Jefferson, up freights and down freights were transported by water to and from Jefferson by barges, flatboats, and skiffs and by land on a low-water road that ran on the north side of the bayou at least as far down as Smithland, six miles below Jefferson.

During extreme low-water periods, the route was converted into a non-route. These were the periods when there was "not enough water to float a mud turtle in the lakes" (*South-Western*, 16 September 1868), Jefferson was said to be "still accessible by water to skiffs and catfish" (*South-Western*, 15 November 1865), and the bayou at Jefferson was said to be "too low yesterday for any purpose whatever, except perhaps for tadpoles to change into frogs" (*Shreveport Times*, 14 October 1875). The consequences, as recorded by the 8 October 1875, *Shreveport Times*, were predictable: "The Jeff. Jimp. has dropped the water question and taken up with—something else. The bayou has ceased to be navigable and the cows that feed along the margins of the lake now give pure milk. There is no water in that section of the country to dilute it. At Mooringsport the smell of whiskey is so strong that the smell of it ten miles off gets a man intoxicated—no water in the lakes is given as the cause."

The route west of Shreveport was essentially a mixed bayou and lake route, or, in the more elaborate language of the 19 June 1875 *Shreveport Times*, a series of "lakes, bayous, swamps, low places, sloughs, mud puddles, duck ponds, meadows, creeks, rivulets, standing water, stagnant pools, etc." There are no good overall descriptions of this route. The principal reason is that the initial federal survey of Cypress Bayou and the lakes, which was conducted in 1871–72, encountered difficulties with the field crew and was provided insufficient funds to determine the steamboat routes through the lakes. The main channel through the lakes was first delineated by Capt. Eric Bergland of the Corps of Engineers in 1885, and the accompanying report by Assistant Engineer F. S. Burrows presents the only systematic description, unfortunately in a brief and highly technical form and for the post-improvement route.

Other federal and state reports offer brief observations on various components of the route. Boat memoranda are few and brief and contain little in the way of route description. There are also a few letters and reminiscences that provide some useful insights. J. Frank Glenn's 1886 "Private Memoranda" contain an elaborate description of the stream portions of the route, but the observations are largely restricted to channel configurations. As a consequence, the features of the route must be reconstructed from bits and pieces of information, primarily from the navigation columns, supplemented by map evidence.

Traditionally, the route has been divided into four segments, which were delineated by Lt. Eugene Woodruff in his 1873 report on Cypress Bayou: (1) Twelvemile Bayou, from Shreveport to the foot of Soda Lake; (2) Soda Lake to the head of Willow Pass, at the foot of Fairy Lake; (3) Fairy Lake to Bois d'Arc Pass, or mouth of Cypress Bayou; and (4) Bois d'Arc Pass to Jefferson. Woodruff also points out that the division would be somewhat different in terms of slackwater conditions, because the level of Fairy (Caddo) Lake extended up to Smithland, above which the bayou was not directly connected with water levels on the lake. The following description of the route will provide a more segmented delineation and will conclude with the secondary routes to Monterey and Clinton.

SHREVEPORT TO SODA LAKE

Boats leaving Shreveport and heading toward Cypress Bayou and the lakes could take either of two paths depending on water conditions. During high-water and low-water periods, Soda Lake was accessible through Twelvemile Bayou. During high-water periods, Soda Lake was also accessible through Cross Bayou and Cross Lake. The latter passage owed its existence to the peculiar circumstances afforded by the raft.

Cross Lake was one of the five lakes produced by the raft at the end of the 1700s. Like Caddo Lake, it formed in an old stream valley, in this case the valley of Cross Bayou. When the lake came into existence, most of the bayou was submerged, with the exception of the downstream portion that flowed past the bluffs on which Shreveport came to be located.

During the 1800s, Cross Lake was hydrologically connected with the lower end of Soda Lake at the boundary line between Townships 18 and 19 North, as shown on Arthur Veatch's 1899 reconstruction of the situation in 1839 (fig. 9-1). Today, Cross Lake terminates on the east about four miles below that point. This connection was not a channel, but rather a floodway on the Red River floodplain squeezed between the natural levee of old Twelvemile Bayou on the east and the

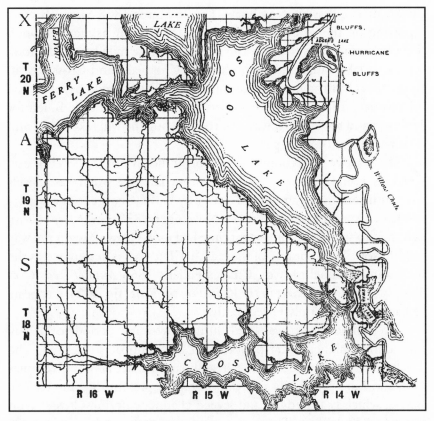

Fig. 9-1. Cross Lake and The Pass. *Source: Louisiana Geological Survey Report No. 4, 1899*

bluffs to the west on which the North Highlands and Cooper Road residential areas are presently located. The western arm of this floodway, as shown on the Veatch map, was the valley of present-day McCain Creek.

During low-water periods, this area was completely dry. During moderate to high-water periods, more water went through this area (and out through Cross Bayou to the Red River) than through Twelvemile Bayou and Red River combined. It was during these moderate to high-water periods that the area was usable by steamboats, and it was appropriately designated "The Pass." The Pass was simply the northeast arm of Cross Lake; therefore, it could be designated either way on maps.

The Pass was a navigation route from the earliest days, having been used by Capt. George Birch in 1825 for skiff passage during the first federal survey of the area. There are only two newspaper accounts of the use of The Pass by steamboats. The 25 March 1868 *South-Western*, reporting on the *Lizzie Hopkins* as she moved downstream through Soda Lake, indicates that "At the head of Twelve mile bayou she took the Cross lake chute and came through Cross lake and Cross bayou, thus cutting off the now dangerous part of Twelve mile bayou." The 23 February 1882 *Shreveport Times* reports that the "Lessie B. left for Jefferson and the lakes by way of Cross Bayou. She will take a route no boat has taken for years past."

The scarcity of accounts is probably indicative of the level of use. Currents would have been too swift within The Pass when water levels were sufficient for steamboats. A letter by W. W. George, a Shreveport resident, that appeared in the 12 November 1858 *Texas Republican* says that no steamboat up to that time had used Cross Lake on the way to Jefferson. Thus, in spite of the fact that The Pass is designated as the high-water channel on Col. Charles Fuller's 1855 *Map of Red River With Its Bayous and Lakes in the Vicinity of the Raft* (**fig. 9-2**), it appears to have been used only infrequently.

Twelvemile Bayou was used during low-water periods or at any time during higher water periods that a steamboat so desired. The Twelvemile Bayou used by the steamboats was actually twelve miles long and bore practically no relationship to present-day Twelvemile Bayou, which is a dredged and leveed channel entering Cross Bayou instead of Red River. The upper portion of present-day Twelvemile Bayou was nonexistent during the steamboat period, the area at that

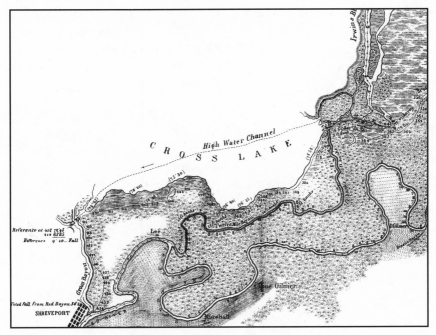

Fig. 9-2. Twelvemile Bayou and The Pass. *Source: S. Ex. Doc. 62, 33rd Cong., 2nd Sess.*

time being occupied by Soda Lake. The lower portion of present-day Twelvemile Bayou is much more closely associated with The Pass than with the historic Twelvemile Bayou.

The upper end of Twelvemile Bayou terminated at the lower end of Soda Lake. Where Soda Lake left off and Twelvemile Bayou began was variable, depending on the amount of water in the lake. During higher water periods, the upper end of Twelvemile Bayou was submerged beneath Soda Lake, with this portion of the channel reappearing during low-water periods. Technically, Soda Lake actually began above the Albany Flats area where there was no indication of any defined channel; but the technical aspects of the hydrologic differentiation were of no interest to steamboatmen who, because of the changing nature of the upstream end, generally envisioned Twelvemile Bayou as originating below Albany Landing on Soda Lake.

The lower end of Twelvemile Bayou has had a complex history (**fig. 9-3**). As shown on Fuller's 1855 map, the bayou originally entered the Red River about 3½ river miles above the confluence with Cross Bayou. The bend of the Red River into which Twelvemile Bayou

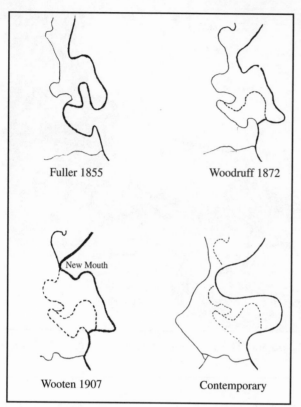

Fig. 9-3. Changes in the mouth of Twelvemile Bayou

Fuller 1855

Woodruff 1872

New Mouth

Wooten 1907

Contemporary

emptied was cut off by a canal at least as early as 1868, because it is shown on Alban and Oliver's *Route to Surround Red River Raft*, and the southern portion of the bend became the downstream portion of Twelvemile Bayou, as shown on Lt. Eugene Woodruff's *Map of the Red River Raft Region and Cypress Bayou*. By 1907, according to Capt. W. P. Wooten's *Cypress Bayou & the Lakes*, a new mouth for Twelvemile Bayou was established above the original mouth by an invasion of the Red River. The present channel enters into Cross Bayou through a manmade diversion.

In spite of these changes, the route taken by steamboats never changed and is shown on Fuller's map **(see fig. 9-2)**. The post-Civil War cutoff simply transformed a portion of Red River into a portion of Twelvemile Bayou. It did not affect the movement of boats. The position of the old channel can be seen by comparing Fuller's map to a modern topographic map **(fig. 9-4)**. The Twelvemile Bayou used by the steamboats is the relict channel generally to the east of present-day

Fig. 9-4. Relict
channel of
Twelvemile Bayou

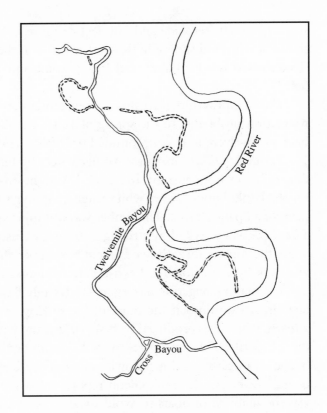

Twelvemile Bayou. The 1907 invasion by the Red River is clearly shown. The lower loop of the relict channel is actually the pre–Civil War bed of the Red River.

Twelvemile Bayou during the steamboat period was not an easy passage. During the lower water periods, it was the sole discharge channel for Soda Lake. Because the Red River was blocked by the raft, most of its water was forced through Soda Lake. H. C. Collins reported in 1873 on the basis of a survey conducted during moderately high water stages that Twelvemile Bayou was about eight times larger than the Red River above the river's juncture with the bayou. This produced a very deep and swift stream with a minimum low-water depth of four feet.

The bayou ran through the alluvial plain of the Red River. The channel was wide (between 200 and 400 feet) and crooked, with large deep places at the bends. The alluvial banks were perpendicular, timbered, and constantly caving, according to H. C. Collins, in "great strips 10 or 20 feet wide and 100 feet or more in length, cracking on the back edge and sliding in slowly, the trees on the bank all getting a slant toward the land side, and finally going into the channel roots first."

The swiftness of the stream and bank and in-stream timber caused navigation problems. In the spring of 1845, the *Cotton Plant* hit the bank in Twelvemile Bayou, rounded broadside, and listed. In January 1867, the *L. Dillard* lost most of her wheel by hitting the bank in a four-mile-per-hour current. In March 1868, the *Fannie Gilbert* "made for the bank, knocking her white-ringed chimneys into the shape and form of a Spanish cross. The timber was not injured in the least." The *Lizzie Lee* was wrecked by striking a stump or cluster of logs six miles above the confluence with Red River in November 1856, and the *Albany* was sunk by a raft floating downstream in August 1878.

The major navigation hazard in Twelvemile Bayou appears to have been in-stream timber, the cause of the sinking of the *Lizzie Lee* and *Albany*, which was produced by bank caving and winds, as reported by the 21 April 1872 *Shreveport Times*: "The timber along Twelve Mile bayou was nearly all blown down, and a good deal in the way of the boats." Although J. Frank Glenn reports a few dangerous stumps, it was the inability of boats to avoid snags in swift currents that caused the major problems, as was the case for the *Gossamer* in September 1868: "the Captain reports Twelve mile bayou in an awful stage of navigation, the current running very swift and the snags as thick as bristles on a hog's back."

SODA LAKE

Cross Lake and Caddo Lake formed in the valleys of Cross Bayou and Cypress Bayou. Soda Lake, Shifttail Lake, and Clear Lake formed in Red River floodplain depressions and therefore were much shallower. Prior to the influence of the raft, the area that came to be occupied by Soda Lake was an intermittent lake formed by spring floods on the Red River. It did not become a permanent lake until the raft caused a permanent diversion of water to the west of the river through distributaries that emptied into the Soda Lake area.

The 1857 report of the Louisiana state engineer correctly characterizes Soda Lake as a mere overflowing bayou. Its southwestern perimeter was fixed by the Albany line of bluffs, but its northeastern

perimeter varied with the amount of water entering the lake through
Willow Pass. As a consequence, the shape of the lake differs in map
representations, depending on the water levels encountered during a
particular survey. Fuller's 1855 map compared to Lt. Eugene
Woodruff's 1872 *Map of the Red River Raft Region and Cypress Bayou*
can serve as an example **(fig. 9-5)**.

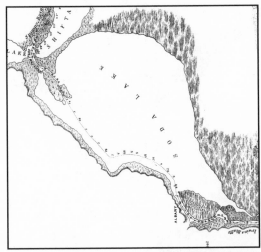

Fig. 9-5. Soda Lake
delineations. *Sources: S. Ex.
Doc. 62, 33rd Cong., 2nd
Sess. (left) and LSU in
Shreveport, Noel Memorial
Library Archives (bottom)*

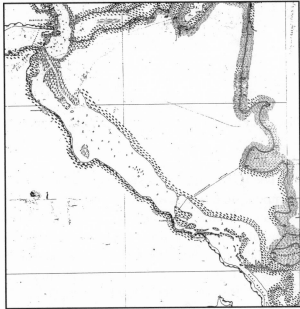

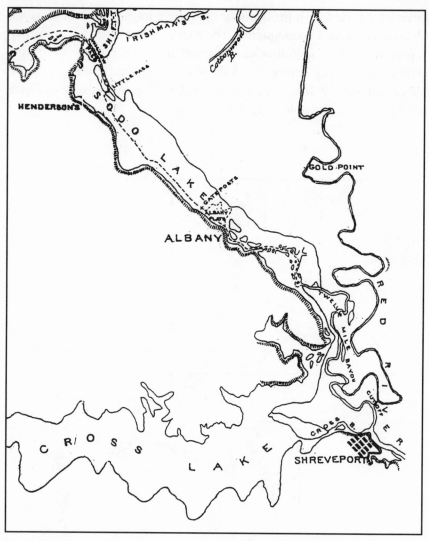

Fig. 9-6. Albany Flats. *Source: H. Ex. Doc. 103, 48ᵗʰ Cong., 2ⁿᵈ Sess.*

The lake formed in a swamp; it was filled with cypress trees and stumps. There were oak trees and oak stumps on the northeastern perimeter derived from the original forests on the Red River floodplain. Soda Lake was filled with mud because it was the main settling basin for Red River sediments. These sediment deposits ranged from six inches to one foot in the vicinity of the Indian mounds at the northeastern perimeter to several feet in the lake proper.

The upper end of Soda Lake began at the foot of Big Willow Pass, which was occupied by islands. At the foot of Little Willow Pass, there was a bar with a depth of about two feet at low water. The water then spread out into a broad, stump-infested area about five miles long with a low-water depth of about three to five feet, no channel, and an imperceptible current. At the lower end of this area, there was a mudbar about one mile across known as Albany Flats that was covered with only one foot of water during low-water periods. The flats are designated on Capt. Eric Bergland's 1885 *Map of Cypress Bayou and the Lakes* (**fig. 9-6**).

At the northwestern edge of Albany Flats, the channel of Twelvemile Bayou began to appear, running to the north of the flats in an arc about two miles in length, with a low-water depth of about two feet. Below the flats, Twelvemile Bayou captured all of the water in the lake during low-water periods and was about two hundred feet wide and four to six feet deep.

Technically, Soda Lake ended at Albany Flats where the channel of Twelvemile Bayou became perceptible. However, during normal water periods and above, the channel was submerged beneath the lake. As a consequence, map representations generally show the lake extending down to the area of The Pass, with Twelvemile Bayou relegated to the area below that point (**see fig. 9-6**).

Boats moving upstream on Soda Lake always used the channel of Twelvemile Bayou in the lower portion of the lake. On reaching the Albany Flats area, which was slightly upstream of Albany Landing, a decision had to be made. In 1854, a steamboat captain named Martin, operating under contract, cut the cypress trees on Albany Flats down during low water, leaving stumps about fifty-four inches high in places. During high-water periods, steamboats could pass through the cutroad over the submerged stumps. During low-water periods, it was necessary to take the channel of Twelvemile Bayou in the arc around the flats, as reported in the 17 March 1872 *Shreveport Times*: "We learn from the officers of the Belle Rowland that navigation between this and Jefferson is slow and tedious work, particularly for a loaded boat. In the cut road across Albany point there are but twenty-six inches of steamboat water. This forces the boats to follow the serpentine channel around."

The cutroad is not named on any maps or in any federal reports, and it is almost always referred to simply as "the cutroad" in the navigation columns. However, it was also known by the name of its maker, as indicated by the 21 February 1872 *Shreveport Times*: "The navigation between this point and Jefferson is pretty good. At least one would think so if he believed all he saw and heard. As long as it suits those most interested, it is not in our province to meddle with it one way or the other, but simply to state facts. At last accounts, per steamer Maria Louise, Cypress bayou, Ferry lake, Willow Pass, Soda lake, Martin's cutroad, Holden cut-off, Keel-boat pass, Houghton's chute, Bois d'Arc pass, three or four blind bayous, and twelve mile bayou were falling slowly, with four feet large over the stumps, logs and other obstructions in the cutroad across the Albany Point. Boats now make the trip down in the usual time, fifteen to eighteen hours."

At the northwest corner of Albany Flats, the channel of Twelvemile Bayou met the high-water channel through the cutroad and the standard route through the upper end of the lake. At this point there was a prominent cypress stump about ten and one-half feet high called the Gate Post. For boats moving upstream during low-water periods, the Gate Post served as the pivot point at the upper end of the arc, pointing the way through the upper end of the lake. For boats moving downstream, the Gate Post was marked to enable boats to determine whether there was sufficient water to move through the cutroad. The markings did not show actual water levels, but rather the depth of water over the stumps with about ten inches deleted to insure clearance.

For boats moving upstream, information on the appropriate route for a particular boat was probably obtained at Albany. The Gate Post markings were needed by boats moving downstream because there was no landing above the flats from which information could be obtained on water levels. The reason for the name was that the cutroad was envisioned as a gate swinging on a post and scribing the arc of Twelvemile Bayou around the flats. During high water, the gate was open, and boats passing upstream and downstream through the cutroad were described as going through the gate, as in the 14 November 1866, *South-Western*: "Capt. Ben. Bonham's Gossamer plumed her wings to-day and took a flight to Jefferson with a first-rate trip of freight. She goes through the 'gate' that you read about, but not the one Peter holds the keys of. The Goosehammer is full-fledged—not a pin feather in sight."

Above Albany Flats, it was a straight shot across Soda Lake into Little Willow Pass during both high-water and low-water periods. All technical reports are in agreement that there was no channel in the

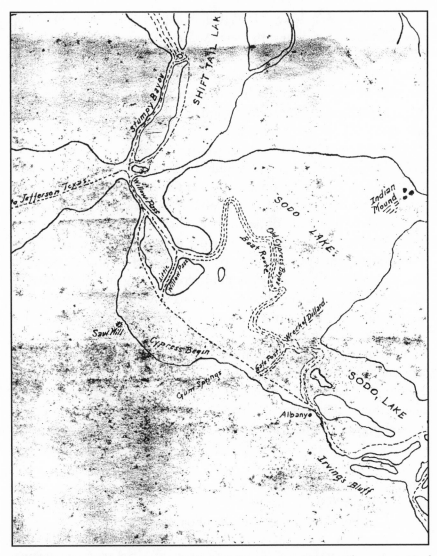

Fig. 9-7. Alternate boat route in Soda Lake. *Source: LSU in Shreveport, Noel Memorial Library Archives*

upper half of Soda Lake. Nevertheless, Alban and Oliver in a map produced in conjunction with their 1868 Louisiana contract to develop a route around the raft show an Old Cypress Bayou boat route in the upper half of the lake (**fig. 9-7**). Although there are no newspaper accounts of any steamboats having used a channel in this area, the Alban and Oliver map was professionally done, and the status of this upper channel remains a mystery.

The Albany Flats area, which was described in the 21 December 1871 *Shreveport Times* as "a muddy bottom, thickly sprinkled with stumps," was the critical point on the entire route. If boats could get past this area, they could almost always reach the vicinity of Jefferson. Even small boats could not begin to use the cutroad unless there was a water depth of at least six feet over the flats, which provided sixteen inches of clearance over the stumps. The channel around the flats did not offer much of an improvement, considering it was filled with sediment and provided only one additional foot of depth.

Running the gate in anything less than high water was called "stumping it," as in the 4 November 1868 *South-Western*: "the No. 8 stumped it a good deal in coming out. The stumps are thick in the lake, and when the mark on the Gate Post indicates thirty inches in the lake no pilot knows where they are until he runs the stem of his boat against them." Under such circumstances, the editor of the navigation column suggests caution, as in the 12 August 1871 *Daily South-Western*:

> Our language is plain;
>> Don't run the cut-roads
> Or you'll be to blame
>> For the damage the steamboat incurs.

Such cautioning was seldom heeded. The 20 December 1871 *Shreveport Times* reports that a boat drawing five feet went over Albany Flats at three feet six inches over the stumps and that the captain said that "he drove her through six inches of mud and liked to have knocked her bottom out on the stumps." The 15 April 1873 *Shreveport Times* provides the following account: "The officers of the C. H. Durfee report thirty-three inches on the Albany flats. The Durfee was drawing that much and dragged through the mud."

The low-water channel around the flats posed its own set of hazards: it was shallow, stump infested, and described as "crooked as a ram's horn." This "serpentine channel" was avoided whenever possible in favor of the cutroad and could only be threaded by an expert when the water in the channel was reduced to three and a half feet. The captain of the *Col. A. P. Kouns* proved himself to be such an expert when the water in the channel reached three feet in September 1875: "there was water enough for the Kouns to crawl along, provided the Captain be a good Christian and don't say any cuss words."

In addition to mud, stumps, and low water, wind was a complicating factor on the shallow lakes of the area for high-profile, lightweight steamboats. Wind problems on the lakes are usually discussed generically, as in the 24 January 1866 *South-Western*: "The prevailing high winds have interfered materially with steamboat navigation, particularly on the lakes, where boats have had to lay up two or three days, waiting for the wind to fall." The 23 December 1871 *Shreveport Times* observes: "With the high winds and low water the boats have a hard time of it in the lakes." The issue of the twenty-fourth states succinctly: "Low water and high winds are death on navigation to Jefferson."

There are only two specific accounts of wind problems on Soda Lake. The first is in a report on the *Starlight* by John Shute, captain of the *Cuba No. 2*, in the 23 January 1867 *South-Western*: "The Cuba drew only three feet and came through the lakes without any detention. She passed the Starlight hard and fast aground just above Albany. From Capt. Shute we learn that the Starlight had laid up for the night, but that a heavy wind broke her from her moorings and blowed her out of the channel. Doubts are expressed whether her officers will be able to get her off before another rise. One of her officers is here now for the purpose of procuring a steamboat to lighter her off." The second account of wind problems on Soda Lake was published by the *Jefferson Democrat* and picked up by the 10 February 1872 *Shreveport Times*: "The Jefferson Democrat of the 8th, speaking of the storm on the lake Monday night says, the May Lowry encountered it near Albany and came near being wrecked. As it was, the water ran completely over her; her upper deck was badly broken in, and Capt. Boley himself blown overboard twice. The first time he succeeded in getting on a part of the wreck and the second time he was picked up by a yawl."

The Albany Flats area, including the cutroad and the bypass channel, was distinguished for its wrecks, groundings, stump hangups, and delays; it was also the place where lightening and offloading were commonly used to enable boats to squeak through or free themselves when they were caught on a stump or mudbar. It tested the mettle and skill of captains and pilots and the durability of boats and provided clear demonstrations of the extremely shallow drafts of many of the boats that operated in the direction of Jefferson. And it was the place that determined whether the route to Jefferson was open or closed.

WILLOW PASSES

At the northern end of Soda Lake, boats entered Little Willow Pass and then Big Willow Pass (**fig. 9-8**). From Big Willow Pass, boats traveling to the upper Red River entered Stumpy Bayou, which led into Clear Lake. Boats heading for points west entered Caddo Lake.

At its foot, Caddo Lake debouched into the Red River floodplain through bluffs only 1,480 yards apart. This discharge was immediately met by the Stumpy Bayou and Shifttail Lake drainage, which received all of the waters diverted by the raft on the Red River. As a consequence, Big Willow Pass was the collecting point for flows from the north and west, with a channel about two miles long and 300 feet wide and a usual depth of from 20 to 30 feet.

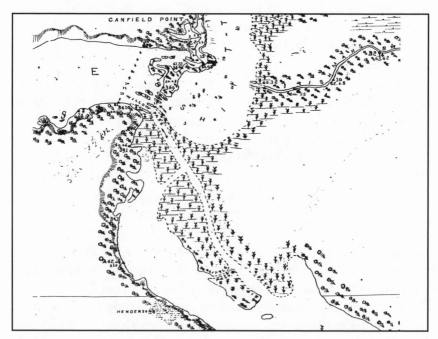

Fig. 9-8. Willow Passes. *Source: LSU in Shreveport, Noel Memorial Library Archives*

Little Willow Pass was about one-half mile long and 200 feet wide. It was also deep but not as deep as Big Willow, which discharged into Soda Lake through channels other than Little Willow. At the foot of Little Willow Pass, there was a bar that caused considerable difficulties, as reported by the 17 March 1872 *Shreveport Times*: "At the mouth of Little Pass there are scant four feet. Boats drawing over that have to be lighted or pull like blazes over logs, stumps, and other obstructions to navigation."

The only description of the area of the passes is given in the 1858 annual report of the Louisiana Board of Swamp Land Commissioners: "The 'Willow Pass' is the only inlet to Soda Lake. It is formed by the simultaneous junction of the waters from Fairy and Cypress Bayou; the Stumpy Bayou, the outlet of Clear Lake; and those of Shift-tail Lake, and is a deep, broad, but sluggish stream. Its banks are low, and the water, even at moderate stages, spreads itself far and wide over the contiguous overflow."

There were only a few stumps in Big Willow Pass and a few more in Little Willow Pass. The depth of water and wideness of the streams allowed fairly easy passage. The only reported difficulty in the passes proper was the June 1856 wreck of the *De De* on a stump in Big Willow Pass. This was during a low-water period when the channel contained only five feet of water. Nevertheless, care needed to be exercised for safe passage, as suggested by J. Frank Glenn's detailed pilot memoranda on stretches, bends, and points to be considered during movement through the passes:

    1. Long Gradual.
    2. Long Round.
    3. Short.
    4. To right of towhead.
    5. False.
    6. False.
       Double opening, on Left.
    7. Little Double.
       Bayou on right.
       "Long Reach."

CADDO LAKE

Caddo Lake was formed in 1800 in the broad, flat-bottomed, forested valley of Cypress Valley. Water levels during the 1800s were generally somewhat higher than they are today and particularly distinguished by violent seasonal water-level fluctuations. The lake was fed by the Cypress Bayou drainage, by its own tributaries, and in part by the Red River. Red River water passing down Stumpy Bayou actually entered the lake at times, dumping sediment in the lower end of the lake and occasionally inducing an upstream current as far as the Texas line. The major function of Red River water, however, was to exert backwater pressure on the Cypress Bayou drainage, thereby functioning as a hydrologic dam.

When the lake came into existence, most of the trees in the valley were killed. The pine, oak, gum, and cottonwood on the outer fringes were the first to go, followed by the water locust and willow adjacent to the bayou, and eventually the cypress adjacent to the bayou. Cypress on the natural levee of the bayou continued to grow, but at a lesser rate, eventually clearly marking the bayou channel as the adjacent trees decayed.

The lake waters also created a new vegetation regime. Dense stands of cypress were created—similar to those of today—but at slightly higher elevations. These trees immediately began to be undermined by wave action and water level fluctuations. The process was gradual, and most grew quite large before toppling on their exposed root systems. The northern end of the lake was probably heavily forested and contained a mixture of old and new cypress. Patches of cypress would have appeared throughout the lake on elevations as they do today, but the stands would not have been as frequent, and the trees would have been more stunted because of higher water levels.

When the first steamboats began penetrating Caddo Lake in the early 1840s, they would have been confronted by a picture of devastation, survival, and new growth, with the most distinctive image being the thousands of decayed tree trunks, which gave rise to false analogies with the earthquake-formed Reelfoot Lake in Missouri. There are two descriptions of the lake from this early period. The first, in Harriet Ames's reminiscences, describes the lake in the late 1830s and early 1840s from a romantic perspective but with good technical detail:

A place more beautiful than Potter's Point it would be impossible to imagine. I never tired of admiring the scenery that lay about my new home. Our house stood upon a jutting promontory, that rose into a hill set in the midst of one of the grandest timber belts in Texas. The level timber lands circled about us, while for more than two hundred feet a steep bank overlooked the most romantically beautiful lake that I've ever beheld. For eight miles one could look across to the opposite shore over a great sheet of sparkling water that washed up into the white beach below the cliff and sang a soft song that the spirits of the forests caught up and carried on unseen wings into the forests depths and tangled music in the meshes of the lofty tree tops. . . .

Islands covered with tall trees rose out of the lake, and these drooped from their shores garlands and loops of wild flowers and graceful vines, like dainty fingers diving into the water to clasp their own beautiful reflection; while towering above the lake the stately trees threw in the afternoon sunlight columns of richest tints all emerald bowered as if to bridge across the space from isle to isle.

A different perspective is provided by the survey crew that established the boundary between the United States and the Republic of Texas in 1841, beginning at the Sabine River to the south and establishing boundary markers every mile. The journal inclusion for 18 May reads as follows:

Advanced the encampment about three miles north, to the shore of Ferry Lake, a short distance to the east of the boundary. Established the forty-fourth and forty-fifth miles. The course of the lake at this point is northeast and southwest, and appears, at some very distant period, from the quantity of large dead cypress standing now in water, ranging in depth from six to fifteen and even twenty feet, to have been once a large cypress swamp, bordering, at various distances, back on each side from one to a half mile, a large bayou called the Cypress, which runs into the lake, or rather forms it, at its northwestern extremity. The channel of this bayou is still traced by its greater depth of water, throughout the whole extent of the lake, and the entire exemption from standing timber within its banks. The numerous arms or bays on this lake, formed at the mouths of its various tributaries, and the great quantity of dead timber and stumps, render its navigation extremely difficult and dangerous.

A later, but still early, description is provided by John T. Coit, who arrived in Jefferson by steamboat and wrote a letter to his wife on 8 May 1858: "Last evening and to day we were passing through Caddo Lake.—In places it is 6 miles wide and is I expect 50 miles the way the boat travelled in length. It is partly grown up with cypress but in places a broad and beautiful expanse of water spreads to a great distance. These lakes have been formed by the great raft and were not here 40 years ago. Sometimes you may see a dead tree standing as they do in a mill pond. Along the lake pine covered hills come up bluff to the shore and were it not for the fact that in dry weather a great part of their bottom is exposed to the sun there would be great temptation held out to one to locate on them."

These accounts include the following lake qualities: dead trees, particularly cypress one-half to one mile on either side of the submerged channel of Cypress Bayou; new, tall cypress spread out and in clusters on rises out in the lake; a well-defined channel of Cypress Bayou beneath the lake, with the channel devoid of trees; deep water at the state boundary line during normal water periods and large portions of the lake dry during the summer, indicating violent water level fluctuations; and white sandy beaches.

Notably absent is any mention of floating or submerged vegetation such as the lilies and lotuses that dominate the Texas side of the lake today. These would have made it impossible for steamboats to move through the lake. They did not dominate the lake during the 1800s because they required permanent water to survive. The shallower areas in which they thrive today would have gone dry during the summer. Also, many are exotic species that were not introduced into the lake until a much later period.

One final difference between the lake of the 1800s and the lake of today was color. The waters of the lake today are brown-stained from tannin in fallen leaves and in cypress bark. The waters of the 1800s are described as clear in an 1873 Corps of Engineers report and an 1858 Board of Swamp Land Commissioners report and as blue by Harriet Ames and an 15 April 1859 *Texas Republican* article on a trip to Caddo

Lake. The difference in color was apparently due to the greater flushing action that took place during the 1800s.

The best delineation of the route through the lake is Eric Bergland's 1885 *Map of Cypress Bayou and the Lakes* (**fig. 9-9**). This delineation was developed on the basis of an 1884 field survey by Assistant Engineer F. S. Burrows using a skiff and sounding rod. The dashed line shows the route, which was equivalent for the most part to the channel of Cypress Bayou. For most of its extent, the route hugged the south shore of the lake, passing close to Mooringsport and Swanson's Landing.

At the western end of the lake, the channel cut sharply to the west, passing above present-day Pine Island, meandered in a loop toward the present-day town of Uncertain, moved back into the lake, looped toward present-day Taylor Island, and then cut to the east, entering Cypress Bayou in the vicinity of the Oxbows. The fairly straight line cutting off the loops between Uncertain and Taylor Island was Withenbury Cutroad, which served as the high-water route. Bergland's map also shows Bois d'Arc Pass Cut (present-day Government Ditch), which was an 1870s Corps of Engineers dredged channel.

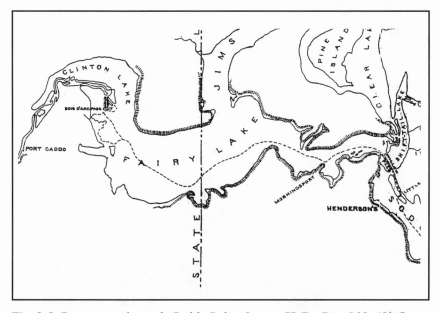

Fig. 9-9. Boat route through Caddo Lake. *Source: H. Ex. Doc. 103, 48th Cong., 2nd Sess.*

A more precise delineation of the channel of Cypress Bayou beneath the lake is given in Capt. J. H. Willard's 1890–91 *Survey of Cypress Bayou and the Lakes,* which was produced in twelve large sheets (scale 1:10,000), five of which cover Caddo Lake. A portion of Sheet 7 is reproduced as **fig. 9-10** to show the fineness of detail, the fact that lake depths are shown on transects, and the closeness of the channel to Swanson's Landing (channel miles marked). Sheet 9 shows Withenbury Cutroad and the federal dredged channel at the northwestern end of the lake.

It should be noted that the channel delineated by Bergland is generally equivalent to the major boatroad on the south side of the lake today. It should also be noted that the delineation of the channel on the Texas side (and the corresponding delineation of the Marion-Harrison County line) on contemporary topographic and sportsman's maps is incorrect. These maps show the eastern end of the channel in Texas as passing between Big Green Brake and Tar Island, when in fact it is much farther to the south.

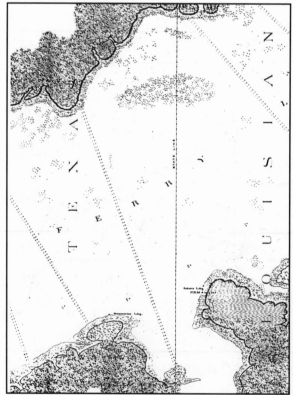

Fig. 9-10. Depth delineation in Caddo Lake. *Source: Louisiana Department of Transportation and Development*

At the northwestern end of the lake, contemporary maps show the channel as heading east from Uncertain into Alligator Bayou and Stumpy Slough, thence into an eastward distributary of Cypress Bayou. This rendition is totally incompatible with all federal survey maps and all descriptions of the route. It has also given rise to the false conception that steamboats headed east toward Potter's Point, when there is no evidence that any steamboat ever went through that area. The steamboat channel (to be specific, the low-water channel) was generally equivalent to the boatroad that loops toward Taylor Island and then heads east into the Oxbows (there is more than one, in spite of what maps say).

There are only two technical descriptions of the route. The first is from Maj. C. W. Howell's 1874 report on improvements to Cypress Bayou: "Fairy Lake, from its head for about half its length, is thickly studded with cypress-trees, stumps, and fallen timber, through which the old channel of Cypress Bayou may yet be traced at low-water, and this, if cleared of logs and stumps, would afford low-water navigation of about 2 feet. . . . In high-water this channel is partly followed by steamboats, and partly avoided by use of what are known as 'cut-roads.' The lower end of the lake affords a navigation of over 6 feet." The second description is by Assistant Engineer F. S. Burrows in Bergland's 1885 report on Cypress Bayou: "The low-water steamboat channel through Fairy Lake is very crooked; has a total length of 16 miles, and a general depth of from 8 to 10 feet. At one time this lake was covered with a growth of heavy cypress timber, the stumps and trunks of much of which still remain. The original channel was cleared out by steamboat men, who cut some of the worst trees and stumps to about the level of low water, and avoided others by making the channel very crooked in places."

From these descriptions, it appears that the channel offered fairly deep water during normal periods, but that it could go as low as two feet during the summer. Burrows is speaking strictly about the low-water route constituted by the channel of Cypress Bayou. Howell mentions cutroads that were used during high-water periods, but does not mention their location.

From Bergland's map, it is obvious that for most of the route through Caddo Lake, steamboats did not diverge from the low-water channel of Cypress Bayou even during high-water periods. There was no reason to do so because the channel was fairly straight and hugged the southern shore, passing near the major commercial points of

Mooringsport and Swanson's Landing. Boats did not need to go in the direction of Potter's Point, because there was no commercial outlet in that direction. Pitts' Landing on the north shore was a short distance from the main channel over deep water. Monterey and Rives' and Bonham's Landings were accessed through the submerged channel of Jim's Bayou.

Boats entered Caddo Lake through Big Willow Pass, moving first through the Red River sedimentary deposits at the foot of the lake, which would have been studded with small cypress, as shown on one of Willard's maps (fig. 9-11). The islands apparently served as a navigation aid—J. Frank Glenn gives the following memorandum on entering the lake and moving toward Mooringsport: "When you circle out from the 3 stumps, get stern on Island and head on lone cypress." As the mile markers on the map indicate, the channel was very close to shore. The only navigation difficulty reported in this area was the wreck of the *Anna* on a stump during low water in 1872.

The channel then headed toward the north shore, as shown on a 1914 Department of the Interior survey map, before looping again and heading toward the south shore peninsula on which Mooringsport was located (fig. 9-12). Glenn speaks of heading toward this point "until abreast of 'Cooper's' house, and head on point at Mooringsport Ferry Ldg." The Department of the Interior map shows how very close the channel came to the Mooringsport peninsula and suggests the location of the landing.

After leaving the Mooringsport peninsula, the channel looped again toward Stormy Point on the north shore, on which Pitts' Landing was located. Glenn's memoranda give the following instructions: "From Mooringsport, get head on Little Island and stern on 'Crooms' warehouse, for Stormy Pt." This was Calvin Croom's warehouse on the north side of the Mooringsport peninsula.

Given its proximity to the channel, Pitts' Landing was probably a regular stopping place for steamboats. The only navigation difficulty reported for this area was the sinking of the *Alida* at Pitts' Landing in 1855. From Pitts', boats proceeded in a wide arc over Rocky Point and headed down toward Swanson's Landing. Boats heading toward Monterey turned off on the channel of Jim's Bayou, which is shown on the Department of the Interior map (see fig. 9-12). The loop shown on the map was an ancient bend of Cypress Bayou that had been cut off before the lake came into existence.

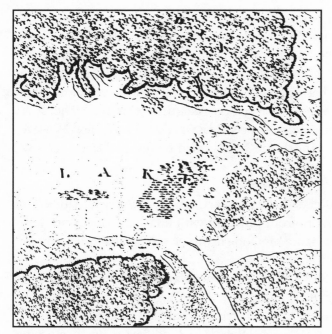

Fig. 9-11. Cypress stands at the foot of Caddo Lake.
*Source: Louisiana Department of Transportation and
Development*

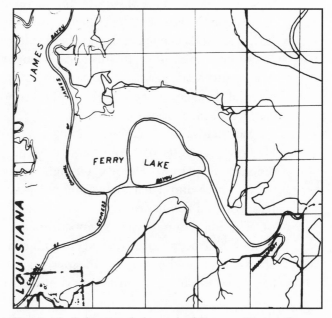

Fig. 9-12. Submerged channel of Cypress Bayou. *Source:
Courtesy of LSU Libraries Special Collections, Baton Rouge*

The channel through the main body of the lake made a broad "V" whose base was near Swanson's Landing (see fig. 9-9). The landing was only a few blocks from the channel, as shown on Willard's map (see fig. 9-10). The channel was accessible to the landing even during low water by a wharf that was built in 1860 to offload railroad iron. There were no reported navigation hazards in this area. The *Mittie Stephens* was not an exception, because it was destroyed by fire. However, winds were a constant threat, as indicated by the 24 December 1871 *Shreveport Times*:

> Just after dark the Flavilla, Capt. Noah Scovell, Matt Scovell, clerk, came in from Jefferson with 604 bales of cotton. From the following memoranda it will be seen that she encountered the tornado in the lake:
>
> MEMORANDA.—Steamer Flavilla left Jefferson Thursday, Dec. 21, 1871, at 11 P.M. Met Carrie A. Thorn at Boone's Bend; passed C. H. Durfee at Smithland; met Fontenelle and Era No. 10, and passed the Ida in Blind Bayou, Friday morning. Ida had laid by for the wind; the others were proceeding on their voyages as best they could; met Wash Sentell laid up at Swanson's on account of wind. Wind increased so that we had to lay up in the lake, two miles below Swanson's. At 11 o'clock P.M., the wind changed to the northeast, blowing a gale, parting all our lines and setting us adrift. We brought up on the other side of the road, against sundry stumps and trees, doing no material damage, as the Flavilla was built under the far famed Cooper's instructions, of 1869.
>
> Saturday, 23d—Laid by six hours in Willow Pass for wind. Had on board 604 bales of cotton at $3 per bale, 12 bales of hides at 75c per cwt. Did not get higher than the bend below town. Three and a half feet water for boats of this class to Jefferson and falling fast.
>
> The Ida sent a messenger aboard for ten pounds of flour, as they had been out a few weeks longer from Jefferson to Shreveport than they anticipated, consequently was out. Rumor has it that the Ida and Durfee are running a race—don't bet.

Just before reaching present-day Pine Island, the route split into high-water and low-water components. The low-water route headed toward shore, passing north of present-day Pine Island, as shown on Woodruff's 1872 map (**fig. 9-13**). Because of time and cost constraints, Woodruff was unable to delineate the route completely through the lake. It should be noted that Pine Island was named Bird Island during the 1800s, as shown on the map and as presented in Woodruff's 1873 survey report.

After passing Bird Island, the low-water channel came close to shore at the present location of Uncertain (there was no landing at this point during the 1800s), moved away and then back to the shore at Taylor Island through a jagged course, and then headed east into the mouth of Cypress Bayou at the Oxbows. The upper portion of this course was roughly equivalent to present-day Boatroad 2-C. It should be noted that Government Ditch was not in existence at the time. This was a project that grew out of Woodruff's survey and was completed after his death.

The convoluted low-water channel from Bird Island to the mouth of Cypress Bayou was bypassed during high-water periods by a cutroad approximately one and a half miles long that was made under contract, but largely at personal expense, in 1854 by steamboat Capt. Robert H. Martin, the same man who made the cutroad on Soda Lake. This

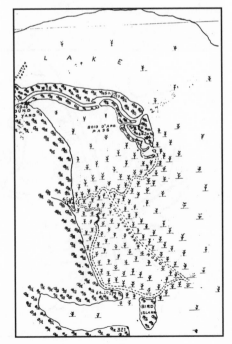

Fig. 9-13. Boat routes at northern end of Caddo Lake. *Source: LSU in Shreveport, Noel Memorial Archives*

303

cutroad is shown on Woodruff's 1872 map **(see fig. 9-13)**, Bergland's 1885 map **(see fig. 9-9)**, Willard's 1890–91 survey map, and Wooten's 1907 map. This was not a dug channel, but rather a cutroad, involving tree removal down to the low-water level.

The northern entrance to this cutroad can be seen on contemporary topographic maps as a beginning channel immediately east of the point at which Government Ditch first crosses the channel of Cypress Bayou in the lake **(fig. 9-14)**. In-field inspection of this beginning channel revealed a slight flow and debris blockage only a short distance within. At the time the cutroad was made, the area was heavily forested by cypress trees that grew up after the lake came into existence, as shown on Woodruff's map. The trees in this area were harvested in the late 1800s and early 1900s, and the course of the cutroad has been obliterated by new cypress growth resulting from the 1914 dam.

The Woodruff, Willard, and Wooten maps name this cutroad Withenberry Road, after Capt. W. W. Withenbury. However, Withenbury's name is not mentioned in connection with the cutroad in any newspaper navigation columns, which generally refer to the cutroads collectively rather than individually. The only mention of this cutroad in the newspaper navigation columns is in the 28 December 1871 *Shreveport Times*, which indicates that the cutroad was also known under the name of its maker:

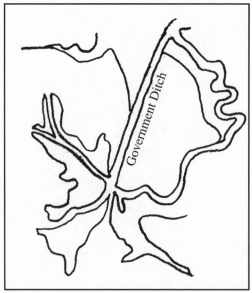

Fig. 9-14. Upper entrance to Withenbury Cutroad

The following is the memoranda of the Flavilla's last trip from Shreveport to Jefferson and back:

Left Shreveport on Monday, December 25, and arrived at Jefferson on Tuesday at 8 o'clock P.M. Laid in port three hours and left for Shreveport. The following boats were in port: Lotus No. 3, Belle Rowland, May Lowry and Wash Sentell. December 27—Passed the Fontenell at Shift Tail Bend, and entered the lakes at 8 o'clock A.M.; met the Clifford at Martin's Cut Road; landed at Mooringsport at 1 o'clock and took on board ten bales of cotton. The wind was blowing a perfect gale. Passed through the Little Pass at dinner time. Found three feet on Albany flats; passed Albany at 2 o'clock P.M.; met the 13th Era at the mouth of Twelve Mile Bayou, and arrived at Shreveport just at dark.

This usage appeared only a few months before Woodruff's survey, indicating that the names Martin and Withenbury were applied to the cutroad simultaneously. This is not an error. Martin and Withenbury ran many steamboats to Jefferson during the same decades, and both were members of the Steamboat Captain's Benevolent Association in New Orleans. Martin apparently named the road after his fellow captain. Woodruff and the later maps could not have provided an independent designation, given the fact that Withenbury retired from steamboating after the Civil War and was living in Cincinnati in 1872. "Withenbury Road" was probably common usage, to distinguish the Caddo Lake cutroad from Martin's Soda Lake cutroad, which was of much greater consequence for the navigability of the route.

Withenbury Cutroad is not mentioned in the navigation columns because it was not the critical high-water passage at the northern end of the lake. That honor goes to Bois d'Arc Pass, which is designated on Woodruff's map (see fig. 9-13). This name has nothing to do with the bois d'arc tree, which never could have grown in the swampy area near the pass. Rather, the pass was named for the steamboat Bois d'Arc, which operated on the route from 1843 through 1845 and obviously was the first boat to chart a course through the pass.

An exact delineation of the route down from the pass cannot be determined at this time because much of it was destroyed by the construction of the Government Ditch, and the whole area is overgrown with trees that came into existence with the 1914 dam.

It is obvious from the configuration of Cypress Bayou in the area of the pass that much of the water would have been thrust out toward present-day Jackson Arm during high-water periods, and early Corps reports suggest that the pass was considered the mouth of Cypress Bayou. There were bars on the edge of the pass, which is understandable because it was an outflow channel, and it does not appear to have been obstructed by trees, which is reasonable because it would have been an ancient outflow channel. In-field inspection indicates that the channel of the pass is presently partly obstructed by soil deposition from the Government Ditch project.

The area of the pass can be seen today as a small outflow channel obstructed by logs on the west side of Government Ditch shortly after it leaves Cypress Bayou. The area is fringed by a few cypress trees that obviously pre-existed the lake and that grew up on the banks of the outflow channel. The pass route ran west of Government Ditch and then crossed over at the lower end, meeting Withenbury Cutroad at the submerged channel of Cypress Bayou **(fig. 9-15)**. It should be noted that the pass pre-existed Withenbury Cutroad. The road ran to

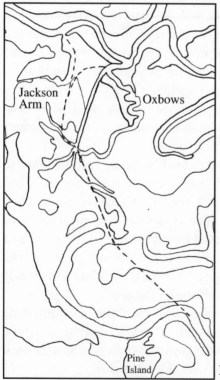

Fig. 9-15. High-water routes

the northwest, crossing the submerged Cypress Bayou at a sharp angle—
it was obviously designed to tie into the pass alignment, providing a
continuous high-water passage from Bird Island into Cypress Bayou.
The configuration of Withenbury Cutroad, which runs from southeast
to northwest, also suggests that the lower portion of the pass route
was constituted by at least a portion of the channel that runs northwest
from the point of intersection of Government Ditch and the submerged
channel of Cypress Bayou.

The pass route was not a dug channel and was not even a formal
cutroad, because it passed through areas of open water. This is the
apparent reason why it is not delineated on maps. Removal of
obstructing trees probably began with the *Bois d'Arc*, was continued
by other steamboats, and was completed by Martin in 1854. That many
trees in this area had been cut to low water is indicated by the fact that
the construction of the upper portion of Government Ditch in 1879
involved the pulling of 563 stumps.

There are no descriptions of any boats actually using the pass route.
That it was a passage for boats is indicated by its name in two senses.
First, it would not have been designated a pass had it not been used for
passage; and second, it would not have been named Bois d'Arc Pass
had it not been used by the boat of that name. That it was a passage for
steamboats, that it was an alternate route to Cypress Bayou in the vicinity
of the Oxbows, and that it was the high-water route is confirmed by
the navigation record, which frequently mentions Bois d'Arc Pass.

There are three texts suggesting passage. The 29 February 1872
Shreveport Times provides an ironic low-water commentary hinging
on the fact that the waters of Caddo Lake were transparent and
depleted during the summer: "After leaving Cypress bayou passing
through Bois d'Arc Pass, we strike Clear lake. It is undoubtedly a
clear lake for it is clear of water. We take mud and approach Ferry
lake. Poorly named, for the reason that shrimp and cat fish hardly
find room to navigate."

The 18 February 1872 *Shreveport Times* refers to "Bois d'Arc
chute." This sense of a downward trending passage from Bois d'Arc
Pass to the submerged channel of Cypress Bayou is made explicit in
the 25 January 1872 *Shreveport Times*: "We have nothing of importance
from Jefferson. Cypress bayou was falling slowly, with seven feet above
the low water mark. In Bois d'Arc pass out to Cypress bayou there
were four and one-half feet."

There are numerous texts in which boats report water levels in the pass, obviously referring to what they experienced while moving through this portion of the route. Most of these reports are made in the context of declining water levels and mention corresponding conditions in the cutroad at Albany Flats, indicating that Bois d'Arc Pass was the high-water route. Two examples will suffice, both of which are from the 1872 *Shreveport Times*, the first from 24 January and the second from 21 May:

> The officers of the Clifford, which boat arrived from Jefferson last evening, report the bayou falling slowly with seven feet above low water mark. She found four and one-half feet in Bois d'Arc Pass and four feet in the cutroad across Albany point.
> The officers of the Carrie A. Thorn, which boat arrived from Jefferson, Sunday night, report the lakes and bayous falling, with five feet in Boon Bend, three feet in Bois d'Arc Pass, six feet on the flats, and four and a half feet in the cut road across Albany Point.

Lastly, there are texts drawing a distinction between the Bois d'Arc Pass high-water route and the Cypress Bayou low-water route. The following quote from the 20 July 1872 *Shreveport Times* cites water level conditions in the pass and bayou that would necessitate use of the low-water route, which would place a burden on the citizens of Jefferson: "The last boat out from Jefferson some days since reported the water falling fast, with three feet in Cypress bayou, twenty inches in Bois d'Arc Pass and thirty inches in the cut road across Albany Point. Boats now have to follow the low water route through the lakes, which is hard on the steamboatmen, but harder on the natives on the frontier."

Woodruff's map also shows an opening from Cypress Bayou above Bois d'Arc Pass leading into the Jackson Arm area **(see fig. 9-13)**, which is also shown on contemporary topographic maps. In-field inspection of this opening indicates that it was a depression that could only be used during very high-water conditions. This route **(see fig. 9-15)** probably joined the Bois d'Arc passage about halfway down to the intersection with the submerged channel of Cypress Bayou. There are no navigation records indicating use of this route.

When the water became too low to proceed through Bois d'Arc Pass, boats could still enter Cypress Bayou at the Oxbows through the channel of Cypress Bayou in the lake. During extreme low-water conditions, the channel of Cypress Bayou through the lake was all that was left of the lake at the northern end and contained only a few feet of water.

The texts of the period indicate that Bois d'Arc Pass, rather than the area downstream of the Oxbows, was considered the mouth of Cypress Bayou. Woodruff, for example, in his 1873 survey report, establishes the pass as the mouth of Cypress Bayou in his divisions of the route:

1. Twelve-mile Bayou, from Shreveport, to the foot of Soda Lake.
2. Soda Lake to the head of Willow Pass, at foot of Fairy Lake.
3. Fairy Lake to Bois d'Arc Pass, or mouth of Cypress Bayou.
4. Bois d'Arc Pass to Jefferson.

The "or" in the third division indicates equivalency and is not a disjunction suggesting a high-water route established by the pass and a low-water route established by the area of the Oxbows, which then would constitute the mouth of the bayou. If Woodruff had wanted to make such a distinction, he would have made it explicitly. This reading is supported by a contemporary account in the 22 March 1876 *Shreveport Times*: "The natives who reside along the banks on Cypress bayou are again made glad with the prospects of first rate navigation. The waters are rising and soon old Cypress will be bank full and steamers can skim along with all ease, much to the delight of the Jimp and its many friends. The lakes this side are filling up fast and a good sized boat with a fair load can strike a bee line for the Cypress bayou outlet or Bois d'Arc Pass without regard to the obstructions brought to daylight in low water."

The wording is similar to Woodruff's; but in this case the "or" cannot possibly be a disjunction. The text is clearly referring to a high-water situation, and it is impossible to strike a beeline from the lakes into the area of the Oxbows. The text is suggesting that boats then had the ability to move straight through Withenbury Cutroad into the route west of present-day Government Ditch that led directly into Bois d'Arc Pass, which was equivalent to the mouth of Cypress Bayou.

The equivalence of Bois d'Arc Pass with the mouth of Cypress Bayou is made explicit in Burrows's survey report contained in

Bergland's 1885 report on Cypress Bayou. Writing about the dredging that had been conducted in previous years at the upper end of the lake, Burrows refers to "Bois d'Arc Pass, being at the entrance of the bayou from Fairy Lake." The importance of this assimilation was that during the 1800s, flows through Bois d'Arc Pass were substantial, giving rise to the opportunity for steamboat passage. Government Ditch has so distorted the historic hydrologic conditions at the head of the lake that it is difficult to conceive that boats ever went through the pass and that it was a passage much preferred to the convoluted Oxbows.

The channel between the pass and the lower end of the Oxbows appears to have been considered a distributary of Cypress Bayou and apparently was named Blind Bayou. This is a probable reading of the 20 July 1872 *Shreveport Times* statement that the *Cuba No. 2* sank at the mouth of Blind Bayou above Swanson's and the 24 December 1871 *Shreveport Times* statement that the *Ida* had laid up in Blind Bayou because of wind on the lake. In addition, Captain Howell's 1874 report speaks about the need for improvements "in the vicinity of the Bois d'Arc Passes and the Blind Bayou, in the upper end of Fairy Lake." A firm conclusion cannot be reached because the submerged channels of Cypress Bayou and Twelvemile Bayou during moderate-water periods were referred to as "blind bayous." Nevertheless, if these texts are referring to the submerged channel of Cypress Bayou in the vicinity of Taylor Island, the reference to the mouth of Blind Bayou makes no sense.

CYPRESS BAYOU TO SMITHLAND

Cypress Bayou up to Smithland at the confluence with Black Cypress was an extension of Caddo Lake in the sense that flat-water conditions prevailed between the confluence and the foot of Caddo Lake. The channel normally had well-defined banks and a width of between two hundred and three hundred feet. However, during spring rains in the Cypress Bayou Basin and backwater pressure from the Red River, the bayou valley would be flooded, converting the stream into a visible lake, as shown on many maps.

The bayou was generally fairly deep, with depth of at least seven feet throughout most of its course up to Smithland. The depth of the water, protection from winds, absence of a strong current, and prevailing lake-like conditions made this a fairly easy passage. Nevertheless, it became narrow and tortuous during low-water periods and held hidden dangers in the form of submerged stumps during moderate-water periods, which produced a few wrecks.

Ironically, the stumps that produced wrecks appear to have been the result of channel improvement projects, of which there were many. The improvements were of two types. In-stream logs were removed, bank timber was cut, and in-stream trees were cut to low water. The remnants of these activities can be seen in the stumps lining the channel with hollow centers and rounded edges (heal collars), the rounding produced by the ability of cypress to continue to grow long after they have been cut. In addition, the channel was straightened and deepened in various places by dredging, and prominent overland cuts were produced in the Little Cypress and Benton areas, where the deposited soil can be seen lining the straight channels. These cuts reduced the channel length to Smithland from twenty-seven to twenty-four miles.

There are no overall descriptions of this passage from the perspective of steamboatmen, although Glenn provides a detailed account of channel configurations. Information from the *Rapides* in the 27 February 1872 *Shreveport Times* mentions a strong current in the bayou when water was falling rapidly on the lakes: "From the officers of the Rapides we learn that the lakes and bayous between this point and Jefferson are falling rapidly. The current in Cypress bayou is very rapid and it takes nice work on the part of the pilots to make any time whatever." In addition, the *Royal George*, which was an ultralight-draft boat, indicates in the 4 September 1873 *Shreveport Times* the degree to which the bayou could be depleted in places during extreme low water: "Found fifteen inches of water in Cypress Bayou and falling: dredge boat stopped work; could not dig as fast as the bayou fell; 10 inches on the Gate Post; 20 inches on the Flats, and falling faster than ever was known."

Boats entered Cypress Bayou through Bois d'Arc Pass in high water and through Blind Bayou past the Oxbows in low water (see fig. 9-13). In either case, the entrance made a sharp turn at Devil's Elbow, a name common to many sharp bends on the Red River and elsewhere and obviously derived from the steamboat period. Moving upstream, boats passed Mound Woodyard on the left and, immediately thereafter, a channel on the right leading into Clinton Lake and thence to the landing at Clinton.

The bayou then dropped southwest in a long, gradual bend with low areas on both sides until arriving at the lefthand bluffs below which

Port Caddo was located (**fig. 9-16**). It is probable that all steamboats stopped at Port Caddo. The bayou turns to the northwest at the bluffs, proceeding in a nearly straight line to the confluence with Haggerty Creek. Capt. J. H. Willard's 1893 benchmark survey map indicates that the elevations north of the creek and bordering Cypress Bayou were called Red Bluffs, at least for the late navigation period.

From Haggerty Creek, the bayou made two large bends before reaching Benton at the confluence with Benton Creek. Immediately above Benton, the situation was complicated. There were two large convoluted bends (**fig. 9-17**) that were cut off by the Corps of Engineers in the 1870s. However, when this work was done, it is clear that the Corps was reworking existing cuts, which must have been made by William Perry through his 1857 state contract for navigation improvements. A stump just above the Benton cutoff wrecked the *Lotus No. 3* in 1873. This was the only wreck on Cypress Bayou for which navigation hazards were the documented cause.

From the cutoff, the bayou ran north with slight bends until reaching a shallow, convoluted area in the vicinity of Little Cypress Bayou (**fig. 9-18**). These bends were also cut off by the Corps of Engineers in the 1870s. Apparently these were fresh cuts, but the area

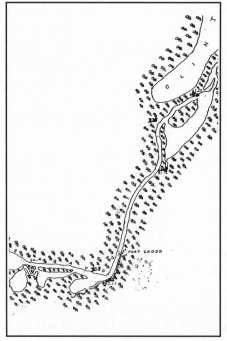

Fig. 9-16. Port Caddo area.
Source: LSU in Shreveport, Noel Memorial Library Archives

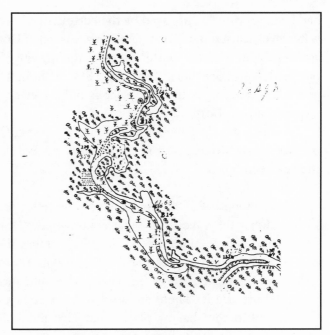

Fig. 9-17. Benton area. *Source: LSU in Shreveport, Noel Memorial Library Archives*

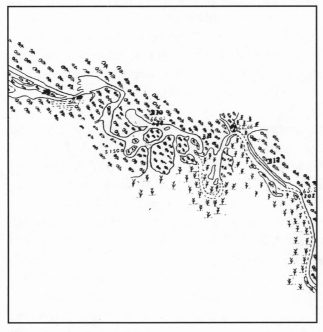

Fig. 9-18. Little Cypress area. *Source: LSU in Shreveport, Noel Memorial Library Archives*

had been previously improved by the cutting of trees down to the low-water level, leaving the stumps. This area was called Dougherty's Defeat, apparently on the basis of the wreck of the *Mary L. Dougherty*, which operated along the route in 1856 and 1857. Although the wreck appears in a steamboat wreck list, the place is only referred to as located on Cypress Bayou above Benton.

This area was described in a 30 June 1874 report by Frank W. Gee, overseer of the dredge boat making federal improvements, just before the cuts were made:

> On the 8th of June I started from Jefferson with the dredge, down the bayou, for what is known as "Dorherty's Defeat," about four miles below Smithland. Here the banks are low, and the bayou spreads out over the country for some distance, and is quite shallow in many places, and makes a number of short bends. There are also many stumps along the channel and in the shallow places that give much trouble to boats, especially in the low-water season.
>
> That portion of the bayou called "Dorherty's Defeat" is from one-half to three fourths of a mile in length, but the whole distance is not low water only in places.
>
> By dredging the channel through the low-water portions and cutting off several short points or bars, thereby making the bayou straighter, and removing the stumps from the channel, the navigation will be materially improved.

The stumps mentioned by Gee were the major hazard in the area and undoubtedly the cause of the wreck of the *Mary L. Dougherty*. They resulted from the navigation improvement efforts of William Perry through his 1854 or 1857 contracts. Boats are mentioned as having difficulties with these stumps. The 4 January 1872 *Shreveport Times* records that the *Belle Rowland* "stumped it a little at Daugherty's Defeat." A memorandum by the *Wash Sentell* in the 1 September 1871 *Daily South-Western* indicates that she "met 13th Era at Dorherty's Defeat hard and fast on a stump waiting for barges to lighter." The constricted channel and shallow depth sometimes made this a critical point of passage on the route, allowing boats of only smaller dimensions to get through, or else providing a need for lightening, as was the case with the *Lotus No. 3* in August 1873.

From Dougherty's Defeat up to Smithland, the bayou was fairly wide and straight, with the exception of the lower end where there was a sharp bend. There are no reports concerning this area other than the wreck of the *Larkin Edwards* in 1860, which involved a stump in the immediate vicinity of Smithland. Smithland was located at the confluence with Black Cypress Bayou. Above this point, the nature of the route changed dramatically.

SMITHLAND TO JEFFERSON

Downstream of Smithland, Cypress Bayou was wide and deep and exhibited a lake-like quality generated by the flat-water conditions extending from the foot of Caddo Lake. Above Smithland, the bayou was shallow and constricted, and water levels were generally dependent on rainfall in the upper bayou watershed. The shallowest place was a shoal about one-half mile below Jefferson that provided only about three feet of clearance.

The original condition of this stretch is difficult to envision, particularly before logs, other debris, and living trees were cleared out by William Perry in 1844. Perry also removed additional obstructions and did some channel deepening in his projects of 1854 and 1857. The stretch was modified by Jefferson's dredge in the early 1870s and more extensively by the Corps of Engineers shortly thereafter.

The stretch was not hazardous, and there were no reported wrecks in the area from in-stream impediments. The major difficulty was low water, which often isolated Jefferson in the summer and gave rise to a system of temporary landings. Jefferson's low-water plight occasioned numerous ironic commentaries in the Shreveport newspapers. Two examples from the *Shreveport Times* will suffice, the first from 5 August 1868 and the second from 4 August 1875:

> The Kouns-Line packet Era No. 8, Capt. Truslow, arrived to-day from a short voyage to Boon Bend, on Cypress bayou, with a light trip, consisting principally of six or seven yahoos in the cabin. Capt. Truslow reports thirty inches of mud and water in the available channel of Soda Lake. Dallas street is at least five miles from water on a natural elevation in Marion County, patiently waiting for the uprising of the waters. A reward of $18,000 is offered for the best method of removing the

settlement to a stream which is navigable at least three months in a year.

The Jefferson papers appear to have ignored the bayou entirely or the dogoned thing has dried up. They never cheep now about the head of navigation. Wait though till the fall rains set in and the branch gets on a rampage and then, ye gods, look out for a voice from the "head of navigation."

The two areas that caused the most navigation difficulties in this stretch were Boon's Bend immediately downstream of The Packery and Potato Bend immediately upstream of The Packery, which are shown on Woodruff's 1872 map (**fig. 9-19**). Boon's Bend was cut off by Jefferson's dredge in August 1872 in connection with the city's project to improve the bayou between Boon's Bend and the city wharf and is shown prior to the cutoff on Woodruff's map.

Potato Bend, which was also known as Esculent Bend and Vegetable Bend, was cut off by Jefferson's dredge in 1871 and is shown as cut off on Woodruff's map. Before the cut was made, there were reports such as the following from the 30 January 1867 *South-Western* indicating

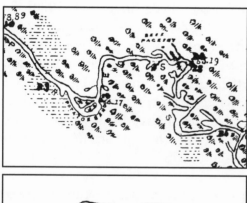

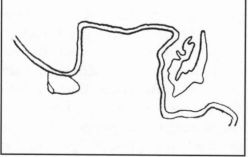

Fig. 9-19. Boon's Bend and Potato Bend. *Source: LSU in Shreveport, Noel Memorial Library Archives (top) and contemporary topographic map (bottom)*

the difficulty of passage through the area: "The Hine was aground 24 hours in Potatoe bend." A new set of difficulties arose after the cut was made, as reported by the 8, 9, and 11 July 1871 *Daily South-Western*:

> The steamer R. J. Lockwood came in from Jefferson yesterday morning bringing us the latest news from Cypress Bayou. Mr. Ike Hunter, her pilot, informs us that there is about three feet in the new cut off below Jefferson, and about three and a half feet on "Albany flats." The bayou and the lakes are falling rapidly. Every steamer that goes to Jefferson now, "receives an introduction" to the bottom of that new cut off before getting through with it, in spite of the desire to form no new acquaintances.
>
> The cut off has from thirty inches to three feet of water in it at Potato Bend, and the channel is very narrow.
>
> The last accounts from Jefferson report Cypress Bayou low and falling. All the steamers that pass up drawing over three feet have to lighten or pull themselves over the shoal water in the new cut off with their steam capstans.

The main route ended at the turning basin in Jefferson, although some boats obviously went upstream as far as Marshall Street, where the meatpackers Stanley & Nimmo had a wharf before the Civil War. No steamboats went above Jefferson, where the channel was even more shallow and constricted and obstructed by a bridge above the landing from the earliest years. However, during periods when there was heavy rainfall in the Cypress Bayou watershed and the roads were impassable to ox-wagons traveling to Jefferson, freight was occasionally transported down the bayou to Jefferson by flatboats and skiffs. The 1 February 1871 issue of the *South-Western* reports the conditions and remedial actions: "At Jefferson, on Saturday, the Bayou was rising fast, with the prospect of getting higher than known for some years past, so says the Times and Republican. Jefferson was entirely cut off from the interior. Three hundred cotton wagons were water bound west of the Cypress, and could not go one way or the other." The newspaper from the eighth offers the following description: "The bayou at Jefferson was falling fast on Saturday, with the banks still under water. For a number of days the Bayou City was cut off from all communication with the interior except by flatboats and skiffs."

ROUTE TO MONTEREY

Besides the main route to Jefferson, there were secondary routes to Monterey on Jim's Bayou and to Clinton on Clinton Lake. Monterey was an important landing on the east bank of present-day Monterey Lake, which was an ancient lake produced by scouring between bluffs by Jim's Bayou (fig. 9-20). Before the advent of the raft, there was only Jim's Bayou, the lake, and the valley through which Jim's Bayou flowed into Cypress Bayou. The raft caused the valley of Jim's Bayou to flood up to the northern end of Monterey Lake, obliterating the lake as a separate entity. Monterey Lake then reappeared after water levels went down on Caddo Lake in the late 1800s.

Monterey Lake is not accessible from Caddo Lake by any but the smallest craft today, so it is difficult to envision Monterey as a heavily used steamboat landing. However, it should be remembered that water levels were higher, producing a deeper, wider, and longer flooded portion on Jim's Bayou than exists today (fig. 9-21). In addition, much of the obstructing vegetation today came about as a result of the 1914 dam. Before 1800, the valley of Jim's Bayou, like the valley of

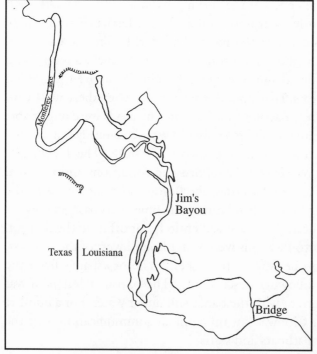

Fig. 9-20. Jim's Bayou and Monterey Lake

Cypress Bayou in which Caddo Lake formed, was forested, but with a greater predominance of cypress. With raft-induced flooding of the Jim's Bayou valley, many of these trees would have been killed. However, remaining trees would have been denser than in the Caddo Lake area, and a new stand of cypress trees would have been established on the fringes of the valley.

Steamboats began traveling to Monterey in the late 1840s and continued until at least the late 1870s. The route to Monterey was constituted by the generally submerged channel of Jim's Bayou. A portion of this channel (up to the northern boundary of Township 20 North) was surveyed and mapped by the Department of the Interior in 1914 (**fig. 9-22**). Steamboats heading to Monterey diverged from the submerged channel of Cypress Bayou northwest of Rocky Point and headed toward present-day Canfield Point.

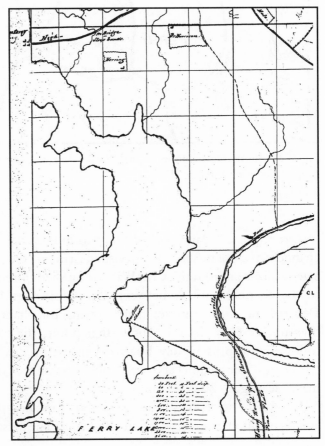

Fig. 9-21. Jim's Bayou during the 1800s. *Source: Louisiana Secretary of State, Division of Archives, Records Management and History*

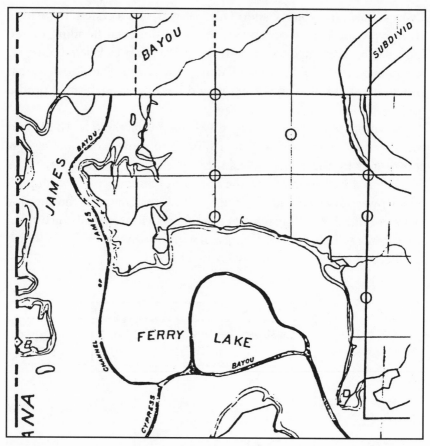

Fig. 9-22. Submerged channel of Jim's Bayou. *Source: Courtesy of LSU Libraries Special Collections, Baton Rouge*

From present-day Canfield Point to present-day Plum Point, the channel ran close to shore. Cottonshed Arm on contemporary maps is a generalization from the Civil War cotton sheds immediately adjacent to the channel halfway between the points (**see fig. 9-21**). The Department of the Interior map showing the channel terminates at present-day Gum Island. Above that point, the channel probably followed the present-day boatroad up to Highway 49, where it terminates. The channel above that point can be seen on contemporary maps (**see fig. 9-20**).

There are no reports by any steamboats moving through this area and no mention of any navigation difficulties. The passage was probably tedious, with boats confined to the channel of Jim's Bayou between flooded areas filled with cypress. The desolate conditions confronted by boats at the lower end of present-day Monterey Lake are suggested by the map and journal of the 1841 United States–Republic of Texas boundary survey crew. The map **(fig. 9-23)** shows the boundary line delineated by mile mounds and the land one-half mile on either side. The text describes the difficulties encountered by the crew as it crossed the flooded area and bayou between the bluffs shown on contemporary maps **(see fig. 9-20)** while advancing north in May:

> 28th.—Encampment stationary. Established 54th and 55th miles. Country poor; timber, oak interspersed with pine.

Fig. 9-23. Route of the boundary survey crew. *Source: S. Doc. 199, 27th Cong., 2nd Sess.*

Measured to half-mile section stake, east of line, and found it to be 66 feet.

29th.—Advanced the encampment a mile and a half, and pitched it a little west of the boundary, on a point of high land bordering the overflow of "Jim's bayou." Traced this day the boundary to the overflow. A part of the men sent around to the lake, to bring the boats to this point, to be used when the depth of water would not admit of operations otherwise. Rafts were constructed, but did not answer so well, owing to the density of the cypress and thick undergrowth.

30th.—Encampment stationary. From the reluctance manifested by the men to go into the water, it became necessary that the officers should lead them. The operations this day in wading and cutting, where the depth of water would admit, through forests of cypress and almost impervious undergrowth, added to the excessive heat of the weather, were very severe upon the party—making, after every effort, only the distance of 1,950 feet, to the bank of Jim's bayou.

31st.—Encampment stationary. Continued our aquatic labors, reaching the high land, after cutting through a deep swamp and overflow almost impenetrable.

The landings on the west side of Jim's Bayou (Rives' and, later, Bonham's) would have been visited by steamboats on the way down from Monterey. Both of these were easily accessed through deep water.

ROUTE TO CLINTON

Clinton was a landing on the north shore of Clinton Lake on the bluffs east of Kitchen's Creek where a road comes down to the lake (**fig. 9-24**) and probably began to be used by steamboats by the late 1840s. The landing was accessed from Cypress Bayou by Clinton Chute on the west, as shown on Woodruff's 1872 map (**fig. 9-25**) and probably by Blind Slough on the east. Clinton Chute was apparently immediately west of present-day Clinton Ditch, if local tradition is correct that Clinton Ditch was a channel dredged in the late 1880s to provide access for lumbering activities on Clinton Lake. "Ditch" suggests a dredged channel.

The relationship between Clinton Chute and Clinton Ditch is shown on Willard's 1890–91 survey Sheet 7. The chute is shown as a smaller

Kitchen's Creek
Clinton Lake
Whistleberry Slough
Judd's Hole
Blind Slough
Clinton Ditch
Clinton's Chute

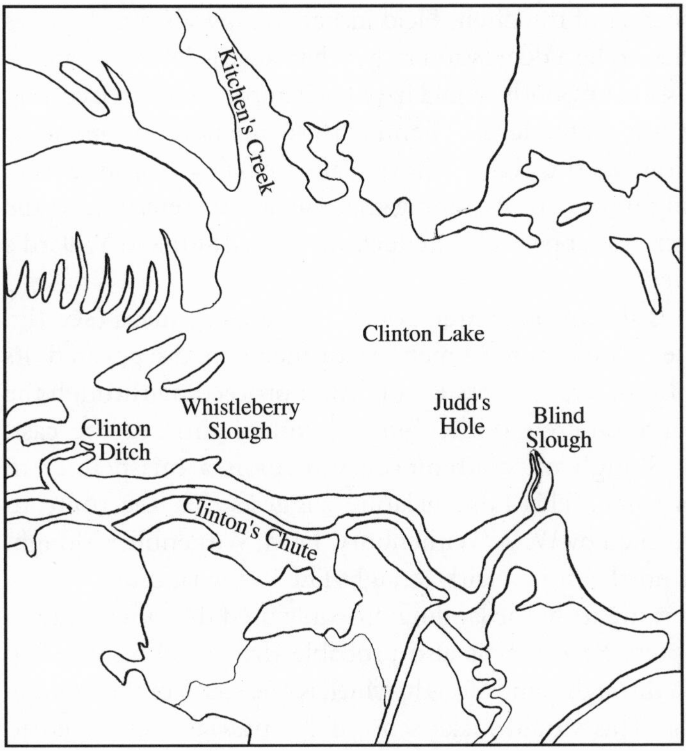

Fig. 9-24. Clinton area

N L A K
CLINTON CHUTE
818
69.58
MOUND WOOD YARD
BOIS D PAS

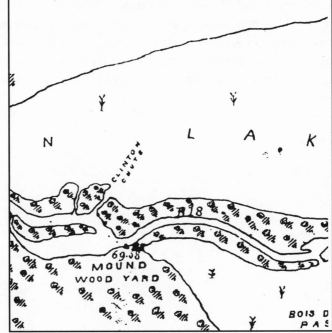

Fig. 9-25. Clinton Chute. *Source: LSU in Shreveport, Noel Memorial Library Archives*

channel to the west of the ditch. Field inspection reveals the chute, as its name implies, to be a depression rather than a well-defined channel, and this depression obviously would have been improved by tree cutting down to the low-water level. Glenn's 1886 memoranda mention "Clinton bayou on the right" shortly after passing "Mound Fish Ground" going upstream. Assuming that Glenn was referring to the chute, the ditch was apparently dredged between 1886 and Willard's 1890–91 survey.

The ditch is shown on contemporary topographic maps (**see fig. 9-24**), but the chute is not. As memory of the chute disappeared, its name was transposed to Cypress Bayou. After proceeding through the chute, the route entered Withenbury Slough slightly to the east. Whistleberry Slough on contemporary maps is a misspelling of Withenbury's name. This nomenclature suggests that the route to Clinton was opened by W. W. Withenbury. From Withenbury Slough, the route was northeast in a fairly straight line to the landing.

Boats returning from the landing probably used the same route to return to Cypress Bayou. It is also probable that boats returned to Cypress Bayou through Blind Slough, which is due south of the location of the landing. This would make sense if the passage were open to steamboats: Clinton would have been visited on the return trip from Jefferson; Blind Slough offers much closer access to the main route down. However, this is purely speculative. The only suggestion that steamboats might have used this passage is Judd's Hole, immediately northwest of the slough, and the fact that there was a Judd's Mark on the wharf at Jefferson, made by John W. Judd, the builder of the 1872 wharf.

·10·
Early Navigation Improvements

ANTEBELLUM EFFORTS

In late 1844, Cypress Bayou between Smithland and Jefferson was cleared of obstructions, allowing the first steamboat, the *Lama*, to reach the newly emerging town of Jefferson in March 1845. This work was conducted under contract through subscriptions amounting to $2,000 and involved the removal of in-stream logs and debris, the removal of bank trees that had fallen over into the water, and the cutting of living and dead cypress trees on the channel fringes down to the low-water level. No digging was involved, and the sawed logs were left in-stream to be carried down by the spring rise on Cypress Bayou.

This was the first of many projects to improve navigation on the Cypress Bayou and the lakes route that involved the citizens of the area, the city of Jefferson, the states of Texas and Louisiana, and the federal government. These efforts extended from 1844 to 1914 and included the building of the dam on Caddo Lake in the latter year. They can be conveniently divided into pre–Civil War and post–Civil War, because the antebellum efforts were based primarily on hand labor and the postbellum efforts used dredges.

Prior to the Civil War, projects were initiated in 1844, 1849, 1854, and 1857. The first three were conducted under contract through private subscriptions, and the fourth was state sponsored with a local subscription match. Thus, there was always interest in and activity with respect to navigation improvements. This interest and activity was not peculiar to the route, but rather a manifestation of the widespread interest in transportation improvements of all types that is reflected in the newspapers of the period.

There is no documentation with respect to who conducted the improvement between Smithland and Jefferson in 1844. However, it appears that the contractor was William Perry. Perry met the *Lama* at Shreveport to provide guidance through the newly opened channel, probably because he was the one who conducted the work and therefore was familiar with stream configurations and the hazards that would be encountered.

The unifying element in the four antebellum improvement projects was William Perry—he was contracted for all of the work in Texas. Perry was born in Massachusetts in 1813 and moved permanently to Jefferson in 1846, where he was accidentally killed by Reconstruction troops in 1869 at the age of fifty-five. During his twenty-three years in Jefferson, he was a land speculator, hotel owner, mayor, steamboat captain, and navigation improvements contractor. He was captain and part owner of the *Bloomer* in 1856–57 and captain of the *Homer* in 1860–61.

Perry was a multifaceted entrepreneur, but he did not initiate any of the navigation projects. This was done by the planters, businessmen, and public officials of the area, directly for the most part, but also through state representation. Given the near absence of Jefferson newspapers for the period, it is necessary to follow these initiatives through the Marshall *Texas Republican*, which was intensely interested in cotton outlets for Harrison County and provides a regional perspective on transportation improvements.

THE 1849 PROJECT

The first issue of the *Texas Republican* appeared on 26 May 1849. A long article was devoted to the advantages of Harrison County and the critical nature of transportation improvements for realizing the county's possibilities, beginning with navigation improvements: "We have navigation four months in the year. For the sum of $10,000 we can have it at all times. Would this not be desirable? Can our planters not spare $10,000? It is only the one-fortieth part of what they now produce in one year. It will return to their pockets again shortly in the way of cheap rates, convenience, and facility. We think it is time to look seriously into this matter—we mean the improvement of the lake."

Government, it should be noted, was not the court of first appeal. The argument was directed toward those whose financial interests were involved with the contention that improvement costs would be exceeded by transportation savings and business efficiency. Transportation savings would be produced by the lower freight rates that would result from quicker travel time for steamboats, reduced steamboat and freight insurance rates, larger loads, and greater steamboat competition.

Money for privately conducted projects was obtained by subscriptions using circulated forms wherein interested parties could sign up for specific amounts. These forms were distributed throughout Harrison and neighboring counties, with an immediate enthusiastic response according to the 8 June 1849 *Texas Republican*: "From the exertions being made in this and neighboring counties, we have strong hopes that Soda Lake will be, by the commencement of the next season, freed from every obstruction that at present intercepts the navigation. During the last winter and spring, steamers of a large class were constantly in the lake, and all the cotton at the different depots has been carried off. Once thoroughly cleaned out, and boats may navigate the lake whenever they can get to Shreveport. The subscriptions for this purpose have already been very liberal. We shall publish, next week, the names of the subscribers and the amounts subscribed."

The next issue published the subscription list along with a notification that William Perry had been chosen to do the work and stipulations by Perry about the nature of his contract. The initial subscription list contained the names of many important Harrison County planters like the Websters, Marshall businessmen like the Perrys, but also cotton merchants like Cobbs and Todd of Port Caddo:

J. J. Webster, 50 cents per bale of cotton of crop 1849
J. B. Webster, the same.

S. M. Haggerty,	$300		W. D. Perry,	50
J. P. Campbell,	100		J. H. Wingfield,	20
Rene Fitzpatrick,	50		J. H. Cole,	25
Seaborn Arnett,	20		J. D. Perry,	50
W. T. Scott,	50		N. Gufton,	25
H. Currie,	50			
B. W. George,	50			
S. Wilkins,	25			

J. D. Todd,	$150	N. B. Cole,	50
C. C. Mills,	100	W. H. Cobbs,	50
W. F. Baldwin,	15	Perry & Spell,	50
C. K. Andrews,	50	A. Jonnegan,	25
W. W. Pridgen,	25	F. Jones,	50
John McCain,	30	H. P. Perry,	50
		Jesse Denson,	20

At the time the initial subscription list was published, $2,000 of the required $3,000 had been raised. Perry promised to "remove the obstructions to the navigation of the lake," but he did not indicate the geographic scope, which was probably quite extensive given the nature of the contributors, including Campbell of Clinton, Gupton of Monterey, and Mills of Benton. Freight savings of $11,250 per year were projected on the basis, in part, of shipment of 15,000 bales of cotton from Harrison County. The project would provide four feet of water navigable depth throughout. Plans were made to obtain the additional sum at the district court, with the observation that: "It is plain, that this is a mere question of dollars and cents; and, generally, it is equally plain, that people work for their own interest. If, in the present case, it should be so the lake will certainly be cleaned of its obstructions."

In the 27 September 1849 *Texas Republican*, the editor reported that Perry had informed him that the public had misperceived the nature of his contract, which called for the cutting of obstructions to the low-water level of 1848. Although he was ready to begin work, he would not be able to unless the water fell to that level. There was still $600 to be raised: "This will not be an objection to him, however, as it will undoubtedly be raised." Nevertheless, this project does not appear to have been undertaken, as is indicated by the 20 May 1854 *Texas Republican*: "When we consider the large number interested in the navigation of the Lake, and the small amount required to clean it out, it is certainly surprising that it has been neglected so long. Had the work been done seven years ago, it would have been a saving to Harrison County alone of thirty or forty thousand dollars over and above the cost."

At the same time that Perry's project was under consideration, the *Texas Republican* published a series of articles on a project to clear out the Sabine River to Fredonia at a cost of $10,000. Although this project was of primary interest to the lower Texas counties along the Sabine, it was also of interest to the lower part of Harrison County, because Fredonia was only about fifteen miles southwest of Marshall. The 7 February 1850 *Texas Republican* reports that the *Buffalo*, at 142 feet by 42 feet, reached Fredonia and returned with 300 bales of cotton and fifteen or twenty passengers, meeting no damage or serious obstacles.

The degree of interest in navigation improvements is best expressed in the 5 July 1851 *Texas Republican*, which describes a forthcoming meeting to consider clearing out Little Cypress Bayou at a cost of $2,000 to make it navigable for keelboats in the hope that it would eventually prove navigable for steamboats. The project was of great interest to Upshur County and was expected to increase land values significantly. The notification for the meeting mentions an added inducement that appears to have been common to all public meetings in Northeast Texas:

> INTERNAL IMPROVEMENTS.
>
> A meeting of the Citizens interested in the navigation of Little Cypress, is requested at the Bluff just above the county line, about a mile and a quarter north of Ray's, on Wednesday, the 16th of July. The object of the meeting is to take some steps to open the above stream so that it may be navigated for keel boats.
>
> The eating part will not be neglected. There will be an extensive fish fry, and a good dinner, for all those who may attend.

THE 1854 PROJECT

Interest in clearing out Cypress Bayou and the lakes was revived early in 1853. A correspondent to the *Jefferson Herald* made an appeal, which was published in the *Texas Republican* on 19 February, along with a commentary by the *Herald* editor. The correspondent stated: "I hope that those interested in the Lake navigation will be aroused to their interest, and take active steps toward clearing out the Lake. There is sufficient water for boats to bring out full loads of cotton if the stumps were removed. The most effectual plan, in my opinion, would be to call meetings of the planters and merchants—say at Jefferson, Smithland, Benton, Port Caddo, Marshall, and in the neighborhood of Swanson's and Mooring's, and get them to sign an article of agreement to pay 50c. a bale on the cotton crop of 1853, the tax to be collected by the warehousemen for the benefit of whoever will clear out the Lake."

The editor of the *Herald* observed: "Either the plan here proposed, or some other and better one should be immediately adopted. We feel confident from conversation with merchants and others here, that an amount of money can be raised by subscription sufficient to clear out the stumps, which now form the only obstruction to the successful navigation of the Lake." It should be noted that the term "clearing out the stumps" did not refer to actual stump removal, but rather to the cutting of dead and living standing timber to the waterline, with the amount of trunk that could be removed dependent on the depth of the water. This is why all such projects were conducted during low-water periods.

When R. W. Loughery, the editor of the *Texas Republican*, visited Jefferson more than a year later in May 1854, he found sentiment strongly in favor of a subscription approach and indicated that a meeting would be held on the twentieth. The 3 June 1854 *Texas Republican* reports that the meeting was held and that a resolution had been adopted to appoint one person in each district who would be responsible for subscriptions, with reports to be presented at a public meeting and barbecue in Jefferson on the Fourth of July. In addition, one thousand copies of an address setting forth the importance of the proposed improvements were distributed.

The 17 June *Texas Republican* published a "Lake Meeting" article that solicited interest in the attendance of a meeting at the courthouse in Marshall on that day "for the purpose of taking measures to assist in cleaning out the Lake." The newspaper warned that the current interest in railroad possibilities should not detract from navigation improvements, because railroads took many years to build: "In the mean time, we have to depend upon the Lake, and the question arises, whether prudence and wisdom do not counsel us to remove the obstructions which interfere with its navigation. It is the opinion of many persons, that if the Lake were cleaned out as far as Port Caddo that steamboats could reach that place, and Benton whenever they can get to Shreveport. Would this not be a great advantage, not alone to Marshall and to Harrison, but to the surrounding counties? We venture the assertion, that before the railroad is built, we will be paid back four-fold the money expended."

Loughery was unable to attend the Independence Day celebration and lake barbecue at Jefferson but reports that subscriptions amounting to $6,000 had been submitted and that other subscription lists were expected. The entertainment was concluded with a ball at the Alhambra Hall and a supper at the Jefferson Hotel. The 15 July *Texas Republican* reports that subscriptions had reached $8,000; the 22 July issue reports that a long list of New Orleans subscribers had appeared in the *Jefferson Herald*, suggesting the strong commercial relationships between New Orleans and the ports and landings along the route; and the 12 August issue reports that "Our Jefferson friends are advertising for one hundred hands to clean out the Lake. Here is a chance for laborers."

This project was definitely conducted and involved activities in Louisiana as well as in Texas. William Perry had the contract for improvements between Jefferson and Port Caddo, and Capt. Robert H. Martin had a contract for improvements between Port Caddo and Albany. The only information on Perry's portion of the project was published in the 9 September 1854 *Texas Republican*. Perry informed the public through the *Jefferson Herald* that he had been engaged with twenty hands in cleaning out the lake, that the work on the banks between Jefferson and Smithland was complete, and that he was waiting for lower water to commence work on the body of the stream. The latter portion of this effort required an unusual procedure. In Perry's words: "We have a dam in progress above the bridge at Jefferson, which will be finished next week, the object of which is to throw all the running water out through a slough or chain of lakes on the Harrison side, which will convey the water some six miles below Jefferson, and will, doubtless, make all the shallow places dry, if the lower lake comes down to near low water mark."

The bridge referred to was Johnson's Bridge at the foot of Houston Street, which crossed over Cypress Bayou on the old road to Marshall, as shown on J. Eppinger's 1850 *Map of Jefferson* (**fig. 10-1**). Perry had built a dam above this bridge with the intention of deflecting the water remaining in the bayou during low water to the south side of the bayou. This water would travel down low areas in the bayou's floodplain to Smithland. The deflection would cause shallow areas of the bayou to be exposed, which could then be dug out by hand.

Whether these actions were taken is unknown. However, it is almost certain that they were, because this was the inception of the most extreme low-water conditions ever encountered by Jefferson. Whether

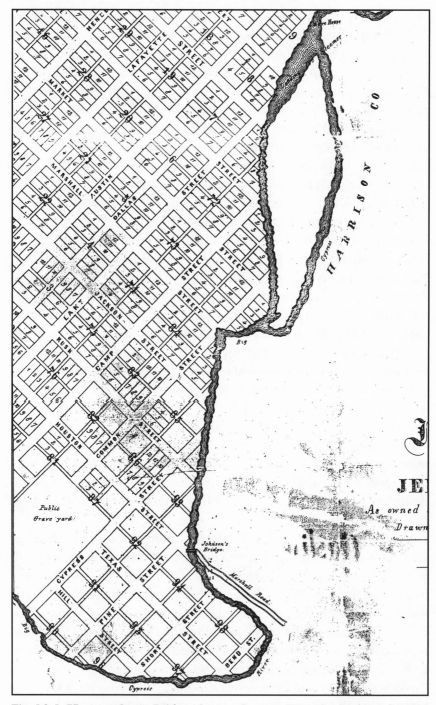

Fig. 10-1. Houston Street Bridge. *Source: Courtesy Texas General Land Office, Austin*

Perry's improvement efforts extended down to Port Caddo is also not known. Any work conducted downstream of Smithland would have involved the cutting of stumps down to the low-water level in the Dougherty's Defeat and Benton areas.

The second portion of the 1854 project was conducted by Robert H. Martin, who first appears in the navigation record in 1851 as captain of the *Osceola*, a boat owned in Port Caddo. Martin operated the *Cleona* from 1852 through 1854, making at least twenty-five trips between New Orleans and Jefferson and Port Caddo. He was, therefore, thoroughly acquainted with the route. The information on his activities is contained in the 4 November 1854 *Texas Republican*, as provided by William Cobbs, cotton merchant at Port Caddo:

> IMPROVEMENT OF THE LAKE.—We learn from our friend, W. H. Cobb, Esq., that Capt. R. H. Martin, is now engaged with some fifteen hands, in cleaning out the obstructions in that portion of the Lake between Port Caddo and Albany. This is one of the most difficult points; but it is believed that the expenditure of fourteen or fifteen hundred dollars upon it, will improve it in such manner as to give us certain navigation throughout the boating season.— Subscription lists will be found at nearly all the stores in Marshall, and planters and others interested, will no doubt avail themselves of the opportunity to aid in paying the expenses of this improvement, as it will be of incalculable advantage to the whole country.

Martin's portion of the project involved major activities in Soda Lake and Caddo Lake. Martin's activities in Soda Lake were preceded by those of Lt. Washington Seawell, whose 1830–31 improvement project established a route around the raft to the upper Red River, including the removal of standing timber and other obstructions in Soda Lake. In addition, in 1847 the Louisiana state engineer was instructed "to finish the improvement, as soon as may be practicable," of Twelvemile Bayou and Soda Lake to the mouth of Black Bayou. This was obviously a modification to the route around the raft.

Martin was the first to tackle the area from the perspective of the needs of the Cypress Bayou and the lakes route, and his particular contribution to the Soda Lake improvements was the building of a cutroad across the Albany Flats area, bypassing the channel loop of Twelvemile Bayou and establishing a straight high-water channel through the lake (**fig. 10-2**). Martin's Cutroad across Albany Flats was about a mile long and involved the cutting of timber down to low water so that boats could pass over in high water. A photograph of Sale and Murphy Canal, which was a late route back to the Red River above the raft, gives some idea of what Martin's Cutroad would have looked like in extreme low water (**fig. 10-3**). However, the canal was a dug channel, whereas Martin's Cutroad was limited to the removal of standing timber.

That Martin actually constructed this cutroad in 1854 is known from the fact that a straight high-water channel through the lake is shown on Charles Fuller's January 1855 *Map of Red River With Its Bayous and Lakes in the Vicinity of the Raft*, along with the fact that it is named Martin's Cutroad in a 21 February 1872 *Shreveport Times* article. In addition, a 16 February 1870 *South-Western* article refers to the major cutroads through the lake (i.e., Soda Lake and Caddo Lake) as having been cut by Martin: "The Rudolph and Rapides report the bayou with 7 feet, and the lakes falling. There are 4 feet 4 inches in the cut roads through the lake, and a boat drawing that much must stick to the channel close as a brother, or run head on upon various and

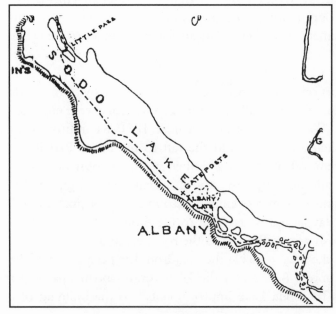

Fig. 10-2. Martin's Cutroad. *Source: H. Ex. Doc. 103, 48th Cong., 2nd Sess.*

Fig. 10-3. Cutroad. *Source: Annual Report of the Chief of Engineers, 1893.*

sundry stumps. These 'cut roads' were made some years ago, we believe, by Capt. Martin, now of the Rapides, by cutting the trees as low as possible when the water was very low, so as to permit the passage of boats over them at an ordinary stage of water."

Martin's second major cutroad was at the northern end of Caddo Lake and is designated Withenberry Road on maps such as W. P. Wooten's 1907 *Cypress Bayou & the Lakes* (**fig. 10-4**). It was a high-water channel allowing the bypassing of a large bend in the channel of Cypress Bayou beneath Caddo Lake. This was not a dug channel, but rather a cutroad, involving tree removal down to the low-water level. Its course has been almost entirely obliterated by cypress trees that grew up in the area as a result of the water regime imposed by the 1914 dam.

Martin made this cutroad in 1854, based on the 1870 *South-Western* article mentioning Martin as responsible for the major cutroads through the lakes and from the fact that it was designated Martin's Cutroad in a *Flavilla* memorandum in the 28 December 1871 *Shreveport Times.*

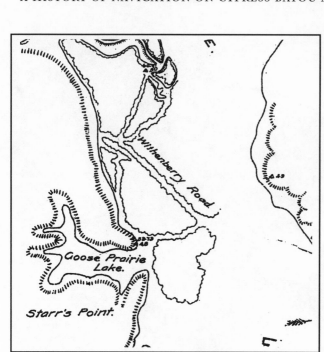

Fig. 10-4. Withenbury Cutroad. *Source: H. Doc. 20, 60ʰ Cong., 1ˢᵗ Sess.*

In addition, it appears on Lt. Eugene Woodruff's 1872 *Map of the Red River Raft Region and Cypress Bayou*, which was prepared before any federal projects were conducted in the area.

The name Withenberry Cutroad was derived from Capt. W. W. Withenbury and should not be taken to suggest that Withenbury constructed the cutroad. If Withenbury had been a participant in the project, it would have been mentioned in the November 1854 *Texas Republican* article describing Martin's efforts, because Withenbury was one of the most prominent captains in the Jefferson trade. Martin probably named the cutroad after his fellow captain, who had been instrumental in opening many passages on the route, and the designation was used to distinguish the Caddo Lake cutroad from Martin's Cutroad on Soda Lake.

Martin's contract was to provide improvements from Albany to Port Caddo. Whether he did any work above Withenbury Road is not known. However, it is probable that he did some timber removal in the area from Bois d'Arc Pass down to the head of the cutroad. Bois d'Arc Pass was the high-water route into Cypress Bayou. Timber removal would probably not have been done in the immediate vicinity of the pass, which carried a sufficient amount of water to prohibit the development of cypress trees. If this work were conducted, it would have been lower down toward the head of the cutroad.

Respecting Perry's and Martin's efforts, the 29 November 1854 *South-Western* says that "Much good has already been done by cutting away the stumps." One of the interesting features of these improvements was that the Martin portion of the project had been conducted almost entirely at Martin's expense, according to the 25 May 1881 *New Orleans Daily Democrat*: "The navigation of the lakes between Shreveport and Jefferson being difficult, slow and tedious by reason of the numerous cypress and post-oak stumps in them, Capt. Martin, in the summer of 1855, we believe it was, the waters being unusually low that year, at his own expense, save $100 contributed by the late John Speake, then of Jefferson, but afterward of New Orleans, hired a force of men and cut out wide, straight lanes through these stumps, taking them off level with the ground. This was a three or four months' job, but he completed it, and thereby wonderfully improved the navigation, every boat in the trade ever since running in what are known to this day as 'Martin's cut roads.'"

The reason why Martin conducted this work at his own expense is unknown. Steamboatmen made minor improvements by occasionally cutting away trees and removing minor obstructions, but large-scale projects were few in number and usually were undertaken only when there was an opportunity to charge tolls, as was the case with the new routes that were developed around the raft. Martin had no way to capture the public benefits of his improvements. He was a resident of Marshall, was to become mayor, and was widely recognized for the high quality of the services provided by the boats he captained. He may simply have been acting for the public good during a period when navigation was suspended, or perhaps assumed that he would eventually be paid.

Another interesting feature of these improvements is that they were initiated by private subscription at a time when the Texas Legislature had already proposed an ambitious state internal improvements effort covering all of the major and many of the minor streams. The proposal's text appears in the 2 July 1853 *Texas Republican* and includes the following appropriations for the area: (1) $12,000 for Ferry Lake from the Louisiana line to Jefferson; (2) $2,000 for Cypress Bayou from Jefferson to Watson's Ferry; (3) $2,000 for Little Cypress Bayou; and (4) $1,000 for Jim's Bayou. Given the fact that the entire area between the state line and Jefferson was covered by the $12,000 appropriation, the section from Jefferson to Watson's Ferry must have been above Jefferson, probably to the Daingerfield area. The idea of extending navigation above Jefferson was, in fact, the subject of much conversation in the Daingerfield area in July 1851.

This proposal was submitted to the voters for approval, as was common for large civil works expenditures in the 1800s. R. W. Loughery, the editor of the *Texas Republican*, objected in the 2 July 1853 issue to the inclusion of numerous minor streams of little conceivable value, rightly pointing out that it was a "log rolling scheme" designed to "appeal to every section, by the promise of some local benefit, which would render voters willing to accept it with all its defects."

THE 1857 PROJECT

Loughery reported on the River Bill, as passed, in the 9 August 1856 *Texas Republican*, remarking that he had read the legislation with care and had found the details admirably drawn. Apparently, many of the initiatives for minor streams were no longer under consideration. The legislation provided for a state contribution of $4,000 for every $1,000 raised by private contributions, not to exceed $50,000 per project. A state engineer office was to be created to examine the work that needed to be done and to contract for its performance.

William Fields of Galveston was appointed the first Texas state engineer to superintend the improvements. Jefferson took the initiative on seeking out a contractor, as indicated by a clipping from the *Jefferson Herald* in the 11 February 1857 *South-Western*: "The time is fast approaching when the above subject must be considered. The benefits to be derived from the $25,000 appropriated will be incalculable to the large country interested, and we hope that the matter will not lose the attention its importance demands at this time. We feel free to say that colonel Fields, the state engineer, will not be able to reach us here at the proper time, and, therefore, we should use every means to ascertain who is best acquainted with the stream, and best qualified to take charge of the undertaking, before making any recommendation to the governor for the appointment of a substitute. Will our oldest citizens who are qualified so to do, begin to canvass the matter among themselves?"

The person selected to do the work was William Perry, who at the time was a resident of Jefferson and captain and co-owner of the New Orleans–to–Jefferson packet *Bloomer*. Perry may have been able to invest in this boat through money obtained from his 1854 improvement project. He operated the *Bloomer* regularly between November 1856 and August 1857. Perry's third improvement project contract was signed 23 July 1857. The contract announcement and a brief description of the nature of the work is given in the 5 August 1857 *South-Western*: "We learn by the Jefferson Herald that the contract for improving the bayou and lake from that place to the Louisiana line, was awarded to captain Wm. Perry, who is to execute the work for $21,298. He is to give a depth of forty inches water throughout, with a channel 50 feet in width to Smithland, and 125 feet in the lake. The work to be completed in eighteen months. The Herald says, 'this will give us perpetual navigation, and may be considered one of the most important enterprises in which the prosperity of Jefferson and northeastern Texas is largely to share.'"

Because the route crossed state boundaries, it was necessary to secure the participation of Louisiana to effect the needed improvements. Matt Ward, a politically influential Jefferson resident, went to Baton Rouge in March to make an appeal, and his success was immediate. Louisiana already had a state engineer office and agreed to commit existing snagboats and laborers to the improvement and to provide supplemental appropriations if needed. These actions were approved enthusiastically by the New Orleans *Daily Picayune*, as indicated in a long "Lake Caddo Improvement" article that was reproduced in the 25 March 1857 *South-Western*.

Perry's contract was for eighteen months, excluding high-water conditions. Fields's November 1857 state engineer's report, which appears in the 13 February 1858 *Standard*, indicates that high water on Cypress Bayou had delayed implementation of the project, but that Captain Perry, who is described as an "energetic man" and a "gentleman of much experience in such improvements," would begin work as soon as water levels allowed. Perry apparently began work in the summer of 1858. The 15 October 1858 *Texas Republican* reports: "The low water during the summer has been of great advantage to those engaged in improving the lake navigation, and many formidable obstructions have been removed." State Engineer E. F. Gray, who replaced the deceased Fields, was in Marshall for several days in November 1858 on his way to inspect the work in the lake. The September 1859 state engineer's report indicates that the work was not yet completed.

The 10 July 1858 *Harrison Flag* reports: "Capt. Perry has machines nearly completed to saw off the stumps under water, and if we understand him aright, a contract for dredge-boats, to deepen the channel." The saws were probably used in the project, which required cutting below low water. There is nothing in contemporary reports to suggest that Perry used a dredge, which certainly would have been noted. Perry's mention of a dredge was in connection with a proposal made by him to extend the project to Shreveport, which would have required dredging to produce continuous navigation. The editor of the *Harrison Flag* apparently thought Perry was referring to the Texas effort.

The specific points of attack were probably the channel to Smithland and the low areas at Potato Bend, Boon's Bend, Dougherty's Defeat, and Benton. Loughery mentions a dam at the lower landing below Jefferson in his August 1860 trip to Jefferson that may have been part of Perry's project. That a great deal of cutting was done in places like Dougherty's Defeat is known from late sources. Frank Gee's 30 June 1874 Corps report indicates that in the Dougherty's Defeat area, there were "many stumps along the channel and in the shallow places that give much trouble to boats, especially in the low-water season." These stumps were undoubtedly the remnants of Perry's activities.

A progress report on Perry's improvement efforts is given in the *Jefferson Gazette*, as quoted in the 20 October 1858 *South-Western*: "We understand that captain Perry has entirely completed his work between Smithland and Benton. He is now working from Smithland up. We have not learned at what time he expects to go into the lake. He has hands at work just below the wharf, straightening a very ugly bend in the bayou, and may have similar improvements going on at different points, we have not inquired. One thing is certain, navigation to this point will be greatly improved this year."

The article goes on to say that improvements were also made on Cypress Bayou between the turning basin and Marshall Street, a few blocks upstream (see fig. 10-1): "Messrs. Bulkley & Stanly have a number of hands now at work on the bayou from opposite Murphy's warehouse up to Stanly & Nimmo's beef packing establishment. They are clearing out the bayou in a most beautiful manner, and have at the foot of Marshall street, a nice location for a wharf. The bank of the bayou from the foot of Marshall street, up to Stanly & Nimmo's is above high water mark, and is peculiarly adapted to shipping purposes. In the course of a year or two we expect to see the entire space occupied by warehouses. The wharf, however, will be finished in a few weeks."

The reason that Perry was not involved in these upstream efforts is that they were a private undertaking and not part of the state contract. The Stanley & Nimmo packery was located immediately east of the Houston Street bridge. The improvements extended up to the packery, and a wharf was constructed at the foot of Marshall Street, where the upstream end of the split channel formed by St. Catherine's Island provided sufficient room for a turning basin. Chester Bulkley was involved in this project because he had recently purchased St. Catherine's Island and was interested in improving the value of his real estate.

The most significant portion of Perry's project was the digging of a channel at Benton. The Benton cutoffs through which boats now pass were Corps of Engineers projects, with the Lower Benton Cutoff dredged in March 1874 and the Upper Benton Cutoff dredged in January 1875. However, the 1 April 1873 *Shreveport Times* states that the *Lotus No. 3* struck a log sticking out of the bank "just above the Benton cut-off," and the 24 May 1873 *Shreveport Times* states, "The captain of the Clifford reports three and a half feet in the upper Benton cut off, and on Albany Point."

Both cutoffs at Benton were obviously in existence before the Corps began working in the Benton area in 1874. This is confirmed by Gee's report at the inception of the Corps effort, which mentions that "the dredge was taken down the bayou some eighteen or twenty miles to the Benton Cut-offs" and that "There are two cut-offs at Benton. Work was commenced on the lower one, it being the shortest." These cutoffs could not have been made by Jefferson's dredge, which did not operate below Boon's Bend. In addition, the dredge was not purchased until 1871, and the existence of cutoffs along the route was mentioned before that time, such as in the 5 January 1870 *South-Western* report: "The last boats out ran all the cut roads and cut-offs without danger."

The Benton area prior to the Corps efforts is shown in Woodruff's 1872 map (**fig. 10-5**), which shows that the bulk of Perry's effort was devoted to the lower Benton cut. Perry would have used hand labor to produce channels 40 inches deep in low water, in keeping with his contract specifications. The cutoffs were later deepened to 5–10 feet by the Corps. The upper cut was about 2,500 feet long and the lower

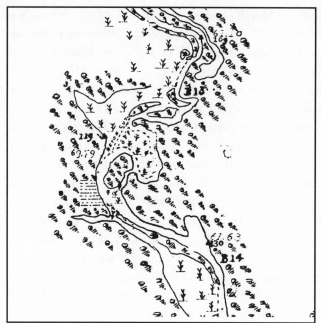

Fig. 10-5. Benton cutoffs. *Source: LSU in Shreveport, Noel Memorial Library Archives*

cut about 400 feet long, as recorded by the Corps in its dredging activities. Together, they saved about two miles in navigation distance. It is unlikely that Perry cut channels 125 feet wide, which would not have been needed. The Corps cuts, which obliterated the signs of Perry's efforts, were made 45 feet wide.

Louisiana was also unable to begin its portion of the project immediately because of high-water conditions. State Engineer Louis Hebert's 1857 annual report (published January 1858) responded to Louisiana Act 173 of 18 March 1857. Hebert was in contact with Fields, his counterpart in Texas. Hebert sent Assistant State Engineer M. J. Fremaux to Soda Lake to conduct a preliminary survey and reported that: "At no time during the year has the stage of the water permitted operations. Lake Sodo is but an overflowing Bayou, as it were. That is, there is a slight channel meandering between the islands at first, and farther on, through a flat ground grown up in trees and covered with stumps. At a low stage of water, the Lake is dry. It is, therefore, at a low stage, that the channel must be cut and staked out."

The 28 July 1858 *Harrison Flag* quotes the *South-Western*: "The Snag-boat Algerine arrived here on Thursday. We understand that she will be put to work in the bayou and lake, removing impediments to

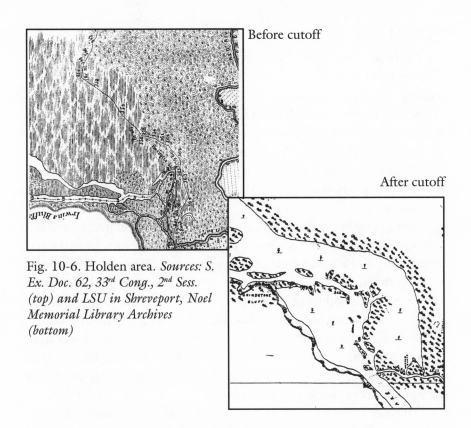

Before cutoff

After cutoff

Fig. 10-6. Holden area. *Sources: S. Ex. Doc. 62, 33rd Cong., 2nd Sess. (top) and LSU in Shreveport, Noel Memorial Library Archives (bottom)*

navigation between this place and the Texas line." The completed Twelvemile Bayou work is described in the 11 September 1858 *Standard*, quoting the *Caddo Gazette*: "Capt. Scott, who commands the State Snag-boat Algerine, has informed us that this bayou has been opened, and every obstruction to navigation removed. The only difficulty which presents itself at this time, is the bottom of the bayou. If there was enough water, we should have good navigation to Jefferson."

The work on the Louisiana side apparently included a channel cut. A Holden Cutoff below Martin's Cutroad is mentioned in the 21 February 1872 *Shreveport Times*. This cutoff involved stream modifications to bypass two large bends in Twelvemile Bayou at the lower end of Soda Lake. The pre-improvement channel is shown in Fuller's 1855 map, and the post-improvement channel is shown in Woodruff's 1872 map **(fig. 10-6)**. The name appears to be connected with the 1859 wreck of the *Joseph Holden*.

SUMMARY

Of the four improvement projects initiated before the Civil War, the first, in 1844, was the most important because it opened Jefferson to steamboat commerce. The second most important was Martin's portion of the 1854 project, which provided a critical passage over Albany Flats that steamboats used whenever possible, as well as Withenbury Cutroad at the northern end of Caddo Lake, which provided large savings in travel distance during high-water periods. The third most important was Perry's portion of the 1857 project, which provided cutoffs of convoluted bends at Benton.

Stump cutting and timber clearing obviously facilitated steamboat passage, but it probably made the route more dangerous by making it faster and at the same time encouraging risk taking by steamboats moving through stump fields. Perry probably contributed to at least one wreck by producing a stump at the head of the Upper Benton Cutoff that snagged the *Lotus No. 3* in 1873. Perry's digging efforts below Jefferson and in the Benton area could not have lasted very long because of rapid siltation. This is probably why the area improved in 1854 needed to be reworked in 1857 and why low water produced continual access problems for Jefferson.

The pre-improvement situation was not as bad and the post-improvement situation not as good as suggested by the newspapers. The *Texas Republican*'s assertion on 27 September 1849 that the route was navigable only four or five months in the year and that improvements could make it "navigable at all seasons" is not borne out by the navigation record. In 1849, for example, boats operated up to Jefferson or Port Caddo in all months except August. Although it is true that boats ceased operating in the direction of Jefferson after July in 1851, this was because the Red River was impassable.

Because the amount of water that entered the lakes from the Red River was the dominant factor in the navigability of the route, improvements could not significantly extend the navigation season. The primary effects were probably to enable a larger class of boats to operate for longer periods and for all boats to operate more efficiently in terms of time and freight loads. All-season navigability could only be accomplished through massive construction projects that could not even be contemplated for the route before the Civil War.

The peculiar features of these early projects were that they were conducted with private subscriptions, including the state-initiated 1857 project, and were based primarily on hand labor, involving contract workers in Texas and the slaves under the authority of the Louisiana state engineer's office. There is no evidence of municipal participation in the funding of any of these projects. Private contributions were secured voluntarily from the direct beneficiaries through community efforts, and the contributions were generally scaled to the degree of benefit. The contributors were planters and businessmen and included cotton merchants in New Orleans. All of the work was done under contract by local favorites such as Perry and Martin because of the high degree of local involvement in decision making.

The pre–Civil War improvements were primarily locally inspired and privately funded in the context of tremendous community support for transportation improvements of all types. The immediate practical interests of the planters and businessmen were combined with a desire for local and regional expansion that would extend beyond their persons and lifetimes. Their contributions, and the efforts of men like Perry and Martin, established the navigational features of the route that served as the base for significant expansions of steamboat activity in the late 1850s and early 1860s and the postwar acceleration of commerce.

·11·
Wrecks

PATTERNS

The steamboats that operated on the tributaries of the Mississippi were wooden-hulled, structurally weak vessels with high-pressure steam engines that carried largely unprotected cargoes through areas characterized by swift currents, shoals, and snags. Boats were run constantly by heavy drinking crews that did not get enough sleep. Freights were at their maximum whenever possible, and boats were pushed to their physical limits to negotiate tight places. The rules of the road were largely informal, and races that tested the capacity of boilers were used to break the tedium of voyages and simply because they were fun.

Because of these factors, it is not surprising that wrecks were common and that the life of a steamboat seldom extended much beyond five years. Wrecks were produced through snagging, explosion, fire, and collision. Snags produced the greatest loss of boats and explosions the greatest loss of life, with the first explosion aboard the *Washington* on the Ohio River in June 1816, when thirteen crewmen were killed and Capt. Henry Shreve was blown overboard.

Many of the boats that were in the Jefferson trade ended their days on the Red River. Wrecks west of Shreveport were not uncommon and involved snagging, explosion, and fire; but there were no collisions. The characteristics of the route were peculiar and segmented.

Twelvemile Bayou was the only portion with a swift current, complicated by caving banks. Soda Lake was mud choked, stump infested, and occasionally windy. Caddo Lake was generally deeper, but also windy, and filled with stumps, logs, and standing rotting timber. Cypress Bayou provided a confined channel fringed with stumps, but without disturbing currents.

Although empirical comparisons are not possible, it appears that Cypress Bayou and the lakes were much safer than the Red and the Mississippi, where currents were swift and dynamic, and shoals and snags constantly changed position. The Cypress Bayou and the lakes route was relatively placid. Ironically, the greatest navigation hazards were the result of navigation improvements, because stumps created by timber removal produced the greatest difficulties. These were fixed hazards; but the conditions for encounter were variable, depending on water levels, boat draft, and freight loads.

Although wrecks are fascinating, they tend to obscure the normal difficulties of navigation and boat operation. Steamboats seldom sank or were totally disabled on the Cypress Bayou and the lakes route. Even so, they were plagued by equipment breakage, minor hull damage, and groundings. These were generally not considered worthy of reporting in the navigation columns of the newspapers unless providing a reason for delay or an illustration of navigation conditions. Some of these accidents that were less than wrecks were nevertheless severe. One example is the *Bloomer*, as reported in the 7 November 1857 *Texas Republican*, quoting the *South-Western*: "The steamer Bloomer, on her recent trip from New Orleans to Jefferson, struck a snag a short distance below the latter place, which caused her to leak so rapidly that there was one foot of water in her hold before the accident attracted attention. Through the exertions of the officers and crew, aided by the passengers, the boat was kept afloat until she reached Jefferson, where the damage was repaired. The cargo was but slightly injured."

Another example of a near wreck was the *Alexander Speer*, as reported in the 3 October 1866 *South-Western*: "The New Orleans and Jefferson packet Alex. Speer, captain John White, arrived from Jefferson to day, with 50 bales of cotton and a fair trip of passengers. We regret to learn from her officers that on her trip she struck a stump near the 'Gate' in Soda lake, and came very near proving a total loss. It was only through the utmost exertions of her crew that she was saved.

But little of her freight was damaged, as most of the cargo in the hold was wet freight."

Near wrecks such as the *Bloomer* and *Alexander Speer* were uncommon. However, they were joined by a multitude of groundings, stump hangings, and mechanical failures that often required minor repairs but more commonly were simply occasions for delay. A few examples will suffice. The 28 February 1855 *South-Western*, citing the *Jefferson Herald*, reports "the little steamboat Augusta to be aground somewhere between this port and Jefferson." The 18 March 1868 *South-Western* reports that the *Frolic* "had the misfortune to knock one of her chimneys down in Cypress bayou, without doing any injury to the trees on the bank." And the 12 January 1870 *South-Western* reports on the *Lotus No. 3* from Jefferson that "She ran the channel through the lakes to keep from stumping it. As it was, she was on a stump some time and was pulled off by the Flavilla."

Although many more boats sank on the Cypress Bayou and the lakes route than has generally been assumed, most of these sinkings were temporary. Steamboats involved significant capital investments and were raised whenever possible. The technology for raising sunken boats went back to ancient times and proceeded apace with the development of steam navigation. It was a relatively simple matter in the shallow waters of Cypress Bayou and the lakes to patch a hull, seal off and pump out the hold, and raise a boat that had been sunk by a snag. For difficult cases there were professional divers and specially designed and equipped bell boats. Wreck reports must be followed by analyses of subsequent newspaper issues to determine the final disposition of a boat: wrecks might be raised weeks and even months later.

If a hull were broken beyond repair, the machinery could at least be salvaged. Many new hulls were outfitted with machinery from sunken boats or, more commonly, from boats whose hulls had simply worn out. Steamboat crews were good at wrecking, and professional salvagers could be employed if needed. These procedures were commonly used to remove valuable machinery and to destroy unusable hulls that constituted navigation hazards. This was particularly important in the relatively confined route west of Shreveport where an in-channel wreck could prohibit the passage of other boats. Again, follow-up work in the newspapers is needed to determine final disposition of a wreck.

THE EVIDENCE

There are three important sources for the initial identification of wrecks on Cypress Bayou and the lakes. Wrecks from the early period of steamboat activity are covered in *Merchant Steam Vessels of the United States, 1790–1868* (generally referred to as the Lytle-Holdcamper list), which is highly reliable because it is based on federal sources. The Works Progress Administration's 1938 *Wreck Reports* is derived from U.S. Customs district records for the Port of New Orleans for the period 1873–1924.

The most comprehensive list of wrecks on the Cypress Bayou and the lakes route is Swain's 1893 *Red River Directory*. A typescript of this list, which is generally reliable, can be found in the Dewey Somdal Papers at Louisiana State University in Shreveport. I have not been able to find any record of the original, which may have been prepared by Andy Swain, a well-known pilot on the Red River. In addition, N. Philip Norman's 1942 essay, "The Red River of the South," contains information on the *Osage* and *Seven Up*. Norman cites Capt. F. W. Wooldridge and the papers of Maude O'Pry as his sources; but the ultimate derivation appears to be Swain's directory, and no additional information is provided.

Wreck lists such as Swain's must be used with care. Locations are generally somewhat vague, and inclusions such as "wrecked at Devil's Elbow" can be misleading because this was a name common to many bends. Lists based on memory are often faulty, and the absence of specific dates for particular wrecks can produce misplaced associations. Most importantly, the Cypress Bayou and the lakes route shared a first leg with the upper Red River trade. A mere enumeration of Twelvemile Bayou and Soda Lake wrecks is out of place in an analysis of steamboat activities west of Shreveport and can produce a false perspective on the relative dangers of various segments of the route. Obviously, upper Red River boat wrecks should be used only to provide supplementary information in an analysis of the route.

The Lytle-Holdcamper list provides information on seven wrecks west of Shreveport:

1. *Cotton Plant*—wrecked by hitting the bank of Twelvemile Bayou on May 29, 1845, with five lives lost.
2. *Jim Gilmer*—snagged on Soda Lake on March 13, 1851, with two lives lost.

3. *Joseph Holden*—snagged on Twelvemile Bayou on April 7, 1859, with no lives lost.
4. *L. Dillard*—snagged on Soda Lake on January 31, 1867, with no lives lost.
5. *Lizzie Lee*—snagged on Twelvemile Bayou on January 13, 1857, with no lives lost.
6. *Marion*—snagged on Soda Lake on January 7, 1859, with no lives lost.
7. *Mittie Stephens*—burned by fire in hay on February 11, 1869, with many lives lost.

Of these seven boats, the *Joseph Holden, L. Dillard, Lizzie Lee,* and *Mittie Stephens* were on their way from or to Jefferson out of Shreveport. According to the 23 May 1845 *Daily Picayune,* the *Cotton Plant* was bound for the upper Red River and sank on Twelvemile Bayou on the seventeenth with three lives lost. According to the 5 January 1859 *South-Western,* the *Marion* was returning from upper Red River when she struck a stump on Albany bar. The *Jim Gilmer* may have been traveling on the route when she was snagged, but I have been unable to obtain a newspaper report that would establish her direction of movement. Newspapers indicate that the *Joseph Holden* wrecked on Soda Lake rather than Twelvemile Bayou, but newspaper accounts are not always correct.

The WPA wreck reports provide information on two boats:

1. *Albany*—struck by a raft on Twelvemile Bayou at Griffen's Place on 8 August 1878.
2. *Lessie B.*—burned by fire in cotton on Cypress Bayou fifteen miles from Jefferson on 21 March 1882.

The *Lessie B.* was on her way back from Jefferson when she burned near Benton. The *Albany* is reported to have been on her way to Albany when she wrecked. However, this boat was a local carrier out of Shreveport and made many trips during 1878. I have not been able to obtain a newspaper wreck report that would confirm the WPA listing.

Swain's directory provides information on thirteen wrecks:

1. *Albany*—sunk at Twelvemile Bayou.
2. *Caddo Belle*—sunk in Cypress Bayou.

3. *Dillard*—sunk at foot of Soda Lake.
4. *Jos. Holden*—sunk in bayou below Albany, 1860.
5. *Lake City*—sunk at Jefferson, Texas.
6. *Lizzie Lee*—sunk in Twelvemile Bayou.
7. *Lessie B.*—burned above Benton, Cypress Bayou.
8. *Mittie Stephens*—burned below Swanson's Landing in Caddo Lake.
9. *Marion*—sunk at Albany.
10. *M. L. Dougherty*—sunk in bayou above Benton, Texas.
11. *Osage*—sunk in Soda Lake.
12. *Seven Up*—sunk in Twelvemile Bayou.
13. *Wm. R. Douglass*—sunk above Benton, Cypress Bayou.

Of these thirteen, the *Albany, L. Dillard, Joseph Holden, Lizzie Lee, Lessie B., Mittie Stephens,* and *Marion* are covered by Lytle-Holdcamper or the WPA. The *Caddo Belle, Lake City,* and *William R. Douglass* are confirmed by newspaper accounts, and the *Mary L. Dougherty* can be inferred from collateral evidence. There is no record of a boat named the *Seven Up.* Although there was an *Osage,* she does not appear in the navigation record as operating west of Shreveport.

The following wrecks are not covered in wreck lists but appear in newspaper articles:

1. *Alida*—Caddo Lake, 1855.
2. *Anna*—Caddo Lake, 1872.
3. *Caroline*—Soda Lake, 1867.
4. *Cuba No. 2*—Caddo Lake, 1868.
5. *De De*—Big Willow Pass, 1856.
6. *Echo*—Soda Lake, 1853.
7. *Larkin Edwards*—Cypress Bayou, 1860.
8. *Lizzie Hopkins*—Soda Lake, 1870.
9. *Lotus No. 3*—Cypress Bayou, 1873.
10. *Lotus No. 3*—Soda Lake, 1876.
11. *Monterey*—Soda Lake, 1850.
12. *Royal George*—Twelvemile Bayou, 1873.
13. *Wamadee*—Twelvemile Bayou, 1865.
14. *Wash Sentell*—Cypress Bayou, 1872.

These wrecks do not appear in the previous lists because they were all raised. All of the boats that wrecked on Cypress Bayou or Caddo Lake were moving from or to Jefferson. The *De De*, which wrecked in Big Willow Pass, was on her way to Jefferson. The *Royal George* and *Wamadee*, which wrecked on Twelvemile Bayou, were on their way to Jefferson. The *Echo, Lizzie Hopkins,* and *Lotus No. 3,* which wrecked on Soda Lake, were on their way from or to Jefferson, and the *Monterey* was destined for Port Caddo. The *Caroline*, which also wrecked on Soda Lake, was probably on her way to Jefferson, but the issues of the *South-Western* covering the specifics of the wreck are missing or unintelligible.

Joining the wreck lists and additional newspaper reports together produces a list of twenty-five wrecks for the route, including five on Twelvemile Bayou, seven on Soda Lake, one in Big Willow Pass, four on Caddo Lake, and eight on Cypress Bayou. Only a few of these wrecks are shown on maps. The exact location of the wreck of the *Mittie Stephens* is shown on a highly reliable map prepared only a few years after the event. The wreck of the *L. Dillard* was a well-known marker on Soda Lake and appears on T. S. Hardee's 1871 *Geographical, Historical and Statistical Map of Louisiana*.

Alban and Oliver's 1868 *Route to Surround the Red River Raft* shows the exact locations of the wrecks of the *L. Dillard, Cotton Plant,* and *Lizzie Lee* and the "state boat" *Sterling*. The *Theodore Sterling* (formerly *Kalbaugh*) was a U.S. government boat employed in raft removal efforts on the Red River in the 1870s. R. E. Jacobs's 1935 *Routes of Steamboats to Surround Rafts in Red River* shows the approximate location of the wreck of the *Mittie Stephens* (derived from the previously mentioned source) and the exact locations of the wrecks of the *L. Dillard, Cotton Plant, Lizzie Lee,* and *Sterling* (all derived from Alban and Oliver). Jacobs's map also shows the exact location of the wreck of the *Joseph Holden*, but the derivation is unknown.

From the 1870s through the early 1900s, the Corps of Engineers conducted a navigation improvement project on Cypress Bayou and the lakes. The 1894 annual Corps report indicates that the upper parts of one wreck on Twelvemile Bayou and three wrecks on Soda Lake were destroyed, leaving only floor timbers and bottom planking, so that the wrecks no longer constituted a navigation hazard. The Twelvemile Bayou wreck was identified as the *Lizzie Lee* and the three Soda Lake wrecks near Albany as the *Marion, Texas,* and *Juberquit*.

The *Juberquit* does not appear in the navigation record. There were many boats named *Texas* and at least two that operated in the direction of Jefferson. However, in the absence of a wreck date in the report and a wreck report for a *Texas* in the newspapers, it is impossible to tell whether this boat was in the Jefferson trade. In addition, an 1899 Corps report on improvements to Cypress Bayou and the lakes indicates that parts of three old wrecks in Twelvemile Bayou were destroyed with explosives.

The twenty-five wrecks involving boats that were operating to the west of Shreveport will be covered sequentially by stream segment.

TWELVEMILE BAYOU

There were five wrecks on Twelvemile Bayou spanning the period 1857–78. This was not the present channel of Twelvemile Bayou, but rather the old channel, which began at the foot of Soda Lake, traveled through areas that are presently land, and emptied into the Red River above Shreveport.

1. The *Wamadee* appears in relation to the route only in conjunction with her wreck and was operating during a low-water period when only the smallest boats were able to reach the vicinity of Jefferson. According to the 29 November 1865 Shreveport *South-Western*, the *Wamadee* had just begun her trip from Shreveport to Jefferson carrying a valuable cargo when she struck a snag about a mile above Shreveport and sank, with boat and cargo reported to be a total loss. Neither the boat nor her contents was covered by insurance. The 6 December 1865 *South-Western* reports that the *Wamadee* had been raised and brought to Shreveport for repairs. This wreck was on the former channel of the Red River that had become a new channel of Twelvemile Bayou through a Red River cutoff.

2. The *Lizzie Lee* was a new 101-ton sidewheeler that made one trip to Jefferson in late November 1856 and was returning to New Orleans from her second trip to Jefferson with a load of cotton when she struck a stump or cluster of sunken logs in Twelvemile Bayou six miles from its confluence with the Red River and sank in a few minutes. The 31 December 1856 *South-Western* (published every Wednesday) says that the sinking occurred the previous Friday evening, that a portion of the cotton had been brought to Shreveport, and that hopes were entertained of raising the boat. The wreck caused considerable

navigation difficulties, but the 18 February 1857 *South-Western* reports: "The steamer Lizzie Lee, sunk a few months since in Twelve Mile bayou, has been raised, and will be immediately repaired and put in running order." The raising apparently was unsuccessful, because this wreck is shown on the 1868 Alban and Oliver map and is reported in the 1894 Corps report to have been partly removed.

3. The *Albany* was described as "a little home packet" and made many local trips out of Shreveport in 1878. The WPA wreck report says that the *Albany*, with Alban as captain, was sunk on 8 August 1878—on her way to Albany—by a raft floating down Twelvemile Bayou at Griffen's Place. There is no report of a wreck for the *Albany* in the *Shreveport Times* for 1878. The boat was seized by the Deputy U.S. Marshal on 6 August at Shreveport to satisfy the claims of some of her employees, occupied space in Cross Bayou on the seventh, was running again on the eighth, and is last reported as laid up at Cross Bayou on the twelfth. This is probably one of the wrecks that was partly removed by the Corps of Engineers in 1899.

4. After the burning of the *Mittie Stephens* on Caddo Lake, the explosion of the *Royal George* on Twelvemile Bayou was the most dramatic disaster in connection with the route. The explosion was covered in detail in the newspapers and in the "Reminiscences of Captain M. L. Scovell, Steamboat Captain on Red River." Matt Scovell was one of three steamboat brothers who were famous Red River captains. Noah and Tiley, who were residents of Louisiana, fought for the Confederacy during the Civil War, and Matt, who was living in Ohio when the war broke out, fought for the Union.

At the age of twenty-two in 1865, Matt went to New Orleans where he received assistance from Tiley in entering the steamboat business, rising rapidly from clerk to chief clerk, pilot, and then captain. In 1873, he was captain of the *Royal George*, which was one of the few boats that continued to serve Shreveport during the yellow fever epidemic of September through November. The *Royal George* was only 135 feet by 27 feet and was said to draw 18 inches with 300 bales of cotton on board when she was first introduced in May 1872.

The *Royal George* made many trips to Jefferson in 1872 and 1873, but she was prohibited from going there during the epidemic. When the quarantine was lifted in November, she immediately began making regular runs between Shreveport and Jefferson. On the evening of 5 December, she left Shreveport with the Jefferson freight of the *Lady*

Lee and *Maria Louise*. It was a bitter-cold night with some ice in Twelvemile Bayou, and the *Royal George* intended to lay up for the night at Albany, just five miles distant, when the boilers exploded at about 8:00.

The explosion occurred on Twelvemile Bayou at Grindstone Bluff about twelve miles above Shreveport according to Scovell and at Quitman Bluffs seventeen miles above Shreveport according to the newspapers. The reason for the explosion was never determined, and the boiler pressure had been checked only a few minutes before. The force of the explosion destroyed the cabin from its forward stair to as far back as the engine room, and the pilot house and officer's cabin fell to the lower deck where the boilers stood. Three men were killed outright, seven were wounded, and two roustabouts were assumed dead under the wreckage. The mate died while being taken to Shreveport. W. C. Ross, the owner of the *Lotta*, was on board with his son. Ross was killed instantly by being blown into the bank of the bayou; the newspaper reported that some effort was required to extricate the body. His son was badly scalded, but he recovered.

Scovell was in charge, but felt ill and went to bed in the hall next to the officer's cabin where it was warmer, leaving the boat under the command of the pilot, Capt. C. F. McLarey. Scovell recounts what transpired in his reminiscences:

> In a minute or so, I heard the explosion. I had time to realize that the boilers had burst and to decide to run aft and get away from escaping steam. This was the last I knew until I landed in the Bayou, fully 100 feet below the boat. I struck the water feet first, and thought I would never quit going down, the water having revived me to consciousness. On coming to the surface, I was congratulating myself that I was not hurt. But I soon found out that I could not see, and concluded my eyes were burned sightless. I was an expert swimmer, and as fast as I came in contact with any of the wreckage, pulled it under me until I had quite a raft sufficient to float on. Suddenly my eye sight came to me, when I slipped off the raft and swam ashore. In the meantime the boat was floating down the Bayou toward me, with all of her cabin, from the Pilot House forward, blown off. I walked up the Bayou and tried to holloa to those on board to throw me a

line and I would make the boat fast. But I could not speak a word. I then discovered that my lower jaw was broken into many pieces. I pulled out most of my teeth that were just hanging by small particles of the gums. The boat had drifted into the bank about where I was standing and made fast. In the place where the boilers had stood, some fire had been left. I was nearly frozen by this time and I got aboard to warm by the fire. There were pork bbls. headed up on the guards, which I climed upon when I became so exhausted I could go no further. Just then I heard the Engineer, John Holsner, and the Clerk, Crate Kouns, coming from aft. Holsner said, "Crate, don't this beat H___. I wonder where the Old Man is." (The Captain of a boat was always called The Old Man, regardless of his age. I was 30 years of age then.) The Clerk replied "I don't know, but probably in the Bayou, dead." By this time they had gotten to where I was and he exclaimed, "Here he is now, wet as a rat and bloody as a stuck pig."

Scovell was brought to Shreveport, where he was a resident, and was able to speak within a month and to walk within two months. Although the upper portions of the *Royal George* were destroyed, the hull was intact and was towed to Shreveport on 7 December by the *Clifford*. Scovell says that she was then brought to New Orleans and outfitted with new boilers and cabin, reentering the Red River trade. Scovell operated many different boats during the following decades; but his account of the explosion of the *Royal George* ends with this comment: "I never made another trip on her."

5. The *Joseph Holden* was a 222-ton sternwheeler that had been operating in the Jefferson trade since 1857. According to the 22 April 1859 *Texas Republican*, the *Joseph Holden* struck a stump and sank about daylight on the thirteenth, two miles above Albany, with no lives lost. The cargo was 1,600 sacks of salt. Because the stern was in deep water, the boat broke in two by her own weight. The 20 April 1859 *South-Western* adds that this boat was moving upstream bound for Jefferson, that she was a total loss and only partly insured, and that the wreck occurred "in the lake, near Albany." The 22 April 1859 *Harrison Flag*, quoting the *Caddo Gazette* through the *Jimplecute*, indicates that the boat sank two miles below Albany in ten feet of water and that aid was given by the *Rescue*.

In spite of what the *Texas Republican* and *South-Western* say, the *Caddo Gazette* is apparently correct in giving the location of the wreck as two miles below Albany, which would place it at the upper end of Twelvemile Bayou, where it is shown on Jacobs's map. It is listed as a Twelvemile Bayou wreck by both Lytle-Holdcamper and Swain. Nevertheless, the lower end of Soda Lake and the upper end of Twelvemile Bayou were undifferentiated, so it could just as easily be classified as a Soda Lake wreck. The important point is Jacobs's location, which appears to be derived from an authoritative source other than the newspapers and is even more plausible if this were the site of the Holden Cutoff. This wreck was probably partly removed by the Corps of Engineers in 1899.

Of the five boats in the Jefferson trade that wrecked on Twelvemile Bayou, three were by snags, one was by a raft, and one was by explosion. The wrecks were evenly distributed over the Twelvemile Bayou portion of the route, and the snaggings occurred in April and November and during low water in December. The explosion was not related to navigation conditions. The *Wamadee* was raised; the *Lizzie Lee* was partly destroyed; and the hull of the *Royal George* was towed back to Shreveport. The dispositions of the wrecks of the *Albany* and *Joseph Holden* are unknown, but they were probably partly destroyed by the Corps of Engineers in 1899.

The only other recorded wreck on Twelvemile Bayou was that of the upper Red River boat *Cotton Plant*, which, after the *Royal George*, was the second-most serious accident on the bayou, as described by Frederic Way in *Way's Packet Directory*: "In the spring of 1845 she took a load of government supplies from New Orleans to Fort Towson, upper Red River, unloaded them, and in returning hit the bank in narrow 12-Mile bayou with disastrous consequences. Her head stuck in the mud, she rounded broadside, and the stern caught on the opposite shore. She listed and filled and the cabin floated off. Five were drowned. A search was made later, after the river fell, for the hull, boilers and machinery, to no avail. Several years later the New Latonia was upbound in the Bayou and the pilot was confronted with a steamboat hull coming toward him, boilers and engine intact, rolling over and over. He prudently landed under a false point, sucked in his breath, and the wreckage passed by without hitting him. It was the missing remains of the Cotton Plant."

SODA LAKE

Soda Lake began at Big Willow Pass near the present foot of Caddo Lake and extended down to the Albany area where it was drained by Twelvemile Bayou. This was an extremely shallow lake that formed in a depression of the Red River floodplain. A cutroad was made through a cypress stand above Albany that served as a high-water passage. During low water, boats followed the old channel of Cypress Bayou that was usually submerged beneath the lake. The point at which the high-water and low-water channels met was called the Gate Post. There were seven recorded wrecks on Soda Lake spanning the years 1850 through 1876. The exact place of half of these wrecks is not known.

1. The *Lotus No. 3* was a 160-foot by 37-foot sternwheeler that had been in the Jefferson trade since 1870 and had already been wrecked on Cypress Bayou in 1873. She was coming back from Jefferson with 1,060 bales of cotton when she struck a stump at the Gate Post at 4:00 on the afternoon of 19 February 1876 and sank in eight feet of water. The water was four to five feet over the main deck with the upper structures protruding. No lives were lost.

As her stern settled, four or five tiers of cotton aft fell off but were recovered. Capt. D. D. Dannals, who was also the principal owner, worked night and day to save the cargo and was assisted by the *Col. A. P. Kouns*, which took 801 bales to Shreveport. The wreck lay straight in the cutroad just below the Gate Post. A marine diver was secured from New Orleans on the twenty-fifth to determine whether she could be raised and, if not, to retrieve the rest of the cotton in the hold.

The little tug *Gussie* set out from Shreveport for the wreck on 2 March with the diver and Dannals on board and towing a flat with all the necessary pumps and other equipment for raising. The *Gussie* came back to Shreveport on the sixth, and Dannals reported that the *Lotus No. 3* had been raised and that he was looking for a pilot to bring her down. Referring to events of the previous day, the 8 March *Shreveport Times* reports: "About dark the steamer Lotus No. 3, Capt. D. D. Dannals, arrived from the scene of her late accident with the two hundred bales of wet cotton in her hold. She does not look a bit worse for her sinking frolic and no stranger to look at her would think she had ever been sunk. She will be repaired here and take out a load of cotton."

2. The *L. Dillard* was built in 1865 and made numerous trips to Jefferson between that year and 1867, when she was wrecked on Soda Lake slightly north of the *Lotus No. 3* on the old channel of Cypress

Bayou looping the cutroad. A fifty-six-ton sternwheeler measuring 107 by 19 feet, this was one of the smallest boats ever to operate on the route and was a local carrier out of Shreveport. Only low-water packets were able to operate on the route in February 1867.

The 6 February 1867 *South-Western* reports that the *L. Dillard* was on the way from Jefferson to Shreveport carrying 397 bales of cotton and a lot of hides when she "got on the stumps in the lake and sank." The cotton was removed by the *Navigator*. Because this boat was inchannel, a wrecking crew was immediately dispatched to work on it. The 30 January *South-Western* reports less than four feet of water in the cutroad, allowing the machinery and upper portions of the boat to be removed, with the hull left intact and serving as a navigation marker for many years thereafter. The machinery of the *L. Dillard* was used on the *Blanton*, as indicated by a constable's sale advertisement in the 24 July 1867 *South-Western*.

3. The wreck of the *Monterey* in 1850 was the first steamboat wreck on the route. The *Monterey* was a 135-foot by 25-foot sidewheeler built in 1846 that made numerous trips to Port Caddo and Jefferson under the captaincy of W. W. Withenbury. The 2 May 1850 *Texas Republican* reports: "The steamer Monterey, about five o'clock on the morning of the 21st ult, 25 miles above Shreveport, on her way to Port Caddo, struck a snag, in the lake, and sunk. A deck hand was unfortunately lost overboard. Cargo total loss." From the mileage figure given, this accident apparently happened in the upper end of Soda Lake. The disposition of the *Monterey* is unknown. She was no longer operative on the route after 1850 and is reported in Lytle-Holdcamper as lost in 1850.

4. The *Echo*, which wrecked in 1853, was the second boat to be lost by Withenbury on the route. This was not the *Echo* that advertised for Fort Caddo in 1842, but rather a new *Echo* built in 1850 and measuring 130 feet by 25 feet. This sidewheeler made many trips to Jefferson under the captaincy of Withenbury in 1851 and 1852. According to the 5 March 1853 *Northern Standard*, "The 'Echo' sank last Friday in the Lake. She ran on a snag, had a load of cotton from Jefferson. If she cannot be raised, she will be destroyed at once to allow the passage of boats." The 5 March *Texas Republican*, quoting the *South-Western*, says that this boat was bound to New Orleans from Port Caddo, that she was carrying 800 bales of cotton and thirty passengers, and that she "struck a stump at the head of Prairie Lake, and sunk. The cotton will be saved,

but it is thought the boat will prove a total loss. The Post Boy has gone up to the wreck." The designation "Prairie Lake" may refer to Soda Lake, but this usage does not appear elsewhere. Apparently this boat was raised, because she is reported in Lytle-Holdcamper as having continued in operation until 1855.

5. The *Jim Gilmer* made only one recorded trip on the route, which was from New Orleans to Port Caddo in 1846. Lytle-Holdcamper indicates she was a 123-foot by 26-foot sidewheeler built in 1846; however, when Josiah Gregg took her out of Shreveport in 1848, he described her as a "dirty little stern-wheel steamer." Lytle-Holdcamper indicates that she was snagged and lost on Soda Lake on 13 March 1851 and that two lives were lost. Frederick Way indicates that the *New Latona* went to get 800 bales of cotton from the sunken *Jim Gilmer* when she encountered the wreck of the *Cotton Plant* tumbling toward her in Twelvemile Bayou. The disposition of this wreck and where she was traveling when she was wrecked is unknown.

6. The 155-foot by 32-foot sternwheeler *Caroline* was built in 1863 and made one trip to Jefferson in 1866. The 6 February 1867 *South-Western* appears to say that the *Caroline* left Shreveport for Jefferson, but this and the next few issues are unintelligible or missing. That the *Caroline* was wrecked in 1867 on Soda Lake around the same time as the *L. Dillard* and was subsequently raised is known from the 27 February and 31 July issues of the *South-Western*:

> We regret to learn that Capt. Bateman has not yet succeeded in raising the Caroline, owing to the sudden rise in the lakes. As she lies perfectly straight, the rise will only retard the work of raising her. Capt. Bateman is still in hopes of seeing her afloat once more. We trust his hopes may be realized.

> The steamer Caroline, Capt. W. D. Bateman, which has been lying on the bottom of Soda Lake for the last six months, made her appearance at our landing yesterday, on her way to the city for repairs. Capt. Bateman deserves credit for the energy he has displayed in raising his boat. She will be ready in a few days to take her place again in the Red River trade.

The *Caroline* operated on the Cypress Bayou and the lakes route in 1869 and 1870, making two trips to Jefferson each year. Lytle-Holdcamper reports her as having been lost in 1870.

7. The *Lizzie Hopkins* was a 453-ton sternwheeler built in 1867 and measuring 159 feet by 36 feet. This was a very heavy boat. Her wreck was brief according to the 26 January 1870 *South-Western*: "We have been furnished the following by Capt. Roots, of the Lizzie Hopkins: 'Hopkins sunk in Soda Lake, on Friday the 21st, with 1561 bales of cotton on board, raised the next day, after getting the Lotus No. 2 to take off 348 bales, came out all right for the down trip; none of her cargo lost and but little damaged; she will soon be repaired and be in place again; the loss by the accident will not be much on either boat or cargo.'" The 19 January *South-Western* reports that the *Lizzie Hopkins* departed for Jefferson on the fifteenth during a low-water period. The wreck obviously occurred on the return trip, because it happened six days later and the boat was carrying cotton. The specific cause of the accident is unknown.

Of the seven wrecks on Soda Lake of boats operating west of Shreveport, all occurred in the first four months of the year. Although some of these were low-water accidents, most appear to have occurred under fairly good navigation conditions. The *Lotus No. 3* wrecked in high water; but this was a large boat carrying a heavy load. All known causes were snags, with the area near the Gate Post apparently causing the greatest difficulties. The wrecks of the *Monterey* and *Jim Gilmer* involved loss of life. Four of the seven Soda Lake wrecks were raised, and one was partly removed.

The only other recorded serious accidents on Soda Lake were the *Hunter* and *Marion*, both of which were passing down through the lake from the upper Red River. The 17 April 1844 *Northern Standard* reports that a few days before the *Hunter* had her bow stove in and was forced to throw overboard five or six hundred bales of cotton. This was probably a serious accident but not a wreck. The 5 January 1859 *South-Western* says that on Sunday the *Marion* struck a stump on Albany bar. No lives were lost and most of the cotton was saved, but the boat proved a total loss. This was one of the wrecks partly removed by the Corps of Engineers in 1894.

WILLOW PASSES

Big Willow Pass between Caddo Lake and Soda Lake produced one major accident. The *De De* was an 80-ton sternwheeler built in Algiers in 1856. It was on her first trip to Jefferson, intending to travel to

Fulton, Arkansas, before returning to Shreveport when, according to the 4 June 1856 *South-Western*, she struck a snag in Big Willow Pass and sank in five feet of water. Two-thirds of the freight was placed on a barge that the *De De* was towing, which was dispatched to Jefferson. The rest of the cargo, including salt, molasses, and whiskey, was on the forecastle and was cast overboard to prevent the boat from breaking in two. The *South-Western* goes on to say that "Through the unremitted exertions of captain Lewis and his officers, the Dede was raised on Saturday, and reached this place Sunday evening. She has been hauled out on Douglass' island and will be thoroughly repaired, and in a few days ready to resume her trips." This boat sank and was raised again at Pecan Point on upper Red River early in 1857, made one trip to Jefferson in June, and is reported by Lytle-Holdcamper as having been lost in 1858.

The wreck of the *De De* was by snag during low water. A possible addition to the Big Willow Pass area was the wreck of the *Alpha*, with B. B. Bonham as captain, at 5:30 A.M. on 20 March 1889 in Stumpy Bayou from an unseen obstruction. The WPA wreck reports indicate that this boat had proceeded from Shreveport to Mooringsport and was on her way to Black Bayou when she sank and proved a total loss.

CADDO LAKE

Caddo Lake was for the most part much deeper than Soda Lake and offered a relatively well-defined channel of Cypress Bayou below the lake for use during low-water periods. The lake was windy at times but generally rather placid. Unseen obstructions such as stumps and submerged logs were a problem; however, the dimensions of the problem should not be exaggerated. Much of the old forest of the Cypress Bayou floodplain was reduced to dead, but standing, timber. The rotting forest and new cypress stands were not much of a hazard because they were visible. Interest in Caddo Lake wrecks has centered on the *Mittie Stephens* because of the dimensions of the tragedy and the mystery surrounding the ultimate fate of the wreck. Nevertheless, it was but one of four wrecks on Caddo Lake, the others of which have receded from memory because they were less dramatic and the boats were raised.

1. The *Anna* was a 156-foot by 32-foot sternwheeler that was one of the Midwest steamers that became important in the Jefferson trade in the early 1870s. She had made one trip to Jefferson in January 1872

and was returning during a low-water period in March with half a load of western produce and furniture when she sank just below Mooringsport from an unreported cause. The 21 March *Shreveport Times* reports that a dispatch had been received the previous day by Stoner Brothers concerning the wreck. This boat was quickly raised. The *Shreveport Times* of the twenty-fourth reports: "We learn from Capt. Hazlett, of the steamer Flirt, that the steamer Anna, lately sunk near Mooringsport, has been raised, and as the Flirt passed, was getting up steam to move up to Mooringsport." On the twenty-sixth, the *Maria Louise* reported having seen the *Anna* on the way to Jefferson to wait for the insurance adjustor from Cincinnati. The *Anna* returned to Shreveport at the end of March.

2. The *Alida* was a 94-ton sternwheeler built in 1853 and measuring 105 feet by 23 feet. The 24 January 1855 *South-Western* reports that the *Alida* had left for Jefferson on Thursday, arrived on Friday, and sank on Monday at Mooring's Landing, with the *Sodo* going to her relief. The 27 January *Texas Republican*, quoting the *Shreveport Democrat*, says that the *Alida* was returning from Jefferson without freight, that she struck a stump in the neighborhood of Pitts' Landing, and that she was run into shallow water by Captain Alban before sinking so that she could be raised without difficulty. The 14 February *South-Western* corrects the location of the wreck and indicates the prospects of raising: "We understand that there is every prospect of raising the Alida, which sunk a few weeks since, at Pitts' landing, and hopes are entertained of getting her afloat during the present week." The fact of raising is established by the issue of the twenty-first: "The steamer Alida has been raised and will be ready to resume her trips on the first rise of water. Her hull was but slightly damaged." This boat continued to operate on the route through 1857.

3. The *Mittie Stephens* was a 224-ton sidewheeler built in 1863 and measuring 170 feet by 29 feet, a fairly large boat for the Jefferson trade. She began running to Jefferson in 1865, appearing for the first time in the extant issues of the *South-Western* on 4 April 1866. She advertised as a regular New Orleans-to-Jefferson packet beginning in 1866 and fulfilled that commitment by making seven trips to Jefferson in 1866, nine in 1867, six in 1868, and two in 1869 before burning on Caddo Lake in February.

Many of the trips made by the *Mittie Stephens* to and from Jefferson were made at night, which was a common practice among steamboats.

The two trips previous to the disaster can be used as examples. On her first trip in 1869, the *Mittie Stephens* departed from Shreveport to Jefferson late at night on 4 January and arrived back in Shreveport early in the evening on the ninth. On the twenty-fourth, she departed for Jefferson late in the evening and arrived back at Shreveport early on the morning of the thirtieth.

Night travel was safe, and the crew was fully acquainted with the route by day and night. The *Mittie Stephens* arrived at Shreveport from New Orleans at 11:00 A.M. on Thursday, 11 February, with her guards flat in the water (indicating that she was fully loaded) and a fair list of passengers. She left late in the evening for Jefferson, for which most of her cargo was consigned. Navigation conditions were ideal. The weather on Thursday and Friday was clear, warm, and spring-like. Reports indicated good navigation for first-class boats with full loads, meaning that the water was very high.

The boat was carrying 274 bales of hay four tiers deep on the guards consigned to federal Reconstruction troops in Jefferson. The hay was extremely dry and insufficiently protected. Iron torch baskets, which were alight, were carried on the bow. A breeze blowing diagonally across the bow carried sparks in the direction of the hay as the *Mittie Stephens* moved through Caddo Lake on the channel of Cypress Bayou shortly after leaving Mooringsport.

At midnight, with the changing of the watchmen, Joe Lodwick, steersman, remarked to William Swain, pilot, that he smelled something burning and at the same time noticed smoke rising from the hay forward on the port side (left side looking forward). This occurred about two and one-half miles below Swanson's Landing according to the 17 February 1869 *South-Western* and about 300 yards from shore according to the 1870 proceedings of the Board of Supervising Inspectors of Steam Vessels.

The alarm was immediately given, the boat headed for shore, and all hands were put to work to extinguish the flames, but without success. In less than five minutes the bow of the boat was run ashore at Jeter's place, with the stern at least 160 feet from shore in 10 feet of water according to the *South-Western*. The inspectors reported that the boat grounded in 3 feet of water forward and from 8 to 10 feet aft.

Most of the passengers and crew were asleep when the fire started and awakened to a scene of immense confusion. Because the front of the boat was enveloped in flames, everyone rushed to the back. Few men of the time could swim, including the people who worked on boats, and women almost never entered the water. A lifeboat was over-occupied, swamped at once, and all in her drowned. Women refused to jump overboard and perished with their children in the flames. Many men jumped overboard at the last minute, some with life preservers; but most were cut to pieces by the paddle wheels, which were left running to force the boat against the shore, a standard operating procedure under such circumstances.

Sixty-two people were lost in the wreck, with forty-three surviving. The lost included thirty-two crew members, seventeen cabin passengers, and thirteen deck passengers. The survivors included thirty-three crew members and ten passengers. The boat was a total loss. This was by far the greatest disaster on the route.

The cause of the accident is clear. The boat should not have been running with lighted fire baskets, which were useful at dock but constituted an impediment to visibility on a running boat. Why the torch baskets were ablaze is not stated in the inspectors' report, and it may be that they were simply not properly extinguished when the *Mittie Stephens* left Mooringsport. The hay should have been better covered. The inspectors determined that the hay was imperfectly protected in the bale (which was the fault of the federal transporters) and on the boat (which was the fault, ultimately, of the captain).

The accident became a disaster for three reasons. It is apparent that the fire was uncontrollable and that the burning bales could not simply be pushed off the guards into the water. It appears that this could not be done because of the intensity of the heat and the quickness of the spread of flames. Although the problem was exacerbated by a stiff wind and the forward movement of the boat, the ultimate cause was the extreme dryness of the hay. The 19 February 1868 *South-Western* indicates that government hay carried to Jefferson was kiln dried. The hay would not have been on board in the first place were it not for the need to supply troops in Jefferson from a Reconstruction headquarters in New Orleans, and the hay would not have been in such a combustible condition had it not been government hay. The sparks generated not just a fire but a near explosion.

The second reason that the accident became a disaster is that it happened at night. A similar accident at the same place during the day would have produced completely different consequences. When the passengers and crew awoke, they did not know where they were; and although the boat quickly reached shore, few could have known that this had occurred. The only thing they could see was an immense wall of fire in front and an immense sheet of darkness in the rear. The moments for decision making were few, and most people either stayed on board or cast themselves indiscriminately into the water and floundered. Disorientation because of darkness was a key element in producing many deaths, since the direction of salvation and the fact that it was only a short distance away were unknown to most. Persons such as William Swain and Joe Lodwick who were among the last to leave the boat but knew where she was in relation to the shore had no difficulty in jumping from the stern and swimming to the safety of shore.

The third reason for the disaster was the unfamiliarity with water on the part of most persons during the 1800s. A skilled swimmer like Matt Scovell could save himself at night in near-freezing water though blinded and with his lower jaw blown off, but many deck hands and passengers on the Red and the Mississippi fell overboard and disappeared without a stroke because they didn't know how to swim. Terror of water appears to have induced many persons, particularly women, to stay on board and face certain death. Many who jumped overboard simply floundered, allowing themselves to be drawn into the paddle wheels.

The documents of the period are very clear that the *Mittie Stephens* was operating in high water, that the fire began about two and a half miles below Swanson's Landing, that the boat quickly reached shore, and that the bow was run ashore in a few feet of water. About two and one-half miles below Swanson's Landing, the old channel of Cypress Bayou, within which the boat appears to have been running, is about one-half mile from shore, inclining toward it. The shore would have been reached within five minutes.

With the formation of Caddo Lake in 1800, a band of cypress trees was formed at the lake fringes similar to what exists today. However, the 1914 Department of the Interior study of the lake demonstrates that by 1869, many of these trees would have been undermined by wave action and dramatic seasonal fluctuations in water levels and would already have fallen over in the water. The *Mittie Stephens* had the capacity to reach shore because she was passing in high water through a stand of cypress trees that had been severely thinned.

A map was prepared a few years later showing the location of the wreck at the shoreline in the area described by the newspapers. This map was based on visual observation of the wreck. Internal evidence from the map revealed that the shoreline where the bow of the wreck was shown was at the 172-foot contour. The boat grounded in 3 feet of water; as a consequence, it can be computed that Caddo Lake was at 175 feet when the *Mittie Stephens* burned. This is compatible with contemporary reports of high water and the fact that 173 feet was the normal high-water level during the 1800s.

A bow at the 172-foot contour would place most of the wreck of the *Mittie Stephens* on land today at the normal dam height of the lake (168.5 feet). A land investigation was made of this area in 1993 that uncovered an immense pile of charred ceramic fragments, melted windowpane glass, and miscellaneous metal pieces such as pipe fittings, hinges, boat nails, and packing box nails. The ceramics have been dated and are all from the right period. It can be safely concluded that the wreck site has been discovered. Whether anything remains of the hull has not yet been determined.

4. The *Cuba No. 2* was a 110-ton sternwheeler measuring 129 feet by 25 feet that was built in 1862 under the name *B. C. Levi* and redocumented on 6 October 1865. She made trips to Jefferson in 1866–68 and briefly sunk in February of the latter year while returning from Jefferson with 450 bales of cotton and a large lot of hides. The 26 February 1868 *South-Western*, quoting the *Jefferson Jimplecute*, says that the sinking occurred from a stump in, or near the mouth of, Blind Bayou, just above Swanson's Landing at six o'clock in the evening. When the *Flicker* passed on the twentieth, the crew had thrown 200 bales overboard and was trying to raise it. She was reported back in Shreveport by the 11 March *South-Western* with the comment that her cotton "did not seem much damaged from a little swimming frolic in the lake." The *Cuba No. 2* continued to make trips to Jefferson in 1868 and is reported lost in 1869 by Lytle-Holdcamper.

Of the four boats that wrecked on Caddo Lake, one was by fire, one by snag, and two by unknown causes. Only the *Mittie Stephens* involved loss of life and loss of the boat. The other three were quickly raised. The fire had nothing to do with navigation hazards. There does not appear to have been any place on the lake that offered peculiar navigation difficulties, and passage across the lake appears to have been effected with ease.

CYPRESS BAYOU

Although Cypress Bayou extended far above Jefferson, there was no steamboat navigation, so that the area of navigation interest extended from Jefferson to the point where Cypress Bayou entered Caddo Lake. The bayou was fairly deep in most places, and a lake-like condition extended from the foot of Caddo Lake up to the confluence of Big Cypress and Black Cypress below Jefferson. The shallow areas were from Jefferson down to Black Cypress and at the Dougherty's Defeat area in the vicinity of the confluence with Little Cypress. The bayou was fringed with stumps resulting from navigation improvements over the decades of steamboat activity.

There were eight reported wrecks on Cypress Bayou, three of which are found only in the newspapers, one of which is derived from the WPA wreck list, and four of which are derived from Swain's directory. I have not been able to find accident reports in the newspapers for three of the Swain boats.

1. The *Lessie B.* was a late boat in the history of the route and the last recorded wreck. She was built in Ohio at the end of 1881 to run between Shreveport and various points on the lakes and up to Jefferson. She made her first trip to Mooringsport on 25 January 1882. She was valued at $7,000, insured for $1,000, and owned by Calvin and W. H. Croom, J. G. Newberry, A. M. Glover, and S. N. Kerley. Her officers were Ben Bonham, captain; T. L. Lyon, clerk; N. A. Bonham, mate; George and Ben Oliver, engineers; and Ben Bonham, pilot.

After returning from Mooringsport on 7 February, she departed for Jim's Bayou on the fourteenth, the lakes on the nineteenth, and Jefferson and the lakes by way of Cross Bayou on the twenty-third. This was the first boat in many years and the last boat ever to travel the high-water route through The Pass. She arrived back from Jefferson on 14 March with "lots of cotton," departed for Jefferson on 18 March, and was reported burned in the 23 March *Shreveport Times.*

> A dispatch was received yesterday morning by Mr. Calvin Croom from Capt. T. L. Lyon, at Scottsville, stating that the Lessie B. was burned Tuesday afternoon at 5 o'clock, fifteen miles below Jefferson, near Benton on Cypress bayou, and boat and cargo was a total loss, also that one life was lost.
>
> Late yesterday evening Capt. Ben Bonham and the crew of the ill-fated steamer arrived here by rail from Scottsville.

Capt. Lyon, clerk, states the boat was discovered to be on fire on the larboard side, near the boilers, and in less than three minutes the boat and cargo, which consisted of 291 bales of cotton, were enveloped in flames. A skiff lying on the bow of the boat was launched, but in the excitement she got away and floated out into the stream, and all hands were compelled to jump overboard. The skiff was subsequently caught, and was of very considerable service. After getting into the water most, if not all, swam to trees and clusters of brush from whence they were taken up by the skiff and carried to the shore fully a quarter of a mile distant. One of the crew, a cabin boy, whose name we could not ascertain, was drowned.

After reaching the shore, Capt. Bonham and crew walked from Benton to Scottsville and came down last evening from that place by rail.

The fate of this wreck is not discussed in subsequent extant issues of the newspaper. The designation fifteen miles below Jefferson as the wreck site indicates that it was two miles below Benton. J. Frank Glenn's 1886 memoranda have an inclusion for the *Lessie B.* as a marker just before a triple bend leading up to Benton. The wreck was not removed immediately, because it was probably off the main channel and did not constitute a navigation hazard; it was in place in 1886 and is probably still there.

Glenn's notations and the newspaper reports place the wreck in the Phillips Slough–Gum Slough area. For the *Lessie B.* to have taken the Cross Bayou route out of Shreveport meant that the water was very high. This is compatible with the newspaper description of the accident, which says that the wreck was a quarter of a mile from shore. The Phillips Slough–Gum Slough area was probably completely flooded. The skiff took the crew to the right-descending bank, and from there they walked up to Benton. The wreck is probably in a swamp, but it could be on either side of the bayou.

2. The *Lotus No. 3* was a sidewheeler built in 1869 measuring 160 feet by 37 feet. She was among the longest-running boats in the Cypress Bayou trade and registered among the highest number of trips, including sixteen in 1870, fifteen in 1871, seven in 1872, eleven in 1873, one in the second half of 1874, eleven in 1875, and five in 1876. These figures were particularly impressive because this was not a local boat, but rather

a New Orleans–to–Jefferson packet. Nevertheless, the recorded figures are underestimates. The wreck report on this vessel, which appeared in the 1 April 1873 *Shreveport Times*, indicates that the *Lotus No. 3* had made sixty-six trips to Jefferson by that time, whereas only forty-one trips are recorded in the navigation columns:

> ACCIDENT TO THE LOTUS NO. 3.—The Lotus No. 3, Capt. D. D. Dannals, met with an accident on her last trip down from Jefferson that came very near being the death of her. Before daylight on the morning of the 29th, while descending Cypress bayou with 565 bales of cotton, when just above the Benton cut-off, she struck a log sticking out of the bank just under the water, on the starboard side just about midships, knocking a large hole in her hull. She commenced filling with water, and before the crew could get a tarpaulin over the hole she had at least four feet of water in her hold. The tarpaulin once over the hole and the four Syphon pumps at work, she was in a fair way of being saved. As soon as she was clear of water, she was listed over until the whole break was above water and then thoroughly repaired, when she went on her way rejoicing. The Lotus No. 3 has made sixty-six trips between New Orleans and Jefferson and this is the first accident to her hull. The log she struck is supposed to be the same one that sunk the Wash Sentell, over a year ago. Passengers are emphatic in their praise of Capt. Dannals and his officers for the judgment and energy displayed in saving the boat and cargo. From the time she sunk until she was under way again all right it was only ten hours.

A note of thanks signed by fifteen passengers appeared on 1 April, and the *Lotus No. 3* arrived back in Shreveport on the fourth. She made many subsequent trips to Jefferson, wrecked on Soda Lake in 1876 with the same captain, was raised again, and burned on the Mississippi River in 1877.

    3. The *Wash Sentell* made two trips to Jefferson in 1870 and does not appear again in the navigation record until the 11 January 1872 issue of the *Shreveport Times*, which reported the arrival of the *Charles H. Durfee* with the crew of the sunken steamer and provided particulars of the accident:

About 5 o'clock Sunday morning Jan. 7th, while descending Cypress bayou with 59 bales of cotton, the boat struck the bank about two and one half miles above Shanghai Landing. Nothing was thought of it, the lick was light and she kept on her way until just below the above landing when she was found to be in a sinking condition. She was landed at once, the off side of the boat sinking up to boiler deck. The officers had no knowledge of the extent of the damage to the hull. All they know is she sunk from her hold being full of water. There were no lives lost though some of the crew and passengers had to swim for their lives. Among the latter was our young friend Buck Chase, who had a tight squeeze for his life. Of the 59 bales on board, the Durfee brought down 58 bales; the other bale was in the hold and of course is lost. We learn that the boat was insured but do not know the amount.

The water was fairly high the week of the wreck. Because Shanghai Landing was two miles above Benton, the accident—which occurred two and one-half miles above the landing—must have been in the Dougherty's Defeat area. The boat then proceeded downstream until just past the landing, where she came to rest.

The hull appears never to have been raised, but all of the machinery was salvaged and brought to Jefferson. The 23 January *Shreveport Times* reports that the *May Lowry* came in from Jefferson carrying the *Wash Sentell*'s chimneys. The 14 December 1873 *Shreveport Times* reports that "Captain Jerry Sullivan has purchased at Jefferson the boilers, shaft, and fire front of the Wash Sentell for the purpose of fixing up the wreck of the Royal George. They will be down on the steamer Durfee and the hull of the Royal George will be towed to New Orleans where she will be made better than new. She will make a capital low water craft with her new machinery on her." Finally, on the sixteenth, the *W. J. Behan* arrived at Shreveport from Jefferson carrying 500 bales of cotton and "a lot of machinery for the steamer Royal George."

4. The *William R. Douglass* was a 229-ton sidewheeler measuring 126 feet by 28 feet built in 1856. She advertised in the *Daily Picayune* beginning in April 1858 as a regular U.S. mail packet to Jefferson and made recorded trips to Jefferson in April under Ben Tarbel and in May under W. W. Withenbury. Swain gives the place of the wreck as above Benton. I have not been able to obtain an accident report on this vessel,

partly because the extant issues of the *South-Western* for 1858 do not begin until 8 September. However, the 17 September 1858 *Texas Republican*, quoting the *South-Western* of Wednesday, says that "The Wm. R. Douglass has been put in complete running order, and is now as good as new." This boat apparently wrecked late in 1858, was repaired, and traveled to Sodo Lake in November according to the *South-Western* of the tenth. The 29 December *South-Western* indicates that the boat was sold to Captain Gwartney, who intended to run her in the Yazoo and Tallahatchie trade. Lytle-Holdcamper reports this boat lost in 1859.

5. The *Mary L. Dougherty* was a 95-ton sidewheeler built in 1853 and measuring 123 feet by 18 feet that made numerous recorded trips between Shreveport and Jefferson and the lakes in 1856 and 1857. She advertised as a transfer boat in conjunction with the *Duke* from New Orleans. Swain indicates that the wreck of the *Mary L. Dougherty* occurred above Benton. I have not been able to find any newspaper records pertaining to this wreck. She last appears in the navigation record in the 22 April 1857 *South-Western*, and the issues for 19 August 1857 through 1 September 1858 are missing. There is good reason for believing that the wreck actually occurred because of the designation "Dougherty's Defeat" for the area of the old convoluted channel of Cypress Bayou near the confluence with Little Cypress. Lytle-Holdcamper shows this boat as having gone out of service in 1859.

6. The *Larkin Edwards* was a tiny opportunistic carrier weighing 67 tons that made frequent trips to Jefferson, Monterey, and landings on Caddo Lake from 1858 on. She is reported in the 13 June 1860 *South-Western*, as quoted in the 23 June *Standard*, as having sunk six miles below Jefferson on the previous Thursday after striking a snag on a return trip from Jefferson. Although there are no extant issues of the *South-Western* from this period, she was probably immediately raised. She operated out of Shreveport in 1861 and made two trips to Jefferson in 1862.

7. The *Caddo Belle* began advertising as a regular Jefferson and the lakes packet in the *Daily Picayune* in December 1857 and is shown as having made one trip from New Orleans to Jefferson in that month and four trips through March 1858 under Capt. A. A. Barnes. She was reported wrecked in the 5 August 1858 Marshall *Texas Republican*, quoting the Shreveport *South-Western*: "The steamer Caddo Belle, from Jefferson bound to this place, while dropping down the Bayou, Sunday

last, swung across the stream about four miles below Jefferson, and it is supposed struck a stump, which caused her to fill and sink. One side of the wreck lies in 13 feet water, and it is feared that the hull broke in two, and will prove a total loss. The Caddo Belle was nearly new, having been built last fall at New Albany, where we understand she was insured for $10,000."

The 8 August *Daily Picayune* elaborated on causation and the prospects of removal: "It appears that she had laid up at Jefferson for some time, and, owing to the effects of the sun and the extreme heat of the weather, the seams opened in her hull, and on wooding her she settled so much that the water poured in through the openings rapidly, sinking her in a very short time. She had no cargo on board. The Caddo Belle was a new boat, and when the river falls she probably will be raised without serious damage."

The 17 September *Texas Republican*, quoting the *South-Western* of Wednesday, indicated that "The Caddo Belle, sunk a few days ago, a short distance below Jefferson, will be speedily raised and renovated." Although this boat does not appear again in the navigation record, she obviously was raised; for given her location a few miles downstream of Jefferson, she would have appeared in later texts, particularly those dealing with channel improvements, if she had remained in place. The *Caddo Belle* was no longer in operation in 1860 according to Lytle-Holdcamper.

8. Little is known about the *Lake City* in connection with Jefferson other than that she was a little packet operating under Captain Dumay that made two trips to Jefferson in December 1869. On the later trip, she was carrying government stores reshipped from the *B. L. Hodge No. 2* and arrived back in Shreveport on 1 January 1870 flying light. The 23 March 1870 *South-Western* indicates that she had been seized on the upper Red River by the United States Marshal for selling liquor to the Indians.

Swain reports her sunk at Jefferson. This sinking could not have taken place in any year before 1871 because the 4 January 1871 *South-Western* mentions the *Lake City* as one of the small boats that had the capacity to reach upper Red River under the prevailing low-water conditions. That the sinking actually took place is substantiated by a clipping from the 4 February 1872 *Jefferson Daily Democrat* that appeared in the *Shreveport Times* on the eighth: "Mr. Shapper has called upon us, and states that the Lilly, the pretty little steamboat now being built at Williams' sawmill, down the bayou, will commence running in a few days, between this point and Shreveport. We are informed by him also, that he is raising the sunken 'Lake City,' now lying opposite our wharf."

The 13 January 1872 *Shreveport Times* identifies this person as Capt. L. J. Shapper. Williams's sawmill was on the south bank of Cypress Bayou about one-half mile above Smithland and is shown on Lt. Eugene Woodruff's 1872 map of Red River and Cypress Bayou. Whether the *Lilly* was built and the *Lake City* raised is unknown because neither of them appear subsequently in the Shreveport newspapers.

Of the eight boats that wrecked on Cypress Bayou between 1857 and 1882, one was burned, one had a hull weakened by heat, two were snagged on stumps, one hit a bank, and three were by unknown causes. The weakened hull and the fire in cotton were not related to navigation hazards. The only places along the bayou that appear to have offered any difficulties were the Dougherty's Defeat area and the Benton Cutoff area, the former of which was convoluted and fairly shallow. The only accident involving loss of life was the *Lessie B.*, where one cabin boy drowned. There were three reported raisings, one salvage, and two probable raisings, and there is good reason to believe that the wreck of the *Lessie B.* is offchannel somewhere below the old site of Benton.

SUMMARY

Assumptions about the navigation hazards of particular steamboat routes are often grounded in the information provided by wreck lists. These lists are usually concerned with documenting where boats finally came to rest. Although providing an important window on the hazards of navigation, they generally disregard the whole dimension of boats that were wrecked and raised and tend to obscure the tremendous variances in causation and severity that attend the end of a boat's operating life. Most importantly, by accentuating the dramatic, they mask the fact that final wrecks fall on a continuum of navigation difficulties that ranged from delay and minor damage to severe damage without sinking, to sinking and raising, and finally to sinking without raising.

There were twenty-five boats that wrecked on the Cypress Bayou and the lakes route (**table 11-1**). Of these, fourteen were by snags, one was by a raft floating downstream, one was by heat weakening a hull, two were by fire, one was by explosion, and six were by unknown

Table 11-1
Wrecks

Boat	Year	Place	Cause	Losses	Disposition
Albany	1878	Twelvemile Bayou	raft	0	partly removed
Alida	1855	Caddo Lake	snag	0	raised
Anna	1872	Caddo Lake	unknown	0	raised
Caddo Belle	1858	Cypress Bayou	heat	0	raised
Caroline	1867	Soda Lake	unknown	0	raised
Cuba No. 2	1868	Caddo Lake	snag	0	raised
De De	1856	Big Willow Pass	snag	0	raised
Echo	1853	Soda Lake	snag	0	raised (?)
Jim Gilmer	1851	Soda Lake	snag	2	unknown
Joseph Holden	1859	Twelvemile Bayou	snag	0	partly removed
L. Dillard	1867	Soda Lake	snag	0	partly removed
Lake City	1871	Cypress Bayou	unknown	(?)	raised (?)
Larkin Edwards	1860	Cypress Bayou	snag	0	raised
Lessie B.	1882	Cypress Bayou	fire	1	unknown
Lizzie Hopkins	1870	Soda Lake	unknown	0	raised
Lizzie Lee	1856	Twelvemile Bayou	snag	0	partly removed
Lotus No. 3	1873	Cypress Bayou	snag	0	raised
Lotus No. 3	1876	Soda Lake	snag	0	raised
Mary L Dougherty	57–58	Cypress Bayou	unknown	(?)	unknown
Mittie Stephens	1869	Caddo Lake	fire	62	unknown
Monterey	1850	Soda Lake	snag	1	unknown
Royal George	1873	Twelvemile Bayou	explosion	7(?)	towed to port
Wamadee	1865	Twelvemile Bayou	snag	0	raised
Wash Sentell	1872	Cypress Bayou	snag	0	partly removed
William R. Douglass	1858	Cypress Bayou	unknown	0	raised

causes. Of the nineteen wrecks by known causes, fifteen were by navigation hazards (snags and raft). The hull weakening, explosion, and fires were unrelated to conditions along the route and could have happened anywhere. Of the fifteen wrecks by navigation hazards, ten occurred below Caddo Lake, indicating that the downstream portion of the route was the most dangerous.

Although steamboats operated along the route from 1840 through 1905, the wrecks occurred between 1850 and 1882. Ten wrecks occurred in the ten-year period between 1850 and 1859, and eleven occurred in the ten-year period between 1865 and 1874 when the volume of traffic was many times greater. This indicates that safety improved over time, probably because of technical improvements in the boats themselves. In the sixty-seven years of steamboat activity, there were only twenty-five wrecks, and of these less than half were of such severity that the boat could not be raised. Given the thousands of trips that were made during that period, the route must be judged as fairly safe.

Of the twenty-five wrecks, five involved loss of life, but only two significant loss of life. Fire and explosion caused almost all of the fatalities. Because the waters of the route were shallow and confined, it is not surprising that navigation hazards produced little in the way of loss of life. Of the seventy-three persons who died in wrecks along the route, about two-thirds were crew members. Steamboat travel along the route was reasonably safe, particularly if person-miles of travel are taken into consideration (which, of course, can only be intuited from scant data). Other modes of travel had their own problems with safety and were not as quick, convenient, and comfortable.

I expected to find a close correlation between low-water conditions and wrecks involving navigation hazards. This proved not to be the case. Low water reduced the volume of traffic and the size of boats, and exposed stumps were not a hazard. It was the unseen stumps in the periods of moderate water that appear to have offered the most difficulties, particularly because moderate water levels induced boats to run the stumps in cutroads and cutoffs. The stumps identified as causing wrecks at the head of the Benton Cutoff and along the cutroad on Soda Lake suggest that most of the stumps that produced wrecks were the result of navigation improvements.

Of the twenty-five wrecks, at least half were raised. Most of these raisings appear to have been conducted by the crews using onboard pumps. The only reported use of specialized equipment was for the raising of the *Lotus No. 3* in 1876, which involved a tug and diver. A brief description of a bell boat is given in connection with the wreck of the *Elnora* on the Red River below Shreveport: "Some kind of a conflutiment, with a bow like a flatboat and a stern like a kick-up-behind, having in tow a barge, came steaming up the river to-day, and after reconnoitering awhile made for the foot of the landing at Texas street. She proved to be a diving bell boat from the wreck of the late steamer Elnora, with fished up treasure on board in the shape of boilers and machinery. She will return to the wreck and fight it out on that line all summer."

A more elaborate description, including equipment and capacity, is given in the 18 May 1870 *South-Western*: "The Dixie, Captain Chas. Lester and J. K. Scott, has been converted with full sets of diving apparatus, armor, bells and Palmer's patent pump, which has a capacity of lifting and discharging four hundred and fifty thousand gallons of water per hour. Capt. Scott has been in the diving business for a number of years, and once went down in a bell to a depth of 94 feet."

Specialized boats were avoided whenever possible because of the high cost: "The steamer Fleta, which we reported sometime ago as sunk near Campte, has been raised. The work was accomplished by a diving bell boat, for $5,000, or one-half of the boat, at the option of the owners of the Fleta."

Most boats on the route were apparently raised by their own crews with the assistance of other steamboats that took off freight. Raisings generally occurred within a few days. Boats unaccounted for include the *Albany* on Twelvemile Bayou; the *Jim Gilmer, Joseph Holden*, and *Monterey* on Soda Lake; the *Mittie Stephens* on Caddo Lake; the *Lessie B.* and *Mary L. Dougherty* on Cypress Bayou; and possibly the *Echo* on Soda Lake and the *Lake City* on Cypress Bayou. Portions, if not all, of the Twelvemile Bayou and Soda Lake wrecks were probably removed by wrecking crews or the Corps of Engineers. Remnants would be off the present channel of Twelvemile Bayou in agricultural areas or even urban areas.

It is unlikely that any steamboats wrecked on Caddo Lake other than the four that were reported, and three of these were raised. The hull and machinery of the *Mittie Stephens* are unaccounted for. Of the eight recorded wrecks on Cypress Bayou, four were raised. The *Lake City* was probably raised. If not, it is unlikely that she would have been allowed to remain in the wharf area at Jefferson, given the extensive dredging conducted by the city and the Corps of Engineers in that area.

Nothing is known about the wreck of the *Mary L. Dougherty*. It appears to have been a permanent wreck, because the boat no longer appears in the navigation record after 1858. If this wreck is extant, it is in the Dougherty's Defeat area downstream from the old site of Smithland. The machinery of the *Wash Sentell* was removed, but her hull is unaccounted for and, if still around, would be downstream of the old site of Benton. The *Lessie B.*, which also wrecked downstream of Benton, offers the greatest possibility for a full wreck discovery. However, the channel of Cypress Bayou, including its old components, was thoroughly investigated for shipwrecks in 1993, and any wrecks or remnants of wrecks would almost certainly be offchannel.

·12·
The Scope of Trade

MARKET AREA

Texas has many rivers that reach far into the interior of the state and that empty into the Gulf of Mexico, suggesting ideal conditions for navigation. If a comprehensive history of navigation in the state should ever be written, it will become clear that steamboats penetrated much farther inland and at much higher levels of activity than has generally been thought. On the other hand, it will be found that high levels of commercial activity were restricted to the lower portions of these rivers. For all practical purposes, the interior of the state was closed to navigation, and the major ports, among which Galveston was preeminent, were located along the coast.

The chief deficiency of the rivers was that they carried high volumes of water for only short periods of time. The Cypress Bayou and the lakes route was peculiar. It was not a river, but rather a bayou and lake route. It did not flow into the Gulf, but rather into the Red River. And unlike the rivers of the state, it did not flow in a general north-south direction but rather in an west-east direction. It provided fairly good conditions for navigation because of the influence of the raft, and it afforded an opportunity for the development of a significant inland port.

The route, at ninety-six river miles, did not penetrate very far into the interior of Texas. It became important because it was geographically isolated and at the same time tied, through the Red River, into the Mississippi, the major artery of national waterborne commerce. Geographic isolation was provided by the fact that the upper reaches of the rivers that penetrated the northern portion of the state and emptied into the Gulf were not navigable. In the immediate vicinity of the route were Little Cypress Bayou, the Sulphur Fork of Red River, and Red River itself. Attempts to make Little Cypress navigable were abortive, and there is no evidence that any steamboat ever traveled up that stream.

Sulphur Fork was, like Cypress Bayou, a tributary to the Red River. Located north of the route, it extended much farther into the interior of Texas than Cypress Bayou. It was navigable in its lower reaches and was improved. However, Sulphur Fork was above the zone of raft influence, and flows were uncertain. It does not appear to have ever developed into a stream of major commercial importance, partly because of its natural qualities, but mostly because it shared in the deficiencies of all navigation on the Red River above the raft.

The Red River was navigable for a great distance above the raft and stretched over the northern perimeter of the state. However, the conditions of navigability were inferior to those on the Red River below the raft, and access was limited. Matt Scovell, who took many boats above the raft, indicates in his reminiscences that the upper Red River was normally navigable only four months of the year. In addition, the route around the raft was difficult and dangerous, giving rise to higher insurance costs. As described in the 23 April 1856 *South-Western*, the voyage around the raft involved "passing through almost interminable lakes, bayous and canals, either thumping the stumps in the bottom or upon the banks, raking the tree-tops above, or the banks on either side."

To complicate matters, the route around the raft changed constantly as the raft moved upstream. When the exit into the Red River from Red Bayou became closed, it was necessary to develop artificial exits progressively upstream. This was done by private companies that charged tolls on the cargoes of steamboats passing through. These artificial exits, in order of development, were Kouns' Canal, Hervey's Canal, and Sale and Murphy Canal. By the time the raft was removed in 1873, all of these canals had been closed, and boats traveled through Posten Lake on the east side of the river at the Arkansas-Louisiana line, crossed over the river, and reentered the old Red Bayou route.

Because of the limited navigability of streams on the north and south, the Cypress Bayou and the lakes route was the dominant factor in a market area that extended for about two hundred miles over the northeastern corner of the state. Ports and landings on the northern perimeter of the route, such as Monterey and Smithland, served the areas to the north reaching up to the Red River. Ports and landings on the southern perimeter of the route, such as Benton and Port Caddo, served Harrison County. Jefferson, as the head of navigation to the west, served a large area extending from the Red River on the north, the Sabine River on the south, and the Trinity River on the west, running roughly in a north-south direction from Sherman to Dallas.

When Josiah Gregg visited Smithland in 1841, he pointed out that if the bayou above to the townsite of Jefferson should ever be cleared out, "Jefferson would take all the western business"; when the town was coming into existence, the Clarksville *Northern Standard* noted that it would "quite definitely concentrate a large amount of commercial business." Once established in 1845, the success of the town in meeting these expectations was immediate, with Edward Smith noting that in 1845 it had only three log houses, but by 1849 had "sixty good houses, and several large well-supplied stores, also one warehouse for the shipment of merchandise, and a small saw and grist steam mill."

Establishment of the full market area geographically was instantaneous, as recognized in a prospectus for a commercial newspaper in Jefferson that was published in the 20 August 1850 *Texas Republican*:

> The commodious and extensive Lake upon which it is situated, being connected with Red River below "the raft," and thus in direct communication by steamers with the great "Father of Waters," is now being visited by the merchants of all countries. And the PORT OF JEFFERSON, extending further than any other into the heart of the rich Cypress Bayou and Sulphur Fork country, will of course concentrate the trade of those regions, which extend in some directions upwards of 150 miles. Indeed, this is naturally the principal Port for a great portion of the vast Red River, Upper Trinity, and "Cross Timbers" regions of Texas. Goods shipped to Jefferson already find their way as far west as the town of Dallas on Trinity river. Indeed Jefferson must ever possess advantage, over every other Port in Eastern Texas, from the obvious and controlling fact

that all the other Ports are either *on* the line, or *beyond* the borders of the State, or else they have tedious and expensive barriers between them and New Orleans, the great heart of Southern Commerce.

The concentration of trade in this market area through Jefferson appears to have been accomplished by at least 1854, as suggested by the 20 May 1854 *Texas Republican*, with due recognition of the potential for trade expansion as the market area developed:

When we consider the large district of country dependent upon Jefferson for trade and commercial facilities, a great portion of which cannot be diverted from it; when we reflect that not one acre in five hundred of the land in this large district is in a state of cultivation, it is evident that our sister town is necessarily bound to become eventually a large commercial place. This territory dependent upon Jefferson reaches back into the interior two hundred and fifty miles, the citizens of which are actively engaged every year in the business of buying and exporting. Jefferson cannot expect always to hold on to this large territory; but she ought to make the most of it while she has it; she ought to do all in her power to increase the value of it; and to promote the settlement of the country.

The market area in its fullness is described in the 16 October 1868 *Texas Republican*: "The 'Jefferson Times' is published at Jefferson, Texas, the head of Red River and Lake navigation; one of the most prosperous cities of the 'Star State.' It commands the entire trade of Northern Texas and the Indian Territory. There are twenty-two counties that trade to this point, embracing an area as extensive as the entire State of Alabama, and containing a large, intelligent, industrious, thrifty, enterprising population. The exports are Wheat, Wool, Cattle, Sheep, Hides, and Cotton. The export of cotton, alone, this season, from the City of Jefferson, it is computed, notwithstanding the short crop, will exceed twenty thousand bales." The 1870 *Digest of the Laws of the City of Jefferson* provides a similar perspective: "A glance at the map will show that Jefferson enjoys the trade of at least twenty counties in Texas, a portion from Arkansas, and a valuable trade from the Indian Nation."

After the *Digest*, the most commonly cited description of Jefferson's market area is that provided by E. Eberstadt in Jefferson and appended to an 1874 Corps report on Cypress Bayou. Eberstadt says that "the territory immediately surrounding and entirely dependent on this outlet for its exports and imports" is comprised of the seven counties of Bowie, Cass, Titus, Upshur, Marion, Hopkins, and Hunt. Eberstadt points out that he has left out "more than that number whose interests will always lead them to seek cheap water-transportation for their shipping when it can be reached." However, this picture is given for a period in which the market area was already in a state of decline.

The market area is best portrayed in Edward Smith's 1849 *Part of North Eastern Texas Shewing the Route of the Inspectors*, which shows the route that he traveled investigating sites for an English colony (**fig. 12-1**). Although the geographic extent of this market area did not change dramatically over the period in which steamboats were the dominant transport mode, it did fluctuate depending on the navigation conditions on the upper Red River. Smith says that the Red was navigable as far as Fort Washita (above Preston on his map), but that in 1849 Pinehill was the head of navigation because of sparse development

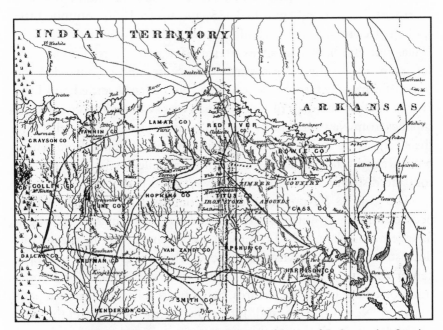

Fig. 12-1. Northeast Texas in 1849. *Source: Archives and Information Services Division, Texas State Library and Archives Commission*

to the west. When the upper Red was navigable, the counties bordering the river could ship and receive directly by steamboat. When it was not, freight was transported overland to Jefferson, Smithland, Monterey, and Shreveport.

The variable nature of these commercial activities is expressed by Scovell in his reminiscences, speaking of the period from 1865 on: "At that time, and up to the latter part of the seventies, all cotton raised in North Texas, as far as Dallas, Fort Worth, Sherman, Gainesville, Paris, Clarksville, etc., was hauled by ox-teams to Shreveport or Jefferson. During the time we had navigation to Upper Red River, which was usually four months in the year, the cotton from Paris, Bonham, Clarksville, New Boston, De Kalb, etc., was hauled to Red River. Naturally, up-freights followed the same channel."

The dimensions of the upper Red River trade should not be underestimated. During the months of March through May 1867, for example, twenty-seven boats arrived at Shreveport from the upper Red River, compared to forty-three from Jefferson and ten from the Red River below the raft. The great commercial center for the upper Red River trade was Clarksville, whose importance was described by the 1 September 1881 *Galveston Daily News*: "This, the oldest town in Northern Texas, was begun in 1835, and up to 1860 continued the leading place in that section, and was such in 1842, when neither Paris, Dallas nor Bonham had an existence. It was to North Texas what Jefferson was to the eastern part of the State, and commanded the trade of a most extensive section then, but sparsely settled and little known. Before the days of railroads in Texas, Clarksville procured its supplies from New Orleans by way of Red River, steamboats delivering their cargoes at Roland's Landing, fifteen miles distant, from which point wagon transportation was used. Clarksville is said once to have sold and distributed her goods as far west as El Paso."

The Cypress Bayou and the lakes route was a conduit by which people and freight were carried into and out of the market area. As a linkage mechanism, it had external components at the upstream and downstream ends. Downstream, New Orleans was the great supply center for the market area, as well as the destination for freight transported out of the market area. Steamboats followed a circular path between New Orleans and Jefferson, bringing up freights for distribution in the market area and carrying down freights of commodities produced in the market area to New Orleans, where they were disseminated to New Orleans' national and international markets through an entirely different set of vessels.

The orientation toward New Orleans was not modified until January 1870 when the St. Louis steamer *Ida Stockdale* arrived at Jefferson. St. Louis and Cincinnati quickly became important competitors to New Orleans for the import and export trade of the market area. Boats from Cincinnati that traveled to Jefferson in the early 1870s included the *Edinburgh* and *Champion*. Boats from St. Louis included the *Anna*, *Emilie La Barge*, *Walter B. Dance*, and *Ida Stockdale* and the Carter Line packets *Henry M. Shreve*, *R. J. Lockwood*, *Oceanus*, *Silver Bow*, *Lady Lee*, and *Belle of Shreveport*. In addition, the Carter Line's *Belle Rowland* was established as a transfer boat at Shreveport, making forty-eight trips to Jefferson from 1871 through 1873.

OVERLAND TRANSPORT

The Cypress Bayou and the lakes route was also a conduit at its upstream end for the movement of freight and passengers into and out of the market area. Freight movements in the market area to and from the conduit were carried out primarily by ox-wagons. These were double-axle, open carriers that were pulled by teams of oxen in yokes of two animals each, with the number of animals determined by the weight of the freight carried in the wagon. These ox-wagons moved in a circular path in the market area, bringing export freights to ports like Jefferson and carrying import freights back to interior settlements on the return trip.

Ox-wagon transport was the primary mode of freight transport throughout the interior of Texas, with similar circular paths oriented on waterborne outlets. In the earliest days, some of this freight carriage was conducted by individual farmers to bring their own produce to market. However, these activities soon became dominated by professional teamsters, who operated alone or as part of transport companies. S. G. Reed in *A History of the Texas Railroads* estimates that there were at least ten thousand teams operating in Texas before the Civil War. J. DeCordova in his 1858 *Texas: Her Resources and Her Public Men* describes the teamsters and their operations: "This wagon-business is a great thing in Texas. His wagon is the home of the driver; his oxen feed on the grass, he eats and sleeps at home. Time is no object. He penetrates the most remote parts of the State, for a consideration, if he can get loaded; if not, he loads himself. He is as free as air, and cares for nobody. These men form a class of themselves, but, with their useful branch of industry, are destined to fade away (like the old bargemen of the Mississippi River) when the snort of the iron horse shall awaken the solitude of the prairies."

The ox-wagons traveled over roads that Smith describes as "universally primitive," with circuitous routes moving through the heads of streams to avoid the deep channels of the rivers. During dry weather, the roads were in fairly good condition, with the exception of deep gutters washed by the rain and creek and river bottoms, which were numerous. During wet weather, the roads were difficult to travel and sometimes impassable. Ox-wagons often became mired, and breakdowns were common.

Ox-wagons were omnipresent on the roads of Northeast Texas. In moving by horseback throughout the area in 1849, Smith noted: "Waggons constantly traverse all the roads over which we traveled." Much of this traffic was moving from or to Jefferson. Reed reports that it was not uncommon for as many as a thousand teams to be at Jefferson at one time; and the 1 September 1881 *Galveston Daily News* reports that the wagon trade at Jefferson was so large that "the roads leading from the west were literally so blocked by the vehicles that passage was difficult." J. M. Keith, a teamster, described the scene at Jefferson in 1870 in the 1928 *Dallas News*, as quoted in T. C. Richardson, *East Texas: Its History and Its Makers:* "I drove one of our teams, hauling cotton. We found a jam of cotton wagons ahead of us and behind us. We got in line early in the morning, but did not reach the scales until almost night. There were six to eight yoke of oxen attached to the wagons from the more distant parts of the country. The merchants had as much business as they could handle. Everybody had money, the hotels and restaurants were turning people away, though the saloons and gambling halls were making shift to take care of everything that came their way. On the water in front of the town were a score or more of steamboats."

Steamboats were part of a transportation system whose weak link was the overland component. Ox-wagons were slow, expensive, and uncertain, averaging 10 to15 miles a day in good weather and 6 to 8 miles a day in bad weather. Smith indicates that the trip from Fannin County, where Bonham is located, to Shreveport took twenty-six days. The route apparently taken in the late 1840s, as shown on Smith's map (see fig. 12-1), was south from Bonham and then directly east to Shreveport. Under the actual conditions of travel, this would be about 260 miles, which would equate to 10 miles per day, with the round-trip between Bonham and Shreveport taking about two months.

Overland freight transport costs appear to have been fairly constant throughout Texas and over time. Reed gives an average of $0.01 per mile per hundred pounds based on 1858 and 1859 *Texas Almanac* figures for overland transport from various points in the interior to coastal ports. Smith gives 1849 rates to Shreveport per hundred pounds of $1.25 from Hopkins County, $1.50–$2.00 from Fannin County, $0.75 from Upshur County (60 miles), and $3.00 from Dallas County. The figure of $2.00 per hundred pounds for the 200-mile trip from Bonham in Fannin County to Shreveport equates to $0.01 per mile per hundred pounds.

Short hauls may sometimes have entailed lower costs per mile than long hauls. The 1861 *Texas Almanac* indicates that wagoners charged $0.75 for transporting a cotton bale 45 miles from Upshur County to Jefferson and $1.00–$1.50 for the 80 miles from Upshur County to Shreveport. A cotton bale weighed four hundred to five hundred pounds; hence, the freight rate for the 45 miles from Upshur County was less than about $0.005 per mile per hundred pounds. There appears to have been a downward pressure on freight rates because farmers and planters in the immediate vicinity of Jefferson could afford the brief time to take their products to market in their own wagons.

Uncertainties in ox-wagon transport were produced by variations in weather. Heavy rains resulted in muddy roads and swollen creek beds that lengthened travel time and occasionally prohibited movement, as reported in the 1 February 1871 *South-Western*: "At Jefferson, on Saturday, the Bayou was rising fast, with the prospect of getting higher than known for some years past, so says the Times and Republican. Jefferson was entirely cut off from the interior. Three hundred cotton wagons were water bound west of the Cypress, and could not go one way or the other."

There were no uncertainties in ox-wagon transport related to security. All early travelers are in agreement with Smith that "The most perfect security to life and property reigns throughout N.E. Texas, far more perfect than can be found in the Eastern States, or in Europe, or indeed in any well-peopled country." Smith notes: "Unprotected loaded wagons, which have been broken down on the highroad, have been known to remain unmolested for many days." The only recorded instance of attacks on wagon trains was during the unusual conditions of civil disorder immediately following the Civil War, as reported in the 4 October 1865 *South-Western*:

> TOO BAD.—We learn from the citizens of Texas, that a good deal of trade is diverted from Shreveport to other points, by reason of the depredations committed on the wagon trains in this vicinity by a gang of highwaymen. They inform us that it is not so dangerous to go to Houston, though it is much further. We have noticed that a number of wagons, instead of camping outside the corporation, come into the town and camp under the protection of the troops. This is a good plan, and we advise all to follow it. In the meantime, something must be done to put a stop to these depredations, and afford protection to our Texas friends.

The costliness of overland transport had a profound effect on the content and geographic boundaries of the market area. Wheat, for example, could not become a significant export commodity through Jefferson because of its relatively low value to weight. Because wheat could not be produced in abundance for export, flour was imported. Most importantly, high overland freight transport costs delimited the areas throughout Texas in which it was feasible to grow cotton. The maximum range was about 150 miles from waterborne transportation. Cotton obviously could be produced beyond Dallas, which was on the perimeter of Jefferson's market area, but it could not be brought to market at a profit. For example, if a five hundred–pound bale of cotton sold at $0.10 per pound and was transported 200 miles at $0.01 per mile per hundred pounds, the initial stage of its journey consumed one-fifth of its value.

PASSENGERS

All of the boats that traveled on the Cypress Bayou and the lakes route carried both freight and passengers into and out of the market area. Passengers were of two types: cabin and deck. Cabin passengers had sleeping accommodations and were fed meals. Deck passengers had no accommodations. They slept on the deck amidst freight as best they could and carried their food with them. Deck passage was preferred by immigrants because it was considerably cheaper than cabin passage.

There are no passenger lists or passenger counts for boats traveling upstream or downstream on the route. However, the Shreveport newspapers provide a sufficient amount of information on the number of people on specific boats to establish a general picture of passenger flows. In many cases the newspapers only mention a "cabin full of passengers" or "a good list of passengers" for specific boats. In many other cases, numbers are given. These are not official counts but rather numbers that are reported by boats to the editor of the newspaper's navigation column. However, they can be considered reliable because captains and clerks knew how many people were on board (although these numbers were sometimes exaggerated).

The downstream passenger movement from ports along the route was much smaller than the upstream passenger movement. Many boats are recorded as carrying only a few people when they reached Shreveport from points west. On the other hand, boats carrying 20–50 people were not uncommon, and the passenger lists were almost always supplemented at Shreveport. A large majority of the persons carried downstream were cabin passengers, apparently businessmen and general travelers on their way to New Orleans.

Upstream passenger loads appear to have been much larger, with numbers above 80 not uncommon. However, this is an impressionistic conjecture. The Shreveport newspapers only record passenger loads for boats docking at Shreveport and destined for Jefferson. Many of these passengers could have departed at Shreveport, although there is nothing in the newspaper accounts to suggest that this was the case. It also appears that the number of deck passengers often outweighed the number of cabin passengers and that most of the deck passengers, and probably many of the cabin passengers, were immigrants.

Passengers were an important source of revenue for boats, and boats obviously served as an important transport mechanism for the movement of businessmen and general travelers. The issue of immigrants is particularly important because it relates to the significance of the Cypress Bayou and the lakes route in the settlement of the West. There can be no question that immense numbers of immigrants passed through Marshall. The 9 December 1854 *Texas Republican*, for example, reports: "For weeks our streets have been lined with the wagons of immigrants. Day after day they pour in upon us." However, many of these people could have come from other states by wagon or from Shreveport overland, bypassing the route.

The Cypress Bayou and the lakes route appears to have been an important immigration channel. When Buck Barry took the second boat to Jefferson in 1845, he reports that there were 130 passengers on board and that most were on their way to Texas. The 6 May 1846 Clarksville *Northern Standard* quotes the Marshall *Soda Lake Herald* to the effect that "The Steamer 'Jim Gilmer,' ORRICK, Master, arrived at Port Caddo on the 18th inst., bringing about 400 Emigrants, also a great deal of property besides." And the 29 March 1875 *Daily Jimplecute* contains an advertisement for the Texas Immigration and Real Estate Agency, with offices in Jefferson, Texarkana, and Denison.

Edward Smith traveled throughout Northeast Texas by horseback in 1849 investigating sites for an English colony and produced, as required by his contract, a formal report on his investigations. One of his primary responsibilities was to determine the best route to Northeast Texas. Smith says that Jefferson is "a more convenient port to the settlers in the interior" because it "enters farther to the west than Shreveport."

Smith recommends the purchase of supplies and buggies at New Orleans because of the much higher cost upstream. For passage from New Orleans, he recommends the *Caddo, Monterey,* and *W. A. Violett,* but not the *Tallahatchie.* Cabin fare to Jefferson is given as $10–$12 for each adult. Smith mentions: "The steerage is a very dirty place, without beds, and the cost is very small." The immigrant will reach Jefferson in about four days, where "he may find ox-wagons which have brought produce to that port" from which he may rent one or two yoke of oxen for the trip inland at "about eighteen miles per day, taking the wagon slowly, but steadily and safely, through the muddy river bottoms."

Smith's observations are important in establishing Jefferson as a point of departure for immigrants. However, his observations cannot be generalized because he was writing for a select group of immigrants who were fairly wealthy in comparison to the masses that entered Texas. Smith does not even quote a price for deck passage, which was favored by immigrants who could afford steamboat travel.

The "River Intelligence" column in the Shreveport *South-Western* provides a number of instances of boats arriving at Shreveport from New Orleans and St. Louis carrying immigrants. Some of these loads were quite large, as in two January 1870 examples. On the twenty-fourth, the *B. L. Hodge* arrived at Shreveport carrying "300 cabin and deck passengers, a number of whom were immigrants, seeking homes in the El Dorado of the west." On the twenty-ninth, the *Selma* arrived, "loaded down to the guards with passengers—so many the clerk couldn't count them. Many of these passengers are emigrants bound for eastern Texas." Although neither of these boats was destined for Jefferson, the immigrants obviously could have transferred to steamboats going in that direction.

There are a few instances in which immigrants are mentioned in connection with boats arriving at Shreveport and destined for Jefferson. The 29 December 1869 *South-Western* reports that the *Era No. 10*, which was bound for Jefferson, arrived at Shreveport with "decks crowded with immigrants." On 31 December, the *Red Cloud* arrived with 350 cabin and deck passengers, most of whom were immigrants to Texas. The 14 December 1870 *South-Western* notes: "Immigrants are pouring into Texas in unprecedented numbers at every point. . . . The Gladiola and Era No. 10 brought up over 500 passengers, most of whom were immigrants to Texas." On 5 January 1871, the *Ida* arrived with "a fine freight and seventy-five cabin and deck passengers—the latter immigrants 'bound for Texas.'" On 17 January, the *Tidal Wave* arrived "crowded with passengers," most of whom were said to be immigrants. And on 21 January, the *Carrie Converse*'s clerk "reported something over a hundred passengers, mostly emigrants."

It is highly likely that most of the immigrants stayed on board to Jefferson, but they certainly also could have departed at Shreveport. There are only three accounts indicating immigrant travel by steamboat to Jefferson, which is not surprising given the fact that Shreveport had no interest in the upstream movement of passengers. The 29 December 1869 *South-Western* reports that the *Lulu D.* arrived from New Orleans with "a good freight and over 200 passengers" and that "Late in the day she continued on her trip to Cypress bayou with her load of living freight." It is inconceivable that a load of 200 passengers to Jefferson would not be composed primarily of immigrants.

There are actually only two records that specifically mention immigrant travel by steamboat to Jefferson. The first was for a St. Louis boat on 19 February 1870: "Not far behind the Texarkana, the Walter B. Dance, all the way from Pike, with Capt. L. T. Belt on the roof, and Oscar Haynes in the office, comes into port. She brings 550 tons of freight from St. Louis, 200 of which are for Jefferson. She had on board 100 immigrants for Texas, about half of whom stop here, the others going on to Jefferson."

The second was a notation concerning immigrants in the 21 December 1870 *South-Western*: "The Bertha brought up some two hundred fine looking German immigrants for Texas, who went on up to Jefferson." The Shreveport accounts are confirmed by one of the handful of extant Jefferson newspapers. The 15 January 1870 *Jefferson Radical* reports: "Navigation is looking up. Steamboats constantly arriving and departing, bringing immigrants and goods, and with them life, trade and prosperity."

It is obvious that a large number of immigrants passed through Shreveport, and it is probable that many of them moved overland through Marshall. Port Caddo and Jefferson both appear to be important points of departure for immigrants from the earliest years, with many immigrants through Port Caddo heading down to Marshall and many through Jefferson heading directly west.

FREIGHT

Freight was the other major factor in steamboat carriage and consisted of up freights (import) and down freights (export). With respect to the up freights, commodity listings for receipts at Jefferson would probably have been fairly similar to those at Shreveport, which are presented for commercial year 1870–71 (1 September 1870–31 August 1871) in an 1873 Corps of Engineers report on Red River and Cypress Bayou:

General merchandise, in packages	201,510
Barrels flour	43,358
Sacks corn and oats	6,891
Bundles iron ties	18,710
Cases boots and shoes	25,104
Barrels and half-barrels molasses	8,111
Sacks coffee	5,125
Barrels and half-barrels whisky	3,116
Bales bagging	1,376
Rolls bagging	2,780
Barrels and half-barrels sugar	2,560
Boxes tobacco	3,100
Wagons, buggies, carriages	671

Casks bacon	2,825
Barrels pork	1,500
Bales hay	250
Hogsheads sugar	351
Coils rope	711
Pianos	45
Total number packages	328,094

Up freights to Jefferson are often given in terms of number of packages, and loads of more than a thousand packages were fairly common, some of which would have been dropped off at other ports and landings along the route. A particularly notable load of over four thousand packages was transported by the *Lizzie Hopkins* to Jefferson on 12 February 1870.

These packages were deposited in the larger warehouses in Jefferson for distribution to commercial establishments and individuals, and most were transported into the interior by ox-wagons that had just offloaded export commodities and were seeking a return load. The geographic dimension of Shreveport's interior trade is fairly easy to follow because every issue of the newspaper contains a column showing the consignees of merchandise carried up by steamboats. I have only been able to find one example for Jefferson, in the 21 May 1867 *Semi-Weekly Jimplecute*, which shows packages (note that *do.* is an abbreviation for ditto) for places as far away as Sherman and Bonham:

CONSIGNMENTS OF MERCHANDISE PER RIVER.
[For three days ending last night]

At J. W. & J. R. Russell & Co's.—L .M. Allan, Daingerfield, 35 pkgs mdz.; Fitch & Loving, Sherman, 1 do.; F. M. Rogers, Sulphur Springs, 2 do.; M. H. Wright, Greenville, 7 do.; J. T. Turner, do. 6 do.; Scott, Dougherty & Co., Gainesville, 12 do.; Follett, Lenox & Reed, Clarksville, 73 do.; Dr. Geo. Gordon, do. 3 do.; Jno. Scaff, do. 6 do.; Miles Reed, do. 3 do.; L. D. Van Dyke, do. 1 do.; R. H. Jackson do. 3 do.; W. J. Avinger & Bro., Hickory Hill, 2 do.; J. J. Hamilton, Paris, 1 do.; W. W. Russell & Co., Bonham, 2 do.; B. S. Walcott, Honey Grove, 65 do.

At Wright, Murphy & Co's.—D .Campbell, Jefferson, 1 case mer.; R. G. Batte, do. 316 sks corn, 42 bales hay, 10 bbls.;

W. C. Batte do. 1 pkg. mer.; B. M. Childress & Bro's, Sulphur Springs, 3 casks bacon; Buford & Harrison, do. 8 pkgs. merc.; diamond N, Daingerfield, 25 do.; Houghton & English, Farmersville, 28 do.; W. M. Bennett, Paris, 3 do.; E. G. Wells, do. 2 do.; J. F. McMurray, do. 101 do.; J. J. Libby, Clarksville, 1 do.; Charles DeMorse, do. 5 do.; T. R. Williams, Bonham, 30 do.; West, Murray & Co., McKinney, 6 do.; W. B. Logon, Jefferson, 6 do.

Commodities were exported from the market area as steamboat down freights. Much more is known about down freights than up freights because the down freights were easier to categorize. The most important export commodities were cotton and cattle and cattle products, particularly beef and hides. Cotton was transported overland by ox-wagon to various ports and landings on the route. Cattle were driven to Jefferson for slaughter or live transport. Animal products, such as hides, were carried overland by ox-wagon to Jefferson and ports and landings on the northern perimeter of the route and were also produced by Jefferson's slaughterhouses.

An 1873 Corps report on Cypress Bayou provides export statistics for Jefferson for commercial year 1870–71. The numbers were compiled by Jefferson's recorder, J. K. Laurance, by order of the city council:

EXPORTS.
Shipped from this port from September 1, 1870,
to September 1, 1871

Cotton (bales)	76,328
Dry hides	84,762
Green hides	18,471
Wool, pounds	87,623
Peltries	48,210
Bois d'Arc seed, bushels	9,721
Cattle	5,381
Lumber, feet	121,000
Pig-iron	amount not ascertained

This would be a good commodity listing were it not for the fact that beef, which was the Jefferson area's second most valuable export commodity, is not mentioned. This may be because The Packery had nearly ceased to function by this time. Alternately, because The Packery was located three miles downstream, its products may never have been included in Jefferson's official export statistics. Bois d'arc seed was used to grow fencerows before the invention of barbed wire in 1874. The pig iron was produced from deposits west of Jefferson and was expected to become an important export commodity, as indicated by the 30 March 1859 *South-Western*, quoting from the *Jefferson Gazette*: "Nash Doyle & Co. made a second shipment on the W. A. Andrew yesterday, of forty tons of iron, manufactured at their forge, 18 miles northwest of this town. Messrs. Leeds & Co. of New Orleans, have tested this iron and pronounce it superior to any now manufactured in the United States. This new article of export though small at present, is destined at no very distant day to comprise a large amount of the shipments from this town." Although raw iron was the basis for significant local industrial activity, it does not appear to have ever become a commercial export commodity. Steamboat transport of raw iron downstream is mentioned in only one place other than the 1857 test load on the *W. A. Andrew*. The 7 June 1871 *South-Western* records that the *C. H. Durfee* arrived back in Shreveport from Jefferson carrying twenty tons of iron, which would have been produced by the Kelly Foundry in Kellyville. This appears to be the "amount not ascertained" in Laurance's compilation of export statistics for commercial year 1871.

Jefferson Nash's facility was important during the Civil War and definitely transported raw iron downstream to Shreveport and beyond for military purposes. There is no evidence for boat transport of Nash's plows as an export commodity before the war. After the war, Kelly's plows had a wide regional distribution. Kelly plows were transported from Jefferson to the Red River area by the *Alexandria* in November 1877 and by the *Col. A. P. Kouns* in December 1877. The *Alexandria* carried four hundred plows, but the dimensions of this export trade are unknown. The *Alpha* carried one hundred plows from Jefferson in 1884, but it is not known whether these were Kelly plows.

Upstream freights are sometimes given in terms of tonnages but are seldom differentiated. The most commonly mentioned up freights are salt—used in Jefferson's beef packing operations—railroad iron, and whiskey, which was drunk by everyone but teetotalers. However, up freights involved practically all commodities needed by farms, plantations, and emerging settlements, including food, clothing, and equipment.

The Cincinnati boat *Edinburgh* made an experimental trip to Shreveport and Jefferson in February 1871. The *South-Western* of the twenty-second provides a listing of the freight (characterized as "fair"), which gives some idea of the types and volumes of up freights that would have been carried by a boat from the Midwest: 400 bedsteads, 84 dozen chairs, 43 bureaus, 40 wardrobes, 41 washstands, 37 tin safes, 168 barrels whisky, 4 horses, 560 sacks malt, 7 bales hops, 4 barrels onion sets, 62 cultivators, 12 barrels sausage, 17 hogsheads bacon, 16 dozen buckets, 31 kegs tar, 16 nests tubs, 9 rolls leather, 40 empty trunks, 92 dozen brooms, 41 reels coil rope, 20 bales oakum, 18 nests willow baskets, 40 boxes starch, 19 dozen sieves, 12 dozen washboards, 100 boxes axes, 50 cases 10 tierces 20 kegs 8 half barrels and 120 buckets lard, 120 boxes soap, 28 plows, 25 half barrels beer, 270 bundles wrapping paper, 10 packages peanuts, 50 rolls bagging, 10 kegs shot, 12 tierces hams, 35 barrels mess pork, 69 bundles bed slats, 7 boxes bacon, 25 bundles hoes, 5 crates earthenware, 350 packages merchandise—altogether 300 tons.

Miscellaneous export commodities mentioned in the navigation record include sheep, mules, pork, horns, skins, leather, tallow, cotton seed, beeswax, and snakeroot, which was believed to cure snake bites. None of these achieved any degree of importance that would necessitate separate consideration. Little is known about the exports of ports and landings on the route other than Jefferson, except that they were all cotton outlets. If any of the ports and landings exported a commodity other than the types that appear in Jefferson's statistics, this fact would surely have been reported in the navigation columns of Shreveport's newspapers. Thus, a discussion of exports can be limited to cotton and cattle and its derivatives.

COTTON

Steamboats never would have operated on the route had it not been for cotton agriculture. Cotton was by far the most valuable export commodity, and it produced the greatest freight revenue for steamboats. In addition, without cotton agriculture, Northeast Texas would have been so sparsely settled that steamboats would not have been able to afford to carry up freights and passengers on the route.

In order to present cotton statistics for the route's market area in **table 12-1**, I have made a guess as to which counties the market area

Table 12-1
Cotton Production: 1849 and 1859
(In Bales)

County	1849	1859
Bowie	1,113	6,874
Cass	1,573	9,968
Collin	1	16
Cooke	0	58
Dallas	44	0
Denton	0	2
Fannin	374	1,499
Grayson	5	220
Harrison	4,581	21,440
Hopkins	8	856
Hunt	5	22
Kaufman	6	381
Lamar	1,055	4,191
Marion	NA	3,708
Red River	579	7,970
Titus	292	5,129
Tarrant	0	0
Upshur	673	7,965
Van Zandt	57	654
Wood	NA	1,108
Total	10,366	72,001
State of Texas	57,596	431,463

NA = Not Applicable (formed by county divisions after 1849).

descriptions are referring to and have included Harrison, whose primary cotton outlets were places like Port Caddo rather than Jefferson. Kaufman and Van Zandt have also been included because their upper portions probably fell within the market area. The numbers are from the 1850 and 1860 censuses, which provide production figures for the previous years. The numbers for 1849 should be compared to Smith's

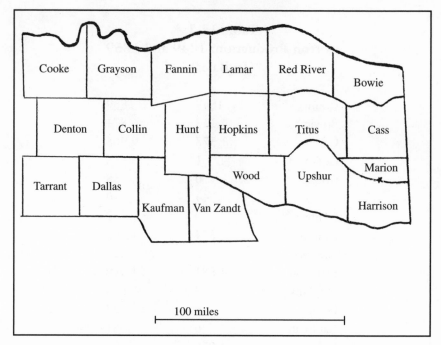

Fig. 12-2. Market area

map **(see fig. 12-1)** and the numbers for 1859 to **fig. 12-2**, which reflects the formation of Wood and Marion Counties.

These numbers illustrate some important points:

1. It is quite obvious why Port Caddo emerged as an important port in the early 1840s and continued to be important at least up to the Civil War. Harrison County ranked second in cotton production in Texas in 1849 and third in 1859.

2. Cotton production before the Civil War was determined by proximity to waterborne transport. All of the major producers in 1859 were either directly on Red River (Lamar, Red River, and Bowie), or else within sixty miles of the route (Cass, Marion, Harrison, Titus, and Upshur). There was a secondary tier of modest producers farther west (Fannin, Hopkins, and Wood) and a rapid falling off of production even farther west (Grayson, Hunt, Van Zandt, Collin, Dallas, Cooke, Denton, Tarrant, and Kaufman).

3. Fluctuations in navigation access to the upper Red River was an important factor in the export trade of the route. The upper Red River counties were high producers. When navigation to the upper Red was

closed, a great deal of cotton was transported to Jefferson, Smithland, and Monterey from Lamar, Red River, and Bowie Counties.

4. The 10 April 1852 *Star State Patriot* states that the ports and landings along the route were shipping out 30,000–40,000 bales a year. The 1859 *Texas Almanac* indicates that these same ports and landings shipped out 60,500 bales during commercial year 1857–58. These numbers are compatible with the census production numbers for the region in 1849 and 1859.

5. The 1859 *Texas Almanac* is particularly important because it provides the only account of the relative weight of the exports of the various ports and landings. Cumulatively, Benton, Port Caddo, and Swanson's Landing are said to have exported 21,000 bales during commercial year 1857–58, which is equivalent to Harrison County's 1859 production. The 25,000 bales through Jefferson are equivalent to production numbers for Cass, Titus, Hopkins, Wood, and Upshur. The 20,000 bales from upper Red River are equivalent to the production numbers for Lamar, Bowie, and Red River.

Cotton was a summer crop. Seed was planted in early April, and the first blooms appeared in June. Picking began in August and extended into the late fall on the largest plantations, with the last cotton often not picked until the beginning of the next year. Ginning began in August and continued into the winter. Light compressing and baling began immediately, producing bales that weighed approximately 400–500 pounds. These were loaded on ox-wagons for transport to the ports and landings, which usually received the first bale in late August or early September. Smith indicates that the common load was five bales of cotton hauled by four yoke of oxen.

A representative large plantation is described in an advertisement in the 15 March 1856 *Texas Republican*:

VALUABLE PLANTATION FOR SALE.

THE undersigned offers for sale, that valuable and well-improved Plantation recently owned by Levi Greer, deceased, late of Harrison County, Texas. Said Plantation is situated in Harrison county, Texas, 3½ miles south-west of Jefferson, and 12 north of Marshall.

There are 1205 acres in the tract; 350 cleared and under excellent fence; all fresh land. Nine negro cabins, gin-house, and mill, dwelling house, kitchen, and all the necessary out-houses on the premises, new, in good order and comfortable repair. For convenience, water, health, and fertility of soil, it is unsurpassed by any plantation in the county. Title warranted.

If not disposed of during the year at private sale, it will be sold at public auction, before the court-house door, in the town of Marshall, on the 1st day of January, 1857.

For terms of sale, apply to

H. N. Greer, on the premises, or to Sam F. Mosely, Jefferson, Texas, or to R. W. Loughery, Marshall.

H. N. Greer.
March 1st, 1856.

A cotton bale was a valuable commodity. The value depended on weight and grade and the current selling price on international cotton markets, which changed daily. A reasonable range for the entire steamboat period would be about $0.10 to $0.20 a pound, with wildly escalated prices immediately after the Civil War. Normal circumstances produced a bale valued from $40 to $100.

When cotton reached a port like Jefferson, it was placed in the hands of receiving and forwarding merchants, who stored the bales until a steamboat arrived and agreement was reached on transport costs. The largest planters had cotton factors in New Orleans, who acted as sellers, suppliers, and bankers, extending long-term credit. There were no cotton factors in Jefferson or Shreveport until after the Civil War. The cotton trade at Jefferson and the other ports and landings on the route was handled by the receiving and forwarding merchants, who normally acted as provisioners, disseminating up freights and selling commodities, often on credit to preferred customers in the interior. These merchants had business connections with cotton factors in New Orleans, who were the ultimate sellers. An early Jefferson example of one of these merchants advertised in the 5 July 1851 *Texas Republican*:

A NEW HOUSE IN JEFFERSON, TEXAS.
Dallas Street, Near the Steam Boat Landing, above high water mark.

J. M. & J. C. MURPHY, *commission and forwarding merchants.* Particular attention given to storing and shipping cotton and to receiving and forwarding all kinds of merchandise, &c.

Dry goods and groceries of all kinds; bagging, rope, and plantation supplies, kept constantly on hand.

Also cash advances made on cotton to be shipped to our friends in New Orleans.

Our warehouse will be completed and the most of our stock in store on or before the 1st September next. At which time and place, we will be pleased to meet and serve our friends and the public generally, and hope by strict attention to business, with low prices and liberal accommodations to merit and receive a liberal share of public patronage.

J. M. & J. C. MURPHY,
Jefferson, Texas, June 21, 1851.

The cotton was then transported downstream to New Orleans, either directly or by transfer operations at Shreveport. A small amount of cotton exported through the ports and landings on the route was sold on the Shreveport market, but this was never an important factor in Shreveport's commerce. At New Orleans, the cotton was sampled, graded, sold, and transported to East Coast and international markets.

As can be seen from **table 12-2**, the post–Civil War recovery of cotton production was slow and did not approximate the prewar level of 72,000 bales until 1869, when more than 69,000 bales were produced in Jefferson's market area (Cass, Marion, and Red River Counties are unreported). The expansion of cotton production was rapid thereafter, as can be seen by comparing the 1869 and 1879 figures. Much of this rapidly increasing production was brought about by the railroads, which provided an export channel for the counties to the west such as Cooke, Denton, Tarrant, Grayson, Collin, and Dallas.

By 1869, almost all of the cotton that was being transported on the route was coming out through Jefferson; in that year about 40,000 bales were exported, which was probably about half of the production. Most of the cotton from the southern tier of counties in the market area was by that time being sent by rail to Shreveport. Cotton exports through Jefferson reached a high of about 90,000 bales in 1871, when the market area was rapidly contracting to seven counties (Bowie, Cass, Titus, Upshur, Marion, Hopkins, and Hunt) identified by Eberstadt as secure in 1874. The reason that exports increased while the market area was contracting was that cotton production was increasing rapidly in the counties still dominated by Jefferson.

Table 12-2
Cotton Production: 1869 and 1879
(In Bales)

County	1869	1879
Bowie	2,990	7,958
Cass	NR	16,181
Collin	4,371	22,145
Cooke	308	11,547
Dallas	3,834	21,469
Delta	NA	4,911
Denton	674	11,568
Fannin	5,699	22,386
Franklin	NA	4,048
Grayson	2,885	19,166
Harrison	8,165	17,619
Hopkins	5,417	8,279
Hunt	4,272	10,805
Kaufman	1,910	10,668
Lamar	6,753	24,673
Marion	NR	7,515
Morris	NA	4,880
Rains	NA	1,915
Red River	NR	17,669
Rockwall	NA	2,630
Tarrant	728	10,950
Titus	7,039	4,923
Upshur	7,362	8,023
Van Zandt	2,926	6,957
Wood	3,919	7,381
Total	69,252	267,832
State of Texas	350,628	805,284

NA = Not Applicable (formed by county divisions after 1869).
NR = Not Recorded.

CATTLE AND CATTLE PRODUCTS

The second major export commodity from the market area that passed downstream on steamboats was cattle and cattle products, particularly beef and hides. Northeast Texas was one of the largest cattle-producing areas in the state. The dimensions of this production are described in Terry Jordan's *Trails To Texas*. When Edward Smith traveled through the area in 1849, he recorded that "Vast herds are driven yearly to the southern market," by which he meant New Orleans. From the earliest years, cattle and hides from local slaughter were brought south to Shreveport and Jefferson for steamboat transport to New Orleans. This movement was soon radically modified by the formation of packing houses in both cities.

Table 12-3 shows cattle production in the counties that probably acted as suppliers to Jefferson. Cattle and hides, along with cotton and bois d'arc seed, appear in the first export records for Jefferson, all of which are found in the Marshall *Texas Republican* and most of which are derived from Jefferson newspaper reports:

1. The 11 March 1854 *Texas Republican* reports: "The Herald says there are 9,000 bales of cotton in the warehouses of Jefferson, and large stocks of hides, peltries, and bois d'arc seed, awaiting shipment."
2. The 15 July 1854 *Texas Republican* cites the *Jefferson Herald* to the effect that "the steamers Cleona and Grenada

Table 12-3
Cattle

County	1849	1859	1869
Fannin	5,671	24,835	12,988
Hopkins	5,701	21,867	14,916
Hunt	2,333	24,623	25,141
Lamar	1,590	20,415	14,249
Red River	5,781	13,438	8,721
Total	25,069	118,361	89,912

left our wharf a few days since, with large cargoes of beef cattle, driven from the upper counties."

3. When Loughery visited Jefferson in February 1855, he observed: "There are several thousand bales of cotton and an immense quantity of peltries, hides, etc., awaiting shipment."

4. The 17 October 1857 *Texas Republican* cites the *Jefferson Gazette*: "The Reub White and Bloomer arrived at our wharf since our last issue. The Bloomer took down about 140 head of beef cattle."

Although some boats such as the *Frolic* were outfitted for the carrying of cattle, there does not appear to have been any functional specialization among steamboats that operated on the route. Cattle were carried on conventional craft along with other typical freight loads such as cotton. This means that deck passengers shared accommodations with cattle. There are no records of such sharing for boats moving downstream on the route; nor, for that matter, is there any mention of downstream deck passengers. There are, however, accounts of boats moving from Shreveport to New Orleans carrying deck passengers and cattle, indicating that it was common practice.

Cattle and hides would have been important export commodities under any circumstances. However, the realm of animal product exports was significantly increased through the formation of slaughter and packing houses in Jefferson that enabled pickled beef in barrels to become a major factor in downstream commodity movements by steamboats. Beef packing made Jefferson a more important destination for cattle drives and dramatically expanded the number of hides transported. It also created a large demand for salt and lime, so that records such as that of the *Hettie Gilmore* carrying 750 sacks of salt to Jefferson in March 1866 were not uncommon.

Beef packing began in Jefferson in 1857 when H. H. Black started an experimental operation with the following advertisement in the *Texas Republican* on 19 September:

IMPORTANT.
I will pay liberal cash prices for all fat, merchantable, and heavy beef cattle, delivered to me at Jefferson, Texas, during the months of November, December, and January ensuing.

I am prepared to receive, slaughter, and pack from forty-five to fifty head per day.

H. H. Black.
Jefferson, Texas, September 19, '57.

That this was the first meatpacking operation in Jefferson is confirmed by the newspaper's commentary: "We call attention to the advertisement of Mr. Black who has commenced the Beef Packing business in Jefferson. He will test it this season as an experiment. If successful, it will be of immense advantage to cattle raisers, as it will enable them to sell their stocks at home, instead of shipping them to New Orleans, with its attendant risks of falling off in weight and a glutted market. We trust he may succeed."

The facility was located on the south side of Cypress Bayou according to the 9 August 1862 *Texas Republican*. This was Black's second operation, with a companion facility opened in Shreveport during the previous year. The Jefferson operation is described briefly in the 7 November 1857 *Eastern Texas Gazette*: "We were down at Mr. Black's beef factory on yesterday. Beeves are slaughtered, skinned and cut up there in quick and scientific style. Mr. Black has made thorough preparations for his work before he commenced killing. We saw some 40 beeves already cleaned and ready to be cut up. It is a sight worth seeing."

The 14 November 1857 *Standard* notes that Black had twenty-five employees and that he intended to pack 3,000 beeves that winter. The 5 February 1859 *Standard* reports that Black had slaughtered 3,000 beeves that season and had begun packing pork on an extensive scale. Black continued to advertise the Jefferson facility until the end of 1859. The facility was sold to the New Orleans firm of Fellows & Company in June 1860. Black apparently continued to be associated with the operation until he left for war. The facility was destroyed by fire in July 1862.

Black's operation was reduced in importance in 1858 through the creation of a much larger firm by Charles Stanley and Samuel Nimmo. The inception of this firm is recorded in the 12 August 1858 *Texas Republican*: "Our enterprising friends, Messrs. Stanley & Nimmo, of Jefferson, Texas, are going extensively into the beef packing business during the ensuing fall and winter. Their large and commodious warehouse has been re-arranged; an important addition to it constructed; barrels made; hundreds of sacks of salt provided; and everything wearing the appearance of abundant means. We wish them every success, for we know they merit it."

Stanley began advertising in January 1855 as a commission and forwarding merchant, and Stanley & Nimmo began advertising in March 1856 as furniture salesmen, with the showroom located in Stanley's warehouse near the Houston Street Bridge. The packery was a modification of the warehouse, and the facilities were located slightly upstream of the business section of town, with animal wastes discharged directly into the bayou. An extensive description of this facility is provided in the 15 October 1858 *Texas Republican* by Loughery on one of his regular visits to Jefferson:

> Among the objects of attraction presented at Jefferson is a visit to the beef-packing establishment of Messrs. Stanley & Nimmo. These gentlemen are entering upon the business on an extensive scale, and from their well known character for prudence and sagacity, we have no doubt that it will be eminently successful. In fact, there is no reason why it should not prove an exceedingly lucrative business. Their close proximity to the prairies will enable them to obtain the choicest beeves at comparatively little cost. The vast extent of the prairies, and the character of the grasses with which they are covered, keep the cattle which roam over them in excellent order all the year, without any cost to the owner, and always in a healthy condition. It is a noted fact that Texas cattle are freer from disease than any in the world. Some of the beef properly packed in this latitude for experiment, has been shipped abroad, and pronounced by competent judges equal to any grass fed beef in the United States. Before engaging in the business, Mr. Stanley spent several months in the North and West, visiting the largest and most successful packeries, collecting all the information that he could gather as to the best method of curing beef to suit the different markets, and full instructions as to packing it after the most approved manner. Having thoroughly informed himself upon every point, his next object was to secure the services of the most competent men to fill the different departments, in which he was successful, as he assured us, beyond even his most sanguine expectations. He also examined

minutely the business arrangements of the best packeries. His establishment is consequently a model of convenience and economy. Everything connected with it seems to contemplate the most rapid dispatch of business with the least loss of time. The building premises for packing, engine, and machinery, cover over three hundred feet square, while the area connected with the business of the establishment embraces several acres. Everything about the premises has an air of thrift and industry. We found the proprietors actively employed in putting their house in order. There are over one hundred thousand staves, which the coopers were working up into barrels. They have a superb steam engine and apparatus for tanking tallow, and in connection with this engine, they have water pipes to convey water to all parts of the building for packing or to use to advantage in case of fire. The tanks are of iron and constructed upon the latest and most improved plan. They have already on hand three or four thousand sacks of salt for commencing, so that they will be ready in a few weeks, or so soon as the weather will permit active operations.

This is an enterprise which will prove of great advantage to this section of country, and particularly stock raisers. Messrs. Stanley & Nimmo are fully prepared and expect to slaughter over one hundred beef cattle a day. The business season for packing will embrace a period of from ninety to one hundred and twenty days, and will enable them, we presume, to dispose of from eight to ten thousand beeves. This establishment is situated immediately on the bayou, and they have nothing to do but to roll the beef when packed from the warehouse on board of a steamboat. That the business will prove a lucrative one, we do not entertain a doubt. As we before observed, the well known prudent character of the men, and the investigations which they made before they went into it, are a sufficient guaranty. We have known them for ten years, and if they are not successful, it will be the first failure they have ever yet made in business.

The first packed beef was produced in January 1859. R. W. Loughery of the *Texas Republican* received a sample, which he describes as follows in the issue for the twenty-eighth: "We received, a few days ago, from the beef packing establishment of our friends Messrs. Stanley & Nimmo, Jefferson, a half barrel of their pickled beef. It is remarkably firm, and richly flavored. Their packers understand the business thoroughly, and the beef which they put up is the finest in the country."

This praise was not unwarranted. By March, Jefferson beef was in New York commanding high prices, as reported in the 29 April 1859 *Texas Republican*, quoting the *Galveston News*:

> TEXAS BEEF.—The New York papers of March 21st report sales of 500 tierces of Texas cured beef at $18.50 per tierce. A tierce we understand is equal to 1½ barrels, which makes the sale equal to $12.33 per barrel. The quality is quoted as good mess, and the price is that which is given for the best brands. We learn that this is probably the first Texas cured beef sold in New York, as Texas beef, though beef from this State has been sold before, with other brands. An experienced beef packer who has been in our city for some time past, informs us that this beef was put up in Jefferson, Cass county, and he entertains no doubt that Texas beef can be cured and shipped to markets abroad in the merchantable condition, so as to compare favorably with beef from any part of the world, and command the highest prices.

The editor of the *Jefferson Gazette* was invited to Christmas dinner at the packery, which was held for some eighty or ninety employees, among whom he found "a pride of conscious merit." His description of the facility at the end of the packing season is contained in the 14 January 1860 *Texas Republican*:

> While on the subject, we may as well state that the slaughtering at this establishment is now pretty well over— four thousand head of cattle having been butchered for the season. And to show with what dispatch they transact business, we will state the fact that the morning of the 24th ult. found them with 177 cattle in the pen, and at 4 o'clock on the evening of the same day every beef was butchered, nicely cleaned, quartered and hanging in the cooling room. The reputation of this establishment with its extensive and convenient arrangements, has gone abroad. Men of experience, who have

visited the best arranged packeries in the world, pronounce its whole construction unsurpassed by any thing of the kind in the country. Their cisterns are capacitated to hold, at the same time, two thousand head of six year old cattle, and every other arrangement is on a scale of equal magnitude. Their pumps are so arranged as to conduct water from the bayou to every department, enabling them to keep all things as clean and nice as their pride, comfort, or fancy may dictate. It is styled by competent judges a model packery, and we have no doubt, justly so. Their beef, we understand, has commanded the highest price in both the New York and Liverpool markets, and, it is well known, has secured an enviable reputation wherever it is known. This is their second season, and it is to be hoped that each succeeding one will bring to them enlarged profits and an extended reputation.

Stanley & Nimmo were in operation for only two packing seasons and failed through gross overextension of debt. The facility was purchased at auction by Elisha Price of New Orleans in October 1860. The 18 November 1860 *Harrison Flag* reports that Price was renovating the facility and planned to begin packing the next week. The firm of Hilliard, Summers & Company from New Orleans advertised in the 21 December 1861 Clarksville *Standard* that it had established a packery in Jefferson. Cattle prices are quoted, and no mention is made of a military relationship. This packery is not noted in the Marshall newspapers. If this was not a new facility, it was probably the old Black plant, because Price continued to operate the old Stanley & Nimmo plant during the Civil War.

Another packery was started during the Civil War, with James B. Dunn operating under contract to the Confederacy and under the supervision of Maj. William H. Thomas, departmental commissary and subsistence officer for the Department of the Trans-Mississippi West, headquartered in Shreveport. The contract was signed in September 1863 calling for the delivery of dried and pickled beef, pickled tongues, and hides. Dunn was responsible for erecting the buildings and machinery needed for slaughtering and packing "at or near Jefferson Texas." The resulting tallow was used by the firm of Nussbaum & Lindsey, also under contract, to produce soap and candles. Although Thomas characterized Dunn as having long experience in the packing business, the barrels of beef distributed to troops in January 1865 were found to be of poor quality.

Dunn's facility did not survive the war. It was replaced by another facility, which was usually referred to as "the packery" in the navigation columns, that was to play an important role in the level of steamboat activity and in the composition of import and export freights. The Packery was located three miles downstream of Jefferson on the north side of the bayou. This facility was apparently in existence by at least 1866: the 16 February *Texas Republican*, quoting the *South-Western*, says that the *National* sank on Red River on the sixth "loaded principally with pickled beef from the Jefferson packery." The name of the firm is not mentioned in the newspapers until February 1868, when it is designated Wilson, Stoner & Company. Stoner left the firm in 1868 and erected his own packery below Shreveport in July. The facility downstream of Jefferson operated under the name John H. Wilson & Company and accounted for about a third of all down freights and substantial up freights. Ownership was transferred to a Colonel Elliott in January 1869. Large quantities of beef were carried out from The Packery during the first two months of 1870 on the basis of the winter packing season, but The Packery is not mentioned in the navigation record after 1870.

There are no firm statistics on beef production at Jefferson. The consignments columns of the New Orleans newspapers cannot be used because they include beef picked up at packeries in Shreveport. There are many mentions in 1866 of boats arriving at Shreveport from Jefferson carrying cattle and hides, and the 21 February *South-Western* shows the *Powell* and *Hamilton* as arriving with salt pork and beef. However, it was not until 1868 that large quantities of beef began to be mentioned. Thereafter, beef and hides are mentioned fairly often. This is probably not reflective of any real production changes, but rather an artifact of reporting procedures in the River Intelligence column of the *South-Western*, which increased in quality over time.

Table 12-4 shows what freight boats were carrying when they returned to Shreveport during the first two months of 1869 carrying freight in addition to cotton. This was a particularly high period in the records of returns and should not be assumed to be representative. Neither should it be considered inclusive, because the Shreveport newspaper was not obligated to provide systematic accounts. It is used merely to show that a large amount of beef was exported from Jefferson

Table 12-4
Beef

Boat	Freight
Gossamer	300 bales cotton, 171 sacks bois d'arc seed, 125 barrels beef
Lotus No. 2	500 bales cotton, 200 barrels beef
Richmond	700 bales cotton, 400 barrels beef
Era No. 9	350 bales cotton, 200 barrels beef
Golden Era	730 bales cotton, 725 tierces beef
Mittie Stephens	413 bales cotton, 643 barrels beef
Enterprise	265 bales cotton, 839 tierces beef, lots of hides
Selma	500 bales cotton, 300 barrels and 100 tierces beef, 50 barrels tallow, 30 barrels pork
Lizzie Hopkins	540 bales cotton, 100 barrels tallow, 322 tierces beef, lots of hides
Judge Fletcher	810 bales cotton, 600 tierces beef
Lotawanna	1,346 bales cotton, 221 sacks bois d'arc seed
Era No. 9	651 bales cotton, 703 sacks bois d'arc seed, 7 bales hides, 4 bales deer skins
Golden Era	200 bales cotton, 600 tierces beef
Richmond	250 bales cotton, 400 tierces beef
Lizzie Hopkins	600 bales cotton, 400 tierces beef
Lotawanna	919 bales cotton, 50 sacks bois d'arc seed, 66 dry hides, 400 bundles green hides, 544 barrels beef
Judge Fletcher	700 bales cotton, 600 tierces beef
Golden Era	250 bales cotton, 400 dry hides, 888 packages beef, 300 bundles green hides
Dora	699 bales cotton, 600 bundles hides, 200 tierces beef, 150 barrels tallow and oil, 250 sacks bois d'arc seed
Caroline	260 bales cotton, 551 bundles green hides, 256 barrels beef
Era No. 9	476 bales cotton, 600 sacks bois d'arc seed
Selma	740 bales cotton, lots of bois d'arc seed

and that The Packery was a significant operation. In reviewing these numbers, it should be kept in mind that a tierce was equivalent to 1½ barrels and held 350 pounds of finished beef.

The last mention of beef in the navigation record is in the 11 May 1872 *Shreveport Times* when the *Charles H. Durfee* is recorded as carrying 600 barrels from Jefferson. The 3 September 1872 *Shreveport Times* annual commercial summary says that Stoner & Company, the large packer in Shreveport, had been idle during commercial year 1871–72 because of low prices on pork and bacon.

VOLUME AND VALUE

The up and down freights that moved along the route constituted a high volume of trade with a high value. Unfortunately, neither volume nor value can be established for any particular year, much less over time; and the situation with respect to Jefferson is not far superior to that of the other ports and landings, about which there is no information other than estimates of cotton exports for a single year.

There are only three contemporary accounts of volume and value. The first was prepared by Jefferson merchants and appears in the 16 October 1868 *Texas Republican*: "Jefferson contains a population of from six to eight thousand, and is rapidly assuming the proportions of a city. . . . Notwithstanding the failure of the cotton crop last year, there were exported from December 1, 1867, to July 1, 1868, twenty-seven thousand bales of cotton; a larger amount than was anticipated. The value of the hides, wool, and peltries shipped is estimated at $155,000. The amount of merchandise sold last year is estimated at $3,500,000. And last year, it will be remembered, was not a fortunate year for business in the South."

Apart from the population figures, these numbers appear to be reliable. The actual count of bales shipped from ports and landings along the route for commercial year 1867–68 was 26,471 bales. In addition, the annual summary for the commercial year published in the *South-Western* gives an estimate of 30,000 bales.

The second account is from the preface to the 1870 *Digest of the Laws of the City of Jefferson*, which provides information that appears to be for commercial year 1869–70 (1 September 1869–31 August 1870): "About seventy-five thousand bags of cotton have been shipped from this place during the past season, about two hundred thousand dollars in hides and peltries, at least one hundred thousand dollars in wool, bees-wax, feathers, etc., to say nothing of cattle, of which there is no estimate, while the trade of this place has advanced within these three years from about three millions to eight millions of dollars."

The preface in which these numbers appear is titled "Jefferson, Its Almost Unexampled Prosperity and the Future Before It." The *Digest* is apparently a promotional piece because it contains advertisements. The numbers are obviously estimates rather than official counts, but they probably provide a reasonable picture of the level of commercial activity for the 1869–70 commercial year.

The third account of volume and value is Eberstadt's "Commercial Statistics" in the 1874 Corps report on Cypress Bayou:

> In 1869 the number of bales of cotton reached 75,352; hides, 160,000; and all other classes of products in like ratio. During the same commercial year the number of packages of merchandise landed here for the interior reached over 350,000, valued at $1,750,000, while the value of merchandise received by the merchants of Jefferson was $20,000,000. At that time the population of the city was 11,000 souls, and business of every class was prosperous in the extreme.
>
> Since that time, from various causes, trade and commerce have been gradually diminishing, and principal among these causes has been the lessening of our navigation, arising from the expenditure of Government appropriations on the Upper Red River in and about the great raft.

These numbers were prepared by Messrs. Johnson & Eberstadt of Jefferson to accompany the report of Assistant Engineer H. A. Leavitt, dated 28 May 1874, on a survey begun in January. They are obviously at least in part estimates rather than official counts and apparently refer to commercial year 1869–70 (1 September 1869–31 August 1870). Raft removal is claimed as the cause of Jefferson's commercial decline since August 1870 in spite of the fact that the raft was not removed until December 1873. A population figure of 11,000 is given for commercial year 1869–70, despite the 1870 federal census report of a population of 4,190. The special city census of March 1872 gives a population of 7,297.

Nevertheless, 75,352 bales appear to be based on a real count and provide an exact number for what the *Digest* called about 75,000 bags of cotton. Although cotton exports were to rise in the next commercial year, Eberstadt is suggesting that the total volume and value of trade through Jefferson reached a peak during commercial year 1869–70. This is borne out by the navigation record and particularly by the number of arrivals at Jefferson, which is a much better index than cotton statistics alone of the overall volume and value of trade (**table 12-5**). During commercial year 1869–70, there were 250 arrivals at Jefferson, compared to 232 in commercial year 1870–71. Although the latter year transported more bales than the former year, there was a dramatic decline in beef exports.

The only other pertinent statistics are Laurance's official city counts for commercial year 1870–71, which provide information on volume of exports alone. These statistics are particularly important because they include the peak cotton export number of 76,328 bales. This is only a few thousand bales above the number that can be compiled for boats returning to Shreveport, which can be accounted for on the basis that the editor of the River Intelligence column did not obtain information for some boats and did not obtain precise information for many boats.

From this analysis, it can be concluded that the volume and value of Jefferson's trade peaked in commercial year 1869–70 and that the statistics provided by the *Digest* and by Eberstadt are generally reflective of the conditions prevailing in that best year.

COMPARISONS

Charles Potts in *Railroad Transportation in Texas* says that "it is estimated that at one time one-fourth of the entire trade of the state passed through Jefferson." This statement, which is based on knowledgeable contemporary opinion, is probably true but cannot be documented, because there are no comparative statistics. It should also be recognized, in attempting to judge the dimensions of Jefferson's importance, that almost all of the trade of Texas passed through ports, of which there were very few, and that prior to the Civil War, there was little in the western half of the state.

Fred Tarpley, in *Jefferson: Riverport to the Southwest*, asserts: "In 1870, only Galveston surpassed Jefferson in commerce and industry."

Table 12-5
Trips and Bales

Boat Records			Other Estimates		
Commercial					
Year	Trips	Bales	Trips	Bales	Source
1866–67	139	22,185		29,518 (J)	9/4/67 *South-Western*
				2,500 (TL)	
1867–68	173	26,471		30,000	9/2/68 *South-Western*
1868–69	193	42,693			
1869–70	250	62,330		75,352 (J)	Eberstadt
				2,500 (TL)	9/7/70 *South-Western*
1870–71	232	73,325		76,328 (J)	Laurance
1871–72	199*	50,470		60,000	9/3/72 *Shreveport Times*
1872–73	155	34,898			
1873–74	NA	NA			
1874–75	34	12,720		11,253	9/2/75 *Shreveport Times*
1875–76	31	14,352	39	15,911	9/1/76 *Shreveport Times*

J = Jefferson
TL = The Lakes
NA = Not Available.
* Boat records plus Laurance's official city counts.

This statement is also probably correct, but there are no comparative commercial statistics for Texas towns. Industrial statistics are available for 1870 from the census, which indicates that Marion County was second only to Galveston County in the volume and value of manufactures. The census lists the following establishments for Marion County: Boots and shoes (3); Bread and other bakery products (1); Bricks (1); Carriages and wagons (4); Men's clothing (2); Furniture (2); Liquors, malts (1); Lumber, sawed (4); Printing, newspapers (2); Saddlery and harness (3); Sash, doors, and blinds (2); and Tin, copper, and sheet ironware (3). The poor quality of the original census tapes makes it impossible to determine which of these facilities were in Jefferson. Moreover, the productions, with the possible exception of lumber, were probably destined for interior markets and therefore were unrelated to steamboat activity.

Shreveport was always a larger port than Jefferson in terms of its import and export trade. Shreveport kept very good export statistics, particularly for cotton. The cotton statistics do not include bales transported from Jefferson, except for the small volumes that were sold at Shreveport. Cotton from the upper Red River was reshipped at Shreveport but was listed separately. Shreveport's cotton statistics reflect only the bales received at its warehouses, apparently most from the southwest.

Commercial year 1870–71 is the only year for which official statistics are available for both Jefferson and Shreveport. During that year, Jefferson shipped 76,328 bales of cotton according to city counts, and Shreveport shipped 104,811 according to the annual summary published in the *Daily South-Western* on 7 September 1871. In addition, Shreveport reshipped 25,000 bales from above the raft, and 2,000 bales were transported directly from wagons to steamboats without touching a warehouse.

During the same commercial year, Shreveport shipped 29,855 head of cattle, compared to the 5,381 recorded by Laurance for Jefferson. Both shipped about 100,000 hides. The 1870 *Texas Almanac* states that Stoner's packery in Shreveport was probably the largest packery in the United States. During sixty working days in commercial year 1870–71, Stoner slaughtered 14,340 beeves, producing 35,000 tierces and barrels of beef, 2,400 barrels of tallow, 2,400 packages of tongues, and 14,340 green hides.

The market area was split into many different segments, with each port and landing capturing the cotton that could be transported to that port or landing by the shortest overland route, which provided the lowest ox-wagon transport costs. There is not a hint of competition among these ports and landings, and they always cooperated to effect navigation improvements. Nor is there any way in which the various ports and landings could have competed—they had no control over steamboat transport costs. These were strictly voluntary agreements between individual shippers and carriers against the background of prevailing transport costs, which themselves were determined by the prevailing water conditions.

Nor was there any competition between the ports and landings on the route and the major external commercial centers of Shreveport and Clarksville. Whether cotton was transported from the upper Red River counties to Jefferson, Smithland, and Monterey or directly downriver was dependent entirely on navigability conditions on the upper Red and around the raft. If Jefferson had not existed, Shreveport would not have captured all of its commerce, because the western limits of cotton production would have been much more restricted.

The traditional emphasis on intra-regional rivalries obscures the fact that the ports and landings on the Red River and on the Cypress Bayou and the lakes route were components of a much larger commercial picture involving the whole of the Mississippi River and tributaries system, with New Orleans as the gatekeeper. For much of the 1800s, this system was the dominant factor in the internal trade of the United States. Agricultural produce (including cotton) was transported downriver to New Orleans, where it was placed on seagoing vessels that ran to the Northeastern ports such as Boston and New York. These Northeastern ports traded with Europe and the British Isles, with most of the cotton sent to the mills of Liverpool. Vessels returning to New Orleans brought manufactured goods from overseas and from the Northeast, which were placed on steamboats for distribution throughout the Mississippi River and tributaries area, which included the Red River region.

A glance at a map of the United States suggests how reasonable and yet how precarious this overall transport system was at the same time. The Mississippi drained the interior of much of the United States and therefore was a natural channel of commerce. This natural quality would not have been realized in its fullness had it not been for the invention of the steamboat, which provided a much more efficient transport mode than the prevailing flatboats and keelboats, particularly because steamboats had the capacity to move quickly upstream against the current. On the other hand, this was a circuitous route, particularly for the upper portions of the Mississippi River valley. Although these areas were much nearer the Eastern seaboard by land than the water route through New Orleans, they were largely isolated by the Appalachian Mountains. It was the resolution of the trans-Appalachian transportation problem that ultimately led to a radical shift in the orientation of the trade of the Red River region, causing the ports and landings of the region to fall into decline.

·13·

The Prewar Years

1856-60

EIGHTEEN FIFTY-SIX

The cotton blooms were promising in June 1855, but the extreme low-water conditions of 1854 through 1855 prevailed until the end of the year. The Red River began a slow rise in September, and the *Jefferson Herald* reported Cypress Bayou rising. However, it was not until November that the river began to rise rapidly and boats were able to get above the falls at Alexandria. By the end of November, the long commercial drought was over at Shreveport, as reported by the *South-Western* on the twenty-eighth: "Our town begins to wear a lively and busy aspect. Merchants are receiving and opening their winter stocks, and long lines of cotton wagons are constantly arriving. Country merchants and planters can now have their orders expeditiously filled, and on reasonable terms."

There were still no boats to Jefferson. A barge laden with cotton arrived at Shreveport from Jefferson late in November, and in late December the *Sodo* attempted to reach Jefferson but could not proceed farther than Smithland because of a large raft in Cypress Bayou. Finally, the 2 January 1856 *South-Western* reports that the *Mary L. Dougherty* and *Hope* had proceeded to Jefferson, and the 9 January issue indicates that the *Hope* arrived back at Shreveport carrying 350 bales of cotton and reporting difficulties with ice in the lakes and bayous. By February, many boats were going to Jefferson, and Judge H. L. Grinsted of the

Jefferson Herald spoke of the prosperity of the place and estimated that 25,000 to 30,000 bales of cotton were awaiting shipment.

The long period in which navigation had nearly ceased was a disaster for planters, merchants, and the general public, as described in the 5 January 1856 *Texas Republican*: "For over eighteen months, there has been a scarcity of money such as we have never known before, owing to the want of navigation, and the inability of our planters to ship cotton. From the same cause, the difficulty and expense of getting articles from New Orleans, all the necessaries of life have been sold at enormous prices."

A local perspective on the problem, just as things were about to change, is given by William S. Logan in a letter to his brother written from Jefferson and dated 20 January 1856:

> We are having a cold winter here. The ground has been frozen 25 days, and two snows in that time. Ground still covered with snow. Our rivers keep low, so we have had no navigation in two years. We have two crops of cotton on hand and no prospect for selling it.
>
> Groceries high and scarce. Corn sells for $1.00 a bushel, pork five cents per pound. Prices for all stock high.
>
> The hire for a negro man is $180 to $200, and for a negro woman $150 to $200. They sell high, too. Women from $1,000 to $1,200; men from $1,500 to $2,000, and hard to get at that.
>
> The town of Jefferson improves some, but slowly, owing to navigation failing. Health good, except a few cases winter fever. The population is about three thousand. You speak of coming to Texas. This is a pleasant place to live in, but you might do better to go West. The land is better and a better range. A man can get 320 acres by settling on it. A good many move from here to get the land. There is no public land here.

Prior to the low-water period of 1854–55, the greatest number of boats to travel to points west of Shreveport was eleven in 1852, and the greatest number of recorded trips was thirty-four in 1853. The year 1856 constituted a large expansion in the level of commercial activity, with twenty-five boats making fifty-two recorded trips.

Boats recorded in the *South-Western* as having made trips to Jefferson in 1856 included the *Alida, Ariel, Bloomer, Camden, De De, Effort, Financier, Grenada, Hope* (**fig. 13-1**), *Julia, Lizzie Lee, Lone Star, Mary L. Dougherty, R. M. Jones, St. Charles, Storm,* and *White Cliff.* The *Storm* made an additional trip to Benton.

Boats recorded in the *Daily Picayune* as having made trips to Jefferson include eleven mentioned in the *South-Western,* but also the *Amanda, Music, Planter, R. W. Powell, Rosa, Swan,* and *William N. Sherman.* This was the second steamboat named *Planter* to travel west of Shreveport. In addition, the *Victoria* went to Petersburg and the *St. Charles* went to Benton.

Boats listed in the *South-Western* but not in the *Daily Picayune* included the *Ariel, De De, Effort, Julia,* and *Mary L. Dougherty.* Because the 1856 issues of the *South-Western* and the *Daily Picayune* are complete, it is obvious that these boats operated strictly between Shreveport and Jefferson during that year.

Only the *Alida, Bloomer, Camden,* and *De De* were sternwheelers. The *Grenada, Storm,* and *Swan* were holdovers from 1852, and the *St. Charles* was a holdover from 1853. All the rest were new additions to the route. Port Caddo is not shown as a destination, which represents a distinct departure from 1854. The trip of the *Victoria* to Petersburg

Fig. 13-1. *Hope,* Vicksburg, Mississippi, ca. 1860. *Source: From the Collection of the Public Library of Cincinnati and Hamilton County*

is the only recorded trip to this variant of Swanson's Landing and suggests its increasing importance with the advent of the railroad.

R. W. Loughery, the editor of the Marshall *Texas Republican*, visited Jefferson in late February. As recorded on 1 March, he noted the revival of commerce from the long drought of 1854–55 and the gradual depletion of the large quantities of cotton that had been stored up:

TRIP TO JEFFERSON.

We have been absent during the past week on a visit to Jefferson, where we were detained until Thursday evening.

The business of the place is rapidly reviving. The immense amount of cotton which has been accumulating in the place for the last two years, is gradually diminishing, and large stocks of merchandise and groceries are coming in. In a few weeks the business prospects of the place will be fully restored.

There is something about Jefferson that we like. The merchants are liberal, high toned, clever men, and there is about them a spirit of enterprize which we admire. . . .

Our trip to Jefferson was in every respect agreeable; so much so, indeed, that we shall be tempted to visit it frequently.

Loughery's second trip to Jefferson, as recorded on 17 May, was unusually muted and did not reflect the expanded commercial activities: "The town was somewhat dull, though there were a good many wagons from the prairies. The bayou had risen about two feet, and was still rising. Two steamboats were expected the evening we left. Conflicting reports, favorable and unfavorable, had been received from the upper Red River. We think the chances are highly favorable to the reopening of navigation for the best steamers."

The *South-Western* provides descriptions of five of the boats that operated along the route in 1856. The *Lone Star* was a 126-ton sidewheeler measuring 112 feet by 26 feet that made three trips to Jefferson in 1856. She was built in Kentucky in 1854, owned by Capt. J. S. Smith and partners in Jefferson, and served the Confederacy during the Civil War. Her modest accommodations are described in the 22 November 1854 *South-Western*: "The Lone Star, capt. Smith's new Red River packet, left Louisville, on the 31st ult., for N. Orleans. She is a neat and staunch craft, and in every way adapted to the lake and up-river trade. Her cabin is very plain, being furnished with open berths in the gentlemen's cabin and comfortable state-rooms for the ladies. In addition to which there is a spacious recess, an excellent nursery, and wide guards around the entire cabin."

The *White Cliff* was a 142-ton sidewheeler measuring 137 feet by 27 feet. Her hull was built in Arkansas in 1856, and her machinery was put in at Shreveport. She made three trips to Jefferson in 1856 and is described in the 13 December 1854 *South-Western*:

> THE WHITE CLIFFS.—We inadvertently omitted to notice the launching of captain Jno. Graham's new steamboat, which took place a few days ago on Little river. She is 137 feet long, has 27 feet beam, and 4¼ feet hold, is of a fine model, and put together in the most substantial manner. She will be brought to the wharf on the first rise of water, when her machinery, cabins, furniture, etc., which are here in readiness, will be put on board. Captain Graham is one of our most experienced and popular commanders, and the White Cliffs, under his auspices, will be a great favorite on Red River. He is entitled to much praise for the enterprise he has displayed in building his boat on our waters, and we are pleased to learn that the citizens in the vicinity of where he built the hull intend presenting to him a section of land, as a token of the estimation in which they look upon his exertions to build up home mechanics and encourage home industry.

The *Lizzie Lee* was a 101-ton sidewheeler built in Kentucky in 1856 but whose dimensions are unknown. She made one trip to Jefferson in 1856, struck a stump and sank in Twelvemile Bayou on the return trip, and was raised in 1857. She is briefly described in the 26 November 1856 *South-Western*: "The new steamer Lizzie Lee arrived on Friday evening from Louisville, via New Orleans. She was built expressly for a Jefferson and Red River packet, and being staunch, very light draught, with great carrying capacity, is admirably calculated for the trade. We wish the Lizzie Lee and her enterprising owners a long and prosperous career."

The *De De* was an 80-ton sternwheeler measuring 118 feet by 21 feet that was built in Louisiana in 1856 and made one trip in the direction of Jefferson in 1856 and one trip to Jefferson in 1857. The first trip was abortive because the *De De* sank in Big Willow Pass, was raised, and returned to Shreveport. The description in the 21 May 1856 *South-Western* emphasizes the *De De*'s extremely shallow draft:

> NEW RED RIVER PACKET.—While in New Orleans we visited the new steamer Dede, built by W. S. Lewis, esq., to run as a summer packet between this place, and the falls, and were highly pleased. She has 119 feet keel, 21 feet beam, and 3½ feet hold, and is propelled by two engines, cylinders 10 inches in diameter with 3 feet stroke, and 1 boiler, 42 inches in circumference and 32 feet long, and is supplied with two steam windlasses, fire-engine, hose, life boat, and all the appurtenances called for by the last act of congress. Her bottom has an extra sheating of two inch oak plank, which makes her unusually staunch. She possesses great carrying capacity, and has an airy cabin for the accommodation of passengers, and is pronounced by our most experienced boatmen to be one of the best low water steamers ever constructed—drawing, with wood and water on board, only 11 inches forward and 14 inches aft. She was built to order, under the personal supervision of her owners, at Algiers, (opposite New Orleans,) and is entirely new, and of Louisiana manufacture. We wish her a long and prosperous career.

The *Bloomer* was a 95-ton sternwheeler measuring 123 feet by 27 feet that made three trips to Jefferson at the end of 1856 and many trips to Jefferson in the following years. This boat is noteworthy because it was the first of two boats captained by William Perry. Perry was half owner of the *Bloomer*, whose entrance into the Jefferson trade is recorded in the 5 November 1856 *South-Western*: "The new steamer Bloomer, captain Perry, arrived here on Friday, from Louisville, via New Orleans. She was built to ply as a packet between this place, Port Caddo, Smithland, Benton, and Jefferson. She is very light draught, although unusually staunch, and possesses great carrying capacity, and is handsomely fitted up for the accommodation of passengers."

EIGHTEEN FIFTY-SEVEN

The year 1857 was a good one for navigation, with the *South-Western* reporting in March that the largest boats could ascend to Jefferson.

This was also the year in which construction of the Southern Pacific was begun at Swanson's Landing, the *Alida* and *Wabash Valley* brought up the locomotive *Louisiana*, H. H. Black established his packery at Jefferson, and Perry received his state contract for navigation improvements.

The excellent conditions for navigation are reflected in the fact that twenty-six boats made seventy-four trips to points west of Shreveport in 1857. The listings for this year are based on the *South-Western* and the *Daily Picayune*, with some minor additions from the *Texas Republican*, quoting the *South-Western*. The reason that more than one source is needed is that extant issues of the *South-Western* end in August, and the Steamboat Register, which provides an inclusive listing of departures from and returns to Shreveport for boats operating along the route, does not begin until 1858.

Boats shown as traveling to Jefferson by these sources include the *Afton, Jr., Alida, Banjo, Bloomer, Caddo Belle, Camden, Col. Edwards, De De, Dick Nash, E. M. Bicknell, Effort, Gossamer, Hope, Joseph Holden, Lafitte, Lecompte* (**fig. 13-2**), *Mary L. Dougherty, Osprey, Reub White, St. Charles, Silver Moon, Southern, Storm, Swan, Wabash Valley,* and

Fig. 13-2. *Lecompte* (second from right) and *Starlight* (fifth from right), New Orleans, Louisiana, 1859. *Source: From the Collection of the Public Library of Cincinnati and Hamilton County*

William N. Sherman. In addition, the *Hope* traveled to Benton, and the *Alida, Dick Nash, Mary L. Dougherty*, and *Osprey* made other trips to Albany, Swanson's Landing, and the lakes. The Albany and Swanson's Landing trips were connected with the development of the railroad. About one-third of these boats were sternwheelers, representing the first significant incursion of this type in the Jefferson trade.

The greatest number of trips was recorded by the *Bloomer* and the *Mary L. Dougherty*. Most of the *Bloomer*'s ten trips were under the captaincy of William Perry. The *Mary L. Dougherty*'s ten trips were the product of her special relationship with the *Duke*. The *Dougherty*, at 95 tons and measuring 123 feet by 18 feet, was a very small boat that operated strictly between Shreveport and points west. She was the transfer partner for the much larger *Duke*, which operated strictly between New Orleans and Shreveport. The formal relationship between the two boats was a matter of some significance and was noted in the 7 January 1857 *South-Western*: "The steamer M. L. Daugherty, captain Lewis, has commenced running as a regular packet between this port and Jefferson, touching at Port Caddo, Smithland, Benton, and all intermediate landings. A boat has long been wanted in the trade, and we hope that captain Smith will be amply repaid for his enterprise. The Daugherty will connect at this place with the Duke for New Orleans."

The *Banjo* was a 105-ton sidewheel showboat measuring 115 feet by 25 feet with a stage and seating for eight hundred. She had tried to reach Jefferson from Shreveport in 1856 carrying Ned Davis and his minstrels but broke a piece of her equipment on Twelvemile Bayou and had to return to Shreveport. The 4 March 1857 *South-Western* indicates that the *Banjo* was going to Jefferson and stopping at Albany, Port Caddo, Benton, and Mooring's Landing. The report on the 1857 trip, which also involved the minstrels, is given in the 11 March issue: "Ned Davis and his Ethiopian minstrels drew crowded audiences at Albany, Mooring's, Benton, Jefferson, &c., and were received with unbounded applause. The boat will return to this place on Friday next, and concerts will be given on that day and Saturday. After which the Banjo will visit Minden, and the landings on lake Bistineau, and thence proceed to Natchitoches."

The *Reub White* was a 110-ton sidewheeler with official dimensions of 104 feet by 27 feet. She was built as an upper Red River packet in late 1856 and traveled in that direction in early 1857 under the captaincy of W. W. Withenbury, but she apparently made the two trips to Jefferson under John Allabaugh. She is described in the 24 December 1856 *South-Western*: "The new steamer Reub White arrived on Sunday from Louisville, via N. Orleans. She was built to run as a packet between this port and the various landings on upper Red River, and is admirably adapted to the trade. She is 108 feet keel, 28 feet beam and 4 feet hold; has two boilers, 22 feet long, 13 inch cylinders with 4 feet stroke, a fine doctor, &c., and will carry between 600 and 800 bales of cotton. She is commanded by captain W. W. Withenbury, one of the most experienced and energetic men on the river."

The *Silver Moon* was a 171-ton sidewheeler built in Kentucky in 1857 that made only a single trip to Jefferson. She is described in the 27 May 1857 *South-Western*:

> THE SILVER MOON.—The Louisville Courier says that captain Greenlaw, the Napoleon of the river, has just added another to his list of boats, the Silver Moon. He had her built expressly for Red river, but at the same time she will prove of service in any river where business is done and low water to contend with. This boat is very staunchly built, with capacity for 450 tons. The hull is 135 feet in length, with 33 feet beam and 5½ hold. She is a regular side-wheeler, and a full grown, fair proportioned, good looking Silver Moon. Her machinery has been tested, and works well, being put up by Roach & Long. The boilers were built by Joe Mitchell, the hull by J. Collins, and the cabin by S. W. Downs. The chandeliers, and a newly invented water gauge, were from the Novelty works. This water gauge is the patent of Mr. Hoyt, of Boston. It is the most simple, and at the same time, ingenious contrivance we have ever seen, consisting of two pipes, one conducting steam from the surface of the boiler, and the other water from the dresser below the boiler. The pipes direct to the sides of the boiler and meet at the waterline, where an index is stationed with pointers, which are elevated or depressed as the water rises or falls in the boilers. The Silver Moon is in charge of captain Greenlaw, her owner.

> The Silver Moon arrived at Shreveport a few days ago, and is one of the most admirable low water boats we have ever examined.

The prosperous conditions of 1857 are reflected in three accounts. Loughery of the Marshall *Texas Republican* visited Jefferson in February and reports on his trip in the issue for the fourteenth:

> The business of Jefferson appears to be looking up. The merchants are receiving and selling goods, and everything wears an air of business and prosperity. When we left, there were two steamboats at the landing and the city was filled with wagons and traders from the upper country.
>
> We know of no place, where one can spend a few days more pleasantly than at Jefferson. There is a life, a sociability, and a thrift about the town which we encounter in but few.
>
> The bayou was falling. Rumors were in town, however of a rise in upper Red River. We hope it may prove true, and that navigation may continue until July.

Ward Taylor purchased the *Jefferson Herald* from Judge H. L. Grinsted in November 1856 and traveled to Shreveport in March 1857. The editor of the *South-Western* reports in the issue of 4 March that "Col. Ward Taylor, Jr., of the Jefferson Herald, and Mr. Nimmo, of the Eastern-Texas Gazette, paid us a visit a few days ago. They speak glowingly of the prosperity of Jefferson."

Loughery of the *Texas Republican* visited Jefferson again on a trip to Linden late in September and reports in the 3 October issue:

> We passed through Jefferson going and coming, and found as much animation in business as we could have expected at this season of the year. There is a large amount of dry goods in the place, and any quantity of groceries. (See our advertisements.) Messrs. Stanley & Nimmo have a large and handsome assortment of furniture which they are selling at New Orleans prices.
>
> The navigation is good for medium size boats, and goods are brought from New Orleans without difficulty. The new crop of cotton is coming in daily for shipment and sale. Business men are looking ahead to a very full and satisfactory fall business.

EIGHTEEN FIFTY-EIGHT

During 1858, eighteen boats made sixty-two recorded trips to points west of Shreveport. The apparent decline from 1857 when there were twenty-six boats and seventy-three trips is deceptive. Extant issues of the *South-Western* extend only from August through December. The *Daily Picayune* does not record local runs on the route, and it is the increasing level of local runs by particular boats that largely accounts for the increasing trip numbers. On the *Daily Picayune* side, there are some boats and many trips that were apparently taken to Jefferson but are recorded as returning from Red River. I have erred in the conservative direction so as to include only boats for which there is a documented arrival from points along the route.

Boats recorded in the *South-Western*, *Daily Picayune*, and *Texas Republican* (quoting the *South-Western*) as traveling to Jefferson in 1858 include the *Afton, Jr.*, *Bloomer*, *Caddo Belle*, *Comet*, *Era No. 1*, *Grenada*, *Ham Howell*, *Joseph Holden*, *Lafitte*, *Linda*, *Osceola*, *Rescue*, *Sallie Robinson*, *Sunbeam*, *W. A. Andrew*, and *William C. Young*. In addition, the *Larkin Edwards* and *William R. Douglass* traveled to Sodo Lake. The major problem with the record for this year is illustrated by the *Larkin Edwards*, which made only one recorded trip in 1858 between August and December. This was a local boat that made at least twenty-eight trips to points west of Shreveport in 1859. If this boat were operating along the route during the early part of 1858, she would have registered a high number of trips.

The *Rescue* was a 77-ton sternwheeler built late in 1858 that made five trips to Jefferson in December. The dimensions of this boat are unknown, but she was one of the smallest tonnages that operated along the route. The 28 October 1858 *South-Western* says that she drew sixteen inches light loaded. She was apparently the first boat to operate on a constant basis between Shreveport and Jefferson. The *Mary L. Dougherty* was a regular packet, but she was dependent on the activities of the *Duke*. The *Larkin Edwards* was an opportunistic carrier that made trips whenever and wherever there was business. The significance of the introduction of the *Rescue* is noted in the 1 December 1858 *South-Western*: "Capt. Crooks intends to run his new, staunch and very light draught steamer Rescue as a regular packet between this place and Jefferson, touching at Albany, Swanson's landing, Benton, Smithland, Port Caddo, Monterey, Pitt's landing, and all intermediate points on the lakes and bayou. A regular packet in this trade has long been needed, and we bespeak for the enterprise a liberal patronage."

That the *Rescue* fulfilled this commitment is indicated by the navigation record for 1858 and 1859. For the months in which she was operating west of Shreveport, the *Rescue* ran back and forth between Shreveport and Jefferson. This was not a fixed schedule. The *Rescue* departed from and returned to Shreveport on all days of the week, apparently laying over only as long as was necessary to obtain a new load of freight and passengers.

The *Era No. 1* was the first of many *Eras* that operated along the route. This line of boats was owned by the Kouns family, which produced many rivermen. Frederick Way in *Way's Packet Directory* says that there was an original, unnumbered *Era* built in Pennsylvania in 1856. This newly completed upper Red River packet is described in the 24 December 1856 *South-Western*. Way also says that this boat wrecked on the Red River in May 1859 and that the *Effort* was bought at that time and renamed *Era No. 1*. However, the *Era No. 1* began operating on the route in 1858. According to the 9 October 1880 *New Orleans Daily Democrat*, George and John Kouns bought the first *Era* in 1855—running her on Red River—and in 1856 built the *Era No. 2* and bought the *Effort* and changed her name to *Era No. 1*. However, the *Effort* was running to Jefferson as late as May 1857.

The boat that ran to Jefferson in 1858 was the *Era No. 1*, appearing under that name as a departure to Jefferson in the 10 November *South-Western* and as an arrival from Jefferson in the 17 November *South-Western*. If Way and the *Daily Democrat* are correct, this was the former *Effort* that was built in 1855 and made six trips to Jefferson in 1856 and 1857. The *Effort* apparently was acquired in late 1857 and renamed *Era No. 1* to distinguish her from the *Era No. 2*, which was constructed in 1857 and never operated along the route.

The *William C. Young* was a 199-ton sidewheeler built in Kentucky in 1854 that made one trip to Jefferson in 1858. This upper Red River boat is described in the 18 February 1854 Clarksville *Standard* quoting the Shreveport *South-Western*: "This new boat, built by captain Fulton, for the upper Red River trade, left Louisville on the 25th ult., for N. Orleans, and as she will make an attempt to get above the falls, may be expected here in a few days. She is said to be admirably adapted to the trade, very staunch and serviceable, with a carrying capacity of about 1000 bales cotton. The cabin is small, but neat and abundantly spacious for the trade. In addition to the main cabin, she has one fitted up expressly for families who are moving, and do not wish to pay full cabin passage. The hull is 140 feet long, with 28 feet beam and 5½ feet hold. The cylinders are 15 inches in diameter, with 5½ feet stroke. She has two boilers, each 24 feet long and 42 inches in diameter."

The year 1858 was the year in which the Southern Pacific was completed from Swanson's Landing to Marshall; William Perry was fully involved in his bayou and lake clearing efforts; and Stanley & Nimmo left retail merchandising and became meat packers. Loughery made two trips to Jefferson during the year. The first was during April when Stanley & Nimmo were still merchants and Stanley was apparently ready to embark on a national tour of meatpacking establishments. A lengthy description of this visit is provided in the 17 April *Texas Republican*:

> TRIP TO JEFFERSON.
>
> We paid a flying visit last week to our neighboring town of Jefferson. The place has considerably improved since we were last there. Many new houses had gone up, and business was very active. The streets were thronged with wagons, carrying off produce and merchandize. Several steamboats were at the landing, and the merchants seemed to be busily engaged. We understand that a very large trade has been done there this season. A friend informed us that 25,000 bales of cotton had been shipped from that point.
>
> We were kindly received. A more hospitable, friendly population is not to be found; and we may add, a more liberal people. We have always found it one of the most prompt in the payment of debts. A people who meet the demands of the editor may be relied upon; for, as a general thing, a printer's bill is the last one paid. Somehow or other there is an aversion to it. Not so, we are pleased to say, in Jefferson.
>
> We had a pleasant time in the revival of old associations; for be it remembered, that our advent in Texas was at Jefferson. We printed the first paper that was ever published in that place. Then it was but a very small town and of little business. Not one at that time believed its present condition would ever be realized.
>
> We spent a portion of our leisure time in the offices of the

Herald and Gazette, and in the charming society of the proprietors of those journals, the hours glided swiftly by. Our friend Ward Taylor, Jr., of the Herald, was not in town, and we regretted to learn, had not yet recovered his health.

There was a charming dinner, or fish fry, at the establishment of Messrs. Stanley & Nimmo. It was, we understood, a "storm" upon friend Stanley, who was about leaving home. These parties, we were informed, are gotten up by the young folks every eight to ten days, and are exceedingly pleasant.

There are two excellent hotels in Jefferson, the Planters' Hotel kept by our old friend Wm. Brooks, and the Jefferson Hotel by James Moore, a very clever gentleman. The hotels are of superior character, and were filled to overflowing.

The second trip by Loughery was during the low-water period of October when the bayou was lower than Loughery had seen it in years, which was proving advantageous to efforts to clear the lake and bayou. This trip is reported briefly in the 15 October 1858 *Texas Republican*: "Business men are making every preparation for the coming season. Houses are going up of a character to warrant the impression that the trade of the place will open upon a more extensive scale than in any former year. In addition to the large brick warehouse of Messrs. J. M. & J. C. Murphy, and the spacious brick building of Mr. Reece Hughes, Mr. W. M. Freeman has just erected a large brick warehouse, and Messrs. J. L. & J. C. Smith are building a spacious brick store-house, which will be finished in a few weeks. We understood that arrangements had been made for erecting five or six other large buildings. In addition to these improvements, the livery stables were being enlarged, and a new one was about to be erected."

The estimate of 25,000 bales of cotton shipped from Jefferson that was provided to Loughery in his first trip in April is generally compatible with statistics presented in the 1859 *Texas Almanac*. The commercial year extended from 1 September through 31 August; therefore, Loughery's informant was referring to shipments from September 1857 through early April 1858.

The *Texas Almanac* was published in the year preceding its title date. The 1859 almanac was published in 1858, and the shipment statistics for "last year's crop," which were given by a knowledgeable Jefferson resident, almost certainly refer to the 1857–58 commercial year. The informant, who may have been the same as Loughery's informant, provides statistics for cotton shipped by Red River to New Orleans: "From Jefferson, 25,000 bales; Smithland, 5,000; Benton, 8,000; Port Caddo, 5,000; Swanson's Landing, 8,000; 5 or 6 Landings on the Lake, 8,000; Monterey, 1,500; Shreveport 60,000; Grand Ecore, 10,000; Above the Raft, 20,000. Total, 150,000."

The only problem of compatibility for the two sources is that they were dealing with different time periods, and boats continued to travel to Jefferson from April through August. The probable explanation of the apparent discrepancy is that most of the cotton had been shipped out by April. This is a distinct possibility given the fact that for later years when monthly shipments of cotton can be computed from boat cargo reports, shipments always declined rapidly as summer approached.

In the latter part of the year, the Louisiana Board of Swamp Land Commissioners developed a proposal to drain Cross Lake so that it could be used for cotton production. This was to be the initial step in reclaiming all inundated Red River lands in Caddo Parish through the removal of the raft. The justification was that all the lakes in the Sodo Lake complex were "mere submerged low lands" owing their transient existence to the raft on the Red River. There was a sharp controversy over the matter, led by the Shreveport *Caddo Gazette* and the *Jefferson Herald*, with the latter maintaining that draining Cross Lake would destroy navigation to Jefferson. Whatever the technical merits of the argument, the *Caddo Gazette* infuriated the citizens of Texas, and particularly those of Jefferson, by making such statements as those quoted in the 25 September 1858 *Standard* that in pursuing its legitimate interests, the State of Louisiana should not consider "the pretensions of an obscure Texas village." Governor Runnels of Texas wrote a letter to Governor Wickliffe of Louisiana, enclosing a protest by Jefferson, and the matter soon came to an end.

The *Jefferson Gazette*, as quoted by the 20 October 1858 *South-Western*, reports that in connection with the establishment of the Stanley & Nimmo packery, the bayou was cleared out from the landing area to the packery at the foot of Houston Street, and a wharf was constructed at the foot of Marshall Street in the small embayment formed by the upper end of St. Catherine's Island. This project was actually conducted by Stanley and Chester Bulkley, who had recently bought St. Catherine's Island and expected it to become occupied by warehouses.

EIGHTEEN FIFTY-NINE

For 1859, I have relied almost entirely on the *South-Western*, whose extant issues extend through 10 August. Most importantly, a Steamboat Register was published each week, showing arrivals and departures at Shreveport for the previous week (i.e., Wednesday through Tuesday, because the paper was published on Wednesday). The completeness of this record is illustrated by the 16 March 1859 issue:

STEAMBOAT REGISTER.
ARRIVED.
Mar. 9— Grand Duke, from New Orleans.
        Hope, from Upper Red River.
        Telegram, from Jefferson.
        Eleanor, from Jefferson.
        Joseph Holden, from Jefferson.
    10— Starlight, from New Orleans.
    11— Larkin Edwards, from Monterey.
    13— Sallie Robinson, from New Orleans.
        Lucy Holcombe, from New Orleans.
        Era No. 3, from Upper Red River.
        Starlight, from Jefferson.
        National, from New Orleans.
    15— W. A. Andrew, from New Orleans.

DEPARTED.
Mar. 9— Telegram, for New Orleans.
        D. R. Carroll, for New Orleans.
        Eleanor, for New Orleans.
        Hope, for Upper Red River.
        R. W. Powell, for New Orleans.
        Joseph Holden, for New Orleans.
    10— Starlight, for Jefferson.
        Grand Duke, for New Orleans.
    11— Larkin Edwards, for Monterey.
    12— Judah Touro, for New Orleans.
    13— Sallie Robinson, for Jefferson.
        Era No. 3, for New Orleans.
        Starlight, for New Orleans.

15— Lucy Holcombe, for New Orleans.
W. A. Andrew, for Jefferson.

During 1859, eighteen boats made ninety-nine trips to points west of Shreveport. These figures are particularly dramatic in that navigation ceased in June and that only three boats are shown as arriving back at New Orleans from Jefferson at the end of December. Boats traveling to Jefferson in 1859 included the *Arkansaw, Bloomer, Comet, Eleanor, Era No. 3, Fleta, Ham Howell, Joseph Holden, Larkin Edwards, Morning Light, Osceola, Rescue, Robert Watson, Sallie Robinson, Starlight, Telegram, W. A. Andrew,* and *Yazoo Belle.* In addition, the *Larkin Edwards* made trips to Monterey and Smithland, and the *Starlight* traveled to Swanson's Landing. Half of these boats were sternwheelers.

The reason for the high number of trips without a dramatic increase in the number of boats is that eight of these boats made more than four trips to points west of Shreveport, including the *Comet, Eleanor, Larkin Edwards, Rescue, Sallie Robinson, Starlight, Telegram,* and *W. A. Andrew.* Chief among these was the *Larkin Edwards,* which made seventeen trips to Jefferson, ten to Monterey (also designated Point Monterey), and one to Smithland. The *Larkin Edwards* was built in Indiana in 1857 and named after the interpreter for the Caddo Indians whose property was instrumental in the formation of Shreveport. This was a tiny boat at 67 tons that normally traveled out of Shreveport on local trips, but occasionally to New Orleans.

The *Era No. 2* never went west of Shreveport. The *Era No. 3,* which was built in Pennsylvania in 1858 and made three trips to Jefferson in 1859, was a 144-ton sternwheeler that was described in the 20 October 1858 *South-Western*: "Capt. Jno. Kouns & Bros., have contracted with Graham, Carr & Co. of Freedom, Pa., for a new boat for the Shreveport trade. She is to be 130 feet keel, 29 feet beam, 28 feet floor, and four feet hold. She is to have three double-flued boilers, 22 feet long and 35 inches in diameter; cylinders 4½ feet stroke and 15 inches in diameter. Her cabin will be neat and commodious, furnished with all the latest improvements. It is calculated that she will carry 1200 bales of cotton. She has been named Era No. 3, and will compose one of the Messrs. Kouns' well known line of light draught packets. The Era No. 3 is to be finished by the 15th November."

The *South-Western* also provides descriptions for two other boats. The *Starlight* (**see fig. 13-2**) was a 280-ton sidewheeler measuring

162 feet by 31 feet that made four trips to points west of Shreveport in 1859. She was built in Indiana in 1858 and operated along the route until 1868. The *Starlight* is described in the 1 December 1858 *South-Western*: "The Starlight, a new steamer daily expected from Louisville, is highly extolled by the papers of that city. She was built expressly for a passenger boat in the New Orleans and Red River trade, and has commodious cabins, elegantly furnished, and supplied with all the latest improvements. Her model is reported to be unusually fine, and the machinery of such power as to make her among the fastest of the fast. The Starlight is commanded by captain Chas. Hayes, and Mr. C. F. Hayes does the honors of the office.—They are well known as the late chief-officers of the Swan, and their old patrons will extend to the new boat a cordial greeting."

The *Telegram* was a 205-ton sternwheeler built in Ohio in 1858 that made seven trips to Jefferson in 1859. She is described in the 29 December 1858 *South-Western*:

> The Cincinnati Commercial furnishes us the following description of the Telegram, now running on Red River: the hull, by Litherbury, is beautifully proportioned, being 151 feet 8 inches in length, 32 feet beam, 30 feet floor, and five feet hold, put together in the staunchest manner, and will carry 1600 bales of cotton. The machinery, by Moore & Richardson, consists of two boilers, 28 feet long and 42 inches in diameter; two engines, cylinders 4½ feet stroke and 20 inches diameter, working a 21½ feet wheel. The cabin is full length, exceedingly tasty and pearly white; the staterooms unusually large, and elegantly furnished throughout, with accommodations for 75 passengers. The cabin is adorned with several of Graciani's beautiful landscapes. The Telegram was built by captain Denslow, to replace the Sunbeam in Red River, and will become popular with travelers and shippers. Her office is occupied by Messrs. J. P. Chandler and F. D. Rogers.

Early in 1859, the Louisiana, Arkansas and Texas Navigation Company was incorporated by the Louisiana Legislature as a private concern to remove the raft. Because the removal would involve various states, it was necessary for the company to secure approval of the incorporation and its purpose from the legislatures of Texas and Arkansas and the U.S. Congress. This time the controversy was primarily within Texas, with Jefferson pitted against Clarksville, the trade center of the upper Red River. Jefferson opposed raft removal on the grounds that it would destroy the navigability of the route. Clarksville supported it on the grounds of economics, land preservation and reclamation, and the fact that the raft was an accident of nature that ought to be removed so that the river could follow its natural course. Shreveport played a secondary role in the controversy but was again accused by Jefferson of trying to capture its commerce by destroying its navigation. Although the bill authorizing the company was reported on favorably by two committees, it was defeated in the Texas House, apparently through the influence of M. D. K. Taylor, a Jefferson resident who was Speaker of the House. Louisiana attempted to pursue an independent course of action in early 1861, but efforts were terminated with the advent of the Civil War.

EIGHTEEN SIXTY

The long period of low water that began in June 1859 broke at the end of December, when the *Daily Picayune* reports that the *Fleta*, *Larkin Edwards*, and *Sallie Robinson* arrived back in New Orleans from Jefferson. By the second week of January, navigation conditions had returned to normal, as reported in the *Texas Republican* for the fourteenth: "During the past week the following boats have arrived at Shreveport: Starlight, Wm. S. Johnson, B. L. Hodge, News Boy, Ceres, Fleta, R. W. Powell, Sallie Robinson, Eleanor, Lecompte, Robert Watson, Era No. 3 from New Orleans; the Era No. 4 and Yazoo Belle, from Alexandria; the Martin Walt, Violett, Rescue, D. R. Carroll and Telegram, from Jefferson. A number of these steamers have gone to Jefferson carrying supplies, and returning freighted with cotton. Business has actively resumed at that place. Red river is rising and the Lake is in fair boating order and also rising rapidly. We have had heavy rains within the last few days thus ensuring permanent navigation."

There are only a few scattered issues of the *South-Western* for August and September 1860, when no navigation was reported. As a consequence, it is necessary to turn to the *Daily Picayune* record, which obviously excludes the local boats out of Shreveport that were beginning to register impressive numbers of trips.

The *Daily Picayune* records that twenty boats made forty-two trips to Jefferson in 1860, including the *Andy Fulton, Arkansaw, E. M. Bicknell, Era No. 1, Era No. 3, Era No. 4, Fleta, Homer, J. D. Swaim, J. M. Sharp, John Ray, Martin Walt, Morgan Nelson, Osceola, Picayune No. 3, Robert Watson, Sallie Robinson, Vigo, W. A. Andrew,* and *William Campbell.* To this list must be added five boats from the *Texas Republican,* with one recorded trip each: *D. R. Carroll, Rescue, Telegram, Violett,* and *National,* the last of which went to Swanson's Landing. The 5 May *Standard,* quoting the Jefferson *Herald and Gazette,* indicates that the *Alligator* went to Jefferson; and the 22 September Alexandria *Constitutional,* quoting the *Herald and Gazette,* indicates that the *Alligator* went to Smithland. The 3 March *Standard* contains a letter mentioning that the *Trio* was at Jefferson on a trip to the upper Red River. The 28 January *Standard,* quoting the *South-Western,* indicates that the *Comet* and *Larkin Edwards* went to Jefferson. The *Standard* records another trip for the *Larkin Edwards* in April; the 23 June *Standard,* quoting the *South-Western,* indicates that the *Larkin Edwards* made a trip to Jefferson before sinking on Cypress Bayou.

The dramatic decline in number of trips from the previous year is caused primarily by the near exclusion of local runs between Shreveport and Jefferson for boats like the *Larkin Edwards.* The *J. M. Sharp* and *Vigo* recorded the most trips, at six each. The *Vigo* was a 144-ton sidewheeler measuring 130 feet by 26 feet that was captained throughout most of the year by W. W. Withenbury. On 29 February, the *Vigo* is recorded as having returned from Jefferson and Monterey, the only time I have encountered a double return record. The *Homer* was captained by Sam Applegate and Robert Watson, but was advertised on 28 December with William Perry as captain.

The *Violett* was an 89-ton sternwheeler measuring 123 feet by 22 feet that was built in Pennsylvania in 1856. She should not be confused with the *W. A. Violett,* which operated on the route in 1851. The *J. D. Swaim* had a particularly unusual name among steamboats that had many strange names. The name of the boat apparently was misspelled when she was first registered: she was redocumented in 1866 as *J. D. Swain.* The three *Era* boats were part of the Kouns line.

The *Sallie Robinson* was a 267-ton sidewheeler measuring 165 feet by 34 feet that was built in Ohio in 1856, advertised for Jefferson in that year, and made recorded trips from 1858 through 1861. It was fairly common for passengers to express their thanks for particularly delightful passages, as they did for the *Sallie Robinson* in the 17 March 1860 *Texas Republican*:

THE SALLIE ROBINSON.

We, the undersigned, passengers on the steamer *Sallie Robinson*, on her present voyage from New Orleans to Jefferson, Texas, hereby tender our sincere thanks and acknowledgments to the officers of said boat, during the voyage, for their constant and uniform care and attention to us as passengers during the entire voyage, and here take the liberty to do them the justice and ourselves the pleasure to invite the travelling public to this boat as one that combines comfort with safety.
February 27th, 1860.

S. D. Pitts,	Sam Fillorely,
J. Cox,	D. A. Bulkley,
J. M. Smith,	Anderson Mills,
A. Morrow,	S. P. Kelly,
S. J. Wooley,	R. B. Wall,
J. Spinck,	C. G. Parsons,
J. T. Mills,	J. Shelton,
Wilfred Terrell,	H. C. Williams,
John Fields,	S. R. Collins,
Wm. E. Hoge,	W. H. Jones,
J. M. Trasson,	E. W. Dougherty,
E. B. Rollins,	H. M. Gleain,
S. J. Mooney,	C. Thetford,
W. Kelly,	John Mayfield,
John Sims,	F. Williams,
Enoch Johnson,	J. S. Stephens,
Joseph Meek,	J. W. Fields,
Wiley Jones,	W. B. Ector,
C. V. Bulkley,	E. A. Fields,
S. W. Jones,	E. A. Jones,
S. P. Ligon,	A. J. Ligon,
M. F. Ligon,	E. I. Moseley.

March 17, 1860.

The *Fleta* was a 95-ton sidewheeler built in Kentucky in 1859, measuring 112 feet by 25 feet. She made trips between New Orleans and Jefferson in late 1859 and early 1860 and then became established as a regular operator between Shreveport and Jefferson in March 1860 according to advertisements that began to appear in the *Texas Republican*:

SHREVEPORT, SWANSON, AND JEFFERSON
Tri-Weekly U. S. Mail Steamer, FLETA.
LEAVING Shreveport Mondays, Wednesdays, and Fridays at 7 o'clock, A.M., tuching at Swanson's at 12 o'clock M., arriving at Jefferson at 8 o'clock P.M. And will leave Jefferson Tuesdays, Thursdays, and Saturdays at 7 o'clock, tuching at Swanson's at 12 o'clock M. Connecting at Shreveport with the following fine passenger packets: Saturdays with the Grand Duke and B. L. Hodge; Tuesdays with the R. W. Powell and Doubloon; Thursdays with the Starlight and Telegram.
This line will be able to put passengers and freight through one day sooner to and from New Orleans than any other way they can travel.
March 10, 1860.

The *Fleta* was the first boat to establish a regular schedule to Jefferson. However, it should be noted that this boat did not operate strictly between Shreveport and Jefferson in 1860, because she is recorded in the *Daily Picayune* as making one trip to New Orleans in May and two in December. The advertisement also suggests the increasing importance of Swanson's Landing, which was serviced by a new locomotive on the Southern Pacific that began to be advertised in February 1860 in the *Texas Republican*:

LOOK OUT FOR SAM HOUSTON!
THE new and splendid LOCOMOTIVE, built for the *Southern Pacific Railroad Company* is now upon the track ready for the transportation of COTTON, FREIGHT, AND PASSENGERS.
Shippers are now requested to forward as there will be no further delay and goods will be forwarded in quick time.
CHAS. E. HYNSON, *Gen. Supn't.*
Marshall, Feb. 25, 1860.

"The large, elegant new passenger car, beautifully painted, and with nicely cushioned seats," as described in the 5 May *Texas Republican*, that accompanied the new locomotive was taken by Loughery from Marshall to Swanson's Landing on 5 March. Describing the new locomotive as "an exceedingly fine one," Loughery disembarked at Swanson's Landing on the *W. A. Andrew* for Shreveport: "Arrived at Swanson's, the next thing was to look around and see what was to be seen. The landing was covered with cotton. I should suppose there was enough on hand to load several steamboats, and it continues to arrive as rapidly as it is taken off. There are a number of hands engaged in constructing a new wharf. About 12 o'clock M., the steamer W. A. Andrew arrived from Jefferson and commenced taking in cotton, which detained her until sometime in the night. She did not leave until daylight the next morning. About 10 o'clock at night, the steamer National came up. I embarked on the Andrew. The trip to Shreveport was pleasant. The fare on the Andrew is excellent, and the officers polite and kind."

This was also the year in which Jefferson aspired to its first rail connection, which was to be a linkage with the Memphis, El Paso & Pacific Railroad. Like the Southern Pacific out of Swanson's Landing, this was accidental undertaking. The Memphis, El Paso & Pacific was to proceed west out of Texarkana, but boats carrying railroad iron could not reach that place because of a shallow area in the Red River above the mouth of the Sulphur Fork. Plans were made to construct a branch line from Moore's Landing to Texarkana, but the passage to the upper Red River became blocked by the Great Raft in May 1860. Railroad officials decided to construct a branch line from Jefferson to Moore's Landing. In spite of the initial enthusiasm for this project, only six miles of track were laid before the Civil War. The report on this project in the *Jefferson Gazette*, as related in the 17 November 1860 *Texas Republican*, gives the only glimpse into Jefferson during that year:

OUR RAILROAD.—The work on the Road to connect this point with the Memphis and El Paso Railroad is progressing rapidly. The grading is already commenced and the prospect of its speedy completion, is very flattering. In the course of next week about three hundred hands will be at work, and Capt. Pratt, who has taken the entire contract, with the exception of furnishing the iron, is daily letting out small contracts, endeavoring to give employment to the hands of every planter who has been so unfortunate as to make a small crop. No man doubts that this connection, the most important in the State, will be completed, and in running order, in less than fifteen months from to-day, giving Jefferson one hundred miles of road through the finest country in the world.

No point, in the State of Texas, can boast of a future so flattering as that of Jefferson, and taking every thing into consideration, no point in the entire South has increased in both business and population, within the past twelve months, as rapidly. Notwithstanding the sorry crops, in every portion of our city new buildings are springing up like magic, new business men are pouring in, and ere another 12 months has rolled around the oldest inhabitant will scarcely recognize the little Bayou City of today.

SUMMARY

During the prewar years of 1856 through 1860, seventy-six boats were operative on the route. All of these went to Jefferson, and some made other special trips to Monterey, Benton, Swanson's Landing, and Smithland. Port Caddo is not listed in any return records, but it appears in all advertisements for boats to Jefferson. Of the seventy-six boats, two-thirds were sidewheelers. The largest was the *R. W. Powell* at 349 tons and measuring 175 feet by 33 feet. The smallest was probably the *Financier* at 53 tons and measuring 93 feet by 18 feet. The average tonnage for all boats was 162.

Boat characteristics did not change very much from the 1845–55 period. The largest and smallest boats for both periods had similar dimensions. The average tonnage for the 1856–60 period was slightly less than for the 1845–55 period. Sternwheelers became more important, but they were still far outnumbered by sidewheelers. The only significant difference between the two periods was an increase in the number of boats and trips per year in the latter period. Although precision cannot be achieved for the latter period because of the diversity of sources, it appears that more than thirty boats were making more than one hundred trips to points west of Shreveport immediately before the advent of the Civil War.

The years 1856 through 1860 present methodological problems that directly affect the interpretation of the data. Through 1855, it is necessary to rely on the New Orleans *Daily Picayune*, because there are few extant issues of Shreveport newspapers prior to August 1854. In addition, it is obvious that the Shreveport *South-Western* increases the quality of its navigation coverage from year to year, culminating in the inclusive coverage provided by the Steamboat Register, which is available for September 1858 onward, with the exception of the missing issues for the last few months of 1859 and the whole of 1860.

Once past the Civil War, the rest of this study, with minor exceptions, will be based entirely on the Shreveport newspapers, which provide the only inclusive coverage of boat movements on the route and the sole insight into local navigation conditions and events. For the transitional prewar years, a mixture of sources must be used, and mixed sources always create problems.

If cumulative figures are used, 1856 appears to be a turning point in the level of commercial activity when compared to 1854, with twenty-five boats making fifty-two trips to points west of Shreveport in 1856 compared to nine boats making thirty trips in 1854. However, if the *Daily Picayune* numbers, which were the sole source for 1854, are used for 1856, the numbers are reduced to nineteen boats and forty-one trips. In addition, there were no recorded trips after the advent of low water in July 1854, so that all trips took place during the first half of the year. As a consequence, there was no distinctive break in commercial activity from 1854 to 1856 but rather an accelerating curve interrupted by the near cessation of boat movements in the second half of 1854 and the whole of 1855.

The distinctive feature of the 1856 to 1860 period compared to years prior to 1855 is the number of trips, as opposed to the increase in the number of boats. In 1859, for example, eighteen boats made ninety-nine trips, compared to the nine boats making thirty trips in 1854. This change is also at least partly deceptive—the change was heavily influenced by local trips out of Shreveport that are not covered by the *Daily Picayune* and therefore do not appear in the record, except by chance, prior to 1855.

Nevertheless, it is unlikely that local carriers of the magnitude of the *Larkin Edwards* were operating on the route prior to 1855; during the 1856 to 1860 period, there were many boats that registered large numbers of trips between New Orleans and Jefferson. As a consequence, the switch in boat-to-trip ratios from 3.3 in 1854 to 5.6 in 1859 appears to be real, representing a consolidation of trade by boats concentrating on business opportunities west of Shreveport at the expense of the occasional trade participants.

This should not be surprising given the fact that the ports and landings along the route exported 60,500 bales of cotton by steamboat in commercial year 1857–58, with 25,000 bales from Jefferson alone. The prewar years were, in fact, the dominant period with respect to the cotton trade. The great expansion of trade after the Civil War was not based on cotton exports. The high point for number of boats and trips was 1870, when fifty-three boats made 295 trips. This tripling of activity over 1859 entailed the export of only 64,000 bales of cotton. Thus, the period 1856–60 (and the first half of 1861) was the high point of cotton-induced steamboat activity.

The large number of boats and trips in 1870 was in large part the result of exports of pickled beef in barrels from the packery downstream of Jefferson, which accounted for one-third of down freights and significant up freights. As a consequence, it can be presumed, in the absence of export statistics for commodities other than cotton, that the two packeries owned by Black and Stanley & Nimmo contributed significantly to the high volume of steamboat activity in the years immediately preceding the war.

This was also the high point for the ports and landings other than Jefferson. The other ports and landings are seldom mentioned in the 1856–60 record. Monterey appears in connection with the special trips made by the *Larkin Edwards* to that area and in a single trip by the *Vigo*. Albany appears as a depot for railroad iron; Swanson's Landing appears in connection with the railroad itself; and Smithland appears in connection with a single trip by the *Alligator*. Apart from these suggestions, the record reveals nothing about the use of the ports and landings other than Jefferson because it only indicates the terminus of a trip.

The use of the various ports and landings by steamboats is better represented by the cotton export statistics in the 1859 *Texas Almanac* and by the assumption that steamboats stopped at all of the major ports and landings on the route. The export statistics show Jefferson at 25,000 bales, Benton and Swanson's Landing at 8,000 bales each, Smithland and Port Caddo at 5,000 bales each, Monterey at 1,500 bales, and five or six landings on the lake at 8,000 bales.

The ranking of Swanson's Landing over Port Caddo is undoubtedly the result of the railroad, which brought cotton to Swanson's Landing at the expense of Port Caddo. Port Caddo does not appear in the navigation record after 1854. This is not because it ceased to exist as a port but because all boats that went to Port Caddo after that year also went above to Jefferson and are recorded as such. Port Caddo obviously continued as an important stop because it was in the third tier of exporters in commercial year 1857–58. The only relative weight that is questionable is that of Monterey, which probably exported more than 1,500 bales when navigation on the upper Red was closed.

After the Civil War when the railroad was built between Shreveport and Marshall and extended progressively westward, the commerce of the southern ports and landings along the route was destroyed, followed soon thereafter by rails to the north that captured the commerce of the northern ports and landings. Monterey and Mooringsport are, in fact, the only places other than Jefferson for which there are indications of cotton export in the early 1870s, and that in very small amounts. The prewar years are, therefore, the period in which the ports and landings other than Jefferson flourished.

With respect to inclusiveness, a high degree of confidence can be placed in the record for the late 1850s, with almost all boats named and modest undercounts in the number of trips. This statement applies to the period but not necessarily to individual years, because steamboats tended to stay in the same trades for at least a few years. If missed in one year, they can be picked up in another.

A few boats from this period need to be checked by other sources. The *C. Hays* and *Sallie Robinson* advertised for Jefferson in the *South-Western* in 1856; the *Belle Creole*, *Marion*, and *Bonita* advertised for Jefferson in the *Daily Picayune* in 1857; the *Moses Greenwood* advertised for Jefferson in the *Daily Picayune* in 1858; and the *T. S. Conley*, *Moro*, and *Bayou Belle* advertised for Jefferson in the *Daily Picayune* in 1860. These boats may have gone to Jefferson. The ones out of New Orleans are generally shown as returning from Shreveport or Red River. That they did not necessarily transfer cargo at Shreveport is indicated by the fact that similar returns are given for some boats that demonstrably (from the records of the *South-Western*) went to Jefferson. Fortunately, such difficulties are relevant only for periods when the Shreveport newspaper record is incomplete.

Different sources tell different stories. The dramatic decline in number of trips in 1860 shows how much is missed by using the *Daily*

Picayune, which for obvious reasons does not record local trips out of Shreveport. The *Larkin Edwards* made twenty-eight trips to points west of Shreveport in 1859 but appears only briefly in the random records for 1860 until her temporary loss in June. The *Fleta* made three trips between New Orleans and Jefferson in 1860 but recorded thirty-nine trips to points west of Shreveport in 1861. Because this boat was advertising regular runs between Shreveport and Jefferson in 1860, it can be assumed that a large number of trips do not appear in the record because of an absence of Shreveport newspapers during that year.

Alternatively, a whole dimension of the Cypress Bayou and the lakes trade has been largely disregarded by this study. Many boats advertised in the New Orleans newspapers for points west of Shreveport that never went in that direction. Instead, they engaged in transfer operations at Shreveport. Following the trail of advertisements is exceedingly complex and would take a great deal of time to accomplish. It would also distort the volume of trade because of double counting. And yet, this particular dimension is a perfectly legitimate component of the story of the Cypress Bayou and the lakes trade and worthy of a separate study.

Wartime Navigation 1861-65

RECONNAISSANCE

South Carolina seceded in December 1860, followed by Louisiana in January 1861 and Texas in February. Lincoln was inaugurated in March, and Fort Sumter was fired on by Confederate forces and surrendered in April. The war was on, but one would never know it from the navigation record concerning the Cypress Bayou and the lakes route, where the only hint of war in 1861 was the occasional movement of troops out of Jefferson by steamboat. Otherwise, it was business as usual, with steamboats operating in their normal capacity as freight and passenger transporters between New Orleans and points west of Shreveport.

The decisive event for the navigation history of the area was the fall of New Orleans in late April 1862, which precipitated a dramatic decline in the level of commercial steamboat activity. Most of the boats operating along the route converted to Confederate service. Some were commandeered; most continued as privately owned military supply and personnel carriers paid by charter for a period or contract by a trip. Lytle-Holdcamper's listing of Confederate registrations, which are not certain indicators of military service, contains the following names: *Ariel, Arkansaw, Banjo, Belle Gates, Comet, D. R. Carroll, Dick Nash, Effort, Eleanor, Era No. 4, Homer, Hope, Lafitte, Lone Star, Osceola, P. E. Bonford, Picayune No. 3, Rescue, Robert Fulton, Sallie Robinson,*

Southern, and *Texas Ranger*. Others with documented service included the *Era No. 6, Fanny Pearson, Fleta, Gen. J. L. Hodges, J. M. Sharp, Lecompte, Robert Watson, St. Charles, Texas, Vigo*, and *William Burton*.

Most of these boats did not operate along the route during the depths of the war following the fall of New Orleans, and many provided services in areas far from the Red River. They were joined in the Red River area by boats that had traditionally operated in other trades and by boats built during the war. Some served as the base for pontoon bridges or were scuttled to prohibit the passage of enemy vessels. Many were scuttled or burned to prevent enemy capture, and many were captured. A few survived to reenter commercial service after the war.

The geographic scope of operations of boats on the lower Mississippi and Red Rivers was increasingly restricted as the war progressed. Federal gunboats ran past the batteries at Port Hudson (above Baton Rouge on the Mississippi) in March 1863, closing the Red River; Port Hudson and Vicksburg fell in July, placing the Federals in full control of the Mississippi. Alexandria on the Red River temporarily fell to Porter's gunboats in May 1863, and Porter's fleet moved up the Red River past Alexandria in March 1864 on an abortive expedition that threatened Shreveport.

The area west of Shreveport did not participate in the war in the sense that there were no military engagements in Northeast Texas; however, it did play a role in the war effort, as a source of recruits, a provisioner for the military, and a conduit for trade through Mexico. Harrison County and Marion County, which was formed in 1860 and in which Jefferson was located, sent many men and boys to war. The isolation of the area from the theaters of combat enabled it to become a supply source for the Confederacy, producing pig iron, beef, soap, candles, leather, shoes, and various foodstuffs.

A Union blockade of the mouth of the Mississippi and the eventual fall of New Orleans caused the trade focus of the states bordering the Red and lower Mississippi Rivers to shift to Southwest Texas, where overland transport to and from Mexico enabled merchants to export cotton and to secure items of commerce. They were soon joined in these activities by the army, which sold cotton through Mexico to secure military supplies. Although the evidence in the readily available sources is fragmentary, it is sufficient to demonstrate that the area west of Shreveport, and particularly Jefferson, served as a place of departure and return for significant quantities of imports and exports.

The area became particularly important from a military perspective after the establishment of the Trans-Mississippi Department in Shreveport in 1863 under the command of General Edmund Kirby Smith. The department was isolated from the rest of the Confederacy because of Union control of the Mississippi; nevertheless, Kirby Smith was an energetic commander who expanded and initiated a wide range of supply functions that increased the value of the area west of Shreveport to the war effort, at least within the confines of the department west of the Mississippi.

A Confederate perspective on the area west of Shreveport is provided by a set of captured Civil War maps that are located in Record Group 77 of the National Archives. **Fig. 14-1** shows the general region, with Jefferson, Smithland, Port Caddo, Swanson's Landing, Mooringsport, Monterey, and Albany represented. **Fig. 14-2** shows the Jefferson area

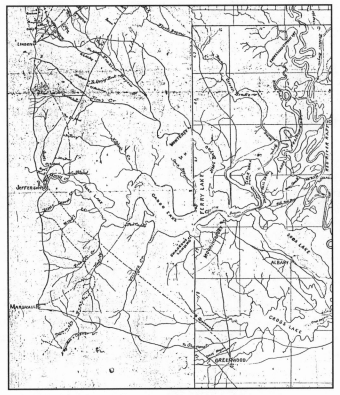

Fig. 14-1. Caddo Lake region. *Source: Louisiana Secretary of State, Division of Archives, Records Management and History*

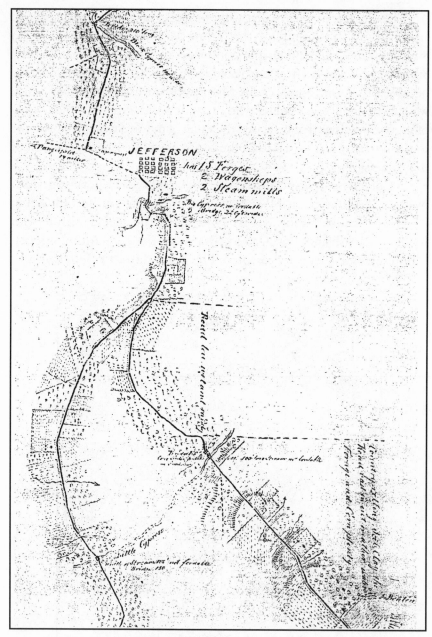

Fig. 14-2. Jefferson area. *Source: Louisiana Secretary of State, Division of Archives, Records Management and History*

in detail, but it does not attempt to delineate the town layout. Roads radiate north to Linden and south over the Houston Street Bridge, which is designated as 22 feet wide. The southern branch out of Jefferson is to Marshall, and the southeastern branch is to Greenwood. The road to Benton is shown heading directly east off the Greenwood Road.

Many of the military-related activities in the area west of Shreveport involved steamboat transport. However, it is impossible on the basis of readily available materials to determine the degree of importance of these activities to the war effort or to determine the level of steamboat activity. After the fall of New Orleans in April 1862, many of the newspapers of the area became nonfunctional because of scarcity of paper and employees. Those that continued to operate exercised a voluntary restraint on reportage of boat movements. No private commercial voyages are reported, and military related boat activities are seldom mentioned.

The newspapers are, nevertheless, suggestive. In 1864, for example, when Kirby Smith's operations were fully underway, there are a significant number of advertisements for bids related to military supply facilities and transport, and there are occasional direct and indirect references to steamboats. With respect to the latter, the 12 January *Semi-Weekly Shreveport News* contains a bid request for the transport of 20,000–30,000 bales of cotton from the Red River to Jefferson and Swanson's Landing; the 5 February issue contains an advertisement for the apprehension of a slave who ran away from the *Era* boats at Albany; the same issue reports "FOR ALEXANDRIA.—The steamer COL. TERRY will leave as above on SATURDAY EVENING at 4 o'clock, February 6th;" and the 7 June *Shreveport News* reports that the *Stella* and *Don Louis* were wrecked by a hurricane at Shreveport and that sundry other boats lost their chimneys.

These hints of a much higher level of steamboat activity than would appear at first sight are confirmed by William H. Tunnard, who arrived at Shreveport on 16 August 1864 aboard the *Lelia*: "One unacquainted with Shreveport at this period, as the great central point, the nucleus of all military operations, could scarcely imagine the activity that prevailed there; the influx and egress of all grades of military officials; the arrivals and departures of steamers and trains, shipment and receipt of stores, etc. Yet outside of military circles there was nothing enticing or attractive about the place, and the mere drone of society would soon tire of its monotony—seek in vain for some amusement to while away the listless hours."

The most important source that I have been able to obtain for documenting boat movements west of Shreveport during the depths of the war is the "Vessel Papers" that comprise National Archives Record Group 109. These are captured documents pertaining primarily to privately owned shipping that carried freight or passengers for the Confederacy. In the thirty-two rolls of microfilm, there is documentation for eight boats that traveled to points west of Shreveport during the war. These documents are particularly interesting because many of the freight receipts can be correlated with war-related production efforts in the Jefferson area.

EIGHTEEN SIXTY-ONE

The winds of war did not blow steamboats off course, with the navigation record for 1861 indicating that twenty boats made 105 trips to points west of Shreveport, compared to twenty-nine boats and 55 trips in 1860. In 1861, seventeen boats made 101 trips to Jefferson, including the *D. R. Carroll*, *Era No. 6*, *Eleanor*, *Fanny Pearson*, *Fleta*, *Fox*, *Gen. J. L. Hodges*, *Harmonia*, *Homer*, *J. M. Sharp*, *Osceola*, *P. E. Bonford*, *Robert Fulton*, *Sallie Robinson*, *Texas*, *Vigo*, and *William Burton*. In addition, the *William Burton* traveled to Albany, and the *Era No. 4*, *Lecompte*, and *Starlight* each made a trip to Swanson's Landing. All of these records are from the *South-Western*.

The cumulative trips for 1861 were much higher than for 1860, but this difference can be accounted for in part by the fact that the 1860 numbers are drawn from the *Daily Picayune*, which does not account for local trips west of Shreveport. The *Fleta* advertised as a tri-weekly mail steamer out of Shreveport in March 1860 and almost certainly began to fulfill this commitment. In 1861 she registered 39 trips to Jefferson, which was the record up to that year. Other boats registering a high number of trips were the *Texas* (10), *P. E. Bonford* (8), and *Homer*, *J. M. Sharp*, and *Sallie Robinson* (7 each).

What was particularly impressive about the recorded 105 trips is that they all occurred during the first six months of the year, after which a low-water period ensued on the Red River until March 1862. The same situation prevailed in 1859 when approximately the same number of trips was made by the same number of boats operating along the route. As a consequence, the figures for 1861 should not be taken to indicate an acceleration of commercial activity during the early months of the war.

Of the 1861 boats, the *Homer* was captained by William Perry during the early part of the year. This 194-ton sidewheeler measuring 148 by 28 feet was the second boat to be captained by Perry. The *Lecompte* made a single trip to Swanson's Landing in 1861. She was wrecked at Campti in April by W. W. Withenbury while returning from New Orleans to Shreveport. The *Homer* was enrolled in New Orleans with Withenbury as captain on 11 May. Withenbury operated this boat in the Confederate service through at least March 1863, in spite of the fact that he was a Union sympathizer from Cincinnati.

The first mention of steamboats in connection with military activities occurred on 1 May 1861, when the Shreveport *South-Western* reported: "The steamer P. E. Bonford arrived here last evening from Jefferson, Texas, with a company of 118 fine and hearty young men, en route to New Orleans." This company was the Marion Rifles under the command of Capt. B. A. Bobo according to the *Shreveport Daily News* of the same date, which has a full listing of the recruits.

The 11 May Marshall *Texas Republican* describes this contingent as follows: "The Marion Rifles, from Jefferson, Texas, left a few days ago for New Orleans, intending to proceed immediately to the seat of war. The company numbered 107 men, embracing within its ranks several of the leading citizens of Jefferson, many of whom we know to be brave, clever fellows. They are the right material for soldiers. Success to them." The *Texas Republican* went on to quote the Shreveport *Caddo Gazette* to the effect that "We cannot too highly commend the conduct of Captains Applegate, Johnson, and Moody, who have so generously offered their fine steamers to convey our troops to New Orleans."

On 2 May, Capt. N. G. Dickinson from New Orleans solicited volunteers from Jefferson in an advertisement that appeared in the *Shreveport Daily News* offering transport by the *Homer*.

WAR UPON THE BORDER! VOLUNTEERS WANTED!
In Captain A. G. Dickinson's company, now forming at Jefferson, Texas.
He desires to enlist ONE HUNDRED AND TWENTY-FIVE MEN, for whom ample provision has been made.

Come forward at once, the company will leave Jefferson on the steamer Homer a few days after her arrival in that port.

Brave Louisianians and Texans will in this company fight side by side.

A. G. DICKINSON
May 2, 1861.

The 3 June *Shreveport Weekly News* reported arrivals from Jefferson of Capt. Fredrick Bass's Marshall Guards aboard the *Fleta* and Capt. Albert Clopton's Cass County Star Rifles aboard the *Texas*. In late July, Capt. William Duke's Jefferson Guards passed through Shreveport en route to Missouri but were ordered to Virginia to fight at Arlington Heights. They were followed in September by Capt. James Jeter's Caddo Lake Boys, which had been formed in the vicinity of the lake, and in November by Captain Cameron's company from Jefferson.

The 1861 recruits appear to have all been transported by steamboat. Mrs. William Roberts of Alabama was visiting in Jefferson and observed the earliest departures of troops, as recounted in a 24 November 1861 letter to her niece: "There have been several companies started from here—the last flag presented had the motto on it—Justice or Death. Tuesday we want to go to the presenting of one. That company will go to Missouri—will leave in the evening. The first company that left here was a new thing to us and a good many of our town folks left. We went in the morning to see the banner presented and again in the evening to see them take the boat."

An early mention of military supplies for Jefferson is in a 17 June 1861 "Vessel Papers" memo from Capt. John Galt in New Orleans to the Third Texas Cavalry Regiment's Col. E. Greer in Jefferson concerning the receipt of public property transported by the *J. M. Sharp* (**fig. 14-3**). The first newspaper mention of military-related production in Jefferson is probably the notice in the 2 December *Shreveport Semi-Weekly News*: "The manufactory of soap has been commenced at Jefferson." However, no additional information is provided in relation to this facility.

R. W. Loughery of the *Texas Republican* visited Jefferson three times in 1861, but he does not mention the incipient hostilities until his third trip in December. The first trip, which occurred in February, simply noted Jefferson's growth in spite of hard times:

Fig. 14-3. John Galt
letter, June 17, 1861.
*Source: National
Archives "Vessel Papers"*

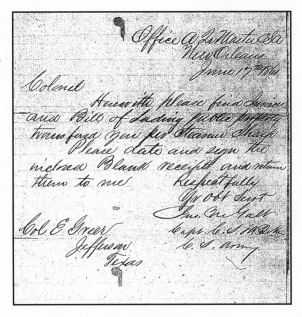

Our neighboring town of Jefferson has improved very much notwithstanding the short crops and hard times. We were agreeably surprised at the number and character of the new buildings. Among them, we noticed a house recently built by Mr. W. M. Freeman, which is forty by one hundred and twenty feet, and surmounted with a belfry or dome, in which the proprietor expects to place a town clock. The upper rooms are devoted to county and law offices. On the second floor there is a large room forty by seventy feet, which is used as a Court room, and in which the recent fairs were held. "Freeman's Hall," as it is called, is emphatically a great house, and we wish we had such a public building in Marshall. We noticed besides, one or two immense warehouses, which have been recently erected.

Mr. J. H. Pratt gave us a very cheering account of the prospects of the railroad from Jefferson designed to connect with the Memphis and El Paso road. This work, when completed, will add largely to the business of our sister town; and, that it will be constructed under the present energetic contractors, we cannot doubt. We hope that before it is finished, our citizens will make the necessary preparations to extend the road to Marshall, to connect with the Southern Pacific.

Our old friend Brooks still keeps up his excellent hotel, where hospitality and attention is dispensed as of yore.

During the second trip in August, Loughery noted: "Jefferson seemed to be lively for the season and times, and the town was improving." On the third trip, which occurred in December after many troops had left Jefferson, Loughery strikes a patriotic note:

On Saturday last we paid a flying visit to Jefferson, and had the pleasure of a few hours social converse with friends in that locality. Among other places we called at the Herald office, and found Messrs. Kirby and Morgan at home, and as agreeable as of yore.

The town is exceedingly dull. Yet, considerable improvement is going on, notwithstanding the hard times. The Messrs. Murphy are building an immense brick warehouse for cotton, over 150 square feet, and which is rapidly approaching completion. Several other new houses are going up. In returning, we spent the night at the residence of Col. C. C. Mills, a gentleman of agreeable manners, and noted for his generous hospitality. The Colonel has given his three sons, (all he has,) to the war, and all the blankets from his beds have been surrendered to our brave volunteers.

Everywhere the spirit of the country is unchangeable. All that our people possess will be freely given, every sacrifice will be endured, and when all is surrendered, the old men of the country will take the places of the young on the battle field.

EIGHTEEN SIXTY-TWO

Jefferson's exceeding dullness in December was as much the result of low water as the fact that many of the young and middle-aged men had left town. The low water on the Red River that began in June 1861 extended through late February 1862, only two months before the fall of New Orleans. During this brief window of opportunity, there was a flurry of steamboat activity in the direction of Jefferson. According to the *Daily Picayune*, *South-Western*, and *Shreveport Semi-Weekly News*, in April the *Rinaldo*, *Larkin Edwards*, *Era No. 5*, and *Fleta* made two trips each to Jefferson, and the *Robert Fulton*, *Moro*, *Col. Terry*, and

Texas made one each. These boats were running to and from New Orleans or in conjunction with New Orleans boats.

A blockade had been established at the mouth of the Mississippi by Union gunboats in May 1861 and farther upstream at the Head of Passes in October. In July and August 1861, cotton factors established a self-imposed embargo on cotton exports in a patriotic, but misguided, attempt to hurt Northern industries and pressure England into support for the Confederacy. The blockade and embargo had no readily noticeable effect on the movement of boats west of Shreveport because low water on the Red and on Cypress Bayou prohibited navigation. Nor, for that matter, were these actions decisive for port activity at New Orleans, which continued at a fairly high level.

When navigation conditions improved on the Red, boats soon began running between Jefferson and New Orleans, and this activity continued right up to the fall of New Orleans. According to the *Daily Picayune*, the *Era No. 5* arrived in New Orleans from Jefferson on 5 April and the *Col. Terry* from Jefferson on the sixth. The *Moro*, with George Sweeny as captain, and the *Jeff. Thompson* (formerly the *Fanny Pearson*), with John Smoker as captain, advertised on the sixteenth for Jefferson, Smithland, Benton, Port Caddo, Swanson's, Mooring's, and Albany. The *Countess*, with W. D. Bateman as captain, advertised for Jefferson, Smithland, Benton, Swanson's Landing, Mooring's Landing, and Albany on the twenty-second. Finally, on the twenty-fourth, the *Texas*, with C. W. Stinde as captain, arrived from Jefferson and advertised for Jefferson and Swanson's. This was the day before the Union gunboats arrived at New Orleans.

Although the blockade and embargo did not have an obvious effect on boat movements west of Shreveport, they did initiate changes in the directional flow of trade, shifting the interest of merchants away from New Orleans and toward Southwest Texas. As early as January 1862, the Marshall *Texas Republican* was reporting that large quantities of cotton were being sent through San Antonio for Mexico and also through Brownsville. The fall of New Orleans in April accelerated this process. By December, Chester Bulkley in Jefferson was advertising for wagons and teams to go west to Navasota, with "Employment given both ways, at good prices."

Whether such activities involved waterborne transport along the route from April 1862 on cannot be documented because private freight bills for this period have not surfaced, and the government freight receipts do not mention cotton. That there was an infrastructure and commodity base for such movements is known. Loughery noted in December 1861 that the firm of J. M. & J. C. Murphy in Jefferson was building an immense brick warehouse for cotton, and this firm advertised in the *South-Western* during the war. In July 1862, the warehouse of Powell & Brother in Jefferson burned with 300 bales of cotton in storage, and, in August, the warehouse of B. J. Terry & Company burned with 4,000 bales in storage.

Cotton storage was not restricted to Jefferson. B. H. Martin, who had sold his Benton facilities to Norsworthy & Kennedy in 1859, resumed operations in January 1862 according to an advertisement in the *Texas Republican* on the fourth:

> RECEIVING, FORWARDING, AND COMMISSION BUSINESS, BENTON, TEXAS.
> The subscriber has resumed the above business, at his old stand, and is now prepared to receive Cotton and other produce. All business entrusted to his care shall receive his best attention.
> B. H. MARTIN
> January 4th, 186(2).

A. P. Hope of Port Caddo is listed as a subscriber in the "Receipts for the Republican" column that appears in the 6 September 1862 *Texas Republican*. This was the brother of Adam Hope, who was a partner with him in the operation of the cotton warehouse in Port Caddo. Adam Hope was away at war and advertised in the 1 April 1863 *South-Western*, indicating cotton storage but apparently without a great deal of commercial activity:

> NOTICE,
> IS here given to all who have Cotton in my warehouse at Port Caddo, on the Lake, that some of the Cotton is becoming damaged from leakage, and not being at home when it was stored, so as to attend to it. I will be responsible for no damaged Cotton, as the owners were told that the house leaked very badly when the cotton was put there.
> ADAM HOPE.
> Port Caddo, March 11, 1863.

Apart from the 24 May 1862 *Texas Republican* mention that Randall's Regiment was being formed at a rendezvous near Port Caddo, the Hope advertisement is the only newspaper mention of Port Caddo during the war. However, the "Receipts for the Republican" column indicates that Port Caddo was at least moderately active during the war, because the following seven people in addition to Hope are listed as subscribers or advertisers between March 1862 and March 1863: W. R. Targart, J. M. Cithrian, S. J. Stuart, Miss Darden, B. F. Sledge, R. H. Hargrove, and J. Hilliard.

Lastly, the military interest in cotton is reflected in a captured Confederate map showing government cotton sheds on the east side of Jim's Bayou below Monterey **(fig. 14-4)**. The remembrance of this facility is manifest in the designation of this area on contemporary maps

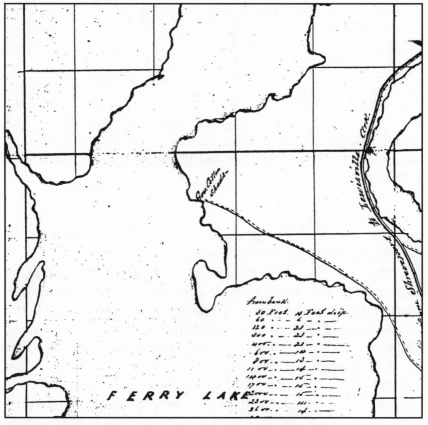

Fig. 14-4. Government cotton sheds. *Source: Louisiana Secretary of State, Division of Archives, Records Management and History*

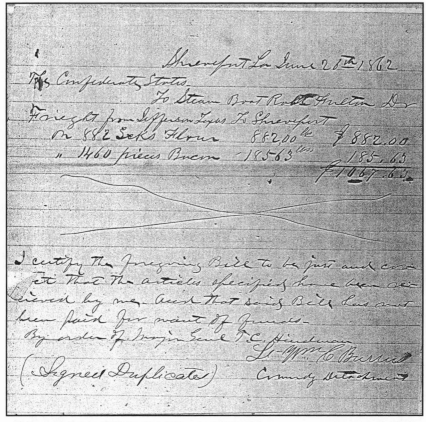

Fig. 14-5. *Robert Fulton* freight bill, June 28, 1862. *Source: National Archives "Vessel Papers"*

as Cottonshed Arm. The placement of the sheds suggests a linkage with boat movements out of Monterey.

After the fall of New Orleans in April 1862, the area west of Shreveport became a stationing place for troops that were in need of supplies. These were brought up to Jefferson from places like Alexandria, Opelousas, and Shreveport, according to the 16 May Jefferson *Confederate News*: "Since our last, there has been four arrivals at our wharf, the P. E. Bonford and Robt. Fulton from Alexandria with sugar and molasses, also the Anna Perret from Opelousas with sugar, coffee and supplies, and the Larkin Edwards from Shreveport with sugar and molasses."

The area west of Shreveport also quickly became an important supply center, drawing on its traditional market region. The 16 May *Confederate*

News reports: "The Texas left for Alexandria with flour, bacon and supplies for the Army." In October, Capt. A. U. Wright, the assistant quartermaster in Jefferson who had been appointed chief purchasing agent for Texas north of Crockett, issued an advertisement in the Marshall, Jefferson, Tyler, and Dallas newspapers for the direct or contract purchase of army cloth, clothing, shoes, hats, leather, hides, and wool. In November, E. Price of Jefferson advertised in the *Texas Republican* for "FOUR thousand head of good pork hogs, to be delivered in Jefferson, Texas, to put up bacon for the government, for which cash will be paid." The dimensions of this supply activity, which included private and military components, were noted in the 14 January *Shreveport Semi-Weekly News*: "During the whole of last week, train after train of movers from Mississippi and adjoining States passed through our city en route for Texas, whose resources are now becoming known, in every direction. We can safely say, without fear of contradiction, that all the beef and pork we eat and the flour we use, is from the industry of the Texans; we could enumerate many other things, but mention only the principal necessaries of life. Cannot we take pattern after our neighbor?"

The military component of these supply activities is reflected in documents contained in the "Vessel Papers." In June, the *Robert Fulton* transported 882 sacks of flour and 1,460 pieces of bacon at a cost of $1,067.63 from Jefferson to Shreveport, where they were signed for by Lt. William Burris of the commissary detachment (**fig. 14-5**); and in September, the same boat was paid $644 for transporting 73 privates, two officers, four mules, and one wagon from Jefferson to Shreveport (**fig. 14-6**). In addition, the government-owned *Cornie* made a trip from Monroe, Louisiana, to Jefferson and back in June–July (**fig. 14-7**) carrying miscellaneous up and down freights. The down freights were mostly from businesses in Shreveport and apparently destined for Camp Moore.

The most important navigation document for 1862 may not be in the "Vessel Papers" but rather in the newspapers. According to the 21 March and 1 April issues of the *Shreveport Semi-Weekly News*, the *Era No. 5* arrived from New Orleans, discontinued her regular trips, made a special trip to Jefferson, and departed for New Orleans from Shreveport on 29 March "with iron for the gunboats." The 5 April *Daily Picayune* notes the arrival of the *Era No. 5* from Jefferson carrying 108 pieces of iron for W. H. McComb and 1,127 pieces for E. Rousseau.

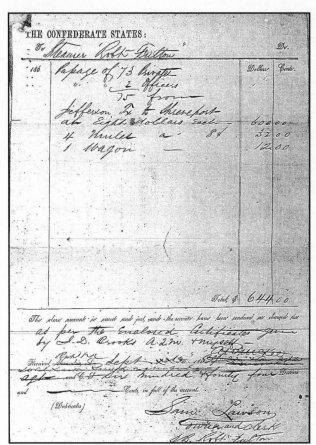

Fig. 14-6. *Robert Fulton* receipt, September 30, 1862. *Source: National Archives "Vessel Papers*

These gunboats were the *Louisiana* and the *Mississippi*, which were being built in New Orleans. With Union threats on the Mississippi River to the north and to the south, the Confederacy was frantically searching for iron to complete these boats. Given this context and the sequence of events recounted in the newspapers, it is possible that the trip of the *Era No. 5* to Jefferson was for the sake of obtaining iron (although it is also possible that the iron for the gunboats was picked up at Shreveport on the return trip). If the *Era No. 5* took iron from Jefferson, it is probable that the load included the six miles of track of the Memphis, El Paso & Pacific, because railroad iron was of the right quality for gunboat plating. However, this track is not shown in the state records as having been abandoned until after the Civil War.

Another contributor to the iron needs of the Confederacy (though not a producer of sufficient quality for gunboat plating) was Jefferson

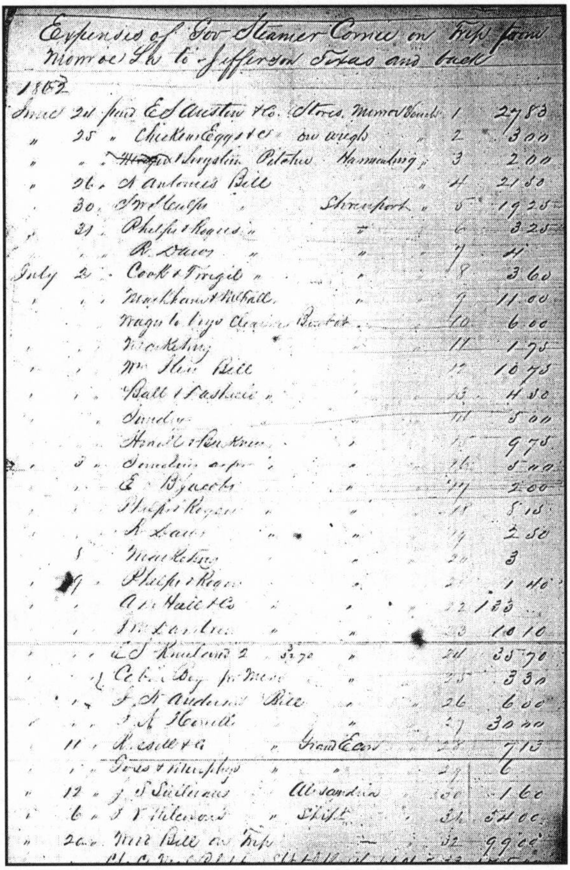
Expenses of Gov Steamer Cornie on Trip from Monroe La to Jefferson Texas and back
1862

Fig. 14-7. *Cornie* expenses, June–July 1862. *Source: National Archives "Vessel Papers"*

Nash's facility, which was located eighteen miles west of Jefferson. Nash began to build the first iron furnace in Texas in 1847 on Alley's Creek, a tributary to Cypress Bayou. This furnace was used for the smelting of ore and for the production of pig and bar iron. A long description of the completed facility was published in the 17 April 1858 *Texas Republican*, which I will take the liberty of reproducing in full because it has not been included in any of the published works on Texas iron:

> COMMUNICATED.
> TEXAS IRON WORKS.
> CASS COUNTY, April 9th, 1858.
> *R. W. Loughery, Esq., Ed. Republican*:
> DEAR SIR.—In compliance with your courteous request to be furnished with information in regard to the character and

extent and prospects of our enterprise, and duly appreciate the interest thus manifested, we proceed to state, that we have commenced at this place the manufacture of "Bar Iron" by what is known, among Iron men, as the "Blumary" process, with a "Catalan Forge."

The works are situated eighteen miles west of Jefferson, and twenty-six or twenty-eight miles North-west of Marshall, in the South-west corner of Cass county and very near the Harrison county line. At and surrounding the "works" are a number of elevated broken ridges or hills, approximating the elevation and dignity of mountains, upon and in which, is one of the most striking deposits of iron ore known in the Mississippi valley. The quantity is doubtless inexhaustible, the quality exceedingly rich, free from deleterious substances, soft, well adapted to the manufacture of "wrought" and "cast" Iron, and easily accessible. Surrounding the mountains and for many miles adjacent thereto, is a splendid "Pine Forest," affording material for a vast amount of the best fuel with which "Iron ore" can be worked. The "forge" is, comparatively, a simple construction, consisting of open fires for working the ore, blast machinery and two German forge hammers for welding up, and drawing the Iron into bars, the power employed is two steam engines driven by steam made chiefly by the waste heat of the forge fires. The process is an old one and likewise simple, the ore after being well roasted is beaten to dust by stampers, running with the machinery and by the foreman used in this form upon his fires, his judgement and skill alone directing him as to time and quantity, in its application. The fuel used in these fires is charcoal. From three to four hours are sufficient to form, in the bottom of the fires, an open porous mass of Iron, called a "*loup*," and weighing from 100 to 150 pounds. This results from the particles of iron having an affinity for each other and coming readily together under the influence of a heat sufficient to weld them into a mass, while the foreign matter in combination becoming liquid at a *lower* heat is drawn off as liquid slag or cinder. The loup is taken out welding hot, with the liquid cinder dripping from it, and under the forge hammer welded into a solid lump, and then drawn into bars. The four fires we are now running, are competent to make, with cold blast, about 1000 pounds of iron per day. The blast heated (by any apparatus in common use) greatly hastens the process and economizes in fuel. Having thoroughly tested the practicability of making Iron of superior quality from our ore, and established the certainty of every question upon which there could be doubt as to making really good Iron at a reasonable cost, it is our present purpose to add the necessary machinery to increase the business, and put our Iron into the various forms necessary to meet the wants of the country, nothing but capital and effort will be necessary to make the business all that may be desired, both to the public and the manufacturer. We shall endeavor to have the works in position during the year, to furnish the Iron wanted in this section(?). The article now manufactured can be found at a number of houses in Jefferson, always on hand at the works, and we shall soon place some of it in your own town in order that your blacksmiths and Planters may try it. We only ask a trial of its quality, and shall expect or desire nothing more than the individual interest of each member of the community may dictate in regard to it. We expect to be able to make and furnish it at a less price than "Iron" can be introduced into the country from elsewhere. We have written you hastily, the writer being at the moment on the eve of a business trip, and indeed on his way, at the place of departure.

Yours very truly,
J. L. NASH & CO.

The firm had been reorganized in 1857 under the name of J. S. Nash and Company, with Nash, his son William, and David Browder as partners. Browder had been brought in from out of state to serve as plant manager, but he did not stay with the firm very long. In the 12 August 1858 *Texas Republican*, Browder indicates that "having by an additional partner placed the 'Texas Iron Works' under more skillful and experienced management than his own, has accepted the proffer of a business situation in the house of Messrs. Fellowes & Co., New Orleans." Browder also indicates that the facility was moving rapidly in the direction of castings: "He informs us that the 'Texas Iron Works' are progressing with their improvements. The Company is now building a 'blast-furnace,' which will be in operation in from sixty to ninety days, when they will be prepared to make castings and pig metal, and in a position to make the heavy castings and machinery necessary to make 'bar iron' of all sizes. We have already spoken of the superior character of this iron. Our readers will recollect the interesting account of these Iron Works, furnished us by Mr. Browder, published in the Republican several months ago, and which was copied by many of our exchanges at home and abroad."

These improvements led eventually to a full-scale foundry that produced molded products, as is indicated by a 10 March 1860 *Texas Republican* advertisement:

> TEXAS PLOWS, ENCOURAGE HOME
> MANUFACTURES.
> I have an agency to sell Nash's Plows. These plows are manufactured at Nash's foundry, 16 miles west of Jefferson, Texas, where the iron is taken out of Texas soil, and the plows are made. They are therefore exclusively of Texas manufacture. It is harder than any other iron made, and is regarded as far superior. These plows speak for themselves. Farmers would do well to look at them before purchasing. If found to fill the bill, they ought, as a matter of State pride, to claim the precedence over plows manufactured abroad. Call and see them.
>
> D. McPHAIL
> Feb. 25, 1860.

EIGHTEEN SIXTY-THREE

The degree of importance of the Texas Iron Works to the war effort cannot be fully determined on the basis of the readily available documents. According to Robert Jones in "The First Iron Furnace in Texas," Nash wanted to produce rifled cannon and shot and shell but apparently produced only a few cannon balls. Shortly after the end of the war, the 8 August 1865 *Shreveport Semi-Weekly News* made the following comment on significance: "The quantity of iron in the several beds discovered near Jefferson seems to be equal to any demand.— The yield of rich ore is immense and the quantity almost boundless. It is proper to state that several furnaces are in operation in the portion of Texas alluded to, one of them for a number of years. They have supplied the country with castings for several years past, and during the war supplied the ore for nearly all the shot and shell manufactured. There is no rolling mill in operation in Texas at present, but this, we presume, will not be much longer neglected."

This passage strongly suggests that Nash produced iron that was used to make shot and shell and not the projectiles themselves. The key passage is equivocal. It certainly cannot be taken to mean that Nash provided the iron for all the shot and shell produced by the Confederacy. The term "country" had strong regional overtones in the 1800s. The statement probably means that Nash and nearby facilities provided the iron for all the shot and shell produced in that portion of the Confederacy. At a minimum, the statement means that the Nash facility was a significant factor in the war effort west of the Mississippi within the confines of the Trans-Mississippi Department.

This regional significance is confirmed by Robert Kerby, in *Kirby Smith's Confederacy: The Trans-Mississippi South, 1863–1865*, who points out that throughout the war, the Nash facility was "the only factory in the Confederate Southwest capable of mass-producing a respectable amount of good-quality pig iron." Kerby also indicates that most of Nash's production was sent to Houston, Austin, Shreveport, and Camden—the four towns in which the department's five large foundries were located. The processed bar and sheet iron produced by these foundries was sent to arsenals at Little Rock, Camden, Arkadelphia, Shreveport, Marshall, Tyler, and San Antonio, to state arsenals at New Iberia and Austin, to the shipyard at Shreveport, and to private arms and ordnance producers throughout the region.

From March 1863 on, the Nash facility operated under the ownership of Nash, his son, James Alley, and Josiah D. Perry (probably the other partner to whom Browder referred). It was a fairly large facility. In the 23 January 1858 Clarksville *Northern Standard*, the Nash facility advertised for fifteen to twenty workmen. From August 1861 through May 1863, the following are listed in the *Texas Republican* in the Receipts for the Republican column as subscribers or advertisers: W. D. Nash (Alley's Mills); C. G. Vandiver (Alley's Mills); J. V. Nash (Texas Iron Works); Nash, Perry & Co.; J. W. Alley; J. M. Hobdy (Texas Iron Works); H. N. Geer (Texas Iron Works); T. R. Mitchell (Texas Iron Works); John Ferguson (Texas Iron Works); and J. C. Perry (Texas Iron Works). In August 1864, the name of the post office was changed from Alley's Mills to Nash's Foundry.

The important points for the present study are that: (1) the Nash facility produced large quantities of iron for the war effort; (2) the facility was operational throughout the war; (3) the iron was used in places in addition to Texas; and, most importantly, (4) the iron used elsewhere was transported out of Jefferson by steamboat. The latter point is confirmed by three 1863 receipts signed by Capt. A. U. Wright, the assistant quartermaster in Jefferson:

1. The first receipt (**fig. 14-8**) indicates that Capt. C. W. Stinde of the *Texas* was paid $800 at Jefferson on 21 May for the 12 May transport of one hundred men and six tons of pig iron from Jefferson to Shreveport.
2. The second receipt (**fig. 14-9**) indicates that Capt. C. W. Stinde was paid $226 at Jefferson on 17 June for the 22 May transport of 15,680 pounds of pig iron and six men from Jefferson to Shreveport.
3. The third receipt (**fig. 14-10**) indicates that Capt. J. B. Goyne of the *Fleta* was paid $419.40 at Jefferson on 23 June for the 23 May transport of nine men and 37,440 pounds of iron from Jefferson to Shreveport.

In the midst of these recorded transport activities, Nash advertised for corn in exchange for salt or castings, apparently to use as animal feed, in the 23 May 1863 *Texas Republican*:

NOTICE. 200 BUSHELS OF CORN WANTED.
The Texas Iron Works, in Marion Co., Texas, will give, in exchange for Corn, Salt or Castings, when delivered at the works. Look at this and bring up your corn without delay.
NASH, PERRY & CO.
May 23, 1863.

Some indication of the dimensions of the iron works near Jefferson is given in a 26 January 1866 *Texas Republican* advertisement for the sale of movable property seized by the government at the end of the war:

PUBLIC SALES OF GOVERNMENT PROPERTY, NEAR JEFFERSON, TEXAS.
C. V. WOODRUFF, AUCTIONEER.
BY order of the Secretary of the Treasury, dated December 8th, ult., I will sell at Public Auction, on TUESDAY,

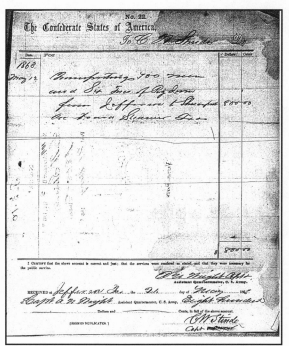

Fig. 14-8. *Texas* receipt, May 21, 1863. *Source: National Archives "Vessel Papers"*

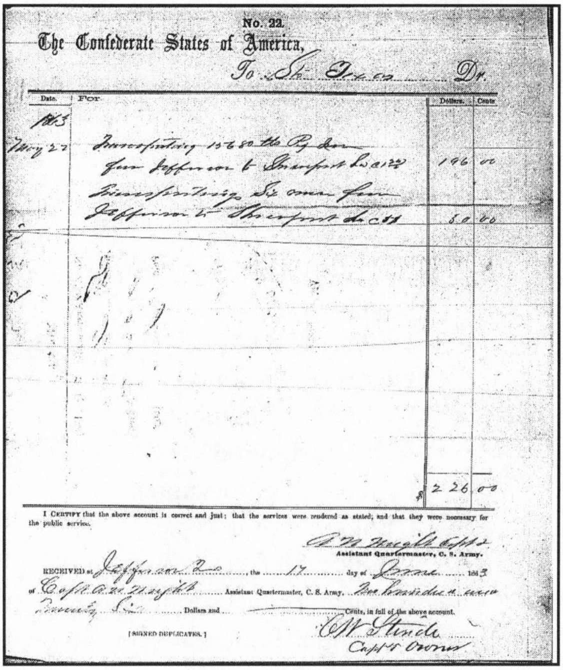

Fig. 14-9. *Texas* receipt, June 17, 1863. *Source: National Archives "Vessel Papers"*

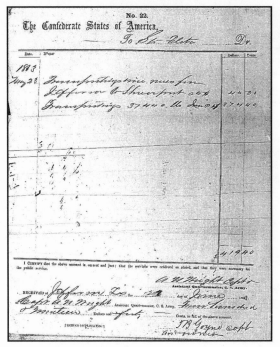

Fig. 14-10. *Fleta* receipt, June 23, 1863. *Source: National Archives "Vessel Papers"*

FEBRUARY 13, at 10 o'clock, A. M., on the premises of the Marion County Iron Works, 18 miles from Jefferson in Cass county, Texas, all the personal movable property at the aforesaid works, heretofore the property of the so-called Confederate Government, and now the property of the United States by capture, viz:

1 Saw Mill,
1 Grist Mill,
1 Engine, 2½ horse power,
1 Engine, 40 horse power,
2 Engines, 30 horse power each,
1 Engine, 40 horse power,
1 Pumping Engine,
1 Doctor Engine,
1 Engine, 20 horse power,
1 Engine, not in repair,
1 Boiler, 20 feet, 42 inch flues,
1 Boiler, 18 feet, double flues,
1 Cylinder Boiler, 36 feet, 36 inch flues,

1 Cylinder Boiler, 32 feet, 34 inch flues,
1 Circular Saw,
1 Iron Turning Lathe,
4 Car Wheels,
1 Fan for Blast Furnace,
2 Log Wagons,
1 Cart,
1 Pair Balances,
1 Pair Platform Scales,
700 tons Pig Iron, estimated,
100 tons Scrap Iron,
1 Kiln Brick, 25 M, (burned),
Lot Moulding Flasks and Patterns,
Lot Timber and Lumber,
2 Swinging Cranes,
1 Suspension Railroad,
6000 Bushels Charcoal,
—ALSO—

Immediately after the above sale on the premises, two miles from the above works, at the Marion County Forge Works, the following described property, viz:

1 Engine, 80 horse power,
1 Engine, 60 horse power,
2 Boilers, 26 feet, 42 inch double flues,
1 Steam Drum,
1 pair Blowing Cylinders,
1 Trip Hammer,
1 Shingling Hammer,
Lot Furnace Castings
10,000 bushels of Charcoal,
TERMS—Cash, in U. S. Treasury notes, at time of sale.

> R. L. ROBERTSON,
> Assist. Superv'g Special Agent, Treas'y Dep't,
> Dist. of Northern Texas.
> Approved.
> O. H. BURBRIDGE,
> Superv'g Special Agent, Third Agency,
> Treasury Dep't, New Orleans.
> January 26, '66.

Jefferson also became a production area for shoes and leather. The first was a military facility established in November 1862 by A. U. Wright, Captain and Assistant Quartermaster, who advertised for workers in the 3 January 1863 *Texas Republican*: "WANTED to work at this place, 100 shoemakers, either white or black, to whom good wages will be given."

This facility is described briefly in the 26 February 1863 *Texas Republican*: "Capt. A. U. Wright of Jefferson, one of the most energetic in the Confederate service, has established a large shoe shop for the Confederate States, in Jefferson, in which he is turning out, we understand, over a hundred pairs of shoes a day. We propose visiting it as soon as we have time."

A private facility was started by D. Lucas & Company to supply leather for the government shoe factory, as indicated by an advertisement in the 5 March *Texas Republican*:

> JEFFERSON TANNERY!!
> *One and a half miles from Jefferson, in Harrison county, Texas.*
>
> OWING to the great scarcity of hides and leather, we propose tanning all the hides we can get on the halves, to the amount of $1,000. We are fully prepared to turn out as good leather as any other establishment in the South, having material sufficient, with full complement of hands, and an experience of 30 years, we confidently expect a liberal share of patronage.
>
> D. LUCAS & CO.
> March 5th, 1863.

The machine for splitting the leather was brought up from Shreveport to Jefferson by the *T. D. Hine* on 23 February (**fig. 14-11**). The receipt was signed on the twenty-sixth at Jefferson by A. U. Wright and L. D. Moore, clerk of the *T. D. Hine*. Captain Pelham, whose name does not appear on the receipt, was master of the boat.

John Porter operated a flour mill in Paradise, the area directly west of Jefferson on the Daingerfield road. His advertisement in the 4 April 1863 *Texas Republican* indicates that he might have been on the verge of going out of business:

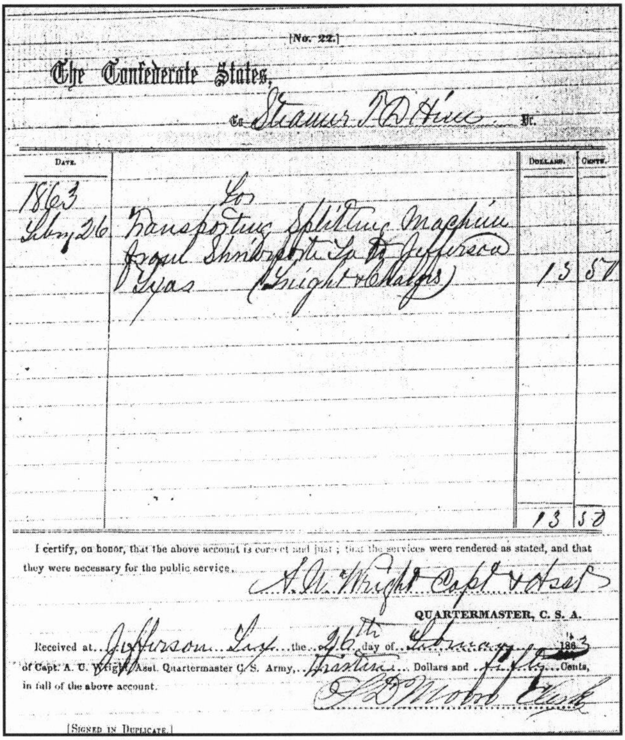
[No. 22.]

The Confederate States,

To Steamer T. D. Hine Dr.

Date.		Dollars.	Cents.
1863 Feby 26	For Transporting Splitting Machine from Shreveport La to Jefferson Texas (Freight & Charges)	13	50
		13	50

I certify, on honor, that the above account is correct and just; that the services were rendered as stated, and that they were necessary for the public service.

A. W. Wright Capt & Asst

QUARTERMASTER, C. S. A.

Received at Jefferson Tex the 26th day of February 1863 of Capt. A. U. Wright, Asst. Quartermaster C. S. Army, Thirteen Dollars and Fifty Cents, in full of the above account.

T. D. Mobe Clerk

[Signed in Duplicate.]

Fig. 14-11. *T.D. Hine* receipt, February 26, 1863. *Source: National Archives "Vessel Papers"*

NOW LOOK OUT!

I have a valuable STEAM ENGINE and BOILER for sale. It is well adapted for a large Flouring Mill, or Manufactory, being Forty-horse power as good as new. I can recommend it, and if sold near my house, I might be induced to put it up for the purchase. Come soon if you want a bargain. I will take Confederate money, negroes, or land, in a situation that would suit me; or on time with approved security.

JOHN PORTER,
Paradise Mills, Jefferson, Texas, April 2, 1863.

Paradise Mills may have contributed to the 8 January shipment of 7,350 pounds of flour from Jefferson to Shreveport by the *Texas* **(fig. 14-12)**. The payment receipt was signed at Jefferson on 14 May by C. W. Stinde, captain and owner of the *Texas*, and by Capt. John W. Thomas, commissary and subsistence officer in Jefferson.

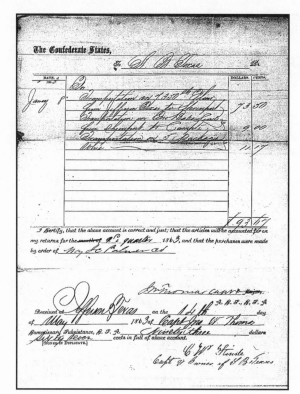

Fig. 14-12. *Texas* receipt, May 14, 1863. *Source: National Archives "Vessel Papers"*

Fig. 14-13. *T.D. Hine* bill of lading, February 27, 1863. *Source: National Archives "Vessel Papers"*

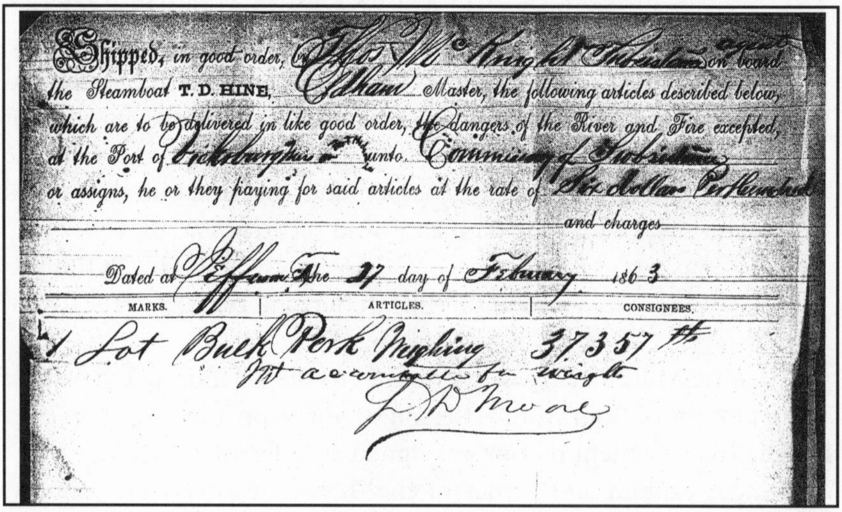

There are freight documents for the transport of pork and bacon out of Jefferson, which may have been related to the firm of E. Price in Jefferson that advertised in November 1862 for 4,000 hogs to supply meat for the military. The first **(fig. 14-13)** was for the 27 February transport of one lot of bulk pork weighing 37,357 pounds from Jefferson to Vicksburg, Mississippi, aboard the *T. D. Hine*, with Pelham as captain and Moore as clerk. This was the return trip for the *T. D. Hine* when she transported the splitting machine to Jefferson. The second **(fig. 14-14)** was for the 15 March transport of twenty casks of bacon weighing 21,249 pounds from Jefferson to Shreveport aboard the *Texas*. In Shreveport, Captain Stinde was paid $212.49 for transport and $5.00 for a warehousing fee for the bacon that he paid in Jefferson.

In addition to these commodity transports, there were substantial troop and related personnel movements from Jefferson to Shreveport by steamboat in 1863:

1. *P. E. Bonford*, 9 February, Lieutenant Johnson and twenty-three privates, Lieutenant Galton and one private, P. M. Spears **(fig. 14-15)**.
2. *P. E. Bonford*, 16 March, E. G. Douglas **(fig. 14-16)**.
3. *Fleta*, 20 March, seventeen men **(fig. 14-17)**.
4. *Fleta*, 10 May, eighteen officers and men **(fig. 14-18)**.
5. *Fleta*, 16 May, troops (Colonel Speight's Brigade) 9–16 May at $2,400 **(fig. 14-19)**.
6. *Texas*, 12 May, one hundred men **(see fig. 14-8)**.
7. *Texas*, 22 May, six men **(see fig. 14-9)**.
8. *Fleta*, 23 May, nine men **(see fig. 14-10)**.
9. *Fleta*, 5 June, six men **(fig. 14-20)**.

There are only two records of freight movements from Shreveport to supply troops in Jefferson. On 9 February, the *P. E. Bonford* brought up two trunks, twenty-seven boxes of merchandise, two bundles, one bag, and one-half barrel for the Eleventh Texas Regiment, along with leather for another recipient **(fig. 14-21)**. This was the up trip for the down trip on the same day carrying troops. On 4 June, the *Fleta* brought up seven packages of empty bags and fifteen barrels of molasses **(fig. 14-22)**. This was the up trip for the *Fleta*'s down trip on the fifth carrying troops.

[No. 22]

THE CONFEDERATE STATES

To Texas Dr.

1863.		Dollars	Cents
March 15	For Transportation twenty Cask bacon from Jefferson Texas to Shreveport La 21249 @ 1/	212	49
	Warehouse Expenses paid	5	00
		217	49

I certify that the above account is correct and just; that the services were rendered as stated; and that they were necessary for the public service.

B M Lewis Major

Received at Shreveport the 15 day of March 1863 of Major R. M. Lewis Quartermaster C.S. Army, the sum of Two hundred seventeen Dollars, forty nine Cents

(Signed in Duplicate.)

C. W. Steele
Capt & owner

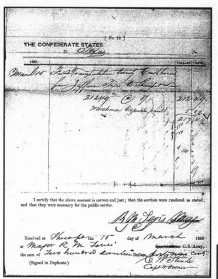

Fig. 14-14. *Texas* receipt, March 15, 1863. *Source: National Archives "Vessel Papers"*

[No. 22.]

The Confederate States,

To Steamer P. E. Bonford Dr.

DATE.		DOLLARS.	CENTS.
1863 Feby 9th	For Transportation of Lt Johnson & 23 Privates from Jefferson to Shreveport	120	00
	Transportation of Lt Patton & One Private from Jefferson to Shreveport	10	00
	Transportation of J M Spears from Jefferson to Shreveport	5	00
		135	00

I certify, on honor, that the above account is correct and just; that the services were rendered as stated, and that they were necessary for the public service.

A. W. Wright
Capt & A Q M C S A

Received Jefferson Feby 9th 1863 of Capt A W Wright One Hundred and Thirty five dollars and — cents, in full of the above account.

(SIGNED IN DUPLICATE.)

J. P. Worley
Capt P E Bonford

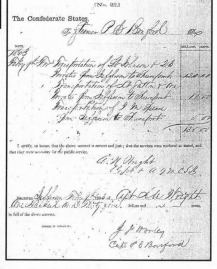

Fig. 14-15. *P.E. Bonford* receipt, February 9, 1863. *Source: National Archives "Vessel Papers"*

No. 22.

The Confederate States of America,

To Str P. E. Bonford Dr

Date.	For	Dollars.
1863 June 15	Transporting E. B. Dwight from Jefferson to Shreveport La	5
		5

I CERTIFY that the above account is correct and just; that the services were rendered as stated, and that they were necessary for the public service.

A. W. Wright

Assistant Quartermaster, C. S. Army

RECEIVED at Jefferson Tex the 15 day of June of Capt A W Wright Assistant Quartermaster, C. S. Army, Five

Fig. 14-16. *P.E. Bonford* receipt, June 15, 1863. *Source: National Archives "Vessel Papers"*

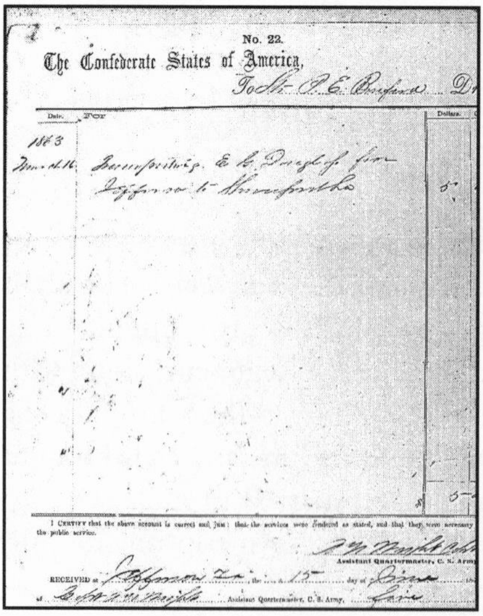

Fig. 14-17. *Fleta* receipt, March 20, 1863. *Source: National Archives, "Vessel Papers"*

[No. 23.]

The Confederate States, To Capt. A. A. Barnes Dr.

DATE.		DOLLARS.	CENTS.
1863 March 20	For Transportation of Seventeen men from Jefferson Texas on board of the Str Fleta to Shreveport La. it being 50 miles at 10 cents per mile	85	00
		85	00

I certify, on honor, that the above account is correct and just; that the services were rendered as stated, and that they were necessary for the public service.

A. H. Wright Capt & Qr. Mr. Quartermaster, C. S. A.

Received at Jefferson Texas the 20 day of March 1863 of Captain A. H. Wright, Asst. Quartermaster, C. S. Army, Eighty five Dollars and Cents in full of the above account.

No. 22.

The Confederate States of America,

To Str Fleta Dr.

Date.	For	Dollars.
1863. May 10	Transporting 18 Officers and men from Jefferson to Shreveport @ 5 $ each	90
		90

I CERTIFY that the above account is correct and just; that the services were rendered as stated, and that they were necessary for the public service.

A. H. Wright Capt. Assistant Quartermaster, C. S. Army.

RECEIVED at Jefferson Tex the 23 day of May 1863 of A. H. Wright Assistant Quartermaster, C. S. Army, Ninety Dollars and Cents, in full of the above account.

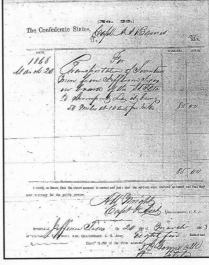

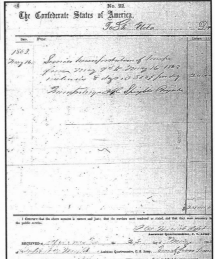

Fig. 14-18. *Fleta* receipt, May 23, 1863. *Source: National Archives "Vessel Papers"*

No. 22.

The Confederate States of America,

To Str Fleta Dr.

Date.	For	Dollars.
1863. May 16.	Services transportation of troops from May 9th to May 16 1863 inclusive 8 days @ 300$ per day Transporting ... Brigade	2400
		2400

I CERTIFY that the above account is correct and just; that the services were rendered as stated, and that they were necessary for the public service.

A. H. Wright Capt. Assistant Quartermaster, C. S. Army.

RECEIVED at Jefferson Tex the 23 day of May 1863 of A. H. Wright Assistant Quartermaster, C. S. Army, Twenty four Hundred Dollars and Cents, in full of the above account.

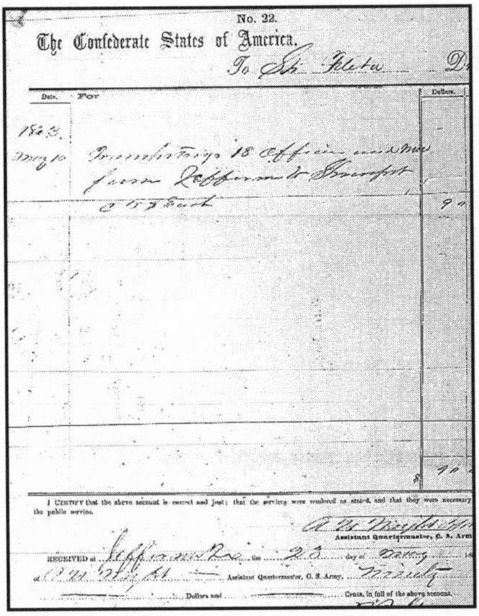

Fig. 14-19. *Fleta* receipt, May 23, 1863. *Source: National Archives "Vessel Papers"*

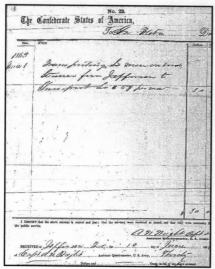

Fig. 14-20. *Fleta* receipt, June 19, 1863. Source: National Archives "Vessel Papers"

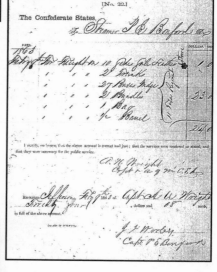

Fig. 14-21. *P.E. Bonford* receipt, February 9, 1863. *Source: National Archives "Vessel Papers"*

Fig. 14-22. *Fleta* receipt, June 4, 1863. *Source: National Archives "Vessel Papers"*

All of the other up freights for 1863 involved the transport of salt from Shreveport to Jefferson:

1. *P. E. Bonford*, 6 January, transport of 317 packages of salt from Shreveport to Jefferson; Capt. J. H. Worley of the *P. E. Bonford* received $250 from Capt. John W. Thomas at Jefferson on 10 May **(fig. 14-23)**.

2. *Texas*, 20 April, transport of 245,883 pounds of salt from Shreveport to Jefferson; Capt. C. W. Stinde of the *Texas* received $2,458.83 from Capt. A. U. Wright at Jefferson on 20 May **(fig. 14-24)**.

3. *Texas*, 13 May, transport of 295 barrels and 55 half-barrels of salt weighing 196,220 pounds from Shreveport to Jefferson; Capt. C. W. Stinde of the *Texas* received $1,962.20 from Capt. A. U. Wright at Jefferson on 13 May **(fig. 14-25)**.

4. *Fleta*, 18 May, transport of 198 packages of New Iberia salt weighing 118,800 pounds from Shreveport to Jefferson; Capt. J. B. Goyne of the *Fleta* received $1,188 from Capt. A. U. Wright at Jefferson on 23 May **(fig. 14-26)**.

Much of this salt was apparently derived from the Avery Island mines near New Iberia, Louisiana, which were a major source for the Confederacy, as is indicated by the *Fleta* receipt. Receipts indicate that salt was transported from Shreveport to Jefferson at one cent per pound; consequently, the total volume delivered from January through May was 585,903 pounds, or a little over 195 tons. Such large quantities of salt could be used only for the preparation of pickled beef. That beef was transported from Jefferson is indicated by a 4 April receipt for $185 signed by Clerk J. B. Goyne of the *Fleta* for Capt. A. A. Barnes and by Capt. A. U. Wright in Jefferson for the 4 April transport from Jefferson to Shreveport of forty barrels of beef weighing 1,800 pounds at one cent per pound and one box of candles **(fig. 14-27)**.

Forty barrels of beef could only have been prepared by a meatpacking plant. Such plants also produced large quantities of tallow, which was used by collateral facilities to make soap and candles. A freight cost of $5 on the candles indicates that the box was a crate containing thousands of candles, suggesting a production facility. The beef and candle production facilities that gave rise to these freight

THE CONFEDERATE STATES,

To Steamer P.E. Bonford Dr.

DATE 1863		DOLLARS	CENTS
Jany 6	For Freight on 317 packages Salt from Shreveport La. to Jefferson Texas	250	
		250	

I Certify, that the above account is correct and just; and that the articles will be accounted for on my returns for the month of 2nd Quarter of 1863, and that the purchases were made by order of Maj. ...

...Thomas Capt. ... Major A.C.S. C.S.A.

Received at Jefferson Texas on the 10th day of May 1863 of Capt. Jno. W. Thomas Commissary of Subsistance, C. S. A., Two hundred & fifty Dollars ... Cents, in full of above account.

[SIGNED DUPLICATE.]

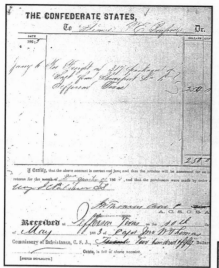

Fig. 14-23. *P.E. Bonford* receipt, May 10, 1863. *Source: National Archives "Vessel Papers"*

THE CONFEDERATE STATES, C.W. Stine, Or...

To Steamer Texas Dr.

1863		Dollars.	C
April 20th	For freight on 245,883 lbs Salt from 1¢ Shreveport La. to Jefferson Texas. Gross Weight	2458	

I CERTIFY, that the above account is correct and just; that the services were rendered as stated; that they were necessary for the Public Service. ...

W.H. Claiborne Capt. ... Major and C...

RECEIVED at Jefferson Tex. the 20 day of May 1863, of ... C. S. Army, the sum of Twenty four hundred fifty eight Dollars Eighty three Cents, in full of the above account.

[Duplicate.]

C.W. Stine

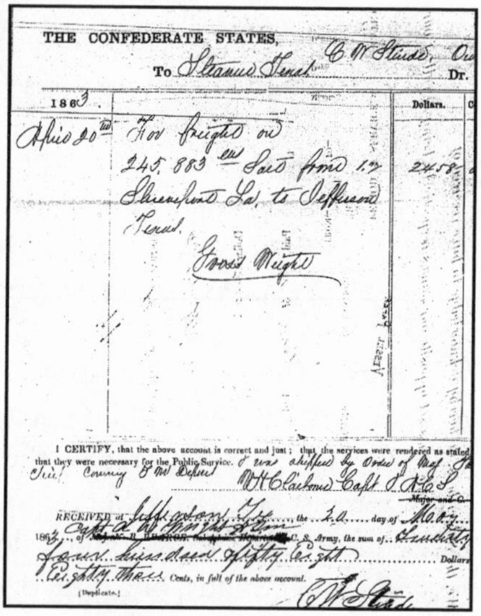

Fig. 14-24. *Texas* receipt, May 20, 1863. *Source: National Archives "Vessel Papers"*

THE CONFEDERATE STATES,

To Steamer Texas Dr.

1863		Dollars.	C
May 13	For Freight on 295 Bbl 455½ Bbl Salt from Shreveport La. to Jefferson Texas, 196,220 pounds ... at 1¢ per pound	1962	

I CERTIFY, that the above account is correct and just; that the services were rendered as stated; that they were necessary for the Public Service.

W.H. Claiborne Capt. ... Major and C...

RECEIVED at Jefferson Tx. the 13 day of May 1863, of Maj. W. B. PEARCE, Subsistence Department, C. S. Army, the sum of Nineteen hundred sixty two Dollars Twenty Cents, in full of the above account.

(Duplicate.)

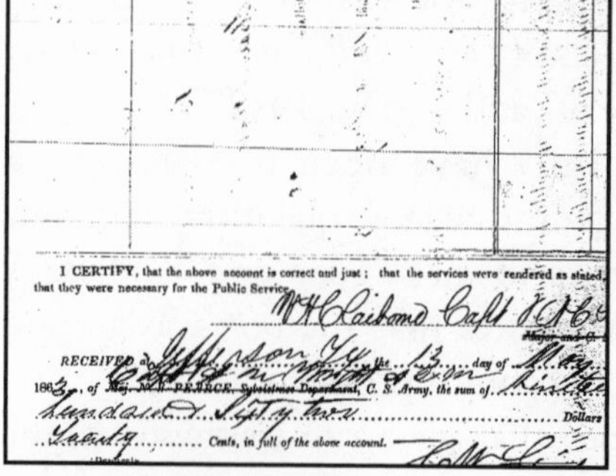

Fig. 14-25. *Texas* receipt, May 13, 1863. *Source: National Archives "Vessel Papers"*

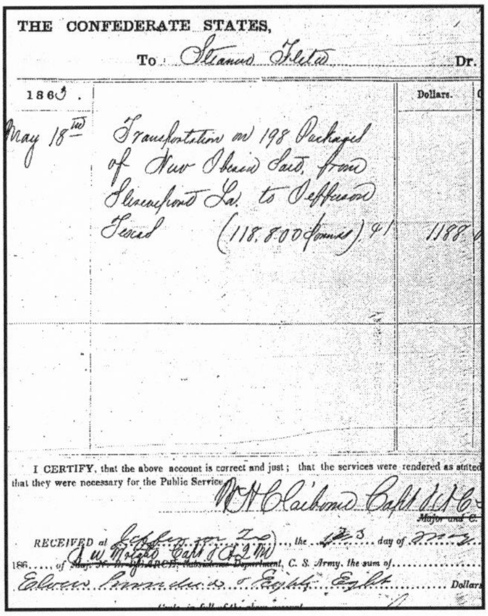

THE CONFEDERATE STATES,

To Steamer Fleta Dr.

1863.		Dollars.
May 18th	Transportation on 198 Packages of New Orleans Salt, from Shreveport La. to Jefferson Texas (118.800 pounds)	1188

I CERTIFY, that the above account is correct and just; that the services were rendered as stated; that they were necessary for the Public Service.

W H Claiborne Capt

RECEIVED at Jefferson Tex, the 23 day of May 186 . of ... C. S. Army, the sum of Eleven hundred & Eighty Eight Dollars

Fig. 14-26. *Fleta* receipt, May 23, 1863. *Source: National Archives "Vessel Papers"*

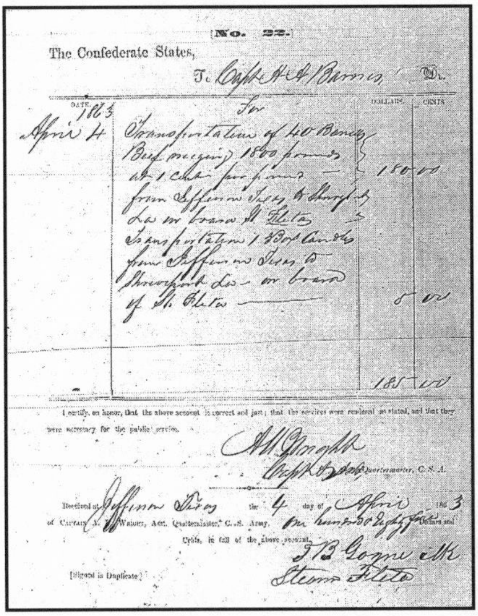

[No. 22.]

The Confederate States,

To Capt H A Barnes Dr.

DATE 1863	For	DOLLARS	CENTS
April 4	Transportation of 40 Barrels Beef weighing 1800 pounds at 1 Cts per pound — from Jefferson Texas to Shreveport La on board St. Fleta	180	00
	Transportation 1 Box Candles from Jefferson Texas to Shreveport La — on board of St. Fleta —	5	00
		185	00

I certify, on honor, that the above account is correct and just; that the services were rendered as stated, and that they were necessary for the public service.

A H Wright
Capt & Quartermaster, C. S. A.

Received at Jefferson Texas the 4 day of April 1863 of Captain A. H. Wright, Act. Quartermaster, C. S. Army, One hundred & Eighty five Dollars and ... Cents, in full of the above account.

[Signed in Duplicate.]

J B Coyne ...
Steamer Fleta

Fig. 14-27. *Fleta* receipt, April 4, 1863. *Source: National Archives "Vessel Papers"*

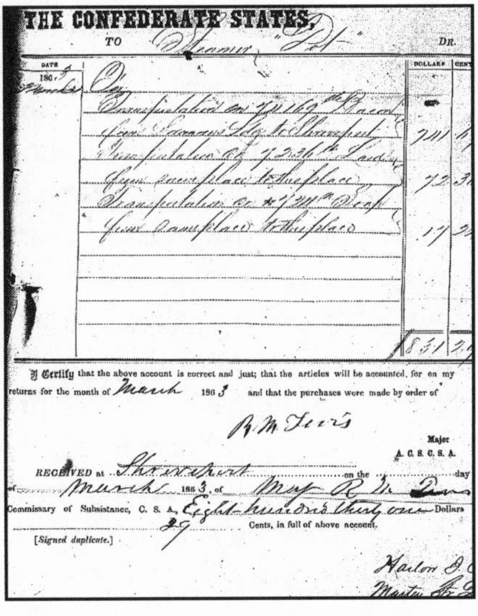

THE CONFEDERATE STATES,

TO Steamer "Dot" Dr.

DATE 1863		DOLLARS	CENTS
March	Transportation on 74169 lbs Bacon from ... to Shreveport	741	
	Transportation of 7236 lbs Lard from same place to the place	72	
	Transportation on 1744 lbs Soap from same place to the place	17	
		831	

I Certify that the above account is correct and just; that the articles will be accounted for on my returns for the month of March 1863 and that the purchases were made by order of

R M ...
Major
A. C. S. C. S. A.

RECEIVED at Shreveport on the day of March 1863, of Maj R. M. ... Commissary of Subsistance, C. S. A., Eight hundred thirty one Dollars 29 Cents, in full of above account.

[Signed duplicate.]

Fig. 14-28. *Dot* receipt, March 1863. *Source: National Archives "Vessel Papers"* receipts cannot have been the well-known ones that were created under contract by the military, because the government-sponsored meatpacking plant was not in existence until the end of 1863, and all of the movements of salt and beef occurred before June. It is apparent that the Stanley & Nimmo packery, which had been acquired by Elisha Price in 1860, was still in operation. The Black packery had been destroyed by fire in July 1862, and Price advertised in October 1862 for hogs to supply meat to the military.

On 19 September 1863, a contract was signed between James B. Dunn and Maj. William H. Thomas, commissary and subsistence officer for the Trans-Mississippi Department in Shreveport. The agreement stipulated that Dunn was to erect before 15 November "at or near Jefferson Texas" the buildings and machinery necessary for slaughtering and packing 150 head of beef cattle a day to produce pickled and dried beef, hides, and tallow. The government agreed to provide Dunn $40,000 for the erection of the facility and $0.06 per pound for the beef, which also covered payment for the hides and tallow. The government also agreed to supply 440,000 pounds of New Iberia salt by 15 November and 4,000 head of cattle from 15 November through 14 January 1864. That this plant was fully operational by the end of 1863 is indicated by the fact that the first products were officially inspected on 5 January 1864 at Shreveport.

Bill Winsor in *Texas in the Confederacy* says that this facility was located at the present intersection of Highways 49 and 59 on the western edge of Jefferson. All of the beef produced by this facility would have been sent out by steamboat, and the first shipment probably occurred at the end of 1863. However, there is no documentation for any beef shipments: the Jefferson record in the "Vessel Papers" comes to an end with the early June voyage of the *Fleta*.

There are only three newspaper records of boats operating west of Shreveport during 1863. The 16 February *Shreveport Weekly News* reports: "The steamer P. E. Bonford, which arrived here yesterday, from Jefferson, had aboard Maj. James Burnet's battalion of sharp shooters, destined for Port Hudson." This is not the 9 February trip recorded in the payment receipt—it did not take six days to travel from Jefferson to Shreveport. The 23 February issue reports that "The Robert Fulton arrived from Jefferson on the 19th inst." No other information is given, and this is the only record for the *Robert Fulton* during 1863.

There were two *Era* boats at Albany in December, as is indicated by an advertisement that appeared in the 22 January 1864 *Semi-Weekly Shreveport News* on the fifth: "RANAWAY. From the steamers *Eras*, at Albany, about December 1st, 1863, the negro man JESSEE, aged 25 years, about 6 feet high, yellow complexion. Said negro was seen in Shreveport on Christmas Eve, and has probably gone to Alexandria. A liberal award will be given for his apprehension."

Isolated mentions like that of the *Era* boats at Albany are important because there is very little information about ports and landings other than Jefferson during the war. D. H. Zachary and C. F. Mosely are listed in the "Receipts for the Republican" column as subscribers in Smithland between March 1862 and April 1863. Who was located at Swanson's Landing is unknown. The same column lists J. M. Swanson as a resident of Palestine in July 1862, and T. F. Swanson had died by April 1861. Nevertheless, Capt. Harlow J. Phelps of the *Dot* received $831.29 from Maj. R. M. Lewis in Shreveport in March 1863 for a March voyage (or voyages) carrying 74,169 pounds of bacon, 7,236 pounds of lard, and 724 pounds of soap from Swanson's Landing to Shreveport **(fig. 14-28)**. This voyage was taken in connection with a *Dot* advertisement that appears in the 16 February 1863 *Shreveport Weekly News*:

STEAMER DOT, HARLOW J. PHELPS,
    In command, being employed by the Confederate States to ply Red River and purchase Bacon, Bulk Pork, Flour, etc., for our army, will pay the highest market price for produce delivered at any point on Upper Red River.
    Will have Sugar, Molasses, Tobacco, Rice, Lowell's, etc., to sell or exchange for any of those articles, or will pay all *Cash if desired*.

The newspaper comments briefly on this advertisement: "We direct particular attention of our readers to the above, and if they have any provision, it behooves them to let Mr. Phelps, an authorized government officer, have what they can spare."

There is also one record for Mooringsport. On 26 January 1863, Capt. C. W. Stinde of the *Texas* received $83 from Maj. R. M. Lewis in Shreveport for the 26 January transport of fifty empty pork barrels from Alexandria to Shreveport and fifty-six and twenty-five pounds of bacon and eighty-three barrels of lard from Mooringsport to Shreveport

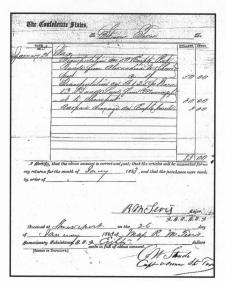

Fig. 14-29. *Texas* receipt, January 26, 1863. *Source: National Archives "Vessel Papers"*

(**fig. 14-29**). Stinde was also reimbursed $3 for the fee charged in Alexandria for the storage of the empty pork barrels.

The only mention of Monterey during the war in the Shreveport and Marshall newspapers appears in the 17 November 1863 *Semi-Weekly Shreveport News*: "We learn that ten negroes, in the employment of the Government, robbed and afterwards burnt the dwelling of Nat Graham, at Monterey, Texas. The negroes were arrested and confined in jail at Jefferson, and upon an investigation, all were released except three, who were committed to jail."

The relevant point is that the government was active in Monterey. Although the nature of these activities is unknown, Monterey was obviously an important place during the war, because the following seventeen persons are listed in the Receipts for the Republican column as residents of Monterey or Point Monterey from September 1861 through April 1863: Daniel Hartsoe, W. Godwin, F. Huffner, T. W. Anderson, Jeremiah Snow, John Maybane, L. C. Graham, Miss L. L. Rives, Mrs. C. D. Marshall, B. C. McReynolds, Robert Lowe, Mrs. E. Childs, Joseph T. Moore, T. M. Horton, N. Perkins, N. Gupton, and Col. M. Hewitt. Monterey may have been playing its traditional role as a cotton outlet, but with boat movements in the direction of Jefferson for overland transport to Mexico, perhaps through persons like C. A. Bulkley in Jefferson, who advertised as follows in the 26 February 1863 Marshall *Texas Republican*: "I wish to buy from 200 to 300 bales of cotton to take to the Rio Grande. Parties having lots to sell will find a purchaser by applying to me, in Jefferson, or Capt. Robt. H. Martin at this place."

EIGHTEEN SIXTY-FOUR

There are no actual records of steamboats operating west of Shreveport in 1864; however, the available evidence is highly suggestive. Kirby Smith made active use of steamboats. General Orders No. 29 from the headquarters of the Trans-Mississippi Department in Shreveport, which appeared in the 9 February *Semi-Weekly Shreveport News*, stipulated that "ALL details upon Steamboats in the Red and Ouachita rivers are hereby revoked." The reason for this revocation is not apparent. Porter's fleet, which eventually moved above Alexandria, did not arrive at the mouth of the Red River until 10 March.

Special Orders No. 168, which appeared in the 12 July *Shreveport News*, indicated that Capt. William McMasters, A.Q.M., had been assigned chief of river transportation and stipulated: "The Captains and owners of steamboats on Red river will by the 20th inst. furnish Capt. McMasters with a list of the men they may require as crews for their boats, for which details will be made especially for each boat." The directive also indicated that a boat "will hereafter make weekly trips between Shreveport and Alexandria, La., upon which troops between the above places will be forwarded."

One of the commodities almost definitely transported by Kirby Smith to points west of Shreveport by steamboat was cotton, as is indicated by an advertisement that appeared in the 12 January *Semi-Weekly Shreveport News*:

> OFFICE CHIEF QUARTERMASTER.
> TRANS-MISSISSIPPI DEPARTMENT, SHREVEPORT, LA.
> TO OWNERS OF STEAMBOATS.
>
> The Cotton Bureau of the Trans-Miss. Department have from Twenty to Thirty Thousand bales of cotton at landings on Red River and Lake Bistinieau and Bodeau, which I desire to have brought to Shreveport, La, and to Jefferson and Swanson's Landing, Texas.
>
> Sealed proposals will be received at this office until 10 o'clock a.m., Monday, the 20th inst, for the transportation of

the whole or any part of said cotton. Persons making proposals can see a manifest of the number of bales of cotton at the various landings on Red River and Lakes at my office. The proposals must specify the number of bales to be carried from and to what points and rate of freight per bale, and time within which the cotton will be delivered.

The proposals will be opened at my office at precisely 2 o'clock, p.m., Monday 25th January, 1864. All bidders are requested to be present. Quarter Master having the right to reject all bids deemed too high.

L. W. O'BANNON,
Lieut. Col. Chief Qr Mr.
Trans-Miss. Dept.
Shreveport, La., January 9, 1864.

Twenty to thirty thousand bales was a lot of cotton, and this was not an isolated incident. Capt. N. A. Birge was the quartermaster for the First Texas Battalion of Cavalry and was agent for the impressment of cotton in 1864–65. A small collection of his papers is available at Louisiana State University in Baton Rouge. One of the documents in this collection is a 5 May 1864 letter from Lt. Col. W. A. Broadwell with the Trans-Mississippi Department's cotton bureau in Shreveport to Birge in Jefferson, instructing him as follows:

Captain,

The Texas office has announced its inability to acquire sufficient cotton (on account of the action and competition of His Excellency Governor Murrah,) to procure the necessary army supplies from Mexico—which demands_____ energy and greater efficiency from this office—You will therefore spare no effort to increase your transportation—if it can be done without embarrassing the movement of the army. Send to "San Antonio" 1000 wagons loaded with cotton—and bring back to this place such loading as the adjut. of the Texas Office (to whom you will deliver the cotton) may be able to furnish—

Because wagons averaged four to five bales, Birge was instructed to transport about 4,000–5,000 bales to Southwest Texas, where it would be brought to Mexico and exchanged for army supplies. This particular shipment was not related to Kirby Smith's advertisement, which appeared many months before. Jefferson was obviously a principal center for cotton export to the west and army supply import from the west. The dimensions of this activity can probably be revealed through a review of the extensive Birge collection at the University of Texas in Austin. It is possible that cotton movements through Jefferson in 1864 rivaled those of the prewar years, although it probably can never be determined what portion of this cotton arrived by steamboat or was simply collected in the area.

The beef packery continued in operation in 1864, and some of the pickled beef and related products such as hides would have been transported out of Jefferson by steamboat. However, an 11 January 1865 letter by Major Thomas indicates that only 500 of the anticipated 3,000 beeves had been slaughtered and that part of the pickled beef was consumed in Jefferson and Marshall. In conjunction with the tallow production of the packery, Nussbaum & Lindsey in Jefferson was contracted to produce soap and candles. The contractors complained in June of deficiencies in machinery, labor, fuel, and provisions and indicated that the entire production of candles could be used in Jefferson. Whether soap and candles were transported by steamboat from this facility is not known.

The existing powder magazine across the bayou from Jefferson was once part of a munitions and armament storage complex that probably included three buildings built in late 1863. The existence of multiple Civil War buildings at this site is confirmed by a clipping from the 21 July 1865 *Trans-Mississippi Bulletin* in Jefferson that appeared in the 26 July 1865 Shreveport *South-Western* shortly after the end of the war. Reporting on Reconstruction troops, the clipping notes: "A detachment of Federal troops, consisting of Co. D, 8th Illinois Infantry, arrived in town last Saturday and reported for duty to the provost marshal, Lieut. Railsback. They are encamped near the ordnance buildings, on the south side of the bayou."

Lt. Col. G. H. Hill was in charge of the Tyler Ordnance Works southwest of Jefferson. His day book, which opens in March 1864 and closes in May 1865, contains various references to the transport of war materials to Jefferson by wagon. The day book would not contain references to boat transport out of Jefferson because such shipments would not be under Hill's authority. However, transport to Jefferson would have been pointless unless the intent was to store at Jefferson and then transport by steamboat, because most of the materials were destined for Shreveport. Shreveport could be reached directly from Tyler by wagon; therefore, the only reason for conveyance to Jefferson was to secure access to water transport.

There are no readily available records for the transport of war materials by steamboat from Jefferson's ordnance storage facilities, which is not surprising given the fact that there are no "Vessel Papers" for the area west of Shreveport after June 1863. Nevertheless, an 18 April 1864 letter from Hill to Thomas G. Rett, chief of ordnance and artillery with the Trans-Mississippi Department in Shreveport, indicates that waterborne transport out of Jefferson was the preferred course of action when sufficient water was available in Cypress Bayou: "For the last two weeks little work has been performed in the Laboratory, the reason being that 21 of my men have been down with the measles. However I will send out a train as I now have on hand 160,000 rounds of small arm ammunition, 1,700 cartridge boxes, cap boxes and belts, and I will have ready by next Saturday, at least 1650 small arms. . . . Shall I send direct to Jefferson or to Shreveport. I believe that by now the river must be down and I think it best to send to Shreveport direct."

EIGHTEEN SIXTY-FIVE

Lee surrendered at Appomattox on 19 April 1865, and Kirby Smith surrendered the Trans-Mississippi forces on 26 May, marking the end of the Civil War. As a consequence, the year 1865 must be divided into two parts, with June marking the return to a peacetime economy.

In January, a shipment of beef from Jefferson's packery reached troop units in the District of Arkansas and was found to be unsatisfactory. This shipment was almost certainly made by steamboat and was probably the first shipment outside the confines of the Trans-Mississippi Department. Major Thomas defended himself, his facility, and Dunn: "The long experience of the Gentleman in charge of the packery in the business is a guarantee to me that we can produce as good an article as ever was made in Cities of the Western States."

Cotton continued to be exported to the west through Jefferson. I have not been able to obtain any documents relating to government cotton. However, there is a document in the N. A. Birge collection that pertains to a private shipment from Jefferson to Mexico. Private sales of cotton through Mexico preceded government sales and always operated in competition with the government. The document is dated 31 January 1865 and is from Maj. A. H. Willie in San Antonio to Peter Dowd, the collector of customs at the port of Rio Grande City: "A. V. Darby is entitled to export into Mexico Six (6) Bales of Cotton . . . weighing 300 pounds, for account of Himsell & Co. said Cotton being exempt from impressment as per Certificate dated Oct 13, 1864 of Capt N. A. Birge aqm and approval of Gen E. Kirby Smith dated Dec 3, 1864 on paying export dues."

On the back of this document, there is a handwritten note by Willie that reads as follows: "This cotton can be exported at any port on the Rio Grande; but the Collector of Customs will first require proof that the same was transported from the vicinity of Jefferson, Texas; and if the permit has been transferred proof must be made that the cotton was transferred with it."

Two of the factors in the private movement of cotton from the Red River area, through Jefferson, and into Mexico are revealed in a 19 April 1864 *Shreveport News* advertisement:

> J. R. Putman   William Henderson
> Putnam & Henderson
> Commission Merchants,
> *Eagle's Pass, Texas, and Matamoras, Mexico,*
> References—G. L. Kouns & Bros, Shreveport, La.

This advertisement appeared for many months in the *Shreveport News*. The reference is to the famous Kouns brothers, who operated many boats on the Red River, including the *Era* series. Besides running steamboats, they operated as receiving, forwarding, and commission merchants in New Orleans through at least January 1862 and apparently moved this operation to Shreveport after the fall of New Orleans. This may explain why two of the *Era* boats were at Albany in January 1864.

The Texas Iron Works continued to supply the Trans-Mississippi Department. The Birge collection contains a 9 January Special Requisition No. 40 for 50,000 pounds of iron that was received by the office of the chief quartermaster at Shreveport and "Approved and respectfully referred to Capt. N. A. Birge aqm Jefferson who will fill this requisition." This iron was almost certainly transported by steamboat from Jefferson to Shreveport. Its destination is unknown, because the name of the person who initiated the requisition is not given.

Also in the Birge collection is a transportation receipt, dated Jefferson, Texas, 7 February 1865, indicating the following: "Received from N. A. Birge and promise to deliver to Capt. William McMasters in Shreveport, quartermaster stores and camp equipment, including 26 bars of iron." The receipt was signed by J. B. Goyne, who was captain of the *Fleta*. This was not a shipment from the Nash facility but a return to Shreveport of a portion of a previous shipment from Shreveport to Jefferson, as indicated by a list of quartermaster's stores dated 17 January 1865. The list indicated that 680 bars of iron and 70,672 pounds of railroad iron were shipped by Maj. George Tucker in Shreveport to N. A. Birge.

The reason that the iron was shipped upstream is that it was being used for the extension of the Southern Pacific Railroad to Shreveport, and Nash did not have the capacity to make any type of railroad iron. Before the war the Southern Pacific extended south from Swanson's Landing to Jonesville then west to Marshall, with an intent to extend east to the Louisiana-Texas line. The right-of-way between Shreveport and the line was owned by the Vicksburg, Shreveport & Texas Railroad, which completed only four miles west of Shreveport before the war.

At the beginning of the war, the people of eastern Texas offered the rails between Swanson's Landing and Jonesville for use in the extension east from Jonesville, as is indicated by the 13 September 1861 *Shreveport Daily News*. In September 1862, the Southern Pacific leased the Louisiana portion of the route from the Vicksburg, Shreveport & Texas Railroad; and on 4 October, E. A. Blanche, chief engineer for the Southern Pacific, advertised for a contractor to lay the track on the twenty-two miles from Jonesville to Shreveport. By early 1862, about six miles were graded and bridged.

In the summer of 1863, Kirby Smith intervened in these private transactions and ordered the Southern Pacific to complete the line to Shreveport for military purposes. The twelve miles of track between Swanson's Landing and Jonesville were pulled up in August. Kirby Smith supplied two hundred laborers and provisions, and by October 1864 the track was completed between Jonesville and Greenwood, Louisiana, slightly over the state line. The section between Greenwood and Shreveport was graded but never completed during the war. That efforts toward completion continued through early 1865 is indicated by the document in the Birge collection that records the only upstream movement of iron during the war.

As the war came to a close and the structure of the Trans-Mississippi Department disintegrated, Maj. William H. Thomas in Shreveport wrote to his friend Maj. John Reid in Jefferson a series of letters expressing first his intent to remain in Shreveport to surrender and second to flee to Houston. Jim Dunn was to be paid for the last beef products with bagging and rope, and Thomas requested Reid to send the remaining salt to Shreveport, where it could be put to good use. Thomas expected to take the *Fleta* in the event of flight, noting, "I will send you and Dunn some coffee by the Fleta." This is the last record of boat movements in the direction of Jefferson before the surrender of the Trans-Mississippi Department on 26 May.

The resumption of commercial steamboat activity on the Red River was immediate and explosive. The 14 June 1865 *South-Western* reports that a large number of strange-looking steamboats had arrived at Shreveport, and the 28 June issue reports that fifteen boats had arrived with full loads, including the *Fleta*, *Texas*, and *Eleanor*. Utilization of the route from Shreveport to Jefferson was also immediate. The 12 July issue reports: "The smaller class of steamboats still reach Jefferson with ease." The 19 July *Daily Picayune* reports the arrival of the *St. Cloud* in New Orleans, the first postwar record of a boat from Jefferson.

This immediate and high volume of commercial activity was precipitated by immense quantities of cotton that had been hidden and hoarded during the war. The wartime source is confirmed by the fact that the initial shipments preceded the availability of the 1865 cotton crop. The 26 July *South-Western* reports that cotton was "coming in with a perfect rush, both by land and water. We do not recollect of any time in the halcyon days of yore when it crowded on us any faster." The 2 August issue reports that 600 bales a day were arriving in Shreveport by wagon and that 30,000 bales had been received since the end of hostilities. The situation in Jefferson is reported in the 16 August issue through a clipping from the *Trans-Mississippi Bulletin* of the eleventh: "The weather still remains excessively warm and dry. The Cypress is falling, with abundance of water, however, for light draught boats to Shreveport. Business is not quite as lively as it has been. Cotton, nevertheless, comes in in large quantities, and every downstream steamer is loaded to the guards."

According to the 30 August *South-Western*, two of the boats that were operating in August to capitalize on these large supplies were the *Blanton* and *Pioneer Era*, apparently operating in that month strictly between Shreveport and Jefferson, because they do not appear in the *Daily Picayune*. On 2 September, the *Fleta* arrived in New Orleans from Jefferson and reports having seen the *Panola* at Jefferson, the *Science No. 2* on Cypress Bayou, and the *Independence* at Rocky Point. The *Blanton* and *Gossamer* were operating in the direction of Jefferson in September, and during the same month the *Panola*, *Science No. 2*, and *Pioneer Era* arrived in New Orleans from Jefferson.

The arrival of the *Pioneer Era* in Jefferson in August was somewhat of a feat, because this boat was 129 feet by 29 feet and weighed 219 tons, and the 23 August *South-Western* reported that Jefferson could only be reached by the "small fry" with careful management. The arrival was noted by the 1 September *Jefferson Jimplecute*, as reported in the 6 September *South-Western*:

> The river continues navigable to this port. We had no idea that so large a boat as the Pioneer Era could reach us on the present stage of water. There is no denying but that the lake navigation gets better each year. Since the first of January, last, there has been no day that boats could not get to Jefferson, and as the time has arrived for the fall rains to commence, we predict and believe that navigation will last the year out.
>
> COTTON.—BUSINESS.—From appearances on the streets we think cotton comes in faster than ever.—There is a large amount in the warehouses here, the most of which we think will be held until next spring. Business of every kind is very brisk, and increasing. Almost every house that will do at all, is now filled with goods, and still they come. Workshops of every kind are going up, and kept busy; prominent physicians and lawyers are coming in, and the prospects of Jefferson were never better.

The predictions on navigation were good, because the *Pioneer Era* continued to operate in the direction of Jefferson in October, as indicated by the *South-Western* for the eighteenth: "The Pioneer Era arrived on Monday night, from Jefferson, with a fair load of cotton. As Jefferson is now accessible to boats of the size of the Pioneer Era, and as the denizens of that burg have plenty of cotton we advise our steamboat friends to give them a call." The arrival of the *Pioneer Era* in New Orleans from this voyage is reported in the *Daily Picayune* of the twenty-fourth.

In November, the *Lizzie C. Hamilton, Beulah, Gossamer, Science No. 2*, and *Carrie Poole* arrived in New Orleans from Jefferson. By 6 December, the *South-Western* was reporting that "We can't touch Jefferson by water with a ten-foot pole." Nevertheless, the *Jefferson Register* was optimistic, as quoted in the 15 December *Texas Republican*: "There is a good prospect for navigation being resumed to our city soon. The Bayou has risen nearly two feet in the last few days, and we learn that White Oak, and Sulphur, and upper Red River are flush and rising. If this be true, we need have no fears from low water during the winter. There is plenty of water to afford navigation for small boats to this place at present, and we expect to hear the frequent sound of the steam whistle soon to cheer the merchant, mechanic, and farmers with their cargoes."

Again, the optimism was justified: the *J. R. Hoyle* and *L. Dillard* left Shreveport for Jefferson on the nineteenth, seeking a portion of the 16,000 bales of cotton reportedly warehoused at Jefferson. That these boats actually reached Jefferson at the end of 1865 is indicated by the fact that they are recorded as having arrived back in Shreveport from Jefferson in the 3 January 1866 *South-Western*. The *L. Dillard*, which was built in Shreveport and named after a local businessman and eventually wrecked on Soda Lake, is described in the 13 December 1865 *South-Western*: "The new steamer L. Dillard, J. J. Hope, master, leaves for New Orleans to-day. The Dillard was built at this place, and is just from the builders hands. She is about one hundred feet long and twenty feet beam—and draws light about 12 inches. She is well built, substantial hull and is well calculated for the present stage of water. She will make a capital Jefferson packet as soon as the water rises a little more—that is to say when it gets a little damp up that way."

The vibrant boat activity from June through December was based on wildly escalated cotton prices, which generated equally exorbitant transport costs. Middling cotton sold at $0.24 per pound on the Shreveport market on 26 September according to the *South-Western* and from $0.25 to $0.27 at Jefferson according to the 1 December *Texas Republican*, quoting the *Jimplecute*. A 500-pound bale at $0.27 was worth $135. According to various issues of the *South-Western*, freight on cotton from Shreveport to New Orleans rose from $4 a bale to $10 a bale in July, reached $15 in August and then $25 in September, fell to $12.50 and then $5 in October, and then went back up to $25 in December. So, a boat carrying 1,000 bales at $25 received $25,000 for the transport of cotton alone. Cabin passage from Shreveport to New Orleans was $60 in December. These were truly "palmy days on Red River," as characterized by Capt. Matt Scovell in his reminiscences:

> I struck Red River in August, 1865, nearly forty-three years ago. This was my first offense at steamboating; and, on the White Collar Line Steamer, "Pioneer," plying between Shreveport and New Orleans. Those were, indeed, "palmy days on Red River."
>
> The freight on a bale of cotton to New Orleans was $25; upstream, freight ran from what would now be considered . . . petty larceny. Passage was $60 between New Orleans and Shreveport. Captains were paid at that time $2000.00 per month, when they stood a watch at the wheel; Pilots $1500.00; first-clerks, mates and engineers $500.00 per month; second-clerks, mates and engineers $250.00; and balance of crew in proportion.
>
> Cotton at that time was worth 75 cents per pound, or, $375.00 per bale.
>
> The banks of Red River, from the mouth of Kiomatia, a distance of one thousand miles, were lined with cotton, and the only question asked by shippers of the Captain was: "How many bales will you take?" The freight on cotton from upper Red River at that time to New Orleans was $50.00 per bale. Boats on Red River were as thick as leaves on Ambrosia.
>
> Tuesdays, Thursdays and Saturdays were the regular days for leaving New Orleans and Shreveport. It was no unusual sight to see as many as half a dozen steamers leaving on each of these days for Shreveport and Jefferson Texas.

SUMMARY

Almost all the work on the naval history of the Civil War is devoted to military operations and to blockade running. Gunboats were, of course, steamboats, but steamboats operating in their traditional role as freight and passenger carriers are seldom mentioned unless they were serving transport functions in conjunction with the movement of gunboats. Gunboats are not mentioned in this chapter because none went west of Shreveport.

E. Merton Coulter in *The Confederate States of America, 1861–1865* states: "Water transportation played little part in the life of the Confederacy, because the blockade made it hazardous along the coast, and the Federal gunboats on the rivers disrupted traffic there." The hundreds of documents in the "Vessel Papers" concerning steamboat transport on the western waters, only a few of which have been covered here, make it clear that Coulter's broad statement must be modified somewhat, at least for the Trans-Mississippi West.

The intent of this chapter has been to demonstrate that the area west of Shreveport played at least a modest role in the war effort, particularly within the confines of the Trans-Mississippi West, and that this role was highly dependent on steamboats operating in their traditional capacity as transport mechanisms. The degree of importance of the area and the dimensions of steamboat activity cannot be determined fully on the basis of the documents that have been reviewed. The "Vessel Papers," which have been fundamental to this analysis, obviously only tell a part of the story. A fuller accounting of the dimensions of military-related activities west of Shreveport and the relationship of steamboats to these activities must await a review of the quartermasters' reports in the National Archives and special collections such as the N. A. Birge Papers at the University of Texas at Austin.

·15·
Seasons of Celebration
1866-71

PROSPECTUS

The burst of activity immediately following the end of the war was anomalous because it was based on pent-up supply and pent-up demand. Cotton prices and transport costs declined to normal levels in 1866. Nevertheless, the burst of activity was fortuitous because it was much more indicative of conditions after the war than before and ushered in a period of sustained high development for Jefferson. From the perspective of navigation to Jefferson, these were seasons of celebration.

This was not the case for the other ports and landings on the route, which never recovered after the war. Jefferson's growth and the demise of the other ports and landings were simultaneous and unrelated. In presenting the sequence of events, I have chosen to deal with the themes of rise and decline in separate chapters because the story of Jefferson's prosperity is complex enough in itself, and the decline of the other ports and landings was a prelude to Jefferson's decline.

The seasons of commercial prosperity in Jefferson were the worst period in its social and political history. Federal intervention in Jefferson was immediate, and the Marshall and Shreveport newspapers began commenting on conflicts between civil and military authorities in Jefferson as early as December 1865. Federal occupation troops began arriving in Jefferson in the first half of 1866 aboard boats such as the *J. R. Hoyle* and the *Una*. Full-scale Reconstruction and military control were established in Jefferson. There were killings, jailings, and trials, many involving Jefferson's prominent citizens.

Because this is a history of navigation rather than a history of Jefferson, these events will hardly be mentioned. Reconstruction and Jefferson's commercial activities were unrelated. The only effect on navigation was a slight increase in boat trips resulting from the movement of federal troops and supplies. Navigation and Reconstruction cross paths dramatically only in isolated instances such as the killing of William Perry and the burning of the *Mittie Stephens.*

Methodologically, the postwar period is also a season of celebration, initiated by the introduction of the "River Intelligence" column in the *South-Western* in January 1866. This column and its successors contain detailed descriptions of navigation conditions on the route and of boat movements and what they were carrying. Without this column, this history could not have been written. Most importantly, the cause and complexity of the decline of Jefferson and the other ports and landings could not be documented and separated from the traditional, but totally unrelated, story of the removal of the Great Raft on the Red River.

Shreveport kept very good records of warehouse cotton receipts and provides an annual summary of commercial activities at the end of the commercial year, which extended from 1 September through 31 August. Jefferson kept similar records, which are not available because of the absence of newspapers but are occasionally quoted in the Shreveport newspapers. The River Intelligence column does not provide a systematic account of what boats were carrying when they arrived at Shreveport from the west, because these shipments were not a part of Shreveport's business activity. Nevertheless, they are of sufficient quality to determine general levels of activity and particularly trends—the boat returns are generally compatible with other information sources.

Most of the boat returns in the River Intelligence column are based on clerk reports or manifests. Although some boats were missed, the reportage on cotton shipments is quite good. These reports use Jefferson as a proxy for all the ports and landings on the route. This is not a problem, however, because newspaper sources indicate that exports from ports and landings other than Jefferson stabilized at 2,500 bales a year during the 1866–71 period. These other ports and landings were, therefore, insignificant contributors to the boat returns.

The number of boats and number of trips west of Shreveport each year was much higher in the 1866–71 period than in the prewar years.

Cotton cannot account for this increase, because it was not until 1870 that cotton exports surpassed the reported 60,500 bales for commercial year 1857–58. It is thus necessary to pay attention to other commodity types, which are not reported at the same level of detail as cotton. The number of times mentioned in the River Intelligence column is a good indication of level of importance. The commodities in descending order of importance by number of times mentioned in boat returns for 1866–71 are: hides (156), beef (59), cattle (30), wool (27), bois d'arc seed (20), sheep (8), tallow (6), lumber (5), snakeroot (4), leather (3), skins (2), salt pork (2), cotton seed (2), and 1 each for pelts, sugar, mules, horses, beeswax, horns, hogs, flour, cow tails, and iron.

H. B. Orton & Company was the major dealer in hides and wool, advertising as the successor to N. G. Tryon, who operated before the war. Beef was produced by Wilson, Stoner & Company. Stoner left the firm to operate out of Shreveport, and the company name was changed to John R. Wilson & Company, until the Wilson Packery was purchased by a Colonel Elliott. Many receiving, forwarding, and commission merchants in the late 1860s dealt in cotton, including the major firms of Wright & Hendricks, Bateman & Brother, and Russell, Rainey & Company. All of these firms were partial cotton factors in that they extended long-term credit against future cotton crops on the authority of their complementary cotton factors in New Orleans. In 1870, full-fledged cotton factors such as W. P. Williams and the expanded Russell, Rainey & Company were established in Jefferson.

EIGHTEEN SIXTY-SIX

In 1866, thirty-six boats made 189 trips to Jefferson, including the *Alone, Alexander Speer, Beulah, Blanton, Caddo, Caroline, Carrie Pool, Cotile, Cuba, Cuba No. 2* (**fig. 15-1**), *Dixie, Doubloon, Fanny Gilbert, Fleta, George, Gossamer, Hettie Gilmore, H. A. Homeyer, Iron City, J. R. Hoyle, L. Dillard, Live Oak, Lotus, Lizzie C. Hamilton, Mattie Cook, Mittie Stephens, Mollie Fellows, Monsoon* (**fig. 15-2**), *Navigator, Pioneer Era, Richmond, Starlight, T. D. Hine, Texas, Thomas Powell,* and *Una.*

Of these boats, only the *Fleta* and *Starlight* had operated along the route before the war, and the *T. D. Hine* and *Texas* had operated along the route during the war. The *Caddo, Gossamer,* and *Live Oak* were the second boats to operate along the route under those names. Three boats had operated under other names during the war, including the

Fig. 15-1. *Cuba No. 2*, New Orleans, Louisiana, ca. 1867. *Source: From the Collection of the Public Library of Cincinnati and Hamilton County*

Fig. 15-2. *Monsoon*, New Orleans, Louisiana, ca. 1867. *Source: From the Collection of the Public Library of Cincinnati and Hamilton County*

Caddo (formerly the *J. T. Stockdale*), the *Cotile* (formerly the *Fair Play*), and the *Cuba No. 2* (formerly the *B. C. Levi*). The *Starlight* had been rebuilt, increasing her length from 162 feet to 167 feet and her width from 31 feet to 34 feet. The *Hettie Gilmore* had been with Porter on the Red River.

Although the number of boats and trips was much larger than in any previous year, the differences should not be exaggerated. In 1861, twenty boats made 105 trips to points west of Shreveport, but all of these trips were made in the first five months of the year. In 1866, boats ran throughout the year, including the summer months, and there were many boats that made a large number of trips, including the *Lizzie C. Hamilton* (48), *Alexander Speer* (12), *Gossamer* (12), *Fannie Gilbert* (11), *Mollie Fellows* (10), and *Pioneer Era* (10).

The *Lizzie C. Hamilton* took the place of the *Fleta* as the primary local carrier. The *Fleta* had been operating as a tri-weekly packet between Shreveport and Jefferson since 1859 and established the prewar record of 39 trips to Jefferson in 1861. In 1866, she made just a single trip to Jefferson, in January, and wrecked at Campti on the Red River on her return trip to New Orleans carrying Jefferson cotton. The *Lizzie C. Hamilton* made trips from Shreveport to Jefferson every other day, even when there was no freight to be carried, and established the all-time record of 48 trips in 1866.

The increased boat activity in 1866 and succeeding years cannot be accounted for on the basis of cotton exports. By actual count, the number of bales from points west of Shreveport in 1866 was 23,781, which was far below the commercial year 1857–58 estimate of 60,500 bales. Other significant export freights for 1866 were hides, cattle, and lumber. In addition, the *Lizzie C. Hamilton*, *Robert Powell*, and *National* took out full loads of salt pork and beef at the end of February without carrying out any cotton. These shipments were the first indicators of the existence of The Packery three miles downstream of Jefferson that was to play an important role in the level of commercial activity through 1870.

Apart from the occasional movement of troops on steamboats, the only effect of military activities on navigation in 1866 was government oversight of cotton shipments, apparently brought about by uncertainties concerning government versus private ownership and ownership within the private sector itself because of wartime disruptions. Bureaucratic delays do not appear to have had any effect on the level of boat activity with the exception of many complaints such as those reported in the 21 February *South-Western*: "Many of the steamboat captains are really discouraged, and talk about paying off and laying up. The time lost in waiting on government officials for a load, and its clearance, leaves no margin for a profit, to say nothing of the annoyances and perplexities they have to encounter. To calculate beforehand the time it will take to make a round trip in, is out of the question. Should any of them come within a week of it, he is at once accounted a prophet, and the balance do him homage. If curses, loud and deep, like buzzards, came home to roost, they would not lack for a full freight of that kind. Push ahead, gentlemen, until another war order comes out."

In January, there was a destructive fire in Jefferson, with losses estimated at $75,000–$80,000. The fire started when a stovepipe ignited the roof of the Violet Saloon and quickly spread to nearby buildings, including the City Hotel and the office of J. A. Carpenter's newspaper. Damages were restricted to commercial establishments, and navigation and navigation-related facilities were not affected.

R. W. Loughery, the editor of the Marshall *Texas Republican*, made a trip to Jefferson in late April and reported on the constriction of commercial activity brought about by interior rainfall and swollen streams:

> On Saturday we paid a visit to our neighboring town of Jefferson, and remained until Tuesday evening. We had not been there since the "break up." Business had been, until recently, very lively; but owing to high water, which has swelled all the streams, and rendered the roads in the interior almost impassable, communication has been measurably cut off, and trade was consequently dull.
>
> The citizens were entertaining high hopes that the railroad from Jefferson to Paris would soon be commenced, under such auspices as to lead to its speedy completion. This will render Jefferson a great place. All that is necessary to achieve this desirable end, is the proper degree of energy, enterprize, and public spirit, which we believe the business men possess. . . .
>
> Wright & Hendricks have the largest establishment West of the Mississippi River. Their warehouse is the most extensive in the State. They have a very large stock of goods. . . .
>
> Many beautiful private residences adorn the place. The bayou was high, but has fallen considerably. Two steamboats

were at the landing, and the streets were thronged with people. Altogether our visit was a pleasant one; so much so that we hope soon to repeat it.

The heavy rainfall indicated by Loughery in late April continued into early May, resulting in one of Jefferson's all-time worst floods. Cypress Bayou had been rising slowly from local rains for a number of days, but on the morning of Wednesday, 9 May, it began rising rapidly at a rate of two inches an hour. By Wednesday night, as reported by the 16 May *South-Western*, quoting the *Jefferson Jimplecute* of the eleventh, "The levee on the left side of Dallas street gave way night before last in front of John Faver's store, corner of Vale street, from the effect of the rapid current."

Still the water rose, increasing to four inches an hour on Thursday. By Friday morning the flood had reached its highest point, which was three and one-half feet higher than the previous record of 1849. The *Jimplecute* reported that "All the lower portion of the city north of the river and east of Vale street is inundated from one to four feet deep."

When the waters began to rise rapidly, the merchants moved all of their stocks to higher ground, but not far enough, for they did not think it would be possible for the water to rise above the record levels of 1849. Jefferson's streets were filled with floating merchandise, including hundreds of bales of cotton.

There was even a fire, as reported by the *Jimplecute*, which occurred on Friday in a vacant storehouse in which lime had been left: "The alarm of fire was given about 8 o'clock this morning, and the fire was soon bursting through the roof of Mr. Turner's storehouse on Dallas street, now occupied by Dr. Huey as a wholesale and retail grocery house. The goods were all removed from the building yesterday except a lot of lime, which coming in contact with water, caused the fire. The water was some four feet deep on the floor, and by great exertion the fire was stopped very soon."

The greatest losses were sustained by the property owners and thirty business establishments, particularly the firms of Batemen & Brother, Wright & Hendricks, W. P. Torrans, W. W. Harper & Company, Bennett & Roberts, John Faver, J. P. Durr and Son, Dr. Huey, W. F. Stilley & Company, and Talbot & Patton. The losses would have been even greater were it not for the fact that steamboats came to the rescue, as reported by the *Jimplecute*: "Yesterday morning the work of removing goods commenced, and was continued throughout the day. The steamer Starlight, the only boat then in port, rendered great assistance, and a large amount of valuable merchandise was saved by her. The Lizzie Hamilton came in from Shreveport about 10 o'clock a.m., and immediately went to work and rendered valuable assistance in moving property. About 2 o'clock p.m., the large brick warehouse of W. M. Freeman's estate, now occupied by Bateman & Bro., gave way to the mighty current of water, and fell in, a large portion of the brick and debris falling on the steamer Starlight, lying alongside taking on goods."

The *Starlight* emerged unscathed, arriving back in Shreveport on Sunday morning carrying 600 bales of cotton and thirty-seven hogsheads of sugar. In its account of the flood, the 16 May Shreveport *South-Western* says: "The Starlight was engaged three days in picking up floating cotton, removing freight, etc. The Lizzie Hamilton was running in the street, trying to save property. The Hine got up before the Starlight left, and lent her assistance in trying to save something from the flood."

The *South-Western* also reports: "The Jefferson packet Lizzie Hamilton arrived from the drowned city on Monday night with a lot of hides and 12 passengers. The Lizzie has been engaged the last five days in ferrying the streets of Jefferson, saving life and property."

It is obvious from these accounts that the *Starlight* and *Lizzie Hamilton*, at least, had been operating on the streets of Jefferson. The *Starlight* was operating in the port area, where Bateman & Brother was located. The *Lizzie Hamilton* was operating farther inland, running the streets.

The capacity of the *Lizzie Hamilton* to accomplish this feat is illustrative of the extreme shallow drafts of many of the boats operating in the direction of Jefferson. During the summer, the "small fry" or "mosquito fleet," as they were called, dominated the Jefferson trade. These boats drew much less than 3 feet of water.

The sternwheeler *Lizzie Hamilton*, at only sixty tons and measuring only 109 feet by 20 feet, was a member of this class. The draft of this boat is unknown. Comparative information from other boats suggests that she would have drawn less than a foot when not carrying freight.

The *Lizzie*, under Captain John Roots of Jefferson, was notorious for her low-water capacities, which were amply demonstrated in 1866 when she made forty-eight trips to Jefferson, including many from July through September. The 15 August *South-Western* jokingly suggested that the *Lizzie* must have carried *water*melons to insure passage when the bayou was nearly dry:

> John Roots' boat came in from Jefferson today with $140 in currency and two watermelons. The currency was the net profit of her last trip, and the watermelons were kept on hand for the purpose of using their contents when the Lizzie got aground in Cypress Bayou.
>
> The Jefferson packet Lizzie Hamilton was off for Jefferson to-day with a first rate trip, reshipped from the "big fellers" that cannot run on water flowing from watermelons. We understood that Capt. Roots has applied for a patent on the watermelon layout.

The *Lizzie Hamilton* had been built in Ohio in 1864 and entered the Jefferson trade in 1866. In 1867 she entered another trade and was abandoned in 1869. Captain Roots reentered the Jefferson trade on the *Lizzie Hopkins* in 1867, apparently without benefit of watermelons.

The *Starlight* was a larger boat at 167 feet by 34 feet. She had been built expressly as a Jefferson packet in 1858 and was one of the longest-running boats in the trade. When the assistance was provided to Jefferson in 1866, the *Starlight* was captained by Charles Hayes. Hayes died in February 1868, and the *Starlight* was sold into another trade. She burned at Algiers, Louisiana, on 23 April 1868.

EIGHTEEN SIXTY-SEVEN

In 1867, twenty-nine boats made 113 trips to Jefferson, including the *Annie Wagley* (formerly USS *Carrabasset*), *Armadillo*, *Caddo*, *Cotile*, *Cuba*, *Cuba No. 2*, *Dixie*, *Elnora*, *Fanny Gilbert*, *Flicker*, *Gossamer*, *Irene* (**fig. 15-3**), *Iron City*, *Lady Grace*, *L. Dillard*, *Live Oak*, *Lizzie C. Hamilton*, *Lizzie Tate* (formerly USS *Victory*), *Lotus No. 2*, *Mittie Stephens*, *Mollie Fellows*, *Monsoon*, *Navigator*, *New Era* (**fig. 15-4**), *Rose Franks*, *Starlight*, *T. D. Hine*, *Texas*, and *Warren Belle* (**fig. 15-5**). In addition, the *Independence* went to the lakes and the *L. Dillard* made a special trip to Jim's Bayou, bringing the total to thirty boats and 115 trips, which carried out 17,212 bales of cotton and significant quantities of hides, beef, and cattle according to the boat reports. The *Starlight* was the first boat to break the four-digit realm for cotton transport,

Fig. 15-3. *Irene* (third from left), Nashville, Tennessee, 1864. *Source: From the Collection of the Public Library of Cincinnati and Hamilton County*

Fig. 15-4. *New Era* and *Era No. 8*, New Orleans, Louisiana, ca. 1867. *Source: From the Collection of the Public Library of Cincinnati and Hamilton County*

Fig. 15-5. *Warren Belle*, Bayou Teche, Louisiana, ca. 1870. *Source: From the Collection of the Public Library of Cincinnati and Hamilton County*

carrying out 1,000 bales in February. The falling off in all categories was caused by a poor cotton crop in the summer, declining cotton prices, swollen streams at the beginning of the year that cut Jefferson off from the interior, and low water at the end of the year.

The trip by the *L. Dillard* to Jim's Bayou was the only commercial trip in 1867 specifically to a port or landing other than Jefferson. The *L. Dillard* went as far as Monterey and arrived back in Shreveport carrying 160 bales of cotton. The trip by the *Independence* also included Jim's Bayou. This was a fishing trip, with freight enumerated as "14 fishing poles, 14 barrels of water, 14 baskets of champagne, 14 natives, and . . . expectations of catching 14 fish and 14 headaches." The party returned without fish but with the story of having caught one 14 feet 7 inches, which was characterized as a whopper: "We don't mean the fish but the story."

In January, G. W. Dillard, editor of the *South-Western*, made a trip from Shreveport to Marshall and then to Jefferson. The ride to Jefferson was by horseback and took four hours through a "poor and thinly settled country." Dillard arrived on Sunday when the businesses were closed and the streets deserted. His impressions, as recorded in the 23 January *South-Western*, included a strong mix of positive and negative elements:

> Great changes have taken place since we last visited this place. From a village, composed of a few shanties, it has grown to be the largest place in Eastern Texas, and has a very flourishing trade. It has some large and substantial business houses, though the majority of them are mere shanties, erected without eye to taste or convenience. Who ever laid off the streets evidently had no idea of the future of the place. The main street is about as wide as a common alley, both sides of which are built up with one-story wooden buildings. Jefferson has yet to go through the severe ordeal through which Shreveport has passed. Some day a fire will break out in those wooden buildings, and no human power at their hands can save the entire street from destruction. It is a little strange to us that merchants occupying these stores should keep such large stocks on hand; but yet it is so, and they will one day have to pay a heavy penalty. Like most small cities, the people are too busy making money to think of improvements. In this respect Jefferson is probably unsurpassed in this region of country. Their steamboat landing is in a worse condition than ours, and those acquainted know we could not find language to give it a worse name. The streets are in almost the same condition as when they came from the hands of the maker, and except perhaps here and there, where some enterprising swine has improvised a wallow. And the sidewalks—what a burlesque! But we will pass on to something more agreeable.
>
> The citizens of Jefferson are generally a mercantile people, and appear to understand the money making part of the business. They keep large and well-selected stocks and dispose of them at small profits—so they tell you. They are up betimes in the morning, and late at night can be found counting their gains. They are a stirring people and deserve and will succeed. This is the place of trade of a large and rich scope of country, which no rival can take from it. The receipts of cotton from the

first of September to the 1st of January were upwards of 11,000 bales. There are now about 2,000 bales on hand, and it is still arriving freely. Business at this time is brisk. An old merchant informed us that more goods were sold last week than in any one in the history of Jefferson. We had ocular demonstration on Monday that it was a business place, and the knowing ones informed us that it was not a good day for business either.

In February, A. D. McCutchen, the editor pro tem of the Marshall *Texas Republican*, made a trip to Jefferson while Loughery was in the same place making plans to open the *Jefferson Times*. McCutchen's report appears in the 16 February *Texas Republican*:

The *pro tem.* made a flying visit to Jefferson a few days ago, and spent half a day very pleasantly in viewing the lions, wonders, and improvements of that flourishing little city. It was our first visit in fifteen months, and we were perfectly astonished at the rapidity of its growth, and the immensity of its improvements. Jefferson is blessed not only with gentlemen of capital and business capacity, but of enterprise and liberality unsurpassed by any town of its size in the Southwest. It is destined, in our opinion, to be the great commercial emporium of Eastern Texas. We may be mistaken, but that is the way it looks to us. Marshall and Shreveport have need to look to their laurels, or they will be outstripped by their perhaps less favorably situated, but more enterprising neighbor. The editor proper of this paper is now on a visit to Jefferson, where he has been since last Saturday. As he will doubtless have a "long say" when he returns, we shall say no more.

Loughery's report appears in the next issue of the *Texas Republican*:

We spent nearly all of the last and the greater portion of the present week in the neighboring city of Jefferson, enjoying the hospitalities and the agreeable society of its citizens. We had not been there since April last. The change in the physical and commercial character of the place has been, in the meantime, very great. A large number of new houses have been built, trade has been unusually brisk, and the population has more than doubled. Among the most notable of these new buildings, is the large and stately brick, on Dallas street, owned by Judge Mabry, now nearly completed.

It is four stories high, and covers the extent of the block south, to Lake street. When finished, it will be one of the most elegant and imposing buildings in the State. We were informed that there were over seventy-five buildings, at this time, in course of erection. To give an idea of the trade of the place, one house, (the Bateman's) we were informed, sold over fifty thousand dollars last month, in addition to its immense warehouse business; another in December last, (Wright & Hendricks, now Wright, Murphy and Co.,) sold over $55,000. Other firms have done equally as well. In fact, the trade has been unexampled. A large number of new buildings are in contemplation, to be put up as soon as the business season closes, so that, when the fall trade opens, Jefferson will possess commercial wealth and advantages such as her most sanguine merchants never contemplated.

Loughery visited Jefferson again in March when the weather was bad in the interior and farmers and planters were at home preparing for the summer crop: "The planting interests demanding the undivided attention of the farmers, there was, consequently, an apparent falling off in the trade of our neighboring city since we saw it last; but not withstanding the absence of farmers, and the unprecedentedly unfavorable state of the weather, she still gave unmistakable evidence of a commercial and trading point of no small importance. Cotton was freely taken at from 17½ to 18 cents, specie; corn was selling at $1.10 per bushel, and gold 134 to 136."

Dillard visited Jefferson again in June to attend a ball at Freeman Hall and reports on the continuing bad weather: "Business was dull, owing to the high water, the city being almost entirely cut off from the interior. The bayou was very high and rising fast when we left, and Dallas street was navigable for skiffs."

Too much water on land during the early part of the year was complemented by too little water in the bayou and lakes during the latter part of the year. The 19 October *Texas Republican* quoted the *Jimplecute* to the effect that the river and lake navigation was closing for the first time in two years, and the next issue reports that Jefferson's freight was passing through Marshall, where the commission merchants were doing "a pretty thriving business in the receiving and forwarding line." The 27 November *South-Western* reports 2,500 bales of cotton in storage at Jefferson that could not move because of low water, and the 18 December issue reports the same conditions with 7,000 to 8,000 bales in storage. Finally, the 7 December *Texas Republican* reports that the *Flicker* was "expected at Jefferson on wheels, having become disgusted with bayou navigation."

The perennial problems connected with low-water conditions provided a strong inducement to action, and Dillard was incorrect in his January observation that Jeffersonians were not interested in infrastructure improvements. There was talk about navigation improvements when Loughery visited Jefferson in February. The 30 October *South-Western*, quoting the *Jefferson Times*, reports preliminary efforts in the direction of an extraordinarily ambitious project: "Judge Mabry and a party of gentlemen left a few days ago to meet Captain Leavenworth and others from Louisiana for the purpose of making a preliminary survey, preparatory to commencing the work of locking and damming the lake and bayou. This work, when finished, will, it is believed, give navigation to Jefferson as long as boats can run in Red River."

Although a survey was conducted, no construction was undertaken. Leavenworth's survey report, dated Jefferson, 31 October, and addressed to the directors of the Lake Lock and Dam Company, appears in an appendix to Lt. Eugene Woodruff's 1873 report on Cypress Bayou. Leavenworth recommended a lock and dam near Albany to resolve the low-water problems on Soda Lake, which were characterized as "the only shoals of any difficulty between Shreveport and the Jefferson packery." Woodruff assumed that the high cost of $160,000 was the reason that the project was not pursued. However, Leavenworth's recommendations were initially adopted by Woodruff, establishing a relationship between the early local initiative and later federal actions.

Dillard, who was from Shreveport and often complained about the condition of the city's dirt landing, observed in his January visit to Jefferson that "Their landing is in a worse condition than ours, and those acquainted know we could not find language to give it a worse name." This must mean that the wharves and docking facilities that had been built prior to 1861 were neglected during the Civil War. Jefferson built a new wharf in 1867, with the contract given to A. U.

Wright according to the city records. The wharf was fully functional at the end of July, as indicated by two boat reports in the 7 August *South-Western*:

> The Gossamer, the smallest of the Kouns' family, entitled to wear two white rings and blow two long whistles, under the command of Jo Green, got off to-day for the new wharf at the foot of Dallas street, with a good fly-time trip, re-shipped from her "big buddy" the Monsoon.
>
> The sidewheeler Dallas street packet Mittie Stephens, Capt. Kellogg, Maurice Langhorne, clerk, came in to-day from the brand new wharf at the foot of Dallas street, with 150 bales of cotton, 40 head of fat cattle, a small list of natives and a copy of the Jimplecute, in which we find the following: "We are indebted to the steward of the Mittie Stephens for the finest sheephead we ever saw." That is more than Mrs. Jimplecute can say.

EIGHTEEN SIXTY-EIGHT

During 1868, thirty boats made 217 trips to Jefferson, including the *Caddo, Cuba, Cuba No. 2* (also called *Gem of the Antilles*), *Dixie, Era No. 8, Era No. 9, Ezra Porter* (**fig. 15-6**), *Fanny Gilbert, Frolic, Flicker, George, Golden Era, Gossamer, Irene, Iron City, J. M. Sharp, Lizzie Hopkins, Lotus No. 2, Lulu D., Mary Ellen, Mittie Stephens, Mollie Fellows, Monsoon, New Era, Pioneer Era, Rantidotler, Richmond, Right Way, Rose Franks,* and *Starlight*. The *Flicker* is actually recorded as having arrived back at Shreveport from Swanson's Landing on one of her trips; however, this trip was to Jefferson and was recorded as Swanson's Landing because the *Flicker* picked up 300 bales of cotton at that place from the wreck of the *Cuba No. 2*. Conversely, the cotton carried back by the *Dixie* on one of her trips to Jefferson was from Mooringsport.

The number of boats was the same as in 1867, but the number of trips was much greater because of the large number of trips by the *Era No. 8* (41), *Gossamer* (24), and *Dixie* (22). Collectively, the 1868 boats carried out 38,954 bales of cotton and large quantities of hides and beef. The *Lizzie Hopkins* was the second boat to break into the four-digit realm, carrying out 1,001 bales of cotton, 600 bull hides, ten horses, five bales of wool, and twenty-nine cabin passengers in March.

Fig. 15-6. *Ezra Porter* (second from right), New Orleans, Louisiana, 1868. *Source: From the Collection of the Public Library of Cincinnati and Hamilton County*

Unusual down freights in 1868 included Lake's Circus, which was transported in March to Shreveport by the *Lulu D.* after having been trapped at Jefferson by heavy rains in the interior; and a March voyage by the *Mittie Stephens* that included "thirty-five Indians from the Nation en route to the North and Europe, to give exhibitions of their skill in ball play, Indian warfare, &c."

The sternwheeler *Rantidotler* was the only square-bowed steamboat to operate on the route and made one trip to Jefferson under Capt. Henry Pitts in September. The dimensions of this boat are unknown, but she was apparently quite small, being the first boat to reach Jefferson at the end of a low-water period. When she docked at Shreveport from Jefferson, she was described as a "square-bowed kick-up-behind pile of boards." The editor of the River Intelligence column in the Shreveport newspaper used the term "kick-up-behind" to refer to sternwheelers.

The *Right Way*, which made eight trips to Jefferson in 1868, is described in the 13 November 1867 *South-Western* when she first arrived at Shreveport from New Orleans:

The Right Way, one of the most complete low water boats that we have seen in many a day, made her appearance at our landing last Thursday, only 7½ days out of the city. She was built expressly for the Red river trade during low water, and no pains have been spared in getting her out. She possesses the requirements of a first-class low water boat—strength and power. Her cabin accommodations are equal to those of many of the larger class of packets. We are indebted to her officers for the following description of the packet:

Hull built at Freedom, Pa.; machinery and outfit at Wheeling, W. Va. Is 135 feet long, 28½ feet floor and 29½ feet beam; has two boilers 24 feet long, 36 inch diameter; 2 steam capstans, 12-inch cylinders, 4 feet stroke; has boiler deck coming out flush with the main deck, thereby protecting cotton from the weather; has hose attached to the doctor, throwing hot or cold water to any part of the steamer; has superior cabin accommodations for 241 passengers, in rooms and open berths. Her timbers are 2½ by 5½, with plank on her bottom 3½ inches thick; all timbers, planks, &c., planed on both sides, and is of the very best Virginia oak.

She was built under the supervision of Capt. Noah Scovill and J. W. Warren, (the former captain and the latter clerk), who are owners. She is the only boat built expressly for above the Raft since 1860, and draws but twenty inches light. Capacity about 1000 bales.

The *Era No. 9* was one of the Kouns sternwheelers measuring 146 feet by 37 feet and weighing 169 tons. She was built in 1868 with the machinery and cabin of the *Fannie Gilbert,* which had wrecked, and ran the route through 1872. She is described in the 2 September 1868 *South-Western* through a clipping from the *New Orleans Bulletin*: "Through a dispatch to Capt. Ben B. Kouns, we learn that the Era No. 9, built by Capt. Geo. L. Kouns for the Red river trade, was launched from the marine ways at Madison, Indiana, yesterday, with machinery, boiler, cabin and everything complete above deck, on a draft of 13 inches aft and 10 inches forward, which, being an average of eleven and half inches under all proves her to be the lightest low water boat ever constructed on the Western waters. The Era No. 9 is to leave

Cincinnati on the 1st of September for this port, and will, on her arrival, enter as a through Jefferson packet."

There were three events in 1868 specifically related to navigation in the vicinity of Jefferson. The first was a freak accident involving the *J. M. Sharp*, which led to the drowning of Major Aulsman with the federal occupation troops, as reported in the 25 March *South-Western*, quoting the *Jefferson Daily Times*: "Capt. H. C. Hynson, Maj. Aulsman, and some others while crossing the bayou yesterday evening had their skiff capsized by waves from the steamer J. M. Sharp, which was just coming into port. Capt. Hynson jumped ashore, and the others of the party saved themselves, but Maj. Aulsman was sucked under the boat and drowned, and at last accounts his body had not been recovered. He was a United States officer on duty at this place, and much esteemed by citizens and soldiers for his many good qualities of head and heart. He leaves a distressed wife to mourn his loss."

The second event was another navigation improvement initiative. The 12 August *South-Western* quotes the *Jimplecute* to the effect that work was soon to begin under appropriations made by the city that would "insure navigation every day in the year." Such an assurance could be achieved only by a project of the dimensions envisioned by Leavenworth in 1867. These appropriations may have been related to the Leavenworth proposal, but that proposal was never enacted. The nature of these appropriations, which probably involved the purchase of the dredge, can almost certainly be clarified through the city records.

The third event was the proposed establishment of a barge line, as reported by the 9 September *South-Western*, quoting the *Jefferson Times*: "Mr. H. H. Woodsmall advertises that he will put a line of light barges on the Bayou, on the 14th, to run between this place and Shreveport. He is an old steamboatman, understands his business, and knows no such word as fail. He will be well supplied with tarpaulins and canvas for the protection of the freight, and proposes to make 'round trips' every week."

Woodsmall apparently established this line, because his advertisement appeared in the *Jefferson Times* on 4 September, and his projected starting date was the fourteenth, which would have been impossible had the barges not already been secured. No mention is made of this line in the navigation record. Because Woodsmall does not mention a steamboat in connection with the line, which would have been necessary for propulsion, it is probable that the barges were rented to normal carriers. References to steamboats pulling barges along the route are quite common.

The high level of steamboat activity along the route in 1868 was intimately related to the expansion of beef packing and the hide trade. Although The Packery three miles downstream from Jefferson was in existence at least as early as 1866, there are only a few records of the movement of salt pork and beef by steamboat in 1866 and 1867. By 1868, The Packery had come into its own, with twenty-three recorded shipments comprising at least 3,143 tierces (at 1½ barrels per tierce) and 1,799 barrels, together containing more than one million pounds of finished beef. No counts are available for four boats that definitely carried beef, including one that carried a full load.

The producer is first identified in the 12 February *South-Western*: "Wilson, Stoner & Co.'s beef packery, near Jefferson, up to the 4th inst, had killed 3000 head of cattle, and had 1000 or 1200 tierces of beef ready for shipment. The Dixie, which arrived in this port Friday morning, brought down 300 tierces."

The product was sampled by Dillard in Shreveport, as recorded in the 11 March *South-Western*: "We have been eating some dried beef and tongues cured at the Jefferson City packery, on Cypress bayou, and pronounce them equal to any we ever tasted. The mess beef put up at the same establishment is equally as good, and comes cheaper than pork."

Stoner left the firm in 1868 and erected his own packery below Shreveport in July, giving as his reason more constant navigation, lower freight rates, and greater proximity to markets. G. W. Stoner & Company became the largest packery in the South and one of the largest in the United States. Although the Jefferson facility of John H. Wilson & Company was more modest, it was extremely important to the regional economy and the level of steamboat activity, as expressed by a *Jimplecute* quote in the 10 December *Daily South-Western*: "To show upon what we base our calculations, we give the figures of Jno. H. Wilson & Co., in this season's business, estimating that only 10,000 head are packed, which is largely under the mark. In the first place, estimating that Wilson & Co., pay only $10 per head for their 10,000 head of cattle, it places $200,000 in gold in the hands of stockraisers. The beef, 20,000 barrels, at $20, brings into the country $400,000, one-third of which, we will estimate, is paid out to the employees of the packery, and thereby finds its way into general circulation. Next, we have 20,000 barrels of beef, besides tallow, hides, horns, &c., as freight and business for our steamers, to say nothing of the many up freights for the concern in the shape of salt, empty barrels, &c."

The 10,000-head projection was made for the 1868–69 packing season (beef was packed in winter). Although only 7,000 head were slaughtered, the general ramifications were as described, and the dollar figures can be proportionately adjusted. Cattle, in fact, sold at $15 per head during this season. The 4 December *Texas Republican* quotes the *Galveston News* to the effect that the Jefferson newspapers were advertising for fifty hands at the beef packery, which was expected to slaughter 7,000 beeves that season. The *Galveston News* also gives a selling price of $20 per barrel but indicates that one beef produced 2½ barrels of finished beef. If these figures are correct, the 7,000 beeves slaughtered in the 1868–69 season produced 17,500 barrels valued at $350,000.

The other important export commodity was hides, which were closely associated with beef production but not completely dependent on it, because hides were produced throughout the interior of Northeast Texas. The numbers of hides carried by steamboats are only occasionally enumerated. Representative numbers for 1868 include the *Dixie* (1,000; 2,000), *Flicker* (100; 1,140; 700 bundles), *Lizzie Hopkins* (600; 523 plus 75 bales), *Lotus No. 2* (1,100 plus 11 bales), *Monsoon* (1,200), *New Era* (100; 5,000), *Pioneer Era* (41), and *Rose Franks* (4,000). A bale contained about 50 hides according to the 2 February 1870 *South-Western*.

Most of the hides were exported by H. B. Orton & Company, which was located in Shreveport and Jefferson. The 16 October *Texas Republican* describes this firm as "too well known to need outside commendation" and points out that they were purchasing "an immense number of hides, peltries, wool, furs, tallow, beeswax, etc." The 11 January *Texas Republican*, quoting the *Houston Telegraph*, indicates that total Texas production was two million hides, that a hide weighed twenty pounds, and that dry hides sold at $0.10 per pound. The Houston trade was valued at $600,000 a year, meaning that Houston exported 300,000 hides a year. The article goes on to say that "the trade of Jefferson and Shreveport in the same line, is fully equal if not superior to that of Houston." The comparison is probably to Jefferson and Shreveport collectively.

When Dillard visited Jefferson in January 1867, he commented on the wooden buildings on both sides of Dallas Street and predicted: "Some day a fire will break out in those wooden buildings, and no human power at their hands can save the entire street from destruction." The buildings were highly inflammable and close together. Jefferson had no fire department, and the only way to fight a fire was to carry barrels of water from the bayou. Dillard's prediction came true on the night of 29 February 1868, as reported in the 4 March *South-Western*:

> DESTRUCTIVE FIRE AT JEFFERSON, Texas.—Loss One Million Dollars.—We learn from different sources that a fire broke out about 11 o'clock last Saturday night, in the store occupied by Rosenberg, on the bayou side of Dallas street, Jefferson, Texas and in a short time the adjoining houses were in flames. The wind was blowing strong from the southwest at the time and the flames spread with great rapidity in the direction of the landing, destroying every house on that side of the street to the landing. The flames crossed the street to H. B. Orton's storehouse and destroyed every building in the direction of the landing down to Messrs. Taylor & Graham's. The Times estimates the loss at one million dollars. The Jimplecute says fifty-one houses were destroyed. This is certainly the most destructive fire that ever visited this section of the country.

Loughery, who was partly established in Jefferson by that time as publisher of the *Times* in addition to the Marshall *Texas Republican*, described the devastation in detail but noted that business adjustments were already being made and that the disruption would have no appreciable effect on the level of trade. In fact, the fire stimulated economic activity through rebuilding and improved the quality of life of Jefferson because the city council passed an ordinance forbidding the erection of frame structures on Dallas and Austin Streets.

The 4 March *South-Western* states that "cotton wagons and Texas bulls were out in strong force." The 18 March *South-Western* quotes the *Jimplecute* to the effect that 1,800 bales of cotton were in storage in Jefferson. The 18 April *Texas Republican* notes that extensive preparations were being made to improve the burned district and that "The bayou was full, and steamboats were arriving and departing daily. Business was brisk, and merchants hopeful." The 27 May *South-Western* quotes the *Jefferson Times* to the effect that "Improvements are rapidly progressing in every section of our city, and Dallas and Austin streets are literally lined with brick, mortar, and lumber, and swarming with intelligent and industrious mechanics, under whose manipulations the various structures in course of erection are progressing most rapidly."

The 29 May *Texas Republican* notes that the bayou was high and trade still good, although not as lively as it had been. The work of rebuilding the scorched area was inspiring: "Several large brick buildings are going up in the burnt district, and it is believed that, during the year the entire burnt district will be filled with brick buildings. When entire blocks are thus built, it looks like liberality and confidence in the permanent prosperity of the place." The 13 June issue notes that all the cotton had come in from the previous season's crop and that business was dull, as was to be expected at that time of year, but that everyone "seemed in good spirits. Already business men are preparing for the coming season. About thirty large brick buildings have been commenced in the burnt district or in the immediate vicinity. The bayou was still high and the prospect is, there will be good navigation until the middle of July."

According to the 24 June *South-Western*, "Dallas street is pretty well lined with wagons this morning—more than we have seen any day during the week." The 16 October *Texas Republican* reports: "About forty new brick buildings have been recently built or are in the course of construction, at an aggregate cost of near, if not exceeding, $400,000." The same issue observes, "All the editors and correspondents who have visited Jefferson recently express their astonishment at the rapid improvement of the place. Our sister city is acting wisely. She is laying the ground work of an enlarged prosperity."

The 21 October *South-Western* cites the *Jefferson Times* to the effect that "cotton is arriving in that port at the rate of 100 bales per day, imparting a new and lively activity to the mercantile trade." The 30 October *Texas Republican* notes: "The city continues to improve. Cotton was coming in, meeting with brisk sales, and the merchants were doing a lively business. The season promises to be unusually brisk. Everything is being done to invite an active trade." "Jefferson is still alive with business. Dallas street was crowded with wagons loaded with cotton," according to the 4 November *South-Western*. By December, when Loughery visited Jefferson, the effects of the fire in February had been almost fully reversed: "The business of the place has greatly improved. The streets are lined each day with cotton wagons, and heavy sales of goods are made. Building still progresses. A number of new houses are going up, and others, started some time ago, are approaching completion. Everything exhibits prosperity and enterprise."

EIGHTEEN SIXTY-NINE

During 1869, thirty boats made 179 trips to Jefferson, including the *Belle, Caroline, Dixie, Dora* (formerly gunboat *Hastings*), *Early Bird, Enterprise, Era No. 9, Era No. 10* (**fig. 15-7**), *Flavilla, Fleta, Flirt, George, Golden Era, Gossamer, Judge Fletcher, Lake City, Leo* (**fig. 15-8**), *Lizzie Hopkins, Lotawanna* (**fig. 15-9**), *Lotus No. 2, Lulu D., Minden, Mittie Stephens, Pioneer Era, Richmond, Right Way, Selma, Texarkana, Travis Wright*, and *Twelfth Era*. In addition, the *Mary Ellen* made a fishing trip to the lakes but took along a little freight.

Collectively, these boats carried out 39,568 bales of cotton. The number of bales exported in 1869 was slightly larger than in 1868, but there were many fewer trips. The decline in trips is accounted for by the fact that there were no prolific carriers with recorded trips beyond

Fig. 15-7. *Era No. 10*, ca. 1875. *Source: From the Collection of the Public Library of Cincinnati and Hamilton County*

Fig. 15-8. *Leo*, Alabama River, ca. 1870. *Source: From the Collection of the Public Library of Cincinnati and Hamilton County*

Fig. 15-9. *Lotawanna*, Ouachita River, ca. 1870. *Source: From the Collection of the Public Library of Cincinnati and Hamilton County*

20, as was the case in 1868. In 1869, the highest number of recorded trips was 15, by the *Dixie* and the *Lotus No. 2*. This produced larger loads per boat, with six boats making trips carrying a thousand or more bales: *Fleta* (1,000), *Lizzie Hopkins* (1,200), *Lotawanna* (1,346), *Lotus No. 2* (1,100), *Right Way* (1,000), and *Selma* (1,500). In addition to cotton, large quantities of hides, beef, and bois d'arc seed were carried out.

The *Enterprise* and *Fleta* were the second boats by those names to operate along the route. The *Mary Ellen* was a tiny craft built in Shreveport that made local runs and was characterized, according to the 1 February 1870 *South-Western*, as "the blow hard, for she makes as much fuss as the biggest of them." The *Belle* made one trip to Jefferson carrying Noyes' Circus on Christmas Day in 1868. She returned to Shreveport in January without the circus, which arrived by the Southern Pacific Railroad. The *Selma* is described in the 28 November 1868 *South-Western* as the largest sidewheel boat in the Red River trade. At 600 tons and measuring 180 by 38 feet, she was the heaviest (but not the longest) boat ever to travel to Jefferson and made 6 trips to that place, all in the first three months of 1869 under ideal navigation conditions. In April, the *Selma* transferred 100 tons of pig iron to the *Dixie* for transport through Jefferson to Kelly's Foundry.

The 203-ton *Flavilla* operated along the route from 1869 through 1873 and is described in the 1 September 1869 *South-Western* on the basis of a Louisville dispatch:

> The Flavilla, Capt. John T. Roots' new sternwheel packet for the New Orleans and Red river trade, will leave for New Orleans at 5 p.m. today on her maiden trip. The Flavilla is a trim, staunch boat of light draught—strength and lightness being the requisites for the trade for which she is intended. Her dimensions are: length 130 feet; beam 32 feet; hold 4½ feet. She has a neat cabin, with accommodations for 30 passengers. The hull and cabin is the workmanship of those skilled workmen, J. R. Stuart & Co., of Madison. She has two engines 13 inches in diameter and four feet stroke; 2 four-flued boilers 22 feet long and 38 inches in diameter. She also has steam capstans and all other modern improvements. Her machinery was built at the Southern Foundry, by Kirk, Dennis & Co., and is perfect in every respect. The Flavilla has a capacity

of 300 tons, and draws only 15 inches light. She is complete in every respect and reflects credit upon her builders.

The *Twelfth Era* was a 205-ton sternwheeler measuring 136 feet by 29 feet that operated on the route only in 1869 and 1870. The 1 December 1869 *South-Western* provides a description:

> THE 12TH ERA.—The last time the 12th Era boat was here, Capt. Isaac Kouns complained that we had not told the people of these diggins what a nice little boat he had, how soon she was built and all about her. So here goes—taken from a Madison paper:
>
> The Red river packet 12th Era, built by J. R. Stuart & Co., for I. H. Kouns, is one of the finest specimens of a steamboat we have seen for many a day. From stem to stern, and from keel to chimney top, she is absolute perfection, reflecting great credit on her builders, and we feel proud of her as the production of Madison mechanics. The hull and cabin by J. B. Stuart & Co.; machinery by Cobb, Stribbling & Co., under the superintendence of H. J. Billings, which is said by experts to be the very best; boilers by N. Winter & Co., said to be the best and neatest ever built in this city; the rivet heads are as smooth as though they had been turned off on a lathe; the sheet iron, tin and copper work, by Hartley & Dorsey. Painting constructed by Sourrier, of Louisville, Ky., and executed by John R. Roler, of this city, is a superior job. The boat was built in just forty-five working days, and her machinery in less than forty. She was ready for delivery in seven days less than contract time.
>
> There, Ike, that is the best we can do for your little pet for the present.

The *Travis Wright* was a 202-ton sternwheeler that operated along the route only in 1869 and 1870. She is described briefly in the 19 May 1869 *South-Western*: "A correspondent writes us from Louisville that Capt. T. J. Reeder has contracted for the building of a stern-wheel steamboat for the Red river trade. She is to be 130 feet in length, 30 foot floor, and not to draw over 13 inches light when delivered, steam up, on the 1st of August."

The two major navigation-related events of 1869 were the killing of William Perry in January and the burning of the *Mittie Stephens* in February. Perry was a steamboat captain, the preferred contractor for improvements to Cypress Bayou, a Jefferson resident and mayor during the Civil War. He had been instrumental in bringing the first steamboat to Jefferson. Perry was accidentally killed by federal occupation troops in Jefferson. The 8 January 1969 *Texas Republican* provides some details on his character and importance:

> Mr. Perry was one of the oldest citizens of the place. We have known him for over twenty years, and a more quiet, orderly, peaceable, useful citizen was not to be found in Jefferson. He was a man of enterprise, a large property owner, and a successful merchant. The place owes much of its prosperity to him. He was a man of temperate habits, and unexceptionable in his bearing, never meddling with other people's business. He was not a secessionist. On the contrary, he was understood to have been opposed to the war, but since its close has never joined or sympathized with the clan of vindictive malcontents, who have endeavored to ruin the country, and the happiness of the people. He was universally respected by all who knew him. His death, under the circumstances, was an outrage.

His funeral, as recorded by the 9 January Daily *South-Western*, quoting the *Jefferson Jimplecute*, was befitting a steamboat man: "Capt. Perry was one of the founders of Jefferson, and has probably done more for the advancement of the place than any other one man. He was a northern man by birth, and has always been a warm and consistent Union man. His loss will be deeply felt, not only by his family and friends, but by the whole community and section. His funeral took place Saturday morning at 10 o'clock, and was attended by an immense throng of people. He was formerly a steamboat captain, and the steamers at the levee all had their colors at half mast, while every business house in the city was closed and all occupations stopped in honor of the deceased."

The Packery was in full operation during the 1868–69 season. The importance of this operation to navigation is described in the 27 January 1869 *South-Western*, quoting the *Jimplecute* of the fifteenth: "John R. Wilson & Co., have this week killed and packed 250 head of cattle per day. We consider this the best work we have ever known. This firm have killed 7000 head up to January 1, and have shipped up to this date, over 4000 barrels and tierces of beef, besides large quantities of tallow, hides, horns, &c. . . . The shipments of this firm is now at least one third of all the down freights of our steamers, and their freights up very heavy. The Judge Fletcher, on her last trip, brought up 2000 packages for the packery."

Another article in the same issue of the *South-Western* says that Wilson & Company had stopped slaughtering at 7,000 head on 25 January because of the poor condition of the cattle, providing a substantially different picture than the *Jimplecute* of operations through January. The 24 November *South-Western* indicates that ownership had been transferred by the next packing season, but that The Packery was still in full operation: "Col. Elliott, now proprietor of the Wilson Packery, is killing cattle extensively. He commenced on the 8th, the same day, we believe, the first were killed last year. We see from one to three hundred head coming in every day."

By May, the increased commercial activity in Jefferson and the improvements induced by the fire were beginning to transform the physical composition of the town from a one-street to a multiple-street business district, as reported by the *Jefferson Times* through the *South-Western* of the twelfth: "Jefferson is no longer confined to Dallas street. Marshall, Austin, Vale, Polk and Walnut streets, all now boast their numbers of large and flourishing business houses; and we are told that twenty more brick stores are under contract, several having been already commenced, to be completed by fall."

Loughery's visit in May was the last to be reported through the *Texas Republican*, because his Marshall and Jefferson papers were consolidated in Jefferson in June as the *Times and Republican*: "Our visit to Jefferson was exceedingly pleasant, for there we mingled with a population with which we feel identified. Socially the place is filled with gloom, but in a business point of view it continues to flourish. During the brief space that we had been absent, a number of brick houses had gone up, or been finished off, and quite a number, including whole blocks, were in prospective. Jefferson is exhibiting more enterprise, liberality, and public spirit than any place this side of the river, outside of New Orleans. All who visit this place are astonished at its progress."

In September, there was yet another meeting in Jefferson to consider improvements to the route, but whether anything came of it is not known, because the only information is what appears in the *South-Western* of the twenty-ninth:

> IMPROVEMENT OF THE LAKE.—We find the following notice in the *Jimplecute* of the 20th, over the signature of the enterprising merchants of Jefferson:
> The merchants of the city of Jefferson are requested to meet at Murphy's Hall, on Wednesday evening, the 22d inst., at 3 o'clock, for the purpose of taking the necessary steps to improve the lake between this place and Shreveport. It is hoped there will be a general attendance, as business of vital importance to the city will be considered. The Mayor and other members of the City Council are invited.

EIGHTEEN SEVENTY

During 1870, fifty-two boats made 294 trips to Jefferson, including the *Bertha*, *Big Horn* (**fig. 15-10**), *Bossier*, *Bradish Johnson* (**fig. 15-11**), *Charles H. Durfee*, *Caroline*, *Carrie Converse*, *Carrie V. Kountz* (**fig. 15-12**), *Cherokee*, *Dixie*, *Dora*, *Enterprise*, *Era No. 9*, *Flavilla*, *Fleta*, *Flirt*, *Fontenelle*, *Frank Morgan*, *Frolic*, *Gladiola*, *Golden Era*, *Ida*, *Ida Stockdale*, *Jefferson*, *Jennie Howell*, *Julia A. Rudolph*, *Lake City*, *Lightest*, *Lightwood*, *Little Fleta*, *Lizzie Hopkins*, *Lotus No. 2*, *Lotus No. 3*, *Lulu D.*, *Minnie*, *R. J. Lockwood*, *Rapides*, *St. John*, *Seminole*, *Silver Bow* (**fig. 15-13**), *Silver Spray*, *Texarkana*, *Texas*, *Thirteenth Era*, *Tidal Wave* (**figs. 15-14 through 15-18**), *Travis Wright*, *Twelfth Era*, *W. F. Curtis* (**fig. 15-19**), *Walter B. Dance* (**fig. 15-20**), *Wash Sentell*, and *Will S. Hays*.

The *Lotus No. 2*, on one of her trips, is actually shown as returning from Monterey, but she went to Jefferson first. Although this boat carried out 450 bales of cotton, it is uncertain what portion came from Monterey. In addition, the *Hornet* made a trip to Jim's Bayou, returning with eleven bales of cotton from Rolla White consigned to Stacey & Poland in Shreveport. Collectively, fifty-three boats made 295 trips to points west of Shreveport in 1870. This was the greatest number of boats and trips for any year on the route.

The number of boats was large, and the number of trips made by particular boats was large, including 25 by the *Julia A. Rudolph*, 23 by the *Era No. 9*, 22 by the *Era No. 10*, and 20 by the *Flirt*. This heightened

Fig. 15-10. *Big Horn* (third from left), St. Louis, Missouri, 1866. Boats crushed by ice. *Source: From the Collection of the Public Library of Cincinnati and Hamilton County*

Fig. 15-11. *Bradish Johnson. Source: From the Collection of the Public Library of Cincinnati and Hamilton County*

Fig. 15-12. *Carrie V. Kountz. Source: From the Collection of the Public Library of Cincinnati and Hamilton County*

Fig. 15-13. *Silver Bow*, Ft. Leavenworth, Kansas, 1869. *Source: From the Collection of the Public Library of Cincinnati and Hamilton County*

Fig. 15-14. *Tidal Wave*, Reeds, Minnesota, ca. 1876. *Source: From the Collection of the Public Library of Cincinnati and Hamilton County*

Fig. 15-15. *Tidal Wave* interior. *Source: From the Collection of the Public Library of Cincinnati and Hamilton County*

Fig. 15-16. *Tidal Wave* exterior. *Source: From the Collection of the Public Library of Cincinnati and Hamilton County*

Fig. 15-17. *Tidal Wave* exterior. *Source: Joseph Merrick Jones Steamboat Collection, Special Collections, Tulane University Library*

Fig. 15-18. *Tidal Wave* exterior. *Source: Murphy Library, University of Wisconsin–La Crosse*

Fig. 15-19. *W.F. Curtis,* Marietta, Ohio, ca. 1871. *Source: From the Collection of the Public Library of Cincinnati and Hamilton County*

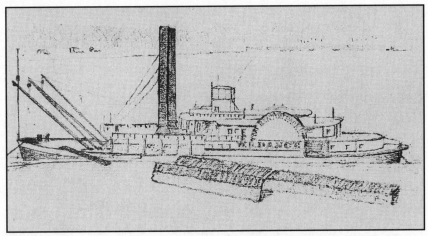

Fig. 15-20. *Walter B. Dance*, Missouri River, 1866. *Source: From the Collection of the Public Library of Cincinnati and Hamilton County*

activity was the result of the export of large quantities of cotton, hides, beef, and cattle. Collectively, the 1870 boats carried out a reported 63,807 bales of cotton. This was the first year in which cotton exports from the ports and landings on the route exceeded the commercial year 1857–58 level of 60,500 bales. Many boats carried out large numbers of bales, including the *Golden Era* (1,500), *Rapides* (1,100), *Julia A. Rudolph* (1,190), *Lizzie Hopkins* (1,250), *Ida* (1,200), and *Lotus No. 3* (1,155).

The *Jefferson* and *Texas* were the second boats by those names to operate along the route. The *Hornet* was a tiny 39-ton screw propeller steamboat that operated along the route from 1870 through 1873. All of her trips were to Jim's Bayou, and she never went to Jefferson. This was the only screw propeller to operate along the route. The *Will S. Hays* (**fig. 15-21**) was a circus boat that carried Dan Rice's Circus to Jefferson in January. The *Carrie Converse* was named after the wife of one of the leading merchants of Shreveport. The *Lightest* was described as "a little beauty—sits the water like a duck and is as light as a feather." The *Frank Morgan* was built on Soda Lake by Captain Tandy during the summer of 1869.

Fig. 15-21. *Will S. Hays* carrying Dan Rice's circus, probably on Ohio River at Cairo. *Source: Ralph Dupae, La Crosse, Wisconsin*

The *Charles H. Durfee* was a 267-ton sternwheeler that operated along the route from 1870 through at least 1875 and is described in the 21 September 1870 *South-Western*:

> The Charles H. Durfee, which made her first appearance at our wharf on Monday night, is admirably well adapted to this trade. While yet new she was burned at the New Orleans wharf last winter. Capt. Aiken subsequently bought the hull, an excellent one, and put new machinery in her and had all her upper works built in New Orleans. Her cabin is very handsome and neatly furnished, and can accommodate fifty passengers with excellent berths, all the bedding of which is entirely new and of the best material. The following are her dimensions: Length, 180 feet; beam 36 feet; hold, 5½ feet. She has 3 large boilers; 15½ inch cylinders and 5 feet stroke. Her carrying

capacity is 2000 bales of cotton, and draws, light, only 20 inches. Capt. J. A. Aiken is in command and Capt. Nat. Puckette, part owner, is in the office. An excellent boat and well officered.

The *Thirteenth Era* was a 298-ton sternwheeler that operated along the route from 1870 through 1873 and is described in the 2 November 1870 *South-Western*: "The 13th Era, which is now on her first trip up Red river, is a finely built craft, has a beautiful cabin and all the modern improvements. She has berth room for thirty-eight passengers and a capacity for twelve hundred bales of cotton. Her draught is 12 inches light. She measures 145 feet in length on deck, 32 feet beam, 3½ feet depth of hold. Her engines and boilers are by Herbertson & Co.; two boilers, 38 inches by 22 feet long; cylinders 12-inch, 4 feet stroke. Cabin by Cromlow & Coon. Painting by Jeffries, of Brownsville. Capt. Truslow will run her for a trip or two, when she will probably be turned over to Capt. Isaac Kouns, her builder. Success to this thirteenth member of the Kouns family."

The *Julia A. Rudolph* operated on the route only in 1870 and is described in the 18 August 1869 *South-Western* on the basis of a dispatch: "Julia A. Rudolph is the name of Capt. H. G. McComas' new Red river packet, intended for a New Orleans, Shreveport and Jefferson packet. The hull was built at California, and is of the following dimensions: Length 150 feet; beam, 34 feet; hold 4½ feet. She is extra timbered and fastened, and is a very substantial affair. Engine cylinders 18 inches in diameter, 24 feet long. The machinery is being fitted up by Jas. Rees, Esq. The cabin will be a handsome one, as W. F. Richardson is doing the joiner work. She will be completed by the 20th of August. Capt. McComas has named his Red river packet after one of St. Louis' favorite daughters. Success to the fair Julia, say we."

The *Jennie Howell* (**fig. 15-22**) operated along the route only in 1870 and is described in the 18 August 1869 *South-Western* on the basis of a Cincinnati dispatch:

> The new sternwheeler Jennie Howell, now lying at the foot of Ludlow street, will be completed a week from to-day. She is being built by Capt. A. M. Holliday for the Red river trade. Her dimensions are as follows: Hull, 146 feet long; beam, 35½ feet; hold 5½ feet. Her wheel is 18 feet in diameter, with 13 buckets 24 feet long. She has three double-flued boilers 22

Fig. 15-22. *Jennie Howell*, Lower Mississippi, 1873. *Source: From the Collection of the Public Library of Cincinnati and Hamilton County*

feet long and 38 inches in diameter; two engines of 4½ feet stroke, with 16-inch cylinders. Her cabin is about 130 feet long; and has 21 commodious state-rooms. Width of cabin ten feet. Space between decks 11 feet. Ceiling of cabin 7½ feet high. She has a Texas 40 feet long and 12 feet wide, containing 10 rooms for officers and crew. Pilot house 11 x 9 feet square. Pilot's wheel 9 feet in diameter. The Jennie Howell, as she lays in the river to-day, draws 14 inches forward and 18 inches aft. When ready for business she will draw 16 inches forward and 20 inches aft. She will be able to carry 600 tuns freight, and can stow 1800 bales cotton. As she is built for Red river, her hull is very staunch. Floor timbers 3¼ by 6 inches; bottom 1½ inches forward and 3½ aft. The entire boat was built under the superintendence of Mr. John P. Shearer, of this city. The hull was built at Millersport by Mr. Shearer; machinery, boilers and chimneys by Capt. C. T. Dumont, Cincinnati; painting by D. Williamson & Co., Cincinnati; ship chandlery furnished by William Shaw; upholstery by Knight & Co.; cabin outfit by Bailey & Co.;

carpets by Drown & Gibson; coffer work by B. Vanduzen; chandeliers by McHenry & Co.

The *Fontenelle* made trips to Jefferson from 1870 through 1872 and is described in the 25 May 1870 *South-Western*:

> At 3½ o'clock P.M. the new steamer, Fontenelle, William Conley, master, John Brooks, clerk, reached here from St. Louis, which port she left Tuesday night the 17th. She brings a fine freight—about equally divided between this point and Jefferson. Her polite clerk supplied us with Western dates of the 17th. The Fontenelle was built expressly for the New Orleans, Shreveport and Jefferson trade, and is entirely new. The following are her dimensions: length on deck 185 feet; breath 33 feet; depth 4½ feet. She has three boilers, 20 feet in length and 30 inches in diameter; 18 cylinders 4½ feet stroke and 14⅝ inches in diameter. W. B. Miller, Inspector of the Board of Underwriters, says of her: "A well built sternwheel boat, good machinery and workmanship used in the construction, and good for Red, Arkansas, or Ouachita rivers, and a No. 1 Mountain boat." She is a nice craft and we welcome her and her gentlemanly officers into our waters.

In contrast to these fair-sized boats was the diminutive *Minnie* (**fig. 15-23**), which operated along the route only in 1870, when she made two trips to Jefferson. She is described in the 13 April 1870 *South-Western*: "And now, following close upon the No. 9, there turns the point below a strange-looking craft, which had the appearance, as 'Jimmie J.' remarked, of a pair of boots sitting in a tub—the boot-legs represented by the chimnies. Upon investigation we found that it was a little stranger in our waters, Minnie by name, and commanded by Capt. William White, Sam Bell 'in the office,' so-called. She is a nice little craft, of light draft and built in 1869. She is 40 tons burthen, and her dimensions are: length 84 feet; 18 feet beam, and 33 inches depth of hold. She has two high pressure engines of 6 inches diameter of cylinder, with 7 inches stroke, and has a five-flued boiler 12 feet long and 40 inches diameter."

The most important commercial event of 1870 was the huge amount of cotton that was transported overland to Jefferson and carried

Fig. 15-23. *Minnie*, Natchez, Mississippi, ca. 1870. *Source: From the Collection of the Public Library of Cincinnati and Hamilton County*

out by steamboat. The 30 March *South-Western* quotes the *Jefferson Times and Republican* of the twenty-fourth to the effect that since the first of September, 58,285 bales of cotton had been received at Jefferson, 53,711 had been shipped, and 4,533 were still on hand. The 7 September annual summary in the *South-Western* indicates that only 2,500 bales had been shipped by all ports and landings on the route other than Jefferson. This means that of the recorded 63,807 bales for 1870, about 61,300 were shipped by Jefferson alone.

Under these circumstances, it is not surprising that 1870 was also the year that marked the emergence of the first cotton factors in Jefferson, with sufficient capital to extend long-term credit, exceeding the storage and transfer capacities of the receiving, forwarding, and commission merchants. This shift was noted in the *St. Louis Democrat*, as recorded in the 13 July *South-Western*: "the former mode of doing business is undergoing a change; and instead of cotton being shipped to New Orleans to be sold on account of the planter to cover advances, it is now sold to merchants and speculators in Shreveport and Jefferson, in great measure."

The most important cotton factor in Jefferson was the firm of Russell, Rainey & Company, successors to the receiving, forwarding, and commission firm of J. W. and J. R. Russell & Company. Russell, Rainey & Company advertised in the 1870 *Digest of the Laws of the City of Jefferson, Texas* as "COTTON FACTORS, RECEIVING, FORWARDING AND COMMISSION MERCHANTS, And Wholesale Dealers in Groceries and Agricultural Implements, ON THE LEVEE AND AUSTIN STREET, JEFFERSON, Texas. CASH ADVANCED ON CONSIGNMENTS." Also advertising in the Digest was "W. P. WILLIAMS, COTTON FACTOR, RECEIVING, FORWARDING AND COMMISSION MERCHANT, AND WHOLESALE GROCER AND LIQUOR DEALER, Corner Soda and Austin Streets. ALSO, HAY, OATS AND CORN FOR SALE. CASH ADVANCES MADE ON CONSIGNMENTS."

The 20 April *South-Western* noted the continuing progress of the town, in spite of the oppression of the federal occupation troops:

> We admire the energy and pluck of the citizens of Jefferson, who, despite the difficulties that beset them, giving outsiders little hope for the future of that city, they are pushing ahead. Success to them, say we. The Times and Republican of the 11th has the following paragraph: "Improvement is the order of the day in Jefferson. Several companies are going into the brick business, and a number of new blocks are in progress and contemplation. The expiration of another season will present as remarkable change as during the past year."

Jefferson obtained a steam fire engine in July, as reported by the *South-Western* of the thirteenth, quoting the *Times and Republican*. The engine cost $10,000. She is described as "9 feet 3 inches high, 18 feet 6 inches long without, and 27 feet long with tongue, 6 feet 2 inches wide." She was designed to discharge 500 gallons of water a minute through any line of hose under 3,000 feet and was claimed never to fail. It was an important factor in the containment of another destructive fire that occurred in Jefferson in August, as reported in a dispatch to the *South-Western* of the thirty-first by Collins of the *Jimplecute*:

DESTRUCTIVE FIRE IN JEFFERSON.
SPECIAL TO THE SOUTH-WESTERN.
JEFFERSON, Texas, August 26, 1870.
To the South-Western:

A fire broke out in the establishment of A. D. Tullis, this morning about two o'clock .The following establishments were burnt out: Towers & Usery; Heilbron; Benners; Pitcher; Russell & Co.; Nichols; Bloomingdale; Tullis; Birge; Nichols & Co.; Lowenthal; Watchholder & Jacobs; Ney & Bro.; Britt & Motley; Stemlein; Eldridge & Bro.; Dodd and several small shops, watchmakers, &c. Loss two hundred thousand dollars; insured for one hundred and twenty-six thousand dollars; mostly by Cotton Bros. Steam fire engine did noble service—the city would have been burnt to the ground but for the same. Russell's building was occupied by Pitcher; Dodd; Nichols & Co. Five or six large new brick buildings burned.

Linda Prouty, in an overview of Jefferson's wharves in a report on archaeological testing in connection with the 1872 wharf, indicates that Lynch and Delivan secured a contract in 1870 to build a wharf at Jefferson that was to tie into the existing wharf (obviously the one built in 1867). The contractors were also responsible for repairing the existing wharf. The completed wharf was to extend from the foot of Camp Street to the foot of Walnut Street. This suggests that the 1867 wharf extended from Walnut Street to the alley between Soda and Washington, which was the probable location of the 1854 wharf. Prouty does not indicate whether the Lynch and Delivan contract was fulfilled, and docking facilities west of Walnut Street would not have been mentioned in the newspapers.

The most significant navigation event of 1870 was the arrival of boats from St. Louis at Jefferson. St. Louis boats had become fully established in the Red River trade during the previous year and transferred freight at Shreveport for Jefferson, but it was not until 1870 that the St. Louis boats actually traveled to Jefferson. The first to arrive was the *Ida Stockdale*, which left Shreveport for Jefferson on 19 January with a fair freight and returned on the twenty-fifth. The day before the *Ida Stockdale* returned, the *Silver Bow*, another St. Louis boat, left Shreveport for Jefferson with a heavy freight, including 190 tons of railroad iron. The *Silver Bow* made an additional trip to Jefferson in

1870, along with single trips by the *Walter B. Dance* and the *R. J. Lockwood*.

These appear to have all been very large boats. *The Silver Bow* at 335 tons and measuring 212 feet by 32 feet was said to be one of the largest boats that had landed at Shreveport up to 1870. The *Ida Stockdale* weighed 377 tons, the *R. J. Lockwood* was 175 feet by 33 feet, and the *Walter B. Dance* weighed 571 tons and was described as "a whale among whales." The 1870 St. Louis boats appear to have been interested almost solely in up freights, with the *R. J. Lockwood*, for example, carrying 800 cooking stoves to Jefferson. Small quantities of cotton were carried out by the *Walter B. Dance* and *Silver Bow* and sold in Shreveport.

Many of the St. Louis boats were members of the Carter Line, with an initial advertisement in the *South-Western* dated 30 June listing the *H. M. Shreve, Silver Bow, Nick Wall, R. J. Lockwood*, and *Mary E. Forsythe*. The advertisement also indicates that these boats made connections with the *Bossier* and *Flirt* at Shreveport for Jefferson. Thus, the volume of trade was much larger than the five trips recorded by the St. Louis boats during the year.

Boats from St. Louis had traditionally operated through New Orleans. The direct trade with Shreveport and Jefferson was in competition with the Port of New Orleans and its merchants. It quickly came to include export as well as import freights and eventually included cotton, St. Louis having greater proximity than New Orleans to markets in the East. The St. Louis boats were also in competition with the Red River boats operating out of New Orleans, which formed the Red River Packet Company in November to set freight rates and assume shared risks and pro rata income. Members of this company included the *Carrie Converse, Charles H. Durfee, D. L. Tally, Era No. 9, Era No. 10, Fleta, Gladiola, Lotus No. 3, Red Cloud, South-Western, Texas, Thirteenth Era*, and *Tidal Wave*. Like most such organizations, it was unstable and disintegrated in June 1871.

EIGHTEEN SEVENTY-ONE

According to 1871 records in the *South-Western, Daily South-Western*, and *Daily Shreveport Times*, thirty-five boats made 158 trips to Jefferson, including the *Belle Rowland, Big Horn, Charles H. Durfee, Carrie A. Thorn, Carrie Converse, Clifford, Edinburgh, Era No. 9, Era No. 10*,

Flavilla. Fleta, Flirt, Fontenelle, Gladiola, Henry M. Shreve, Hamilton, Ida, La Belle (**fig. 15-24**), *Lady Lee* (**fig. 15-25**), *Little Fleta, R. J. Lockwood, Lotawanna, Lotus No. 3, Lulu D., Maria Louise* (**fig. 15-26**), *May Lowry, Oceanus, Rapides, Red Cloud, Right Way, Salado, Silver Bow, Texas, Thirteenth Era,* and *Tidal Wave.* The *May Lowry* made an additional trip in March to Jim's Bayou, carrying out 184 bales of cotton, which raises the number of trips to 159.

Boats registering a high number of trips included the *Charles H. Durfee* (15), *Lotus No. 3* (15), *Carrie Converse* (13), and *Tidal Wave* (13). On the way back from one of her trips to Jefferson, the *Tidal Wave* stopped off at Jim's Bayou, where she took out about 100 bales of cotton. Collectively, these boats carried out a recorded 69,442 bales of cotton, averaging 437 bales per trip. Excluding 35 trips for which there are no cotton records, the average load was 560 bales. Boats carrying large loads of cotton included the *Lotus No. 3* (1,050; 1,300; 1,350), *Carrie Converse* (1,175; 1,150), *Tidal Wave* (1,637), *Lotawanna* (1,171; 1,126), *Red Cloud* (1,333), *Charles H. Durfee* (1,653), *Red Cloud* (1,089), *Texas* (1,068), *Gladiola* (1,024), and *Ida*

Fig. 15-24. *La Belle*, New Orleans, Louisiana, 1877. *Source: From the Collection of the Public Library of Cincinnati and Hamilton County*

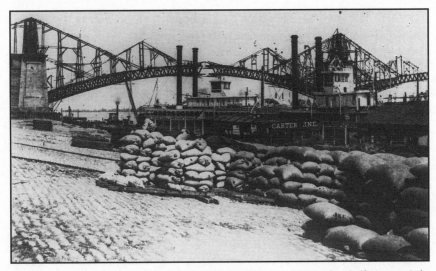

Fig. 15-25. *Lady Lee*, St. Louis, Missouri. *Source: From the Collection of the Public Library of Cincinnati and Hamilton County*

Fig. 15-26. *Maria Louise* at New Orleans, Louisiana. *Source: Ralph Dupae, La Crosse, Wisconsin*

(1,200). The *Charles H. Durfee*'s load of 1,653 bales was the largest recorded load ever taken out of Jefferson.

This is not all of the story for 1871. Unfortunately, there is a three-month gap (13 September–15 December) in the Shreveport newspapers that must be filled by the *Daily Picayune*. During the gap, 22 additional trips were recorded, as well as four new boats: *Cherokee, Garry Owen, Hesper*, and *Ruth*. The boat list for 1871 is almost certainly inclusive. However, the *Daily Picayune* records do not encompass local trips between Shreveport and Jefferson. This problem is easily resolved because in March 1872, Jefferson's Recorder's Office provided a count of 226 steamboat arrivals in 1871.

There was also additional cotton transported out of the area during the gap. Collectively, the boats returning to New Orleans from Jefferson during the gap carried 16,585 bales. It is impossible to tell how much of this cotton was from the area west of Shreveport, because some of the cotton was picked up at Shreveport and at various landings on Red River on the return trip to New Orleans. On the other hand, the recorded bales do not include cotton transported to Shreveport from the west by local carriers. Fortunately, Jefferson provided a count of 46,661 bales shipped from 1 September 1871 through 30 March 1872 that appeared in the 3 April *Shreveport Times*. Subtracting recorded boat returns of 26,543 bales for this period produces a figure of 20,118 bales for the gap.

This means that the total cotton exports from the area west of Shreveport were about 89,560 bales in 1871, which was by far the high point in the history of the route, exceeding the 1870 record by more than 25,000 bales. These huge quantities of cotton were carried out by fewer boats (39) making fewer trips (226) than in 1870, when fifty-three boats made 295 trips. Larger loads in 1871 only partly explain the tremendous falling off of the level of steamboat activity from 1870 to 1871. The major cause was the demise of The Packery.

Large quantities of beef were carried out from The Packery in the first two months of 1870 on the basis of the winter packing season. Yet The Packery is not mentioned in the navigation record after 1870. Large quantities of salt were carried up to Jefferson by the *Julia A. Rudolph* in May and July, apparently for use in the next packing season. However, the only record for beef export in 1871 was an insignificant five barrels by the *Charles H. Durfee* in June. Because beef exports from The Packery accounted for about one-third of all down freights as well as heavy up freights, the disappearance of commercial activity connected with The Packery was the obvious cause of the large reduction in boat trips from 1870 to 1871.

The reason for the demise of The Packery is not mentioned in the Shreveport newspapers. Stoner in Shreveport shipped tremendous quantities of beef in early 1871 but is reported as idle during the 1 September 1871 through 31 August 1872 season and does not appear to ever have revived. A generic explanation for the decline of both of these facilities is given in the annual commercial summary of the *Galveston News* as quoted in the 11 September 1872 *Shreveport Times*.

According to the *News*, beef packing in Texas was quite good in 1868, 1869, and 1870. Stock raising was a disaster in 1871 because of a lack of rain. Many cattle died in the winter because no forage had been produced in the summer. Low prices on bacon during the 1871–72 commercial year caused many plants to be idle, as was the case with the Stoner Packery. These temporary problems could have been overcome were it not for the fact, according the *News*, that Texas was simply too hot for the adequate curing of meats. The *News* reports the abandonment of meatpacking facilities throughout the state, with the exception of minor production for local markets. The newspaper also assumes an attendant large decline in the production of wet salted hides.

What the *News* meant by "too hot" was that Texas suffered from competitive disadvantages in relation to the traditional Midwestern meatpacking centers like Chicago, where cooler temperatures enabled a longer packing season. Meatpacking was viable in Texas only as long as Texas cattle were not available to the Midwestern meatpackers. Things changed rapidly in the late 1860s with the expansion of rail lines into the Kansas Territory. The first Texas cattle were transported out of Abilene by the Union Pacific (later Kansas Pacific) in September 1867. This marked the beginning of the great cattle drives and the beginning of the end of the Texas meatpacking industry.

The turning of Texas cattle to Midwestern markets is recorded in the 10 February 1872 *Daily Shreveport Times*, citing the St. Louis *Republican*. According to the *Republican*, the number of Texas cattle transported over the Kansas Pacific had risen from 34,700 head in 1867 to 51,320 in 1869; but the big jump was in 1870, when 131,360 were transported, increasing to 161,320 in 1871. To facilitate this enormous business, the railroad company had prepared a guide map of the Texas cattle trail from several points in Texas to several points on the railroad, particularly Abilene.

The *Salado* was a 110-ton sternwheeler that made only one trip to Jefferson, in 1871. She is described in the *Cincinnati Enquirer*, as quoted in the 2 December 1868 *South-Western*: "The Salado, a new boat built at Wheeling for Red River, arrived here yesterday. She derives her name from a river in Brazil. Her length is 130 feet; beam 26 feet; half-length cabin, with 12 state-rooms. She has but one boiler, 20 feet long, 40 inches in diameter, with six flues. With 200 bushels of coal aboard and 80 tons of freight, she drew only 20 inches. She will carry 250 tons, and has now 170 tons, principally Wheeling manufactures, for New Orleans. She is owned by Capt. Jas. Taylor, and others, and is in command of Capt. T. L. Taylor, formerly of the Annie White."

The *Red Cloud* (**fig. 15-27**), a 599-ton sternwheeler measuring 161 feet by 39 feet, made nine trips to Jefferson in 1871 and is one of the many very large boats that operated on the route during that year. She is described at Shreveport in the 7 December 1870 *South-Western*: "FOR NEW ORLEANS.—The new and magnificent packet Red Cloud, has her flag flying for the city to-day. To all who are skeptical on the

Fig. 15-27. *Red Cloud*, Red River, ca. 1870. *Source: From the Collection of the Public Library of Cincinnati and Hamilton County*

subject we would suggest that they take a look at this elegant steamer, and if they do not agree with us that she is a beauty and one of the most completely appointed boats they have ever seen, we will stand treat—to cigars—and make the barkeeper pay them. Her cabin is lovely, if not divine, and everything about her is in the most superb style. Capt. Brinker on the roof and Messrs. Russ and Mitchell in the office will assure safety and comfort."

The *May Lowry* traveled to Jefferson from 1871 through 1873 and in 1876. She was originally 138 feet long but was reported in September 1872 to be undergoing an extension. This produced a boat that was 210 tons and measured 196 feet by 31 feet. She is described as she originally appeared at Shreveport on her arrival from New Orleans in the 15 February 1871 *South-Western*: "Early this morning the new steamer May Lowry, Capt. Boley, came in from the city, four days out, with a fair trip. She left for Jefferson early in the forenoon. The May Lowry is a new boat, built at Pittsburg for the Upper Red River trade, and is one of the more complete low water boats that we have ever seen. She only draws twelve inches light and will carry one thousand bales of cotton on three feet. She has low pressure machinery and runs like a scared dog. She only carries one smoke stack, which gives her rather an odd appearance."

During 1871, there was a large increase in the St. Louis traffic, with twenty-four trips collectively by the *Belle Rowland*, *Henry M. Shreve*, *Lady Lee*, *R. J. Lockwood*, *Oceanus*, and *Silver Bow*. All of these boats were members of the Carter Line, which also included in the Red River trade the *Mary Forsythe* and *Mary E. Poe*. However, the latter two boats never went west of Shreveport. The *Flirt* was still operating in a transfer capacity for this line in the early part of the year, but she was replaced in July by the line member *Belle Rowland*, which made six trips to Jefferson in 1871, thirty-one in 1872, and eleven in 1873.

Cincinnati entered the competition against both St. Louis and New Orleans by introducing the *Edinburgh* to the Red River region in February on an experimental basis. This was also an extremely large sternwheeler at 393 tons and measuring 210 feet by 30 feet. This boat arrived at Shreveport on 20 February with a fair freight and a good passenger list and left shortly thereafter for Jefferson. She arrived back on the twenty-fifth carrying eighty-one bales of cotton, dropped the cotton off at Shreveport, and left the same day for Cincinnati. The trip was successful and was repeated three times by the *Edinburgh* in 1871. However, the Cincinnati boats were never as important as the St. Louis boats, and the only other trip by a Cincinnati boat to Jefferson was the *Champion* in 1872.

The Midwestern boats caused great consternation among New Orleans merchants and public officials in 1871. Import freights were a serious matter, but in 1871 the Midwestern boats began to take out cotton to places other than New Orleans. Of the boats operating west of Shreveport, the first step in this direction was taken in March by the *Silver Bow*, which came in from Jefferson on 4 March flying light and left during the night with a load of cotton for Memphis. On 9 June, the *Edinburgh* arrived from Jefferson carrying 660 bales of cotton, picked up 125 at Shreveport, and left for Cincinnati on the next day. On 7 July, the *R. J. Lockwood* arrived from Jefferson with 667 bales of cotton, picked up 250 bales from Shreveport, and left for St. Louis in the evening. The boat report notes that this cotton was to be shipped out of St. Louis to New York by rail. The reason for this shift was not mysterious and was noted by the editor of the Shreveport *South-Western* on 21 June, with a final comment on why the St. Louis boat traffic would be short-lived:

> We were surprised by a statement made to us by one of the largest and most intelligent cotton buyers, to the effect that he could ship cotton from this place via the Carter Line to St. Louis and New York cheaper that he can by the way of New Orleans. Our informant states there is a difference of eighty cents per bale in favor of the new route. Those of our people who are pouting about and always trusting to natural advantages as superior to railroads will do well to consider the significance of this one fact. Who would have believed a recognized prophet on a prediction of this fact five or ten years ago? And yet, by the operation of well known laws, that trade seeks the direct in preference to the circuitous route, and the speediest always of even competitive routes, it is an "accomplished fact" today. And if we had a road to Duvall's Bluff and Memphis, with the Mahone consolidation extended west of the Mississippi, a cheaper and quicker route to Liverpool would be had than even the Carter Line.

On 18 January, the editor of the Shreveport *South-Western* chided Loughery of the *Jefferson Times* on estimates of wagons in Jefferson and the implications for the amount of cotton entering the town: "The Jefferson Times says that there were between five and six hundred wagons in that place on the 10th. A lively and enterprising city is Jefferson, we cheerfully admit, but couldn't our contemporary be induced to fall a wagon or two? Five hundred wagons. Let us see. They must have averaged four bales of cotton, which would give us two thousand bales as the receipts for one day. Don't you see this won't do, friend Loughery."

Loughery was probably writing about the number of wagons in town, not the number that had arrived on a particular day. The volume of incoming traffic, as represented by the number of wagons in town, was compatible with the extraordinary amount of cotton that was shipped out of Jefferson during that year. The 1 February *South-Western* quoted the Jefferson *Times and Republican* to the effect that between 1 September 1870 and 27 January 1871, 19,271 bales had been received at Jefferson, 17,329 had been shipped, and 1,922 were on hand. The 29 March *South-Western*, again quoting the *Times and Republican*, indicates that up to the twenty-fifth, 34,085 bales had been received, 31,359 had been shipped, and 3,255 were on hand. The shipment numbers closely parallel the Shreveport boat return records, providing a cross-confirmation of the validity of both sources.

Reconstruction continued as a serious social and political problem, but without any deleterious effects on commercial activity. In fact, the 8 March *South-Western* claimed that Jefferson had a better reputation than Shreveport as a place of business "from the very causes that were regarded as prostrating to her interests. The fact of its being the seat of the notorious military commission, and the point where a large number of troops were quartered, gave it a prominence which it might not otherwise have acquired. These troops not only disbursed a large amount of money in the place, but their letters to friends all over the North familiarized it to thousands of people, who, but for this, would scarcely have known of its existence."

In early February, Jefferson experienced its fourth major fire since the Civil War, as reported in the 8 February *South-Western* through a dispatch from the *Times and Republican*:

BY TELEGRAPH.
FOR THE SOUTH-WESTERN.
Special to the South-Western.

DESTRUCTIVE FIRE IN JEFFERSON.
JEFFERSON, TEXAS, Feb. 7th, 1871

A fire broke out last night in the Russell Building, on Austin street. The whole block was consumed, including the houses of the following firms: Grinnan & Wayland, S. W. Stone, D. J. Shohan, Faulkner & Shyrock, Birge, Nichols & Co., J. P. & J. C. Alford, and Pinski. The Daily Democrat was also burned. The total loss is probably not less than three hundred thousand dollars; about two hundred thousand insured.

J. H. McEACHERN.

The fire engine again did good service, but only after a delay in putting it back in operation after it had run into Cypress Bayou seeking water—Jefferson did not have a municipal system. A new Hook and Ladder Company also did well, in spite of little experience. Both of the firefighting mechanisms were soon given a new home, as reported in a 19 April letter from Jefferson that appeared in the 26 April *South-Western*:

According to promise, we give you some jottings which may be of interest to you and your readers. The bayou here is receding, and has fallen since Monday 4½ inches, but is still six feet above low water mark. The lakes are also falling steadily, but with plenty of water for the boats running here. Business yesterday and to-day was tolerably lively, receipts of cotton about 400 bales each day, for which there seemed to be an active demand, yet almost everybody complains of the dullness of the times and the scarcity of money. No doubt the farmers are now too busy planting to come in with cotton. There are many evidences of improvements going on here; quite a number of new dwellings—some of considerable claims to architectural display—are being erected, also stores, etc., in place of those recently burned, and the city authorities are about to erect a large building for the use of the fire engines, etc., to cost $3500.

Yet another fire occurred at the end of June, as reported in the 5 July *South-Western*. This time there was understandable, but never proved, suspicion of the work of an incendiary:

ANOTHER FIRE IN JEFFERSON.

JEFFERSON, TEXAS, June 30.—A fire broke out last night between Austin and Dallas streets, in Jean Buron's storehouse. In the vicinity were mostly old frame buildings. The flames spread rapidly consuming all the buildings on two blocks except Schluter & Smith's brick storehouses. Total loss estimated at $55,000; insurance $13,000. The following are among the losses: W. W. Sloan, loss $5000, insurance $2500; F. A. Schluter, $4000; W. E. Penn, agent, $1500; W. B. Ward, $2000, insurance $1000; E. Klienbach, $12,000, insurance $4000; Gus Hodge, $5000; Watt's corner, $1000; Mrs. Brinck, $2500; Louis Vehon's stock, $350; Simons & Eberstadt, City Hotel, $3000, insurance $2000; Raymond & White, $5000; Dan Heyn & Co., $5000, insurance $2500; R. Waterhouse $5000; Jack Gill $1800, insurance $1200; Jacobs & Dimitry's stock is a total loss; amount unknown. It is supposed to have been fired by an incendiary.

McEACHERN

With respect to navigation improvements, 1871 was the year in which Jefferson's dredge began operations. The *Lone Star* was of a bucket variety and was built at a cost of $20,000, with the machinery supplied by Atkins & Burgess in Chicago and the hull built in Jefferson. The machinery appears to have been brought to Shreveport from New Orleans in late August 1869 by the *Enterprise* and then to Jefferson by the *Lotus No. 3*. The dredge is shown in operation in Brosius's 1872 *Bird's Eye View of Jefferson, Texas* (**fig. 15-28**) and was described in an 1873 Corps report after she was put in operation as "an excellent machine for dredging sand and clay" and was said to have done "good service in pulling stumps—a kind of work for which a dredge is not specially adapted."

As the *Lone Star* was nearing completion, she was described in the *Jefferson Herald*, as quoted in the 25 January 1871 *South-Western*: "This splendid piece of workmanship is fast assuming huge proportions, and when completed will be as fine and staunch in every respect as was ever built. It is expected that this dredger is to do very difficult work, and from the timbers in it, she will most certainly prove a complete success. The machinery will, in a few days, be ready to set in position, and in a short time the work of dredging will be commenced."

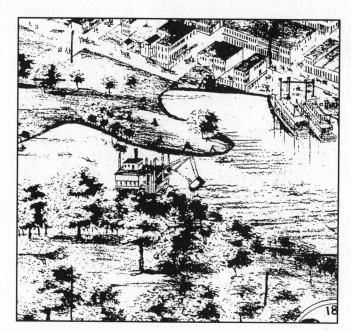

Fig. 15-28.
Jefferson's
dredge.
*Source: Library
of Congress*

The *Lone Star* appears to have begun work at Potato Bend between the town and The Packery, where a cutoff was completed in late June. Boats immediately began using the narrow cutoff in spite of falling waters, and most had to use their steam capstans to pull themselves through. The first boat to report having passed through was *La Belle*, at 510 tons and measuring 178 feet by 40 feet. Her account of the new passage, which appeared in the 30 June 1871 *Daily South-Western*, explained part of the difficulty: "There is only four feet at the foot of the Potato Bend cut-off. There is six feet in Potato Bend, but the dredge boat filled up the end of it, or, in other words, made a dam across the regular channel to throw the water through the cut-off. There is about ten feet through the cut-off until you get to the foot, where the dredge boat left, unfinished, a ridge all the way across it, on which there is only four feet."

The editor of the *Daily South-Western* was much amused about the improvement efforts and skeptical about the results, as expressed in the 22 July issue: "The Jefferson people seem determined to have a channel in their bayou if they have to knock the bottom out of it. They have a large dredge-boat hard at work now, attempting to accomplish that object. The question is, if they do knock the bottom out, will it stay out? We opine not. The next rise will deposit sediment in the channel again, so that, when the Bayou gets low they will have to repeat the digging-out operation again. We would advise the Jefferson folks to move their town down here where we have good navigation the entire year."

The Potato Bend improvement was, however, permanent and used by all subsequent boats, apparently without the need for additional dredging. The officers of the *Carrie Converse* reported in the 12 August *Daily South-Western* that "the lump or reef which annoyed the boats so much at the foot of the new cut-off has been worn away by the constant pulling of boats over it, and there is now plenty of water through the cut-off from head to foot."

SUMMARY

The key navigation feature of the 1866–71 period was the high number of boats and trips, culminating in 1870 when fifty-three boats made 295 trips to points west of Shreveport. The number of boats operating along the route and the number of trips made by those boats was much higher in the 1866–71 period than in the 1856–60 prewar period. However, the acceleration of commerce in the prewar period that reached its high point in the first year of the war found its natural culmination in 1866. Activity in 1865 after the war ended offered a suggestion of what was to come; but this year was anomalous because of the peculiar circumstances that had been generated by the suspension of commercial activity during the war.

The postwar expansion of commerce was not based initially on cotton exports. The war had a devastating effect on cotton production, and postwar labor difficulties made recovery slow. It was not until 1870 that cotton exports reached the levels apparently sustained in the immediate prewar years. The postwar high levels of steamboat activity were based on export items other than cotton and on increased imports to meet the needs of a rapidly expanding population to the west. Among export items other than cotton, beef was the commodity that generated the most activity. The demise of The Packery in 1870 triggered a sharp decline in boats and trips.

The decline would have been much larger had it not been for the fact that 1871 was the high year for cotton exports. Of the 89,560 bales that were exported in 1871, all but approximately 2,500 were from Jefferson. Advertisements for navigation-related commercial facilities at the other ports and landings on the route were prominent before the war and absent after the war; other ports and landings are not mentioned in steamboat advertisements after early 1867. Although boats apparently continued to stop at these other ports and landings, they did not play a part in the postwar expansion of commerce. Their decline was unrelated to Jefferson's expansion.

The boats operating after the war were much larger than those before the war. Boats longer than 200 feet were not uncommon; however, it was the smaller craft like the 109-foot *Lizzie C. Hamilton* that registered the largest number of trips. The most dramatic change in the fleet composition was the switch from sidewheelers, which were dominant before the war, to sternwheelers. Of the 125 boats that operated along the route during the 1866–71 period, approximately two-thirds were sternwheelers.

The boat list for the 1866–71 period is complete. All boats that went west of Shreveport stopped at Shreveport, and the newspaper column dealing with navigation provides detailed coverage of boat movements. There is only one small gap in the record, in the year 1871, and this is filled by the *Daily Picayune*, because it is nearly impossible that any local carrier would have operated out of Shreveport only during the missing period. The introduction of the Midwestern boats was an important phenomenon, but that did not affect the level of steamboat activity. Of the 126 boats that operated along the route during the 1866–71 period, only the tiny screw propeller *Hornet* never made a trip to Jefferson.

The dramatic increases in commercial activity after the war were restricted to Jefferson and marked the decline of the intermediate ports and landings. The cause of their decline was soon to catch up with Jefferson, precipitating a rapid falling off of cotton exports and steamboat activity. Reconstruction and devastating fires did not affect the bright promises of the future that were conveyed by every visitor to Jefferson during the postwar period. It was a new transport mode that swept steamboats off the waters of the Western rivers after the Civil War and destroyed towns such as Jefferson whose commercial primacy was based on navigation.

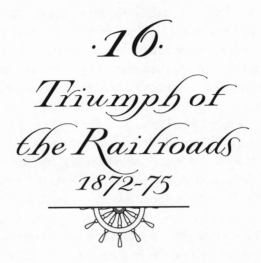

·16·

Triumph of the Railroads
1872-75

OVERVIEW

This new transport mode was the railroad. It was, of course, an old technology and one that had knocked steamboats off the waters of the Eastern rivers before the Civil War. It played a similar role after the war in the lower Mississippi River valley and in states to the west such as Texas. Within a few years after the war, the southern and northern ports and landings on the route were destroyed, and in another few years Jefferson was devastated.

The local events were part of a much larger drama involving hundreds of ports and landings. Shreveport's steamboat activity fell into a spiral of decline, closely paralleling that of Jefferson. The trade of the Red River area was oriented away from New Orleans and toward Midwestern cities such as St. Louis, with direct rail connections with the Eastern seaboard manufacturers and the sea route to England from New York. It was no longer necessary to pursue the circuitous route out of New Orleans through the Gulf and up the East Coast. St. Louis became a cotton center replacing New Orleans as the destination for Texas and Arkansas cotton. The steamboat trade of the Midwestern cities with places like Shreveport, which had risen to fifty-eight arrivals in commercial year 1871–72, was extinguished by competition from the rails.

The expansion of the rail system to the west was rapid after the war, and the newspapers were filled with information on the progressive development of the rails. Every town, including Jefferson, wanted to be on a rail line. Emissaries were sent by the railroad companies; deals were made to acquire property; towns bickered over where the rails should go; men and equipment arrived by steamboat; road beds were prepared; tracks were laid; and locomotives were put in operation.

Interior towns such as Dallas benefited greatly. New towns such as Longview emerged from nowhere along the rails. Cotton agriculture expanded rapidly to the west beyond Dallas, and immigrants flooded the area. Towns such as Jefferson, whose commercial activity was predicated on the old transport mode, suffered. But, the triumph of the railroads was not simply over the steamboats, which they hardly noticed; the rails opened the West and transformed an existing economic and social structure whose day had passed.

The place of the rails in Jefferson's demise has already been demonstrated by Ben Cooner in a 1965 thesis on "The Rise and Decline of Jefferson, Texas." But Cooner's thesis has had little effect on the prevailing assumption that Jefferson's decline was caused by the removal of the raft on the Red River. The assumption that raft removal was the cause arose out of the observation that the decline appeared to have begun around 1873, the same year as raft removal, and it was widely known that raft removal would ultimately have consequences for the navigability of the route. The correlation is reasonable but incorrect. The objective of the present chapter is to demonstrate that the rails were the cause through the perspective of the people who lived through the events.

RAILROAD EXPANSION

Before the Civil War, there were only a few hundred miles of railroad track in Texas, all of which was in Northeast Texas and in the Houston-Galveston area. The most important rail in Northeast Texas was the Southern Pacific, which extended from Swanson's Landing on Caddo Lake south to Jonesville then west to Marshall. This rail greatly enhanced the importance of Swanson's Landing but unintentionally. The Southern Pacific was envisioned as an east-west line. The north-south portion between Swanson's Landing and Jonesville was built to supply materials by steamboat for the east-west route when the Vicksburg, Shreveport & Texas Railroad, which was under other ownership, failed to construct a rail from Shreveport west to connect with the Southern Pacific at the state line.

The Vicksburg, Shreveport & Texas Railroad, which was under charter in Louisiana, completed a rail from the Mississippi River opposite Vicksburg to Monroe prior to the war. Fifteen miles were graded west of Monroe in the direction of Shreveport. At Shreveport, work on the line west to Greenwood, Louisiana (at the state line where the tie-in was to be completed with the Southern Pacific), ran into difficulties. Only five miles of track were completed prior to the war, although grading was completed to the state line.

The only other rail in the area was the six-mile track of the Memphis, El Paso & Pacific, which headed north out of Jefferson. This railroad was envisioned as a transcontinental that would proceed from Fulton, Arkansas, down the west bank of the Red River to El Paso, thence to the Pacific Ocean. Like the Swanson's Landing–to–Jonesville spur of the Southern Pacific, the track out of Jefferson was built inadvertently. The original intent was to bring supplies to Fulton by steamboat on the Red River. However, this intent was stymied by navigation problems. As a consequence, it was decided to bring supplies to Jefferson by steamboat and proceed north to Fulton, a decision about which Jefferson was ecstatic.

During the war, efforts were made to complete the Southern Pacific from Jonesville to Shreveport but without any final success. By early 1862, the Southern Pacific had graded about six miles east of Jonesville. In September, it leased from the Vicksburg, Shreveport & Texas the area between Shreveport and the state line. A Southern Pacific advertisement for bids for laying track between Jonesville and Shreveport appears in the 3 October *Semi-Weekly Shreveport News*, but it is unlikely that any work was accomplished given the absence of manpower and the need for using railroad iron for other purposes.

When Kirby Smith established the Trans-Mississippi Department at Shreveport in 1863, he ordered completion of the rail for military purposes and supplied men and equipment for getting the job done. The twelve miles of track between Swanson's Landing and Jonesville were pulled up in August and were relaid east out of Jonesville. The 12 January 1864 *Semi-Weekly Shreveport News* reports the track nearly completed to Greenwood; the 28 October *Texas Republican* reports completion; and the 11 April 1865 *Shreveport News* reports completion three miles east of Greenwood.

The war ended in May 1865. The 1 July *Shreveport Semi-Weekly News* reports that the road was fully graded to Shreveport, and the 27 October *Texas Republican* reports that only thirteen to fourteen miles of track remained to be laid. The 1 August 1866 *South-Western* reports that the gap was closed on Saturday (28 July) and that the first train went through from Shreveport to Marshall on Sunday. Marshall, through its 4 August *Texas Republican*, stated that it had been transformed overnight from a retail trade to a wholesale trade center and that the rail from Shreveport was "the first practical movement in Eastern Texas, the commencement of a series of enterprises, that will be rapidly carried forward." An advertisement that appeared continuously in the 1867 *South-Western* for L. C. DeLisle, commission and forwarding merchant and wholesale and retail dealer in general merchandise at Marshall, shows a Southern Pacific locomotive at the siding **(fig. 16-1)**.

The first bale of cotton at Shreveport from Marshall by train arrived early in September. In October, the River Intelligence column of the Shreveport *South-Western* ended with the following notification: "The New Orleans and Shreveport weekly packet Navigator will in all probability be in a port this morning at an early hour, and leave again for the city on the arrival of the cars." The "cars" referred to were railroad cars, whose arrival would determine the departure time of the

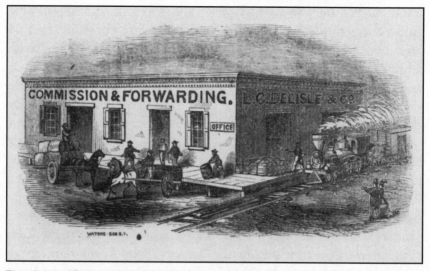

Fig. 16-1. Train at Marshall. *Source: Courtesy of LSU Libraries Special Collections, Baton Rouge*

Navigator. This was the first instance of an expression that became extremely common in subsequent years in the navigation column and in steamboat advertisements, with the place mentioned changing as the Southern Pacific extended farther to the west.

In January 1867, G. W. Dillard of the *South-Western* took the train from Shreveport to Marshall and found the track in a wretched condition. The engine stalled three or four times on down grades, and the trip took six and a half hours. Marshall was found to be thriving, but there were 1,000 bales of cotton at the depot that could not be shipped because of the condition of the rail. Nevertheless, the 17 April *South-Western* reports that "Most of the cotton arriving now comes by rail," and the 20 November issue reports that the road was fully repaired and in good order.

From the beginning of the rail connection, the Marshall *Texas Republican* had been extremely sensitive to Jefferson's concerns. But in October, low water suspended Jefferson's commerce, which automatically accrued to Marshall's benefit through its Shreveport rail connection: "In consequence of the low stage of water in the Lake and Bayou between Shreveport and Jefferson, the greater portion of the freight for the latter place, now passes through and pays duty in Marshall, and our commission merchants are doing a pretty thriving business in the receiving and forwarding line." The newspaper remarked that this was "an ill wind that blows nobody good."

In 1868, the Louisiana portion of the road was purchased and repaired. The 19 February *South-Western* reports large loads of cotton arriving at Shreveport by rail: "Trains on this road have been making trips for the past week or so with regularity, the 'Johnson' engine, with all the available rolling stock on the road, making the round trip to Marshall and back every day, with full loads. The receipts of cotton by this route will average from 1200 to 1500 bales a week."

By late October, the Marshall *Texas Republican*, as quoted by the Shreveport *South-Western*, was reporting large advances in rolling stock and freight: "For the past week the Public Square of this city has been crowded with cotton wagons. The Southern Pacific Railroad has been taxed to its capacity in carrying off the great staple of Texas. A new locomotive, the 'Marshall,' built expressly for this road, and twenty additional freight cars, now on hand, will be put in operation in a few days. This fact, with the improved condition of the track, ensures the prompt transportation of freights, which are daily increasing."

In early November, Dillard made a second trip to Marshall that provided a glowing account of the rail and its significance to Shreveport: "On Sunday the train consisted of eight cars, one a passenger car, and brought down two hundred bales of cotton. How encouraging to our people and merchants who have hitherto seen a train of only three open cars, and have never known more than 140 bales to be brought here on any one trip. The bed of the road is being rapidly improved; new platform and box cars rapidly constructed. We say for ourselves, and were convinced that the road is now under the management of those who have the determination and power to develop its capacity, to push it forward beyond Marshall at an early day, and thus in the most essential and important conceivable manner aid in advancing the progress, growth, and welfare of our city and portion of the country."

The 11 November *South-Western* quotes the Marshall *Harrison Flag* to the effect that 200 bales of cotton were arriving daily and the streets thronged with wagons and the Marshall *Texas Republican* to the effect that "Eight cars leave Marshall every morning; one passenger and seven freight cars, which return in the evening. There is also a night train. Over six hundred bales, if necessary, can be carried off every day, and back freights brought in." It is not surprising under these circumstances that eight boats advertised in the 18 November *South-Western* that they would leave Shreveport for New Orleans on the arrival of the cars from Marshall.

The 21 July 1869 *South-Western* reports that Hallsville (actually Hallville in the earliest records), which was fourteen miles west of Marshall, was being developed as the rail was extended in that direction. The 17 November issue reports that the first train arrived in Shreveport from Hallsville on the fifteenth. Boats immediately began indicating that they would leave Shreveport on the arrival of the cars from Hallsville. By 22 December, as the new cotton crop began to arrive in abundance, the railroad began to exceed Shreveport's capacity to handle the incoming freight: "This institution is now doing an excellent business. From two hundred and fifty to three hundred bales of cotton are brought in daily, and more would be sent forward but from the inconvenience of getting it out of the way when it reaches here. There is certainly a great demand for labor in Shreveport at this time. We the other day noticed two car loads of cotton standing on the track which there was not enough available labor to handle."

The effect of these developments on the southern ports and landings such as Benton, Port Caddo, and Swanson's Landing must have been devastating. It should be remembered that Harrison County was the market area for these ports and landings, and the Southern Pacific ran right through this market area, extending from Shreveport to Marshall in July 1866, Marshall to Hallsville in November 1867, and Hallsville to Longview in January 1871.

The Southern Pacific carried between 1,200 and 1,500 bales of cotton a week in early 1868; 11,500 bales in January 1870; and 55,168 bales in the twelve months preceding September 1871. In the twelve months preceding September 1858, Benton, Port Caddo, and Swanson's Landing exported 21,000 of the 35,500 bales of cotton exported by all ports and landings on the route other than Jefferson. Cotton exports for all ports and landings other than Jefferson were only 2,500 bales for the twelve months preceding September 1867 and 2,500 bales for the twelve months preceding September 1870. This appears to be a constant for the immediate postwar years. It is probable that little of even this small amount was exported from the southern ports and landings, because Monterey to the north continued to show some life.

The major ports and landings other than Jefferson along the route continue to appear in steamboat advertisements in 1865 and 1866, but they disappear after early 1867, and there are no postwar advertisements for any cotton merchants. September 1870 is the last time that cotton export statistics are given collectively for these other ports and landings. Although they continued to be mentioned from time to time as commercial places, it is probable that they were distributing import freights to local planters and no longer played a significant role in the cotton trade.

For Jefferson, the events of 1866-70 connected with the development of the Southern Pacific did not appear to have had any detrimental effect. The year 1871 was to prove the best year for cotton exports from Jefferson, when thirty-nine boats carried out nearly 90,000 bales. Nevertheless, 1871 was deceptive because the seeds of destruction had already been planted and were to grow with amazing speed and strangle Jefferson in a few short years. By 1875, only nine boats were operating, and fewer than 12,000 bales were carried out.

In order to understand what happened, it is best to look at the key elements in the development of the railway system affecting Jefferson through a map **(fig. 16-2)** in the 3 August 1873 *Shreveport Times*. This map displays existing and proposed roads. Although it contains a few minor errors, it presents an excellent picture of the relationship between the rails of Northeast Texas and lines in other states.

The key rails in this picture are the Houston & Texas Central heading north out of Houston to Red River City; the Missouri, Kansas & Texas proceeding out of Indian Territory on the north to Red River City (no longer in existence); the Cairo & Fulton from Little Rock to Texarkana; and the Texas & Pacific (successor to the Southern Pacific in 1872), running west from Shreveport to Dallas and from Texarkana to Sherman and between Marshall and Texarkana through Jefferson.

The Texas Central was important because it entered Jefferson's market area from the rear, providing a trade route to the south through

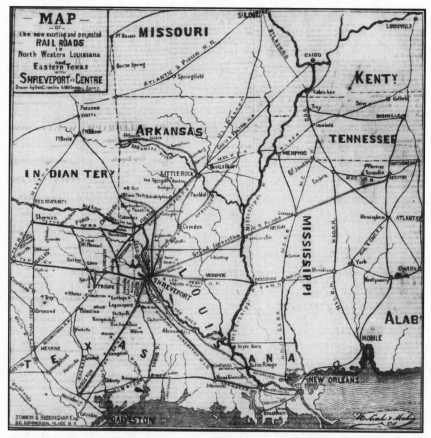

Fig. 16-2. Northeast Texas railways. *Source: Courtesy of LSU Libraries Special Collections, Baton Rouge*

Galveston. This line reached Hearne in 1868; Groesbeck (between Bremond and Corsicana) in 1870; Corsicana on 5 November 1871; Dallas in August 1872; and Red River City in 1873. This line caused only a temporary disturbance to Jefferson's commercial activity.

The Missouri, Kansas & Texas was important because it entered Jefferson's market area from the rear, providing rail access to St. Louis, thence to the Eastern seaboard. This line reached Denison (between Red River City and Sherman on the map) on Christmas Day 1872. This line was also of temporary importance in Jefferson's demise.

The Cairo & Fulton did not, in itself, have any direct effect on Jefferson's commercial activity. It was important because it provided a linkage between the Texas & Pacific system in Texas and Cairo and St. Louis to the northeast, thence to the Eastern seaboard. The Cairo & Fulton was completed through to Texarkana in February 1874.

The Southern Pacific reached Longview in January 1871 and was absorbed by the Texas & Pacific on 21 March 1872. The sections from Longview to Dallas, Marshall to Texarkana (through Jefferson), and Sherman to Brookston (nine miles west of Paris) were completed in 1873. Although the section between Paris and Texarkana was not completed until 1876, this was merely icing on the cake. Trains were running to Dallas on the southern portion of the system in August 1873. The first train reached Texarkana through the Marshall-Jefferson-Texarkana section on 29 December 1873. With the completion of the Cairo & Fulton bridge over the Red River in February 1874, continuous rail service was available from Dallas to St. Louis.

The first signs of difficulty for Jefferson began to appear in the newspapers in 1871. The rail to Longview was completed in early January, and the first load of freight arrived on the sixteenth. The first bale of cotton was shipped from Longview to Marshall on 1 February. By May, boats began notifying that they would leave Shreveport for New Orleans on the arrival of the cars from Longview. However, this was not the problem. The problem was to the southwest with the Texas Central and to the northwest with the Missouri, Kansas & Texas and the capture of a portion of Jefferson's market area by the Midwestern cities.

Jefferson's market area was fully developed early on and remained the same until the late 1860s. It is last described in its fullness in the 16 October 1868 *Texas Republican*: "The 'Jefferson Times' is published at Jefferson, Texas, the head of Red River and Lake navigation; one of the most prosperous cities of the 'Star State.' It commands the entire trade of Northern Texas and the Indian Territory. There are twenty-two counties that trade to this point, embracing an area as extensive as the entire State of Alabama, and containing a large, intelligent, industrious, thrifty, enterprising population. The exports are Wheat, Wool, Cattle, Sheep, Hides, and Cotton."

By 1871, this market area had become severely restricted according to an article on Jefferson and its trade by C. D. Morris that appeared in the *Jefferson Herald* and was reprinted in the 4 January 1871 *South-Western*:

> The City of Jefferson is at this time the natural commercial business point for thirteen counties, composing a territory of square miles half the size of Tennessee. As large as is this territory from which Jefferson derives its present support it is but little more than half the number of counties that contributed ten years ago to its commercial support. We have lost in that short period of time, the entire trade of several of our wealthiest Northwestern counties, and one-half the trade of others; the question then is: where has this trade gone? You have but to look at the map of Texas, and trace out the long line of the Texas Central Railroad, or visit the present terminus of that road, and ask the teamsters what county they are from, and you will at once learn that they are from the counties that once sent their produce to this market.
>
> Now citizens of Jefferson, will you please refer to the map of Texas again and trace the projected line of the Central, and see the counties it is soon destined to pass through, terminating within two and a half years more at Preston, in Grayson county, where it will meet the Missouri, Kansas & Texas Railroad coming into our state through the Indian Nation. Then I ask you again where are the counties you will have to support your "brick and mortar?" Even Bowie and Red River will go to the Texas Central; their hauling will be surer and cheaper; there will be no impassable Sulphur streams to cross; teamsters can buy their forage for one-half the price along the road to Central; there will be no uncertain navigation to rely on in getting their goods up at any and all seasons of the year by the interior merchants.

Again, freights and insurance are cheaper from New York to Galveston than from New York to New Orleans. It costs the merchant from the interior after reaching New Orleans but fifty-five dollars to go on to New York, where he finds a better market in every respect than in New Orleans; besides the time from latter place to New York is now reduced to seventy hours. But it is unnecessary for him to go by way of New Orleans; he has an outlet by the Missouri & Kansas Railroad direct to the North and East and can reach New York as soon and cheaper than he can reach New Orleans.

What is particularly surprising about this document is that it was written before the railroads penetrated Jefferson's market area. The Texas Central had not yet reached Corsicana. The Missouri, Kansas & Texas was even farther away, not yet having reached Fort Gibson on the Arkansas River in what was to become Oklahoma. And yet, the western counties in Jefferson's market area had already been partly split off. The contraction of the market area was not reflected in cotton exports, which continued to increase through 1871. Increasing cotton production in a contracting market area gave rise to a false sense of prosperity in Jefferson.

The major element in the picture at this time was Galveston through the Texas Central. Galveston had always carried on trade with New Orleans but also traded directly with the East Coast. Even before the Texas Central reached Jefferson's market area, it provided a cheaper route to New York through Galveston than was available to New York through New Orleans; and it was obvious to the Jefferson proponent who wrote the newspaper article what would happen after the Texas Central advanced even farther north. There was also a hint of the looming importance of the rail system advancing out of the Midwest, which eclipsed the Galveston route after it was fully developed.

One of the major weaknesses of the ox-wagon–steamboat transport system was that storage was required between the two transport phases. This was necessary because neither steamboats nor ox-wagons were constantly arriving at a port like Jefferson. Storage was expensive and entailed a commission. There were also costs connected with the use of drays to transport freight between warehouses and landings. Storage was a secondary problem for the railroad-steamboat transport mode because trains arrived constantly, even if steamboats didn't; and it was no problem at all for the railroad mode alone, which provided continuous service between demand and supply points, particularly with the expansion of spur lines.

The 11 August 1871 *Daily South-Western* contains a letter from a correspondent to the *Bonham News* (Bonham is in Fannin County between Sherman and Paris on the railroad map) claiming that Jefferson's merchants were extortioners, citing as an example a storage and handling charge by Bateman and Brother of Jefferson of $92.75 on a small portable engine that had been transported from Zanesville, Ohio, for $110.50. The specific charge that the engine had not been warehoused may have been incorrect. The important point of the letter was the impending revolution in the direction of trade that would be brought about through the rails advancing from the Midwest, spearheaded by the Missouri, Kansas & Texas, which was projected to cross the Canadian River (a tributary to the Arkansas entering from the southwest) in January 1872: "I came down last week from St. Louis. I went up in May; since that time fifty miles have been added to the railroad, over which the cars now run; and if the rate of building continues, the road will cross the Canadian by the 1st of January next. The cars already bring good freights for Northern Texas. I passed over thirty wagons from this county and Grayson heavily laden for our region. But that the whole trade is about the 'shift shoulder' is evident by the numerous trains laden with *cotton*—yes, COTTON! I met more than two hundred bales on its way up, in the space of two days. One year's more work on the railroad, and those remorseless extortioners on Cypress Bayou may close their grinding shops, so far as Northern Texas is concerned."

The *Shreveport Times* was unwilling to judge the specific charges but felt that the letter was worth reprinting because of its implications for the future: "We do not know the merits of the case, or whether the correspondent may not be too severe in his cauterizing; but this we do know, that the people of Texas are bent upon having railroad connections with the great commercial centres of the country, and that there will never more be a quiet acquiescence in exorbitant steamboat freights, or their more vexatious warehouse and handling accompaniments. We give the communication to the News alluded to, which speaks for itself, and may open the eyes of the people to the changes taking place in the matter of transportation for the people in the back country."

In December, Shreveport merchants complained about freight being sent to Galveston over the Texas Central; and Galveston merchants complained that they were being hurt by the rails because they allowed interior merchants to deal directly with St. Louis. A Louisville firm indicated in the *Courier-Journal*, as cited in the 16 December *Shreveport Times*, that it was receiving cotton from the area near Sherman. The cotton was wagoned nearly 200 miles to Gibson's Station, where it was put aboard the Missouri, Kansas & Texas for shipment to St. Louis, thence to Louisville. The firm claimed that it could get cotton cheaper this way than by Red River through Jefferson.

At the end of 1871, the trade of Northeast Texas and Northwest Louisiana was on the verge of a fundamental reorientation away from the ox-wagon–steamboat transport mode to New Orleans to a rail transport mode to the Midwest. The first phase of this reorientation was the incursion of Midwestern boats into New Orleans' trade territory, an event of great significance to New Orleans, but none to Shreveport and Jefferson, because the level of steamboat activity was not affected.

The second phase was constituted by the development of the rails. The first portion of this phase involved the extension of the Southern Pacific (later the Texas & Pacific) to the west. This did not affect the level of steamboat activity at Shreveport, because it simply replaced ox-wagon transport by rail. The extension of the Missouri, Kansas & Texas from the north had only a minor effect on the reorientation. It was merely a prelude to more direct rail connections with the Midwest.

The extension of the Texas Central from the south (and later the International Railroad from Hearne to Longview and the Houston & Texas Central from Houston to Palestine) had a more dramatic effect on Shreveport and Jefferson, but it was also short-lived. The principal effect was on New Orleans. Rail access to Galveston with its oceangoing fleet provided cheaper access to the Eastern seaboard than the rail/ox-wagon–steamboat access to New Orleans, thence to the East Coast on oceangoing vessels. In addition, it was not burdened by seasonal navigation problems on the route and on Red River.

The final portion of the rail phase in this reorientation was the completion of the Texas & Pacific linkage to the Cairo & Fulton at Texarkana in February 1874 and a collateral line between Shreveport and Texarkana. The Texas & Pacific by this time encompassed the whole of Jefferson's market area, and the linkage provided direct rail access to the Midwest. Consequently, New Orleans lost Northeast Texas and

Northwest Louisiana. Steamboat trade between the region and the Midwest disappeared, and steamboat trade between the region and New Orleans was eclipsed.

EIGHTEEN SEVENTY-TWO

The Texas Central reached Dallas in August and McKinney in December. The Missouri, Kansas & Texas reached the Canadian River (a southern tributary to the Arkansas River) in April and Denison, Texas, on 31 December. Trains were running on the Cairo & Fulton from Little Rock to the Little Red River in February, and construction farther south of Little Rock began in April. The Southern Pacific was absorbed by the Texas & Pacific in March.

In January, when the Missouri, Kansas & Texas had crossed the Arkansas River but not yet the Canadian River, the *Shreveport Times* noted: "The trade between Northern Texas and St. Louis seems to be immense and should attract the attention of our people. Upwards of six hundred wagons are engaged in transporting the freight between the town of Sherman and the southern terminus of the road." Galveston claimed that it could provide cheaper rates but that St. Louis merchants had their agents all over northern Texas.

In May, a correspondent from the *St. Louis Democrat* writing from McKinney reported: "A large crop of cotton has been planted, and if the season continues favorable and the M. K. and T. railroad is pushed forward with the same vigor that has built it from Vidalia, Mo., to the interior of the Indian Territory, it will be to Red river in time to carry the bulk of our cotton this fall to our city." The 5 June *Shreveport Times*, which carried this quote, commented: "Here is another item, which is threatening to Jefferson, as Collin and adjoining counties have heretofore been the most profitable customers to that city."

In 1872, twenty-eight boats made 130 trips to Jefferson, and the *Hornet* made one fishing trip to Jim's Bayou. The boats that went to Jefferson included the *Anna, Belle Rowland, Bossier, Carrie A. Thorn, Champion, Charles H. Durfee, Clifford, D. L. Tally* (**fig. 16-3**), *Emilie La Barge, Era No. 9, Era No. 10, Flavilla, Fleta, Flirt, Fontenelle, Gladiola, Hesper, John T. Moore, La Belle, Little Fleta, Lotus No. 3, Maria Louise, May Lowry, Rapides, Right Way, Royal George, Texas,* and *Thirteenth Era.* In addition, the *Clifford* made 3 fishing trips to Jim's Bayou, and the *Belle Rowland* made 1.

Fig. 16-3. *D.L. Tally*, Gainesville, Alabama, ca. 1895. *Source: From the Collection of the Public Library of Cincinnati and Hamilton County*

The *Bossier* was the second boat along the route by that name. The *Champion* was the second boat from Cincinnati, which made a strong bid to capture a portion of the Red River trade in 1872. The *Anna* and *Emilie La Barge* were from St. Louis and made 3 trips collectively to Jefferson. However, the bulk of the St. Louis trade was carried by the Carter Line's *Belle Rowland*, which operated in a transfer capacity at Shreveport and made 30 trips to Jefferson.

This was a year of unusual navigation events. The *Emilie La Barge*, at 218 feet, appears to have been the longest boat ever to travel to Jefferson (**fig. 16-4**). The *Emilie La Barge* was a sidewheeler built in Illinois in 1869 for the Missouri trade that was purchased by the Carter Line in 1871. She made a single trip to Jefferson, at the end of June 1872, during a brief period of unusually high water.

The *Royal George* had the lowest recorded draft of all the boats that operated along the route and was captained by James Crooks of Jefferson. She is first described in the 21 May 1872 *Shreveport Times*.

Fig. 16-4. *Emilie La Barge* (second from left), St. Louis, Missouri, 1873. *Source: From the Collection of the Public Library of Cincinnati and Hamilton County*

The new steamer Royal George is rather a nondescript looking affair as she now lies at the landing, with a cabin just planted, but her hull is one of the best. It was built by Capt. James Crooks, at Hood's Landing, on Little river, from the native white oak. She is 135 feet long in the keel, 27 feet beam, and three feet hold. She will carry 800 bales of cotton. She brought out the weight of 300 bales on eighteen inches of water. She has the machinery of the old George, and, when finished, will be one of the most complete low water boats in the trade. As she was built away up in the woods, the Captain was often put to his "stumps" to get all the material he stood in need of. For instance a whistle was the one thing he was bound to have. It was but the thought of a moment and out of a small paint keg sprung an improvised whistle which answers a very good purpose. Some of the bystanders remarked that the captain built to the whistle, like a cooper building a new barrel to an old bung hole, but that is a vile slander, for he built to the old pilot house, which is the only thing that we recognize as belonging to the old craft. She is not named in honor of anybody, but honors her name, and goes in on her own merits, backed by the indomitable energy of Captain James Crooks.

The *Royal George* made 28 trips west of Shreveport from 1872 through 1874, when she exploded on Twelvemile Bayou. Her initiation to the Jefferson trade was in August 1872 during a low-water period in which she immediately proved her worth: "The Royal George is now in clover and has it all to herself. She draws only eight inches light and will carry one thousand barrels on twenty inches. What a god-send she is for Jefferson, to say nothing about what she is for her owners."

In September, the *Royal George* arrived in Shreveport from Jefferson drawing eighteen inches loaded on one occasion and sixteen inches "with all the freight she wanted" on another. The *Shreveport Times* was impressed: "There are still about twenty inches for the steamer Royal George between this point and Boon's Bend, the head of navigation on Cypress bayou. She is the only boat that finds it profitable to continue in the trade, but we don't know how long she will find it so; possibly as long as the heavy dews continue, unless the grass in the channel gets too long and too thick."

The most significant navigation event from the perspective of the Jeffersonians was the single trip made by the *John T. Moore* in May. The *John T. Moore* was a 497-ton sternwheeler measuring 177 feet by 42 feet that was built in Cincinnati in late 1870 at a cost of $80,000. She owed her fame to the fact that she was one of the very small number of commercial iron-hulled steamboats; her uniqueness was accentuated by the fact that much of her decking and superstructure were also made of iron.

Special technical features included 4-inch clinker-lapped hull plating with double riveting, iron deck frame, iron deck underneath the boilers to prevent fires, and eleven independent iron bulkhead compartments to prevent sinking. Accommodations featured a full-length cabin, forty staterooms, gas lighting, and steam heat.

The *John T. Moore* was named for a New Orleans merchant and was built to run between New Orleans and Shreveport. This was a large, fairly heavy boat with a capacity of 1,200 tons, or 4,000 bales of cotton. However, as a Red River boat, it was also essential that she be able to run in fairly shallow water. The 23 November 1870 *South-Western* indicates that when sitting at the wharf in Cincinnati with water in her hold, she was drawing 14 inches forward and 16 inches aft. The 22 February *Daily Picayune* notes that the boat's draft "will not exceed twenty-four inches, with fifty tons to trim her."

The *John T. Moore* made many trips between New Orleans and Shreveport in 1871 and 1872; however, it was not until May 1872 that she made her first trip to Jefferson, as recorded in the *Shreveport Times* of the ninth: "The only sign of business on the landing yesterday forenoon was in the vicinity of the gangway of the iron steamer John T. Moore. During the night she had covered a full square with miscellaneous freight which caused the drays to congregate there in large numbers. She stayed with us until late in the forenoon when she left for Jefferson, situated on Cypress Bayou. She had a fair freight for that point and a goodly number of passengers. Although the Moore had been running two seasons in this trade, this is her first visit to Jefferson. We hope that the iron horse or the 'cock of the walk' as she proclaims herself will not become alarmed at the sight of the natives and run away."

The *John T. Moore* returned to Shreveport four days later, departing from Smithland and taking Bois d'Arc Pass. An account of the trip is contained in the 12 May *Shreveport Times*: "About the middle of the day the great iron steamer John T. Moore came in from Jefferson, with 200 bales of cotton and a good list of passengers. Capt. Boardman informs us though water was low, he never made an easier trip to Jefferson than he did with this Moore. She made the run down from Smithland to this point in about eleven hours, although she was drawing four feet. The people of Jefferson were highly delighted with the appearance of the Moore, and extended to her a pressing invitation to call again. John, the polite old gent, promised to do so at the earliest opportunity, river and water permitting."

Jefferson's dredge, the *Lone Star*, was back at work on Cypress Bayou in August. The nature of the work was described in the *Jefferson Democrat*, as quoted by the 22 August *Shreveport Times*: "The dredge boat is at work on Boon's Bend, and we learn that she is doing well. We had the pleasure of forming the acquaintance of Mr. Fasser, the engineer. We find him quite intelligent. He has a great deal of experience with dredge boats. He pronounces it one of the best he has ever seen, and that we only require a derrick to make it a success. We hope he may be able to get the river open to Jefferson. If the water was two feet higher, he could soon accomplish the work. When he gets to Jefferson, there is nothing in the way from the head of the lake, except Dougherty's Defeat."

The 27 August *Shreveport Times* continued to poke fun at Jefferson's efforts to improve Cypress Bayou: "The Democrat of the 24th reports navigation pretty well over until another rise or the dredge-boat works her way up from Boon's Bend to the wharf. We would rather take our chances on the rise." The last newspaper report from 1872 was in the 6 September *Shreveport Times*: "The dredge boat doing good work in Cypress bayou between Boon's Bend and Jefferson. As soon as she gets through with that section she will drop down to Daugherty's defeat and give the stumps there a tussel." Although the *Lone Star* eventually worked downstream, it was not a city effort. The dredge was working her way upstream, having reached The Packery in December, when she was acquired by the Corps of Engineers for a more ambitious federal project.

The boats that traveled to Jefferson in 1872 carried out only 22,694 bales of cotton, a precipitous decline from the previous year. An 27 October *Shreveport Times* clipping from the *Galveston News* reports "much of the produce now seeking an outlet through Galveston that formerly went via Red River;" and the 16 November *Shreveport Times* reports that cotton was going from Canton, Texas, to Galveston. However, the problem in the latter half of the year was not with the Texas Central to the south or the Missouri, Kansas & Texas to the north. Jefferson was nearly inaccessible during the second half of 1872 because of low water; and the *Jefferson Times*, as cited by the 17 August *Shreveport Times*, reported cotton crops in Harrison, Marion, Cass, Titus, and a portion of Bowie County almost completely ruined by drought. The cotton that was produced was diverted to Galveston because of Jefferson's inaccessibility, and there was no apparent cause for alarm.

Before the low water set in, the *Jefferson Daily Times* of 30 March, as cited by the *Shreveport Times* of 3 April, indicated that since 1 September 1871, Jefferson had received 47,122 bales and shipped 46,661, with 1,601 on hand. The boat count reveals 50,470 bales from commercial year 1871–72 (1 September 1871–31 August 1872); and the 3 September annual summary in the *Shreveport Times* gives an estimate of 60,000 bales for the same period. Because Jefferson measured its business success by the commercial rather than the calendar year, this was a respectable volume of trade, nearly duplicating the situation in the 1869–70 commercial year.

Nevertheless, there were some signs of change. In June, before the low water set in, there were reports of plenty of water to Jefferson, but nothing to ship, a theme that was to be repeated continuously in later years. Although it was not unusual for Jefferson's commercial activities to begin to decline rapidly by June, this was certainly not the case in 1871. In addition, rail competition appears to have begun exerting some downward pressure on Red River freight rates. This is the apparent source of the comment in the 3 September *Shreveport Times* annual commercial summary that most boats suffered during the season because of low rates.

If Jefferson was concerned, there is no indication in the Shreveport newspapers. Attitudes were still highly optimistic, as indicated by a quote from the *Jefferson Democrat* contained in the 14 April *Shreveport Times*: "Jefferson is every day gaining ground. Its locality, the liberality of its people, their enterprise, what they have already accomplished, and what they are endeavoring to achieve, and will unquestionably realize, is not only recognized by our own people, but is appreciated abroad. We are all in a hurry; we are all impatient; the wheels move too slow. But let us be patient. We are on the eve of a new prosperity, if our leading men will act in harmony, and push the ball already set in motion."

As in previous years, this optimism was not quenched by three drastic fires that occurred in Jefferson in 1872. The first, in January, broke out in the agricultural warehouse of J. N. Needham, consuming the entire block with the exception of two structures. Losses were estimated at $122,000, and one person was killed by a falling wall. In July, a fire broke out in the Freeman Building on Dallas Street and swept both sides of the street from Market to Vale. Losses were estimated at $150,000. In September, a fire consumed the house of Conley & Prewitt on the upper part of Dallas Street. It leaped to the adjoining buildings on Lake Street and then extended across Dallas to the National Hotel, which was saved. Losses were estimated at $40,000.

As in previous years, rebuilding was immediate. The business district that emerged from the series of postwar conflagrations is shown in Brosius's 1872 *Bird's Eye View of Jefferson, Texas*, with many large, multiple-story brick buildings between Henderson on the north, the bayou on the south, Soda on the east, and Market on the west (**fig. 16-5**). Three boats are shown in port, with one arriving and one leaving, including the *Maria Louise*, *Lotus No. 3*, and *Charles H. Durfee*. The city's dredge, the *Lone Star*, is shown at work in the harbor area, indicating a strong commitment to the navigation future. This was Jefferson at the height of its commercial activity and the beginning of its commercial decline.

The Brosius sketch was done in the spring of 1872 and does not show a wharf that was constructed in the latter part of the year by John W. Judd. Judd's contract was for a wharf from the western edge of Walnut Street to the middle of the block between Soda and Washington Streets. The wharf was to be 20 feet wide and 590 feet long and was to consist of pile and framework constructed of sound timber and iron, with the front to be 2 feet below the level of the existing wharf.

EIGHTEEN SEVENTY-THREE

The Texas Central out of Houston reached Sherman in late February and Denison in the middle of March, providing (through the Missouri, Kansas & Texas linkage) a through line from Galveston to St. Louis.

Fig. 16-5. Jefferson during its primacy. *Source: Library of Congress*

Shreveport complained in May about Galveston cutting into its business, and Galveston reported extraordinary receipts of cotton in December.

The Missouri, Kansas & Texas from the north was running semi-daily trips on the 620 miles to St. Louis by January. In February, a St. Louis commission merchant in Denison issued a circular to cotton shippers advertising reduced rates over the Missouri, Kansas & Texas of $0.60 per hundred pounds of cotton to St. Louis with no charge for railroad handling and no commission fee. Much cotton from the upper Red River counties was being taken out by the Missouri, Kansas & Texas in May.

Trains were running on the Cairo & Fulton to Fulton by April, and pilings were being placed on the Red River for a bridge in October. In February, a Washington, Arkansas, merchant wrote to the firm of Sale & Murphy in Shreveport recommending freight and insurance reductions to compete with the Cairo & Fulton, or else the entire trade of the upper Red River would be lost by Shreveport. In March, Capt. Matt Scovell, who was in the upper Red River trade, indicated that it was widely believed in that area that with the completion of the Cairo & Fulton, steamboats would be a thing of the past.

In 1873, the Texas & Pacific was being developed west to Dallas, east out of Sherman, and northeast out of Marshall, with an intended connection through Jefferson with the Cairo & Fulton at Texarkana. The northern tier of this system was constructed out of Sherman to the east, with building toward Bonham and Honey Grove beginning in February. The northern tier was completed from Sherman to Brookston—nine miles west of Paris—during the year, but the section between Paris and Texarkana was not completed until 1876, providing connection with the Cairo & Fulton.

The southern tier of the system was formed by the continuing extension of the line west out of Shreveport, which had reached Longview in 1871. Construction proceeded east from Dallas in 1873, and the connection was made in the first week of August. Boats advertised that they would leave Shreveport on the arrival of the cars from Dallas. Shreveport expected that it would receive the cotton of Wood, Van Zandt, Kaufman, and Dallas Counties. The first train from Dallas arrived at Shreveport on 11 August, and freight was being shipped from Shreveport to Dallas by 23 August.

Jefferson's market area was being encompassed by the Texas Central and Missouri, Kansas & Texas on the west and by the Texas & Pacific on the north and south and extending to the western perimeter. The final element in this picture was the construction of the Texas & Pacific from Marshall, through Jefferson, to Texarkana, where the Texas & Pacific met the Cairo & Fulton, providing direct rail service from Northeast Texas to the Midwestern cities such as St. Louis.

The *Jefferson Democrat*, as quoted in the *Shreveport Times*, reported in January concerning a railroad bridge over Black Cypress Bayou above Jefferson: "The two thousand feet of piling from where the railroad crosses the bayou above the city to the cut near Broadway, is almost completed, a gap of only about twenty yards still remaining, which is fast being filled." The same publications in March reported that the contract for building the bridge over Cypress Bayou had been awarded to Crump and Hunsucker and was expected to be completed in May.

The section of the road between Marshall and Jefferson was completed on Saturday, 29 June, and Jefferson prepared for a grand celebration, as reported in the 5 July *Shreveport Times*.

> THE JEFFERSON RAILROAD CELEBRATION.—We had the pleasure of a call yesterday morning from our old friend, Mr. G. W. Dillard, formerly of the South-Western, and at present of the Jefferson Daily Tribune. Mr. Dillard in behalf of the committee of arrangements, requests us to extend a formal invitation to the citizens of Shreveport to attend the grand railroad festival in Jefferson on the 8th inst., in honor of the completion of the railroad between that city and Marshall. There will be a grand barbecue, steamboat excursion in the afternoon, fireworks and a splendid ball at night. Mr. Dillard yesterday received a dispatch from Mr. J. Campbell, stating that on the morning of the celebration a special train at 7 o'clock, will leave Shreveport for Jefferson, arriving in the latter city at 11 A. M. Fare half-rate each way. We hope a large delegation will attend the celebration of our Jefferson friends in whose new era of prosperity we sincerely rejoice. That the affair will be a splendid one, all who are familiar with the liberal and hospitable character of the Jeffersonians need not be told.

Unfortunately, the editor of the *Shreveport Times* was unable to attend the event, so a full account is not available of what obviously was a grand affair, as reported by the 10 July *Shreveport Times*.

THE JEFFERSON CELEBRATION.

We very much regret that we were unable to visit our friends in Jefferson and participate in their railroad celebration on Tuesday last. We have however met a number of our citizens who were there, and without an exception they express themselves highly pleased with their reception. Everything went off splendidly. Thousands of people were present; an abounding and excellent barbecue dinner was spread; the ball, fireworks, etc., were elegant. Indeed, our friends say Jefferson surpassed herself on the occasion, and that no effort was spared to make the vast crowd comfortable, cool and happy. One of our friends says he tried to spend two and a half, but everything was free to visitors and he failed after a prolonged effort. We congratulate our sister city on the success of her railroad festival.

By early August, the road had been completed nine miles northeast out of Jefferson toward Texarkana, reaching the newly established town of Monterey. The old town of Monterey was still in existence, because it is mentioned in the 22 March *Shreveport Times*. The new town, which appears in railroad advertisements, was started by the Texas & Pacific, as indicated by the 27 July *Shreveport Times*: "A new town is being laid out on the Texas and Pacific nine miles beyond Jefferson called Monterey. The company are arranging to settle a large number of German families in and about the town."

By mid-August, the rail was being developed from Monterey northeast and from Texarkana southwest, heading toward the Sulphur River. Cars were running twenty-two miles north of Jefferson in late August and three miles beyond Atlanta (thirty-one miles from Jefferson) in early September. The rail reached Moore's Landing on the Sulphur River on 2 October, and the 19 November *Shreveport Times* reports cars running between Jefferson and Moore's Landing. By 30 December, cars were running to Texarkana.

In February, Shreveport indicated that it would have a rail connection to northern Texas through the Marshall-Jefferson road, which connected with the east-west lower tier of the Texas & Pacific at Marshall. In April, Shreveport boasted that it would get the produce of the northern counties through the Marshall-Jefferson road and that Jefferson's trade would be brought to Shreveport. In July, in the midst of the railroad celebration, Jefferson freight was carried by rail to

Jefferson, and Jefferson's newspaper was delivered by rail at Shreveport on the same day that it was printed. By November, boats from New Orleans and St. Louis were turning over Jefferson freight to the rail at Shreveport, and the rail was shipping cotton from Jefferson to Shreveport at $1.25 per bale.

The navigation picture for 1873 was complicated by low water hanging over from the past year, a poor cotton crop in some counties during the previous summer, the national financial panic beginning in September, and a yellow fever epidemic in Shreveport that prompted Jefferson to establish a quarantine from 3 September through 7 November. Nevertheless, the record was much better than the previous year, with thirty-seven boats making 162 trips to Jefferson and two other boats making 4 trips to Jim's Bayou.

The low-water barrier from the previous year was broken by the *Bossier* on 18 January. There are two views of this arrival. The first is presented in a memorandum by the *Bossier* that appeared in the 23 January *Shreveport Times*: "landed at the Jefferson wharf at 10½ P.M., amidst the firing of cannon and the glare of sky-rockets; the deafening and prolonged cheers of the citizens were tremendous in honor of the arrival of the first boat for six months. Champagne flowed like water." The second is from the *Jefferson Democrat*, as quoted in the same issue of the *Shreveport Times*: "About half-past eleven o'clock last night, the little steamer Bossier, Capt. C. J. Boardman, landed at our wharf, flying light, having only 162 packages aboard. She was greeted with a brilliant display of fire works, and many shouts from the large crowd of people drawn thither by the shrill notes of her whistle, to witness the arrival of the first steamer of the season."

Boats that traveled to Jefferson in 1873 included the *Andrew Ackley* **(fig. 16-6)**, *Bannock City, Belle of Shreveport, Belle Rowland, Bossier, Carrie A. Thorn, Charles H. Durfee, Clifford, Era No. 10, Flavilla, Fleta, Flirt, Frank Morgan, Frazier, Gladiola, Huntsville, John T. Moore, Katie P. Kountz, La Belle, Lady Lee, Leo, Lessie Taylor, Little Fleta, Lotus No. 3, Maria Louise, May Lowry, R. T. Bryarly, Rapides, Right Way, Royal George, Ruby, Seminole, Shamrock, South-Western, Texas, Thirteenth Era*, and *W. J. Behan*. In addition, the *Lotta* made 1 trip to Jim's Bayou, and the *Hornet* made 3.

The *Ruby* and *Shamrock* were the second boats by that name to operate along the route. The latter was a circus boat. The *South-Western* was named in honor of the Shreveport newspaper. The *Belle of Shreveport*

Fig. 16-6. *Andrew Ackley* (middle), Sioux City, Iowa, 1868. *Source: From the Collection of the Public Library of Cincinnati and Hamilton County*

and *Lady Lee* were Carter Line steamboats operating out of St. Louis. The *Belle Rowland* continued to operate in a Carter Line transfer capacity out of Shreveport and made 11 trips to Jefferson during the year.

The *R. T. Bryarly* is described in the 15 October 1872 *Shreveport Times*:

> This steamer, just completed at the Falls of the Ohio, cost over $20,000, according to the Louisville Courier. She is now on her way to Upper Red river. Her capacity is 1,500 bales of cotton when fully loaded, and will carry 800 bales on thirty inches of water. The following are her dimensions: length, one hundred and fifty feet; beam, thirty-three feet; hold, three feet in the clear in the shoalest place; ten-inch crown to the deck; engines, twelve inches in diameter and four feet stroke, working a water-wheel fourteen feet in diameter, twenty-four and a half length of buckets and fourteen inches wide. She has two boilers twenty-two feet long and thirty-eight inches in diameter; also double engines forward for working a steam capstan. She is very roomy between decks, and is admirably suited for the storage of cotton and other freight. The R. T. Bryerly has been built and is owned by Capt. Noah Scovill and Jo. T. Bryerly, expressly for the Upper Red river trade. Capt. Scovell will command. Mr. Thomas Howard, late chief of the Katie, and a

gentleman not only well known to our people, but those of the Red River country, will have charge of the office.

The most important navigation events of the year after the arrival of the *Bossier* were trips made by the *Belle of Shreveport* and the *John T. Moore* to Jefferson. The *Belle of Shreveport* (figs. 16-7 and 16-8) was a 581-ton Carter Line sternwheeler built in Metropolis, Illinois, in 1872 and operated by Capt. Tom Rea. She is described in the 28 February *Shreveport Times*:

> As the Belle is a stranger in our waters, and as both captain and clerk are old friends, we must say a word descriptive and in praise of her. She was built under the personal supervision of Capt. Rea expressly for the St. Louis and Shreveport trade. She is a model of steamboat architecture and the largest sternwheel boat that ever entered Red river. Her length, from stem to stern, not counting her wheel, is 200 feet; length of beam 44 feet, depth of hold 7 feet. She has 19 inch cylinders with 6 feet stroke; four new boilers, 28 inches in diameter, 24 feet long and double riveted, securing additional safety.
>
> Capt. Rea does not know her actual carrying capacity, but says he has had on her 1100 tons which did not bring her down entirely to her work. She cost $57,000, although the captain economised by using a portion of the machinery of the Silver Bow and some of the appurtenances of that boat and of the Carrie Converse.
>
> In short, the Belle is a complete steamboat. There is nothing particularly gaudy about her, but everything is substantial and comfortable. The lady's cabin is in more elegant style than the other portions of the boat, which shows a proper appreciation of the sex by the builder. We give welcome to our city's namesake and wish her all prosperity.

Although shorter than the 218 by 38-foot *Emilie La Barge*, the *Belle of Shreveport* at 202 feet by 43 feet was much wider, making her the largest boat ever to travel to Jefferson. Nevertheless, as was typical of the western river steamers, she had an impressively shallow draft. The *St. Louis Democrat*, as reported in the 20 October 1872 *Shreveport Times*, gives her light-loaded (without freight) draft as 24 inches forward

Fig. 16-7. *Belle of Shreveport*, Mississippi River, ca. 1872. *Source: From the Collection of the Public Library of Cincinnati and Hamilton County*

Fig. 16-8. *Belle of Shreveport* (on left), Carondelet, Missouri, ca. 1881. *Source: From the Collection of the Public Library of Cincinnati and Hamilton County*

and 30 inches aft. The 16 November 1872 *Shreveport Times* says that she drew 7⅔ feet loaded to the guards (that is, with a full freight).

The *Belle of Shreveport* made only one trip to Jefferson, in May 1873. This trip could not have been accomplished were it not for the fact that water levels on the route were extremely high from rains throughout the Red River region. The *Belle of Shreveport* arrived at Shreveport from St. Louis on 25 May, discharged freight the next day, and left for Jefferson at 5:00 in the evening of the day after. She lay overnight at Twelvemile Bayou and arrived at Jefferson within twenty-four hours.

She was reported at Jefferson on Thursday (along with the *John T. Moore*, *Lotus No. 3*, and *Seminole*), but she may actually have been at a point slightly downstream of the Jefferson landing where iron for the Texas & Pacific was unloaded and where she was observed by the *Seminole*. The trip back to Shreveport took fifteen hours, including a small layover on Twelvemile Bayou. She arrived at Shreveport at 4:00 in the morning on the last day of May heavily laden but carrying only two bales of cotton for local merchants. She left for St. Louis at 2:00 in the afternoon.

That this was the largest boat that ever traveled to Jefferson is confirmed by the 31 May *Shreveport Times*, which says in regard to the trip to Jefferson that the *Belle of Shreveport* was "the largest that ever made the run up there," accomplishing "a feat of which Capt. Thos. W. Rea may well feel proud."

The second and third trips to Jefferson of the iron boat *John T. Moore* were made in 1873. The *John T. Moore* departed for Jefferson from Shreveport on the night of Wednesday, 28 May, carrying 2,600 bars of railroad iron, for which she got $9 per ton freight, and a pleasure party of Shreveport citizens who paid $7 for the round trip. She reached the railroad iron landing below Jefferson on Friday, and a party was held that night, which was attended by Jeffersonians and described in a "dispatch" by Captain Boardman: "Last night the Jeffersonians stormed the out-posts and finally boarded us. Terrible contest—excitement intense—more girls than you could make love to in a week. During the Terpsichorean battle we had a waltzing engagement between two belles of the rival cities. Thermometer one hundred and twenty in the shade, and on the rise. Jefferson was lightning on the heel, but old Shreveport held her own; and no matter how they danced, we could bear it. Many waste places made glad."

The *John T. Moore* went upstream to Jefferson on Saturday to take on cotton, left Jefferson at 1:00 Sunday morning, and arrived back at Shreveport at 4:30. This trip was so successful that another pleasure excursion was planned for the next month. The *John T. Moore* left Shreveport for Jefferson on the night of Monday, 16 June, carrying 300 bars of railroad iron, an excursion party, and a band. She returned to Shreveport shortly after noon on Wednesday carrying fifty-seven bales of cotton.

Jefferson had its normal fare of fires in 1873. On 23 April, a fire broke out at 3:00 in the afternoon in Schluter's establishment on Dallas Street. The building and a stock of dry goods were consumed, along with Sam Moseley's law office, the Texas & Pacific Railroad office, and the railroad telegraph office. The response observed by the *Shreveport Times* was the same as in previous years: "It will be seen by a special in our telegraphic columns that our sister city has again been visited by a fire, though it has had a longer respite than usual. Less resolute and less enterprizing people than those of Jefferson would have become disheartened by these repeated destructive visitations. Nothing daunted, however, they immediately commence the erection of new buildings upon the sites of those lately destroyed. Their energy and pluck certainly deserve a higher reward."

Yet another fire occurred in July, as reported in the *Shreveport Times* of the seventeenth:

FIRE IN JEFFERSON—LOSS OVER $200,000.
JEFFERSON, TEXAS, July 16.—Great conflagration Tuesday night. Three two-story buildings burned, occupied by A. Gilham and Russell, Rainey & Co., commission merchants. The buildings were worth forty-five thousand dollars, and were insured for fifteen thousand. A. Gilham's stock of consigned goods was sixteen thousand; Russell, Rainey & Co.'s stock and consignments were one hundred and fifty thousand. Insurance on these goods forty-five thousand. The fire was without doubt the work of an incendiary. Other buildings were in imminent peril, but the fire was fortunately confined to these buildings by the persevering efforts of the fire department. These buildings were on the levee, in fifty feet of the bayou, therefore water was plentiful. The only casualties were two firemen, Charles McDougal and Dan Coffeld, badly

scorched by the flames breaking through a window while they were on a ladder with the hose. This district will be rebuilt at once. Nobody hurt.

During the latter part of the year, Shreveport experienced its worst yellow fever epidemic. Jefferson established a quarantine on 3 September, as was common during a period when the cause of yellow fever was unknown and it was thought to be contagious. There was little in the way of boat movements until October, when a few boats managed to get to Jefferson, and the quarantine was raised on 7 November.

With respect to cotton shipments, 1873 was a fairly good year, with 41,582 bales exported from Jefferson. This may actually be a slight undercount, because the 31 August commercial summary in the *Shreveport Times* indicates that some boats from Jefferson did not stop at Shreveport on the way down. The primary observable effects of the rails on navigation were the continuing downward pressures on freight rates and the continuing reductions in cotton exports.

It is impossible to determine the precise effects of the rails in bringing about reductions in Jefferson's cotton exports by water because no statistics are available, and there are only a few brief mentions of cotton transports out of Jefferson's traditional market area, which in any case was shared by Shreveport in its southern portions and, depending on the navigability of the Red above the raft, in its northeast portion. Nevertheless, the Texas & Pacific established rates of $4 a bale of cotton from Dallas to Shreveport, a price with which ox-wagons that might have wanted to carry cotton to Jefferson could not compete. It can be presumed that the continuing cotton export reductions from Jefferson in 1873 were highly dependent on the activities of the rails.

With the completion of the Texas & Pacific to Jefferson in June, cotton could be brought into Jefferson by rail for transport to New Orleans by steamboat. Conversely, cotton brought into Jefferson by ox-wagon could be transported out by rail to Shreveport, Galveston, or St. Louis. The Texas & Pacific advertised freight rates on a bale of cotton from Jefferson to Shreveport at $1.25, which was highly competitive with steamboat rates; and the *Jefferson Tribune*, as reported in the 20 December *Shreveport Times*, indicated that the rate of a bale of cotton from Jefferson to Shreveport was $1.

The rail rates provided strong downward pressure on steamboat rates from March onward. The impact was particularly disturbing during the low-water periods when steamboat rates were traditionally higher, as in this 27 August *Shreveport Times* comment: "The Royal George is the only packet now running in the Cypress Bayou trade, and she don't get half enough to do. . . . The freight rate by rail to Jefferson won't allow the steamboats to gouge the natives much longer."

The first word from Jefferson that something had gone wrong came at the beginning of September, only two months after the grand railroad celebration. The correspondent was Louis "Spence" Flatau, one of the best known of the Red River pilots and a longtime Jefferson resident. His comments appeared in a lengthy communication to the *Jefferson Daily Democrat* and were briefly excerpted in the 4 September *Shreveport Times*: "The great Pacific railroad that we had all looked so fondly to for succor, that we hopefully imagined would build us up and make us a great place, has gone by and alas, we are but a way station! We liberally and generously donated lands for a depot and bonds by thousands to it and it has not helped us. On the contrary, unless we do something that will enable us to profit by it, we are hopelessly ruined."

The great Pacific railroad that Flatau was referring to was the Texas & Pacific, which was intended for development all the way to the West Coast. Like most other towns seeking a rail, and in this case participation in a transcontinental rail, Jefferson thought that the railroad would only enhance its status as an import and export center, extending its range farther to the west. Like most other ports, it almost certainly thought that the rails would complement and enhance its navigation activities.

Flatau saw that this was not the case when the rail was only about twenty-five miles northeast of Jefferson. In referring to Jefferson as a way station, he had probably observed import freights coming in from Shreveport by rail through Marshall and being shipped through Jefferson to the upper Red River counties without even stopping at Jefferson. He probably also observed cotton from those counties being brought to Jefferson by rail, compressed at the Texas & Pacific facility that was in place in April, and sent on to other points without in any way contributing to the economic life of the city.

Flatau's letter is important because it was written before the full force of the railroads was felt and because it recognized that Jefferson's commercial viability was intimately tied to its existence as a port. His proposed solution to the impending crisis was to establish a steamboat line between Jefferson and New Orleans that could compete with the rails. This suggestion was later partly implemented but had only a modest short-term effect on the course of events.

EIGHTEEN SEVENTY-FOUR

This was the pivotal year in Jefferson's history because it was in February that the Cairo & Fulton bridge over the Red River at Texarkana was completed, providing direct access to the Midwest, thence to the East Coast. Unfortunately, there are no extant Shreveport or Clarksville newspapers for the first five months of the year, and there is no way to estimate the amount of cotton shipped by steamboats during the year. However, a fairly good estimate can be made of the number of boats operating along the route and the number of trips.

According to New Orleans *Daily Picayune* records, eleven boats made 27 trips to Jefferson from January through May 1874, including the *Belle Rowland, Charles H. Durfee, La Belle, Lessie Taylor, Lotus No. 3, Maria Louise, R. T. Bryarly, Sabine, Seminole, Texas,* and *W. J. Behan*. According to *Shreveport Times* records, five boats made 13 trips to Jefferson from June through September, including the *Clifford, Lessie Taylor, Lotus No. 3, Royal George,* and *W. J. Behan*. The *Clifford* also made a trip to Jim's Bayou. In addition, the *Clifford, Frank Morgan,* and *Royal George* made trips to Albany, Clear Lake, and Rocky Point on Caddo Lake to obtain paving materials for Shreveport streets.

Cumulatively, fourteen boats made 44 trips to points west of Shreveport in 1874. This was an extraordinary decline from the previous year, when thirty-nine boats made 166 trips. Although there is probably some undercounting of trips because of lack of information on local runs during the first five months, the undercounting would be insignificant, and it is unlikely that any other boats went west of Shreveport during the year. The only possible significant complicating factor would be the Midwestern boats, including their transfer operations at Shreveport, which had been important factors in the navigation record for previous years. However, the Midwestern boats on the Red River were the first to fall victim to the rails, and these operations had been extinguished by at least February, as reported by the 16 September 1874 *Shreveport Times*: "Most of our readers are well aware that the Carter line, composed of the heaviest tonnage ever in this river, was well established and doing all our Western produce carriage at a very low rate. As soon as railroad communication was established between this point and St. Louis this line was compelled to withdraw. It could not load one of its boats in a month's time. In other words it could not compete with the rail."

The dimensions of this collapse are better measured by the situation at Shreveport than at Jefferson. During commercial year 1871–72, there were 467 arrivals at Shreveport, of which 52 were from St. Louis and 6 were from Cincinnati; during commercial year 1872–73, there were 375 arrivals at Shreveport, of which 40 were from St. Louis and 3 were from Cincinnati. The strategy to extinguish Midwestern boat competition pursued by the rail was quite simple according to the 16 September 1874 *Shreveport Times*: "All the latter asked was steamboat rates and insurance added, quick transit giving them the preference." The advertised trip time by rail from Shreveport to St. Louis in 1874 was only thirty-five hours.

From June though December of 1874, only 1,672 bales of cotton were shipped from Jefferson by steamboat, almost all by the *Royal George*, with the largest load at 261 bales. Even if all the cotton that arrived in New Orleans from January through May on boats that had been to Jefferson were added to the picture, the amount would still be insignificant. This appears to be the result of three factors: not much cotton was arriving at Jefferson by ox-wagon; cotton arriving at Jefferson by rail was simply shipped through after compression, if compression had not taken place beforehand; and most of the cotton that reached Jefferson's storage facilities by ox-wagon was transported out by rail rather than by steamboat.

For obvious reasons, 1874 was the year in which the impact of the rails on navigation became topical in the *Shreveport Times* navigation column. The effects were felt at Jefferson, Shreveport, and New Orleans. With respect to Jefferson, the 10 July *Shreveport Times* reports: "The last boats out from the lakes found about three and one-half feet at Gum Springs flats, and falling. A light boat might reach Jefferson but there is so little freight offering it is not likely the experiment will be tried this week. River business above this point seems to have been completely killed off for some reason or other. Perhaps the railroad did it. Don't all speak at once! Poor Fulton has got no organ to speak for her, so that we can lam 'her sort' to our heart's content. Of course Jefferson will show fight."

With respect to Shreveport, comments are made on up freights and down freights in relation to New Orleans. Concerning up freights, boats in New Orleans had been informed of a rise on Red River but did not respond according to the 24 September *Shreveport Times*: "All the light draught boats in New Orleans have been notified of the rise, and the prospects for good low water navigation; but as yet we have not heard of any of them going on berth. The fact is just this: to compete successfully with the rail they will have to put rates down so low that it would look hazardous to make the attempt. . . . If it were not for the rail and river freight was five card rates, there would be no end to the boats in the trade. The fact is there has been more water in the river all along than there has been business."

Similar problems were experienced with down freights, as reported in the 26 September *Shreveport Times*: "The Bastrop, Captain Gus Hodges, gets off to day. . . . She has been at the landing about one week offering to take cotton at $2.50 per bale, but has not met with any success to speak of, although during that time some four hundred bales have been shipped by rail; and there is a stock now on hand of some thousand bales. This is the first time that such a thing has occurred in the history of low water in Red river. It is all owing to the rail and the authorities say the half is not told yet. It is reported that the rail will take cotton to New York as soon as the river gets high at one dollar per hundred, and perhaps as low as seventy-five cents per hundred. The object is to take all the cotton for the eastern market. The rail is built and it must do business at some price or other."

The decline of river navigation was not of severe consequence for Shreveport, which was emerging as a cotton market. Low rail rates to the East Coast from Shreveport contributed to this emergence. The severest effect was on New Orleans, which was losing one of its primary market areas, as reported in a *Daily Picayune* extract that appeared in the 18 October *Shreveport Times*:

> Steamer Carrie A. Thorn left Shreveport October 9 a.m., with 204 head cattle and 347 bales cotton; the cotton having been obtained at the low figure of $1.50 per bale, and only 3½ feet water in the river. The cause of such a price on such a stage of water is certainly not on account of too much river tonnage, but is directly attributable to railroad competition, as Northern, Eastern and Western capital is there on hand, ready and willing to purchase, and in such quantities as to make it an inducement for the railroad to give a rate to St. Louis of $3.50 per bale, and

to New York at $1.20 per 100 pounds, and no insurance necessary, placing cotton in the above markets at a cheap rate of transportation, and where it is sold at an equal if not better rate than it would bring in the New Orleans market. With a limited supply of capital, and a heavy rate of insurance, New Orleans can expect to receive but little of the North Louisiana and Texas cotton. This is a subject which demands the immediate and serious consideration of our merchants and insurance companies.

These changes were primarily the result of straightforward economic considerations, with lower freight costs and quicker transit time giving the advantage to rails over steamboats. The 15 and 16 September *Shreveport Times* commercial column gives an elaborate analysis of cost differentials. Cotton was shipped from Shreveport to Providence, Rhode Island, by rail at $6.07 per bale. The cost by steamboat during high water, when freight costs were at their lowest, was $7.35 per bale by way of New Orleans. To New York by rail was $5.85 compared to $6.40 by steamboat by way of New Orleans.

Rates established by the Texas & Pacific for transport to St. Louis from Jefferson were $3.25 per compressed cotton bale and $4.00 per uncompressed cotton bale. The same rates from Shreveport were $2.75 and $3.50. The *Jimplecute* complained about the discrepancy and about the *Shreveport Times* supporting rail over water. The Shreveport newspaper said it was not running the railroad and that it had been surprised by the advantages of the rail when the analysis was conducted.

The flexibility of the rail in establishing rates is shown by a Texas & Pacific offer, as reported in the *Jimplecute*, to take compressed cotton from Jefferson to St. Louis for $2.50 per bale and uncompressed for $3.25 per bale, provided 1,000 bales were shipped within sixty days. The first shipment of cotton from Jefferson to New York was reported in the *Jimplecute*, as cited in the 24 September *Shreveport Times*. By September, Jefferson was shipping by rail to New York, St. Louis, and Galveston and by steamboat to New Orleans.

EIGHTEEN SEVENTY-FIVE

In 1875, eight boats made 31 trips to Jefferson, including the *Belle Rowland, Charles H. Durfee, Col. A. P. Kouns, Era No. 10, Frank*

Morgan, Lotus No. 3, Maria Louise, and *R. T. Bryarly.* In addition, the *Lotus No. 3* made one trip to Mooringsport, and the U.S. government boat *Sterling* made a reconnaissance trip up Cypress Bayou to Jefferson. These boats carried out only 11,785 bales of cotton. The number of boats and number of trips had declined to the level of the early 1850s but with much less cotton.

The *Col. A. P. Kouns* (**fig. 16-9**) was a 309-ton sternwheeler built in 1874 that made many trips to Jefferson from 1875 through 1878. She is described in the 5 November 1874 *Shreveport Times:* "The Colonel A. P. Kouns is 165 feet in length, 33 feet beam with 3 feet 4 inches clear in the hold. Her cylinders are 14 inches in diameter, with 4 feet, 8 inches stroke. She has two double-flued boilers, 24 feet long and 40 inches diameter. With her machinery and cabin on she draws 14 inches. Her carrying capacity is 1800 bales of cotton. Her cabin has all of the modern improvements. Captain Mart Kouns is one of our old time steamboat men and his return to the river again after an absence of some years will be hailed with delight by his many friends."

The Great Raft on the Red River was removed in December 1873. During 1874 and 1875, water level fluctuations on the route followed

Fig. 16-9. *Col. A.P. Kouns,* Jefferson, Texas, 1875. *Source: From the Collection of the Public Library of Cincinnati and Hamilton County*

traditional seasonal patterns. In order to demonstrate that the decline of navigation on the route was not caused by raft removal, but rather was a direct consequence of the development of the rails, it is necessary to consider a post-raft year with good navigation, little steamboat activity, and a local contemporaneous perspective on the cause. These criteria are fulfilled by 1875 and the *Shreveport Times* navigation column, which derived information on Cypress Bayou from the *Jefferson Leader* and from Ward Taylor, editor of the *Daily Jimplecute*. I will simply quote from the texts, which speak for themselves and provide a running commentary on an usually high-water season.

> The Jeff. Jimp., of Thursday, says there is plenty of water in the bayou but that Jefferson has got precious little use for it. The Jimp. has got the dumps. The people have gone for the railway much to the disgust of the Jimp., and steamboats. . . . The Jimp. is disconsolate. It is an old time steamboat Jimp., and hates innovations—particularly railway innovations. Jimp., old fel., we condole with you and would go for these railroad magnates but it is no use. They have got an undoubted right to carry freight as cheap as they please. (9 January)
>
> The Jeff. Jimp. mourns the loss of boats at that port. It says the railway has bluffed them all off with low freights. It thinks it very doubtful the rail will allow any more boats to pass Shreveport at present or not. Give em goss Jimp., we'd back you. (10 January)
>
> We continue to hold out good navigation from this point to Jefferson on Cypress bayou. Without going into arithmetic, we should feel safe in saying there is more water than business. There cannot be less than six feet through the lakes, and we don't believe there is six feet of business up that way. (24 February)
>
> The lakes this side furnish plenty of water for the steamers to run everything and rising. There is a long ways more water up that way than there is business, and for that matter that is pretty much the case no matter which way we turn. (24 March)
>
> Our shippers follow the simplest rules in the world and ship by the lowest route. They are fond of competition and never go back on fifty cent cotton when they cannot get it lower. This may look a little strange to our Cypress bayou

friends, but it is nevertheless so. They have an idea that cheap freights are a great desideratum. (31 March)

There appears to be no end to the water that has fallen about Jefferson. . . . The lakes this side are plumb full and rising fast. There is no trouble about navigation, as boats can run anywhere. (3 April)

The lakes this side are falling fast, with plenty of water for the class of boats that find it profitable to ply in that trade. There is a long ways more navigation than there are uses for it. (9 May)

The officers of the Lotus found four feet in Bois d'Arc pass as they came out, and six feet and six inches at Gum Springs, in Soda Lake, with the water falling slowly. There is a long ways more water than business. (21 May)

The Lotus No. 3 left the city last night and is due here next Sunday night or Monday morning. No hurry now. Don't know about her going to Jefferson. Nothing to go for. (10 June)

The lake is now in fine boating condition, but owing to the want of business the boats have little use for it. One boat a week is more than enough. (17 June)

The Leader of Thursday reports Cypress bayou at Jefferson falling slowly, with four feet two inches above Judd's low water mark. The lakes this side are falling fast, but there is plenty of water for most any sort of boat to run to Jefferson that finds it profitable. Business has played out up that way, and the water will soon follow suit. Then the average Jeffersonian will be much vexed. As long as there is plenty of water in the bayou no matter about the business, he is all right, but just let that ditch run short of water and then h__l's to pay. (3 July)

The Jefferson papers don't seem to put much stress on the thin water in Cypress bayou and merely gives it a passing notice. It is too low up that way for steamers of any size, and we have no small chap fellows to feed them with. From this out the rail will attend to Jefferson business. The lakes this side are still navigable and the pool line carries out all its contracts with the lake landings. This state of affairs never existed before. Boats years ago in going above here if they could get through the lakes, would go to Jefferson if they had to pull over dry land. There was business there then but now how changed. (10 July)

Jefferson sends no greetings in the shape of a rise in the bayou and we feel for the bayou city. There is not much use for navigation but as Mrs. Toodles remarked about the coffin it is so handy to have in the family. (6 August)

Cypress bayou literature does not appear to be giving any attention to navigation at this time. From a casual glance at the last at hand a stranger would not know it emanated from the head of navigation. Never mind, when the new crop comes in, should there be no water in the bayou, the Jimp. will put up a howl that will make the railway magnates quake from the bottom of their feet to the top of their heads. As it is now, the denizens have no use for water, except to mix with their whisky, and that requires very little. (7 August)

The Jeff. Jimp. of last Saturday discourses as follows about Cypress bayou: "The river at this point has risen three inches more since yesterday, showing 26 inches by the new gauge. The rise is from backwater. Nothing to keep boats away now but the want of freights. If our merchants will send their orders to New Orleans instead of St. Louis we will soon hear the steamers whistle." Man alive, what do you mean? Your merchants understand their business best, and will buy where they can buy the cheapest! Steamers can be hanged when St. Louis will undersell New Orleans and the railway will "tote fair." (11 August)

The lakes above here in the direction of Jefferson are navigable for light draught boats, but as there is no business offering the water is thrown away. Cypress bayou, on which there are three or four commercial centres, viz: Port Caddo, Benton, Smithland and Jefferson, is navigable for light draught vessels as high up as the latter encampment, but as there is no trade with the natives at this season of the year, it is an utter waste of water privileges. (14 August)

Cypress bayou and the lakes furnish water plenty for a light draught boat, but there is no business to draw them out of their summer retirement. (21 August)

The Jeff Jimp of the 11th reports a rise in the bayou for the preceding twenty-four hours of one inch. This would leave the drink navigable for light water boats. The lakes this side offer plenty of water for all the business offering. (14 September)

Navigation is open to Jefferson for any class of boats it will pay to keep in the trade. There is plenty of water and still rising. The lakes furnish at least four feet in the low water channel. (21 September)

The last Jeff. Jimp. at hand reported less than thirty inches in the bayou at that point. The Col. A. P. Kouns found about thirty-three inches in the low water channel in the lakes and the water falling fast. It will take another rise before a packet the size of the Kouns will make the attempt to reach Jefferson. Smaller boats though could make the riffle like a knife. (3 October)

Jefferson literature of late is quiet on the subject of water. The bayou, or river, which they sometimes call it, is dead low—too low for navigable purposes. Catfish will run aground on the bar just below that point, if they are fools enough to venture up that far. (10 October)

The natives along what was once the borders of the Cypress bayou, have forgotten to what nation of people they have sprung from, it has been so long since they have seen anybody from another land. They now live within and for themselves. Their children know not what navigation means. (21 November)

The Jefferson Jimp. is in ecstasies. Cypress bayou was rising fast on Wednesday, and navigation was assured. We copy as follows from the Leader on Thursday: "The bayou is rising rapidly and navigation is now secured. We join with our jubilant neighbor the Jimplecute and cry 'carry the news.' A boat may be expected early in the week, when business on the levee will be lively." (25 December)

So far Jefferson has played a poor hand. According to the "Jimp." all the cotton has gone East per rail, and a rise in the river, as they call it—God save the name—makes no difference. We did think that a dose of water would save them, but alas, we were mistaken. Up goes that settlement! (29 December)

There is plenty of water for any size packet to go to Jefferson, when there is money in sight for the boat. Speaking of Jefferson reminds us that old man Kolster came here to see a steamboat. He saw one and left for Jefferson, to report progress to Ward Taylor. Let us hear from the Jimp. (31 December)

SUMMARY

The southern ports and landings on the route were destroyed a few years after the war by the extension of the Texas & Pacific west out of Shreveport into their market area. The northern ports and landings fell a few years later by the development of the Texas Central from the south and the Missouri, Kansas & Texas from the north to the western perimeter of Jefferson's market area. Jefferson's market area was progressively encompassed by these three rails from 1871 on, culminating in the extension of the Texas & Pacific through Jefferson to Texarkana in 1873 and its linkage with the Cairo & Fulton in February 1874, providing direct rail access from Northeast Texas to Midwestern cities and the East Coast.

The postwar navigation statistics are presented in **table 16-1**. These data apply almost entirely to Jefferson, because the other ports and landings made insignificant contributions to trip numbers and cotton exports after the war. The high point of navigation along the route was 1870, when more than fifty boats made nearly 300 trips. The reduction in boats and boat trips from 1870 to 1871 was a result of the

Table 16-1
Boat Activity: 1866–75

Year	Boats	Trips	Bales Shipped
1866	36	189	23,781
1867	30	115	17,212
1868	30	217	38,954
1869	31	180	39,568
1870	53	295	63,807
1871	39	226*	89,560
1872	28	134	22,694
1873	38	165	41,582
1874	14	44	NA
1875	9	32	11,785

* Laurance's official city counts.
Source: Computed from newspaper records.

disappearance of The Packery. The high point for cotton exports was 1871, when almost 90,000 bales were sent out of the route, with about 2,500 provided by ports and landings other than Jefferson. Commercial activity, as measured by trips and cotton exports, rose fairly steadily after the war, reaching a peak during 1870 and 1871 and declining rapidly into insignificance thereafter.

The decline began before the Great Raft was removed on Red River in December 1873 and tracks closely the development of the rails. The rails were identified as the causative agent in the decline of navigation along the route by contemporary sources in Jefferson and by the navigation column in the *Shreveport Times*, which tracked activities west of Shreveport on a daily basis. The long-term effects of raft removal on the navigability of the route were topical. However, the effects did not enter into the analysis of the experienced decline of navigation activity through 1875 when it had become obvious to everyone that the railroads were triumphant.

Jefferson's population declined from 4,180 in 1870 to 3,260 in 1880. As late as April 1872, confidence was still being expressed in the future of Jefferson, a confidence bolstered by the railroad celebration in July 1873 and manifest in capital improvements after fires as late as July 1873. Flatau raised a cry of alarm in September 1873, predicting the imminent demise of Jefferson if action was not taken to combat the influence of the rails. By July 1875, the town had undergone a traumatic change, as revealed by a Jefferson dispatch to the *Galveston News* on the twenty-third: "It is quite melancholy to see the number of fine business blocks vacant here. Depopulation is imminent."

The abandonment of portions of the business district is not directly related in the dispatch to the influence of the rails and can be presumed to be at least partly related to the national financial panic of 1873. Nevertheless, contemporary sources are clear that besides destroying navigation, the rails captured Jefferson's trade, destroying the commercial activity on which the town was based, thereby leading to Jefferson's demise. The various factors are assimilated in a 1 September 1881 *Galveston Daily News* commentary on the decline of Jefferson:

> Jefferson was once the trade center, the metropolis of Eastern Texas, and the point of distribution for a region 200 miles in extent to the west and northwest. Fifteen years ago, and before the advent of railroads in this section, Jefferson sold

her goods as far west as Dallas and Sherman, and points far in the interior of the Indian Territory, whence also she drew the products of the country. She was then the center of a wagon trade so large that the roads leading from the west were litterally so blocked up with vehicles that passage was difficult. But the building of the Texas and Pacific worked an era of decline for Jefferson which has depreciated her property 70 per cent since 1874; forced half her population to move away; left her finest buildings without a tenant; and partially made her the Palmyra of Texas. The railroads, by opening up the country tributary to Jefferson to other markets, instead of increasing the trade of the town, cut it off. Railroad competition for freights has also forced steamboats out of the bayou, which they now rarely ever ascend as in former days, but stop at Shreveport. The decline of the place will illustrate the power of railroads.

Jefferson's demise was not an isolated phenomenon. The rails destroyed many ports and landings throughout the Red River region and, indeed, throughout the nation. The one closest to home was Clarksville, the locus of navigation-related activities in the upper Red River region (see railroad map). Clarksville was affected by the Texas & Pacific in exactly the same way as Jefferson, as recounted in the same issue of the *Galveston Daily News*: "Before the days of railroads in Texas, Clarksville procured its supplies from New Orleans by way of Red River, steamboats delivering their cargoes at Rowland's Landing, fifteen miles distant, from which wagon transportation was used. Clarksville is said once to have sold and distributed her goods as far west as El Paso. Like Jefferson, the trade of the town came to a standstill simultaneously with the railroad era, because most of the country tributary to Clarksville then began to patronize other markets opened up."

Shreveport's experience was similar but different. Shreveport's primary market area was to the southwest. This market area was lost to Galveston through the completion of the International to Longview in January 1873. However, Shreveport was emerging as a cotton trade center and secured additional supplies from east of the Red River by wagon and down the Red River to Coushatta by steamboat, placing itself in direct competition with New Orleans. Much of the cotton that arrived at Shreveport was sent downstream by steamboat, but much was also sent by rail to the Midwest and the Eastern seaboard. This mixture of events—combined with the disappearance of the Midwestern steamboats because of rail competition—led to an extraordinary decline in Shreveport's navigation but did not destroy its commercial viability. The effect of the rails on steamboat activity at Shreveport, which fell from a high of 467 arrivals in commercial year 1871–72 to 218 arrivals in commercial year 1874–75, is described in the 1 September 1875 *Shreveport Times*:

> The completion of the Cairo and Fulton railway to Texarkana, making a quick through connection between this point and St. Louis, was a severe blow to our river business. As soon as the business of the road was well under way our river connection with St. Louis and Cincinnati was completely severed and that of New Orleans terribly crippled. In the St. Louis and Cincinnati trades we lost forty-three arrivals with a registered tonnage of 16,485 tons. In the New Orleans trade we lost 126 arrivals with a registered tonnage of 23,398 tons. Our business connections with St. Louis were more than kept up through the facilities offered by the railroad but our Cincinnati business was pretty much lost while the New Orleans trade suffered a severe blow. . . .
>
> Before the railway made any inroads upon us, the shipments of cotton down Red river from Shreveport and points above amounted to 125,000 bales and some seasons 150,000. One season, 1870–1871, they were nearly 200,000 bales, and for the last season the shipments did not exceed 75,000 bales. Taken in this light, our railway system has more effectually demolished our river business than any other trade we have a knowledge of. The rail crosses Red river at two different points and taps in at a third point, where its presence is most sensitively felt. The completion of the International road to Longview had no little to do in robbing the river of a portion of its business. To that, Galveston and Houston is in a great measure indebted for all the cotton they get from the Red river country.

The local events in Jefferson, Clarksville, and Shreveport were part of a much larger picture in which the trade of Northeast Texas and Northwest Louisiana shifted away from New Orleans and steamboats and toward the Midwest and Eastern seaboard and rail. The big loser in this process was New Orleans, and the big winner was St. Louis. New Orleans owed its commercial primacy to the fact that it was the locus of all trade activity in the Mississippi River valley as long as that trade was based on navigation. This was, in a sense, an artificial primacy, because New Orleans was remote from the great manufacturing and population centers of the nation. The rapid development of rails west of the Mississippi after the war and linkages to the Midwest and East Coast produced a transportation network with which New Orleans and its river navigation could not compete; and rail access to the rich cotton lands of Texas and Arkansas led to the emergence of St. Louis as a major cotton center, as reflected in **table 16-2**.

The most striking feature of the story that unfolds in the newspapers from 1872 through 1875 is the rapidity with which rails supplanted steamboats as the dominant transport mode serving the area of Northeast Texas and Northwest Louisiana. This was caused in part by the rapid development of the rails after the war. However, rails showed their most dramatic effect when critical linkages were established, such as the tie-in between the Texas & Pacific and the Cairo & Fulton in February 1874, which extinguished the Carter Line of boats from St. Louis overnight. Such a dramatic change in transport modes can only be explained in terms of the immense competitive advantages of the rails and the corresponding weaknesses of steamboats and the economic structure in which they operated.

Although steamboats demonstrated an amazing capacity to move through areas of low water, they obviously could not operate on land.

Table 16-2
Cotton Receipts at St. Louis

Commercial Year	Bales	Commercial Year	Bales
1869–70	18,518	1875–76	245,209
1870–71	20,270	1876–77	NA
1871–72	36,421	1877–78	266,314
1872–73	59,700	1878–79	331,000
1873–74	103,741	1879–80	470,000
1874–75	133,966		

Source: *Annual Report of the Chief of Engineers, 1880*, page 1281.

The upper limits of steamboat activity west of Shreveport were set by the northern and southern shores of Caddo Lake and by Cypress Bayou as far as Jefferson on the west. The market areas served by steamboats extended far inland where the farmers, planters, and communities that required these services were located. These three elements constituted the demand factors for import freights carried by steamboats. The first two elements constituted the supply factors for export freights, particularly cotton, carried by steamboats.

Import and export freights were carried over land by ox-wagons. This was a slow-moving and extremely expensive transport mode for the distance covered, and wagons often got bogged down on muddy roads, sometimes for weeks at a time. Transit times prohibited the quick realization of returns on commodities such as cotton in which a great deal of capital was invested. Ox-wagons arrived at ports and landings with export freights such as cotton and carried back import freights. This was not a continuous movement. Instead, wagons followed the seasonal demand for cotton transport in the fall. The interior was cut off from import freights during much of the year because ox-wagons could afford to operate only when they were able to carry freights from and to the interior.

The fragility of the overland transport system was pointed out in 1859 by George Pierce of Georgia, a bishop of the Methodist Episcopal Church, South, who traveled from Shreveport to Marshall when the Southern Pacific was first under construction:

> After inquiring the way to Marshall, we drove through; and as we had been told to follow the telegraphic wires, we found no difficulty in sticking to the right track. The posts and wires seemed like old acquaintances, after our long sojourn amid prairies and woods; and they indicated, too, that we had returned to the highways of a progressive people. But this is a new country; and although the citizens have availed themselves of the electric news-carrier, yonder comes a relic of the past— a primitive medium of transportation—a cotton-wagon drawn by oxen. For forty miles we were rarely out of sight of these clumsy vehicles and their slow-moving teams. But their days are numbered: one more season of toil, and the patient ox will rarely travel beyond his owner's broad acres, and the cumbrous wagon will stand still in its shed. There upon the right is an

embankment, and just ahead an excavation. These footprints of the engineer are the forerunners of an iron track, the iron horse—his speed and his burden. When once the steam-whistle wakes the echoes of these woods and vales, and the country commands all the facilities of a well-managed railroad, emigration from the East will receive a new impetus, and capital and intelligence will work new wonders in the West.

A port like Jefferson was not an agricultural center in the sense that interior farmers and planters brought their produce to town and purchased supplies for their operations. Rather, ports like Jefferson were primarily transfer mechanisms. Import freights were carried to Jefferson by steamboats, stored, and distributed to the market area by ox-wagons. Export freights were carried to Jefferson by ox-wagon, stored, and sent out by steamboat. Almost all of the business activities in town were intimately connected with these transfer operations. The dominant economic entity was the receiving, forwarding, and commission merchant, who dealt with freight moving in both directions.

Steamboats were limited in the geographic scope of their operations to waterbodies that contained sufficient water for navigation. They had to follow the circuitous paths afforded by waterbodies, which often required a long trip to reach a point on another stream that was fairly close by land. There were seasonal limitations on navigation, with additional low-water periods that restricted the flow of trade. Although steamboats generally were able to move fairly quickly, the sinuosity of streams produced travel times that were not impressive for point-to-point, straightline distances.

Ironically, when the conditions for navigation to Jefferson were good, the conditions for overland transport by ox-wagon were bad, so that Jefferson suffered at both ends of its transport system. The ability to reach the landing at Jefferson with ease was highly dependent on rainfall in the Cypress Bayou basin; unfortunately, it was precisely at this time that the roads became impassible, so that ox-wagons could not reach the landing from the interior. Because boats could almost always reach Jefferson with effort, the problem of interior transport was more significant, as demonstrated by the 22 February 1871 *South-Western*, quoting the *Jefferson Herald*: "Cotton and other produce has almost ceased to come in—high water and the bad condition of the roads are the great drawbacks to our prosperity. Our ox teams wont do to depend on when the earth is dampened by the dews of heaven—at least such as fall in this section."

Steamboats did not operate on regular schedules, and departure and arrival times were uncertain. Standardization of freight rates was impossible because boats were independent operators. Freight rates were never posted by boats because they were voluntary, on-the-spot agreements between shippers and carriers. Capital costs for steamboats were low, but operational costs were high, primarily because of crew salaries. Large crews had to be carried on board because of the complexity of steamboat operations and the fact that stops involving freight handling were frequent. High operational costs necessitated fairly high freight costs and produced freight cost floors below which boats could not operate without losing money.

Railroads were not limited in the geographic scope of their operations and could penetrate directly into areas of demand of import freights and areas of supply of export freights. Because they could travel over land and water, their lines were built in such a fashion as to establish the shortest transport distance between points. They were fairly fast, ran on straight tracks, and established much lower travel times than steamboats from one point to another.

Railroads operated during all seasons, under regular schedules, with specific departure and arrival times, and with posted rates. Low operating costs enabled railroads to run constantly on fixed schedules, regardless of freight offerings, and to provide highly competitive freight rates that would secure a return on capital over the long term. This competitiveness was increased by the fact that railroads were operated as systems. Freight rates could be set on particular segments of the system to secure competitive advantages in relation to alternative transport modes.

When the rails penetrated Northeast Texas, ox-wagons were immediately replaced as the dominant interior transport mode. Import freights could be brought directly into the interior where the elements of demand such as farmers, planters, and communities were located. This gave rise to the development of interior merchandise stores and deprived Jefferson of its position as the conduit for import freights into its market area.

While penetrating the demand areas, the rails were also penetrating the supply areas that produced the export freights, particularly cotton, out of Jefferson's market area. Once a bale of cotton was put on a train, there was no reason to take it off at a place like Jefferson. This would not have been the case if New Orleans had maintained dominance of Jefferson's cotton trade. There was no rail to New Orleans, so it would have been necessary to ship by steamboat out of Jefferson. However, because the flow of cotton had shifted toward the Midwest and Northeast, whatever cotton arrived at Jefferson by rail simply passed through, usually with compression, which contributed little to the economic life of the city. Cotton could not be transported by rail to Jefferson then placed on steamboats for carriage to the Midwest because this circuitous route took more time and was more costly than the direct rail to St. Louis. Thus, Jefferson was also deprived of its position as the conduit for export freights out of its market area.

It is obvious from the texts that have been cited that navigation to Jefferson declined because there was little demand for steamboat services; there was little demand for steamboat services because there was little in the way of freights at Jefferson for outshipments and little demand at Jefferson for inshipments; and import and export freights had largely disappeared from Jefferson because its market area had been captured by the rails.

The effect on Jefferson was devastating because most of its business activity was intimately connected with its status as a port—that is, as a transfer mechanism for import freights moving into its market area by steamboat and then by ox-wagon and export freights moving out of its market area by ox-wagon and then by steamboat. When this mediating function was lost, Jefferson as the locus of trade in Northeast Texas collapsed.

Steamboats assumed a minor secondary role in the transport system. Some cotton was still brought into Jefferson by ox-wagon from immediately surrounding areas and shipped out by steamboat to New Orleans. But even this meager flow of cotton by water was to be replaced in time by rails, so that the twilight of steamboat activity on the route, which extended into the next century, was characterized by local freight carriage.

The vibrant period of steamboat activity west of Shreveport came to an end in 1873, a mere third of a century after the first cotton was carried out of Port Caddo. Early in 1875, when the transition to rails was complete, the editor of the navigation column in the *Shreveport Times* provided a fitting epitaph for the steamboat era: "Everybody has his day. Look out for the engine when the bell rings."

·17·
The Raft Destroyed

INTERIM EFFORTS

After Henry Shreve removed the Great Raft on the Red River in May 1838, he stipulated that four years of maintenance work would be required to keep the raft from reforming. New rafts formed in the vicinity of the old raft's previous head in July 1838 and April 1839, both of which were removed by Shreve. Another raft formed in August 1839 and was removed by Arkansas citizens. Yet another formed that the State of Louisiana was unsuccessful in removing. In October 1840, Shreve reported navigation permanently closed pending additional congressional appropriations.

Shreve was never able to realize his objective of a Red River free of the raft for navigation. He was relieved of his duties as superintendent of Western River Improvements, and Col. Stephen H. Long was placed in charge of operations for dealing with the raft. Long was directed in March 1841 to survey the raft region, to devise a plan for dealing with the raft, and to provide an estimate of costs. This gave rise to Long's 1841 survey report, which was the third (after Birch and Shreve) federal reconnaissance of the raft region.

Long's report contains a map (**fig. 17-1**) that shows the upper Red River cutoff made by Shreve, an overland portage to the east that was used briefly in the late 1830s and early 1840s to circumvent the raft, and the raft in two segments of about a mile each. The lower

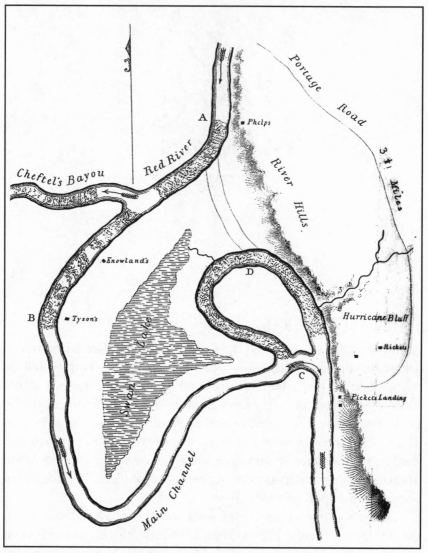

Fig. 17-1. The raft in 1841. *Source: S. Doc. 64, 27ᵗʰ Cong., 1ˢᵗ Sess.*

segment was the one attacked unsuccessfully by the State of Louisiana. The reason for the formation of the post-Shreve raft at this point is also clear, because discharges through Cheftel's Bayou (formerly Coushatta Bayou, later Shifttail Bayou, then Peach Orchard Bayou, now extinct) created a slackwater situation immediately downstream on the Red in which raft materials could accumulate.

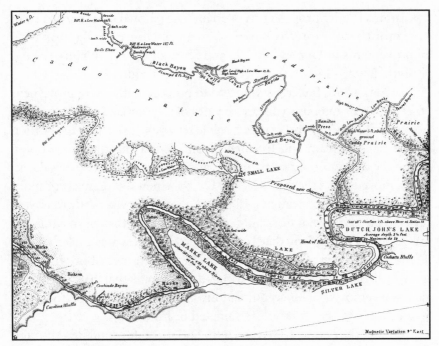

Fig. 17-2. The raft in 1855. *Source: S. Doc. 62, 33rd Cong., 2nd Sess.*

Long recommended that the work of raft removal be carried out by a private contractor under the superintendence of the Corps. The contract was awarded to Thomas T. Williamson, who conducted the work under the supervision of Capt. T. B. Linnard using Shreve's old snagboat *Eradicator.* Although the contractor was diligent and the effort successful, the cost of removal was greater than had been anticipated, and the work was not completed on time. The raft reformed in 1842, was removed, and reformed to an even greater extent in 1843. By January 1844, Williamson announced his intention to abandon the work. The effort was continued by Captain Linnard, but by July 1844 the entire workforce was disabled by sickness. Operations were suspended with one thousand yards of raft remaining.

A new survey of the raft region was initiated by Congress in August 1852 and completed by Col. Charles A. Fuller in November 1855. Fuller's survey report of March 1855 contains a map **(fig 17-2)** showing the head of the raft just below Elmer's Bayou and its foot just below Cowhide Bayou at the point where Linnard had suspended his operations. Fuller proposed an overland cut (shown on the map) from the mouth of Elmer's Bayou down to Dooley's Bayou, with improvements to Dooley's Bayou and Shifttail Lake, tying into the old Stumpy Bayou–Soda Lake–Twelvemile Bayou route.

In May 1855, Fuller was directed to proceed with the improvement to Dooley's Bayou but to discard the idea of the overland cut. To provide access to Dooley's Bayou, it then became necessary to remove the portion of the raft upstream and to catch incoming raft materials by a boom across the river at Elmer's Bayou. The raft portion above Dooley's Bayou was removed using the snagboat *Gopher*, but a new raft segment of about a mile formed in the vicinity of Elmer's Bayou. This was partly removed, and the materials were stored in Dutch John's Lake through a cut in the banks of the Red River that later came to be known as Fuller's Inlet. During the winter of 1857, a new raft segment formed above the inlet, complementing the segment farther downstream that had only been partially removed. The accumulations proved too rapid for the small workforce, and the work was terminated in June 1858.

During the period 1838 through 1858, the raft prohibited through navigation on the Red, but it was not an absolute impediment to commercial activity. The Old River trade between the foot of the raft and Shreveport was vibrant, extending up to Hurricane Bluffs and then to Carolina Bluffs after Linnard had completed his work. The upper Red River was accessible through the old Seawell route, which passed through Twelvemile Bayou, Soda Lake, Stumpy Bayou, Clear Lake, Black Bayou, Sewell's Canal, Red Bayou, and then back into Red River. However, this passage was treacherous and not usable for large portions of the year—sometimes for whole years—and insurance rates were high.

In addition, the raft continued to extend upriver. Fuller's last report, which was prepared in September 1858, noted that the head of the raft was within four hundred yards of Red Bayou. It can be assumed that the Red Bayou route ceased to be operational in the spring of 1859. Artificial cuts, such as Kouns' Canal, Hervey's Canal, and Sale and Murphy Canal, were made progressively upstream of the raft's head, tying back into the old Red Bayou–Black Bayou route (**fig. 17-3**). These were short-lived passages constructed under state charters by private companies that charged tolls, considerably reducing the profitability of the Arkansas cotton crop.

When Fuller's efforts came to an abrupt halt in 1858, a group of planters above the raft met in Washington, Arkansas, and determined

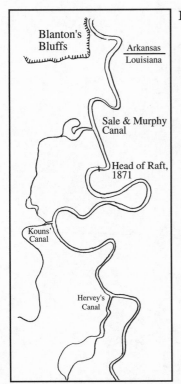

Fig. 17-3. Artificial cuts

that the cost of raft removal would be about half the additional expense sustained annually through increased freight rates, freight damage, and insurance resulting from navigation difficulties caused by the raft. Under their president, C. M. Hervey, who cut Hervey's Canal in the fall of 1861, they petitioned the Louisiana Legislature for a charter to remove the raft. Although the charter was granted, no action was taken because of the advent of the Civil War. After the war, the same group petitioned the U.S. Congress to either remove the raft or else grant a charter to enable them to do so.

In the late 1860s, a new route was developed on the east side of the Red River through an emergent raft-formed waterbody called Posten Lake that crossed over from Arkansas to Louisiana (**fig. 17-4**). This route passed through Posten and McWillie Lakes, crossed over the Red River between two raft segments, and reentered the old Red Bayou route. By the early 1870s, the raft was only a few miles from the Arkansas line, threatening the entrance to the Sale and Murphy route on the west side of the river. There were no opportunities for additional cuts upstream because the Red touched Blanton's Bluff just past the Arkansas

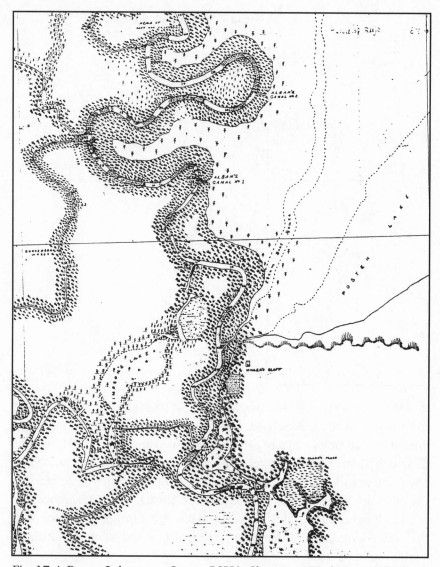

Fig. 17-4. Posten Lake route. *Source: LSU in Shreveport, Noel Memorial Library Archives*

line, and an artificial channel through the bluff was not feasible. In a few more years, the raft would close the northern entrance to Posten Lake.

The navigation situation was critical but probably could be surmounted by the ingenuity of steamboatmen, who always seemed to be able to chart a passage through whatever conditions were posed by the raft. Of even more importance than the navigation problem was flooding caused by the raft, which had already devastated the agricultural productivity of the fertile lands of Caddo Prairie to the west of the river between Blanton's Bluff and Shreveport. The flooding effects of the raft extended many miles above its head, and the upriver planters in Northeast Texas and Southwest Arkansas lived in absolute certainty that their investments would eventually be destroyed as the raft moved upstream. A letter from T. P. Hotchkiss appended to an 1873 Corps report may serve as an example: "As soon as the raft reaches Blanton's Bluff, which is again on the west side, and near the Louisiana line, the same phenomena will be observed in the valley of the Sulphur, as were about the valley lands of the Bayou Pierre, Bistineau, Bodceau, Cass, Cypress, and Black Bayous, forming immense lakes. All the swamplands of the Sulphur and Posten's Bayous are destined in their time to become shallow lakes, and unless this barrier is removed, the old and wealthy settlements of Long Prairie are destined to become a waste, like its rival in richness, Caddo Prairie."

It is widely believed that Shreveport was a prime mover in efforts to remove the raft, with the intention of destroying Jefferson as a competitor. No evidence has been offered to substantiate this opinion, other than the fact that Shreveport was an advocate of raft removal, which is understandable given its close commercial relationships with the upper Red River. Shreveport would have been in favor of raft removal even if Jefferson had never existed.

Pressure on Congress to appropriate funds to deal with the raft came primarily from the Territory, and later the State, of Arkansas and secondarily from the State of Louisiana in response to the navigation interests of its commercial center, New Orleans. These pressures began to be exerted in the 1820s, long before Shreveport came into existence, and were continuous over the decades leading up to final removal of the raft in 1873. The reasons remained the same as those articulated by Joseph Paxton in 1828: improved navigation, land protection, and land reclamation.

THE 1871–72 SURVEY

In the second session of the Forty-first Congress (1869–70), a new congressman, B. Frank Whittemore of South Carolina, introduced House Resolution 1289 "To provide for the improvement of Red river,

Caddo Lakes, and Big Cypress bay, between the cities of Shreveport, Louisiana, and Jefferson, Texas." What Whittemore had in mind is unclear, because the wording is vague, and there was no discussion on the floor of Congress. Whittemore did not stay around long enough to see action on his resolution. He was expelled from the House when it was found that he had been selling cadet appointments to West Point.

Whittemore's resolution was not for a survey but to secure appropriations for immediate improvements. The resolution was referred to the Committee on Appropriations, which referred it to the Committee on Commerce, apparently in recognition that direct action was inappropriate. A joint resolution (House Resolution 243) was then introduced by William T. Clark of Galveston "Providing for a survey of Red river and the lakes and bayous between Jefferson, in Texas, and Shreveport and Alexandria, Louisiana."

Again, the wording is unclear with respect to specific intent, and there was no discussion. In any case, the joint resolution gave rise to a provision in the River and Harbor Act of 11 July 1870 for a survey of Cypress Bayou and in the River and Harbor Act of 3 March 1871 for a survey of the Red River, with the latter including the raft area and Tone's Bayou below Shreveport, which was siphoning water out of the Red River into Bayou Pierre.

In the absence of committee hearing transcripts, Congress' reason for initiating a threefold survey of the raft area, Cypress Bayou, and Tone's Bayou can only be surmised. Any improvements to navigation on the Red needed to take the raft and Tone's Bayou into consideration. It was also widely understood that the raft was instrumental in securing the navigability of the Cypress Bayou and the lakes route, so that any consideration of its removal needed to address potential effects to the west. In providing for a joint survey, Congress clearly expressed an intent to improve navigation on the Red while at the same time protecting the interests of the ports and landings on the route west of Shreveport.

Responsibility for the Cypress Bayou survey was given to Capt. C. W. Howell of the New Orleans District Corps of Engineers, and Lt. Eugene A. Woodruff was directed to conduct the survey. Woodruff proceeded to Jefferson in January 1871 to begin work, but he was prevented from doing so by high water in the bayou. Congressional action in March expanded Howell's survey responsibilities to include the Red River, and this effort was also delegated to Woodruff, producing the combined 1871–72 survey of Cypress Bayou and the lakes, Red River in the vicinity of the raft, and Tone's Bayou.

Woodruff felt that it would be unwise to conduct the joint survey during the unhealthy seasons of summer and autumn, so most of the year passed without action. Arrangements were made to begin on 15 October, at which time the survey crew was ordered to assemble at Shreveport, which was to serve as headquarters for the work effort. Because of extreme low water, the Red was not navigable, and Woodruff had to travel overland from New Orleans to Vicksburg, then to Monroe and Shreveport. The road from Monroe to Shreveport was in bad condition, and a week was lost in transporting instruments and camp equipment. It was not until 31 October that the first party could be sent into the field.

The survey crew was divided into four teams, each consisting of a transit man and levelers, with rodmen, oarsmen, and a cook. H. C. Ripley was placed in charge of the Red River and raft survey, which extended from Blanton's Bluff (just above the Arkansas line) to Shreveport. H. C. Collins was placed in charge of the survey for the Red River valley from Blanton's Bluff to Shreveport, which encompassed the various bayous and lakes that served as navigation routes around the raft. J. O. Fox was placed in charge of the Cypress Bayou survey, which began at Jefferson and was intended for completion down to the head of Big Willow Pass. S. H. Calhoun was placed in charge of the Tone's Bayou survey.

After two months of work at Tone's Bayou, the Calhoun party was reassigned to survey the area between Shreveport and Carolina Bluffs and met the Ripley party working downstream on 1 February 1872. Errors were found in Calhoun's survey at Tone's Bayou and on Red River, and he was dismissed. Fox's party on Cypress Bayou was proceeding at a very slow pace, and he was dismissed before reaching the Louisiana line. Ripley reworked the Calhoun survey on Red River, and Collins, who had been covering the valley area west of the river, proceeded to Swanson's Landing. Woodruff completed the process by surveying Dooley's Bayou, which Fuller had recommended as a navigation alternative to raft removal.

The survey effort was completed in about five months and resulted in two reports and a number of maps. Preliminary results were published in the 1872 annual report of the chief of engineers, and the completed survey was described the next year. The final report contains an overview of the history of the raft and its effects on the Red River area that will remain an important document for anyone interested in the hydrologic development of the area west of Shreveport.

A large map was produced in two parts, one covering Red River and the other covering Cypress Bayou and the lakes from Jefferson to Shreveport. The latter part was the first federal survey of Cypress Bayou and Caddo Lake and contains valuable historic information but with a regrettable deficiency noted by Woodruff: "Thanks to the energetic co-operation of Assistants Ripley and Collins and their parties, the most important part of the topography and hydrography of the field are secured, the deficiency being chiefly in the survey of the lakes, in which the location and depth of the ancient bayous and the steamboat routes could not be obtained in the time for which the funds held out."

Woodruff was given wide latitude on recommendations concerning the raft, but there were only two major alternatives—either to remove the raft or improve the bypass. On reading Fuller's report, he was initially predisposed to the idea of improving the route around the raft, but the survey quickly changed his mind. His conclusions, as stated in the final survey report, were unequivocal:

> As between the main river and any side-route, the question in my mind hardly admits of discussion.
>
> The river to be opened should not only afford passage for boats at moderate stages of water, but should have sufficient capacity, particularly depth, to carry the drift which will continue to come from the upper river till the sources of its supply are destroyed. To give such capacity to any of the side-routes would require extensive excavations in the clay formations found at some part of all such routes. All of such routes would be shorter than the main river, and therefore would have a greater fall per mile. The different levels in these routes would be connected by rapids, as in Dooley's Bayou, and nothing short of locks and dams would make them passable at all seasons when boats could navigate the main channel if opened.
>
> The present routes, by Posten Bayou on the east, and Kelly's Bayou on the west, afford navigation in high water. If nothing more were needed, the raft might remain. But such navigation is uncertain and expensive, and if the raft be allowed to continue its formation even this will fail. Besides this, valuable plantations

have been ruined by the overflows caused by the damming up of the waters by the raft.

The need of a cheap mode of transportation of the products of the upper river, the relief of plantations made worthless by overflows, and the prevention of the ruin of more valuable plantations above, are of sufficient importance to warrant appropriations for these ends, provided the work be judged practicable within reasonable limits of expenditure.

By removing the raft, and only in this way, can these ends be attained.

The practicality of the effort was rooted in an assessment of the raft. Woodruff found that the raft was discontinuous, with large open spaces of water between the raft segments, as shown on one of his survey maps (**fig. 17-5**). When the open spaces were excluded from the computation, the total length of the raft was only about seven miles. Between its head and Dooley's Bayou, the raft was composed primarily of floating logs, estimated at 290 acres (**fig. 17-6**). Below Dooley's Bayou, the raft was composed primarily of towheads, which were masses of silt and debris that collected around stumps whose roots rested on the bottom of the river and whose trunks broke the water surface (**fig. 17-7**). The area of towheads was computed at 103 acres.

On the basis of this analysis, Woodruff concluded that the difficulties of raft removal had been grossly exaggerated and that the work could be accomplished in one year. The plan of action was threefold: (1) Towheads would be removed by a specially constructed double-hulled scow with equipment for raising logs and saws for dismembering them. The cut timber would be transferred to a steamboat with crane that would place the materials on the banks. (2) A sawboat would be used to cut up floating raft. Buoyant pieces would float off downstream, and waterlogged pieces would be placed on the banks. (3) Axmen would clear the banks for hundreds of miles above to eliminate the influx of raft materials.

Woodruff was fully conscious of the effect that raft removal would have on the route to Jefferson, which was the presupposition for the conduct of the dual survey. Raft removal would obviously cause a decline in the navigability of the route, because it was the raft that deflected water into the lakes. However, Woodruff thought that the process would be very gradual, because the distributaries would fail to capture

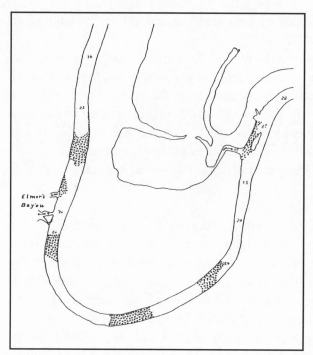

Fig. 17-5. Raft segments. *Source: LSU in Shreveport, Noel Memorial Library Archives*

Fig. 17-6. Floating logs. *Source: LSU in Shreveport, Noel Memorial Library Archives. Photographer: R.B. Talfor*

Fig. 17-7. Towheads. *Source: LSU in Shreveport, Noel Memorial Library Archives. Photographer: R.B. Talfor*

significant amounts of water only after the Red scoured out its sediment-laden bed.

Nevertheless, his preliminary and final reports proposed corrective actions that would eliminate the potential threat to the navigability of the route that would result from raft removal. The corrective actions would involve improvements to Cypress Bayou and a dam, with or without a lock, at Albany that would actually improve the route by resolving the traditional low-water problems at the lower end of Soda Lake. Woodruff requested funds for these corrective measures at the same time that he requested funds for raft removal.

As a result of Woodruff's preliminary survey report, Congress appropriated through the River and Harbor Act of 10 June 1872 $150,000 for raft removal, $10,000 for improvements to Cypress Bayou, and $20,000 for improving Tone's Bayou. The River and Harbor Act of 3 March 1873 appropriated another $80,000 for removing the raft and $50,000 for improving Cypress Bayou and dredging and the construction of a dam at the foot of Soda Lake. These were the first in a series of appropriations that were directed to raft removal and channel maintenance on the Red and reciprocal improvements to Cypress Bayou and the lakes.

Woodruff was instructed to conduct a survey, not to come up with a proposal for raft removal, an idea that he did not initially favor. The survey addressed Cypress Bayou and the lakes as well as the Red River, in full recognition of the hydrologic unity of the area. In opting for raft removal, Woodruff provided recommendations for corrective actions that would insure the navigability of the Cypress Bayou and the lakes route. All of Woodruff's recommendations were affirmed by congressional appropriations. There is nothing in this record to suggest that the interests of the ports and landings on the Cypress Bayou and the lakes route were not taken fully into account; it is fitting that the resolution that eventually gave rise to the initial appropriations for raft removal was submitted by J. Hale Sypher of New Orleans, rather than by a representative from the Shreveport area.

WOODRUFF AT WORK

Woodruff had originally intended to build a double-hulled scow to serve as the main workboat. When the congressional appropriations were less than he had requested, he left New Orleans in August 1872 to visit the upper Mississippi River ports to find an appropriate vessel. The wrecking boat *Aid*, which had been built in Pittsburg in 1869, was found in St. Louis and purchased for $19,000.

The *Aid* was 136 feet long with a total width (including the 14-foot space between the two hulls) of 44 feet and drew 3 feet. She had spent most of her life removing machinery from wrecks and, with a few modifications, was well suited to raft removal (**fig. 17-8**). The *Aid* left for New Orleans in October under the command of Capt. Thomas Rogers and carrying 2,500 pounds of blasting powder. Smallpox had been prevalent in St. Louis, and a single case was discovered among the crew of the *Aid* on the way to New Orleans.

A brief quarantine in New Orleans did not cause any delay, because the Red was at a low stage and impassable. While waiting in New Orleans, the *Aid* was further outfitted with steam saws and a steam pump and hoses for washing mud from logs. A thousand pounds of dynamite was taken on board, which, like the blasting powder, was to be used on an experimental basis. The *Aid* started up the Red River on 25 November with two craneboats (*No. 1* and *No. 2*) in tow and a crew

Fig. 17-8. *Aid. Source: LSU in Shreveport, Noel Memorial Library Archives. Photographer: R.B. Talfor*

of 17 lumbermen from Michigan who were to be replaced by a new crew in Shreveport and assigned to different duties.

The *Aid* did not arrive in Shreveport until 10 January. In the meantime, on 1 December Woodruff organized a shore party of about 20 men to begin chopping surface logs and growing trees on the towheads constituting raft segment three in the vicinity of Carolina Bluffs. Two similar parties were organized on 9 December, one of which began chopping towheads at the foot of the raft, and the other of which began removing logs that were part of the floating raft in segment twenty-eight at Miller's Bluff. Attempts to burn the floating raft failed.

The rise in the Red River that enabled the *Aid* to reach Shreveport on 10 January also enabled her to proceed upriver toward the raft on 20 January, accompanied by two smaller steamers, the *Kalbaugh* and the *Hornet*, which had been hired to tow the two craneboats to Carolina Bluffs. The *Hornet* was a tiny 39-ton screw propeller steamboat that had been active in the Old River (the Red above Shreveport and below the raft) and Jim's Bayou trades. It does not appear in the raft removal record after this point.

The *Aid* reached Carolina Bluffs on 27 January and began pulling snags slightly downriver of the raft. The craneboats began attacking the towheads at Cowhide Bayou with the intent of opening a passage for the *Aid*. This was accomplished in two days, and the *Aid* proceeded into the area of minor towheads below the raft proper, with one of the craneboats working ahead. Two weeks were required to work through these initial towheads, after which the *Aid* broke through to open water below raft segment one and began the full assault on the raft itself.

When fully implemented, the components of the work force involved 150 men and officers and ten vessels. The workers were assigned to one of four shore parties (**fig. 17-9**) that worked at various points along the raft or else served as crews for the various vessels. The components of the fleet are pictured in the photographic album that was developed as the work progressed:

1. The *Aid* was the mainstay of the work effort. Her powerful steam capstans were used to pull embedded logs onto the sloped, iron-reinforced apron between the hulls, where they were washed with steam hoses and the initial dismemberment took place with steam saws (**fig. 17-10**). The *Aid* was initially under the command of Captain Rogers, who was replaced by Capt. I. B. Hiserman in June.

2. The *Kalbaugh* was a supply boat that ran between the raft and Shreveport and broke up incipient jams. She was purchased in April at a cost of $2,500, renamed the *Thomas F. Sterling*, and placed under the command of Capt. J. S. Tennyson. Nothing is known about this steamboat other than her photographic documentation (**fig. 17-11**).

3. Craneboats *No. 1* and *No. 2* were scow vessels 65 feet long and 25 feet wide that were equipped with boom-cranes, steam saws, and cabins for the crews of 12 (**fig. 17-12**). These boats were particularly useful in opening passages for the *Aid* and in dismembering raft components that were not touched by the *Aid* as she moved upstream.

4. The five sawboats were flatboats measuring 55 feet by 16 feet and 65 feet by 15 feet. They were equipped with portable steam saws that were used to dismember the large logs generated by the *Aid* and other smaller logs that were pulled from the raft (**fig. 17-13**). Cut materials were

Fig. 17-9. Shore party. *Source: LSU in Shreveport, Noel Memorial Library Archives. Photographer: R.B. Talfor*

Fig. 17-10. *Aid. Source: LSU in Shreveport, Noel Memorial Library Archives. Photographer: R.B. Talfor*

Fig. 17-11. *Kalbaugh. Source: LSU in Shreveport, Noel Memorial Library Archives. Photographer: R.B. Talfor*

Fig. 17-12. Craneboat. *Source: LSU in Shreveport, Noel Memorial Library Archives. Photographer: R.B. Talfor*

Fig. 17-13. Sawboat. *Source: LSU in Shreveport, Noel Memorial Library Archives. Photographer: R.B. Talfor*

allowed to float downstream or else were deposited in off-channel areas such as lakes and distributaries.

5. The shearboat *Essay* (**fig. 17-14**) was outfitted with a crab, a pair of spears at the bow for hoisting snags, a small cabin, a kitchen, and a storeroom and followed closely in the wake of the *Aid*.

The best description of the work done by these boats is in the 13 May 1873 *Shreveport Times* in a long article by the editor based on in-field inspection of the progress to that date, which was up to raft segment twenty-five of the forty-two segments:

AT WORK.

A description of the attack to day made by the fleet on the raft or tow head No. 25, one-eighth mile long, may not be without interest. There it lays one solid bed of logs embedded in mud upon which live cotton woods grow and flourish. Capt.

Fig. 17-14. *Essay. Source: LSU in Shreveport, Noel Memorial Library Archives. Photographer: R.B. Talfor*

Rogers has examined the map and formed his plan of attack. The signal is sounded by two long whistles, when the steamer Aid with her steam capstans, and immense purchase power, moves to the attack, followed at intervals of one hundred yards by one crane boat and two flats armed with glittering saws. An old log, perhaps one hundred feet long, first attracts the attention of the commanding officer, who at once orders the skiff men in advance to hitch "onto him." This is done quickly and soon the steam capstan is tugging away. If he prove refractory and won't yield, another capstan is called in, when he generally succumbs and is dragged from his sandy bed with many more hanging to him, forming quite a mass of logs, dirt, roots and growing cotton woods. This mass is pulled to pieces and the logs turned loose to be picked up by the steam saw boats in the rear and cut into small pieces which are allowed to float off and eventually find a resting place in the lakes supplied by Dooley bayou outlet. Sometimes the Aid moves up and hitches on to three or four different parts of the raft as she is able to do, having a front of forty or fifty feet and then backs out with all her weight and force. Sometimes she makes three or four efforts before the mass moves. Once moved the water soaks through, the dirt crumbles and the mass is easily pulled to pieces and the logs allowed to float off. In this way she has been eating into raft No. 25 all day and as the whistle sounds for the close of the day's work, the Aid is over half way through. It is in this way she has worked through twenty-four patches of solid raft and in this way will finish the remaining ones. Of course some of them were much harder to get through than others, but the Aid has never yet hitched to anything in the raft that did not respond to her summons. It will be seen that the removal of this raft has been accomplished, by simple but powerful means—industry and main strength. This description of the removal of raft No. 25, will answer for all, as there has been little or no variation in the removal or cutting a channel through the others.

The only thing that needs to be added to this picture is the use of explosives. The dynamite deteriorated en route and was entirely worthless, and it was difficult to get the blasting powder deep enough into the towheads because of the compactness of the masses; however, nitroglycerin proved its worth on a trial run at the end of May at Alban's second canal, which was to provide access to Posten Lake for the disposal of raft materials:

> Part of the work of opening this canal consisted of the removal of growing trees in deep water. One large cypress was a complete barrier to the passage of any but the shortest drift; and on this tree our first experiment was made. The tree stood in 12 feet of water, was 30 inches in diameter at the water-surface, and perfectly sound, having been dead but one year. To allow the passage of drift required that the tree should be cut off at least 6 feet under water. The cartridges, containing in all 5 pounds of nitro-glycerine, were suspended in the water on the up-stream side of the tree, 6 inches from the bottom, the current holding them in contact with the trunk. Electric exploders and the Smith's battery were used, and the charge

exploded. The tree, which stood with a hundred feet of trunk and a full top of branches above the water, was lifted about 10 feet in the air, and the bottom of the trunk thrown at the same time about that distance from the stump, away from the cartridges, causing the tree to fall in a direction opposite to that toward which it was leaning. The trunk was found to have been cut squarely off at the bottom, the upper end having a broomed and shattered appearance.

Twenty pounds of nitroglycerin were exploded the same day, with equally satisfactory results. Despite these impressive qualities, nitroglycerin was slow to be introduced in the work process, partly because only one battery was available at first, but mostly because the workmen distrusted its safety. It was used successfully by shore parties and the *Kalbaugh* to break up pieces of incipient jams, but it did not become a part of the *Aid's* armory until September when the project was nearly over.

A month-by-month account of the progress of the work effort is given in Woodruff's 1873 and 1874 reports. But apart from the fact that a few men drowned and a few others became ill and had to be taken to Shreveport, the work, as the *Shreveport Times* recognized, was fairly repetitious, however impressive. The only significant milestone was the opening of Red River up to the Red Bayou outlet in May, which enabled steamboats to avoid Clear Lake and Black Bayou, moving upriver on the Red from Shreveport, thence into Red Bayou and the Sale and Murphy route around the raft. The event and its significance are described in Woodruff's 1873 report:

> The 16th of May opened an era in upper Red River navigation. Mr. Kent's party had opened a narrow channel through raft No. 26, below Red Bayou, and the Aid began the work of enlarging it the 15th.
>
> A party of gentlemen from Shreveport Chamber of Commerce, with ladies, had come up to see the work of raft-removal, and in anticipation of the event of opening navigation to Red Bayou, by which the shoal and dangerous mouth of Black Bayou would be avoided.
>
> The steamer R. T. Bryarly, with a heavy load of freight for the upper river, came up the night of the 15th, expecting to go

through Red Bayou, and thence by the Sale and Murphy route to Fulton, Ark. Only a few heavy logs remained to be pulled; and, after an hour's work on the morning of the 16th, the Aid backed out of the still narrow channel to make room for the Bryarly to pass through. She went through without stopping, and, with jubilant whistling from both boats, passed into Red Bayou, the first boat in twenty-nine years to take freight for upper Red River past Carolina Bluffs.

This passage was recorded in the photographic album (**fig. 17-15**) and in the Bryarly's 13 May advertisement in the *Shreveport Times* in anticipation of the event:

FOR UPPER RED RIVER VIA CAROLINA BLUFFS.
Leaves THIS DAY, May 13.
    The Sale & Murphy line packet R. T. BRYARLY, Capt. W. T. SCOVELL, will leave as above, going through the raft channel lately cut by Lieut. Woodruff. For freight or passage apply on board or to SALE & MURPHY, Agents.

Fig. 17-15. *R.T. Bryarly. Source: LSU in Shreveport, Noel Memorial Library Archives. Photographer: R.B. Talfor*

The return trip of the *Bryarly* is recorded in the 20 May *Shreveport Times*:

> At 3 o'clock in the morning the R. T. Bryarly, Capt. W. T. Scovell, Tom Howard, clerk, came in from the head of the raft, with 1000 bales of cotton. This is the first arrival to come out through the channel cut in the old raft, from Red bayou down, in twenty-nine years. As a matter of record we give the date in full—Monday, May 19, 1873. She got six hundred bales of her cotton at Flavilla landing on Kelly bayou, brought to that point by the Royal George from Rowland. The balance she got at the head of Red bayou, brought to that point from Bargetown by the steamer Royal George. The Flavilla first brought it to Bargetown from the Upper river. We congratulate the citizens above the raft on the success of Lieut. E. A. Woodruff, so far, and have no fears but that he will remove the five miles of floating raft this summer, when the whole route will be open up to navigation.

The end was accomplished, but not by Woodruff and not during the summer, which was the occasion for the great yellow fever epidemic of 1873 in Shreveport.

DEATH OF WOODRUFF

Eugene Augustus Woodruff was born in Independence, Iowa, in 1842 and attended the U.S. Military Academy, where he graduated seventh in a class of forty-one in July 1862. He became a second lieutenant in the Corps of Engineers in June 1866 and was promoted to first lieutenant in March 1867. He engaged in project work on the Tchefuncte and Tangipahoa Rivers in Louisiana and at Corpus Christi and Aransas Pass in Texas and was appointed to conduct the survey of the raft region in 1871. The survey was completed in 1872, and the work of raft removal began late in that year. During August 1873, while working on the raft, Woodruff went to Shreveport, where he died at the age of thirty-one during the 1873 yellow fever epidemic.

Woodruff's field reports and his cadet photograph (**fig. 17-16**) reveal him to be a man of insight, energy, and determination, mixed with charm and kindness. The technical work displayed in his maps

Fig. 17-16. Eugene Woodruff. *Source: United States Military Academy Library, Special Collections and Archives*

and reports is impeccable, insightful, well reasoned, forcefully stated, and elegantly presented. In spite of his youth, he successfully commanded and gained the respect of large field crews and was quick to dismiss anyone who did not live up to his responsibilities. He quickly gained the hearts of the people of Shreveport, which served as his base of operations, by organizing trips to the work areas at the raft above Shreveport and at Tone's Bayou below.

Woodruff apparently arrived at Shreveport from the raft on 30 August aboard the *Sterling*, which was seeking provisions. This was when the first few cases of yellow fever were reported and it was not yet certain that an epidemic was beginning. On 3 September, the Shreveport Howard Association was formed "to relieve the sick as nurses as far as may be in their power and to solicit contributions from the citizens of this and adjoining places, for the relief of the needy." This was a local chapter of the Howard Association, which had begun in 1837 in New Orleans for the relief of yellow fever victims.

Woodruff did not leave Shreveport. Instead, he joined the Howard Association and was appointed on 4 September to patrol the Second Ward to identify yellow fever victims and maintain civic order. Within two weeks he became ill, as reported in the 17 September *Shreveport Times*: "We regret to learn that this gallant gentleman has been taken down with the fever. He came down from the work on the raft last week, and seeing our deplorable condition, at once tendered his services to the sick, and nursed and waited upon them until taken down. May he have a speedy recovery is the earnest wish of all our citizens."

Within another two weeks, he was dead, as reported in the 2 October *Shreveport Times*.

> LIEUT. E. A. WOODRUFF,
> Of the United States Engineers Corps, died of the fever Tuesday night, September 30th. Although death is busy taking off our best citizens, many of whom pass to the grave without a tribute notice from us, yet we should be derelict in our duty to pass him by without a brief paragraph. He came among us about two years ago a perfect stranger, sent by his government to remove the raft in Red river. By his courtesy to our people, stern integrity and unflinching industry and perseverance, he won the esteem of this community, and his death is looked upon as a public calamity. Some three weeks since hearing of our affliction he left the work on the raft and gave his whole attention to our sick and dying. In about a week he was taken with the fever and the hope was universally expressed that he might recover; but alas, the ways of providence are inscrutable, and he rests in his grave. He died a martyr to the blessed cause of charity, and may his reward be great in the world to come.

Why didn't Woodruff leave Shreveport? His commander, Capt. C. W. Howell, was of the opinion that he had gone to Shreveport to begin a survey of Soda Lake to determine the feasibility of constructing a lock and dam; "Finding himself in the midst of an epidemic; unable to get assistants; having been exposed to disease; and unwilling to risk carrying that disease among his employees at work on Red River raft, he did what was proper, prudent, and humane, though his action cost him his life."

This opinion is not plausible. The *Sterling* went back to the raft and returned to Shreveport for more provisions. The medium for infection of the work crew was present without Woodruff. He could have proceeded to Soda Lake, with plenty of assistants, because the city was being rapidly abandoned. Or, he could simply have left. That leaves only one possible explanation, the *Shreveport Times*'s tribute that "he died a martyr to the blessed cause of charity." The newspaper's 15 November retrospective on the epidemic speaks of "the gallant Woodruff, allied with us by no tie save that of a common humanity, he resolved to share our fate."

During the epidemic, about two-thirds of the population of 9,000 abandoned the city and 759 people died, including many members of the Howard Association and most notably priests who flocked to the city to care for the sick. A picture of the city during the height of the epidemic is given in the 17 September *Shreveport Times*:

> THE EPIDEMIC
>
> Exhibits but little change. While the number of new cases are not so numerous, owing to the want of material to work on, the number of deaths are fearful to contemplate. The mortality is beyond precedent, and it looks as though comparatively few would get well. Thus far very few have got about, while some linger along between life and death. In some few instances whole families have been swept out of existence in the short space of one week. The change in the weather Saturday night sent scores to their beds, which accounts for the large number of interments in the last day or two. In the language of one of the New Orleans physicians, they dropped off like sheep dying of the rot. Medical treatment of the most skillful kind does not appear to do any good in a great many cases, while in many others the temporary relief afforded is quickly followed by death. Our stores are all closed and all our dwellings turned into hospitals. In fact Shreveport is one great hospital—one great charnel house, and the TIMES merely a death record.

Woodruff's actions were particularly praiseworthy because he was thought by many to be the cause of the disaster. At this time it was unknown that yellow fever was transmitted by mosquitoes. Four different explanations were offered. A circus from Mexico had recently left the city and could have provided transmission by a carrier. The other three were versions of the commonly accepted idea that yellow fever was caused by decaying matter. One possible cause under this theory was the unsanitary conditions in Shreveport. A second was the rotting carcasses of cattle that had stampeded aboard the *Ruby* and caused her to sink. A third was that the removal of the raft caused the epidemic, a theory summarized by the *New Orleans Republican*, as reported by the 17 September *Shreveport Times*: "Another theory is that the dislodging of the great raft has let loose immense quantities of decayed vegetable matter which eliminates malarial poisons all along the course of Red river until all is absorbed by the atmosphere."

In attempting to dispel this notion on more than one occasion by pointing out that the 150 raft workers were in excellent health, the *Shreveport Times* suggests that this was the most widely held explanation. Given the prevalent concepts of miasma as the causative agent, an extraordinary and unique disruption like raft removal was a likely explanation for the devastation. Patrolling the streets in Shreveport and caring for the sick was an extraordinary act of courage on Woodruff's part.

The records of condemnation are silent. His fellow officers prepared a tribute that appeared in the 23 October *Shreveport Times*:

> LIEUT. E. A. WOODRUFF.
>
> At a meeting of the officers employed on the Red River Raft, the following preamble and resolutions were adopted:
>
> WHEREAS death has in the person of Lieut. E. A. Woodruff, deprived us of a dear friend, the Army of an efficient officer, the country of a devoted patriot, and humanity of an ornament to the race,
>
> THEREFORE, Be it resolved, that while we deplore his loss as irreparable, we gladly testify to the excellent quality of his character, his sturdy integrity, the lively interest which he felt and expressed in all those with whom he associated, his fine social qualities, which rendered him an ornament to any society, his love for and interest in the advancement of the race, his lively sense of the brotherhood of man, and his consistent Christian life, which rendered him an ideal man.
>
> Resolved, that the manner of his death proclaims him a worthy follower of Howard, the Philanthropist—an act requiring a loftier courage than any displayed on the field of battle.
>
> Resolved, that we tend our deepest sympathy to the bereaved family, especially to his mother, whose future hopes so justly depended on the fruit of the mature years of him, whose early manhood had already accomplished so much.

Woodruff is buried in the Oakland Cemetery at Shreveport. His grave is marked by a tall grey monument with an arched top and a relief of a crown with a cross passing through it. The epitaph is by his widowed mother:

> To my beloved son, Eugene A. Woodruff, Lieutenant of Engineers, U.S.A. A member of the Howard Association during the Great Epidemic. Died September 30, 1873, Aged 31 years. "I was sick and you visited me."

END AND AFTERMATH

When Woodruff became ill in the middle of September, work continued on segment thirty-nine, through which an opening was achieved by the end of the month. Nitroglycerin was used for the first time in direct connection with the activities of the *Aid*. Cans containing ten to twenty pounds of nitroglycerin were sunk to the bottom of the river and exploded with the effect of breaking the long logs and loosening the tangled masses in the immediate vicinity. Small charges were also used to cut long logs and stumps too far beneath the water surface to be reached by other means.

After Woodruff died at the end of the month, his brother George, who had been part of the workforce from the beginning, was placed in charge of the raft removal operations. Rafts forty and forty-one were removed without difficulty. Work began on segment forty-two, the last in the series, which was found to have increased in size by two-thirds of a mile since the time of the initial survey. Nitroglycerin was used liberally, and the work of raft removal was completed at the end of November: "Operations upon raft No. 42 were continued until the evening of the 26th. The river at that time was rising rapidly, and at daylight on the 27th the remaining portion of the raft obstructing the channel went out, and Red River was relieved of a serious obstruction to its navigation."

For obvious reasons, there was no one from Shreveport to greet the event as there had been for the opening of the river up to Red Bayou. The "River and Weather" column in the 3 December *Shreveport Times* also reported the event in a rather subdued fashion: "Last Thursday the steamer *Aid* pulled out the last of the great Red River raft, and steamed up to Spring Bank, twelve miles above Bargetown, on the head of the Old Raft. Navigation is now open to the Upper River Straight, the main channel, for the first time in thirty years."

A more elaborate tribute was given in the 8 December issue, but even this appeared in the "Local Intelligence" column, perhaps not surprising given the fact that the city had not yet recovered from the epidemic, which had nearly destroyed the newspaper by killing off its employees:

> IT IS FINISHED.
>
> Capt. Tennyson, of the steamer Sterling, called on us last night, bringing a small bale of cotton, two inches thick and four inches long, neatly done up with wire, which he intends as a compliment to our river man, but who, at the time of the Captain's visit, had retired to his dreams of steamboats and low middling. This bale is one of five, the first that have been shipped through the raft. It is from the plantation of A. I. Williams, at Spring Bank, situated on the main river, and eighteen miles above the head of the old raft.
>
> In other words, the great work has been accomplished, and now any boats that can go to Carolina Bluffs can go to Fulton. The opening was completed on the 27th of November, since which time the Aid, after going through to Spring Bank, has been engaged in widening out the channel. Captain Tennyson informs us that most of the water has been drawn away from the lakes and is now in the main channel. At Carolina Bluffs the water is even now within three and a half feet of the highest water mark of the past season.
>
> This is, indeed, a grand achievement, though the triumph of those who have accomplished it is marred—the lamented Woodruff did not live to witness the result of his faithful labors.

The key element in Shreve's failure was the unwillingness of the federal government to provide the necessary funds for maintenance after the channel had been cleared. This was not the case in the 1870s. For many years after 1873, large appropriations were made to insure that the raft did not reform.

The nitroglycerin that proved so successful in dealing with the raft was used concurrently by Woodruff in improvements to Tone's Bayou and Cypress Bayou, the two other components of his overall work effort in the region. The nitroglycerin was produced for Woodruff by Charles D. Chase, a chemist who had been taught by G. M. Mobray, a nitroglycerin manufacturer in St. Louis who had used the product successfully in blasting the Hoosac tunnel.

Nitroglycerin was not transported for long distances and therefore had to be produced on-site. According to the 24 December 1873 *Shreveport Times*, Woodruff's nitroglycerin was produced on an island opposite the ice house on Cross Bayou, a reasonable place given the fact that ice was essential to manufacturing, transport, and storage. The nitroglycerin used on the raft was stored at a facility near raft number eight (**fig. 17-17**). Although there is no documentation, the nitroglycerin used on Cypress Bayou was almost certainly stored in the powder magazine at Jefferson.

After the raft was destroyed at the end of 1873, the remaining nitroglycerin was divided between the Cypress Bayou facility and a small house at the foot of Twelvemile Bayou, which was also used to store dynamite and blasting powder. This division was the apparent reason for a trip by the *Aid* to Jefferson at the end of December. Although no problems had been encountered in using nitroglycerin

Fig. 17-17. Nitroglycerin facility. *Source: LSU in Shreveport, Noel Memorial Library Archives. Photographer: R.B. Talfor*

during the work, on 12 June 1874, the storehouse on Twelvemile Bayou exploded, as recorded in the 13 June *Shreveport Times*: "Shortly after 12 o'clock yesterday our citizens were startled out of their boots and propriety by the loudest report ever before heard in this part of the continent. The concussion was so great that many thought that their houses were tumbling about their ears, and, we believe, in some instances glass was shivered. Everybody rushed out into the streets to learn whence came this reverberating thunder, in comparison with which heaven's artillery were but a pop-gun."

It was first thought that a boiler must have exploded on the *Charles H. Durfee* or at one of the sawmills or at the cotton seed oil factory. When it was determined that it was none of these, people rushed to the conclusion that it must have been a boiler explosion aboard the *Clifford*, which had gone to Albany with a cabin full of Shreveport's leading citizens who were looking for materials to pave the streets. However, it was soon realized that it must be the nitroglycerin camp, particularly after steamboatmen insisted that no boiler explosion could make such an impact. Many of the curious traveled to the site by skiff and steamboat, including the editor of the *Shreveport Times*, who records: "We soon after reached the spot and the scene presented was a curious one. Not a vestige of the house remained, but where it stood was a perfectly circular hole in the earth, in shape resembling a bowl, about ten feet deep and twenty in diameter. There was not a leaf on the trees for twenty yards around, but the ground was literally strewed with their "remains" having been reduced almost to a green powder. A small tree had been completely upset, while several presented the singular appearance of having been perforated by, say twenty thousand wood-peckers."

No one was hurt, and it was later assumed that the explosion of the nitroglycerin had been set off by the spontaneous combustion of old dynamite.

During 1874 and 1875, the *Sterling* kept the river free from jams and transported supplies to the workers on the crane, shearboats, and sawboats, which removed remaining portions of the raft and felled bank timber. "Having become worn out in service, and almost totally unfit for the duty required of her," the *Sterling* was retired in June 1875 and replaced by the *Thomas B. Florence* in November.

The *Florence* was an iron-hulled steamboat that continued, under Captain Tennyson, to engage in the same operations as the *Sterling*. In

June 1877, the *Florence* was sunk near Benton on her way to assist the dredge that had sunk while making improvements to Cypress Bayou, but she was soon raised. In 1879 she was sent to St. Louis for repairs and was soon back in service.

In January 1877, the shearboat *Essay* was at work on Tone's Bayou as part of a fleet of eight boats under Captain Tennyson:

> The Essay, a flatboat now attached to the government fleet, recalls to the memory of Captain Tennyson many pleasant recollections of the past. She was built by the Captain in the raft region some two or three years ago, and was conveniently fitted up with a bedroom, dining room and kitchen for his comfort and convenience whilst he was engaged in the work of clearing out the raft. Every vestige of improvement has been removed from her, and she has been converted into an ordinary flat. Notwithstanding her demolishment she to-day stands high in the estimation of the Washington authorities and is ranked with the government steamer Aid—an event which the Captain never dreamed of for a moment when he was building her— and has a commander appointed for her at remunerative wages, we assume.

In 1879, the *Essay* and craneboats *No. 1* and *No. 2* were found to be worn out and were dismantled. The *Aid*, which had led the attack on the raft, was grounded in front of Shreveport in March 1878. In 1879, her engines and part of her machinery were taken out and shipped to St. Louis, to be used in other boats and for other purposes. The hull, cabin, and boilers were sold at public auction in Shreveport.

ASSESSMENT

The Woodruff raft removal effort stayed on schedule and took twelve months to complete at a cost of $230,000. Henry Shreve's raft removal effort was always off schedule and took five years to complete at a cost nearly $100,000 greater. These basic facts have led to the assumption that Woodruff conducted a more successful project, with nitroglycerin providing the decisive advantage. However, nitroglycerin was actually used in conjunction with the *Aid* only during the last two months of the project.

The basic facts are deceptive. Shreve's men and boats were in the field only seventeen months during the five years. Moreover, the Shreve raft was longer and more difficult, because it was eighty years old. The raft attacked by Woodruff was less than half that age. Technically, both projects were conducted with energy and efficiency.

The major difference between the projects was that Woodruff's improvements were permanent, but they soon became implicated in a different type of failure. Reviewing Woodruff's project in 1894, Capt. J. H. Willard stated the following: "Looking at photographs of the raft before and during operations, one would say that it had been easier to cut through rock than to make a navigable river through such a mess of tangle, that grew higher and larger with every flood, yet to-day there flows in the channel marked out for it a broad and deep river, safe at all stages, except for an occasional snag that drifts from above or a log that rises from the bottom as it scours."

The only problem with this picture is that it does not contain any boats. Woodruff's efforts provided a cleared channel that was immensely important to the Red River trade and particularly to the upper Red River trade. But Shreveport's steamboat business suffered the same decline as that of Jefferson's; in 1894, when Willard was writing only twenty years after the raft had been removed, there were only seventeen boats operating on the Red River, and only nine of these made trips to Shreveport.

So passeth the glorious works of the hand of man. But the work of the spirit, as exemplified by Woodruff in Shreveport, participated in and passed into the eternal. In this he had the better part.

·18·
Twilight of the Steamboats

THE SETTING

Jefferson's decline was caused by the rails, which captured the town's market area, depriving it of its function as an import and export center and thereby destroying its commercial activity, including its steamboat activity. The decline was assisted by the financial panic of 1873, which weakened many of the town's businesses, and by the fact that the town was financially overextended by Reconstruction administrations, as indicated by the 8 March and 7 June 1871 Shreveport *South-Western*:

> Those of our citizens who visit Jefferson are not reluctant to admit that, in some respects, it is a more prosperous place than Shreveport, while at the same time we have good reason to know that some of the leading men of that place regard its property as fictitious, or at least think that it has grown beyond the limits justified by the trade seeking it.
>
> Our neighboring city of Jefferson is saddled with an imported mayor and extemporized Board of Aldermen; and the press of the town is fearful that financial affairs are somewhat mixed. The Times and Republican, of the 30th ult., reviews a financial statement made by the Board, which is designed to leave the impression that the city is out of debt, but which the Times says can be found not to be the case upon close inspection.

It predicts that if relief does not come in the shape of railroads, Jefferson will be bankrupted to pay obligations to the amount of $120,000—in the shape of taxes and outstanding city debts. We sympathize with our neighbor, but see no remedy for the evil so long as municipal affairs are administered by a carpet bag element. We doubt not that our contemporaries have their hands full in watching the leaks in their city treasury.

The idea that removal of the raft on the Red River caused Jefferson's decline by destroying the navigability of Cypress Bayou and the lakes is not unreasonable. The function of the raft in thrusting water to the west is well known, and Jefferson's commercial decline appears to have begun shortly after the raft was removed. However, this was a correlation of dramatic events that suggested a false causation. The real cause, which was understood by contemporary observers, was the development of the rails, culminating in the completion of the Texas & Pacific tie-in with the Cairo & Fulton in February 1874, only two months after the raft was removed.

Jefferson's attitude toward the proposal to remove the raft is unknown. Only two expressions of concern appeared in the Shreveport newspapers. The 22 March 1871 *South-Western* contains part of a letter from a non-resident correspondent to the *Jefferson Herald*:

This raft matter is an old subject, and there never has been a doubt expressed by steamboatmen or others but that its opening would badly damage, if not entirely destroy the Lake navigation. But with this understanding it has created little fear, because the universal opinion is that it could never be done.

Now, I am one of those who have within the last few years arrived at the conclusion that there is nothing impossible to American enterprise and energy. Therefore would it not be well for some of your citizens who are most interested to examine into the matter? I believe there is something in the Constitution of the United States that might stay a work calculated to injure one section for the benefit of another.

The commentary by the editor of the *South-Western* was not defensive: "We have heard river men argue that the removal of the raft would not injure navigation to Jefferson. Be that as it may, we do not see how the

Constitution of the United States could prevent the opening to navigation of streams such as Red River. Congress has before now voted appropriations for the same work."

An 18 February 1873 communication from a Jefferson resident to the *Jefferson Democrat* appeared in the 21 February *Shreveport Times*. The writer of the letter had spoken to C. E. Forshey, commissioner and levee engineer for the State of Louisiana. Forshey said that raft removal would be ruinous to Jefferson's navigation, that Jefferson should protest, and that he would be happy to come to Jefferson to speak to the Chamber of Commerce if they were interested in taking action.

Because the raft was already being removed, this suggests that Jefferson had not taken a position of opposition. In addition, there was a peculiar quarrel mentioned in the *Shreveport Times* between the editor of the *Shreveport Times* navigation column and his *Jefferson Democrat* counterpart, with the former arguing that raft removal would materially injure navigation in the lakes and the latter arguing that it would not. Apparently Jefferson was not concerned because it was confident in its railroad prospects, which would resolve the traditional problems with overland ox-wagon transport, and corrective action to reverse the detrimental effects of raft removal was part of Woodruff's plan.

Shreveport was in favor of raft removal because the cotton from upper Red River was brought to its warehouses, which contributed to its economic activity. The upper Red River ports in Texas and Arkansas were in favor of raft removal for obvious reasons. As was the case with Shreve's removal efforts, Arkansas was the primary mover behind federal appropriations for the 1873 removal efforts, as reported in the 13 May 1873 *Shreveport Times*: "The people of South Western Arkansas are likely to be the most benefited at this time and it is to them that we are mainly indebted for the last four appropriations made by the general government."

Southwestern Arkansas benefited from the flood protection afforded by raft removal. The upper Red River ports and Shreveport benefited for only a very short period of time. The rails were triumphant over Shreveport and Clarksville as well as over Jefferson.

Woodruff did not make any direct comments on the potential for raft removal to diminish Jefferson's trade. Instead, he confined his observations to issues of navigation and navigability, which he thought would be affected over the long term. Later comments in some Corps of Engineers reports after the raft had been removed were not as guarded. Capt. W. H. Benyaurd, for example, in an 1875 report on improvements to Cypress Bayou, stated that the removal of the raft had already caused a decline in Jefferson's commercial activity and that the rail was a secondary cause.

Such comments should be understood in light of the fact that they appear in requests for congressional appropriations to rectify the harmful consequences to the navigability of the route that would ultimately result from raft removal. The only Corps technical report to address the issue was that of Assistant Engineer F. S. Burrows, dated 26 December 1884, which appears in Capt. Eric Bergland's 1885 survey report on Cypress Bayou. In evaluating the cause of the decline of Jefferson's trade, Burrows maintained: "The construction of railroads, which furnish other and more convenient means of outlet, assisted to a very limited extent by the partial deterioration of the navigable condition of the bayou, has had an almost disastrous effect on the town."

Jefferson's position, as stated in many places over the decades and maintained by many persons up to the present, was that the removal of the raft caused the navigability of the route to decline, which led to the decline of commercial activity. It has already been demonstrated that the initial dramatic shocks were experienced in 1874 and 1875 when there is no evidence for declining water levels and consequent reductions in boat activity. However, this does not mean that raft removal did not have an effect in subsequent years, producing water level declines and a shortened navigation season and thereby contributing to later reductions in boat activity and related commercial activity.

There was widespread agreement that removal of the raft would cause the bed of the Red River to scour, that this would produce lower water levels on the Red, that these lower water levels would reduce the supply to the lakes (particularly at the critical point of Albany Flats), and that eventually the level on the Red would generally fall below the entrances to the distributary channels. Woodruff maintained that the process would be gradual, but only if the outlets from the Red River that enabled water to enter the area of the lakes were left open.

Unfortunately, there was no stream gauge at Albany Flats that would enable the tracking of water level changes. The few Corps surveys provided only point-in-time readings and therefore are non-comparable.

In the absence of comparative data, F. S. Burrows in his 1884 survey report presents a balanced perspective reflecting current technical thought on the matter:

> The stage of water at Shreveport, at the time of the examination, was 6 feet above low-water mark, and yet . . . it was found to be less than 1 foot above low water on Albany Flats and through Soda Lake. On a 6 to 8 feet stage of water, very lightest draught boats are unable at the same stage to make the trip to Jefferson with any degree of safety. It is claimed that in former years navigation to Jefferson opened almost simultaneously with that to Shreveport. The reason most generally assigned for the present shortening of the navigable season is the removal of the raft from Red River above Shreveport, and the closure of some of the outlets of that stream. That these circumstances have had a limited adverse effect upon the navigation of the lakes is no doubt true, for the following reason: The slope of Upper Red River is much greater than through Twelve-mile bayou and the lakes; and so long as the bed of the river was filled with a jam of logs the water was forced through the openings and over the banks into the lakes, which caused and maintained an increased elevation of their water-surface whenever there was any considerable rise in Upper Red River. As nearly all of the large outlets still remain open, most of the water supply of the lakes is still derived from Red River; but as the concentration of the water has doubtless caused a gradual deepening of Red River, and a consequent lowering of its water surface, the height of the water in the lakes has perhaps likewise been decreased without the compensating advantage of scouring action.

Burrows's survey was conducted exactly eleven years after the raft was removed in December 1873. By December 1884, the scouring action in the bed of the Red consequent to raft removal had lowered the water surface elevation of the Red, producing a modest decline in the water surface elevation of the lakes. The only change in the navigability of the route was a modest extension of the period of non-navigability during low-water periods, which usually occurred during summer.

This is not the picture of devastation carried by the popular imagination concerning the effects of raft removal on the navigability of the route; such modest reductions could hardly have had any significant effect on the level of boat activity west of Shreveport. And yet, according to Burrows's report, during commercial year 1883–84, "the only craft in the trade was a small stern-wheel steamboat, drawing only 2½ feet of water, which made irregular trips from Shreveport to Jefferson." The reason for this situation was obvious to Burrows: "Although the commerce of the bayou during the last ten or fifteen years has decreased from a large and paying traffic to almost nothing, this state of affairs is not chargeable wholly, nor even to any considerable extent, to the fact that the navigation of the bayou has become more difficult and dangerous. As stated before, the building of railroads has furnished more convenient outlets for a large section of country which had been tributary to Jefferson, and thus caused its decline as an important commercial center."

It remains to determine whether these technical observations are borne out by the navigation record. The question at issue is whether, after the initial shock caused by the rails in 1874 and 1875, there is evidence to suggest that water levels declined on the route and that these declines resulted in diminished boat activity. This question can be answered only within the context of the waning years of the 1870s, for after that time boat activity to Shreveport and to the west of Shreveport had been diminished to such a degree that the navigation column in the Shreveport newspapers no longer provides detailed commentary on water levels, particularly in the direction of Jefferson.

Complicating the picture for this period were factors positive and negative. On the positive side was the formation of the New Orleans and Red River Transportation Company in April 1875 "for the purpose of harmonizing conflicting interests, regulating the supply of tonnage in accordance with the demands, and the maintenance of rates." This company, generally known as the Pool Line, encompassed most of the boats on Red River from 1875–80, including the *St. Mary, Maria Louise, Texas, Bonnie Lee, Lotus No. 3, Col. A. P. Kouns, W. J. Behan, La Belle, Belle Rowland, Carrie A. Thorn, C. H. Durfee, Dawn, Bart Able, Silver City, Kate Kinney, Joe Bryarly, Danube, Alexandria, Frank Willard, Cornie Brandon, Ashland, Jewel,* and *Laura Lee.* Most of these boats traveled to Jefferson.

The reason for the formation of the line was to establish freight rates that would be followed by all members to avoid competitive downpricing, which in the context of railroad competition was leading to bankruptcies. Scovell in his reminiscences indicates that the boats remained privately owned but were strictly regulated. All earnings went into a common fund and were pro-rated according to shares. Rates for cotton to New Orleans were set at $1.50 per bale through an agreement with the merchants at Alexandria. There were other competitive lines such as the Merchants and Planters Reform Line, which included the *R. W. Dugan*, and there were also some independent boats. One of the main effects of the Pool Line was to assure a competitive transport mode so that railroad rates would not become exorbitant, which is why the line was given some degree of public support.

On the negative side, there were serious navigation problems on the Red River that have sometimes been mistaken as indicating that the removal of the raft was a disaster for Shreveport as well as for Jefferson. Indeed, if one looks at the decline of navigation to Shreveport, it is easy to make a case for Shreveport similar to the one that traditionally has been made for Jefferson. Nevertheless, navigation to Shreveport was destroyed by the rails, and the removal of the raft had only one minor effect on the navigability of the Red River.

When the raft was removed, the scouring of raft-deposited sediments lowered the bed of the Red and therefore the water surface level. The depth of water did not change, although it is easy to misinterpret Corps reports on water surface elevations in this way. One unintended consequence was that old stumps emerged as serious navigation hazards in some places.

The idea that the lakes served as a reservoir for the replenishment of lower Red River during low-water periods and that raft removal would destroy this function could never be tested, because any possible effects were overshadowed by events at Tone's Bayou below Shreveport. This bayou connected the Red to Bayou Pierre, one of the early channels of the Red, and threatened to recapture the flow of the Red. This is why it was part of Woodruff's overall project. Dams were built, but they constantly failed. When more water entered Bayou Pierre through Tone's Bayou, water depths on the lower Red decreased, and navigation became difficult.

There was an equally serious problem at the mouth of the Red where it entered the Mississippi. This area was an old bend of the

Mississippi where the Red River was a tributary to the Mississippi and the Atchafalaya was a distributary. Henry Shreve cut off this bend before he removed the raft in the late 1830s. The Red River began to send more water into the Atchafalaya, and the cutoff bend, which still served as the entrance of the Red into the Mississippi, experienced increasing shoaling, which became a serious problem for the passage of boats in the late 1870s.

The existence of the Pool Line did not revive boat activity, although it did lessen the rate of decline. However, there were so few boats operating in the direction of Jefferson in the late 1870s that subtle changes in water levels or a contraction of the navigation season cannot be deciphered on the basis of boat movements. Moreover, any emerging disparities between the navigability of the route and the navigability of Red River, which would provide firm evidence for harm to the route caused by raft removal, were obscured by difficulties on the Red caused by Tone's Bayou and Shreve's cutoff. Nevertheless, the navigation record is sufficient to demonstrate that the issue of water level declines on the route, though technically indeterminable with any precision, was in any case irrelevant to the continuing decline of boat activity and that the reduction of the route to a condition of non-navigability occurred late in the story and was essentially unrelated to the removal of the raft.

EIGHTEEN SEVENTY-SIX

During 1876, ten boats made thirty-four trips to Jefferson carrying out 13,928 bales of cotton, approximating the commercial activity of the previous year. The boats included the *Bonnie Lee*, *Carrie A. Thorn*, *Charles H. Durfee*, *Clifford*, *Col. A. P. Kouns*, *Dawn*, *Fontenelle*, *Lotus No. 3*, *May Lowry*, and *R. T. Bryarly*. The *Col. A. P. Kouns* registered the highest number of trips at thirteen. Large loads of cotton included the *Col. A. P. Kouns* (1,201), *Lotus No. 3* (1,230), and *R. T. Bryarly* (1,091). On her second trip to Jefferson, the *May Lowry* stopped at Monterey to pick up about 100 bales of cotton. In addition, the tugboat *Gussie* made a trip to Albany.

The *Dawn* operated along the route only in 1876, making two trips to Jefferson. She is described in the 2 September 1975 *Shreveport Times* on the basis of a clipping from the *Cincinnati Commercial*: "Captain Charley Truslow's new Red river packet Dawn, built at

Madison, Ind., attracted considerable attention at the levee. She received her cabin outfit and considerable freight yesterday, and departs for New Orleans this evening. The hull is 160 feet long, 32 feet beam, with 4 feet hold, and will carry 1500 bales of cotton. She has two new boilers, 38 inches in diameter and 26 feet long. Her cylinders are out of the Thirteenth Era, and are 12¼ inches in diameter, with 4 feet stroke. She was tested by the Louisville inspectors, and is allowed 152 pounds of steam. She draws 18 inches of water. She cost $13,000."

The theme of lots of water but little business was prevalent throughout the first half of the year, applying to Shreveport as well as to Jefferson. A few examples from the *Shreveport Times* will set the stage:

> The Lotus No. 3, the last packet out from Jefferson, found seven feet on the flats with the water rising very fast. The Jimp. can now send up a yell, but then all the cotton goes east and there is none for the boats. (22 January)
>
> The largest packets could reach the Jefferson settlement, if sufficient inducements were held out. As it is, the Kouns and the Lotus No. 3 are sufficient to do the water business, the rail getting the largest slice. All the Lake landings are acceptable to steamboats on account of the large supply of water on hand. (17 February)
>
> A boat could go to Monterey on Jeem's bayou without any trouble, if any inducements were held out. (10 February)

With respect to the effects of raft removal, the 16 January *Shreveport Times* noted that the lakes were filling up with sediment from Dooley's Bayou, which entered into Shifttail Lake, down to the head of Twelvemile Bayou. The 27 February *Shreveport Times* notes that the *Jimplecute* had become concerned about the swiftness with which water was being depleted in Cypress Bayou: "The Jimp. howls for more rain and is for pitching into the men who allowed the surplus water to run out fast, greatly to the detriment of lake and bayou navigation."

However, it is apparent that this rapid depletion was caused by extreme low water on the upper Red, producing a situation in which local rains in the Cypress Bayou watershed were not contained by backwater pressure from the Red. Ironically, the *Jimplecute*'s comments came at the inception of one of the highest water periods on record, caused primarily by heavy volumes of water from the upper Red River. All landings on the route became accessible to large boats, and the Polk Street bridge at Jefferson was threatened. According to descriptions in the *Shreveport Times*, the route was transformed into a lake:

> The officers of the C. H. Durfee report Cypress bayou very high at Jefferson. It was all over the wharf as well as the country this side of the town. There were no banks in sight and it was like running through the woods. The current was very strong all the way down to the lakes and all a boat had to do was to keep out of the woods. Capt. Boardman says the bayou is higher than he ever saw it before. The lakes this side are full and steamers can take all the short cuts and by-paths without danger of getting hurt. (31 March)
>
> The Jeff Jimp of the 29th reports Cypress Bayou rising at the rate of twelve inches in twenty-four hours, being then upwards of sixteen feet above dead low water. The natives look for the highest water of this or any other season since 1866. The Cypress bottom is a vast sea of water and the wooden wharf at Jefferson under water. The bayou, with the exception of the strong current, is more like the lakes than a river. The lakes this side of Port Caddo are nearly full, and if the rise holds out many more days will spill over. Of course navigation is good to all points of the compass. (1 April)

Unfortunately, these immense volumes of water could do nothing to improve the business prospects for boats, as reported in the 11 April *Shreveport Times*: "The Jefferson papers of last Saturday reported the bayou at that point rising fast, with the prospect of getting higher than at any time before this season, which was the highest for several years. The wharf at Jefferson was all covered with water and all the low country along the serpentine slough. There is very little to damage in the Cypress bottom, no matter how high the stream gets, as there is not much land in cultivation. The lakes this side are brim full, but there is little danger of hurting anything as there is nothing to hurt. All this water is of little practical use as there is very little freight to move one way or the other."

The highest mark was not achieved, and the bayou began to recede on 17 April. A few trips were made by boats to Jefferson in May and

June. By the middle of July, navigation conditions were still much better than business opportunities: "There is plenty of water in the lakes and bayou for light draught boats, but little or no business offering." In late July, rains on the upper Red produced a backwater rise on Cypress Bayou up to Jefferson: "Eight feet and rising from back water was the Wednesday report from Jefferson. The lakes this side are chug full and threaten to spill over."

This was an unusual rise for the inception of summer and provided a sufficient reserve for the *R. T. Bryarly* to make trips to Jefferson in early and late August. By the end of August, navigation was practically closed to Jefferson; yet there was still sufficient water to emulate previous low-water exertions if there were a reason for going: "No doubt if sufficient inducements were offered our boats would go to Jefferson, but there is no business offering."

All of the trips to Jefferson in 1876 were made during the first half of the year. The second half of the year was characterized by extreme low water on the Red. No unusual conditions were reported for the route. The very high water along the route during the first half of the year may have been partly produced by an incipient raft on the Red that was of sufficient dimensions to prohibit the passage of boats.

EIGHTEEN SEVENTY-SEVEN

During 1877, six boats made twenty-two trips to Jefferson carrying out 10,065 bales of cotton, which was a decline in all categories from the previous year. The boats included the *Alexandria, Col. A. P. Kouns, Danube* (fig. 18-1), *Lotus No. 3, R. W. Dugan* (fig. 18-2), and *W. J. Behan*. Large loads of cotton included the *Col. A. P. Kouns* (1,486, 1,400, and 1,300), *R. W. Dugan* (1,000), and *Alexandria* (1,247). The *Alexandria* and *Col. A. P. Kouns* carried shipments of Kelly plows in November and December. In addition, the tugboat *Gussie* made a fishing trip to Jim's Bayou, and the *Albany* made a trip to Albany and the lakes. As in the previous year, the *Col. A. P. Kouns* registered the largest number of trips at eleven. In one of her three trips in March, the *Col. A. P. Kouns* carried our cotton from Jefferson to New Orleans at $0.25 per bale, an all-time low.

The *Danube* was a sternwheeler built in Cincinnati for the Red River trade in 1877. She traveled to Jefferson from 1877 through 1879 and is described in the 15 August 1877 *Shreveport Times.*

Fig. 18-1. *Danube* (on left), Algiers, Louisiana, 1889. *Source: From the Collection of the Public Library of Cincinnati and Hamilton County*

Fig. 18-2. *R.W. Dugan*, Hermann, Missouri, ca. 1875. *Source: From the Collection of the Public Library of Cincinnati and Hamilton County*

CHARLEY THORN'S NEW BOAT.—We received yesterday a letter from our friend George A. Ditton, dated Cincinnati, August 5th, in which he gives the following particulars of Captain Thorn's new Red river packet Danube. If no unforeseen occurrence prevents, the launch of the hull will take place Tuesday. She is as perfect a model of shape, skill and workmanship as ever floated or made a name in the Sunny South. She is 178 feet long, 34 feet beam, 33 foot floor, 4½ foot hold, full length cabin with 24 staterooms, 28 foot boiler deck, 2½ foot guards, outside of staterooms. She has a 28 foot forecastle, and is 13½ feet between decks. Will have a Texas and observatory. She will be provided throughout with all the modern improvements. The boiler deck is now on. The day after the launch she will be towed down to S. B. James' shop to receive her machinery, now complete and ready to be placed aboard.

W. Ehler, the experienced and popular cabin builder, will finish the cabin within twenty days. The Danube will be completed, trial trip made and leave Cincinnati for New Orleans September 1, there to enter the New Orleans and Red River Transportation Company. Come on with your beautiful Danube, genial Charlie, and may you both live long and prosper.

The low water during the second half of the previous year broke on the Red River in late January and on the route in early February, and the first boats traveled to Jefferson during that month. In March, the Red River contained "oceans of water"; in April, the *Jimplecute* reported plenty of water in the bayou for large steamers. During the middle of July, boats were still traveling to Jefferson, and navigation was still good on the Red River. As was often the case, Soda Lake was impassable during the middle of September: "The Steamer Florence, Capt. Tennyson, returned to Jefferson yesterday after an unsuccessful attempt to reach the city. She only found fourteen inches of water at Gum Springs in Soda lake. From this it would look like the old frog pond leading to Jefferson was pretty near dried up. The renowned gate post is there but instead of being useful to steamboats it is now used as a scratching post for stock to rub against. It is said that the latter frequently suffer for drinking water. We don't vouch for the latter."

Low water ended on Red River in late October and on the route by early November, when it was reported that there was sufficient water for the largest class of boats to reach Jefferson. These conditions prevailed through December, but only six trips were made by boats to Jefferson during the last two months of the year. Four reports in the November *Shreveport Times* strike the same somber notes as in previous years:

> There is more navigation between this point and Jefferson than there is business. (10 November)
> Jefferson is accessible to all sorts of crafts but there are no inducements held out for a boat to go there. (11 November)
> There is good navigation to Jefferson but the people up that way don't seem to know it, or if they do, don't appreciate it. Jimp, come down here and see a steamboat. (14 November)
> We now have fine navigation to all points on the river above and below, and on all the tributaries that lay claim to navigation. Some of the points, such as Jefferson, Benton, Port Caddo, Monterey and Bellevue have very little use for boats at this time. Skiffs do them to hunt and fish in, and that is all the use they have for water. (18 November)

EIGHTEEN SEVENTY-EIGHT

In 1878, five boats made sixteen trips to Jefferson carrying out 7,358 bales of cotton. The boats included the *Bonnie Lee, Col. A. P. Kouns, Danube, Frank Willard* (**fig. 18-3**), and *Joe Bryarly* (**fig. 18-4**). Large loads were carried out by the *Col. A. P. Kouns* (1,400 and 1,300) and the *Bonnie Lee* (1,168). In addition, the *Albany* made one trip to the lakes, and the *Vicksburg* made one trip to Mooringsport, both carrying out a few bales of cotton.

All trips other than that of the *Vicksburg* to Mooringsport were made during the first half of the year. Jefferson was described in January as "a place once of considerable importance, but now almost lost to view." Good navigation conditions did not produce commensurate business, for "all accounts agree that she is better served with navigation than with business." This situation continued in March: "From this point to Jefferson on Cypress Bayou we have more water than business." At the end of June, the *Jimplecute* reported unusually high water for

Fig. 18-3. *Frank Willard* (left front), Gallipolis, Ohio, 1870. *Source: From the Collection of the Public Library of Cincinnati and Hamilton County*

Fig. 18-4. *Joe Bryarly. Source: From the Collection of the Public Library of Cincinnati and Hamilton County*

the inception of summer: "The rise in the river to-day has reached one inch per hour and the gauge shows over 16 feet of water in the channel. If this morning's rain extended above, as we feel satisfied, the rise will reach the highest mark for six years."

The *Jimplecute* indicates that the rise was from local rains and from Red River backwater, which was produced by rains on the upper Red. Navigation conditions were excellent on the Red but had little effect on the level of steamboat activity at Shreveport: "Business in steamboat circles has almost played out, and the boats only run now to keep up appearances. If we had business in proportion to the stage of water there would be 'millions in it' for the boats and something for us."

Jefferson experienced a modest degree of returning prosperity by the end of the year as a result of wholesale trade with the little towns that were springing up along the East Line & Red River Railroad. This railroad was formed in June 1876 to run between Jefferson and Sulphur Springs, passing through "some eight or ten thrifty little towns . . . on the road—Kellyville, Lassater, Avinger, Hughes Springs, Daingerfield, Cason, Pittsburg, Leesburg and Winnsboro." The road had reached Winnsboro in 1878 and was projected to reach Sulphur Springs in January 1879, with the promise of "making Jefferson the entrepôt for the two sections of country lying between the two branches of the Texas and Pacific."

EIGHTEEN SEVENTY-NINE

In 1879, 3,162 bales of cotton left Jefferson on five boats, including the *Cornie Brandon, Danube, Frank Willard, Jewel,* and *Joe Bryarly.* These boats logged a total of twelve trips to Jefferson that year. A lengthy description of the *Jewel* appears in the 26 October 1878 *Shreveport Times*, quoting the Louisville *Courier Journal*:

> Many large and many fine boats have been built here during the past year, but in our humble opinion, the most complete and perfect stern wheel boat of her class that was ever built is the Jewel, now ready to go south and take her place in the New Orleans and Red River trade. She is owned by Capt. O. P. Truslow, her commander, and Mr. C. W. Drown, her clerk. She is of 500 tons burden, and has capacity for carrying 1,800 bales of cotton. Her hull is strongly built, of easy and graceful

model. She is 177 feet long, 33 feet beam and 5 feet deep. The cabin is of good proportion, beautifully designed, with eighteen rooms in the main, including recesses, in the rear of which is a saloon cabin containing four large rooms and gang-ways. The Texas is fifty feet long, and on top of this is a handsome pilot house. The cabin and rooms are most elegantly furnished with the best of material; the furniture is splendid; the mirrors are elegant; the looking-glasses fine; the beds splendid; the tables and pantry-ware elegant—everywhere and everything is the picture of comfort, convenience and elegance. The painting throughout is an excellent job. Mr. McIlvain, the "boss" of the joiners' department, and Williams, boss of the painting department of the Howards' mammoth concern reflected credit upon themselves in their work on the Jewel and upon the Howards.

She has two Otis steel boilers, each 26 feet long and 40 inches in diameter; two engines, each with 12-inch cylinders, 5 feet stroke, besides doctor and other engines. She works a wheel 15 feet in diameter and 25 feet bucket. The boilers, machinery, sheet iron work, stoves, etc., are all first class. She was built and furnished by the following firms: Hull, cabin and painting, Howard & Co.; boilers, M. Zier & Co.; furniture, bedding, etc., J. Shrader, Sr.; carpets, etc., J. Shrader, Jr.; blankets, &c., New Albany Woollen Mills; chandeliers, tableware, &c., Bridgeford & Co.; mirrors, looking-glasses, &c., Fitch & Lindsey; books, printing, &c., R. W. Meredith & Co. The office, bar, and forward hall are "beauties," and Captain Truslow has not wanted for anything that will make the pretty Jewel all that will constitute speed, comfort and safety, and if the passengers and shippers up "old Red" are not pleased with the Jewel, there is no use in wasting time and money in trying to please them in the building of a first-class fine steamboat. She leaves for Cincinnati this morning to load for the south. To Capt. Truslow, Mr. Drown and their Jewel we tip our hat, and say "bon voyage."

In the middle of January, the *Joe Bryarly* tried to get to Jefferson but found only 13 inches of water on Albany Flats. At the end of January, the *Frank Willard* found 30 inches in the channel through the lakes and was able to reach Jefferson. By early February, navigation was good on the route and on the Red. In the middle of February, the *Jimplecute* complained about a statement in the *Shreveport Times* that the *Danube* had obtained only a part of a load of cotton. The *Jimplecute* contended that she could have got all that she wanted if she had not been part of the Pool Line and requesting rates higher than shippers were willing to pay.

Water levels fluctuated on the Red, with lots of water but no business reported at Shreveport during the high-water periods. The 30 April *Jimplecute* reported high water in Cypress Bayou: "At 3 o'clock this evening the gauge showed 13 feet and 8 inches of water, a rise of 11 feet in all. It is still rising at the rate of 1½ inches an hour and the Polk street bridge will soon be in danger. Captain J. M. Thomas is doing all that he can, with the limited force he has to keep the drift broke loose and is strengthening the end abutments."

During the high water in May and early June, the *Jewel* made two trips and the *Danube* one trip to Jefferson, carrying out modest amounts of cotton. The extant newspaper records end on 13 June. There were apparently no boats to Jefferson during the second half of the year, because the 6 March 1880 *Shreveport Times* reports the first departure for that point during the season, which began on 1 September 1879.

EIGHTEEN EIGHTY

In 1880, four boats—the *Alexandria, Caddo Belle, Cornie Brandon,* and *Frank Willard*—made seven trips to Jefferson. In addition, the *Caddo Belle* made one trip to Mooringsport, and the *Gussie* and *Thornbush* made one trip each to Mooringsport. Only 1,427 bales of cotton were carried out, most of which was from Mooringsport. The *Gussie* carried a load of merchandise for Croom & Noel in Mooringsport. Three of the four trips made by the *Frank Willard* were primarily to Mooringsport, the first of which carried Col. Calvin Croom and lots of his freight; the trip by the *Thornbush* was commissioned by Croom. Thus, even the small amount of commercial activity during this year was not enacted primarily at Jefferson.

The *Caddo Belle* is described in the 5 August *Shreveport Times* on the basis of a clipping from the 30 July *Cincinnati Commercial*:

> The Caddo Belle arrived from Portsmouth and received
> her insurance papers from Inspector Frank Pierce yesterday

morning, and will be ready to proceed on her voyage Saturday night. She is bound for Red River, and goes through to Shreveport. She has engagements for almost a full trip already made, but may be induced to contract here for a few special lots. Capt. Al. Ketchum, her owner, is in command. He lately owned the Trout, which met with success while he ran up Red river last season. The Belle is designed to take the Trout's place, and being a larger and better boat, the people of Red river cannot help being well pleased over the change. She is 130 feet long, 26 feet beam, and 4 feet depth of hold. She has 10-inch cylinders, with 4 feet stroke. She has one steel boiler 24 feet long, 48 inches in diameter, and having six 10-inch flues. For a boat of her size, she is very light, trimming on 14 inches, with 20 tons on board. Her cabin is not completed. The staterooms and the cabin outfit have been left out to make room for a furniture trip. She will carry a big lot of furniture out of the river. She is built like all cotton boats, having her upper guards cut off. She will carry 800 bales of the staple. She is a neat boat, and promises to have all the substantial comforts when she is finally completed to her staterooms and outfit. She will leave for Red river Saturday.

The trip by the *Alexandria* in early March was the first trip to Jefferson during the navigation season, which had begun on 1 September of the previous year. The Pool Line had high expectations for the remainder of the season, as reported by the 11 March *Shreveport Times*, quoting the *Jimplecute*: "We interviewed Captain Boardman yesterday, and he informs us that there is three feet of water in the channel, and that he will take 300 bales of cotton away from Jefferson, and will arrive in Shreveport with 500 bales. He says the Alexandria is the pioneer boat of the Red River Transportation Company, always being sent out to 'break the ice' for the regular navigation, being the lightest draft of the fleet. The Captain assures us there will be a boat here every week from this on."

These expectations were not met. The arrival of the *Alexandria* in March was, in fact, the last arrival of a steamboat at Jefferson directly from New Orleans and involved in the cotton trade, and even this trip was not a round trip. The *Alexandria* returned to Shreveport, transferred to the *Jewel* for New Orleans, and set out for Minden.

Three trips were made by the *Frank Willard* to Mooringsport in May and June, with Jefferson included as an afterthought. The reason for this disregard is revealed in the account of the first trip in the 9 April *Shreveport Times*: "The Dandy Frank, Capt. T. E. Jacobs, H. D. LaCossit clerk, arrived yesterday from Jefferson. To judge from the encouragement with which the Willard met at the hands of the Bayou City it would seem as though the merchants there don't care whether the steamboats sink or swim. Her freight out of Jefferson consisted of one sugar kettle consigned to New Orleans. On the way down, however, she picked up one head of cattle and forty or fifty bales of cotton." In May, the *Cornie Brandon* went to Jefferson, returning at Shreveport with only twenty bales of cotton. The *Thornbrush* went in June to Mooringsport. W. W. Withenbury (the captain of the first steamboat to Jefferson) died in Cincinnati on 17 July, and his obituary appeared in the *Cincinnati Commercial* two days later:

> Capt. W. W. Withenbury, who died on Walnut Hills, on Thursday, was an old-time steamboatman, well known to the veterans. He will be remembered as Commander of the Echo, Vigo, Texana, and other boats. He commenced his career as a steamboatman in the New Orleans and Red River trade before the war. During the "unpleasantness," his northern sympathies got him into trouble, and at one time he was under sentence of death at Louisiana. He was a shrewd, active man, of fine conversational abilities, and skillfully engineered his way to freedom. He wrote a number of letters to the Commercial several years ago, which were extensively copied. His "Red River Reminiscences" were highly interesting, and full of witty and intelligent observations. Nearly ten years ago he retired from the river and returned to Cincinnati, his old home. He was stricken with paralysis several years ago, and was a patient sufferer up to the time of his death. The colors on the Public Landing will be displayed at half-mast to-day, in respect of the memory of the deceased. The funeral will take place to-day at 3 P. M., from the family residence, 411 McMillan street, Walnut Hills.

The Pool Line had experienced heavy financial losses in the second half of 1879 while running six boats on the Red River during low water. The line was dissolved on 31 August, and some of its boats were put up for sale. In November, the *Jimplecute* reported that there was plenty of water in Cypress Bayou for a good class of boats if there were any inducements for them to go to Jefferson. In December, the *Frank Willard*, now operating as an independent, made one trip to Jefferson, leaving with 379 bales of cotton; the *Caddo Belle* made one trip to Mooringsport and one to Jefferson, carrying out 175 bales and 225 bales, respectively. The cotton was carried to New Orleans but not by these boats.

LOCAL TRAFFIC

Steamboats continued to operate along the route from 1881 through 1905; however, this traffic was almost entirely local in nature, with boats traveling between Shreveport and various landings on the lakes and Cypress Bayou, including Jefferson and Mooringsport, or between the various landings themselves. Much of the small amounts of cotton that were brought out apparently came from Mooringsport. The cotton appears to have been transported to New Orleans through transfer operations at Shreveport. With the completion of the Texas & Pacific from Shreveport to New Orleans in 1881, even these transfer operations were dominated by rails.

For 1881–89, I have continued to rely on the *Shreveport Times*, with information incorporated from annual reports of the Corps of Engineers concerning improvements to the Red River and Cypress Bayou. For 1890–1905, I have relied on the Corps annual reports, because the newspaper record is lengthy, the navigation column does not appear to contain much of interest, and the reports are thorough. The annual reports cover the fiscal year (through 30 June of the year of the report).

1881
Only four boats ran west of Shreveport during 1881. These were the *Caddo Belle*, which made two trips to Mooringsport; the *Cornie Brandon*, which made one trip to Mooringsport; the *Frank Willard*, which made two trips to Mooringsport, one of which included a side fishing trip to Jim's Bayou; and the tug *Gussie*, which made one trip to Albany and one to Mooringsport. These boats carried out only 779 bales of cotton. Navigation on the Red River was good during the first

half of the year, but the lower Red was depleted by Tone's Bayou during the second half of the year and was obstructed by stumps that emerged as the Red scoured out its bed after raft removal.

The Red River Packet Company (later called the Red River and Coast Line) was formed in July and included the *Cornie Brandon*, *Alexandria*, *John D. Scully*, *Yazoo Valley*, *Jesse K. Bell*, *Danube*, *Jewel*, *Maria Louise*, *Silver City*, and *Kate Kinney*. Scovell in his reminiscences indicates that this was a joint stock company that operated on the Red River until 1902. It concentrated on trade along the fringes of the Red River below Shreveport, generally referred to as the Coast. Only one of these boats (the *Cornie Brandon*) subsequently went west of Shreveport. At the end of October, the *Jefferson Democrat* noted the emergence of excellent navigation conditions on Cypress Bayou and the lakes. Nevertheless, no boats went west of Shreveport in the latter part of the year, in spite of the fact that there were a modest number of arrivals at Shreveport.

1882

The *Lessie B.* appears to be the only boat that operated along the route during 1882. The *Lessie B.* was built in Cincinnati in late 1881 and was owned and operated by Capt. Ben Bonham to run between Shreveport and the lakes and Jefferson. According to extant issues of the *Shreveport Times* through June 1881, she made approximately six trips between Shreveport and points west, including Jefferson, Mooringsport, and Jim's Bayou. The trip to Jefferson in March resulted in a down freight of "lots of cotton." During a second trip to Jefferson at the end of March, this boat burned on Cypress Bayou below Benton.

1883

During 1883, the *Alpha* made three trips to Jefferson and three trips to the lakes; the *Cornie Brandon* made two trips to Mooringsport and a fishing trip to Jim's Bayou; and the *John G. Fletcher* made one trip to Mooringsport. The *Alpha*, which replaced the *Lessie B.*, was a small sternwheeler at 125 tons captained by Ben Bonham. In November, an article appeared in the *Shreveport Times* on Jefferson with the subtitle "The Town not Dead but Growing—The Spirit of Enterprise Visible Everywhere." The article pointed out that although "a great many people say and think Jefferson is dead," there was still a lot of capital in the town, and improvements were being made to private property. The Red River Planters and Merchants Transportation Company and the Red River Consolidated Pool Line were formed during this year.

1884

During 1884, the *Alpha* made seven trips to Jefferson, two to Mooringsport, and one to the lakes; the *Ranger* made one trip to Mooringsport; and the *Shields* made a fishing trip to Jim's Bayou. On her first trip of the year in early January, the *Alpha* carried out 29 bales of cotton, 625 sacks of cotton seed, one hundred plows, seven corn mills, forty bundles of hides, one steam cotton press, and a lot of miscellaneous freight. The *Alpha* was windbound for two days in Caddo Lake, with waves of ten feet reaching the banks. On her second trip a week later, the *Alpha* encountered ice in Cypress Bayou and "large fields of ice in the lake and was compelled to put out fenders over the bow of the boat in order to break her way through." Jefferson was flooded in early May.

A Corps report on Cypress Bayou by Assistant Engineer F. S. Burrows dated 26 December 1884 states that the cotton compress at Jefferson was handling about 60,000 bales annually, but that during the past year only 500 bales were shipped by boat, with 600 tons of up freights received. Below Jefferson, 1,500 bales of cotton were shipped, and 1,600 tons of freight were received. Cotton was shipped from Jefferson to New Orleans at $1.25 a bale.

1885

During 1885, the *Alpha* made seven trips to Jefferson and two to Mooringsport, and the *John G. Fletcher* made a fishing trip to Jim's Bayou. This was the sixteenth annual fishing trip from Shreveport to Jim's Bayou. The *Alpha* was refitted in September.

1886

During 1886, the only newspaper report of travel west of Shreveport was a fishing trip to Jim's Bayou by the *John G. Fletcher*. However, the 1886 Corps report on Cypress Bayou indicates that a 125-ton steamboat navigated Cypress Bayou and the lakes, making thirty trips from January to July, with up freights of 600 tons of general merchandise and plantation supplies and down freights of 4,500 bales of cotton and 16,000 sacks of cotton seed. This boat must have been the *Alpha,* apparently making runs between local points, which would not have been reported in the Shreveport newspapers.

1887

The *Alpha* made one trip to the lakes in February, one trip to Jefferson and Mooringsport in March, and one trip to Mooringsport in April. According to the 1888 Corps report on Cypress Bayou, the only boat to travel to Jefferson during the fiscal year (July 1887–June 1888) was the U.S. snagboat *Florence,* which made the trip in July 1887 and March 1888. An unnamed boat (obviously the *Alpha*) went as high as Mooringsport, carrying out 1,800 bales of cotton and 1,000 tons of cotton seed. The owner stated: "Boats could have run to Jefferson ten months in the year, but no business for them to do."

1888

In April, the *Alpha* went to Mooringsport and Jeter's Landing, the first mention of the landing in the navigation record. A visitor to Jefferson in June reported that some of the vacant stores on Dallas and Austin streets from a few years before were now "occupied by thrifty, energetic business men and the city has a decidedly improved commercial aspect," as exemplified by the Jefferson Lumber Company and the woolen and flouring mills.

1889

In an 1889 Corps report on improvements to Red River, the Board of Trade of Jefferson indicated that the route had been navigable for ten months during the fiscal year, but that navigation did not commence until February. Through June 1889, the Farmer's Alliance *G. W. Sentell* (**fig. 18-5**) made one trip to Jefferson in February; the *Marco* made six trips to Jefferson from February through April; and the *Friendly* made three trips to Jefferson in May and June. The *Friendly*, with John Boardman as captain, and the *Marco* linked at Shreveport with the New Orleans packet *Dacotah,* operating under Capt. W. T. Boardman.

The trip of the *G. W. Sentell* in February was the first arrival at Jefferson direct from New Orleans in nearly a decade and gave rise to the second documented photograph of a steamboat at Jefferson. Although this photograph usually appears with the inscription "pictured in Cypress Bayou about 1891," the *G. W. Sentell* made only one trip to

Fig. 18-5. *G.W. Sentell*, Jefferson, Texas, 1889. *Source: From the Collection of the Public Library of Cincinnati and Hamilton County*

Jefferson, and the shot was actually taken in the second week of February 1889. From this picture, it is clear that the wharf was no longer in existence. Nevertheless, the landing is covered with boxes and barrels, and the boat is covered with people and loaded with lumber for the return trip to New Orleans.

These appear to be unusual circumstances for 1889, and in fact they were. The photograph was sketched and appears in the 3 August 1889 *Frank Leslie's Illustrated Newspaper* with a background photographic sketch of Polk Street **(fig. 18-6)** and an accompanying article on "JEFFERSON TEXAS. One of the Gems of the Lone Star State." The article points out that Jefferson's commerce had been destroyed by the rails, but that it was now beginning to revive on the basis of extensive iron deposits, five large sawmills, and aggressive actions on the part of businessmen. The reason for the arrival of the *G. W. Sentell* at Jefferson and an explanation for what appears in the picture is also given:

Fig. 18-6. Polk Street and *G.W. Sentell* at Jefferson. *Source: Frank Leslie's Illustrated Newspaper, August 3, 1889*

A Board of Trade has been organized and is hard at work. The first thing it did was to incorporate a company to sell groceries at wholesale, and $50,000 was put up with which to commence operations. The steamboat scene represented in this issue shows the landing of the steamer, with the goods on the wharf, and as it marks a new era in the history of the city, the people generally turned out to see it done. These groceries were all purchased in New Orleans, making in the aggregate twenty-four car-loads, on which was saved $3,300 in freight by having them shipped by steamboat instead of by rail. This, the merchants claim, gives them an advantage over both Dallas and Fort Worth, which they propose to give to the benefit of the retail dealer, and by this means re-establish the commercial supremacy of the city.

The *Friendly* (**fig. 18-7**) was significant because she was owned by the Jefferson and New Orleans Navigation Company, which had been formed by Jefferson merchants. The purchase of this boat was heralded by the 12 April *Shreveport Times* as:

JEFFERSON'S AWAKENING.

In the ante-bellum days Jefferson had as many live and enterprising citizens to the square foot as any other town of its size in the country. They struggled manfully against adverse fate but her location was against her when railroads came upon the scene. Recently her people have been encouraged to hope much from her iron interests, but it will be seen from the following special to the Times-Democrat that they do not propose to idly await, and rely solely upon, the development of those interests:

This has truly been a red letter day in the history of Jefferson and marks the dawn of a new era. The merchants of this city, after a long and dreary sleep brought about by extortionate freight rates, have decided to control their own transportation, and with this end in view the board of trade, at a called meeting yesterday, appropriated $5,000 for the purchase of a new boat which will connect with the independent steamer Dacotah at Shreveport. A suitable boat has been purchased and the deal consummated to-day. This places Jefferson and the surrounding country in cheap communication with New Orleans, St. Louis and the East, and gives her a forward place in the march of progress.

These were exaggerated claims. The purpose of the purchase, as revealed in the 6 July *Shreveport Times*, was to provide a competitive

Fig. 18-7. *Friendly*, Monroe, Louisiana, ca. 1891. *Source: From the Collection of the Public Library of Cincinnati and Hamilton County*

transport mode that would result in reduced freight rates from the Texas & Pacific Railroad. During her four years of service, the *Friendly* operated between Shreveport and Jefferson in conjunction with various boats in the Red River and Coast Line (rather than Boardman's independent *Dacotah*), and some of the boats in this line traveled between Shreveport and Jefferson. Although this produced a fairly significant volume of traffic, the carriage was primarily of up freights from New Orleans and down freights to Shreveport.

1890
The Corps reports indicate that the route was navigable throughout the fiscal year. The *New Haven*, a 93-ton sternwheel measuring 136 feet by 24 feet and captained by Ben Bonham, made fourteen trips between Shreveport and Jefferson; and the *Friendly*, a 68-ton sternwheel measuring 120 feet by 27 feet, made nineteen trips. The principal freights were 3,300 tons of merchandise from New Orleans. Down freights consisted of 200 tons of cotton and 25 tons of cotton seed.

1891

The Corps reports indicate that the route was navigable from 1 December 1890 through the end of the fiscal year. The 303-ton sternwheel *Nat F. Dortch*, which measured 164 feet by 29 feet, made ten trips between Shreveport and Jefferson; and the *Friendly* made twenty-eight trips. Up freights were 700 tons, and down freights consisted of 625 tons of cotton and 200 tons of cotton seed.

1892

The Corps reports indicate that the route was navigable from 1 February through the end of the fiscal year. The *Friendly* made ten trips between Shreveport and Jefferson, and the *New Haven* made four trips. The 149-ton sternwheel *Rosa Bland*, which measured 113 feet by 23 feet, made twelve trips between Shreveport and Jefferson and six trips between Shreveport and Mooringsport. The 112-ton sternwheel *Blue Wing* (**fig. 18-8**), which measured 119 feet by 24 feet, made two trips between Shreveport and Mooringsport. There were only 272 tons of up freights. Down freights consisted of 467 tons of cotton, 60 tons of cotton seed, and hides, skins, and livestock.

Fig. 18-8. *Blue Wing*, Kentucky River, ca. 1890. *Source: From the Collection of the Public Library of Cincinnati and Hamilton County*

1893

The Corps reports indicate that the route was navigable from 24 November 1892 through the end of the fiscal year. The *Rosa Bland* made fourteen trips between Shreveport and Jefferson, and the *Nat F. Dortch* made thirteen trips. There were 732 tons of up freights; down freights consisted of 1,115 tons of cotton, 105 tons of cotton seed, and hides, skins, and livestock. Capt. J. H. Willard's Cypress Bayou survey report for this year describes the water-related facilities at Jefferson and the general orientation of the town's business: "The wharves and buildings that were on the bayou when the water route was the chief dependence have been abandoned and have gone to decay, and the business part of the town has moved towards the railroads." A benchmark survey map accompanying the report shows the silting-in of the turning basin **(fig. 18-9)**.

1894

The Corps reports indicate that the route was navigable from the early part of November 1893 through the end of the fiscal year. The *Rosa Bland* made seventeen trips between Shreveport and Jefferson. There were 605 tons of up freights. Down freights consisted of 320 tons of cotton, 65 tons of cotton seed, and hides, skins, and livestock.

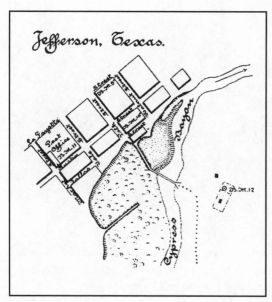

Fig. 18-9. Turning Basin siltation. *Source: Annual Report of the Chief of Engineers, 1893*

1895
The Corps reports indicate that there was no traffic on the route because of extraordinarily low water.

1896
The Corps reports indicate that the *Rosa Bland* made six trips between Shreveport and Mooringsport, but the amount of freight could not be ascertained. Jeffersonians complained about the obstruction of the Kansas City, Pittsburg & Gulf Railroad Bridge across Caddo Lake at Mooringsport. Railroad officials stated that the obstruction was caused by temporary piling preparatory to putting the draw of the bridge in place and that if a boat had desired through passage, they would have removed whatever pilings were necessary.

1897
The Corps reports indicate that the *Rosa Bland* made three trips between Shreveport and Jefferson, and the sternwheeler *Nellie L.* made two trips with barges between Jefferson and Shreveport. Down freights consisted of 90 tons of cotton (or 355 compressed bales at 760 pounds per bale), 200 tons of cotton seed, and 100 tons of seed meal.

1898–1902
The Corps reports indicate that there was no traffic on the route. The year 1898 was the first fiscal year in twenty-six years that twelve months had elapsed without sufficient water to move the Corps' dredge across Albany Flats.

1903
The Corps reports indicate that there was no traffic between Shreveport and Jefferson and that the dredge was still not able to cross Albany Flats. A 12-ton gasoline boat drawing 16 inches light and 18 inches loaded made 52 trips between Jefferson and Shanghai, 100 between Shanghai and Benton, and 15 between Jefferson and Caddo Lake. Freight consisted of 20 tons of cypress logs, 1,200 tons of lumber, 10 tons of provisions, 10 tons of grain, 1,310 tons of telephone poles, and 2,000 tons of cord wood.

1904
The Corps reports indicate that Cypress Bayou between Jefferson and

the lakes was navigable throughout the year for light-draft boats, but that only in the latter part of June could a boat ascend from Shreveport. The *Nellie G.*, a 15-ton gasoline boat drawing 18 inches light, made 100 trips between Jefferson and the lakes, moving 120 tons of saw logs and 1,725 tons of telephone poles. The *Anna Tardy*, a 71-ton sternwheel measuring 81 feet by 18 feet and drawing 3 feet loaded, made a trip between Shreveport and Jefferson carrying seven passengers, but she did not return.

1905
The Corps reports indicate that Cypress Bayou between Jefferson and the lakes was navigable throughout the year for light-draft boats, but that only during June could a boat ascend from Shreveport. The *Nyma May*, a 14-ton gasoline boat drawing 21 inches loaded, made five trips between Jefferson and local points. The *Anna Tardy* is reported as operating between Jefferson and local points. Freight included 70 tons of cotton, 280 tons of cotton seed, 2 tons of grain, and 5,544 tons of miscellaneous commodities. The operations of the *Anna Tardy* between Jefferson and local points from 1 July 1904 through 30 June 1905 were the last reported movements of a steamboat along the route.

SUMMARY
The newspaper navigation columns and the Corps reports reveal three distinct periods for the years 1876 through 1905. From 1876 through 1880, navigation along the route was similar to that of previous decades, with boats operating between New Orleans and Jefferson, but at diminished and diminishing rates. Water levels do not appear to have posed a problem, and no effects of raft removal are noted by the newspapers. The route continued to be characterized by plenty of water but little business. Continuing declines in the meager level of boat activity from 1875 were produced by the paucity of commercial opportunities and the inability of the Pool Line to stay the inevitable.

From 1881 through 1898, the route was still navigable. Through 1888, there was little boat activity. There was a modest revival from 1889 through 1894 when traffic increased through the formation of a steamboat line that capitalized on emerging opportunities for local freight carriage. There was no traffic in 1895 anywhere on the route because of low water, but during 1896 and 1897 there were a few trips between Shreveport and Mooringsport and Shreveport and Jefferson.

From 1898 through 1905, the route was not navigable between Shreveport and Jefferson because of a scarcity of water on Albany Flats. In 1904 and 1905, there was a modest amount of activity between local points on Cypress Bayou, but only one trip from Shreveport to Jefferson. Most of these trips were made by the gasoline-powered boats *Nellie G.* and *Nyma May.*

The distinction of making the last commercial steamboat run between Shreveport and Jefferson goes to the 71-ton sternwheeler *Anna Tardy*, which carried seven passengers to Jefferson in June 1904. She was built and owned by Capt. Frank Tardy of Evansville, Indiana, and was transferred to the Red River trade in 1901 under the ownership of W. E. Cravens and Frank Knudson. She apparently became trapped upstream at Jefferson because she is reported to have made only a half round trip in 1904, when the route was navigable only in June, and is listed as engaged in trade between Jefferson and local points down to Caddo Lake in fiscal year 1905 (i.e., through June 30). However, she did manage to get out after summer because she was snagged on the Red River in November 1905, suffering a total loss.

It is clear from the navigation record that a modest number of boats operated along the full route from Shreveport to Jefferson from 1876 through 1894 and that the long-expected non-navigability of the route did not occur until 1895. This confirms two observations made by Woodruff. The first was that the decline of water levels along the route would be very gradual. The second was that the process of gradual diminishment would continue to be played out as long as the Red River outlets of the distributaries that fed the lakes were not closed by human action. The reduction of the route to a condition of non-navigability in 1895 was not the end result of the gradual process induced by raft removal but rather the immediate result of the closure of the distributaries.

There were forty-three outlets from the Red River above Shreveport, including the artificial outlets such as the Sale and Murphy Canal. The first closure occurred in 1884, but it failed and was re-closed in 1891. Cottonwood Bayou, which was the first distributary to supply water to the lakes, was the last to be closed, in 1900. However, the vast majority of the outlets were closed between 1892 and 1894, producing the observed condition of non-navigability on the route from 1895 on.

Contemporaneous with these outlet closures was the building of levees along the Red River, which was initiated by the River and Harbor Act of 1892 and eliminated overbank flooding as a potential contributor to the water supply in the lakes.

These were joint efforts on the part of the Corps of Engineers, the Louisiana State Board of Engineers, and the Caddo Levee District. The Corps was responsible for closure of most of the large outlets, an effort undertaken to increase water depths and scouring action in the Red River and thereby improve its navigability. Most of the levee work was done by the Louisiana Board of Levee Commissioners and the Caddo Levee District for the purposes of flood control and land reclamation. The last stretch of levee, between the Sale and Murphy and Scott Slough outlet closure dams, was completed shortly after the turn of the century. The levees and outlet closure dams together formed a continuous levee system that completely cut off the lakes from the Red River.

The decline of the waterbodies and their associated navigation west of Shreveport was discussed in numerous Corps reports shortly after the turn of the century. The relative contribution of the removal of the raft and the construction of the levee system in this decline was judged in favor of the latter, as in the last major survey report on the route, which was prepared by Capt. T. H. Jackson of the Corps in 1913: "A prevalent error appears to be that communication by water to Jefferson, Tex., ceased upon removal of the Red River raft. Steamboat men state that boats continued to run to Jefferson, Tex., for several years after removal of this obstruction in Red River and ceased only when, owing to levee building, the supply of water to the Shreveport-Jefferson waterway was cut off by these measures of land reclamation."

That Woodruff's technical prognostications proved to be correct was a moot point. The number of boats desiring to travel west of Shreveport from the late 1870s onward was so small that reduced water levels and a shortened navigation season would have had no effect on the level of boat activity, and the extinction of the route's navigability in 1895 was not a matter of commercial consequence.

The route, its ports and landings, and the steamboats that served them had ceased to play an important role in the affairs of the world years before. That role was based on cotton export to New Orleans. The condition for its existence came to an end in early 1874 through rail linkage with the Midwest, and its formal end was marked by the trip of the *Alexandria* from New Orleans to Jefferson in March 1880.

The Pool Line boats, which included the *Alexandria*, were the last steamboats to compete directly with the rails for the cotton produced west of Shreveport and carried out through the ports and landings along the route. They were also the last boats to maintain the traditional ties of the cotton trade between Northeast Texas and New Orleans.

The dissolution of the Pool Line in 1880 was a consequence of the anticipated completion of the Texas & Pacific between Shreveport and New Orleans in 1881, after which Red River cotton was carried to New Orleans by rail rather than by steamboat. Successors to the Pool Line were regional carriers such as the Red River and Coast Line, which concentrated on the trade of the coast of the Red River below Shreveport. West of Shreveport, steamboats operated in geographic isolation, carrying up freights and passengers and down freights of cotton seed, a by-product of the cotton trade.

A saying common in the 1800s is that commerce has no friends. It will seek the most efficient and least-costly transport mode and will favor the best markets, indifferent to the effects on a town such as Jefferson and oblivious to the nostalgia for paddlewheels. Observing the progressive withdrawal of the New Orleans boats from the Red River trade in the late 1870s, the editor of the navigation column in the *Shreveport Times* remarked, "One by one the roses fall." After the *Alexandria* reached Jefferson in March 1880, the route was bare of blossoms, and its historic importance disappeared, with Withenbury's death during the same year placing a seal of closure on the story.

·19·

The Cypress Bayou
and Waterway Project

RESTITUTION

Eugene Woodruff clearly understood that the removal of the raft would ultimately lead to the destruction of the navigability of the Cypress Bayou and the lakes route. But, as an engineer, he also knew that the process would be gradual and long term. The bed of the Red was filled with raft-induced sediments that would take many years to scour, and the distributaries that fed the lakes were strong competitors for Red River water. It would be many years before bed scouring in the Red reduced surface water levels to such a degree that water would no longer pass through the distributaries during moderate-water periods.

Nevertheless, he was adamant that the ultimate result of raft removal should never come to pass and that corrective actions at modest cost could sustain the navigability of the route. If Woodruff had lived to express an opinion on the matter, he would have said that the grounds for restitution were unrelated to the decline of Jefferson's commerce. For him, the matter was one of elementary justice: when the federal government damaged the navigability of a waterway, it had a responsibility for restoration. This position was expressed in his final survey report: "The injury to the Jefferson navigation will be gradually increased, and justice to the people of that section will require that some means be taken to remedy it." The same position was expressed in one of Woodruff's field reports shortly before he died: "It remains to be seen how much the removal of the Red River raft will affect the lake and bayou navigation to Jefferson. The injury will probably be gradually increasing as the channel at Red River capacitates itself to carry a larger portion of the water. The city of Jefferson has therefore a just claim, apparently, to measures of relief from the injury unavoidably inflicted by the raft removal."

Woodruff's plan of restitution was twofold, involving improvements to Cypress Bayou and structural measures that would insure the navigability of the route. As expressed in his initial survey report, "The improvements of which the route is susceptible consist of removing stumps and snags, dredging (which is required near Jefferson), and giving slackwater navigation in Sodo Lake and Fairy Lake by dams, alone or with locks." Woodruff's recommendations gave rise to the Cypress Bayou and Waterway Project, a late coinage by the Corps to express the unitary nature of the efforts expended on Cypress Bayou and the lakes. This project, which extended from 1872 through 1918, entailed three different efforts:

1. The improvements portion of the project involved the removal of obstructions, the dredging of Cypress Bayou, and the dredging of overland cuts to bypass convoluted bends. These cuts are observable on the ground today. The most well known is Government Ditch at the head of Caddo Lake.

2. Woodruff recommended structural measures such as locks and dams to provide slackwater navigation on Soda Lake and Caddo Lake. These recommendations encountered technical difficulties. Woodruff's successors considered various structural proposals in survey reports that extended over many decades, but no adequate formulation was achieved.

3. In continuity with these early survey reports, another set of reports was issued at the beginning of the 1900s to address an emergent problem that threatened the navigability of the route. These reports led to the construction of a dam at the foot of Caddo Lake that preserved navigation above but that prohibited through traffic.

IMPROVING CYPRESS BAYOU

The improvements to Cypress Bayou and the lakes that were made between 1872 and 1918 involved channel dredging, the removal of obstructions, and overland cuts. These cuts are shown, as completed, on Capt. Eric Bergland's 1885 *Map of Cypress Bayou and the Lakes* (**fig. 19-1**). The work was begun on 18 December 1872 with a $10,000 congressional appropriation and involved the use of Jefferson's dredge, the *Lone Star*. The city had initiated a dredging effort from Boon's Bend to the city wharf and had reached The Packery by December. Jefferson was anxious to have responsibility for the improvements shifted to the federal government because of the "low condition of the city finances." Woodruff assumed charge of the dredge in December, the same month in which he began to remove the raft. He appointed Frank W. Gee to superintend the work.

Woodruff's initial efforts involved a continuation of the city plan, which was to dredge a 45-foot channel in such a fashion that a constant depth of water would prevail between Boon's Bend and the city wharf. Woodruff found that the city had simply deposited spoil and logs and stumps on the bank, which would slip back into the channel during high water. The logs and stumps were pulled from the spoil and hauled farther inland; however, Gee continued to deposit spoil immediately on the bank because the dredge would not reach any higher. In June

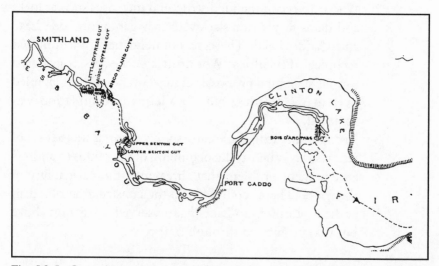

Fig. 19-1. Corps improvements. *Source: H. Ex. Doc. 103, 48ᵗʰ Cong., 2ⁿᵈ Sess.*

1873, the hoisting drum on the dredge broke, work was suspended, and a new drum was ordered from Atkins & Burgess in Chicago. During the first six months of operation, 44,000 cubic yards of dredged material were removed.

In the meantime, in March, Congress appropriated an additional $50,000. One purpose of this large appropriation was to obtain a scow with hoisting machinery to remove the stumps and logs, because the dredge was not well suited to that activity. In addition, a boom-derrick was to be established on a movable tram on the bank to remove the spoil farther away from the channel. It is not reported whether this machinery was ever purchased and employed.

The new hoisting drum arrived in Jefferson in July aboard the *Huntsville,* and work was resumed at the city wharf, because the water in the bayou had fallen too low to move the dredge downstream. The 2 August *Shreveport Times,* quoting the 30 July *Jefferson Tribune,* indicates that in testing the new machinery, "The first lick turned up a big cypress stump, three hoop skirts, one pair high gaiters and a yearling alligator, all in a good state of preservation." The 16 August *Jefferson Tribune,* as quoted in the 20 August *Shreveport Times,* indicates: "We interviewed Capt. Gee, of the dredge boat, yesterday, and he informed us that it would take some time to finish the work he is now engaged upon, near the powder magazine; that the bottom of the bayou is filled with roots, and old hewn logs, heavy and solid. He has a channel cut to a width of forty feet, but will widen it to sixty, with a depth of nine feet at this stage of the water."

The drum broke again in late August. A stronger drum was ordered; Woodruff died in September; the new drum arrived in October; and the dredging between Boon's Bend and the city wharf was completed in December. The dredge was then taken some eighteen to twenty miles downstream to the cutoffs at Benton that apparently were made by William Perry in the late 1850s using hand labor. Although these cuts were very shallow, they had been used by steamboats. Gee's efforts were devoted to widening and deepening. Work on the Lower Benton Cut was completed in March 1874. This channel was 400 feet long, 45 feet wide, and 7–10 feet deep, requiring the removal of 4,400 cubic yards of earth and reducing the navigation distance by one mile (**fig. 19-2**).

High water prohibited dredging of the longer cut, and the dredge was brought back to Jefferson for repairs. In June, the dredge proceeded

Fig. 19-2. Benton cutoffs

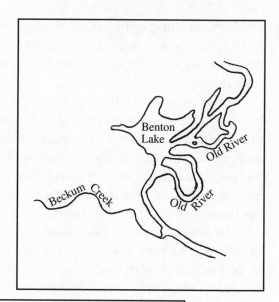

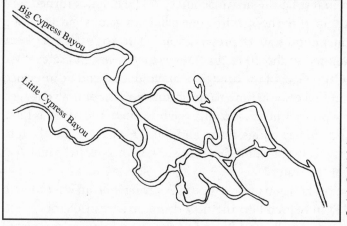

Fig. 19-3. Little Cypress Bayou area cutoffs

to the Dougherty's Defeat area about ten miles below Jefferson where the bayou was shallow and convoluted and the banks were ill defined. At this place, whose name suggests the difficulties posed to navigation, the Little Cypress Cut was completed in July **(fig. 19-3)**. This cut was approximately 2,500 feet long, 40 to 50 feet wide, and 5 to 10 feet deep, requiring the removal of 22,000 cubic yards of earth. A number of logs and stumps were removed with nitroglycerin, which had proved useful in the destruction of the raft.

The Upper Benton Cut was completed in January 1875 under a new superintendent, Joseph Burney. It was 45 feet wide and required the removal of 25,000 cubic yards of earth. The work party then moved upstream, dredging and removing logs and stumps, until reaching the Dougherty's Defeat area, where three cuts (Middle Cypress and the two Sisco Island cuts) similar to the others were completed in June. These efforts entailed the removal of 63,400 cubic yards of material.

Additional work was performed on the Upper Benton Cut in July. The dredge sank in the winter of 1876 and was outfitted with a new hull in October 1877. The dredge was then outfitted with new machinery in July 1878, thereby becoming fully owned by the federal government. Dredging resumed in December, and the Dougherty's Defeat cuts were improved. The dredge then moved to Bois d'Arc Pass in February 1878, where more than a thousand stumps were removed or cut to low water, and the upper portion of the channel that came to be known as Government Ditch was dredged. This cut was 7,000 feet long and required the removal of 28,000 cubic yards of earth (**fig. 19-4**).

The various cutroads made by the steamboatmen were surveyed, and a best route was chosen and marked. In August 1879, a work party was assembled under the command of George Alban to remove cypress stumps and other obstructions in the selected channel. (This was the George Alban who piloted the *Lama* on the first voyage to

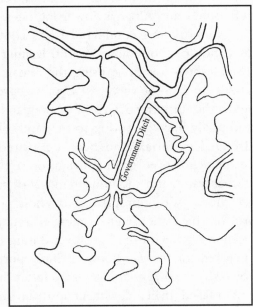

Fig. 19-4. Bois d'Arc Pass cut

Jefferson.) The award of the contract to Alban is mentioned in the 15 March *Shreveport Times*: "Capt. George Alban has been awarded the contract of putting up mile posts along the route between this place and Jefferson. He nailed his first sign to a china tree at the ferry landing yesterday which reads: 'Jefferson 65 miles.' The route was surveyed by Lieut. Woodruff, deceased, in 1872-3. Capt. Alban states that the distance is barely 65 miles, notwithstanding it has been computed by steamboatmen at ninety miles. The route is across Albany Point straight to Bois d'Arc Pass. The captain will begin the work of putting up the signs and blazing the channel in a few days."

Working from Bois d'Arc Pass through the lakes to Cross Bayou, Alban and his crew removed 2,102 stumps and snags and 3,267 overhanging trees and put up sixty-six posts with painted sign boards to designate the route across the lakes. Alban apparently retired the next year (1880), which was the same year in which Withenbury died. A brief biographical sketch is given in the *New Orleans Democrat,* as quoted in the 6 October 1880 *Shreveport Times*: "Capt. Geo Alban made his first appearance in Red river about the time Capt. H. M. Shreve was removing the great raft, and is the oldest Red River pilot alive in this section of the country to day. In 1845 he was captain of the Little river and afterwards of the Alida, White Cliffs, Corinne, Marion, Wm. Terry and others. Since the war he has steamboated but little, but superintended the work of clearing the channel through the lakes to Jefferson. Capt. Alban is now living on a farm near Shreveport."

No work was conducted from 1880 through 1886, with the exception of the removal of 150 leaning trees on Cypress Bayou in 1884, which was done using the remaining project funds from the 1870s. In 1884, a survey of Cypress Bayou and the lakes conducted under the authority of Capt. Eric Bergland found that many of the cuts had partly filled in, owing to the sandy alluvial soil and the fact that dredged materials had been deposited on the banks. Bergland recommended redredging, extension of the Bois d'Arc Pass Cut into deeper water, and additional removal of hazards to navigation.

Money was appropriated for these purposes in 1886 and 1888, part of which was used to completely rebuild the *Lone Star*, which had been in service on the Red River during the interim. A new hull was prepared for the *Lone Star* at Shreveport in June 1887, which was towed by the snagboat *Florence* to Jefferson, where the new machinery was installed. In her movement upstream on Cypress Bayou, the *Florence* encountered heavy rafts of timber that had to be broken up to secure passage.

The refurbished dredge began operations in August 1887 under the superintendence of M. B. Lydon. The previously dredged areas were reworked from August 1887 through May 1888, with the exception of the two Benton cuts, which were still in good condition. Extensive dredging was done near Jefferson, and the Bois d'Arc Pass Cut was extended 1,000 feet. Included in this work were improvements to the Boon's Bend cutoff, which had been made in August 1872 by the dredge while it was still under the authority of Jefferson.

Work in 1889 and 1890 shifted to downstream areas. The snagboat *Howell* was employed in May 1889 in removing snags, stumps, and leaning trees from Twelvemile Bayou. The snagboat *Florence* and the dredge *Lone Star* proceeded from Shreveport to the Gate Post in December and made a cut 827 feet long and 42 feet wide at the upstream end of Albany Flats. After making minor improvements on Cypress Bayou, the *Florence* and *Lone Star* returned to Shreveport.

No work was conducted in 1891 and 1892. In 1893, Congress made a small appropriation for channel work, while at the same time requesting a survey of Cypress Bayou and the lakes, which was conducted by Capt. J. H. Willard. The appropriation was used at the end of 1893 to operate the snagboat *Breck* on Twelvemile Bayou and to enable a chopping party aided by explosives to move upstream all the way to Jefferson.

Additional appropriations were made in 1894 and 1896. Willard envisioned using the money to refine the previous cuts and to extend the Bois d'Arc Pass Cut several hundred yards to connect with the bayou channel in the lake. The *Lone Star* had been rebuilt twice and repaired three times and was no longer serviceable. She was replaced by a used ladder dredge, but this dredge was never able to make it over Albany Flats because of lack of water.

As a consequence, another party was sent out from Jefferson, working downstream during the closing months of 1898 using tools, tackle, and explosives to remove minor obstructions. The Corps report for 1901 recommended that the unexpended funds be returned and the work of improvement cease. The ladder dredge was sold in 1903.

No work was conducted between 1899 and 1905. Work during the last period differed dramatically from the previous periods. A dam at the foot of Caddo Lake was authorized in 1910 and constructed in

1914. There was no dredging during this period, other than that required for construction of the dam. Navigation improvements consisted of removal of obstructions and the posting of channel markers on Caddo Lake. The work was conducted by two quarterboats. Quarterboat *No. 1* sank in 1912 and was replaced by *No. 2*, which was wrecked in March 1918. Hand labor was continued until May, after which all project appropriations were allocated to the maintenance of Caddo Lake dam, thus effectively ending the improvements portion of the Cypress Bayou and Waterway Project.

STRUCTURAL PROPOSALS

The key element in Woodruff's plan of action did not involve the improvements. These could do nothing to affect water levels on the route, which necessarily had to decline in the long term with removal of the raft, ultimately leading to the destruction of navigability. This problem could be resolved only through structural measures that would capture basin drainage. All of the proposals along these lines were directed to resolving navigability difficulties in Soda Lake, which was always the major impediment to steamboat traffic. All fell into technical and cost difficulties, with the latter being the most disturbing element as commercial traffic declined on the route.

Woodruff initially thought that the problem could be resolved by wing dams at Albany Point that would confine the flow of water to a narrow chute, insuring a sufficient amount of water above. This proved infeasible because there wasn't a sufficient amount of water to be captured during low-water stages. Woodruff then proposed a lock and dam at the same place, which would capture all of the water, providing navigability to Jefferson when Twelvemile Bayou was navigable to Albany, which was nearly at all times when the Red River was navigable to Shreveport.

Woodruff's superior, Capt. C. W. Howell, was skeptical about the proposed plan, which was not based on a detailed survey. Congress appropriated $50,000 for construction of the dam and dredging at the foot of Soda Lake, but this money was directed by Howell to Cypress Bayou improvements until an adequate assessment could be made. Woodruff was instructed to conduct an investigation of Soda Lake in the fall of 1873, but he died in Shreveport. Assistant Engineer H. A. Leavitt proceeded with the investigation, which was completed in March 1874.

On the basis of this investigation, Howell considered a number of proposals and recommended a dam at the foot of Soda Lake combined with a dredged channel between Soda Lake and Gold Point to the northeast on the Red River. This project was technically feasible because the water level on Red River at Gold Point was normally six feet higher than on Soda Lake. This would cause water to flow through the channel into Soda Lake, where it would be captured by the dam. Under these circumstances, the route would proceed up the Red River above Shreveport and down through the channel into Soda Lake. Although the dam was to be composed of untrimmed cypress trees ballasted with stone, the total project was unacceptable to Congress because of the estimated cost of $372,580.

The River and Harbor Act of 19 September 1890 directed the secretary of war "to cause a survey to be made of Cypress Bayou and the lakes between Jefferson, Tex., and Shreveport, La., in order to ascertain if the navigation of the said bayou and lakes can be materially and permanently improved by the construction of such dams, and locks and dams, as may be necessary." The survey was conducted by Capt. J. H. Willard, who recommended that a dam be placed at the foot of Soda Lake, but that Cottonwood Bayou be used rather than Howell's proposed dredged channel.

Cottonwood Bayou was the first large distributary above Shreveport and the apparent site of the break in the banks of the Red River that brought the Sodo Lake complex into existence. Use of the bayou would require a lock at the Red River end. Willard proposed his plan "with half-hearted recommendations and considerable misgivings, because the probable useful life of the improvement cannot be estimated." The cost of $375,000 was found unacceptable by Congress, and no action was taken.

The River and Harbor Act of 13 June 1902 directed an examination of "Cypress Bayou, and especially Cypress Bayou with the lakes between the city of Jefferson, Tex., and the Red River, with a view to ascertaining whether the same can be made navigable by means of a dam put below Albany flats, and by cutting a ditch in a northeasterly direction into Red River." This examination was conducted by Capt. Charles Potter, who notes in his report that the congressional directive was initiated by the Jefferson Commercial Club. Potter reviewed previous reports and concluded his own 1902 report with a terse judgment: "As the law calls for my opinion as to the advisability of the improvement, I have to state that in my judgment water transportation between Shreveport and Jefferson can not be maintained by building a dam below Albany Flats and by cutting a ditch in a northeasterly direction to Red River unless there be added an expensive system of locks and dams, upon which half a million dollars or more might be spent with small return of business. It is my opinion, therefore, that Cypress Bayou and the lakes are not worthy of further improvement by the United States."

The initial attempts from 1872 through 1902 to address the issue of navigability through structural measures had led nowhere. With the decline of steamboat activity on the route, the only justifications that could be posed for the necessary large expenditures were the debt to Jefferson owed by the federal government and the reduction of railroad freight rates that would result from competitive waterborne commerce. However, as soon as Potter's report was prepared, a new problem was discovered that threatened the remaining navigation and would forever have destroyed the possibility of restoring the route. This problem was resolved by the construction of a dam at the foot of Caddo Lake in 1914.

DAMMING CADDO LAKE

There have been two dams at the foot of Caddo Lake. The first was completed in December 1914. The second, which was a replacement for the first, was completed in June 1971. This is the dam that is at the foot of Caddo Lake today.

The reason why these dams were built has not been investigated. The traditional story concerning the first dam is that the waters of the lake had receded and that the oil companies were experiencing difficulties in getting men and equipment to the offshore rigs. They therefore requested that the lake either be fully drained or else reconstituted to a depth to permit boats to operate.

This story cannot be true. Gulf Refining Company secured its drilling lease in November 1910, and Ferry Lake No. 1, the first offshore drilling rig, was not completed until May 1911. The dam, however, was proposed in December 1905 and authorized for construction by Congress in June 1910. The dam was not constructed to resolve the difficulties of Gulf's service fleet but rather to protect the integrity of the route.

When the distributaries that fed the lakes west of Shreveport were closed in the 1890s, the waters of the lakes rapidly receded. Caddo Lake was protected from extinction by a shoal of Red River sediments at its foot. These were the deposits first noted by Woodruff's assistant, H. C. Collins, in the 1872 survey of the raft region. The emergent components of these deposits are shown on Woodruff's map (fig. 19-5) and, although now submerged, are accessible during extreme low-water periods today. By raising the drainage elevation of Caddo Lake, the deposits formed a catchment basin for the waters of Cypress Bayou that enabled Caddo Lake to continue to exist, although in an attenuated form, as shown by one of Arthur Veatch's 1905 photographs (fig. 19-6).

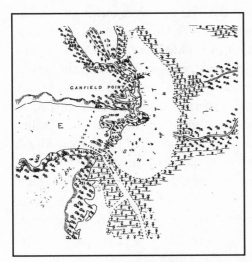

Fig. 19-5. Sediment deposits at foot of Caddo Lake. *Source: LSU in Shreveport, Noel Memorial Library Archives*

Fig. 19-6. Caddo Lake in the early 1900s. *Source: H. Doc. 488, 59th Cong., 1st Sess.*

The protecting shoal, however, was jeopardized in the early 1900s by an event occurring downstream in the Soda Lake area. During the raft period, Soda Lake was the site of tremendous depositional activity that obliterated the old channel of Cypress Bayou. When the distributaries were closed and the waters of Soda Lake began to recede rapidly, a headcut formed at the lower end of the lake at the entrance to Twelvemile Bayou. This headcut was gradually eating its way upstream through the soft sediments in the bed of Soda Lake, seeking to reconstitute the ancient hydrologic regime of Cypress Bayou.

The headcut took the form of a small waterfall (**fig. 19-7**). As the falls moved upstream, the remaining waters in Soda Lake were progressively depleted, as can be seen by Capt. W. P. Wooten's rendition of the situation in 1907 (**fig. 19-8**). The falls were moving upstream at a rate of one-tenth of a kilometer per year. Given this rate of recession, they would have reached the foot of Caddo Lake by the early 1940s, rapidly eating through the sediment deposits and draining the lake.

In 1903, this phenomenon was brought to the attention of Capt. J. M. DeWare, president of the Jefferson Navigation Company, an organization created to continue the cause of restitution of navigability on Cypress Bayou and the lakes. He contacted Congressman Morris Sheppard, and they conducted a brief survey of the falls in September. In April 1904, a hearing was held before the Committee on Rivers and

Fig. 19-7. Soda Lake falls. *Source: H. Doc. 236, 63rd Cong., 1st Sess.*

Harbors in which Congressman Sheppard and Captain DeWare provided testimony, asking for a survey by the Corps to determine the implications of the falls for navigation and what should be done about the situation.

This survey was approved by the River and Harbor Act of 3 March 1905, which directed the secretary of war to "survey Cypress Bayou and the channels connecting Shreveport, Louisiana, with Jefferson, Texas, including an examination of the falls near Little Pass." Section 1 of the Act stipulated that the survey effort should be conducted with the funds remaining in the budget for improvements to Cypress Bayou and the lakes. The survey was conducted under the authority of Capt. W. P. Wooten by Assistant Engineer Walter Polk.

In his December 1905 report, Wooten addressed the problem of the falls within the context of the historic efforts to secure through navigation from Shreveport to Jefferson. Wooten concluded that the

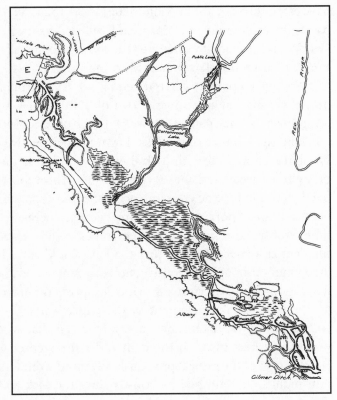

Fig. 19-8. Soda Lake falls. *Source: H. Doc. 220, 60th Cong., 1st Sess.*

only feasible solution to the problem of the falls that also would secure navigation was to construct a lock and dam at the foot of Caddo Lake and dredge out the channel below to provide navigation through the Soda Lake area by backwater from Red River. However, he recommended against this plan in the light of high costs ($525,000) and low benefits: "The present commercial importance of Jefferson would not in my opinion justify anything like the expenditure necessary to render the waterway to Shreveport navigable, nor do I believe that the prospective commerce which the improvement might develop would justify it. I have to report therefore that, in my opinion, the Cypress Bayou and the lakes are not worthy of further improvement by the United States."

The River and Harbor Act of 2 March 1907 instructed the Corps to take another look at the situation but this time to determine the advisability of constructing only the dam at the foot of Caddo Lake (no lock, no dredging below). Captain Wooten also conducted this examination and found that the falls "are working their way upstream, and the lower end of Soda Lake has already been drained. After they have eaten through about 4 kilometers more they will have entered the passes, where the water is deep, and will at once begin at the foot of Caddo Lake, eventually draining that and destroying all navigation now existing between Jefferson and Mooringsport."

Wooten's report, which is dated 27 July 1907, supported the dam-only alternative, at an estimated cost of $100,000, as a viable measure for preserving navigation between Jefferson and Mooringsport by blocking the advance of the falls. From the perspective of navigability, Wooten preferred the with-lock alternative, pointing out that the dam-only alternative would cut off navigation to Shreveport. Nevertheless, the dam would have no consequences for commercial steamboat activity between Shreveport and Jefferson, because there was none by that time. Wooten also pointed out that a lock could be installed through the dam at a later date and that the falls would assist in the required dredging: "Although the construction of a dam would at present destroy navigation from Jefferson and Mooringsport to Shreveport, it would not prevent the improvement of the entire waterway later if such a course should be determined upon, since all that would be needed would be a lock through the dam and a dredged channel below. In fact, the cost of the project previously advanced would not be increased, but might be diminished by constructing the lock and dredging the channel several years later, since the inroads of the falls would certainly diminish the amount of dredging."

Wooten made a feeble attempt to justify the expenditure of $100,000 by citing recent increases in sawmill activity and the potential exploitation of iron ore deposits. This dramatic reversal of perspective on benefits and the attendant justification of the dam-only alternative was seconded by the division engineer's office, the chief of engineers office, and the Board of Engineers for Rivers and Harbors. It is obvious that a decision to preserve navigation, even if only in part for the time being, had already been made in the halls of Congress and that the decision was related to the perceived injustice done to Jefferson by the removal of the raft, which is mentioned in the reports by the reviewing agencies.

Supporters of the reestablishment of the navigability of the entire route were dissatisfied with the limitations of this half-measure, and the River and Harbor Act of 3 March 1909 instructed the Corps to investigate the feasibility of constructing a lock in the proposed dam and providing a navigable channel below. This investigation was conducted by Capt. A. E. Waldron.

Waldron reviewed Wooten's original dam-lock–dredged-channel proposal and came to the conclusion that the expenditure of $525,000 could be justified on the basis of reductions in rail freight rates that would be induced by water competition. He also stated emphatically that without the lock and dredged channel, the dam should not be built, because the amount of traffic that would be generated above the dam would be insufficient to justify the expenditure of even $100,000.

Waldron's recommendation for a dam with lock and dredged channel was rejected by the division engineer's office, the chief of engineers office, and the Board of Engineers for Rivers and Harbors. They recommended the dam alone. It was this recommendation that gave rise to the Congressional Act of 25 June 1910 authorizing the construction of the dam at the foot of Caddo Lake but stipulating that the dam should be built in such a fashion as to admit a lock when deemed necessary.

One last attempt was made to secure through navigation. The River and Harbor Act of 11 February 1911 instructed the Corps to investigate the feasibility of establishing a lock in the approved dam and providing downstream improvements that would secure year-round navigation. Maj. T. H. Jackson conducted this investigation. A public meeting was held in Shreveport that was attended by approximately 350 people, including a former governor of Louisiana, the mayor of New Orleans, and Congressman Sheppard. All comments were favorable to the proposal, with the discussion of benefits centering on the reduction of rail rates rather than the revival of steamboat commerce.

This would have been an extremely expensive project ($2.2 million) involving two locks, vast quantities of dredging below the dam, and the diversion of Twelvemile Bayou into Cross Lake, which would become the new route. The vast quantities of dredging were needed to secure navigation on Twelvemile Bayou and the Soda Lake area during low-water periods on the Red. This went far beyond any proposal that had been made before and far beyond the moral argument for restoration of the navigability that had been destroyed by federal actions—the route had never been navigable year-round.

Jackson's report of 8 June 1912 recommended against the project on the basis of its high costs and low demonstrable benefits, and in this opinion he was seconded by higher authorities. The authorized dam, which did not include downstream improvements, was completed in December 1914 at a cost of $100,000. This was a crib dam with sheet-piling foundations (**fig. 19-9**), a design unusual for the Corps after the turn of the century, but one that fully met the congressional directive to build in such a fashion as to admit a lock when deemed necessary. The cheapness of the construction was also undoubtedly an element in securing congressional approval for a project whose benefits were questionable.

If the oil companies had any position on the dam, they did not express it in the public record. This is not surprising given the fact that the 1905 proposal for building the dam was made four years before

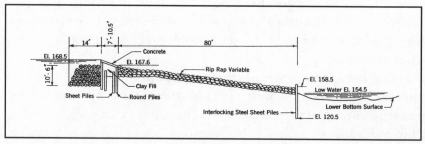

Fig. 19-9. 1914 dam. *Source: Vicksburg District, U.S. Army Corps of Engineers*

the Caddo Field had proven itself, and the dam was authorized by Congress before the oil companies had seriously considered drilling into the bottomlands of Caddo Lake. However, it can be assumed that they were not indifferent to the authorized project in the period between 1910 and 1914 because offshore drilling required large capital investments to implement new technologies.

SUMMARY

The efforts from 1872 through 1918 were carried out under various titles in the Corps annual reports until the inception of the dam, after which they were referred to as the Cypress Bayou and Waterway Project. The work connected with the project came to an end in 1918 with the last in-field improvement work. The title was actually carried on the books for many decades thereafter but only with an annual summary of local boat traffic. The total cost of the project through 1918 had reached nearly $300,000, as shown in **table 19-1**, covering improvements, surveys, and the dam.

The improvement effort between 1872 and 1918 involved the dredging of 19,700 feet of channel, the consequent removal of 348,000 cubic yards of earth, the destruction of 37,000 channel stumps and logs, the removal of 36,000 leaning trees and shore snags, and the cutting of 100,000 square yards of willows and brush. The dredging produced seven major cuts, reducing the navigation distance from Jefferson to Shreveport from ninety-six to sixty-five miles. Potato Bend and Boon's Bend could be added, but they were improvements to preexisting cuts. Nearly 220,000 cubic yards of earth were removed to produce a channel through Bois d'Arc Pass and from the Benton Lake area to Jefferson with a minimum configuration of about forty-five feet wide and seven feet deep.

The results of this effort are clearly visible in the contemporary landscape. From Caddo Lake to Jefferson, Cypress Bayou is wide and open, with fairly clear banks—quite different from the tortuous, heavily forested portion of the bayou above Jefferson. The overland cuts are observable on topographic maps, with most serving as the preferred route for boat traffic. Close observers traveling through these cuts will notice that the banks along the cuts are formed by two layers of earth, one of which is the original land surface and the other of which is overlying dredged material.

Table 19-1
Congressional Appropriations
Cypress Bayou and Waterway Project

10 June 1872	$10,000.00
3 Mar. 1873	50,000.00
14 Aug. 1876	13,000.00
18 June 1878	15,000.00
3 Mar. 1879	6,000.00
5 Aug. 1886	18,000.00
11 Aug. 1888 (from Red River appropriations)	5,000.00
19 Sept. 1890 (survey)	10,000.00
13 July 1892 (survey)	2,000.00
13 July 1892 (from Red River appropriations)	1,701.33
18 Aug. 1894	10,000.00
3 June 1896	5,000.00
2 Mar. 1907	10,000.00
3 Mar. 1909 (allotted 2 Apr. 1909)	6,000.00
25 June 1910	5,000.00
25 June 1910 (construction of dam)	100,000.00
27 Feb. 1911	2,500.00
25 July 1912	5,000.00
4 Mar. 1913	500.00
2 Oct. 1914 (allotted 7 Oct. 1914)	2,000.00
4 Mar. 1915 (allotted 1 Apr. 1915)	5,000.00
27 July 1916	5,000.00
8 Aug. 1917	5,000.00
18 July 1918 (allotted 29 Aug. 1918)	<u>5,000.00</u>
Total	$296,701.33

Source: *Report of Chief of Engineers, 1918.*

Although memory of the origin of the cuts has disappeared and most remain unnamed, Government Ditch, whose name suggests its origin, is a well-known feature at the head of Caddo Lake whose official name was Bois d'Arc Pass Cut. The lake is still heavily infested with stumps, but it is not difficult to imagine what the situation would now be had the Corps not removed thousands of others in earlier decades. The main east-west boatroad on the south side of the lake is roughly the route worked extensively by the Corps.

Below the dam, the works of improvement are no longer visible. Soda Lake no longer exists, having been gradually depleted of its water through raft removal, closure of the Red River outlets, and the construction of a drainage channel. This latter effort was conducted by the Caddo Levee District in the 1920s. Most of the original channel of Twelvemile Bayou was not incorporated in the drainage channel and now lies on land. As had been proposed in Jackson's 1912 report, the drainage channel that now constitutes Twelvemile Bayou flows down toward Cross Lake.

The 1914 dam was replaced by the present dam in 1971. Without the 1914 dam, Caddo Lake would have disappeared before World War II, with its bed used as a cotton field, which was the indignity suffered by Cross Lake before it was reconstituted as a water supply source for Shreveport in the 1920s. The situation in 1913, when the dam was already under construction, was concisely stated by Frank Leverett of the U.S. Geological Survey: "Now that the raft has disappeared, the lake is maintained by a barrier of sediment which was built across the eastern end by floods discharging down Red River. It will persist until this barrier has been cut through by the headward recession of Twelvemile Bayou. It would then be drained as in the pre-raft stage if there were no dam constructed to prevent its drainage."

The dam was not built to save Caddo Lake as a natural entity. There is nothing in the public record to suggest that this was a matter of concern to anyone. In fact, the reports of the period reflected strong desires for drainage of the lake so that the land could be reclaimed. Support for the dam was based strictly on the desire to maintain navigation, and it was on the basis of navigation that the dam was proposed and authorized. It would not have been built without strong congressional representation and without continuous pressure from interests in Jefferson who at least wished to keep the potential for navigability of the route alive.

The 1914 dam was an impediment to navigation, but it was built in such a fashion as to admit a lock when this might be deemed necessary. Although obviously prohibiting through traffic by commercial vessels, it was crossed over by small craft during high-water periods. The Corps, in its careful rendering of every scrap of waterway activity, records the following passages over the dam in its 1916 annual report:

Boats	Downstream	Upstream	Total
Motor boats	11	5	16
Barges	1	0	1
House-boats	0	1	1

Woodruff's structural proposals were designed to insure that ultimate destruction of the route would not be a consequence of raft removal. Although his proposals, and those of Howell and Willard, did not result in any actions, they led directly into the survey reports by Wooten, Waldron, and Jackson. Although these reports were precipitated by the issue of the falls, they addressed this issue only within the context of the desire to restore the navigability of the route.

The quest for navigability did not end with Jackson's 1916 report. A series of reports was issued in the 1900s that were continuous with the earlier reports. The last of these was the Shreveport-to-Daingerfield Study. The failure of this study to produce a justifiable project gave rise to the present Caddo Lake Initiative. Thus, the activities of the present are a direct outcome of processes set in motion by Lt. Eugene Woodruff in 1872 to provide "measures of relief from the injury unavoidably inflicted by the raft removal."

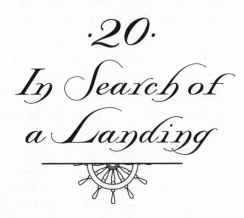

·20·

In Search of

a Landing

OIL ON THE WATERS

The *Anna Tardy* was the last commercial steamboat to operate along the route. She made one trip from Shreveport to Jefferson in 1904, operated between Jefferson and local points in early 1905, ran down to Shreveport during the latter part of the year, and wrecked in November on the Red River. Even before this time, commercial activity, such as it was, was beginning to be captured by gasoline-powered vessels. This shift was intimately connected with the expansion of the lumber industry.

Lumber had always been an important commercial product for Jefferson because of nearby pine and cypress stands, but most of this lumber appears to have been produced for local use or shipped to the west by ox-wagon. The first mention of the export of lumber by steamboat was in 1866, when the *Alexander Speer* made one trip carrying an unspecified amount and the *Lizzie Hamilton* made two, one of which carried a full load. J. K. Laurance, Jefferson's recorder, lists 121,000 feet of lumber as an export commodity for commercial year 1871, and Woodruff's 1872 *Map of the Red River Raft Region and Cypress Bayou* shows Williams' Saw Mill on the south side of the bayou above Smithland.

A large expansion of the lumber industry took place in the late 1800s and early 1900s. The 3 August 1889 *Frank Leslie's Illustrated*

Newspaper indicates that five of the largest sawmills in the world were located in the Jefferson area. The Corps reports on Cypress Bayou for 1884–96 indicate that huge quantities of logs were rafted to Jefferson. The 1884 report indicates production of 20 million feet of lumber by these mills, and the 1889 *Frank Leslie's Illustrated Newspaper* indicates that production had risen to 140 million feet in 1888, which was transported to northern markets by rail. This large-scale production was based primarily on yellow pine.

Lumber was not an export commodity by boat during this late period, and boats were not connected with most of the lumbering activity. The few instances of log and lumber movements by boat were restricted to small gasoline-powered craft that pulled barges, a combination far more suitable than steamboats to local runs carrying lumber products.

In fiscal year 1903, an unnamed 12-ton gasoline boat drawing sixteen inches light and eighteen inches loaded made fifty-two trips between Jefferson and Shanghai, one hundred between Shanghai and Benton, and fifteen between Jefferson and Caddo Lake transporting 20 tons of cypress logs, 1,200 tons of lumber, 1,310 tons of telephone poles, 2,000 tons of cord wood, 10 tons of provisions, and 10 tons of grain, at an estimated value of $27,150. In fiscal year 1904, the 15-ton gasoline boat *Nellie G.*, which drew eighteen inches light, made one hundred trips between Jefferson and the lakes carrying 120 tons of saw logs, 1,725 tons of telephone poles, and 4 tons of miscellaneous freight at an estimated value of $9,100.

In fiscal year 1905, the 14-ton gasoline boat *Nyma May*, which drew twelve inches light and twenty-three inches loaded, made five trips between Jefferson and local points carrying passengers and miscellaneous freight. No commercial statistics are reported for fiscal year 1906. In fiscal year 1907, unnamed gasoline boats pulled barges carrying 960 tons of livestock, 420 tons of pilings, 213 tons of shingles, 50 tons of railroad ties, 30 tons of feed and provisions, and 30 tons of miscellaneous freight. No commercial statistics are reported for fiscal years 1908 and 1909.

The moribund condition of local traffic was shocked into vibrancy by the emergence of the oil industry in the Caddo Lake area, which dominated the final phase of commercial navigation along the route. The first successful oil well in Caddo Parish was completed by the Savage brothers in March 1905 in an area that later came to be known as Oil

City. Standard Oil, the Texas Company, and Gulf all had drilling programs underway by 1907, and by 1909 there were 183 wells in the Caddo Field. In spite of this rapid development, many of the wells were gassers, there were numerous blowouts, and cratering destroyed many of the rigs. Trees No. 4, which was completed late in 1909 on the west side of Jim's Bayou, was the first big producer, demonstrating the field's potential by early 1910.

J. B. McCann followed a gas seepage across Caddo Lake, discovering a productive area near Mooringsport. By 1910, successful production on three sides suggested that there must be something underneath the water. The Caddo Levee District, which had the authority to lease Caddo bottomlands, advertised for bids on the 8,000-acre bed of Caddo Lake in Louisiana, and the lease was obtained by the Gulf Refining Company on 4 November 1910.

Although there had been some offshore drilling in California, this was from piers that extended out from the shore. Ferry Lake No. 1, which was completed in early May 1911, was the first freestanding offshore well. Seven more wells had been drilled in the lake bed by the end of 1911. In order to service the offshore wells, Gulf eventually maintained a large fleet consisting of three tugboats, ten barges, a floating piledriver, and thirty-six small boats. The division superintendent in charge of these operations was called "admiral."

The oil industry is first mentioned in a Corps of Engineers report for fiscal year 1910 (ending 30 June 1910), when two gasoline vessels with barges were reported carrying the following commodities:

Article	Amount	Value
	(short tons)	
Railroad ties	60	$480
Livestock	42	4,200
Lumber	400	4,800
Oil well supplies	1,435	287,000
Miscellaneous	175	1,750
Total	2,112	$298,230

There was an explosion of activity during the second half of 1910, evident in the Corps report for fiscal year 1911 showing ten gasoline vessels and ten barges transporting the large commodity listings and tonnages shown in **table 20-1**. The report notes that this is an

Table 20-1
Commodities and Tonnages, Fiscal Year 1911

Article	Amount (Units)	Amount (Short Tons)	Value
Angle irons	15 tons	15	$1,200
Boilers	150,000 pounds	75	30,000
Brick	10 tons	10	30
Casing	1,517,488 pounds	759	151,800
Cement	344,000 pounds	172	1,590
Crude oil	1,000 barrels	158	1,500
Drilling rigs	430,000 pounds	215	86,000
Grain	2,500 bushels	75	1,875
Gravel	75 tons	75	113
Hay	47 tons	47	705
Ice	2,000 pounds	1	8
Livestock	224 head	140	4,480
Lumber	1,356,109 ft. b.m.	2,712	27,120
Lumber	7,500 ft. b.m.	18	280
Machinery	937 tons	937	374,800
Miscellaneous	285 tons	285	5,700
Oil-well supplies	280 tons	280	7,000
Piling	200 (number)	125	500
Pipe	4,889 tons	4,889	977,800
Pipe fittings	111 tons	111	27,750
Provisions	56 tons	56	5,600
Pumps	24,000 pounds	12	4,800
Rivets	10 tons	10	1,600
Rods	2,100 pounds	1	75
Sand	30 tons	30	30
Tank steel	662,000 pounds	331	52,960
Tubing	9,200 pounds	4	800
Total		11,543	$1,629,496

incomplete list because many of the oil companies did not give an account of their activities. The report also noted that "The opening of oil wells in this territory has caused a considerable increase in the amount of commerce on this waterway. Its existence has been a great convenience in bringing supplies to the oil-well drillers." However, much of this waterborne transport was merely across Jim's Bayou to the western edge of the Caddo Field on land.

By the end of 1911, the development of the offshore platform complex was well underway. The commodity listings show only minor changes from the previous year, indicating that offshore structures were fairly similar to those on land, particularly because the status of "land" in the Jim's Bayou area was somewhat uncertain, and the earliest incursions into bayou and lake waters were made by platforms with ramps to land. Transport to the offshore structures as well as across Jim's Bayou was carried on by gasoline launches and gasoline towboats with barges. Representative vessels for 1911–12 are listed in the Corps report for 1912: "*Willie*, with barges *No. 1* and *No. 2*; *Lillie Lucille*, draft 17 inches, with barge; two launches and barges, unnamed; *Poco No. 1*, draft 36 inches, net tonnage 1 ton, towboat; *Poco No. 2*, draft 26 inches, net tonnage 1 ton, foreman's runabout; *Poco No. 3*, draft 18 inches, net tonnage 400 pounds, foreman's runabout; *Poco No. 4*, draft 24 inches, net tonnage 1,000 pounds, foreman's runabout; *Poco No. 5*, draft 36 inches, net tonnage 1,500 pounds, towboat; *Poco No. 6*, draft 18 inches, net tonnage 1,000 pounds, runabout; *Texas*, barge, draft 36 inches, net tonnage 20 tons; *Leonard, Dan Walker, Emer M., Victor, Chloe* and barges; *Petrolia, Rastus, Gulf, Mable S., O.K., No. 2, Scout, Dan Patch, Gypsy* (and four barges); *Ferro* and barges; *Sun, Edna.*"

Throughout the second decade of the twentieth century, the freight listings in the Corps' annual reports did not show much change in commodity types, though by volume there was a rise from 14,000 short tons in 1911 to a maximum of 44,000 short tons in 1913. The most interesting change in the freight listings was an increase from 666 wood pilings in 1911 to 10,696 pieces in 1914, accompanied by 1,000 pieces of cement piling. Because each offshore platform required 140 pilings, 1914 was apparently the height of offshore construction in the early period of development. In addition, many millions of feet of board lumber were transported by water for use on land and water.

The Corps' statistics on freight movements provide only a small window on the extraordinary amount of activity and excitement connected with the development of the Caddo Field, which included hundreds of wells on the lake. Although freight movements declined as the construction phase ended, vessel trips reached a high point of

3,806 in 1957. The centers of action shifted from the old ports and landings to new towns like Oil City and to transformed towns like Mooringsport. Jefferson was the recipient of a large boost in its commercial activity. The oil-induced population expansion replicated the cotton expansion of sixty years before, and the lumber needs of the oil industry transformed the environment in a manner similar to the land-clearing efforts of the early settlers.

Although gasoline-powered vessels do not generate the same interest as steamboats, it should not be forgotten that steamboats were essentially freight and passenger carriers. Like the vessels that replaced them, they were workboats. Just as steamboats were essential features of the cotton trade, so were Gulf's service boats in the implementation of offshore technology. There was, however, a decided change in the scope of movement—all of the later traffic was local in nature, as noted in Capt. T. H. Jackson's 1913 report on the Jefferson-Shreveport Waterway: "The navigation on the Jefferson-Shreveport waterway at present is all on Caddo Lake, Cypress Bayou, and James Bayou. The latter is not literally a part of the above-named waterway, but is a tributary of the lake. This navigation consists principally of boats in the fishing business, the shipping of lumber from the sawmills on Cypress Bayou to the oil fields, and the barging of oil well and pipeline construction materials from Mooringsport, Louisiana, to the oil fields on James Bayou."

THE PAST AS PRELUDE

The decisive change in the navigation history of the area west of Shreveport was not the move from steamboats bearing cotton for New Orleans to the offshore service vessels carrying supplies and equipment locally but rather the supplanting of the offshore service vessels by recreational craft, which now dominate the navigation picture. Although the practical aspects of navigation have changed from commerce to leisure, there has been a continuing effort to revive commercial navigation in the form of barge tows. This effort is continuous with the proposals begun in 1872 to restore the navigability of the route that was lost through federal actions. The recent failure of these efforts has provided the opportunity for the emergence of new forms of commercial activity in which recreational navigation and the navigation history of the area will play a significant role.

Pleasure boating in the area west of Shreveport extends back to the steamboat period, but it is only during the last few decades that recreational craft have proliferated and that recreational boating has become an important factor in the local economy. These craft include motor boats, airboats, powered barges, jet skis, and canoes that provide opportunities for fishing, hunting, sightseeing, bird watching, and water sports.

The recreational craft include tour boats on Cypress Bayou and Caddo Lake. The most interesting of these from a structural perspective is the *Graceful Ghost* (**fig. 20-1**), a sternwheel steamboat that formerly operated on Cypress Bayou out of Jefferson but now operates on Caddo Lake out of Uncertain. When this boat moved from Cypress Bayou to Caddo Lake in 1994 under Capt. Lexie Palmore, she was the first steamboat to travel that route since the *Anna Tardy* in 1905.

The present tour boats themselves have historical predecessors. Among these should be mentioned the *Queen of Cypress* and *Cypress Queen*. The *Queen of Cypress* was originally a barge pulled by the tugboat *Irby Grey* that carried logs to Jefferson for the Clarke and Boice Lumber Company. Around 1920, a second story was added to the barge along

Fig. 20-1. *Graceful Ghost. Source: Lexie Palmore McMillen, Uncertain, Texas*

with decks and railings to make her resemble a steamboat—but without a paddlewheel—and during the 1920s and 1930s she operated as a party boat for Jeffersonians. The *Cypress Queen* was a miniature paddleboat that provided excursions on Cypress Bayou out of Jefferson in the late 1960s.

One of the key factors in the maintenance and promotion of recreational boating was the 1971 replacement of the 1914 dam on Caddo Lake. When the dam at the foot of Caddo Lake that was to be built in 1914 was authorized in 1910, a public hearing was held in Shreveport to consider the proposal to place a lock in the dam and to provide downstream dredging. At that time, the Caddo Levee District was opposed to the dam because a permanent lake would interfere with their traditional sectoral leasing practices, and they feared legal implications concerning their right to lease the bed of the lake. However, they supported the proposed project, while retaining a formal position of opposition to the dam, because they were interested in the land reclamation possibilities that would be afforded by downstream dredging.

After the dam was constructed without a lock and without downstream dredging, the Caddo Levee District proceeded with its land reclamation objectives during the 1920s by dredging and leveeing the Soda Lake and Twelvemile Bayou areas. Most of the original channel of Twelvemile Bayou was abandoned, a new mouth upstream of the one used by steamboats that was formed by an invasion of Red River was cut off, and the stream was diverted into Cross Bayou. Present-day Twelvemile Bayou has little in common with the natural channel used by steamboats and is essentially a drainage ditch.

It is well known that the 1914 dam leaked, with a major failure occurring in June 1922 through seepage and undermining. This leakage was the result of foundational deficiencies exacerbated by the Caddo Levee District's downstream dredging. Riprap and fill were placed by the levee district and the Corps of Engineers, but it was obvious by the late 1950s that a new dam was needed: the dam was old, a portion of the spillway was moving downstream at about an inch a year, and a large hole had been scoured downstream of the spillway riprap. The dam was in danger of failure. The Senate Committee on Public Works adopted a resolution on 2 January 1962 directing the Corps to investigate the feasibility of replacing the dam; a favorable report was issued in June 1965.

The 1914 dam was justified on the basis of nonexistent navigation benefits. The justification for the dam replacement was even more peculiar. There was clearly no federal interest in dam replacement, as navigation on the lake was negligible other than for pleasure boats and oilfield workboats, and recreation was a purely local concern. Nevertheless, in the 1965 report "Caddo Dam, Louisiana," the district engineer, his superiors, and review organizations such as the Red River Valley Association argued for dam replacement on the basis of a moral obligation to the local inhabitants who had invested in the area because of the conditions induced by the 1914 dam: "The threat of the loss of the present lake levels through failure of the existing dam is sufficient to justify replacement of the present dam. Although the benefits are largely local in nature, they have developed as a result of a Federal project constructed to serve navigation needs which no longer exist. The Federal Government has a moral obligation to reconstruct the dam to its present level to insure continuation of the benefits now being derived from the lake."

The primary benefits, as the report points out, were the continuation of the recreational importance of the lake and the maintenance of property values, which themselves were largely dependent on water-based recreational opportunities. Recommendations for local assumption of authority over the dam and for a drawdown structure within the dam to control aquatic vegetation on the lake were rejected, and the dam was completed on 18 June 1971, with a 2,400-foot concrete wall, 860 feet of which has a crest elevation of 168.5 feet. The Corps of Engineers is responsible for maintaining the dam but has no authority over the lake. The dam prohibits through navigation. However, when the waters of the lake rise dramatically, pleasure craft occasionally pass over the crest, as they did with the 1914 dam.

With respect to commercial navigation, the Cypress Bayou and Waterway project initiated in 1872 was never taken off the books. Its authority was incorporated into the New Orleans District's 1965 Comprehensive Basin Study for the Red River below Denison Dam. This report found a favorable benefit-to-cost ratio for navigation to Shreveport and bank stabilization on the Red River and a favorable, but modest, benefit-to-cost ratio for navigation on the Cypress Bayou and the lakes route up to Daingerfield, Texas. This new formulation would incorporate into the route Cypress Bayou above Jefferson through Lake O' the Pines, which had been created by a dam in 1959.

The accent would shift from steamboats to barges, but the emphasis would still be on commercial navigation. Traditional low-water problems on the Red and the route would be resolved by a system of locks and dams.

The New Orleans District recommended both the Red River and Shreveport-to-Daingerfield reach projects for construction, which were authorized by Congress through the 1968 River and Harbor Act. Construction began on the Red River and is now complete. The district conducted a reanalysis in 1980 of the transportation benefits for the Shreveport-to-Daingerfield reach and recommended a project reformulation study that would take a closer look at transportation benefits and include a complete environmental analysis. It was this recommendation that gave rise to the Shreveport-to-Daingerfield Navigation Study.

The Cypress Valley Navigation District was created in 1965 at the request of the Red River Valley Association to serve as a local sponsor for the Shreveport-to-Daingerfield reach of the overall Red River project. CVND has authority over the Cypress Bayou Basin and Caddo Lake portions of Harrison and Marion Counties. It was created by the Texas Legislature under an existing Texas Water Development Board program with powers to "promote, construct, maintain, and operate . . . navigational canals and waterways and all navigational systems or facilities auxiliary thereto, using the natural bed and banks of the Cypress River, its tributary streams and Caddo Lake."

These are broad powers, obviously providing the opportunity for a much greater range of activities than simply serving as the local sponsor for a federal navigation project. These powers have enabled CVND to play a representative role in the late history of navigation, with its heavy emphasis on recreational navigation, but with a continuing interest in the revival of commercial navigation. The organization has functioned as an advocate of commercial navigation but never had the opportunity to become a local sponsor because of the failure of the federal navigation project. Its practical activities have been restricted to the realm of recreational navigation, to which it has made important contributions.

Caddo Lake and Cypress Bayou are heavily used areas for water-based recreation. This high level of use, which is important to the local economy, could not have been achieved without the provision and maintenance of access, particularly on the western half of Caddo Lake. In fact, were it not for the activities of CVND, much of the western side of the lake would now be closed to recreational boating. This is because the western half of the lake is choked with aquatic vegetation, including indigenous and introduced species, the most recent and threatening being the water hyacinth.

During the 1800s, the growth of aquatic vegetation was checked by the continuous flushing action of water level rises and declines and, most importantly, by the drying up of much of the lake bed during the summer. There is no mention of aquatic vegetation in any of the texts of the 1800s, which would have prohibited the passage of steamboats. In particular, it is not mentioned by Harriet Ames, who would have noted its occurrence from her romantic perspective. The dam at the foot of Caddo Lake is essential to its existence, but it provides continuous moderate water levels in which aquatic vegetation flourishes.

The efforts of the CVND have been devoted to establishing and maintaining a system of recreational boatroads by dredging, stump cutting, and marking and by keeping them open through maintenance dredging, debris removal, and vegetation control. These efforts are similar to those of the Corps of Engineers in its improvements to the steamboat route, but with the addition of vegetation control. The geographic scope of activities ranges from Lake O' the Pines through Caddo Lake, with a concentration of activities in the upper end of the lake. Funding is provided locally through Harrison and Marion Counties and by the state through the Texas Parks and Wildlife Department.

Two major access canals have been created through dredging. Carney Canal, which provides access from Cypress Bayou to the lower end of Carter's Lake, required the dredging of an existing slough. Bradley Canal, which provides access from Cypress Bayou to Caddo Lake through Jackson Arm, required the dredging of an overland cut through Mossy Brake. The existing Government Ditch was redredged and cleared of debris in an improvement to the federal navigation project of the 1800s. These cuts have required continuous dredging because of siltation and the sandy nature of the soils, which produces bank sloughing.

The cuts are part of an elaborate network of boatroads that extends from Jefferson through Caddo Lake. The boatroads were constructed largely on the basis of existing usage patterns. Construction of the boatroad network involved stump cutting, stump and log removal, removal of overhanging and fallen trees, debris clearance, and vegetation cutting. Pilings were driven along the established routes, and sign boards were posted. These activities have been continuous, because vegetation and debris continue to accumulate, and siltation continues to occur. In addition, the marker system has been improved.

The spread of aquatic vegetation poses the most serious problem. Vegetation has been cut mechanically and treated by herbicides, and at one point the use of grass carp was considered. In addition to channel cutting and boatroad establishment and maintenance, CVND has been involved in a wide range of issues affecting navigation, such as flood control, pollution control, navigation hazards, navigation safety, collateral water resources projects, usage conflicts, environmental concerns, mapping, and archeological preservation. However, the major function continues to be maintenance and enhancement of the recreational boatroads.

Although statutorily designated as the local sponsor, CVND did not take a proactive role in the promotion of the Shreveport-to-Daingerfield navigation project. This is because the board is composed of local citizens who have a strong interest in maintaining the integrity of Caddo Lake and, like many other people in the area, were waiting to see the final Corps plans and attendant environmental consequences before making a final decision on the project. However, the board formally, and unanimously, endorsed the basic concept of the project in its April 1992 meeting and established a liaison committee to work with the Corps. A final decision was never required because the project proved to be infeasible.

The Shreveport-to-Daingerfield Navigation Study was conducted in the early 1990s by the Vicksburg District, which had assumed joint authority over the area with the Fort Worth District because of a change in the boundaries of the New Orleans District. The study was a reevaluation of the feasibility of extending the Red River Waterway project from Shreveport through Lake O' the Pines by constructing a 9-foot by 200-foot channel with locks that would enable barges to travel along the old route and above. In determining feasibility, equal weight was to be given to environmental concerns because of changes in federal policy.

Funding for the study was spearheaded by Congressman Jim Chapman, who was interested in the economic development of the area. The study, as an objective analysis, was widely supported. However, area residents were divided over the idea of navigation through Caddo Lake. Proponents and opponents of the idea of navigation were both concerned with maintaining the integrity of the lake, but the latter assumed that nothing could be designed that would maintain that integrity. This issue never came to a head because the Corps found the project to be infeasible on economic and environmental grounds.

Congressman Chapman immediately proceeded to another approach to economic development called ecotourism, which centers on the capacity of environmental and cultural resources to attract tourists. A plan was developed jointly with the Texas Parks and Wildlife Department and is being implemented through the Caddo Lake Initiative, whose goal is to protect and promote the natural and cultural attributes of Caddo Lake and the Cypress Bayou Watershed.

The part that navigation will play in this initiative is as yet uncertain, but will probably be large. For the foreseeable future, commercial navigation will play a role only through remembrance of the past. Ecotourism by its very nature must concentrate on recreational, as opposed to commercial, navigation. Recreational boating and boat tours on Cypress Bayou and Caddo Lake are already important elements in the local economy and will become increasingly important. The bayou frontage at Jefferson is being rehabilitated, and an educational and interpretive center has been established that will emphasize the ecology and history of the area, including its navigation history. This book was sponsored by the Cypress Valley Navigation District as a contribution to these efforts and a testimony to the dominant role that navigation has played in the history of the area west of Shreveport.

Appendix A

Steamboats at Work

THE WORKING BOAT

The popular image of steamboats as floating palaces originated during their period of operation. For many of the people who traveled and worked on them, they were palatial; and in terms of comfort and convenience, they were far superior to the alternative transport modes of horseback, ox-wagon, stagecoach, flatboat, and early rail. However, when this image is read back into time, it leads to distortion.

By modern standards, the general conditions of life in the immediate past were wretched, and steamboats were no exception. The modern traveler, if he could go back in time, would be shocked by the dirt, danger, and disease; extremes of heat and cold; insects; the stench of fellow passengers and cargo; primitive-to-nonexistent sanitary facilities; clutter; indifference to life; widespread heavy drinking; lack of running water; the poor quality of the food; the conditions of work; inefficiencies in operation; and the tedium of the voyage.

Accommodations, such as they were, were designed for cabin passengers. Deck passengers, who constituted the bulk of the traveling public, slept amidst the cargo and were given nothing to eat. Deck crews had no place to sleep, were on call twenty-four hours, were driven by curses and blows of the mate, and ate the table scraps. Wharves were uncommon. Freight and passengers were loaded and offloaded by planks hand placed between the boat and dirt landings that turned to muck with rain and that were constantly stirred by the movement of wagons on shore.

The image of the floating palace also obscures the fact that steamboats were not pleasure craft but rather commercial freight and passenger carriers. As such, they were workboats operated as businesses. They should generally be thought of as independent small businesses operating in a highly competitive environment, largely unregulated, unable to control freight rates, opportunistic, unscheduled, eclectic in the type of freight carried, constantly on the move, unable to expand, constrained by the seasonal conditions of navigation, and subject to the dangers imposed by high-pressure engines and external hazards.

Steamboats were fun to work on precisely because they were not floating palaces. Work was difficult because business was risky; the conditions of navigation were hazardous; boats were demanding; and the movement of freight required hard physical labor. But, these were challenges that were immediate and tangible and afforded a high degree of satisfaction when they were successfully met. Common effort was directed toward the demands of an idiosyncratic moving structure that served as a temporary home and upon which everyone's fate depended. It is not surprising that steamboats were personalized, as in Capt. W. H. Daniell's comment on the *Latona,* as reported by Frederick Way: "She made barrels of money and was very popular—she was my home and I loved her, and when she was dismantled in 1857 I thought I had lost my best friend."

THE WORKERS

The persons who worked on steamboats were divided into officers and crew. The officers included the captain, clerk, pilot, engineer, and mate. The crew included the cabin crew, the deck crew, and the firemen.

Captains are sometimes thought of as boat operators, but this was a function fulfilled by the pilot. The captain was in charge of overall operations of the boat, but because these were businesses, most of his time was spent on business operations, with an occasional turn at the wheel. He worked closely with the clerk, who was in charge of soliciting and recording freight and passengers. There was often a second clerk. Scovell in his reminiscences records that in the early 1870s, boats destined for Jefferson dropped one clerk off at Shreveport to deliver freight, collect bills, and receive cotton for the down trip.

The fate of the boat was largely in the hands of the pilot, who operated the wheel and was the mediator between the external and internal conditions of the movement of the boat. Because boats operated constantly, there was usually a second pilot. The pilot was in contact with the engineer, who was in charge of the machinery that provided the power for the movement of the boat. There was usually a second engineer. At least two firemen operated in shifts to keep the boilers stocked with fuel.

The cabin crew was similar to the staff of a small hotel and was responsible for food preparation and other domestic services. Bars appear to have been generally run by independent operators. The mate was in charge of the deck crew. Although generally known for their prowess and profanity, mates exercised considerable intelligence in the placement of freight to maximize loads and insure boat stability. Deck hands were manual laborers. Their task was not an easy one, because there were no mechanical devices for lifting and they were on call around the clock for freight carriage and wooding. This is why they are generally pictured sleeping on freight when a boat was in port.

Steamboats were labor intensive, with the number of workers dependent on the size of the boat and therefore its carrying capacity. I have not seen any crew lists for a boat operating in the direction of Jefferson. However, the Dewey Somdal Papers at LSU in Shreveport have crew lists for the *Flicker* for various trips from New Orleans to Thibodeaux, Louisiana. This boat, which was representative of the medium range of boats that operated along the route, carried the following personnel on a January 1867 voyage: captain, two clerks, two pilots, two engineers, mate, watchman, painter, roustabout, two firemen, steward, cook, pantryman, two cabin boys, chambermaid, and ten deck hands.

There were no fixed wage rates or full-time jobs. Compensation was modest, and employment was unsteady. Compensation and job continuity were dependent on skill levels. Captains and clerks might be associated with a particular boat over the years, particularly if the captain was an owner. But captains normally operated more than one boat during a year, which is why it is difficult to track captains in the navigation record. Other officers were associated with particular boats to varying degrees. Officers appear to have had fairly steady employment, at least during periods of navigability when their services were in demand. Crews were itinerant workers hired by the trip and subject to discharge when the trip was over.

For the unusual circumstances following the Civil War when transport demands were high and boats and skilled personnel were few, Scovell cites wages of $2,000 a month for captains, $1,500 a month for pilots, $500 a month for first clerks, mates, and engineers, and $250 a month for their assistants. However, these were unusual times. For the *Flicker* in 1867, daily wages were $3.33–$5.00 for first officers, $2.00–$2.50 for second officers, $1.50 for firemen, $1.17–$1.33 for deckhands and the cook, and $0.40–$0.50 for cabin boys and chambermaids.

The salaries of Red River pilots were controversial because of limited entry established by an apprentice system and the later licensing of pilots for operation on particular streams and the formation of an association in New Orleans that was fairly effective in establishing rates. These matters became particularly controversial when they were perceived as offering competitive disadvantages to the New Orleans boats when the Red River trade began to the invaded by Midwestern boats in the early 1870s. A Cincinnati correspondent cited in the 4 January 1871 *South-Western* claimed that Red River pilots made $500 a month. A respondent in the 25 January issue claimed that no Red River pilot made more than $400 a month. This was more than the $250 a month paid by the St. Louis boats. Yet the St. Louis pilots operated under yearly contracts, whereas the Red River pilots sometimes worked only four months in the year according to the respondent.

There is a great deal of information in the newspapers on captains and some of the other officers that operated along the route, should anyone wish to develop composites. The 12 October 1875 *Shreveport Times* claimed that "as a class we know of none that has made a better impression on the community." This was probably not an exaggeration. The captains had a high level of responsibility, and because they dealt with the public and other businessmen in a relation of trust, it was generally necessary for them to be gracious and equitable.

For obvious reasons, little is known about crew members who operated along the route, and they are seldom mentioned as individuals unless some unusual circumstance captured a newspaper's attention, as in this 2 March 1872 *Shreveport Times* account: "A white deck-hand on the steamer La Belle performed a remarkable feat of strength— considering the unhandy weight lifted—when she was in port at Jefferson a few days since. On a wager he carried on his back a bale of cotton weighing 408 pounds from the landing to the engine room of that boat and back to the landing. He had some assistance, however, in getting the bale up."

The work was heavy and dangerous, pay was low, accommodations were nonexistent, and sleep was intermittent. As a consequence, ship jumping was not uncommon, with the requirements of wooding and freight movement sometimes assumed by the cabin crew, officers, and passengers. Ship jumping at Jefferson is mentioned in the 16 February

1870 *South-Western*: "The Era No. 9 came in from Jefferson at 6 o'clock flying light, as she hurried down to meet the Selma here to take her Jefferson freight. She reports that it is almost impossible to get hands at Jefferson to work at fifty cents an hour in specie. Crews have got into the habit of jumping at that point." Ship jumping appears to have become much more common after the Civil War when blacks replaced whites as deckers and steamboat officers received little assistance from civil authorities in enforcing actions against crews.

SIZE OF BOATS

Public concepts of steamboats are dominated by the Mississippi River vessels. The most famous of these were the *Natchez* and *Robert E. Lee*, both of which were about 300 feet long. Boats of this size never traveled on the Cypress Bayou and the lakes route. The vast majority were in the range of 100 to 200 feet and were shallow-draft vessels built specifically for the Red River trade or for negotiating the small rivers, bayous, and lakes of the lower Mississippi River valley. Although most of these boats traveled on the Mississippi to reach New Orleans, they were not regular Mississippi River steamers.

Table A-1 shows the average length of boats by year. There was little change in the size of boats operating along the route before the Civil War. After the war, boats increased in size fairly rapidly. The late period was again characterized by modest-sized boats, although it should be kept in mind that the 303-ton *Nat F. Dortch*, which measured 164 feet by 29 feet, was still operating along the route as late as 1891.

The dimensions of many of the smaller boats are unknown because they were often locally built and operated and never went to New Orleans. Examples of very small boats include the 46-ton *Little Yazoo* (80 x 20), the 61-ton *Dime* (NA x 18), the 27-ton *Augusta* (NA), the 53-ton *Financier* (93 x 18), the 67-ton *Larkin Edwards* (NA), the 40-ton *Minnie* (83 x 18), and the 42-ton *Independence* (75 x 17). The smallest boats generally operated in a transfer capacity for larger boats that traveled to New Orleans. Besides operating along the route, they also traveled to Cross Lake, Old River, and the upper Red.

The larger boats are the most surprising. Although water levels were somewhat higher (about 2½ feet) on Caddo Lake during the 1800s, and similar water levels prevailed up to Smithland, Cypress Bayou was even more restricted and convoluted. The bayou as it is seen today

Table A-1
Average Length of Boats by Year (in feet)

Year	Boats*	Length	Year	Boats	Length
1841	3	130	1862	5	132
1842	4	142	1863	5	113
1843	5	141	1864	NA	NA
1844	5	132	1865	12	113
1845	11	127	1866	33	137
1846	11	134	1867	30	143
1847	9	135	1868	28	146
1848	8	142	1869	25	144
1849	10	142	1870	43	150
1850	5	138	1871	34	158
1851	9	145	1872	22	157
1852	12	137	1873	28	158
1853	11	140	1874	11	155
1854	11	131	1875	7	156
1855	3	118	1876	8	173
1856	24	127	1877	6	165
1857	22	126	1878	3	168
1858	11	131	1879	2	176
1859	14	137	1880s	5	125
1860	20	135	1890s	5	130
1861	17	143			

* For which data are available.

NA = Not Available.

Source: Computed from Appendix B.

is a large improvement over the channel followed by the steamboats. Thus, it is difficult to envision large boats traveling as far as Jefferson. Nevertheless, boats over 150 feet were very common, and there were about forty boats over 170 feet, including the well-known 170 x 29 *Mittie Stephens* and the 177 x 42 *John T. Moore*.

Boats of 200 feet or more were nonexistent on the route before the Civil War and uncommon after. The two largest boats prior to the war were the *R. W. Powell* and the *D. R. Carroll*, both of which were 175-foot sidewheelers. The first two boats in excess of 200 feet were the *Frolic* in 1868 (205 x NA) and the *Fontenelle* in 1870 (206 x 34). Both of these boats operated out of New Orleans and were the only 200-plus New Orleans boats to travel to Jefferson.

A new size class of boats appeared in the early 1870s through the entrance of St. Louis and Cincinnati in the Jefferson trade. These boats were designed for travel on the Mississippi, Missouri, and Ohio and therefore were very large. Many were 200 feet or better, including the 571-ton *Walter B. Dance* (200 x 34), the 335-ton *Silver Bow* (212 x 32), the 393-ton *Edinburgh* (210 x 30), the 218 x 38 *Emilie La Barge*, and the 581-ton *Belle of Shreveport* (202 x 43).

The *Emilie La Barge* was a sidewheeler built in Illinois in 1869 for the Missouri trade that was purchased by the St. Louis Carter Line in 1871. She made only one trip to Jefferson, at the end of June 1872, during a period of unusually high water. The *Belle of Shreveport* was shorter than the *Emilie La Barge*, but it was 5 feet wider, making it the largest boat ever to travel along the route.

The *Belle of Shreveport* was a St. Louis sternwheeler built in 1872 at a cost of $57,000 and operated by Capt. Tom Rea as part of the Carter Line. When she first arrived at Shreveport in 1873 carrying 1,100 tons of freight, which was not a full load, she was described as "a model of steamboat architecture, and the largest sternwheel boat that ever entered Red river."

As her name implies, she was designed specifically to operate between St. Louis and Shreveport, requiring considerable travel on the Mississippi. She was described as substantial and comfortable, but with nothing particularly gaudy about her, and she was said to be as handsome as she was fast. At 202 feet by 43 feet (excluding the sternwheel), she encompassed 8,686 square feet of water surface; and she drew without freight only 24 inches forward and 30 inches aft.

The *Belle of Shreveport* made only one trip to Jefferson, in May 1873, heavily laden with Midwestern goods. This feat could not have been accomplished were it not for the fact that water levels on the route were extremely high from rains throughout the Red River region, producing a minimum depth of 12 feet on Cypress Bayou.

The *Belle of Shreveport* arrived at Shreveport from St. Louis on Sunday, 25 May 1873, carrying a large freight. She began discharging freight on Monday morning, a process that was completed on

Tuesday, when she left for Jefferson at 5:00 in the evening. She lay overnight at Twelvemile Bayou and arrived at Jefferson within twenty-four hours.

She was reported at Jefferson on Thursday, along with the *John T. Moore*, *Lotus No. 3*, and *Seminole*, but she may actually have been at a point slightly downstream of the Jefferson landing where iron for the Texas & Pacific Railroad was unloaded and where she was observed by the *Seminole* on Friday. The trip back to Shreveport took fifteen hours, including a small layover on Twelvemile Bayou. She arrived at Shreveport at 4:00 Saturday morning carrying two bales of cotton for local merchants and left for St. Louis at 2:00 in the afternoon.

That this was the largest boat that ever traveled to Jefferson is confirmed by the 31 May *Shreveport Times*, which says in regard to the trip to Jefferson that the *Belle of Shreveport* was "the largest boat that ever made the run up there," accomplishing "a feat of which Capt. Thos. W. Rea may well feel proud." This was the last Midwestern boat to travel the route.

BOAT DRAFTS

The most distinctive feature of the steamboats that operated on the Mississippi River and its tributaries was their extreme shallow draft. The draft of a boat is basically dependent on weight, hull structure, and horizontal dimensions. Steamboats on the Mississippi River system were lightweight, with large, almost flat hulls. Running drafts were dependent on these factors plus the amount of freight carried.

There are four sources of information in the navigation record concerning the draft of boats that operated along the route. The most prominent of these are the claims made in advertisements, construction notices, and commentaries. Although there is no reason to doubt the validity of these claims, it should be noted that the drafts are not representative but are provided for their distinctiveness. In addition, the drafts cited are mostly for light-loaded conditions, which means essentially without freight. Operational drafts are given in a few instances, but these appear to be claims rather than observed running conditions. The examples are arranged by date of draft citation, with tonnage and dimensions added. Tonnages for prewar boats should be increased by forty-five percent to assure comparability.

1. *Express Mail*: 244 tons; 165 x 25; 23 inches light (*Daily Picayune*, 19 June 1841).
2. *Lama*: 68 tons; 100 x 24; 24 inches (*Daily Picayune*, 27 October 1844).
3. *Little Yazoo*: 46 tons; 80 x 20; 14 inches (*Daily Picayune*, 29 January 1845).
4. *De De*: 80 tons; 118 x 21; 11 inches forward and 14 inches aft with wood and water on board (*South-Western*, 21 May 1856).
5. *L. Dillard*: 56 tons; 107 x 19; 12 inches light (*South-Western*, 13 December 1865).
6. *Right Way*: 291 tons; 134 x 28; 20 inches light (*South-Western*, 13 November 1867).
7. *Flicker*: 147 tons; 125 x 26; 12 inches light (*Daily Picayune*, 16 November 1867).
8. *Era No 9*: 169 tons; 146 x 37; 13 inches aft and 10 inches forward with machinery, boiler, cabin and everything complete above deck, "which, being an average of eleven and half inches under all proves her to be the lightest low water boat ever constructed on the Western Waters" (*South-Western*, 2 September 1868).
9. *Mollie Fellows*: 224 tons; 139 x 25; 30 inches with bulkheads in and wood and water on board (*South-Western*, 12 February 1868).
10. *Travis Wright*: 202 tons; 129 x 32; 13 inches light (*South-Western*, 19 May 1869).
11. *Jennie Howell*: NA; 146 x 36; 16 inches forward and 20 inches aft (*South-Western*, 18 August 1869).
12. *Flavilla*: 203 tons; 129 x 30; 15 inches light (*South-Western*, 1 September 1869).
13. *Bossier*: NA; NA; 12 inches light (*South-Western*, 13 July 1870).
14. *Thirteenth Era*: 298 tons; 150 x 33; 12 inches light (*South-Western*, 2 November 1870).
15. *May Lowry*: NA; 138 x 31; 12 inches light and carries 1,000 bales on 3 feet (*South-Western*, 15 February 1871).
16. *Belle of Shreveport*: NA; 202 x 43; 24 inches forward and 30 inches aft light; 7⅔ feet fully loaded (*Shreveport Times*, 20 October and 16 November 1872).

17. *Col. A. P. Kouns*: 309 tons; 165 x 33; 14 inches with machinery and cabin on (*Shreveport Times*, 5 November 1874).

18. *Dawn*: NA; 160 x 32; 18 inches (*Shreveport Times*, 2 September 1875).

19. *Caddo Belle*: NA; 125 x 25; trimmed on 17 inches with 20 tons on board (*Shreveport Times*, 5 August 1880).

The second source of information concerns observed running conditions. Operational drafts were greater than light-loaded drafts because they involved the increased weight of freight and passengers. Comparisons are possible because in a few instances light-loaded and operational drafts are given for the same boat. However, it should be noted that there was no such thing as a standard operational draft for a particular steamboat. That depended entirely on what the boat was carrying:

1. *Sodo*: NA; 108 x 20; "With wood, water, and provisions on board, she draws less than 11 inches; and left here for the falls, with 151 bales of cotton, drawing under 18 inches." (*South-Western*, 13 December 1854).

2. *Lulu D.*: 245 tons; 135 x 35; drew 30 inches with 160 head of cattle and a fair list of passengers (*South-Western*, 12 August 1868).

3. *Dixie*: 102 tons; 131 x 24; drew 30 inches at the bow with a good freight (*South-Western*, 12 August 1868).

4. *Era No. 8*: 62 tons; 122 x 25; drew 2 feet at the bow with a light freight (*South-Western*, 12 August 1868).

5. *Rose Franks*: 240 tons; 126 x 29; drew 30 inches with 150 head of cattle and a small list of passengers (*South-Western*, 12 August 1868).

6. *Richmond*: 339 tons; 143 x 35; drew about two feet with 125 head of cattle, fifteen passengers, and ten bales of cotton (*South-Western*, 19 August 1868).

7. *Pioneer Era*: 219 tons; 129 x 29; ran fully loaded on 30 inches (*South-Western*, 30 September 1868).

8. *Salado*: 110 tons; 128 x 25; "With 200 bushels of coal aboard and 80 tons of freight, she drew 20 inches" (*South-Western*, 2 December 1868).

9. *Silver Bow*: 335 tons; 212 x 22; was drawing three feet at Shreveport with a "good freight of Western produce" (*South-Western*, 8 December 1869).

10. *Charles H. Durfee*: 267 tons; 178 x 36; 20 inches light (*South-Western*, 21 September 1870); drew 30 inches with a good load of passengers and freight (*Shreveport Times*, 6 August 1872).

11. *John T. Moore*: 497 tons; 177 x 42; 24 inches with 50 tons to trim her (*Daily Picayune*, 22 February 1871); drew 5 feet with a good freight (*South-Western*, 10 May 1871); ran fully loaded on 6 feet (*South-Western*, 17 May 1871).

12. *Royal George*: NA; 135 x 27; "She draws only eight inches light and will carry one thousand barrels on twenty inches." (*Shreveport Times*, 1 September 1871); "She brought down the weight of 300 bales on eighteen inches of water." (*Shreveport Times*, 21 May 1872); she was drawing 18 inches loaded on one occasion and 16 inches "with all the freight she wanted" on another (*Shreveport Times*, 11 and 17 September 1872).

13. *Cherokee*: 260 tons; 131 x 33; drew 16 inches light and was reported running on 20 inches (*Shreveport Times*, 10 September 1872).

14. *R. T. Bryarly*: 331 tons; 150 x 33; 12 inches light (*Shreveport Times*, July 6, 1872); 30 inches with 800 bales of cotton on board (*Shreveport Times*, 15 October 1872).

15. *Katie P. Kountz*: NA; NA; took out 1,250 bales of cotton on less than four feet (*Shreveport Times*, 21 February 1873).

16. *Lotus No. 3*: NA; 160 x 37; carried 240 bales of cotton on 30 inches (*Shreveport Times*, 4 May 1873).

17. *Huntsville*: 213 tons; 159 x 33; carried 600 bars of railroad iron on three feet (*Shreveport Times*, 26 July 1873).

The navigation columns generally give the water levels encountered by boats on the last trips out. Although these are usually not specifically correlated with drafts, the reports can be used to determine which boats made it through various places under specific water level conditions. In addition, because what boats were carrying is usually reported, the weight of a boat on a particular trip can be roughly compared to its ability to pass through water levels of various types.

The *Tidal Wave* in December 1870 can be used as an example of the level of specificity that can be found in some instances. This boat was 160 feet by 36 feet and therefore about 10 feet longer than the average boat operating during that year. It went up to Jefferson with "a good passenger and freight list" and returned with 594 bales of cotton. The navigation column for the seventh reports the following: "Capt. Scovell, of the Tidal Wave, reports 4 feet at Potato Bend for a very narrow boat, though his boat had to pull on 3 feet."

Lastly, a series of Corps reports on improvements to the Red River in the 1890s provides light and loaded draft information for the boats that operated along the route during the final period of steamboat activity:

1. *Nat F. Dortch*: 303 tons; 164 x 29, 1 foot, 6 inches light; 4 feet loaded.
2. *Friendly*: 67 tons; 120 x 27; 11 inches light; 3 feet loaded.
3. *New Haven*: 93 tons; 136 x 24; 2 feet, 6 inches light; 4 feet loaded.
4. *Rosa Bland*: 149 tons; 113 x 23; 1 foot, 3 inches light; 3 feet, 6 inches loaded.
5. *Blue Wing*: 112 tons, 119 x 24; 1 foot, 8 inches light; 3 feet, 6 inches loaded.
6. *Nellie L.*: NA; NA; 1 foot, 10 inches light; 3 feet, 6 inches loaded.

STERNWHEELERS AND SIDEWHEELERS

Table A-2 shows the relative distribution of sternwheelers and sidewheelers along the route by enumerating the percentage of boats that were sternwheelers. Sidewheelers were dominant before the Civil War. From 1840 through 1854, only one sternwheeler, the *Ellen*, was active along the route (in 1847, when nine boats were operative). The year 1855 was anomalous because low water on the Red River restricted the route to a few local boats.

It was not until 1859 that sternwheelers began to constitute even half of the boats. The decline in 1861 appears to be related to the shifting of sternwheelers to the war effort. Immediately after the war, they accounted for two-thirds of the boats operating along the route, rising fairly steadily thereafter. The *La Belle* was the last sidewheeler to travel to Jefferson, in 1874. This was a very large boat at 510 tons and

Table A-2
Rig Type

Year	Boats*	Sternwheelers	Percent Sternwheelers
1841–46	36	0	0
1847	9	1	11
1848–54	68	0	0
1855	4	3	75
1856	25	4	16
1857	25	8	32
1858	17	5	29
1859	17	9	53
1860	26	12	46
1861	20	5	25
1862–64	CW	CW	CW
1865	12	8	67
1866	34	20	59
1867	29	16	55
1868	28	18	64
1869	26	18	69
1870	50	40	80
1871	35	29	83
1872	24	21	88
1873	31	28	90
1874	11	10	91
1875–1905	26	26	100

* For which data are available.

CW = Civil War.

Source: Computed from Appendix B.

178 feet long. Through 1905, there were nothing but sternwheelers. Thus, it is easy to see why it has commonly been assumed that only sternwheelers went west of Shreveport.

The switch from sidewheelers to sternwheelers along the route was part of a trend for the entire steamboat fleet on the Western rivers. Sidewheelers were initially preferred for their elegance and maneuverability. The form of the sternwheeler was more ideally suited to the shallow and restricted streams of the Western rivers and also provided capacity for greater freight storage. However, the advantage of this form could not be achieved until maneuverability was improved. This improvement was brought about by incremental technical modifications and finally by the introduction of a new type of rudder. The degree to which this was an incremental process is suggested by the gradualness with which sternwheelers replaced sidewheelers along the route.

UNUSUAL BOATS

All of the steamboats that traveled west of Shreveport were conventional sternwheelers and sidewheelers, with the exception of the iron boat *John T. Moore*, the screw propeller *Hornet*, and the square-bowed *Rantidotler*. The *John T. Moore* was one of a very small number of commercial iron-hulled boats, but with the added feature that much of the decking and superstructure was also made of iron. She was a 497-ton sternwheeler measuring 177 feet by 42 feet that was built in Cincinnati in late 1870 at a cost of $80,000. With a capacity for 1,200 tons or 4,000 bales of cotton, she was nevertheless of shallow draft, running on 24 inches with 50 tons to trim her and up to only six feet fully loaded.

The *John T. Moore* made many trips between New Orleans and Shreveport in 1871 and 1872, but it was not until May 1872 that she made her first trip to Jefferson, arriving back at Shreveport with 200 bales of cotton and a good list of passengers. A second trip to Jefferson was made in 1873. Up freights included railroad iron, but the major purpose of the trip was a pleasure excursion. This trip was so successful that a second pleasure excursion was made in June. The *John T. Moore* is shown in Brosius's 1872 *Bird's Eye View of Shreveport, Louisiana.*

Screw propeller steamboats like the *Hornet* were uncommon on the shallow waters of the Mississippi River and tributaries system. Paddlewheels were continuously damaged by snags but easily repaired by a ship's carpenter. Propellers were also easily damaged, as they are today; but repair shops were distant, and replacement propellers might take weeks to obtain. The *Hornet* was a tiny 39-ton craft built in Shreveport in 1870 and locally operated out of Shreveport on Jim's Bayou and on Old River (the stretch of the Red below the raft). She made five recorded trips to Jim's Bayou from 1870 through 1873, including one that carried out Ben Bonham's first cotton crop. This boat never went to Jefferson.

The sternwheeler *Rantidotler* was the only square-bowed steamboat to operate along the route and made one trip to Jefferson under Capt. Henry Pitts in September 1868. The dimensions of this boat are unknown, but it apparently was quite small, being the first boat to reach Jefferson at the end of a low-water period. When she docked at Shreveport from Jefferson, she was described as a "square-bowed kick-up-behind pile of boards."

The *Beaver* should probably be mentioned in the context of unusual boats, because she was a recessed-wheel sternwheeler. This was why she was described as "queer-looking" when she arrived at Shreveport in November 1843. Although intended for the Port Caddo trade, the *Beaver* never traveled the route—she was found to be without the requisite papers for entering the Republic of Texas. Instead, the *Beaver* traveled to upper Red River around the raft and burned at Shreveport when she returned.

The only other unusual boat mentioned in the newspapers was not propelled by steam but demonstrated the lengths to which some persons were willing to go to move cotton during low water, as reported by the 17 November 1869 *South-Western*: "A queer looking craft came in to-day from Cypress bayou with 46 bales of cotton, which she wanted to reship. She got $6 per bale through. This, we believe, is the only water craft now plying between Jefferson and this point. From appearances, we should judge that her motive power was not sufficient for an up stream boat. Said power consists of two grown up men vigorously applied to a grindstone apparatus near the stern. The Levee boys will have her photograph taken to-day and forwarded to the Jimplecute office as a specimen of 'naval architecture.'"

BOAT BUILDING

Of the boats that operated along the route, eighty-seven percent were built in the four Midwestern states of Indiana (twenty-six percent), Pennsylvania (twenty-three percent), Ohio (twenty-two percent), and Kentucky (sixteen percent). In addition, ten boats were built in Louisiana, eight in Virginia, six in West Virginia, five in Arkansas, four in Missouri, two each in Iowa and Illinois, and one each in Tennessee,

Minnesota, and Wisconsin. The only thing that changed over time was the rank order, which prior to the Civil War was Ohio, Kentucky, Pennsylvania, and Indiana. Of the boats produced in Ohio, three-fourths were produced before the war; of the boats produced in Kentucky, four-fifths were produced before the war.

The dominance of these four states was not unusual, because the great boatbuilding centers were all along the Ohio River, including Pittsburg, Cincinnati, Louisville, and Jeffersonville. The location of these centers was not determined by the availability of wood to make the hulls but rather by the availability of raw materials, foundries, and technical expertise needed to make the machinery. There was also a minor boatbuilding center in New Orleans, where most of the Louisiana boats that operated along the route were built.

There are reports of boatbuilding activity at Shreveport (probably on Cross Lake), Albany, Clear Lake, and Cypress Bayou below Jefferson. The nature and scope of this activity is unclear, but probably minor. The unfinished hull of a steamboat was advertised for sale in 1865 at Barr's Mill on Clear Lake, and it is known that the hull of the dredge *Lone Star* was built at Jefferson. The only documented local building of steamboats that operated along the route was for the *Sodo* at Shreveport in 1854, the *L. Dillard* at Shreveport in 1865, the *Mary Ellen* at Shreveport in 1868, the *Frank Morgan* on Soda Lake in 1869, and the *Hornet* at Shreveport in 1870. These were all small boats that were locally owned and operated. The *Mary Ellen*, for example, was described as "just the thing to run in the small lakes and bayous."

The steamboats that were built locally would probably have employed machinery from wrecks or worn-out boats. However, the 29 July 1868 *South-Western* reports the *Tom Poland*, built at Albany but never appearing on the route, as "entirely new." Glenn's 1886 memoranda mention the Alpha Shipyard on the right-ascending bank of Cypress Bayou between Port Caddo and Benton. Ben Bonham may have been connected with this facility, because his *Alpha* was one of the few boats operating along the route in the middle 1880s.

DEPARTURES

Steamboats seldom left when advertised—they waited until sufficient freight was obtained to justify a trip. The 29 December 1869 *South-Western* was incredulous that anyone would take the advertisements seriously: "We wish to call the attention of the Associate Press reporter at New Orleans, to the fact that his reports of the departures of steamboats for Red River are hardly ever correct. In fact, they are oftener wrong than right. A six-year old boy, who was only half-way good at guessing, could beat him all hollow. He appears to make up his departures from the boats advertised in the papers. That steamboats do not always leave as advertised is well known to everybody, it would appear, but our press reporter at New Orleans. As long as he is well paid, we think he might, once in a while, send us a correct report. See if you can't do better in the future."

The situation was similar at Jefferson in 1865, as reported by John Anderson in *Red River Dust*: "Left Clarksville and arrived at Jefferson on the morn of 24th October. Friday: went on board the *Lizzie Hamilton* and paid $10 passage to Shreveport, then found she will not sail til Saturday evening. Went on board the *Sciene No. 2*. Was told she would not sail on Friday evening. She did not start until Saturday night and then only got as far as the packery. Started on Sunday morning, took on more freight—already had about 300 bales of cotton. Made about 12 miles on Sunday and about 20 during the night."

ON THE WAY

The number of boats operating in the direction of Jefferson at any one time was highly variable, depending on transport demand and seasonal navigation conditions. The low point was constituted by zero, which was not unusual. During the good times, a substantial number of boats operated simultaneously in the direction of Jefferson, as in the following instances:

> The following boats have arrived from Jefferson: Lizzie Hamilton, Dillard, and Powell. The Fanny Gilbert had made two trips. A gentleman who came passenger on the Fanny Gilbert, reports having passed the Texas in the lake. She will probably be in port to-day. He also counted seven boats in the lake, bound for Jefferson. (*South-Western*, 24 January 1866)
>
> The following steamers were above here in the direction of Jefferson last night: Ruby, 13th Era, Flirt, Era No. 10, May Lowry, Belle Roland, Huntsville, Andrew Ackley, and Bossier—nine in all. (*Shreveport Times*, 5 February 1873)

There is no information in the newspapers on how boats communicated so as to be able to assure that boats moving upstream and downstream did not block each other in narrow places such as Cypress Bayou.

AT PORT

The newspapers do not contain any descriptions of the port area at Jefferson, which would need to be reconstructed on the basis of elaborate descriptions of facilities and activities at Shreveport's landing. The teamster J. M. Keith said that in 1870 one could find a score or more of steamboats on the water in front of Jefferson. This appears to be an exaggeration, because there is nothing in the navigation record to suggest the possibility of this number of steamboats at Jefferson at any one point in time.

The typical situation during good times is represented in Brosius's 1872 *Bird's Eye View of Jefferson, Texas*, which shows three boats at the wharf and one leaving and one coming. The few mentions in the newspapers concerning the number of boats at Jefferson correspond to the picture presented by Brosius. Charles DeMorse reports in the 10 April 1858 *Standard* that there were five boats in port at one time when he visited Jefferson late in March. The 8 January 1869 Jefferson *Home Advocate* reports: "Navigation is good, and our wharf often crowded with boats, as many as six at a time." The 2 June 1869 *South-Western* reports that the *Enterprise* left three boats at Jefferson when it departed for Shreveport. The *Flavilla*'s 28 December 1871 memorandum in the *Shreveport Times* notes that the *Lotus No. 3*, *Belle Rowland*, *May Lowry*, and *Wash Sentell* lay in port during the three hours she was at Jefferson.

MEALS

There are no accounts of meals on boats west of Shreveport. However, the *R. W. Powell*, with Robert H. Martin as captain, made one trip to Jefferson in 1856. A bill of fare for this boat was provided by R. W. Loughery in the 19 April 1856 *Texas Republican*:

DINNER ON BOARD THE STEAMER R. W. POWELL.
Soup—Oyster. Fish—Baked Red, maitre d' hotel sauce;

barbecued and broiled Trout, parsley sauce. Boiled—Chicken; Leg Mutton, caper sauce. Turkey; Corned Beef; Tongue; Ham. *Entrees*—Pate cheand of Kidneys, fine herb sauce; Cassar role of Rice, a la Windsor; Fillet of Chicken, a la Conti; Barbecued Venison Chops, piquant sauce; Turkey Wings, tomato sauce; Chicken, a la royal; braised hogs head, find herb sauce; stuffed shoulder of mutton, a la Anglais; beef-steak, au pomme de tene; braised breast of mutton, caper sauce; braised beef tongue, a la Anglais; oyster pies; giblet patties. *Roast*—Beef, mutton, turkey, chickens, ducks, pork. Vegetables of the season. *Game*—Saddle of venison, cranberry jelly; French ducks, with turnips; black duck, with Guava jelly. *Pastry and Dessert*—Blackberry, plum, mince, apple and cranberry pies; tartlets, pound cake, rum and Madeira jelly, bell fritters, pound and flour pudding, vanilla and boiled custard, floating island, cream cake, blackberry, Italian and Russian cream, blanc menges, vanilla ice creams. *Fruits*—Pine apples, oranges, bannanas, English nuts, apples, prunes, raisins, Brazil nuts, almonds, pecans, figs, filberts. *Coffee*—Java, with cream.

Such fare was available only to cabin passengers and would have been available when the *R. W. Powell* went to Jefferson. However, it was not representative of the food normally obtainable on boats that traveled the route. The *R. W. Powell* was well known for the unusually high quality of its table, and Loughery notes that "the table is not equalled by the first class hotels of New Orleans." Dinner on board the *R. W. Powell* was probably near the best that a steamboat could offer. Lesser boats probably ranged downward to the bread and bacon that was standard at most meals on land, even at some of the hotels. In addition, Louis Hunter in *Steamboats on the Western Rivers* notes that dining was not elegant. Food was generally consumed voraciously by hand from the serving tables.

WHISTLES

Steamboat whistles broke the silence of rural areas and were particularly welcome when they marked the advent of navigation after a low-water period, as in the 15 December 1865 *Texas Republican* quote from the *Jefferson Register*: "There is plenty of water to afford navigation for small boats to this place at present, and we expect to hear the frequent sound of the steam whistle soon to cheer the merchant, mechanic, and farmer, with their cargoes." However, they were generally considered a nuisance in port and were attacked in the New Orleans and Shreveport newspapers, as in the 18 January 1871 *South-Western*:

> A small amount of whistle would not be so intolerable, but most pilots appear to take a fiendish pleasure in splitting the ears of the groundlings by continuous screams, apparently deluding themselves, too, with the idea that the movements of their boat is a matter of profound and startling interest to everybody for miles around. A modest whistle upon arriving and on the eve of departure, no one could reasonably object to, but to keep the thing up, at intervals, by the hour, involves too great a strain upon the nerves and patience of landsmen. If we are not misinformed, some town in the West makes it a finable offense for a boat to whistle while lying at the wharf. If so, the Fathers of that town deserve a monument higher than that of Bunker Hill, as the greatest philanthropists of their day and generation.

The town in the West with a prohibition on whistles was not Jefferson, because it had no ordinances to that effect.

COMMUNITY RELATIONS

In the trades connected with the smaller streams of the Mississippi River system, steamboats were integrated into the life of the communities they served. Participation of a boat in a particular trade tended to be fairly personal, and the ability to attract large numbers of cabin passengers was highly dependent on reputation. Boats might be locally built or built by locals, and captains were often from the communities they served. Overlying these factors was an immense system of trust without which the long-term and long-distance features of the cotton economy could not have been functional.

In the absence of Jefferson newspapers, the nature and degree of the involvement of steamboats in the communities they served must remain largely hidden, particularly because community relations were largely manifestations of business self-interest and therefore would appear in subtle forms as they do today. Examples from common practice include the widespread illegal carriage of mail for private individuals and the provision of newspapers and gifts for the editors of navigation columns.

The 1 June 1870 *South-Western* reports the following: "The Sunday school children of Jefferson had a picnic excursion on the 24th of May, aboard the Lotus No. 3. They were conveyed down the Bayou and disembarked under the shadow of the grand old trees fringing that stream, where they had a 'nice time' generally. Capt. Dannals and the other officers of the Lotus are spoken of in terms of highest praise by the press of Jefferson for their care and attention to the little folks on the occasion."

In 1871, the ladies of Jefferson organized a benefit for the Catholic Church that involved an indigo-blue flag fifteen feet long and five feet wide, with a white wreath and enclosed star and the words "Our" on one side of the flag and "Own" on the other. All of the steamboats that arrived at Jefferson between May and July flew the flag for various periods of time, after which it was presented permanently to the *Charles H. Durfee* as "Our Own," with the proceeds from the voting for favorite steamboat going to the Catholic Church.

CRIME

Petty crime was probably fairly common on steamboats, but it is unreported in the newspapers, just as it is unreported in the newspapers of today. Boats could not be held up or hijacked because they were protected by large crews; however, thefts from wrecked boats on the Red River were common. Serious crime aboard boats was apparently fairly uncommon, because it would have been reported in the newspapers and seldom is. The opportunity for serious theft appears to have been most available when a boat was in port and the officers were not vigilant because they were asleep, as in this Shreveport example from the 28 March 1866 *South-Western*: "The safe of the steamer Caddo was robbed of some fifteen hundred dollars in currency and a bag of gold, on last Friday, by some adroit thief. The gold was afterwards recovered; but the greenbacks are no longer the property of the Caddo. The thief first stole the key of the safe from the clerk, who was asleep in the ladies' cabin, and at his leisure quietly examined the safe, and gobbled up what he wanted. The second clerk was asleep at the time in the office."

Murders and killings were extremely common on land, so much so that the editor of the Marshall *Texas Republican* stated that if he were to describe all of them, there would be no room for the reportage of anything else. There are no reports in the newspapers of any murders on steamboats that operated on the Red River or along the route, apparently because it was easy to escape on land but nearly impossible on a boat. The only reported killing aboard a steamboat concerned the *Telegram* in May 1859. A steward and a cabin boy got into a fight with barrel staves when the cabin boy refused to follow orders. The captain broke up the fight, and it was thought that the blows received by the cabin boy were not serious, but he later died. The steward was turned over to the authorities in New Orleans.

Conflicts between crew members seldom resulted in serious violence aboard steamboats because of the tight command system that was exercised in a relatively isolated environment. Crew members settled differences on land at port, as in this example from the 13 July 1858 *Texas Republican* regarding William Perry's *Bloomer*: "We learn from the Jefferson Herald, that the body of a man was discovered floating in the Bayou, opposite the steamboat landing, on Friday morning last. The head, breast, and arms were mangled in a shocking manner. It appears that he had been beaten to death by the mate and second mate (L. A. Johnson and _____ Wilcox) of the steamer Bloomer, and his body thrown into the Bayou. The deceased was an Irishman, a deck-hand on the boat. The preliminary trial of the accused had been postponed for a day, and they were taken under guard to the steamer. While at dinner, the second mate escaped. Parties were out after him in all directions, and it was believed he would be captured."

BOATS AT PLAY

Steamboats were workboats, not recreational craft, although they were obviously fun to operate, particularly when a trip was lucrative. Nevertheless, they were not restricted to freight carriage. Boats that operated along the route included the showboat *Banjo* and the circus boats *Belle* and *Will S. Hays*. Paid pleasure excursions to Jefferson were conducted by the *John T. Moore* in 1872 and by the *Col. A. P. Kouns* in 1875 and 1876 in connection with the Queen Mab Celebration. Annual paid fishing excursions were made by various boats in the 1870s and 1880s from Shreveport to Jim's Bayou, "where perch and white trout do most congregate." There are no reports of steamboat races on the route, which would have been a physical and practical impossibility even if it had been desired.

NEGOTIATING SHALLOW WATERS

Steamboats had a number of different means for negotiating shoal places, particularly the bars that increased in prominence during low-water periods. The most common was ramming through. Warping involved the use of a capstan, which was a vertical rotating drum around which a cable was turned. The cable was anchored upstream or attached to a tree, and the boat was pulled over the impediment. Force was applied by the deck crew until the 1850s, when the steam capstan was introduced. Sparring involved the use of spars planted at an angle in the bed of the stream toward the front of the boat along with block and tackle and the capstan. The boat was walked over the impediment, much like the action of crutches. Lightening involved offloading of freight and sometimes passengers to a companion vessel (a lighter, therefore lightering) or to shore, with the weight reduction allowing the boat to move over the impediment.

The route had few shoal places and nothing in the way of extensive bars. The primary shoal places were on Soda Lake and between Smithland and Jefferson. These places were different from the typical bar situations encountered on the Red and were sufficiently different from each other to require a different set of responses. As places to be negotiated, both were geographically extensive. The area between Smithland and Jefferson was, for example, six miles in length. This geographic extensiveness made some techniques more suitable than others. The dissimilarities lay in the fact that the area between Smithland and Jefferson was simply shallow, whereas the Soda Lake area was mud choked and stump infested.

There are no examples of sparring in the navigation record concerning the route. Sparring was not an effective technique in mud, and the sandbars along the route were not large enough to make this practice necessary.

Ramming through was very common and occurred in places with and without stumps. An example of the without-stump scenario is found in the 15 April 1873 *Shreveport Times*: "The officers of the C. H. Durfee report thirty-three inches on the Albany Flats. The Durfee was drawing that much and dragged through the mud." An example of the with-stump scenario is found in the 20 December 1873 *Shreveport Times*, when a boat drawing five feet went through three and a half feet at Albany Flats and the captain said that "he drove her through six inches of mud and liked to have knocked her bottom out on the stumps." Running the stumps was referred to as "stumping it."

The use of steam capstans also appears to have been quite common, particularly in the area between Smithland and Jefferson. The cutoff at Potato Bend was made in July 1871 at the inception of low water. The 11 July *Daily South-Western* reports: "All the steamers that pass up drawing over three feet have to lighten or pull themselves over the shoal water in the new cutoff with their steam capstans." Also in July, the *Texas* reported shoal water from the Boon's Bend cutoff to Jefferson. The 5 July *South-Western* reports: "The steamer had to bring her steam capstan and lines into requisition and pull herself through the cut-off just below the town." The length of these pulling operations was sometimes quite extensive. The 30 June 1871 *Daily South-Western* reports that *La Belle* had to negotiate low water from Potato Bend to Jefferson: "We had to 'barge' our freight going up and coming down, and took the boat to the wharf light after pulling eight hours over shoal water with our steam capstan."

Load lightening was also very common. There is no mention of discharge of passengers along the route in the navigation columns—an event that probably would have been mentioned if it had occurred. Discharge of freight to shore occurred infrequently and is usually mentioned in the context of double tripping, a process involving the partial offloading of freight, movement to destination, return to the point of offloading, and return to destination. An example that enabled a boat to carry its full load to Jefferson in installments is in the 1 August 1873 *Shreveport Times*: "the Lotus No. 3 had to double trip it from Daugherty's Defeat up."

Load lightening to companion vessels was extremely common. Steamboats with heavy loads were sometimes accompanied by other steamboats to make certain that freight reached its destination. An example of tendering is given in the 17 and 18 July 1873 *Shreveport Times*, where the *Lessie Taylor* is said to have been accompanied by the *Clifford* as a tender to enable the *Lessie Taylor* to reach the wharf at Jefferson. Such practices were uncommon for obvious reasons. Most steamboat-to-steamboat load lightening did not involve companion vessels, but rather occurred under emergency circumstances, such as when one boat came to the rescue of another that was stuck in mud or hung up on a stump.

The most common means of negotiating shallow places involved the use of barges. These were towed rather than lashed to the sides of steamboats, as in the 21 February 1866 *South-Western*: "The Texas was ten days above here, wallowing about in the lakes and bayou, with a barge in tow, on which there was about four hundred bales of cotton." Barges were effective transporters during low-water periods because they drew even less water than steamboats. A barge might be towed with freight on it to diminish the draft of the steamboat or towed empty to serve as a lighter if the steamboat ran into difficulties. Barges were also available along the route, particularly in the vicinity of Jefferson, to provide an alternative transport mode for boats that were unable to proceed farther. They also appear regularly in accounts of lightering to enable a boat to get out of mud or off a stump.

Many of the examples of the use of barges for freight transport were in the stretch between Smithland and Jefferson during the summer and involved up freights, probably because down freights were generally not heavy until the fall. These barges are not reported to have been pulled by steamboats. Their mode of operation is not described in the newspapers. An example is given in the 18 September 1867 *South-Western*, which uses the common designation "Dallas Street" for Jefferson: "Capt. John T. Root's sidewheel packet T. D. Hine came in today from Cypress bayou flying light. She barged her freight from the packery to Dallas Street."

Examples of the use of barges to assist stranded steamboats are given in a memorandum by the *Wash Sentell* that appeared in the 1 September 1871 *Daily South-Western*: "Water on flats above new cut-off 18 inches; met 13th Era at Dorherty's Defeat hard and fast on a stump waiting for barges to lighter; Little Fleta in Blind Bayou; Belle Roland in Albany flats, hard aground, lightering on barge—only 20 inches water to be found. Met Hesper at the head of Twelve Mile Bayou."

In addition to barges that were undoubtedly owned and operated by particular steamboats, there were at least two barge companies that operated along the route out of Jefferson. H. H. Woodsmall advertised in the *Jefferson Times* in September 1868 that he would run a regular line of barges between Jefferson and Shreveport. There was also a barge at Jefferson that could be used as a lighter by steamboats attempting to reach Jefferson during low water, as described in the 17 July 1872 *Shreveport Times*, quoting the *Jefferson Times*: "In connection with the subject of low water, which is close at hand, we will mention the fact that our esteemed friend Major Allen has just landed and fully equipped, a first class barge, 100 by 30 feet, to lighten steamers over the bars and shoals of our bayou, capable of carrying 1000 barrels or about thirty tons of freight, on from ten to twelve inches of water. In consequence of her extreme beam and gracefulness of form this boat has been named the 'Tobias Nix.'"

DAY OF TRAVEL

The economics of steamboat operations provided strong incentives for continuous operation. As a consequence, one should expect to find an absence of pattern in the days of arrival and departure at a port like Jefferson. Scovell in his reminiscences indicates that Tuesdays, Thursdays, and Saturdays were the normal days of departure from Shreveport to Jefferson in the immediate aftermath of the Civil War. No reason is given, and this is not the case in succeeding years.

Most steamboat ports had laws prohibiting business operations on Sunday. Jefferson had such a law before the Civil War, which established a fine of $50 for the discharge of freight from steamboats on Sunday. Whether the ordinance was regarded, or perhaps fines paid, is not known. Steamboats were exempted from Sunday prohibitions in the 1870 *Digest of the Laws of the City of Jefferson, Texas*. Shreveport had such a law until well after the Civil War, but it was disregarded. After enumerating the large number of arrivals and departures at Shreveport the previous Sunday, the *South-Western* makes the following comment: "The foregoing will do for one Sunday, considering its 'agin' the law to do business in this city on the 'Sabba' day. The divine person who gathered corn on the 7th day, because he was hungry, would have been in a bad fix if he had attempted such a thing in this city, provided it belonged to one of our aldermen."

There are no arrival and departure records for Jefferson. However, the *South-Western* provides a detailed record of departures to Jefferson from Shreveport and arrivals at Shreveport from Jefferson. The departures and arrivals for commercial year 1869–70 (1 September 1869–31 August 1870) are shown in **table A-3**. This table confirms

Table A-3
Day of Departure and Arrival
Boats at Shreveport to and from Jefferson
Commercial Year 1869–70

Day	Departures	Arrivals
Monday	20	16
Tuesday	30	32
Wednesday	46	34
Thursday	35	45
Friday	15	42
Saturday	22	28
Sunday	40	48

Source: *South-Western*, 1869–70.

the expected randomness of departures and arrivals, which would have been duplicated at Jefferson.

TIME OF TRAVEL

There are many memoranda in the *South-Western* and *Shreveport Times* of trips from New Orleans to Shreveport demonstrating that boats were in a constant state of movement, including at night, in traveling from one port to another. The memorandum of the *Era No. 3* in the 8 December 1869 *South-Western* may serve as an example: "Left New Orleans, Tuesday, Nov. 23, at 6 P.M.; met Richmond at Red Church at 10 P.M.; 24th, met Gladiola at White Hall saw-mill at 3 A.M., Lotus No. 2 at Point Pleasant at 8 A.M. and Rapides at Baton Rouge at 11 A.M.; 25th, met Nick Wall at Grand Point at 4 A.M. and Jennie Howell at Rappions at 7 A.M.; 26th, met 12th Era at Bartlett's at 11 A.M. and Lotus No. 3 at Bayou Pierre at 3 P.M.; 30th, met Rose Franks at A. W. Baird's at 7 A.M. and Era No. 10 at W. W. Williams' at 11 A.M.; Dec. 1st. met Julia A. Rudolph laying up at Reub White's at 3 A.M."

When a New Orleans boat reached Shreveport, it partly offloaded and proceeded up to Jefferson or above the raft. At Jefferson, boats offloaded and loaded and proceeded back to Shreveport, where they acquired additional loads and went down to New Orleans, thence back to Shreveport. Boats operating strictly between Shreveport and Jefferson went back and forth, taking time in port only to offload and load.

Times of departure at Shreveport to Jefferson and of arrivals at Shreveport from Jefferson for commercial year 1869–70 are shown in **table A-4** by broad categories. The departures confirm the expected randomness, but the arrivals do not. The arrivals count tracked the departures count until May, when high water and short trips resulted in a heavy predominance of day arrivals. I have no idea why this should be the case. In any case, it should be clear that night travel was common west of Shreveport and that boats did not leave on mornings and arrive back in evenings, which would be the expected pattern if day travel were preferred. Unfortunately, there are only eight memoranda of trips to and from Jefferson, and five of these are small. The three large ones all mention night travel. The first, which is partly quoted, is from the 24 December 1871 *Shreveport Times*: "Steamer Flavilla left Jefferson Thursday, Dec. 21, 1871, at 11 P.M. Met Carrie A Thorn at Boone's Bend; passed C. H. Durfee at Smithland; met Fontenelle and Era No. 10, and passed the Ida in Blind bayou, Friday morning." The *Flavilla* arrived in Shreveport and quickly left again, providing this 28 December 1871 *Shreveport Times* memorandum on its second trip: "Left Shreveport on Monday, December 25, and arrived at Jefferson on Tuesday at 8 o'clock P.M. Laid in port three hours and left for

---

Table A-4
Time of Departure and Arrival
Boats at Shreveport to and from Jefferson
Commercial Year 1869–70

Time	Departures	Arrivals
Morning	37	29
Day	77	137
Evening	34	40
Night	55	29

Source: *South-Western*, 1869–70.

Shreveport. The following boats were in port: Lotus No. 3, Belle Rowland, May Lowry, and Wash Sentell. December 27—Passed the Fontenelle at Shift Tail Bend, and entered the lakes at 8 o'clock A.M.; met the Clifford at Martin's Cut Road; landed at Mooringsport at 1 o'clock and took on ten bales of cotton. The wind was blowing a perfect gale. Passed through the Little Pass at dinner time. Found three feet on Albany Flats; passed Albany at 2 o'clock P.M.; met the 13th Era at the mouth of Twelve Mile Bayou, and arrived at Shreveport just at dark."

The third memorandum is from the 23 January 1873 *Shreveport Times* and records the breaking by the *Bossier* of a navigation impasse caused by low water:

> The steamer Bossier left Shreveport for Jefferson with a light trip, on Friday, January 17th at 9 A.M. Landed at Albany at 2½ P.M.; found the 13th Era, Little Fleta, and Ruby tied up, wind bound. The Ruby went out at 3 P.M., and gave the lake a trial, reaching the Gate Post by dark. The rest of the Tea-party lay by all night at Albany. . . . Saturday, January 18th.—The Bossier took the lead at daylight, and kept it all the way; found 30 inches at the Gum Spring, and 30 inches at the mouth of Little Pass; landed at the Jefferson wharf at 10½ P.M., amidst the firing of cannon and the glare of sky-rockets; the deafening and prolonged cheers of the citizens were tremendous in honor of the arrival of the first boat for six months. . . .
>
> DOWN TRIP.—Left Jefferson Monday night, January 20th, with 328 bales of cotton and sundries. . . . Tuesday, January 21st.—Met the steamer Ruby below Daugherty's Defeat; tied up for the night at Mooringsport. . . . Wednesday, January 22d.—Met the steamers 13th Era and Flavilla above the Dead Breake; found 30 inches and falling slowly; landed at Albany at 10 A.M.; wooded and took on cotton; landed at Shreveport at 6 P.M.

How were steamboats able to travel at night before the introduction of electric searchlights in 1878? Fire baskets were used for illumination when loading or offloading at landings. They were extinguished when the boat got underway again and would in any case have been less than worthless when a boat was moving. Intuition suggests starlight and moonlight, but this appears to be the opposite of the case. In the Dewey Somdal Papers at LSU in Shreveport, there is a record of an interview with Capt. Ben White at Shreveport concerning navigation on the Red River that makes the following point: "Before electric lights were used on boats, oil lamps and reflectors were used by pilots to pick up landings or obstructions in the river. Prior to the use of oil lamps, the pilot depended entirely on his own eyesight in navigating and preferred a dark night to a moonlight or starlight night, as shadows from the bank or trees on the bank would give a false picture of the river and many wrecks resulted from the shadows cast by the moonlight. Experienced pilots knew the river so well that they needed no help from spotlights at all and could navigate with comparable safety when visibility would hide the bow of the boat."

Fog was a much greater impediment to navigation than darkness. The high volume of night traffic indicates that White's observation was correct and that boats operated quite well without any sort of illumination. Thus, comments such as the following by Capt. James Crooks of the *George*, although somewhat exaggerated, are fairly close to the truth: "Soon after Capt. Jeems ate his dough (sometimes called duff for short), he backed his muley out for Cypress bayou with a good freight at $1 per bbl. Capt. Jeems says the George knows her way to Esculent Bend by herself in the dark" (*South-Western*, 10 October 1869).

TRIP DAYS

Although steamboats tried to accomplish their business as quickly as possible, the amount of time that it took to run from Shreveport to Jefferson and back to Shreveport was highly variable, depending on the boat, its freight, the nature of its business, and water and weather conditions. **Table A-5** provides information on trip days for commercial year 1869–70, a portion of that year, and the early part of 1859 for comparative purposes.

As can be seen from column 1 of the table, boats that left Shreveport for Jefferson could generally be expected to arrive back within two to six days. Column 2 of the table shows the distribution for the last quarter of column 1 when there was unusually high water in the summer. During good navigation conditions, boats could be expected to arrive back at Shreveport within two to four days. Column 3 shows that the general pattern in column 1 pre-existed the Civil War.

Trip Days	Sept. 1869–Aug. 1870	May–Aug. 1870	Jan.–May 1859
Table A-5			
Trip Days			
Round Trips from Shreveport to Jefferson			
1	7	7	0
2	35	23	3
3	38	21	3
4	46	10	11
5	28	3	9
6	10	1	3
7	9	0	6
8	2	0	1
9	3	0	2
10	4	0	4
11	4	0	1
12	0	0	0
13	0	0	1

Source: *South-Western*, 1859, 1869, and 1870.

It should be noted that trip days in the table were computed by subtracting date of departure from date of return (e.g., if a boat left on the second and returned on the fifth, it was recorded as a three-day trip). However, these were not standard twenty-four-hour-long days, because boats departed and arrived at different hours. Many of the one-day trips appear to be thirty-six hours or above. However, there are examples such as the *Fleta*, which arrived at Shreveport at 3:00 in the morning on Monday, 22 August 1870, offloaded until leaving for Jefferson at 8:00 in the morning, and arrived back at Shreveport at 11:00 in the morning on Tuesday, 23 August. This was a twenty-seven–hour trip.

Before the route was improved by cutoffs in the 1870s, it was ninety-six actual river miles. Up trips were slower than down trips. The usual time for a down trip was fifteen to eighteen hours according to the 21 February 1872 *Shreveport Times*. The record for this stretch was established by the *Lizzie Hamilton* on Saturday, 23 June 1870, as reported in the *South-Western*: "The Jefferson packet Lizzie Hamilton was the only arrival to-day. She made the trip from Jefferson to this point in 6 hours, bringing 20 bales of cotton, 400 hides, and a cabin full of passengers." This boat averaged sixteen miles an hour.

The record round-trip does not appear to have been identified. The 22 April 1872 *Shreveport Times* reports: "About the middle of the afternoon the Belle Rowland, under the command of her new Captain, came in from Jefferson flying light. She made the trip from this point to Jefferson, with seventy tons of freight and back, in thirty-eight hours,—the best time on the books." This statement is incompatible with a 4 July 1866 *South-Western* report that the *Lizzie Hamilton* made the round-trip in less than 30 hours. It is also incompatible with the computed twenty-seven hours for the *Fleta*, unless the newspaper made a mistake in the date of arrival or departure by the *Fleta*.

The *Fleta* also established one of the fastest trips from New Orleans to Jefferson, as recorded in the 24 August 1870 *South-Western*: "Speaking of your lightning packets, the Fleta, on her last trip up, made the run from New Orleans to Jefferson in the remarkably short time of 3 days, 23 hours and 5 minutes! This was her time from port to port, and she lost two hours towing a barge some distance from the mouth of the river, made 7 freight landings, and lay four hours at Shreveport. Capt. Poff asks, 'how is that for a 13-inch cylinder?' Pretty well, we should say."

The 22 April 1868 *South-Western* reports that the *Ezra Porter* made the round-trip from New Orleans to Jefferson and back within seven days.

After the route was shortened by cutoffs in the early 1870s, quicker trips were possible. On 26 June 1875, the *Lotus No. 3* arrived back at Shreveport carrying twenty-five bales of cotton from a twenty-eight–hour round-trip that included a four-hour layover in Jefferson. High water all along the route enabled the *Lotus No. 3* to "run all the cut off and short cuts like a deer."

SEASONALITY

The New Orleans newspapers indicate that there was a drastic decline in boat movements throughout the lower Mississippi valley during the summer months, as reflected in the paucity of boat returns and advertisements. This was the case for the Red River in general and for the Cypress Bayou and the lakes route in particular. It was during the summer months that lower Mississippi Valley steamboats entered other trades or were laid up for repairs.

Prior to the Civil War, the Cypress Bayou and the lakes route was often closed to navigation in the months of July through September; there were even some years such as 1854 and 1855 in which drought produced conditions of non-navigability that extended across the seasons. The navigability of the route was determined by conditions on the Red River. Local rains in the Cypress Bayou basin could affect the ability of boats to reach the landing at Jefferson, but they had little effect on Soda Lake water levels, which were the primary determinant of the ability of boats to travel west of Shreveport.

Soda Lake water levels were determined by water levels on Red River. As a consequence, when boats could reach Shreveport on the Red River, they could almost always travel west of Shreveport. Conversely, when navigation was closed to Shreveport because of low water on the Red, the movement of boats west of Shreveport was prohibited. The primary low-water impediment on Red River was the falls at Alexandria. There was also a secondary impediment at the mouth of Red River constituted by sandbars in an unfortunate cutoff of a Mississippi River bend made by Capt. Henry Shreve.

Table A-6 shows the number of boat trips west of Shreveport by month for the first five years after the war. It is obvious that there were no summers in which boats did not travel west of Shreveport. One important reason for this change was the progressive reduction in the draft of boats, which allowed smaller boats to operate on very shallow water. In addition, there were improvements to the Red and the route. But these factors were probably overshadowed by increased incentives for pushing through, combined with an increased number of boats participating in the Cypress Bayou and the lakes trade. Postwar summer travel was not related to favorable navigation conditions. The boats that reached Jefferson during the summer generally did so through extraordinary exertions induced by economic incentives.

The monthly distributions show a pattern of high levels of boat activity during the first three months of the year, lower activity during the three months preceding and following summer, and lowest during the three months of summer. This suggests that seasonal water level fluctuations were the primary determinant of the number of boats

Table A-6
Trips per Month to Points West of Shreveport

Month	1866	1867	1868	1869	1870
January	18	20	6	23	29
February	36	12	32	16	29
March	35	15	32	24	37
April	11	15	21	15	25
May	18	13	19	12	16
June	14	9	18	19	24
July	9	13	21	13	16
August	15	10	7	10	27
September	5	10	1	13	18
October	8	3	13	13	27
November	11	2	16	8	27
December	11	2	30	14	20

Source: *South-Western*, 1866–70.

moving on the route. The anomalies appear to prove the case. October–December 1867 and January and September 1868 were low-water periods that resulted in diminished boat activity. Conversely, August 1870 had unusually high water, producing a high level of boat activity in a normally dull month.

Table A-7 shows the number of bales of cotton by month on boats arriving from points west. The pattern is fairly similar to the overall boat pattern, suggesting that bales shipped were a function of boat trips, which themselves were determined by water levels. Nevertheless, it is impossible to determine from the two tables whether bales shipped were a function of boat trips or vice versa. The anomalous December 1868 suggests that bales determined boats; yet, in August 1870, only 106 bales were carried by twenty-seven boats.

This quandary can be resolved. Spring rises did not provide the occasion for the greatest volume of traffic. Moreover, after a certain threshold was reached allowing passage for the regular packets through Soda Lake, the amount of water was irrelevant. If boat trips were a

Table A-7
Bales of Cotton Shipped from Points West of Shre

Month	1866	1867	1868	1869
January	2652	6114	452	10855
February	7714	2022	10528	8431
March	3517	2955	9716	6519
April	1501	2894	4416	2761
May	1830	1019	1192	1258
June	674	974	133	262
July	597	780	0	39
August	393	327	7	0
September	7	9	40	602
October	550	0	1321	1003
November	2178	0	3697	1522
December	2205	121	7552	6062

Source: *South-Western*, 1866–70.

Table A-8
Cotton Receipts and Shipments at Shrevep

Month	Commercial Year 1869–70 Receipts	Shipments	Commercial Ye Receipts
September	2932	2399	463
October	7446	5232	1596
November	13482	9499	10118
December	19736	16487	13635
January	18905	18278	11404
February	17327	17413	13378
March	13811	14610	17356
April	6521	9106	11249
May	4889	7022	12944
June	4521	7492	5521
July	1359	995	4895
August	589	1005	2447

Source: *South-Western*, 7 September 1870; *Daily South-*
7 September 1871.

:t function of water levels, trips should be more evenly distributed
ng the non-summer months.

Cotton receipts at Jefferson determined the overall pattern of boat
. This should not be surprising, given the fact that steamboats
: commercial freight transporters and that cotton was the dominant
,ht. This can be seen by comparing **table A-6** to **table A-8**, which
vs cotton receipts and shipments by month at Shreveport for two
:al commercial years (such data are not available for Jefferson).
on was obviously shipped soon after it was received. Receipts were
from June through October and high for November through May,
December through March constituting peak months.

Receipts were determined by production, preparation, and inland
sport patterns. Cotton was a summer crop, and the first bale was
:rally received at ports like Shreveport and Jefferson in late August
irly September. However, the bulk of the staple took a long time
et to outlets such as Jefferson because it needed to be harvested,
.ed, baled, and transported over great distances by slow-moving
vagons. Receipts picked up in the latter months of the year and
hed a crescendo in the first few months of the next calendar year.
Seasonal fluctuations in boat movements were, therefore, primarily
rmined by the flow of cotton to ports like Jefferson, providing a
:al transport demand situation. The number of boats operating
g the route declined in summer because the cotton crop of the
ious summer had largely been received and shipped. The effect of
:otton cycle was not dramatic because of Jefferson's high volume
ade to the west. Most of the boats returned to Shreveport without
on, indicating that up freights in themselves were sufficient to
itain a significant level of boat activity.

This overall pattern and its up-freight modification should not
ure the influence of water levels. When water was insufficient for
: movements, navigation was suspended no matter what the
sport demand, as shown by October–December 1867. In addition,
iths like August 1870 with anomalously high water levels produced
. levels of boat activity.

The seasonality of cotton production and distribution produced
onal changes in the economic life of a town like Jefferson, but in a
:tion exactly the opposite of that of an agricultural community.
commercial year began in September. Wagon arrivals, cotton
ige and transactions, and boat movements began to pick up in the

latter part of the calendar year. The height of economic activity occurred in winter and began to fall off in the spring as cotton stocks from the previous summer's production were depleted. Summers were commercially dull. This framework of expansion and contraction is confirmed by Loughery's observations on what he saw in Jefferson on his many trips, broken only by unseasonably high- or low-water levels and by interior rains that caused the movement of cotton wagons toward Jefferson to be suspended.

COST OF BOATS

Steamboats were not expensive. A fine mid-sized boat could be built for under $25,000. For example, the 150-foot *R. T. Bryarly* cost $20,000 and the 160-foot *Dawn* cost $13,000. Economies in construction were available through the use of machinery from boats that were out of service, and used boats at very low cost were readily available. At the upscale end of boats that operated along the route were the *Belle of Shreveport*, which cost $57,000 and was the largest boat to travel to Jefferson; and the *John T. Moore*, which was of special iron construction and cost $80,000. The cost of locally built home packets such as the *Albany* was probably under $10,000.

Boats were often owned by the captains who operated them, either in whole or in part. With dual shareholders, one might serve as captain and the other as clerk. Multiple shareholding was also very common, making the opportunities for investment available even to people of modest resources, as reported in the 18 July 1872 *Shreveport Times*: "Any industrious man of small income, who has saved a thousand dollars, can purchase an eighth or sixteenth interest in a steamboat."

FREIGHT RATES

There were no such things as standard freight rates. The few meager attempts to establish rates through steamboat combinations were not effective and usually came to quick ends. Freight rates for any specific commodity were trip-specific and were determined by voluntary agreements between shippers and carriers. Nevertheless, these decisions were not arbitrary, because they operated in the context of prevailing rates, which were understood by everyone and often published in the newspaper, particularly for cotton.

Prevailing rates were simply the reflection of voluntary transactions, expressing the price for which a particular commodity was generally being carried at a particular point in time. Prevailing rates could remain constant over a number of weeks, but they could change from week to week or even from day to day. They are generally stated as whole dollars or as whole plus half dollars. Freight costs for cotton were by bale rather than by weight. An example from the 9 October 1867 *South-Western*: "RATES OF FREIGHT.—From New Orleans to Jefferson, $2.50 and $3.00 per barrel; from New Orleans to Shreveport, $1.50 and $2.00. From Shreveport to New Orleans—Cotton, per bale, $4. Cattle, per head, $8. Passage, $30."

The primary determinant of prevailing rates was competition. When there were many boats in operation, freight costs tended to be low, as reported in the 18 May 1870 *South-Western*: "The large amount of tonnage in the trade, and the consequent competition has brought freight down to $1 bale on cotton." High water enabled more boats to operate, increasing competition and suppressing rates, as indicated in the 19 January 1870 *South-Western*: "The bayou is rising, and in the twenty-four hours previous to this writing it has risen about eight inches. There have been heavy rains in the regions of the head waters of the tributaries of Red river, and we may look for a rise equal to the one we had in December. This is cheering in the extreme, and makes the heart glad. Such news is the mother of smiles to those interested. Plenty of water, therefore plenty of boats; *ergo* cheap freights."

Low water reduced the number of boats in operation, which produced higher freight costs. This was explained in a tongue-in-cheek manner by the 6 January 1872 *Shreveport Times*, referring to the ostensible delight of Jefferson shippers in stamping cotton with high freight rates: "Our friends at Jefferson are in the uninterrupted enjoyment of low water navigation and high freights. We do not 'begrudge' their happiness and trust it may never be less. Whenever they have to pay three dollars per bale on cotton the court can safely say that the water is low and navigation exceedingly tedious, for never within the memory of the 'oldest inhabitant' were they known to come down so liberally with their stamps, unless forced to by circumstances beyond their control."

As reflections of voluntary agreements, the prevailing rates were not posted rates and were usually expressed in terms of what the boats had been able to secure during the previous week. In addition, the prevailing rates established the general parameters in which decisions were made and are not necessarily indicative of what a particular boat had been able to secure. It was the function of the clerk to secure the highest rate possible and the function of the shipper to secure the lowest rate possible. If agreement on a freight cost could not be reached, the clerk would try another shipper, which might involve another commodity type. Lack of agreement could result in reduced or even absent loads, with the intent of pursuing opportunities downstream. The dynamics of these free market transactions are illuminated by the 31 January 1866 *South-Western* during a postwar period in which freight rates were high and unstable:

> The rates of up-freight are very irregular, and it is impossible to give any settled quotations. It is landed here from 62½ c. and $2 bbl. There don't appear to be any regular prices whatever. The rates of passage are in the same fix. It looks as though all the shipper had to do was set his own price, provided there were plenty of boats in port. Freight for Jefferson is in the same category. Freight on cotton to the city is still held at $5; from Jefferson to the city, $10 per bale; from Spring Bank to this place, $10 per bale. A lot of hides were shipped from Jefferson to the city, for $2.50 per hundred lbs. A lot of cattle were shipped from this point to the city for $15 per head. The steamer Texas took out cotton from Jefferson for $15 bale. She refused to take any at this point for less than $10, and of course got but few bales. The Fleta received $12 per bale from Jefferson, but took some at this place for $5.
>
> Our merchants are not quite fools enough to pay a premium of five dollars on a bale of cotton, to be allowed the privilege of shipping even on the Jefferson packet Texas, Stinde, commanding.

There is little in the way of freight cost information prior to the Civil War. Edward Smith provides rates for 1849 of $1 a bale from Jefferson to New Orleans, $0.625 to $1 a bale from Shreveport to New Orleans, and $2 to $2.50 a bale from upper Red River to New Orleans. The 1858 *Texas Almanac* provides figures of $1.50–$1.75 a bale from Benton and Port Caddo to New Orleans. During 1855–56, cotton was shipped from Shreveport to New Orleans at rates of $1–$7 a bale.

The immediate aftermath of the Civil War was characterized by high transport demand and low transport supply, the latter occasioned by the destruction of boats during the war, the death of skilled crew members, and the absence of an apprentice program during the war years. Cotton transport costs from Shreveport to New Orleans in the latter half of 1865 were high, moving from $4–$10 a bale in July to $15 a bale in August and $25 a bale in September, then dropping to $12.50 a bale and $5 a bale in October, then rising back to $25 a bale in December.

It was near the end of this inflated price period that a fairly continuous record for Jefferson begins, as shown in **table A-9**. The normal range was from $1 to $8 a bale after the postwar inflation, with fairly low rates achieved from 1870 on. The cited rates for individual boats are a little higher, but they apparently were cited precisely because they exceeded prevailing rates. Rates from Shreveport tended to be about one-third less than from Jefferson. After railroad competition fully set in, rates from Shreveport were generally not more that $1 a bale, and some boats even took out cotton at $0.50 and $0.25 a bale. The only price given for Jefferson to Shreveport was $1 bale on 30 January 1867.

Prices for commodities other than cotton are seldom quoted. Barrels were taken from Shreveport to Jefferson during the postwar period at $0.75 to $2.00 and from New Orleans to Jefferson at $1.00 to $3.50. Tierces were shipped from Shreveport to New Orleans at $1.00 to $4.00. Cattle ranged from $5.00 to $12.50 a head from Shreveport to New Orleans, and sheep are quoted at $1.00.

COTTON LOADS

There is a well-known photograph of the *Col. A. P. Kouns* with an inscription indicating at the Jefferson wharf in 1875 and loaded with 2,000 bales of cotton. The load figure is unlikely. The 3 November 1874 *Shreveport Times* says that this boat had a 1,800-bale capacity. The figure of 2,000 bales is way out of line with all boat records. Although the newspaper record is incomplete for 1875, the largest recorded load for the *Col. A. P. Kouns* in that year was 1,256 bales in January.

The largest recorded load of cotton from west of Shreveport was 1,653 bales by the *Charles H. Durfee* in May 1871. This load was

Table A-9
Cotton Transport Rates from Jefferson to New Orleans

Date	Cost Per Bale
24 January 1866	$10.00
31 January 1866	10.00
31 January 1866	15.00 (*Texas*)
31 January 1866	12.00 (*Fleta*)
7 February 1866	10.00
14 March 1866	5.00 (Kouns line)
23 January 1867	3.00
30 January 1867	3.00
19 June 1867	1.00–1.50
18 December 1867	7.00 (*Gossamer*)
19 February 1868	3.50
26 February 1868	8.00
4 March 1868	3.50
15 September 1869	5.00 (*Lotus No. 2* from Boon Bend)
6 October 1869	7.50 (*George* from Potato Bend)
24 November 1869	6.00
8 December 1869	10.00 (*Flavilla* from Smithland)
8 June 1870	2.50
7 December 1870	2.00
21 December 1871	2.00–3.00
6 January 1872	3.00
13 January 1872	1.50
20 January 1872	1.25
30 January 1873	5.50
20 February 1873	3.00
13 March 1873	2.50
20 March 1873	2.00
11 November 1873	3.50

Source: *South-Western*, 1866–71; *Shreveport Times*, 1871–75.

probably entirely from Jefferson, because cotton exports from the other ports and landings on the route were negligible after the Civil War. Whether it was the largest all-time load cannot be determined because accounts of number of bales carried do not begin to appear in the Shreveport newspapers until 1866. Returns at the Port of New Orleans cannot be used because boats that went west of Shreveport picked up cotton at Shreveport and at landings along the Red and Mississippi Rivers on the return trip to New Orleans. Nor can it be presumed that large loads would only have been taken out after the Civil War, because extraordinary freights were seen at New Orleans before the war that were not reattained until many years after the war. The 22 September 1880 *New Orleans Daily Democrat* says that the *Latona* brought a load of 1,549 bales of cotton from Port Caddo in 1846, but it is not certain that all of this cotton was actually taken from Port Caddo, rather than being supplemented with bales from downstream on the Red River.

There was no such thing as a typical load of cotton taken out of the area west of Shreveport. What a boat carried in the way of cotton depended on availability of stocks, willingness of suppliers to ship particular volumes at particular prices, willingness of the carrier to ship particular volumes at particular prices, alternative freight opportunities, and anticipated or already secured opportunities for obtaining cotton at Shreveport or farther downstream on the return trip. The only adequate generalizations for the decade after the Civil War (the only period for which there are records) are that cotton loads from west of Shreveport ranged from zero to 1,653; loads above 1,000 were uncommon; and boats seldom carried capacity loads.

Table A-10 shows the average number of bales carried by boats carrying cotton for 1866 through 1880. These numbers indicate two trends: an increase in cotton loads over time, with a decline in the last two years; and increased loads from 1875 through 1878 as cotton exports declined. **Table A-11** shows cotton loads greater than 1,000 bales. These fifty-two loads represent a little more than five percent of the total loads carried during the decade. Only five loads were at 1,500 or greater bales. The yearly distribution reflects total cotton exports and increases in loads over time. The monthly distribution reflects the pattern of cotton receipts at Jefferson.

Table A-10
Average Bales per Trip

Year	Total Trips	Trips Carrying Cotton**	Total Bales	Average Bales Per Trip
1866	189	115	23,781	207
1867	115	61	17,212	282
1868	217	144	38,954	271
1869	180	111	39,568	356
1870	295	174	63,807	367
1871*	159	110	69,442	631
1872	134	63	22,694	346
1873	165	89	41,582	467
1874	NA	NA	NA	NA
1875	32	28	11,785	421
1876	35	30	13,328	464
1877	24	15	10,065	671
1878	18	12	7,358	613
1879	12	10	3,162	316
1880	10	6	1,427	238

* Through July 12.
** Recorded loads only.
Sources: *South-Western*, 1866–71; *Daily South-Western*, 1871; and *Shreveport Times*, 1871–80.

PASSENGER RATES

Passenger accommodations were of two types: cabin and deck. Cabin passage provided a room and meals; deck passage provided neither. Smith indicates that in 1848 cabin passage was $12 between Jefferson and New Orleans and $10 between Shreveport and New Orleans. The only later records are $10 cabin from Jefferson to Shreveport (7 February 1866), $30 cabin from Jefferson to New Orleans (19 June 1867), $5 cabin from Jefferson to Shreveport (13 January 1872), and $25 cabin from Jefferson to New Orleans (13 January 1872).

There is no information on deck passage to Jefferson. Cabin passage between Shreveport and New Orleans ranged from $15 to $20 in 1855–

Table A-11
Cotton Loads Greater Than 1000

Year	Month	Boat	Bales
1867	February	*Starlight*	1000
1868	March	*Lizzie Hopkins*	1001
1869	January	*Right Way*	1000
1869	January	*Lotawanna*	1346
1869	January	*Selma*	1500
1869	December	*Lizzie Hopkins*	1200
1869	December	*Lotus No. 2*	1100
1869	December	*Fleta*	1000
1870	January	*Golden Era*	1500
1870	February	*Rapides*	1100
1870	February	*Julia A. Rudolph*	1190
1870	February	*Lizzie Hopkins*	1250
1870	February	*Ida*	1200
1870	May	*Lotus No. 3*	1155
1871	January	*Lotus No. 3*	1050
1871	February	*Carrie Converse*	1175
1871	February	*Lotus No. 3*	1300
1871	March	*Tidal Wave*	1637
1871	April	*Lotawanna*	1171
1871	May	*Red Cloud*	1333
1871	May	*Lotawanna*	1126
1871	May	*Lotus No. 3*	1350
1871	May	*Charles H. Durfee*	1653
1871	May	*Carrie Converse*	1150
1871	May	*Red Cloud*	1089
1871	June	*Texas*	1068
1871	December	*Gladiola*	1024
1871	December	*Ida*	1200
1872	February	*Charles H. Durfee*	1350
1872	March	*Lotus No. 3*	1005
1872	March	*Rapides*	1023
1873	March	*R. T. Bryarly*	1118
1873	March	*Charles H. Durfee*	1012

Table A-11 continued
Cotton Loads Greater Than 1000

1873	March	*Maria Louise*	1625
1873	March	*Rapides*	1450
1873	March	*Charles H. Durfee*	1250
1873	March	*Maria Louise*	1033
1873	May	*Seminole*	1000
1875	January	*Col. A. P. Kouns*	1256
1875	January	*Col. A. P. Kouns*	1098
1875	January	*Lotus No. 3*	1066
1876	January	*Col. A. P. Kouns*	1201
1876	January	*Lotus No. 3*	1230
1876	February	*R. T. Bryarly*	1091
1877	February	*Col. A. P. Kouns*	1300
1877	February	*R. W. Dugan*	1000
1877	March	*Col. A. P. Kouns*	1486
1877	December	*Alexandria*	1247
1877	December	*Col. A. P. Kouns*	1400
1878	January	*Col. A. P. Kouns*	1400
1878	February	*Col. A. P. Kouns*	1300
1878	March	*Bonnie Lee*	1168

Source: *South-Western*, 1866–71; *Shreveport Times*, 1871–78.

56. In the immediate aftermath of the war, cabin passage between Shreveport and New Orleans rose to $60 (13 December 1865). Normal prices during the postwar period were $15 to $30 for cabin passage and $5 to $10 for deck (slightly below cattle rates). Adding one-fifth (based on the cabin differential for 13 January 1872), deck passage from Jefferson to New Orleans probably ranged from $6 to $12.

When numbers are given for cabin and deck passengers arriving at Shreveport on a boat, the number of deck passengers is always much greater than the number of cabin passengers. A boat carrying fifty cabin passengers, for example, might carry two hundred deck passengers.

Although cabin passengers paid more, the cost of services for them was equivalent to the receipts. Steamboats made their passenger money on the high-volume deck passengers who were provided no services or accommodations.

PROFITABILITY

Steamboats, in general, appear to have been modestly profitable operations until late in the steamboat period when rail competition caused many boats to reduce rates to such a degree that they could not accommodate the hazards of navigation. Some captains and owners died wealthy but apparently never on the basis of the operation of a single vessel. Most suffered the fate of small businesses unable to expand or to increase market share. The captains and pilots who retired from the route did not retire to leisure but to other endeavors such as farming, merchandising, and even gold digging in California.

Trip income figures are mentioned from time to time in the newspapers, as in the 18 May 1870 *South-Western*: "At 10 last night the Bradish Johnson got off with a brag trip—1200 bales of cotton, 56 cabin passengers, 40 head of cattle and 100 head of sheep. She had about a $2500 trip." However, income figures alone are not particularly useful, as pointed out by the 16 December 1871 *Shreveport Times*: "Mr. Watson, passenger agent, informs us that the John T. Moore left with 2200 bales of cotton, 58 cabin passengers and 29 deckers. The cotton was taken at $1.50 a bale, cabin passengers at $20, and the deck passengers at $5. This gives her an aggregate down trip of $4605. To those not familiar with steamboating, this would seem to be a large amount for a boat to make in so short a time, but the expenses of such a boat as the Moore are terrific."

The profitability of a particular voyage was dependent on income minus expenditures for the round-trip. The major sources of income were freight and passengers, with the former usually the most important. Cabin passengers paid more than deck passengers, but they did not contribute to profitability because of the high cost of services that were provided to them. Wages were the major expense, followed at a distance by wood, provisions, and wharfage. Freight insurance was covered by the shipper, not the carrier.

As businesses, boats kept detailed records of their income and expenditures. Unfortunately, most of these have disappeared because they had no use after a boat was out of service, and I have not seen any for a boat that operated along the route. The quality of detail can be seen in the Arthur Hinckley Papers at the Louisiana State Archives in Baton Rouge, which contains such things as freight lists and charges, names and room assignments for cabin passengers, pay rates and total pay by person, and cost of wood at each station.

The profitability of a boat as a business venture was dependent on the capital costs and the cumulative income and expenditures of its various trips. Steamboats were not expensive, but they were continuously repaired and generally did not last over five years. Boats were insured but apparently always underinsured, as indicated by numerous wreck reports. Extraordinary costs were not a problem, because crew and passengers worked and traveled at their own risk and could not sue for damages. Capital costs, repairs, and insurance were offset to some degree by insurance compensation, resale, or salvage.

The level of profitability was highly dependent on the business acumen of the officers. However, the margin for bargaining was slim because negotiations took place within the context of prevailing freight and labor rates, which were set by market forces. Because this was an open entry system, transport supply generally met transport demand, so that freight costs remained fairly low. Even during the period immediately after the Civil War when there was a great disparity between supply and demand, boats were apparently not able to make a killing because escalated freight and passenger rates were offset by high labor costs.

Steamboat operational costs were high because they were labor intensive. The utility of labor could be maximized only by keeping a staffed boat constantly on the move or engaged in the discharge and receipt of freight. The 7 April 1867 *South-Western* provides a typical picture of a New Orleans boat at Shreveport and destined for Jefferson: "The New Orleans and Jefferson packet Live Oak, Captain John White, Gilham, clerk, came in to-day from the Crescent City, with her guards in the water and her cabin full of passengers. She was busy the better part of the day and nearly all night in discharging the freight consigned to this place. About daylight she left for Dallas street Camp, for which point she had a hunkadora trip."

When there was a lull in activity, crews were immediately discharged. An example for Jefferson is contained in the 7 February 1873 *Shreveport Times*: "The Democrat says the Ruby has paid off her crew and laid up at that point." An example for Shreveport is contained in the 14 August 1867 *South-Western*: "Business with our steamboat men has been nothing near as good for the past week as its predecessor. Most of the packets have had light up trips, and if they had anything like a good down trip they had to stay in port four or five days to pick it up. Most of the boats discharge their crews as soon as they discharge their up freight, and employ them again as soon as they get a fair down freight engaged."

Because officers could not be discharged, delays in securing freight were nevertheless costly, as reported in the 4 September 1867 *South-Western*: "The packets have not been troubled with much business, though some of them have been able to pay expenses, while others have lost money. This visiting in port four or five days to pick up a trip eats up all the profits. It is close work for our river men to make both ends meet."

Particularly galling for the steamboatmen were the attorney-instigated lawsuits that became prevalent after the Civil War ostensibly involving disputes over compensation for deck hands. Boats could be seized and become inoperable under such circumstances. There is little reason to doubt that the newspapers were correct in identifying most of these cases as instances of an extortion racket.

Appendix B

Steamboats by Year

The following is a list, by year, of the steamboats that operated along the route from 1841 through 1905. Most of the inclusions are from arrival records at Shreveport. Advertisements were employed in some cases before 1855 and are not firm indicators that a boat traveled along the route during the year. Of the 2,629 confirmed trips, 2,426 were to Jefferson.

Boat data are taken from William Lytle, *Merchant Steam Vessels of the United States, 1807–1868* (generally referred to as the Lytle-Holdcamper list); WPA, *Ship Registers and Enrollments of New Orleans, Louisiana*; and Frederick Way, *Way's Packet Directory*. A few dimensions and tonnage figures are taken from the newspapers.

KEY

Name: The name as it generally appears in the newspapers, with a few modifications to conform to Lytle-Holdcamper. When a boat first appears in the record, it is underlined. A (2) after a boat name indicates that this is the second boat by that name to operate along the route.
Source: Indicates where the information was derived on name, place, and trips.

R = Record (newspaper-listed arrivals at Shreveport or New Orleans)

A = Advertisement

O = Other, as noted in list of sources

Place: Refers to where the boat went, which does not mean that it did not stop elsewhere.

AL = Albany

BN = Benton

C = Caddo

JB = Jim's Bayou (may include Monterey)

JF = Jefferson
MP = Mooringsport
MT = Monterey (also Point Monterey)
PC = Port Caddo (also Fort Caddo)
SM = Smithland
SW = Swanson's Landing (also Petersburg)
TL = The Lakes

Trips: Refers to the number of trips made by that boat during that year. I have not attempted to estimate the number of trips that might be suggested by advertisements.

Place Built: By state designations.

Year Built: All in the 1800s.

Type: Rig type.

H = Sidewheel
W = Sternwheel
S = Screw (applies to only one boat, the *Hornet*)

Tons: As registered. For comparability, add forty-five percent to the pre-Civil War figures.

Dimensions: Hull length and width, rounded for convenience. Excludes guards and paddlewheels.

NA = Not Available.

YEAR	NAME	SOURCE	PLACE	TRIPS	PLACE BUILT	YEAR BUILT	TYPE	TONS	DIMEN-SIONS
1841	Brian Boroihme	A	PC	~	KY	36	H	187	135 x 24
	Farmer	A	BN	~	KY	39	H	180	121 x 23
	Miami	R	C	1	VA	39	H	114	133 x 13
1842	Echo	A	PC	~	OH	36	H	158	152 x 18
	Georgia	A	C	~	PA	37	H	135	137 x 19
	South Western	R	C	1	IN	39	H	202	139 x 24
	Star	R	PC	2	KY	41	H	138	141 x 22
	"	A	SM	~	"	"	"	"	"
1843	Bois d'Arc	R	PC	1	KY	43	H	182	136 x 26
	Ontario	R	PC	2	PA	36	H	133	149 x 19
	Robert T. Lytle	R	PC	2	OH	42	H	159	158 x 22
	Swan	A	PC	~	OH	40	H	93	118 x 21
	Telegraph	R	PC	1	PA	40	H	165	143 x 22
1844	Bois d'Arc	R	PC	9	KY	43	H	182	136 x 26
	Planter	A	PC	~	OH	43	H	166	120 x 23
	"	R	TL	1	"	"	"	"	"
	Republic	R	PC	1	OH	42	H	147	140 x 22
	Robert T. Lytle	R	PC	1	OH	42	H	159	158 x 22
	"	R	TL	1	"	"	"	"	"
	Sabine	R	PC	5	KY	43	H	106	108 x 21
1845	Bois d'Arc	R	PC	9	KY	43	H	182	136 x 26
	Col. Harney	A	PC	~	IN	44	H	132	112 x 26
	Douglas	A	PC	~	IN	41	H	263	167 x 26
	Gazelle	O	JF	1	OH	44	H	82	104 x 20
	J. E. Roberts	A	PC	~	VA	44	H	118	128 x 24
	Lama	O	JF	1	OH	44	H	68	100 x 24
	"	R	PC	1	"	"	"	"	"
	Little Yazoo	A	PC	~	OH	43	H	46	80 x 20
	Maid of Kentucky	R	PC	4	OH	40	H	192	NA
	New Brazil	A	PC	~	OH	41	H	166	144 x 22
	Panola	A	PC	~	OH	44	H	120	120 x 25
	Rodolph	R	PC	4	IN	44	H	213	156 x 25
	Yazoo	R	PC	1	OH	42	H	304	151 x 28
1846	Belle of Ouachita	A	JF	~	IN	43	H	103	NA
	Enterprise	R	PC	1	OH	44	H	106	109 x 22
	Express Mail	A	PC	~	OH	41	H	244	165 x 25
	Frankland	A	PC	~	TN	45	H	96	138 x 18
	J. E. Roberts	R	JF	1	VA	44	H	118	128 x 24
	"	A	PC	1	"	"	"	"	"
	Jim Gilmer	R	PC	1	OH	46	H	115	123 x 26
	Latona	O	PC	1	IN	46	H	197	155 x 26
	Live Oak	A	JF	~	LA	45	H	64	113 x 15
	Rodolph	A	PC	~	IN	44	H	213	156 x 25

YEAR	NAME	SOURCE	PLACE	TRIPS	PLACE BUILT	YEAR BUILT	TYPE	TONS	DIMEN-SIONS
	<u>Vesta</u>	A	JF	~	IN	45	H	92	117 x 21
	"	A	PC	~	"	"	"	"	"
	<u>Yalobusha</u>	R	PC	1	OH	44	H	116	115 x 24
	Yazoo	A	JF	~	OH	42	H	304	151 x 28
	<u>Wheel of Fortune</u>	A	PC	~	KY	45	H	165	NA
1847	<u>Belle of Illinois</u>	A	PC	~	PA	45	H	78	100 x 20
	<u>Buffalo</u>	A	JF	~	KY	47	H	136	123 x 22
	<u>Ellen</u>	R	JF	2	KY	46	W	99	129 x 20
	"	R	PC	1	"	"	"	"	"
	Latona	A	PC	~	IN	46	H	197	155 x 26
	<u>Monterey</u>	R	JF	1	OH	46	H	143	135 x 25
	"	A	PC	~	"	"	"	"	"
	Rodolph	A	PC	~	IN	44	H	213	156 x 25
	Vesta	A	JF	~	IN	45	H	92	117 x 21
	<u>Victress</u>	R	JF	1	OH	41	H	190	155 x 25
	"	A	PC	~	"	"	"	"	"
	<u>Yazoo City</u>	R	PC	1	OH	43	H	229	146 x 28
1848	<u>Belvidere</u>	A	PC	~	OH	48	H	197	168 x 26
	<u>Caddo</u>	R	PC	2	KY	48	H	188	150 x 24
	<u>Creole</u>	R	JF	1	KY	47	H	122	125 x 22
	<u>J. T. Doswell</u>	A	PC	~	KY	48	H	190	155 x 25
	Latona	A	JF	~	IN	46	H	197	155 x 26
	"	A	PC	~	"	"	"	"	"
	<u>Monroe</u>	A	PC	~	IN	48	H	183	127 x 25
	Monterey	A	JF	~	OH	46	H	143	135 x 25
	"	A	PC	~	"	"	"	"	"
	Vesta	A	PC	~	IN	45	H	92	117 x 21
1849	Belvidere	A	PC	~	OH	48	H	197	168 x 26
	Caddo	A	JF	~	KY	48	H	188	150 x 24
	"	R	PC	1	"	"	"	"	"
	<u>Corinne</u>	R	JF	1	OH	49	H	121	134 x 22
	<u>D. B. Mosby</u>	R	PC	3	OH	49	H	164	140 x 25
	<u>Dime</u>	A	JF	~	OH	45	H	61	NA x 18
	<u>Duck River</u>	R	JF	8	OH	47	H	132	124 x 26
	"	R	PC	1	"	"	"	"	"
	Latona	R	PC	2	IN	46	H	197	155 x 26
	Monterey	R	JF	5	OH	46	H	143	135 x 25
	"	R	PC	2	"	"	"	"	"
	<u>Shamrock</u>	R	JF	1	KY	48	H	139	164 x 26
	<u>Tallahatchie</u>	R	PC	1	IN	47	H	163	132 x 24
	<u>W. A. Violett</u>	R	JF	2	PA	48	H	162	120 x 23
	"	R	PC	1	"	"	"	"	"
1850	Caddo	A	JF	~	KY	48	H	188	150 x 24

YEAR	NAME	SOURCE	PLACE	TRIPS	PLACE BUILT	YEAR BUILT	TYPE	TONS	DIMEN-SIONS
	Duck River	R	JF	8	OH	47	H	132	124 x 26
	Medora	R	PC	7	IN	45	H	198	155 x 25
	Monterey	R	JF	1	OH	46	H	143	135 x 25
	"	R	PC	5	"	"	"	"	"
	R. C. Oglesby	R	JF	2	IN	49	H	115	126 x 23
1851	Caddo	R	JF	1	KY	48	H	188	150 x 24
	"	R	PC	4	"	"	"	"	"
	Corinne	R	JF	1	OH	49	H	121	134 x 22
	Echo (2)	R	JF	5	OH	50	H	161	130 x 25
	"	R	SM	1	"	"	"	"	"
	Latona	R	JF	2	IN	46	H	197	155 x 26
	Osceola	R	JF	11	PA	49	H	125	125 x 23
	Red River	R	PC	1	OH	50	H	276	174 x 29
	Southern	A	JF	~	NA	NA	NA	NA	183 x 31
	Tallahatchie	R	PC	1	IN	47	H	163	132 x 24
	W. A. Violett	R	JF	1	PA	48	H	162	120 x 23
1852	Caddo No. 2	A	JF	~	KY	51	H	273	170 x 29
	Caspian	R	JF	2	PA	51	H	248	115 x 31
	Cleona	R	JF	7	PA	50	H	185	128 x 27
	"	R	PC	1	"	"	"	"	"
	Echo	R	JF	4	OH	50	H	161	130 x 25
	Frances Jones	R	JF	1	KY	51	H	62	116 x 16
	Grenada	R	JF	4	IN	51	H	217	140 x 28
	Lucy Robinson	R	PC	1	IN	51	H	239	121 x 27
	Pitser Miller	R	JF	2	PA	48	H	158	126 x 26
	"	R	TL	1	"	"	"	"	"
	Post Boy	R	JF	2	OH	51	H	157	140 x 24
	Red River	R	JF	3	OH	50	H	276	174 x 29
	"	A	PC	~	"	"	"	"	"
	Storm	R	JF	1	OH	48	H	247	172 x 28
	"	R	PC	1	"	"	"	"	"
	Swan (2)	R	PC	1	IN	51	H	127	109 x 22
1853	Alabama	R	JF	6	PA	52	H	213	NA
	Caddo No. 2	A	JF	~	KY	51	H	273	170 x 29
	Cleona	R	JF	9	PA	50	H	185	128 x 27
	"	R	PC	1	"	"	"	"	"
	Compromise	R	PC	1	PA	51	H	270	173 x 27
	Grenada	R	JF	1	IN	51	H	217	140 x 28
	John Strader	R	JF	3	PA	52	H	205	137 x 28
	Pitser Miller	R	JF	3	PA	48	H	158	126 x 26
	Post Boy	R	TL	1	OH	51	H	157	140 x 24
	S. W. Downs	R	JF	1	IN	51	H	236	165 x 27
	"	R	PC	3	"	"	"	"	"

YEAR	NAME	SOURCE	PLACE	TRIPS	PLACE BUILT	YEAR BUILT	TYPE	TONS	DIMEN-SIONS
	St. Charles	A	JF	~	OH	50	H	311	126 x 30
	"	R	PC	1	"	"	"	"	"
	Texas Ranger	R	JF	3	IN	51	H	159	137 x 22
	Venture	O	JF	1	LA	51	H	61	102 x 20
1854	Allen Glover	R	JF	1	PA	47	H	241	NA
	B. E. Clark	R	JF	3	OH	53	H	199	150 x 27
	Belle Gates	R	JF	3	IN	51	H	278	174 x 28
	"	R	BN	1	"	"	"	"	"
	C. Hays	A	JF	~	PA	51	H	240	170 x 27
	Caddo No. 2	R	JF	2	KY	51	H	273	170 x 29
	"	R	PC	1	"	"	"	"	"
	Cleona	R	JF	8	PA	50	H	185	128 x 27
	Grenada	R	JF	2	IN	51	H	217	140 x 28
	Ruby	A	JF	~	PA	51	H	103	116 x 20
	St. Charles	R	JF	4	OH	50	H	311	126 x 30
	Storm	R	JF	4	OH	48	H	247	172 x 28
	Texas Ranger	R	PC	1	IN	51	H	159	137 x 22
	Unicorn	A	JF	~	PA	53	H	188	126 x 30
1855	Alida	R	JF	1	PA	53	W	94	105 x 23
	Augusta	R	JF	1	PA	53	W	27	NA
	Grenada	R	JF	1	IN	51	H	217	140 x 28
	Sodo	R	JF	1	NA	54	W	NA	108 x 20
	"	R	SM	1	"	"	"	"	"
1856	Alida	R	JF	2	PA	53	W	94	105 x 23
	Amanda	R	JF	1	KY	52	H	142	130 x 26
	Ariel	R	JF	2	OH	54	H	169	98 x 13
	Bloomer	R	JF	3	KY	56	W	95	123 x 27
	Camden	R	JF	2	KY	55	W	122	122 x 24
	De De	R	JF	1	LA	56	W	80	118 x 21
	Effort	R	JF	1	LA	55	H	114	125 x 25
	Financier	R	JF	2	LA	55	H	53	93 x 18
	Grenada	R	JF	4	IN	51	H	217	140 x 28
	Hope	R	JF	2	KY	55	H	193	128 x 34
	Julia	R	JF	1	KY	48	H	99	93 x 26
	Lizzie Lee	R	JF	1	KY	56	H	101	NA
	Lone Star	R	JF	6	KY	54	H	126	112 x 26
	Mary L. Dougherty	R	JF	3	PA	53	H	95	123 x 18
	Music	R	JF	3	IN	50	H	273	172 x 29
	Planter (2)	R	JF	1	IN	52	H	182	133 x 26
	R. M. Jones	R	JF	1	KY	51	H	193	136 x 27
	R. W. Powell	R	JF	1	IN	55	H	349	175 x 33
	Rosa	R	JF	2	KY	51	H	265	116 x 28
	St. Charles	R	JF	1	OH	50	H	311	126 x 30

YEAR	NAME	SOURCE	PLACE	TRIPS	PLACE BUILT	YEAR BUILT	TYPE	TONS	DIMEN- SIONS
	"	R	BN	1	"	"	"	"	"
	Storm	R	JF	3	OH	48	H	247	172 x 28
	"	R	BN	1	"	"	"	"	"
	Swan	R	JF	4	IN	51	H	127	109 x 22
	Victoria	R	SW	1	KY	55	H	161	133 x 30
	White Cliff	R	JF	3	AR	56	H	142	137 x 27
	William N. Sherman	R	JF	1	IN	55	H	194	130 x 30
1857	Afton, Jr.	R	JF	3	KY	56	H	155	134 x 28
	Alida	R	JF	2	PA	53	W	94	105 x 23
	"	R	AL	1	"	"	"	"	"
	Banjo	R	JF	1	OH	55	H	105	115 x 25
	Bloomer	R	JF	10	KY	56	W	95	123 x 27
	Caddo Belle	R	JF	1	IN	57	H	134	NA
	Camden	R	JF	1	KY	55	W	122	122 x 24
	Col. Edwards	R	JF	1	KY	56	H	216	155 x 31
	De De	R	JF	1	LA	56	W	80	118 x 21
	Dick Nash	R	JF	4	LA	56	W	127	134 x 22
	"	R	TL	1	"	"	"	"	"
	E. M. Bicknell	R	JF	1	OH	57	H	203	135 x 30
	Effort	R	JF	5	LA	55	H	114	125 x 25
	Gossamer	R	JF	1	NA	NA	NA	NA	NA
	Hope	R	JF	3	KY	55	H	193	128 x 34
	"	R	BN	1	"	"	"	"	"
	Joseph Holden	R	JF	3	OH	56	W	222	NA
	Lafitte	R	JF	2	KY	56	H	95	107 x 19
	Lecompte	R	JF	1	OH	56	H	250	155 x 32
	Mary L. Dougherty	R	JF	8	PA	53	H	95	123 x 18
	"	R	TL	1	"	"	"	"	"
	"	R	SW	1	"	"	"	"	"
	Osprey	R	JF	3	LA	56	W	109	115 x 24
	"	R	SW	1	"	"	"	"	"
	"	R	AL	1	"	"	"	"	"
	Reub White	R	JF	2	VA	56	H	110	104 x 27
	St. Charles	R	JF	2	OH	50	H	311	126 x 30
	Silver Moon	R	JF	1	KY	57	H	171	124 x 28
	Southern (2)	R	JF	1	VA	57	W	126	118 x 27
	Storm	R	JF	1	OH	48	H	247	172 x 28
	Swan	R	JF	2	IN	51	H	127	109 x 22
	Wabash Valley	R	JF	5	KY	53	H	136	NA
	William N. Sherman	R	JF	2	IN	55	H	194	130 x 30
1858	Afton, Jr.	R	JF	1	KY	56	H	155	134 x 28
	Bloomer	R	JF	9	KY	56	W	95	123 x 27
	Caddo Belle	R	JF	4	IN	57	H	134	NA

YEAR	NAME	SOURCE	PLACE	TRIPS	PLACE BUILT	YEAR BUILT	TYPE	TONS	DIMEN- SIONS
	Comet	R	JF	2	KY	57	H	183	130 x 29
	Era No. 1 (Effort)	R	JF	1	LA	55	H	114	125 x 25
	Grenada	R	JF	6	IN	51	H	217	140 x 28
	Ham Howell	R	JF	4	VA	57	W	144	120 x 30
	Joseph Holden	R	JF	9	OH	56	W	222	NA
	Lafitte	R	JF	1	KY	56	H	95	107 x 19
	Larkin Edwards	R	TL	1	IN	57	NA	67	NA
	Linda	R	JF	1	OH	55	H	167	NA
	Osceola	R	JF	1	KY	58	H	157	NA
	Rescue	R	JF	5	KY	58	W	77	NA
	Sallie Robinson	R	JF	4	OH	56	H	267	165 x 34
	Sunbeam	R	JF	1	OH	57	W	167	NA
	W. A. Andrew	R	JF	9	NA	57	H	229	132 x 30
	William C. Young	R	JF	1	KY	54	H	199	140 x 28
	William R. Douglass	R	JF	1	KY	56	H	229	126 x 28
	"	R	TL	1	"	"	"	"	"
1859	Arkansaw	R	JF	1	KY	57	W	131	132 x 29
	Bloomer	R	JF	1	KY	56	W	95	123 x 27
	Comet	R	JF	6	KY	57	H	183	130 x 29
	Eleanor	R	JF	5	OH	58	W	206	150 x 31
	Era No. 3	R	JF	3	PA	58	W	144	129 x 36
	Fleta	R	JF	1	KY	59	H	95	112 x 25
	Ham Howell	R	JF	4	VA	57	W	144	120 x 30
	Joseph Holden	R	JF	4	OH	56	W	222	NA
	Larkin Edwards	R	JF	18	IN	57	NA	67	NA
	"	R	MT	10	"	"	"	"	"
	"	R	SM	1	"	"	"	"	"
	Morning Light	R	JF	3	PA	58	H	198	144 x 30
	Oceola	R	JF	1	KY	58	H	157	NA
	Rescue	R	JF	11	KY	58	W	77	NA
	Robert Watson	R	JF	3	PA	58	W	137	129 x 28
	Sallie Robinson	R	JF	8	OH	56	H	267	165 x 34
	Starlight	R	JF	4	IN	58	H	280	162 x 31
	"	R	SW	1	"	"	"	"	"
	Telegram	R	JF	7	OH	58	W	205	158 x 31
	W. A. Andrew	R	JF	6	NA	57	H	229	132 x 30
	Yazoo Belle	R	JF	1	IN	55	H	138	134 x 28
1860	Alligator	R	JF	1	NA	NA	NA	NA	NA
	"	R	SM	1	"	"	"	"	"
	Andy Fulton	R	JF	1	PA	59	W	146	125 x 27
	Arkansaw	R	JF	1	KY	57	W	131	132 x 29
	Comet	R	JF	1	KY	57	H	183	130 x 29
	D. R. Carroll	R	JF	1	KY	58	H	300	175 x 34

YEAR	NAME	SOURCE	PLACE	TRIPS	PLACE BUILT	YEAR BUILT	TYPE	TONS	DIMEN-SIONS
	E. M. Bicknell	R	JF	1	OH	57	H	203	135 x 30
	Era No. 1 (Effort)	R	JF	1	LA	55	H	114	125 x 25
	Era No. 3	R	JF	1	PA	58	W	144	129 x 28
	Era No. 4	R	JF	2	PA	59	W	103	134 x 22
	Fleta	R	JF	3	KY	59	H	95	112 x 25
	Homer	R	JF	2	VA	59	H	194	148 x 28
	J. D. Swaim	R	JF	2	IN	59	H	228	151 x 30
	J. M. Sharp	R	JF	6	IN	59	H	218	147 x 29
	John Ray	R	JF	1	OH	59	W	86	100 x 24
	Larkin Edwards	R	JF	3	IN	57	NA	67	NA
	Martin Walt	R	JF	1	OH	59	W	64	NA
	Morgan Nelson	R	JF	2	PA	59	H	109	120 x 22
	National	R	SW	1	NA	NA	NA	NA	NA
	Oceola	R	JF	1	KY	58	H	157	NA
	Picayune No. 3	R	JF	2	PA	59	W	136	NA
	Rescue	R	JF	1	KY	58	W	77	NA
	Robert Watson	R	JF	2	PA	58	W	137	129 x 28
	Sallie Robinson	R	JF	5	OH	56	H	267	165 x 34
	Telegram	R	JF	1	OH	58	W	205	158 x 31
	Trio	O	JF	1	KY	58	W	150	NA
	Vigo	R	JF	6	PA	59	H	144	130 x 26
	Violett	R	JF	1	PA	56	W	89	123 x 22
	W. A. Andrew	R	JF	2	NA	57	H	229	132 x 30
	William Campbell	R	JF	1	MO	56	H	322	NA
1861	D. R. Carroll	R	JF	2	KY	58	H	300	175 x 34
	Era No. 4	R	SW	1	PA	59	W	103	134 x 22
	Era No. 6	R	JF	1	PA	60	W	83	NA
	Eleanor	R	JF	3	OH	58	W	206	150 x 31
	Fanny Pearson	R	JF	1	IN	60	H	137	123 x 26
	Fleta	R	JF	39	KY	59	H	95	112 x 25
	Fox	R	JF	2	AR	55	W	74	110 x 22
	Gen. J. L. Hodges	R	JF	3	KY	60	H	252	162 x 31
	Harmonia	R	JF	1	PA	56	W	151	NA
	Homer	R	JF	7	VA	59	H	194	148 x 28
	J. M. Sharp	R	JF	7	IN	59	H	218	147 x 29
	Lecompte	R	SW	1	OH	56	H	250	155 x 32
	Osceola	R	JF	1	KY	58	H	157	NA
	P. E. Bonford	R	JF	8	IN	60	H	231	140 x 30
	Robert Fulton	R	JF	3	PA	60	H	158	137 x 29
	Sallie Robinson	R	JF	7	OH	56	H	267	165 x 34
	Starlight	R	SW	1	IN	58	H	280	162 x 31
	Texas	R	JF	10	OH	59	H	170	138 x 20
	Vigo	R	JF	5	PA	59	H	144	130 x 26

YEAR	NAME	SOURCE	PLACE	TRIPS	PLACE BUILT	YEAR BUILT	TYPE	TONS	DIMEN-SIONS
	William Burton	R	JF	1	OH	57	H	253	151 x 29
	"	R	AL	1	"	"	"	"	"
1862	Anna Perrett	R	JF	1	IN	57	W	NA	133 x 32
	Col. Terry	R	JF	1	NA	NA	NA	NA	NA
	Cornie	O	JF	1	PA	60	W	69	100 x 23
	Era No. 5	R	JF	2	PA	60	W	115	NA
	Fleta	R	JF	2	KY	59	H	95	112 x 25
	Larkin Edwards	R	JF	2	IN	57	NA	67	NA
	Moro	R	JF	1	KY	NA	H	132	122 x 25
	P. E. Bonford	R	JF	1	IN	60	H	231	140 x 30
	Rinaldo	R	JF	2	NA	NA	NA	NA	NA
	Robert Fulton	R	JF	3	PA	60	H	158	137 x 29
	Texas	R	JF	1	OH	59	H	170	138 x 20
1863	Dot	O	SW	1	NA	NA	NA	NA	NA
	Fleta	O	JF	7	KY	59	H	95	112 x 25
	P. E. Bonford	R	JF	4	IN	60	H	231	140 x 30
	Robert Fulton	R	JF	1	PA	60	H	158	137 x 29
	T. D. Hine	O	JF	1	IN	58	H	131	148 x 30
	Texas	O	JF	6	OH	59	H	170	138 x 30
	"	O	MP	1	"	"	"	"	"
1864	NO BOATS								
1865	Beulah	R	JF	1	WV	65	W	339	128 x 24
	Blanton	R	JF	2	NA	NA	NA	NA	NA
	Carrie Poole	R	JF	1	IN	65	W	154	119 x 21
	Fleta	R	JF	1	KY	59	H	95	112 x 25
	Gossamer (2)	R	JF	1	PA	65	W	144	123 x 23
	Independence	R	JF	1	LA	63	H	42	75 x 17
	J. R. Hoyle	R	JF	1	IN	65	W	115	101 x 20
	L. Dillard	R	JF	1	LA	65	W	56	107 x 19
	Lizzie C. Hamilton	R	JF	1	OH	64	W	60	109 x 20
	Panola (2)	R	JF	1	OH	63	H	89	132 x 22
	Pioneer Era	R	JF	2	IN	63	W	219	129 x 29
	St, Cloud	R	JF	1	MN	61	H	25	90 x 13
	Science No. 2	R	JF	2	PA	60	W	116	135 x 27
1866	Alone	R	JF	2	WI	64	W	80	110 x 27
	Alexander Speer	R	JF	12	PA	64	W	171	139 x 26
	Beulah	R	JF	3	WV	65	W	339	128 x 24
	Blanton	R	JF	1	NA	NA	NA	NA	NA
	Caddo (2)	R	JF	1	PA	63	W	188	152 x 32
	Caroline	R	JF	1	IN	63	W	198	155 x 32
	Carrie Poole	R	JF	7	IN	65	W	154	119 x 21
	Cotile	R	JF	1	IN	59	H	162	139 x 27
	Cuba	R	JF	1	VA	64	W	168	149 x 28

YEAR	NAME	SOURCE	PLACE	TRIPS	PLACE BUILT	YEAR BUILT	TYPE	TONS	DIMEN- SIONS
	Cuba No. 2	R	JF	1	PA	62	W	110	129 x 25
	Dixie	R	JF	1	OH	60	H	102	131 x 24
	Doubloon	R	JF	1	OH	59	H	293	172 x 34
	Fanny Gilbert	R	JF	11	IN	64	W	145	130 x 26
	Fleta	R	JF	1	KY	59	H	95	112 x 25
	George	R	JF	2	IO	65	H	105	118 x 21
	Gossamer	R	JF	12	PA	65	W	144	123 x 23
	Hettie Gilmore	R	JF	1	OH	59	W	78	110 x 22
	H. A. Homeyer	R	JF	1	IN	63	W	222	165 x 33
	Iron City	R	JF	1	WV	64	W	190	150 x 29
	J. R. Hoyle	R	JF	6	IN	65	W	115	101 x 20
	L. Dillard	R	JF	6	LA	65	W	56	107 x 19
	Live Oak (2)	R	JF	1	KY	63	H	356	176 x 37
	Lotus	R	JF	2	NA	NA	NA	NA	NA
	Lizzie C. Hamilton	R	JF	48	OH	64	W	60	109 x 20
	Mattie Cook	R	JF	1	IN	60	W	120	124 x 24
	Mittie Stephens	R	JF	7	IN	63	H	224	170 x 29
	Mollie Fellows	R	JF	10	OH	64	H	224	139 x 25
	Monsoon	R	JF	1	OH	63	H	267	180 x 34
	Navigator	R	JF	3	PA	62	W	243	154 x 39
	Pioneer Era	R	JF	10	IN	63	W	219	129 x 29
	Richmond	R	JF	3	KY	66	W	339	143 x 35
	Starlight	R	JF	6	IN	58	H	477	167 x 34
	T. D. Hine	R	JF	9	IN	60	H	205	148 x 30
	Texas	R	JF	3	OH	59	H	170	138 x 30
	Thomas Powell	R	JF	9	KY	65	H	109	101 x 20
	Una	R	JF	3	KY	63	H	121	NA
1867	Annie Wagley	R	JF	1	KY	63	H	202	153 x 31
	Armadillo	R	JF	1	PA	65	W	453	157 x 33
	Caddo	R	JF	5	PA	63	W	188	152 x 32
	Cotile	R	JF	3	IN	59	H	162	139 x 27
	Cuba	R	JF	1	VA	64	W	168	149 x 28
	Cuba No. 2	R	JF	3	PA	62	W	110	129 x 25
	Dixie	R	JF	2	OH	60	H	102	131 x 24
	Elnora	R	JF	1	IN	65	W	332	152 x 33
	Fannie Gilbert	R	JF	5	IN	64	W	145	130 x 26
	Flicker	R	JF	4	PA	66	W	147	125 x 26
	Gossamer	R	JF	10	PA	65	W	144	123 x 23
	Independence	R	JB	1	LA	63	H	42	75 x 17
	Irene	R	JF	7	KY	64	W	211	156 x 32
	Iron City	R	JF	1	WV	64	W	190	150 x 29
	L. Dillard	R	JF	6	LA	65	W	56	107 x 19
	"	R	MT	1	"	"	"	"	"

YEAR	NAME	SOURCE	PLACE	TRIPS	PLACE BUILT	YEAR BUILT	TYPE	TONS	DIMEN-SIONS
	Lady Grace	R	JF	2	IN	65	W	387	160 x 33
	Live Oak	R	JF	10	KY	63	H	356	176 x 37
	Lizzie C. Hamilton	R	JF	1	OH	64	W	60	109 x 20
	Lizzie Tate	R	JF	1	OH	63	H	160	158 x 30
	Lotus No. 2	R	JF	5	PA	66	W	230	135 x 26
	Mittie Stephens	R	JF	9	IN	63	H	224	170 x 29
	Mollie Fellows	R	JF	1	OH	64	NA	224	139 x 25
	Monsoon	R	JF	7	OH	63	H	267	180 x 34
	Navigator	R	JF	1	PA	62	W	243	154 x 39
	New Era	R	JF	1	IN	60	H	259	162 x 32
	Rose Franks	R	JF	1	OH	66	W	240	126 x 29
	Starlight	R	JF	5	IN	58	H	477	167 x 34
	T. D. Hine	R	JF	15	IN	60	H	205	148 x 30
	Texas	R	JF	3	OH	59	H	170	138 x 30
	Warren Belle	R	JF	1	IN	65	H	242	144 x 25
1868	Caddo	R	JF	4	PA	63	W	188	152 x 32
	Cuba	R	JF	1	VA	64	W	168	149 x 28
	Cuba No. 2	R	JF	6	PA	62	W	110	129 x 25
	Dixie	R	JF	22	OH	60	H	102	131 x 24
	Era No. 8	R	JF	41	IN	67	H	162	122 x 25
	Era No. 9	R	JF	1	IN	68	W	169	146 x 37
	Ezra Porter	R	JF	4	PA	66	H	451	179 x 36
	Fannie Gilbert	R	JF	4	IN	64	W	145	130 x 26
	Flicker	R	JF	5	PA	66	W	147	125 x 26
	Frolic	R	JF	5	VA	60	H	393	205 x NA
	George	R	JF	6	IO	65	H	105	118 x 21
	Golden Era	R	JF	1	PA	66	W	208	156 x 32
	Gossamer	R	JF	24	PA	65	W	144	123 x 23
	Irene	R	JF	1	KY	64	W	211	156 x 32
	Iron City	R	JF	2	WV	64	W	190	150 x 29
	J. M. Sharp	R	JF	6	IN	59	H	218	147 x 29
	Lizzie Hopkins	R	JF	13	OH	67	W	453	159 x 36
	Lotus No. 2	R	JF	7	PA	66	W	230	135 x 26
	Lulu D.	R	JF	4	IN	67	W	245	135 x 35
	Mary Ellen	R	JF	3	LA	68	NA	NA	NA
	Mittie Stephens	R	JF	6	IN	63	H	224	170 x 29
	Mollie Fellows	R	JF	12	OH	64	NA	224	139 x 25
	Monsoon	R	JF	6	OH	63	H	267	180 x 34
	New Era	R	JF	4	IN	60	H	259	162 x 32
	Pioneer Era	R	JF	5	IO	63	W	141	129 x 29
	Rantidotler	R	JF	1	NA	NA	W	NA	NA
	Richmond	R	JF	5	KY	66	W	359	143 x 35
	Right Way	R	JF	8	PA	67	W	291	134 x 28

YEAR	NAME	SOURCE	PLACE	TRIPS	PLACE BUILT	YEAR BUILT	TYPE	TONS	DIMEN-SIONS
	Rose Franks	R	JF	8	OH	66	W	240	126 x 29
	Starlight	R	JF	2	IN	58	H	477	167 x 34
1869	Belle	R	JF	1	NA	NA	NA	NA	NA
	Caroline	R	JF	3	IN	63	W	198	155 x 32
	Dixie	R	JF	15	OH	60	H	102	131 x 24
	Dora	R	JF	9	PA	60	H	293	180 x 34
	Early Bird	R	JF	2	IN	67	H	174	126 x 26
	Enterprise (2)	R	JF	7	IL	64	W	293	160 x 33
	Era No. 9	R	JF	13	IN	68	W	169	146 x 37
	Era No. 10	R	JF	12	IN	68	W	176	136 x 31
	Flavilla	R	JF	8	IN	69	W	203	129 x 30
	Fleta (2)	R	JF	5	IN	69	W	NA	132 x 31
	Flirt	R	JF	4	NA	NA	NA	NA	NA
	George	R	JF	10	IO	65	H	105	118 x 21
	Golden Era	R	JF	10	PA	62	W	208	156 x 32
	Gossamer	R	JF	1	PA	65	W	144	123 x 23
	Judge Fletcher	R	JF	4	PA	60	H	260	NA
	Lake City	R	JF	1	NA	NA	NA	NA	NA
	Leo	R	JF	4	IN	68	H	349	165 x 40
	Lizzie Hopkins	R	JF	13	OH	67	W	453	159 x 36
	Lotawanna	R	JF	12	OH	67	W	479	155 x 35
	Lotus No. 2	R	JF	15	PA	66	W	230	135 x 26
	Lulu D.	R	JF	4	IN	67	W	245	135 x 35
	Mary Ellen	R	TL	1	LA	68	NA	NA	NA
	Minden	R	JF	1	NA	NA	NA	NA	NA
	Mittie Stephens	R	JF	2	IN	63	H	244	170 x 29
	Pioneer Era	R	JF	9	IO	63	W	141	129 x 29
	Richmond	R	JF	1	KY	66	W	359	143 x 35
	Right Way	R	JF	2	PA	67	W	291	134 x 28
	Selma	R	JF	6	PA	67	H	600	180 x 38
	Texarkana	R	JF	1	IN	69	W	343	136 x 36
	Travis Wright	R	JF	2	IN	69	W	202	129 x 32
	Twelfth Era	R	JF	2	NA	69	W	205	136 x 29
1870	Bertha	R	JF	3	PA	63	W	218	136 x 32
	Big Horn	R	JF	3	IN	65	W	312	154 x 34
	Bossier	R	JF	1	NA	69	W	NA	NA
	Bradish Johnson	R	JF	3	IN	69	H	NA	122 x 34
	Caroline	R	JF	3	IN	63	W	198	155 x 32
	Carrie Converse	R	JF	10	PA	70	H	NA	160 x 33
	Carrie V. Kountz	R	JF	1	MO	69	W	NA	187 x 40
	Charles H. Durfee	R	JF	5	PA	69	W	267	178 x 36
	Cherokee	R	JF	1	IN	70	W	260	131 x 33
	Dixie	R	JF	5	OH	60	H	102	131 x 24

YEAR	NAME	SOURCE	PLACE	TRIPS	PLACE BUILT	YEAR BUILT	TYPE	TONS	DIMEN-SIONS
	Dora	R	JF	3	PA	60	H	293	180 x 34
	Enterprise	R	JF	5	IL	64	W	293	160 x 33
	Era No. 9	R	JF	23	IN	68	W	169	146 x 37
	Era No. 10	R	JF	22	IN	68	W	176	136 x 31
	Flavilla	R	JF	7	IN	69	W	203	129 x 30
	Fleta	R	JF	13	IN	69	W	NA	132 x 31
	Flirt	R	JF	20	NA	NA	NA	NA	NA
	Fontenelle	R	JF	4	PA	70	W	NA	206 x 34
	Frank Morgan	R	JF	9	LA	69	W	108	124 x 26
	Frolic	R	JF	3	VA	60	H	393	205 x NA
	Gladiola	R	JF	5	IN	69	W	277	137 x 35
	Golden Era	R	JF	5	PA	62	W	208	156 x 32
	Hornet	R	JB	1	LA	70	S	39	NA
	Ida	R	JF	5	MO	66	H	326	172 x 32
	Ida Stockdale	R	JF	1	PA	67	W	377	NA
	Jefferson	R	JF	3	IN	58	W	146	120 x 30
	Jennie Howell	R	JF	6	NA	70	W	NA	146 x 36
	Julia A. Rudolph	R	JF	25	PA	69	W	NA	154 x 34
	Lake City	R	JF	1	NA	NA	NA	NA	NA
	Lightest	R	JF	8	IN	70	W	NA	136 x 29
	Lightwood	R	JF	1	OH	68	W	156	130 x 26
	Little Fleta	R	JF	3	IN	70	W	209	NA
	Lizzie Hopkins	R	JF	5	OH	67	W	453	159 x 36
	Lotus No. 2	R	JF	16	PA	66	W	230	135 x 26
	Lotus No. 3	R	JF	17	PA	69	W	NA	160 x 37
	Lulu D.	R	JF	2	IN	67	W	245	135 x 35
	Minnie	R	JF	2	PA	69	W	40	83 x 18
	R. J. Lockwood	R	JF	1	PA	70	W	NA	175 x 33
	Rapides	R	JF	4	OH	69	W	415	154 x 38
	St. John	R	JF	1	IN	69	W	464	176 x 34
	Seminole	R	JF	1	IN	69	W	420	158 x 44
	Silver Bow	R	JF	2	PA	69	H	335	212 x 32
	Silver Spray	R	JF	1	PA	64	W	352	NA
	Texarkana	R	JF	6	IN	69	W	343	136 x 36
	Texas (2)	R	JF	5	IN	69	W	NA	136 x 35
	Thirteenth Era	R	JF	4	PA	70	W	298	150 x 33
	Tidal Wave	R	JF	6	PA	70	W	NA	160 x 36
	Travis Wright	R	JF	2	IN	69	W	202	129 x 32
	Twelfth Era	R	JF	7	NA	69	W	205	136 x 29
	W. F. Curtis	R	JF	1	WV	64	W	211	NA
	Walter B. Dance	R	JF	1	KY	66	H	571	200 x 34
	Wash Sentell	R	JF	2	NA	NA	NA	NA	NA
	Will S. Hays	R	JF	1	IN	65	H	340	NA

YEAR	NAME	SOURCE	PLACE	TRIPS	PLACE BUILT	YEAR BUILT	TYPE	TONS	DIMEN- SIONS
1871	Belle Rowland	R	JF	6	PA	71	W	NA	160 x 35
	Big Horn	R	JF	2	IN	65	W	312	154 x 34
	Carrie A. Thorn	R	JF	2	IN	71	NA	247	NA
	Carrie Converse	R	JF	15	PA	70	H	NA	160 x 33
	Charles H. Durfee	R	JF	18	PA	69	W	267	178 x 36
	Cherokee	R	JF	1	IN	70	W	260	131 x 33
	Clifford	R	JF	1	IN	71	NA	121	NA
	Edinburgh	R	JF	4	KY	65	W	393	210 x 30
	Era No. 9	R	JF	6	IN	68	W	169	146 x 37
	Era No. 10	R	JF	8	IN	68	W	176	136 x 31
	Flavilla	R	JF	4	IN	69	W	203	129 x 30
	Fleta	R	JF	5	IN	69	W	NA	132 x 31
	Flirt	R	JF	3	NA	NA	NA	NA	NA
	Fontenelle	R	JF	1	PA	70	W	NA	206 x 34
	Garry Owen	R	JF	1	WV	70	W	289	131 x 33
	Gladiola	R	JF	3	IN	69	W	277	137 x 35
	Hamilton	R	JF	1	OH	67	W	123	NA
	Henry M. Shreve	R	JF	3	IN	67	H	567	198 x 35
	Hesper	R	JF	1	OH	66	W	184	127 x 35
	Ida	R	JF	3	MO	66	H	326	172 x 32
	La Belle	R	JF	3	IN	69	H	510	178 x 40
	Lady Lee	R	JF	4	PA	71	W	417	176 x 35
	Little Fleta	R	JF	3	IN	70	W	209	NA
	Lotawanna	R	JF	6	OH	67	W	479	155 x 35
	Lotus No. 3	R	JF	17	PA	69	W	NA	160 x 37
	Lulu D.	R	JF	3	IN	67	W	245	135 x 35
	Maria Louise	R	JF	1	IN	71	W	521	180 x 34
	May Lowry	R	JF	7	PA	71	NA	NA	138 x 31
	"	R	JF	1	"	"	"	"	"
	Oceanus	R	JF	4	PA	70	W	365	180 x 41
	R. J. Lockwood	R	JF	6	PA	64	H	NA	175 x 33
	Rapides	R	JF	2	OH	69	W	415	154 x 38
	Red Cloud	R	JF	9	OH	70	W	599	161 x 39
	Right Way	R	JF	1	PA	67	W	291	134 x 28
	Ruth	R	JF	1	PA	70	W	NA	140 x 35
	Salado	R	JF	1	WV	68	W	110	128 x 25
	Silver Bow	R	JF	1	PA	69	H	335	212 x 32
	Texas	R	JF	7	IN	69	W	NA	136 x 35
	Thirteenth Era	R	JF	3	PA	70	W	298	150 x 33
	Tidal Wave	R	JF	13	PA	70	W	NA	160 x 36
1872	Anna	R	JF	2	PA	64	W	NA	156 x 32
	Belle Rowland	R	JF	30	PA	71	W	NA	160 x 35
	"	R	JB	1	"	"	"	"	"

YEAR	NAME	SOURCE	PLACE	TRIPS	PLACE BUILT	YEAR BUILT	TYPE	TONS	DIMEN-SIONS
	Bossier (2)	R	JF	1	IN	71	W	115	NA
	Carrie A. Thorn	R	JF	5	IN	71	NA	247	NA
	Champion	R	JF	1	PA	64	W	292	146 x 27
	Charles H. Durfee	R	JF	9	PA	69	W	267	178 x 36
	Clifford	R	JF	8	IN	71	NA	121	NA
	"	R	JB	3	"	"	"	"	"
	D. L. Tally	R	JF	3	OH	70	W	NA	161 x 37
	Emilie La Barge	R	JF	1	IL	69	H	NA	218 x 38
	Era No. 9	R	JF	1	IN	68	W	169	146 x 37
	Era No. 10	R	JF	5	IN	68	W	176	136 x 31
	Flavilla	R	JF	2	IN	69	W	203	129 x 30
	Fleta	R	JF	4	IN	69	W	NA	132 x 31
	Flirt	R	JF	2	NA	NA	NA	NA	NA
	Fontenelle	R	JF	2	PA	70	W	NA	206 x 34
	Gladiola	R	JF	2	IN	69	W	277	137 x 35
	Hesper	R	JF	2	OH	66	W	184	127 x 35
	Hornet	R	JB	1	LA	70	S	39	NA
	John T. Moore	R	JF	1	OH	71	W	497	177 x 42
	La Belle	R	JF	4	IN	69	H	510	178 x 40
	Little Fleta	R	JF	6	IN	70	W	209	NA
	Lotus No. 3	R	JF	7	PA	69	W	NA	160 x 37
	Maria Louise	R	JF	6	IN	71	W	521	NA
	May Lowry	R	JF	5	PA	71	NA	210	196 x 31
	Rapides	R	JF	5	OH	69	W	415	154 x 38
	Right Way	R	JF	4	PA	67	W	291	134 x 28
	Royal George	R	JF	7	AR	72	NA	NA	135 x 27
	Texas (2)	R	JF	1	IN	69	W	NA	136 x 35
	Thirteenth Era	R	JF	4	PA	70	W	298	150 x 33
1873	Andrew Ackley	R	JF	4	PA	68	W	207	162 x 25
	Bannock City	R	JF	2	IO	66	W	150	150 x 28
	Belle of Shreveport	R	JF	1	IL	72	W	581	202 x 43
	Belle Rowland	R	JF	11	PA	71	W	NA	160 x 35
	Bossier	R	JF	9	IN	71	W	115	NA
	Carrie A. Thorn	R	JF	1	IN	71	NA	247	NA
	Charles H. Durfee	R	JF	14	PA	69	W	267	178 x 36
	Clifford	R	JF	7	IN	71	NA	121	NA
	Era No. 10	R	JF	2	IN	68	W	176	136 x 31
	Flavilla	R	JF	2	IN	69	W	203	129 x 30
	Fleta	R	JF	2	IN	69	W	NA	132 x 31
	Flirt	R	JF	5	NA	NA	NA	NA	NA
	Frank Morgan	R	JF	6	LA	69	W	108	124 x 26
	Frazier	R	JF	2	NA	NA	NA	NA	NA
	Gladiola	R	JF	2	IN	69	W	277	137 x 35

YEAR	NAME	SOURCE	PLACE	TRIPS	PLACE BUILT	YEAR BUILT	TYPE	TONS	DIMEN-SIONS
	Hornet	R	JB	3	LA	70	S	39	NA
	Huntsville	R	JF	9	IN	64	W	213	159 x 33
	John T. Moore	R	JF	2	OH	71	W	497	177 x 42
	Katie P. Kountz	R	JF	1	PA	71	W	NA	NA
	La Belle	R	JF	1	IN	69	H	510	178 x 40
	Lady Lee	R	JF	1	PA	71	W	417	176 x 35
	Leo	R	JF	1	IN	68	H	349	165 x 40
	Lessie Taylor	R	JF	5	IN	70	W	434	157 x 38
	Little Fleta	R	JF	5	IN	70	W	209	NA
	Lotta	R	JB	1	NA	NA	NA	NA	NA
	Lotus No. 3	R	JF	11	PA	69	W	NA	160 x 37
	Maria Louise	R	JF	3	IN	71	W	521	180 x 34
	May Lowry	R	JF	3	PA	71	NA	210	196 x 31
	R. T. Bryarly	R	JF	4	IN	72	W	331	150 x 33
	Rapides	R	JF	2	OH	69	W	415	154 x 38
	Right Way	R	JF	2	PA	67	W	291	134 x 28
	Royal George	R	JF	12	AR	72	NA	NA	135 x 27
	Ruby (2)	R	JF	17	IN	71	W	117	NA
	Seminole	R	JF	5	IN	69	W	420	158 x 44
	Shamrock (2)	R	JF	1	OH	63	W	217	NA
	South-Western	R	JF	1	NA	70	W	411	180 x 42
	Texas	R	JF	1	IN	69	W	NA	136 x 35
	Thirteenth Era	R	JF	4	PA	70	W	298	150 x 33
	W. J. Behan	R	JF	1	IN	73	W	NA	165 x 33
1874	Belle Rowland	R	JF	2	PA	71	W	NA	160 x 35
	Charles H. Durfee	R	JF	6	PA	69	W	267	178 x 36
	Clifford	R	JF	1	IN	71	NA	121	NA
	"	R	AL	1	"	"	"	"	"
	"	R	JB	1	"	"	"	"	"
	"	R	TL	1	"	"	"	"	"
	Frank Morgan	R	TL	1	LA	69	W	108	124 x 26
	La Belle	R	JF	1	IN	69	H	510	178 x 40
	Lessie Taylor	R	JF	1	IN	70	W	434	157 x 38
	Lotus No. 3	R	JF	5	PA	69	W	NA	160 x 37
	Maria Louise	R	JF	1	IN	71	W	521	NA
	R. T. Bryarly	R	JF	2	IN	72	W	331	150 x 33
	Royal George	R	JF	9	AR	72	NA	NA	135 x 27
	"	R	TL	1	"	"	"	"	"
	Sabine	R	JF	2	NA	NA	NA	NA	NA
	Seminole	R	JF	1	IN	69	W	420	158 x 44
	Texas	R	JF	3	IN	69	W	NA	136 x 35
	W. J. Behan	R	JF	3	IN	73	W	NA	165 x 33
1875	Belle Rowland	R	JF	1	PA	71	W	NA	160 x 35

YEAR	NAME	SOURCE	PLACE	TRIPS	PLACE BUILT	YEAR BUILT	TYPE	TONS	DIMEN-SIONS
	Charles H. Durfee	R	JF	2	PA	69	W	267	178 x 36
	Col. A. P. Kouns	R	JF	11	OH	74	W	309	165 x 33
	Era No. 10	R	JF	2	IN	68	W	176	136 x 31
	Frank Morgan	R	JF	1	LA	69	W	108	124 x 26
	Lotus No. 3	R	JF	10	PA	69	W	NA	NA
	"	R	MP	1	"	"	"	"	"
	Maria Louise	R	JF	2	IN	71	W	521	180 x 34
	R. T. Bryarly	R	JF	2	IN	72	W	331	150 x 33
1876	Bonnie Lee	R	JF	2	IN	75	W	316	165 x 30
	Carrie A. Thorn	R	JF	1	IN	71	NA	247	NA
	Charles H. Durfee	R	JF	1	PA	69	W	267	178 x 36
	Clifford	R	JF	1	IN	71	NA	121	NA
	Col. A. P. Kouns	R	JF	13	OH	74	W	309	165 x 33
	Dawn	R	JF	2	IN	75	W	NA	160 x 32
	Fontenelle	R	JF	1	PA	70	W	NA	206 x 34
	Gussie	R	AL	1	NA	NA	NA	NA	NA
	Lotus No. 3	R	JF	5	PA	69	W	NA	160 x 37
	May Lowry	R	JF	2	PA	71	NA	210	196 x 31
	R. T. Bryarly	R	JF	6	IN	72	W	331	150 x 33
1877	Albany	R	TL	1	NA	NA	NA	NA	NA
	Alexandria	R	JF	3	NA	77	W	NA	165 x 28
	Col. A. P. Kouns	R	JF	11	OH	74	W	309	165 x 33
	Danube	R	JF	1	OH	77	W	NA	175 x 34
	Gussie	R	JB	1	NA	NA	NA	NA	NA
	Lotus No. 3	R	JF	4	PA	69	W	NA	160 x 37
	R. W. Dugan	R	JF	2	OH	73	W	NA	160 x 32
	W. J. Behan	R	JF	1	IN	73	W	NA	165 x 33
1878	Albany	R	TL	1	NA	NA	NA	NA	NA
	Bonnie Lee	R	JF	4	IN	75	W	316	165 x 30
	Col. A. P. Kouns	R	JF	4	OH	74	W	309	165 x 33
	Danube	R	JF	3	OH	77	W	NA	175 x 34
	Frank Willard	R	JF	1	OH	73	W	75	NA
	Joe Bryarly	R	JF	4	NA	NA	W	NA	NA
	Vicksburg	R	MP	1	NA	NA	NA	NA	NA
1879	Cornie Brandon	R	JF	2	NA	NA	NA	NA	NA
	Danube	R	JF	2	OH	77	W	NA	175 x 34
	Frank Willard	R	JF	5	OH	73	W	75	NA
	Jewel	R	JF	2	IN	78	W	500	177 x 33
	Joe Bryarly	R	JF	1	NA	NA	W	NA	NA
1880	Alexandria	R	JF	1	NA	77	W	NA	165 x 28
	Caddo Belle (2)	R	JF	1	OH	80	NA	NA	125 x 25
	"	R	MP	1	"	"	"	"	"
	Cornie Brandon	R	JF	1	NA	NA	NA	NA	NA

YEAR	NAME	SOURCE	PLACE	TRIPS	PLACE BUILT	YEAR BUILT	TYPE	TONS	DIMEN-SIONS
	Frank Willard	R	JF	4	OH	73	W	75	NA
	Gussie	R	MP	1	NA	NA	NA	NA	NA
	Thornbush	R	MP	1	NA	NA	NA	NA	NA
1881	Caddo Belle	R	MP	2	OH	80	NA	NA	125 x 25
	Cornie Brandon	R	MP	1	NA	NA	NA	NA	NA
	Frank Willard	R	MP	2	OH	73	W	75	NA
	Gussie	R	AL	1	NA	NA	NA	NA	NA
	"	R	MP	1	"	"	"	"	"
1882	Lessie B.	R	JF	2	OH	81	NA	NA	NA
	"	R	MP	1	"	"	"	"	"
	"	R	JB	1	"	"	"	"	"
	"	R	TL	1	"	"	"	"	"
1883	Alpha	R	JF	3	NA	NA	NA	125	NA
	"	R	TL	3	"	"	"	"	"
	Cornie Brandon	R	MP	2	NA	NA	NA	NA	NA
	"	R	JB	1	"	"	"	"	"
	John G. Fletcher	R	MP	1	IN	77	W	NA	121 x 26
1884	Alpha	R	JF	7	NA	NA	NA	125	NA
	"	R	MP	2	"	"	"	"	"
	"	R	TL	1	"	"	"	"	"
	Ranger	R	MP	1	AR	82	NA	NA	95 x 17
	Shields	R	JB	1	NA	NA	NA	NA	NA
1885	Alpha	R	JF	7	NA	NA	NA	125	NA
	"	R	MP	2	"	"	"	"	"
	John G. Fletcher	R	JB	1	IN	77	W	NA	121 x 26
1886	John G. Fletcher	R	JB	1	IN	77	W	NA	121 x 26
1887	Alpha	R	JF	1	NA	NA	NA	125	NA
	"	R	MP	1	"	"	"	"	"
	"	R	TL	1	"	"	"	"	"
1888	Alpha	R	MP	1	NA	NA	NA	125	NA
1889	Friendly	R	JF	3	WV	88	W	67	120 x 27
	G. W. Sentell	R	JF	1	IN	82	W	NA	NA
	Marco	R	JF	6	NA	NA	NA	NA	NA
1890	Friendly	O	JF	19	WV	88	W	67	120 x 27
	New Haven	O	JF	14	NA	NA	W	93	136 x 24
1891	Friendly	O	JF	28	NA	NA	W	67	120 x 27
	Nat F. Dortch	O	JF	10	IN	89	W	303	164 x 29
1892	Blue Wing	O	MP	2	KY	82	W	112	119 x 24
	Friendly	O	JF	10	NA	NA	W	67	120 x 27
	New Haven	O	JF	4	NA	NA	W	93	136 x 24
	Rosa Bland	O	JF	12	AR	89	W	149	113 x 23
	"	O	MP	6	"	"	"	"	"
1893	Nat F. Dortch	O	JF	13	IN	89	W	303	164 x 29

YEAR	NAME	SOURCE	PLACE	TRIPS	PLACE BUILT	YEAR BUILT	TYPE	TONS	DIMEN-SIONS
	Rosa Bland	O	JF	14	AR	89	W	149	113 x 23
1894	Rosa Bland	O	JF	17	AR	89	W	149	113 x 23
1895	NO BOATS								
1896	Rosa Bland	O	MP	6	AR	89	W	149	113 x 23
1897	Nellie L.	O	JF	2	NA	NA	NA	NA	NA
	Rosa Bland	O	JF	3	AR	89	W	149	113 x 23
1898	NO BOATS								
1899	NO BOATS								
1900	NO BOATS								
1901	NO BOATS								
1902	NO BOATS								
1903	NO BOATS								
1904	Anna Tardy	O	JF	1	IN	NA	W	71	NA
1905	Anna Tardy	O	JF	~	IN	NA	W	71	NA

SOURCES

1841: *Daily Picayune; Miami* from *New Orleans Price Current.*

1842: *Daily Picayune; Georgia* from *New Orleans Commercial Bulletin.*

1843–44: *Daily Picayune.*

1845: *Daily Picayune; Lama* and *Gazelle* from 10 July 1878 *Daily Democrat.*

1846: *Daily Picayune; Latona* from article in 22 September 1880 *Daily Democrat; Live Oak* from *Caddo Gazette.*

1847–48: *Daily Picayune.*

1849: *Daily Picayune; Caddo* to Jefferson from *Texas Republican.*

1850: *Daily Picayune; Caddo* from *Caddo Gazette.*

1851: *Daily Picayune; Southern* from *Texas Republican.*

1852: *Daily Picayune; Caddo No. 2* from *Texas Republican.*

1853: *Daily Picayune; Venture* from article in 12 April *Caddo Gazette.*

1854: *Daily Picayune.*

1855: *South-Western.*

1856: *South-Western* and *Daily Picayune.*

1857–58: *South-Western; Daily Picayune; Texas Republican.*

1859: *South-Western* through 10 August; *Daily Picayune* through end of year.

1860: *Daily Picayune; D. R. Carroll, Rescue, Telegram, Violett* from 14 January *Texas Republican; National* from article on Swanson's Landing in 10 March *Texas Republican; Comet, Larkin Edwards,* and *Trio* from *Standard; Alligator* from *Standard* and Alexandria *Constitutional.*

1861: *South-Western.*

1862: *Larkin Edwards, Rinaldo, Robert Fulton* from *South-Western; Col. Terry* and *Texas* from *Daily Picayune; Era No. 5, Fleta, Moro* from *Semi-Weekly Shreveport News; Cornie* and additional trips for *Robert Fulton* from "Vessel Papers." *Anna Perrett* from 16 May *Confederate News.*

1863: *P. E. Bonford* and *Robert Fulton* from *Shreveport Weekly News;* rest from "Vessel Papers," including additional trips for *P. E. Bonford.*

1864: No boats.

1865: *Daily Picayune; South-Western* from 7 June to end of year.

1866–70: *South-Western.*

1871: *South-Western,* 9 January through 12 July; *Daily South-Western,* 13 July through 12 September; *Daily Picayune,* 14 September through 19 December; *Shreveport Times,* 19–31 December.

1872–73: *Shreveport Times.*

1874: *Daily Picayune,* 1 January through 7 June; *Shreveport Times,* 30 June through end of year.

1875–89: *Shreveport Times.*

1890–1905: Annual reports of the chief of engineers.

Appendix C

Alphabetical Listing

This is an alphabetical listing of all of the steamboats for which there is documentation or good reason to believe that they traveled on the route. It uses the convention employed in all steamboat listings to place the boat names that begin with initials first under each letter of the alphabet.

For the spelling of boat names, I have used the Lytle-Holdcamper renditions, which are derived from enrollment records. For the vast majority of boats, the newspaper renditions (excluding nicknames, shortened versions, and occasional discrepancies within a newspaper or among newspapers) are the same as Lytle-Holdcamper. Most discrepancies are trivial (for example, the newspapers use *Dede* rather than *De De* and *12th Era* rather than *Twelfth Era*), and most occur when the newspapers use the initials rather than the full name of the boat (for example, *C. H. Durfee* rather than *Charles H. Durfee*). The newspaper renditions may represent the name as it appeared on the boat when this differed from the more formal enrollment name. However, no firm conclusions can be drawn because of contrary examples (for example, the newspapers use *H. M. Shreve* rather than the *Henry M. Shreve* that appeared on the boat and in the enrollment papers and the *Walter B. Dance* that appears in the enrollment papers rather than the *W. B. Dance* that appeared on the boat).

There are only four non-trivial discrepancies, all of which are from the 1850s:

1. *Lecompte*—This boat may have been named for a famous racehorse of the period, generally rendered Lecomte in the newspapers, and it is this spelling that is used in hundreds of newspaper boat records and advertisements in the New Orleans and Shreveport newspapers. However, it may also have been named for the prominent Red River planter Ambrose LeCompte. Lytle-Holdcamper and Way use *Lecompte*. Both renditions are used in the enrollment papers.

2. *Mary L. Dougherty*—The Shreveport newspapers use *Daugherty* for this local boat. It appears as *Dougherty* in Lytle-Holdcamper, Way, *Ship Registers and Enrollments of New Orleans*, the *Daily Picayune*, and the enrollment papers.

3. *S. W. Downs*—Solomon Downs was a well-known New Orleans official, which is the spelling used in Way and the newspapers. Lytle-Holdcamper mistranscribed the enrollment papers and use *Downes*.

4. *White Cliff*—This boat was built in Arkansas for the upper Red River trade and is named for a well-known landing and geographic feature rendered White Cliffs in the newspapers, which was also the name of the boat in the newspapers. The singular appears in Lytle-Holdcamper, Way, *Ship Registers and Enrollments of New Orleans*, and the enrollment papers.

It should also be noted that Way uses *Lowery* for the *May Lowry* that appears in the newspapers, citing the name of the company for which the boat was built. In the absence of enrollment documents, I have retained the newspaper usage.

There are 350 boats on this list, including 10 with duplicate names and one that was renamed. Of the 350, 324 have documented trips on the route. The rest are based on advertisements, which were necessarily incorporated through the year 1854. Of the 350, 297 went as high as Jefferson. Of these, 288 are documented.

Persons wishing to supplement this list should keep in mind that advertisements are not reliable indicators that a boat went west of Shreveport, for reasons explained in the text. Additions should be based on concrete evidence, such as bills of lading.

KEY

Name: Derived from Appendix B.
Year: Year that the boat began operating on the route.
Status: C = Certain (derived from firm record).
    U = Uncertain
Port: Highest point reached in all trips made by that boat.
    BN = Benton
    JB = Jim's Bayou
    JF = Jefferson
    MP = Mooringsport
    PC = Port Caddo

SM = Smithland
SW = Swanson's Landing
TL = The Lakes
Place Built: By state designations.
Year Built: All in the 1800s.
Type: Rig type.
H = Sidewheeler
W = Sternwheeler
P = Screw
Tons: Pre- and post-Civil War not comparable.
Dimensions: Length and width, rounded for convenience.
NA = Not Available

NAME	YEAR	STATUS	PORT	PLACE BUILT	YEAR BUILT	TYPE	TONS	DIMENSIONS
Afton, Jr.	1857	C	JF	KY	56	H	155	134 x 28
Alabama	1853	C	JF	PA	52	H	213	NA
Albany	1877	C	TL	NA	NA	NA	NA	NA
Alexander Speer	1866	C	JF	PA	64	W	171	139 x 26
Alexandria	1877	C	JF	NA	77	W	NA	165 x 28
Alida	1855	C	JF	PA	53	W	94	105 x 23
Allen Glover	1854	C	JF	PA	47	H	241	NA
Alligator	1860	C	JF	NA	NA	NA	NA	NA
Alone	1866	C	JF	WI	64	W	80	110 x 27
Alpha	1883	C	JF	NA	NA	NA	125	NA
Amanda	1856	C	JF	KY	52	H	142	130 x 26
Andrew Ackley	1873	C	JF	PA	68	W	207	162 x 25
Andy Fulton	1860	C	JF	PA	59	W	146	125 x 27
Anna	1872	C	JF	PA	64	W	NA	156 x 32
Anna Perrett	1862	C	JF	IN	57	W	NA	133 x 32
Anna Tardy	1904	C	JF	IN	NA	W	71	NA
Annie Wagley	1867	C	JF	KY	63	H	202	153 x 31
Ariel	1856	C	JF	OH	54	H	169	98 x 13
Arkansaw	1859	C	JF	KY	57	W	131	132 x 29
Armadillo	1867	C	JF	PA	65	W	453	157 x 33
Augusta	1855	C	JF	PA	53	W	27	NA
B. E. Clark	1854	C	JF	OH	58	H	199	150 x 27
Banjo	1857	C	JF	OH	55	H	105	115 x 25
Bannock City	1873	C	JF	IO	66	W	150	150 x 28
Belle	1869	C	JF	NA	NA	NA	NA	NA
Belle Gates	1854	C	JF	IN	51	H	278	174 x 28
Belle of Illinois	1847	U	PC	PA	45	H	78	100 x 20
Belle of Ouachita	1846	U	JF	IN	43	H	103	NA
Belle of Shreveport	1873	C	JF	IL	72	W	581	202 x 43
Belle Rowland	1871	C	JF	PA	71	W	NA	160 x 35

NAME	YEAR	STATUS	PORT	PLACE BUILT	YEAR BUILT	TYPE	TONS	DIMENSIONS
Belvidere	1848	U	PC	OH	48	H	197	168 x 26
Bertha	1870	C	JF	PA	63	W	218	136 x 32
Beulah	1865	C	JF	WV	65	W	339	128 X 24
Big Horn	1870	C	JF	IN	65	W	312	154 x 34
Blanton	1865	C	JF	NA	NA	NA	NA	NA
Bloomer	1856	C	JF	KY	56	W	95	123 x 27
Blue Wing	1892	C	MP	KY	82	W	112	119 x 24
Bois d'Arc	1843	C	PC	KY	43	H	182	136 x 26
Bonnie Lee	1876	C	JF	IN	75	W	316	165 x 30
Bossier	1870	C	JF	NA	69	W	NA	NA
Bossier (2)	1872	C	JF	IN	71	W	115	NA
Bradish Johnson	1870	C	JF	IN	69	H	NA	122 x 34
Brian Boroihme	1841	U	PC	KY	36	H	187	135 x 24
Buffalo	1847	U	JF	KY	47	H	136	123 x 22
C. Hays	1854	U	JF	PA	51	H	240	170 x 27
Caddo	1848	C	JF	KY	48	H	188	150 x 24
Caddo (2)	1866	C	JF	PA	63	W	188	152 x 32
Caddo Belle	1857	C	JF	IN	57	H	134	NA
Caddo Belle (2)	1880	C	JF	OH	80	NA	NA	125 x 25
Caddo No. 2	1852	C	JF	KY	51	H	273	170 x 29
Camden	1856	C	JF	KY	55	W	122	122 x 24
Caroline	1866	C	JF	IN	63	W	198	155 x 32
Carrie A. Thorn	1871	C	JF	IN	71	NA	247	NA
Carrie Converse	1870	C	JF	PA	70	H	NA	160 x 33
Carrie Poole	1865	C	JF	IN	65	W	154	119 x 21
Carrie V. Kountz	1870	C	JF	MO	69	W	NA	187 x 40
Caspian	1852	C	JF	PA	51	H	248	115 x 31
Champion	1872	C	JF	PA	64	W	292	146 x 27
Charles H. Durfee	1870	C	JF	PA	69	W	267	178 x 36
Cherokee	1870	C	JF	IN	70	W	260	131 x 33
Cleona	1852	C	JF	PA	50	H	185	128 x 27
Clifford	1871	C	JF	IN	71	NA	121	NA
Col. A. P. Kouns	1875	C	JF	OH	74	W	309	165 x 33
Col. Edwards	1857	C	JF	KY	56	H	216	155 x 31
Col. Harney	1845	U	PC	IN	44	H	132	112 x 26
Col. Terry	1862	C	JF	NA	NA	NA	NA	NA
Comet	1858	C	JF	KY	57	H	183	130 x 29
Compromise	1853	C	PC	PA	51	H	270	173 x 27
Corinne	1849	C	JF	OH	49	H	121	134 x 22
Cornie	1862	C	JF	PA	60	W	69	100 x 23
Cornie Brandon	1879	C	JF	NA	NA	NA	NA	NA
Cotile	1866	C	JF	IN	59	H	162	139 x 27
Creole	1848	C	JF	KY	47	H	122	125 x 22

NAME	YEAR	STATUS	PORT	PLACE BUILT	YEAR BUILT	TYPE	TONS	DIMENSIONS
Cuba	1866	C	JF	VA	64	W	168	149 x 28
Cuba No. 2	1866	C	JF	PA	62	W	110	129 x 25
D. B. Mosby	1849	C	PC	OH	49	H	164	140 x 25
D. L. Tally	1872	C	JF	OH	70	W	NA	161 x 37
D. R. Carroll	1860	C	JF	KY	58	H	300	175 x 34
Danube	1877	C	JF	OH	77	W	NA	175 x 33
Dawn	1876	C	JF	IN	75	W	NA	160 x 32
De De	1856	C	JF	LA	56	W	80	118 x 21
Dick Nash	1857	C	JF	LA	56	W	127	134 x 22
Dime	1849	U	JF	OH	45	H	61	NA x 18
Dixie	1866	C	JF	OH	60	H	102	131 x 24
Dora	1869	C	JF	PA	60	H	293	180 x 34
Dot	1863	C	SW	NA	NA	NA	NA	NA
Doubloon	1866	C	JF	OH	59	H	293	172 x 34
Douglas	1845	U	PC	IN	41	H	263	167 x 26
Duck River	1849	C	JF	OH	47	H	132	124 x 26
E. M. Bicknell	1857	C	JF	OH	57	H	203	135 x 30
Early Bird	1869	C	JF	IN	67	H	174	126 x 26
Echo	1842	U	PC	OH	36	H	158	152 x 18
Echo (2)	1851	C	JF	OH	50	H	161	130 x 25
Edinburgh	1871	C	JF	KY	65	W	393	210 x 30
Effort	1856	C	JF	LA	55	H	114	125 x 25
Eleanor	1859	C	JF	OH	58	W	206	150 x 31
Ellen	1847	C	JF	KY	46	W	99	129 x 20
Elnora	1867	C	JF	IN	65	W	332	152 x 33
Emilie La Barge	1872	C	JF	IL	69	H	NA	218 x 38
Enterprise	1846	C	PC	OH	44	H	106	109 x 22
Enterprise (2)	1869	C	JF	IL	64	W	293	160 x 33
Era No. 1 (Effort)	1858	C	JF	LA	55	H	114	125 x 25
Era No. 3	1859	C	JF	PA	58	W	144	129 x 28
Era No. 4	1860	C	JF	PA	59	W	103	134 x 22
Era No. 5	1862	C	JF	PA	60	W	115	NA
Era No. 6	1861	C	JF	PA	60	W	83	NA
Era No. 8	1868	C	JF	IN	67	H	162	122 x 25
Era No. 9	1868	C	JF	IN	68	W	169	146 x 37
Era No. 10	1869	C	JF	IN	68	W	176	136 x 31
Express Mail	1846	U	PC	OH	41	H	244	165 x 25
Ezra Porter	1868	C	JF	PA	66	H	451	179 x 36
Fanny Gilbert	1866	C	JF	IN	64	W	145	130 x 26
Fanny Pearson	1861	C	JF	IN	60	H	137	123 x 26
Farmer	1841	U	BN	KY	39	H	180	121 x 23
Financier	1856	C	JF	LA	55	H	53	93 x 18
Flavilla	1869	C	JF	IN	69	W	203	129 x 30

NAME	YEAR	STATUS	PORT	PLACE BUILT	YEAR BUILT	TYPE	TONS	DIMENSIONS
Fleta	1859	C	JF	KY	59	H	95	112 x 25
Fleta (2)	1869	C	JF	IN	69	W	NA	132 x 31
Flicker	1867	C	JF	PA	66	W	147	125 x 26
Flirt	1869	C	JF	NA	NA	NA	NA	NA
Fontenelle	1870	C	JF	PA	70	W	NA	206 x 34
Fox	1861	C	JF	AR	55	W	74	110 x 22
Frances Jones	1852	C	JF	KY	51	H	62	116 x 16
Frank Morgan	1870	C	JF	LA	69	W	108	124 x 26
Frank Willard	1878	C	JF	OH	73	W	75	NA
Frankland	1846	U	PC	TN	45	H	96	138 x 18
Frazier	1873	C	JF	NA	NA	NA	NA	NA
Friendly	1889	C	JF	WV	88	W	67	120 x 27
Frolic	1868	C	JF	VA	60	H	393	205 x NA
G. W. Sentell	1889	C	JF	IN	82	W	NA	NA
Garry Owen	1871	C	JF	WV	70	W	289	131 x 33
Gazelle	1845	C	PC	OH	44	H	82	104 x 20
Gen. J. L. Hodges	1861	C	JF	KY	60	H	252	162 x 31
George	1866	C	JF	IO	65	H	105	118 x 21
Georgia	1842	U	PC	PA	37	H	135	137 x 19
Gladiola	1870	C	JF	IN	69	W	277	137 x 35
Golden Era	1868	C	JF	PA	66	W	208	156 x 32
Gossamer	1857	C	JF	NA	NA	NA	NA	NA
Gossamer (2)	1865	C	JF	PA	65	W	144	123 x 23
Grenada	1852	C	JF	IN	51	H	217	140 x 28
Gussie	1876	C	MP	NA	NA	NA	NA	NA
H. A. Homeyer	1866	C	JF	IN	63	W	222	165 x 33
Ham Howell	1858	C	JF	VA	57	W	144	120 x 30
Hamilton	1871	C	JF	OH	67	W	123	NA
Harmonia	1861	C	JF	PA	56	W	151	NA
Henry M. Shreve	1871	C	JF	IN	67	H	567	198 x 35
Hesper	1871	C	JF	OH	66	W	184	127 x35
Hettie Gilmore	1866	C	JF	OH	59	W	78	110 x 22
Homer	1860	C	JF	VA	59	H	194	148 x 28
Hope	1856	C	JF	KY	55	H	193	128 x 34
Hornet	1870	C	JB	LA	70	S	39	NA
Huntsville	1873	C	JF	IN	64	W	213	159 x 33
Ida	1870	C	JF	MO	66	H	326	172 x 32
Ida Stockdale	1870	C	JF	PA	67	W	377	NA
Independence	1865	C	JF	LA	63	H	42	75 x 17
Irene	1867	C	JF	KY	64	W	211	156 x 32
Iron City	1866	C	JF	WV	64	W	190	150 x 29
J. D. Swaim	1860	C	JF	IN	59	H	228	151 x 30
J. E. Roberts	1845	C	JF	VA	44	H	118	128 x 24

NAME	YEAR	STATUS	PORT	PLACE BUILT	YEAR BUILT	TYPE	TONS	DIMENSIONS
J. M. Sharp	1860	C	JF	IN	59	H	218	147 x 29
J. R. Hoyle	1865	C	JF	IN	65	W	115	101 x 20
J. T. Doswell	1848	U	PC	KY	48	H	190	155 x 25
Jefferson	1870	C	JF	IN	58	W	146	120 x 30
Jennie Howell	1870	C	JF	NA	70	W	NA	146 x 36
Jewel	1879	C	JF	IN	78	W	500	177 x 33
Jim Gilmer	1846	C	PC	OH	46	H	115	123 x 26
Joe Bryarly	1878	C	JF	NA	NA	W	NA	NA
John G. Fletcher	1883	C	MP	IN	77	W	NA	121 x 26
John Ray	1860	C	JF	OH	59	W	86	100 x 24
John Strader	1853	C	JF	PA	52	H	205	137 x 28
John T. Moore	1872	C	JF	OH	71	W	NA	177 x 42
Joseph Holden	1857	C	JF	OH	56	W	222	NA
Judge Fletcher	1869	C	JF	PA	60	H	260	NA
Julia	1856	C	JF	KY	48	H	99	93 x 26
Julia A. Rudolph	1870	C	JF	PA	69	W	NA	154 x 34
Katie P. Kountz	1873	C	JF	PA	71	W	NA	NA
L. Dillard	1865	C	JF	LA	65	W	56	107 x 19
La Belle	1871	C	JF	IN	69	H	510	178 x 40
Lady Grace	1867	C	JF	IN	65	W	387	160 x 33
Lady Lee	1871	C	JF	PA	71	W	417	176 x 35
Lafitte	1857	C	JF	KY	56	H	95	107 x 19
Lake City	1869	C	JF	NA	NA	NA	NA	NA
Lama	1845	C	JF	OH	44	H	68	100 x 24
Larkin Edwards	1858	C	JF	IN	57	NA	67	NA
Latona	1846	C	JF	IN	46	H	197	155 x 26
Lecompte	1857	C	JF	OH	56	H	250	155 x 32
Leo	1869	C	JF	IN	68	H	349	165 x 40
Lessie B.	1882	C	JF	OH	81	NA	NA	NA
Lessie Taylor	1873	C	JF	IN	70	W	434	157 x 38
Lightest	1870	C	JF	IN	70	W	NA	136 x 29
Lightwood	1870	C	JF	OH	68	W	156	130 x 26
Linda	1858	C	JF	OH	55	H	167	NA
Little Fleta	1870	C	JF	IN	70	W	209	NA
Little Yazoo	1845	U	PC	OH	43	H	46	80 x 20
Live Oak	1846	U	JF	LA	45	H	64	113 x 15
Live Oak (2)	1866	C	JF	KY	63	H	356	176 x 37
Lizzie C. Hamilton	1865	C	JF	OH	64	W	60	109 x 20
Lizzie Hopkins	1868	C	JF	OH	67	W	453	159 x 36
Lizzie Lee	1856	C	JF	KY	56	H	101	NA
Lizzie Tate	1867	C	JF	OH	63	H	160	158 x 30
Lone Star	1856	C	JF	KY	54	H	126	112 x 26
Lotawanna	1869	C	JF	OH	67	W	479	155 x 35

NAME	YEAR	STATUS	PORT	PLACE BUILT	YEAR BUILT	TYPE	TONS	DIMENSIONS
Lotta	1873	C	JB	NA	NA	NA	NA	NA
Lotus	1866	C	JF	NA	NA	NA	NA	NA
Lotus No. 2	1867	C	JF	PA	66	W	230	135 x 26
Lotus No. 3	1870	C	JF	PA	69	W	NA	160 x 37
Lucy Robinson	1852	C	PC	IN	51	H	239	121 x 27
Lulu D.	1868	C	JF	IN	67	W	245	135 x 35
Maid of Kentucky	1845	C	PC	OH	40	H	192	NA
Marco	1889	C	JF	NA	NA	NA	NA	NA
Maria Louise	1871	C	JF	IN	71	W	521	180 x 34
Martin Walt	1860	C	JF	OH	59	W	64	NA
Mary Ellen	1868	C	JF	LA	68	NA	NA	NA
Mary L. Dougherty	1856	C	JF	PA	53	H	95	123 x 18
Mattie Cook	1866	C	JF	IN	60	W	120	124 x 24
May Lowry	1871	C	JF	PA	71	NA	138	138 x 31
Medora	1850	C	PC	IN	45	H	178	155 x 25
Miami	1841	U	PC	VA	39	H	114	133 x 13
Minden	1869	C	JF	NA	NA	NA	NA	NA
Minnie	1870	C	JF	PA	69	W	40	83 x 18
Mittie Stephens	1866	C	JF	IN	63	H	224	170 x 29
Mollie Fellows	1866	C	JF	OH	64	H	224	139 x 25
Monroe	1848	U	PC	IN	48	H	183	127 x 25
Monsoon	1866	C	JF	OH	63	H	267	180 x 34
Monterey	1847	C	JF	OH	46	H	143	135 x 25
Morgan Nelson	1860	C	JF	PA	59	H	109	120 x 22
Morning Light	1859	C	JF	PA	58	H	198	144 x 30
Moro	1862	C	JF	KY	NA	H	132	122 x 25
Music	1856	C	JF	IN	50	H	273	172 x 29
Nat F. Dortch	1891	C	JF	IN	89	W	303	164 x 29
National	1860	C	SW	NA	NA	NA	NA	NA
Navigator	1866	C	JF	PA	62	W	243	154 x 39
Nellie L.	1897	C	JF	NA	NA	NA	NA	NA
New Brazil	1845	U	PC	OH	41	H	166	144 x 22
New Era	1867	C	JF	IN	60	H	259	162 x 32
New Haven	1890	C	JF	NA	NA	W	93	136 x 24
Oceanus	1871	C	JF	PA	70	W	365	180 x 41
Ontario	1843	C	PC	PA	36	H	133	149 x 19
Osceola	1851	C	JF	PA	49	H	125	125 x 23
Osceola (2)	1858	C	JF	KY	58	H	157	NA
Osprey	1857	C	JF	LA	56	W	109	115 x 24
P. E. Bonford	1861	C	JF	IN	60	H	231	140 x 30
Panola	1845	U	PC	OH	44	H	120	120 x 25
Panola (2)	1865	C	JF	OH	63	H	89	132 x 22
Picayune No. 3	1860	C	JF	PA	59	W	136	NA

NAME	YEAR	STATUS	PORT	PLACE BUILT	YEAR BUILT	TYPE	TONS	DIMENSIONS
Pioneer Era	1865	C	JF	IN	63	W	219	129 x 29
Pitser Miller	1852	C	JF	PA	48	H	158	126 x 26
Planter	1844	C	TL	OH	43	H	166	120 x 23
Planter (2)	1856	C	JF	IN	52	H	182	133 x 26
Post Boy	1852	C	JF	OH	51	H	157	140 x 24
R. C. Oglesby	1850	C	JF	IN	49	H	115	126 x 23
R. J. Lockwood	1870	C	JF	PA	70	W	NA	175 x 33
R. M. Jones	1856	C	JF	KY	51	H	193	136 x 27
R. T. Bryarly	1873	C	JF	IN	72	W	331	150 x 33
R. W. Dugan	1877	C	JF	OH	73	W	NA	160 x 32
R. W. Powell	1856	C	JF	IN	55	H	349	175 x 33
Ranger	1884	C	MP	AR	82	NA	NA	95 x 147
Rantidotler	1868	C	JF	NA	NA	NA	NA	NA
Rapides	1870	C	JF	OH	69	W	415	154 x 38
Red Cloud	1871	C	JF	OH	70	W	599	161 x 39
Red River	1851	C	JF	OH	50	H	276	174 x 29
Republic	1844	C	PC	OH	42	H	147	140 x 22
Rescue	1858	C	JF	KY	58	W	77	NA
Reub White	1857	C	JF	VA	56	H	110	104 x 27
Richmond	1866	C	JF	KY	66	W	339	143 x 35
Right Way	1868	C	JF	PA	67	W	291	134 x 28
Rinaldo	1862	C	JF	NA	NA	NA	NA	NA
Robert Fulton	1861	C	JF	PA	60	H	158	137 x 29
Robert T. Lytle	1843	C	PC	OH	42	H	159	158 x 22
Robert Watson	1859	C	JF	PA	58	W	137	129 x 28
Rodolph	1845	C	PC	IN	44	H	213	156 x 25
Rosa	1856	C	JF	KY	51	H	265	116 x 28
Rosa Bland	1892	C	JF	AR	89	W	149	113 x 23
Rose Franks	1867	C	JF	OH	66	W	240	126 x 29
Royal George	1872	C	JF	AR	72	NA	NA	135 x 27
Ruby	1854	U	JF	PA	51	H	103	116 x 20
Ruby (2)	1873	C	JF	IN	71	W	117	NA
Ruth	1871	C	JF	PA	70	W	NA	140 x 35
S. W. Downs	1853	C	JF	IN	51	H	236	165 x 27
Sabine	1844	C	PC	KY	43	H	106	108 x 21
Sabine (2)	1874	C	JF	NA	NA	NA	NA	NA
Salado	1871	C	JF	WV	68	W	110	128 x 25
Sallie Robinson	1858	C	JF	OH	56	H	267	165 x 34
Science No. 2	1865	C	JF	PA	60	W	116	135 x 27
Selma	1869	C	JF	PA	67	H	600	180 x 38
Seminole	1870	C	JF	IN	69	W	420	158 x 44
Shamrock	1849	C	JF	KY	48	H	139	164 x 26
Shamrock (2)	1873	C	JF	OH	63	W	217	NA

NAME	YEAR	STATUS	PORT	PLACE BUILT	YEAR BUILT	TYPE	TONS	DIMENSIONS
Shields	1884	C	JB	NA	NA	NA	NA	NA
Silver Bow	1870	C	JF	PA	69	H	335	212 x 32
Silver Moon	1857	C	JF	KY	57	H	171	124 x 28
Silver Spray	1870	C	JF	PA	64	W	352	NA
Sodo	1855	C	JF	LA	54	W	NA	108 x 20
South Western	1842	U	PC	IN	39	H	202	139 x 24
South-Western	1873	C	JF	NA	70	W	411	180 x 42
Southern	1851	U	JF	NA	NA	NA	NA	183 x 31
Southern (2)	1857	C	JF	VA	57	W	126	118 x 27
St. Cloud	1865	C	JF	MN	61	H	25	90 x 13
St. Charles	1853	C	JF	OH	50	H	311	126 x 30
St. John	1870	C	JF	IN	69	W	464	176 x 34
Star	1842	C	PC	KY	41	H	138	141 x 22
Starlight	1859	C	JF	IN	58	H	280	162 x 31
Storm	1852	C	JF	OH	48	H	247	172 x 28
Sunbeam	1858	C	JF	OH	57	W	167	NA
Swan	1843	U	PC	OH	40	H	93	118 x 21
Swan (2)	1852	C	JF	IN	51	H	127	109 x 22
T. D. Hine	1863	C	JF	IN	58	H	131	148 x 30
Tallahatchie	1849	C	PC	IN	47	H	163	132 x 24
Telegram	1859	C	JF	OH	58	W	205	158 x 31
Telegraph	1843	C	PC	PA	40	H	165	143 x 22
Texarkana	1869	C	JF	IN	69	W	343	136 x 36
Texas	1861	C	JF	OH	59	H	170	138 x 30
Texas (2)	1870	C	JF	IN	69	W	NA	136 x 35
Texas Ranger	1853	C	JF	IN	51	H	159	137 x 22
Thirteenth Era	1870	C	JF	PA	70	W	298	150 x 33
Thomas Powell	1866	C	JF	KY	65	H	109	101 x 20
Thornbush	1880	C	MP	NA	NA	NA	NA	NA
Tidal Wave	1870	C	JF	PA	70	W	NA	160 x 36
Travis Wright	1869	C	JF	IN	69	W	202	129 x 32
Trio	1860	C	JF	KY	58	W	150	NA
Twelfth Era	1869	C	JF	NA	69	W	205	136 x 29
Una	1866	C	JF	KY	63	H	121	NA
Unicorn	1854	U	JF	PA	53	H	188	126 x 30
Venture	1853	C	JF	LA	51	H	61	102 x 20
Vesta	1846	U	JF	IN	45	H	92	117 x 21
Vicksburg	1878	C	MP	NA	NA	NA	NA	NA
Victoria	1856	C	SW	KY	55	H	161	133 x 30
Victress	1847	C	JF	OH	41	H	190	155 x 25
Vigo	1860	C	JF	PA	59	H	144	130 x 26
Violett	1860	C	JF	PA	56	W	89	123 x 22
W. A. Andrew	1858	C	JF	NA	57	H	229	132 x 30

NAME	YEAR	STATUS	PORT	PLACE BUILT	YEAR BUILT	TYPE	TONS	DIMENSIONS
W. A. Violett	1849	C	JF	PA	48	H	162	120 x 23
W. F. Curtis	1870	C	JF	WV	64	W	211	NA
W. J. Behan	1873	C	JF	IN	73	W	NA	165 x 33
Wabash Valley	1857	C	JF	KY	53	H	136	NA
Walter B. Dance	1870	C	JF	KY	66	H	571	200 x 34
Warren Belle	1867	C	JF	IN	65	H	242	144 x 25
Wash Sentell	1870	C	JF	NA	NA	NA	NA	NA
Wheel of Fortune	1846	U	PC	KY	45	H	165	NA
White Cliff	1856	C	JF	AR	56	H	142	137 x 27
Will S. Hays	1870	C	JF	IN	65	H	340	NA
William Burton	1861	C	JF	OH	57	H	253	151 x 29
William C. Young	1858	C	JF	KY	54	H	199	NA
William Campbell	1860	C	JF	MO	56	H	322	NA
William N. Sherman	1856	C	JF	IN	55	H	194	130 x 30
William R. Douglass	1858	C	JF	KY	56	H	229	126 x 28
Yalobusha	1846	C	PC	OH	44	H	116	115 x 24
Yazoo	1845	C	PC	OH	42	H	304	151 x 28
Yazoo Belle	1859	C	JF	IN	55	H	138	134 x 28
Yazoo City	1847	C	PC	OH	43	H	229	146 x 28

Bibliographical Essay

OVERVIEW

The easiest way to write a navigation history for an area is to have a continuous newspaper record for a primary port. Jefferson had many newspapers during the 1800s, but almost all of the issues have disappeared. The few remaining ones, for the most part, are not commercially oriented.

New Orleans has a continuous newspaper record, and because it was the focus of the trade of the ports and landings west of Shreveport, it would seem that the New Orleans newspapers would provide the best source for a local navigation history. However, there are four major limitations in the use of the New Orleans newspapers. Because New Orleans dealt with many different trade areas, the coverage of local events in those areas is not extensive, particularly with respect to the conditions of navigation. Advertisements in the New Orleans newspapers are useful for determining which boats were in the Cypress Bayou and the lakes trade, but they cannot be used to determine which boats actually went to that area because of the problem of transfers at Shreveport and, to a lesser extent, at Alexandria. The Consignments column in the New Orleans newspapers, which shows the commodities transported for various firms, is misleading, because boats arriving at New Orleans from the area picked up additional freight at Shreveport and other Red River and Mississippi River ports on the return trip. Lastly, Midwestern boats that went directly to the area are not reported in the New Orleans newspapers.

This navigation history could not have been written were it not for the fact that Shreveport was a port, that all boats that went west of Shreveport stopped at that place on the up and down trips, that Shreveport has a fairly continuous newspaper record from late 1854 on that is available on microfilm, and that the columns that cover navigation activities provide a detailed account of boats, navigation conditions on the route, and the major commodities carried by boats moving from the Cypress Bayou and the lakes area. Scattered issues of various Shreveport newspapers are available prior to 1854. Extant issues of the weekly Shreveport *South-Western* begin in August 1854. A Steamboat Register, providing a simple list of arrivals and departures, was instituted in September 1858; and a River Intelligence column, providing detailed information on the route and its boats and commodities, was instituted in January 1866. The *South-Western* became a daily briefly at the end of 1871, after which the record is picked up continuously by the daily *Shreveport Times.*

To provide a complete record of navigation events, it was necessary to use a number of sources. For the earliest period, I relied on the steamboat arrivals section of the *New Orleans Commercial Bulletin* and the arrivals and departures column and steamboat advertisements in the New Orleans *Daily Picayune.* Fortunately, the advertisements are organized by trade area, the boats that went west of Shreveport are listed under "Red River," and it is not necessary to read the advertisements in every issue because the inclusions are repeated over a number of days. For 1855 on, I switched to the Shreveport newspapers, using the New Orleans newspapers to fill in the gaps.

Navigation information in the *South-Western* prior to September 1858 appears in the masthead column. The Steamboat Register, from September 1858 to May 1861, provides arrivals and departures, after which navigation information becomes scarce with the advent of war. For the war years, I relied primarily on the thirty-two rolls of microfilm designated the "Vessel Papers" by the National Archives. The full-fledged navigation columns in the Shreveport newspapers from January 1866 on were carefully reviewed for information on the route, its boats, and their commodities, a task that obviously became more time consuming with the inception of dailies in 1871. For 1890–1905, I used the Corps of Engineers reports on improvements to the Red River and Cypress Bayou, which provide good coverage of boat movements during a period in which the navigation columns are tedious to read because there was little in the way of boat activity.

The year 1855 proved to be fruitful from a methodological standpoint. The Shreveport newspapers reported little in the way of boat movements, and I became curious as to what the New Orleans newspapers had to say about the lack of activity. Surprisingly, there were hundreds of advertisements for boats to Jefferson, but all of these were shown, correctly, as arriving back from Alexandria or the Red River, since the falls at Alexandria were impassable because of low water. This was a very clear demonstration that advertisements are not reliable for establishing a navigation history, if one is concerned about which boats went to which ports. However, it also demonstrated that many boats participated in the Jefferson trade that never docked at Jefferson, a dimension of the story that I have not touched.

Except for the earliest years, I have not attempted to provide the names of captains. The last names are available in the Shreveport and New Orleans newspapers, and many full names are available through newspaper advertisements. The problem is that captains switched boats, so that more than one captain is often associated with a particular boat during a single year.

The steamboats that traveled along the route did not operate in a vacuum, but rather in a particular economic and social context. Thus, in order to provide a history of navigation, it was necessary to understand something about the ports and landings, interior and exterior markets and market mechanisms, and the production components for various commodities such as beef. Again, the newspapers proved to be most valuable, particularly the Shreveport newspapers and the Marshall *Texas Republican*. Like most newspapers published in what were the major metropolitan areas of the day, they provided regional coverage. More importantly, the newspapers of the period had an exchange system. Editors read other newspapers and lifted articles of interest verbatim for their own publications. I have used many quotes from the Jefferson newspapers, almost all of which are derived from external sources. In addition, Robert Loughery, the editor of the *Texas Republican*, had a special interest in Jefferson, since this is where he began in the newspaper business in Texas. His coverage of Jefferson, and particularly his accounts of visits, provide a running commentary on events to the north.

To establish the context in which boats operated, I scanned each issue of the newspaper consecutively, covering the *Texas Republican* from 1849 to 1869 and the Shreveport newspapers from 1854 to 1889. Also helpful were the Clarksville *Northern Standard* (later *Standard*) and the Marshall *Harrison Flag*. The business advertisements proved to be particularly important because they enabled a tracking of navigation-related activities in some of the lesser ports and landings, about which there is very little information. I have incorporated into the text every scrap of information I found with respect to ports and landings other than Jefferson. Much of the information available on Jefferson from the newspapers has been left out, since there is a great deal that is not related to navigation.

There are important newspaper sources that were not used or were used only slightly. The Galveston newspapers provided statewide coverage from the earliest years, with emphasis on navigation-related activities because Galveston was the state's most important port. The Dallas newspapers would probably provide important information for the post–Civil War period. The New Orleans newspapers could also be reviewed with profit.

The historic reports of the Corps of Engineers are fundamental for anyone wishing to conduct a navigation history of any area. They usually do not contain much information on boat movements; but they are essential for understanding the hydrologic conditions under which boats operated and the transformation of the conditions of operation through navigation improvements. Unlike the modern reports that are collective, guarded, and highly technical, the old reports were written by highly opinionated and insightful individuals, are interesting to read, and reveal a lot about the people in charge of the projects. Most are readily available in the annual reports of the Chief of Engineers.

Maps become increasingly important as one moves toward definitive analysis of a particular geographic area. The most valuable for this analysis were the early Corps of Engineers survey maps, because they deal with navigation and are technically precise. The second most important set of maps was that produced by the General Land Office for the 1839 Louisiana survey, which included portions of Texas. These maps provided a wealth of information on the early development of the area and are as important for what they don't show as for what they do. Contemporary topographic maps also proved important, particularly when used for comparison with the older maps.

The early travel accounts for the area are readily available in published sources. They must be used with caution in light of the usages of the period and the dramatic shifts that have taken place in the geographic designators for the area. One of the key elements in the interpretation of some of these early texts has been the realization that the lake was conceived, correctly, to have extended up to Smithland on Cypress Bayou.

The finest book on steamboats is Louis Hunter's *Steamboats on the Western Rivers: An Economic and Technological History*, which deals with the Mississippi River and its tributaries. It is a highly technical work that clarifies the mechanics of steamboat operations. There are also a number of good popular works on steamboats, among which I found Frank Donovan's *River Boats of America* to be useful.

Boat data were obtained from four sources. William Lytle's *Merchant Steam Vessels of the United States, 1807–1868* (generally referred to as the Lytle-Holdcamper list because of an extension by the latter) is a comprehensive listing based on enrollment documents in the National Archives. *Way's Packet Directory* by Frederick Way contains descriptions of most of the boats that operated along the route. The Works Progress Administration's *Ship Registers and Enrollments of New Orleans, Louisiana* is a six-volume work that provides detailed information on boats that docked at New Orleans. Most of the boat descriptions in the text were obtained from the Shreveport newspapers, usually on the basis of clippings from New Orleans newspapers or the Midwestern cities where the boats were built. Detailed descriptions of this type are available in the New Orleans newspapers for most of the boats that operated along the route, but would take a great deal of time to extract.

It is pointless to look for boat photographs until after one has a firm record, has collected boat data, and has some sense of the types of craft that are being looked for. The names of boats are not clearly visible on most photographs; and when the are, one runs into the problem that most names were used by more than one boat. I found the collection at the Public Library of Cincinnati and Hamilton County to be the most useful for boats that operated west of Shreveport, but also reviewed the collections at the University of Wisconsin at LaCrosse and Tulane University in New Orleans.

CHAPTER 1: NAVIGATION'S NATURAL SETTING

The two most important sources for understanding the early hydrologic and environmental development of the area are the works of Arthur Veatch and the 1914 Department of the Interior study. Veatch was a Louisiana geologist who dealt with the hydrologic history of the Shreveport area in Gilbert Harris and A. C. Veatch, *A Preliminary Report on the Geology of Louisiana* (Louisiana Geological Survey Report No. 4, 1899). See also his comments on the formation and destruction of the lakes in the Red River Valley in A. C. Veatch, *Geology and Underground Water Resources of Northern Louisiana and Southern Arkansas*

(Professional Paper No. 6, U. S. Geological Survey, 1906, published as House Document 488, 59th Cong., 1st Sess.).

The 1914 Department of the Interior study is composed of documents, maps, and photographs prepared by a surveyor, a geologist, and an ecologist in conjunction with disputed ownership of oil-rich lands on the Louisiana side of Caddo Lake. The studies had never been published because they were confidential documents used for many years in court cases. I obtained the entire Ferry Lake file from the National Archives, selected the most pertinent documents, and placed copies under the title "Examination of Ferry (Caddo) Lake" in depositories in the Caddo Lake area, including the Cypress Valley Alliance in Jefferson. A similar study, which I have not seen, was done for the Soda Lake area and is available through the National Archives.

Corps reports are usually obtainable in the annual reports of the Chief of Engineers (formerly Chief of Topographical Engineers), with the date of the report usually corresponding to the year of the Chief's report. Some reports are published as Senate and House documents. The reports used in this chapter were: Linnard (1844), "Report on the Improvement of the Navigation of Red River" (annual report); Fuller (1855), "Col. Fuller's Survey of Red River" (House Executive Document 90, 33rd Cong., 2nd Sess.); Woodruff (1872), "Cypress Bayou" in "Improvement of Navigation in Red River Above Shreveport, Louisiana" (annual report, 1873); Collins (1872), "Geological Notes of Assistant H. C. Collins" in Woodruff (1873), "Survey of Raft Region, Louisiana; Cypress Bayou, Texas; and Tone's Bayou, Louisiana" (annual report); Howell (1874) "Improvement of Cypress Bayou and Construction of Dams and Dredging at the Foot of Soda Lake, Texas" (annual report); Willard (1893), "Survey of Cypress Bayou and the Lakes Between Jefferson, Tex., and Shreveport, La." (annual report); and Potter (1902), "Report of Capt. Chas. L. Potter, Corps of Engineers" in "Preliminary Examination of Cypress Bayou, Texas, Including the Lakes Between Jefferson, Texas, and Red River, Louisiana" (annual report, 1904).

DeWare's comments were presented before the Committee on Rivers and Harbors and are contained in the committee report "Improvement of Certain Rivers and Waterways in Louisiana and Texas" (microcard HRi 58-N). Smith provides a comprehensive picture of Northeast Texas in *Account of a Journey Through North-Eastern Texas Undertaken in 1849*. Gregg's comments are in Maurice Fulton, ed.,